Marriage and Family Therapy

Linda Metcalf, PhD, LMFT, is a tenured professor of education and director of the School Counseling Program at Texas Wesleyan University in Fort Worth, Texas. Dr. Metcalf has been a licensed marriage and family therapist for 17 years and has taught marriage and family therapy (MFT) since 2004. Her approach to teaching MFT incorporates skill building and application of theoretical constructs in experiential exercises, which resulted in this work. She has used the systemic approach in work with schools as a school counselor and frequently consults internationally with schools and school districts. She is a former president of the Texas Association for Marriage and Family Therapy and the current president of the American Association for Marriage and Family (2011–2012). She has been married to Roger Metcalf for 36 years, and together, they have reared three children—Roger Jr., Kelli, and Ryan.

She is the author of nine books: *Counseling Toward Solutions: A Practical Solution-Focused Program for Working with Students, Teachers, and Parents*; *The Field Guide to Counseling Toward Solutions: The Solution-Focused School*; *Parenting Toward Solutions: How Parents Can Use Skills They Already Have to Raise Responsible, Loving Kids*; *Teaching Toward Solutions*; *Solution-Focused RTI: A Positive and Personalized Approach to Response to Intervention*; *Solution Focused Group Therapy: Ideas for Groups in Private Practice, Schools, Agencies, and Treatment Programs*; *The Miracle Question: Answer It and Change Your Life*; *How to Say It to Get Into the College of Your Choice: Application, Essay, and Interview Strategies to Get You the Big Envelope*; and the coauthor with Elliott Connie of *The Art of Solution Focused Therapy*, by Springer Publishing.

Marriage and Family Therapy
A Practice-Oriented Approach

Linda Metcalf, PhD, LMFT
Editor

SPRINGER PUBLISHING COMPANY
NEW YORK

Springer Publishing Company, LLC
11 West 42nd Street
New York, NY 10036
www.springerpub.com

Acquisitions Editor: Jennifer Perillo
Senior Production Editor: Diane Davis
Composition: Absolute Service, Inc.; Gil Rafanan, Project Manager

ISBN: 978-0-8261-0681-0
E-book ISBN: 978-0-8261-0682-7

11 12 13 14 15/ 5 4 3 2 1

Library of Congress Cataloging-in-Publication Data

Marriage and family therapy : a practice-oriented approach / Linda Metcalf, editor.
     p. cm.
  Includes index.
  ISBN 978-0-8261-0681-0
  1. Marital psychotherapy. 2. Family psychotherapy. I. Metcalf, Linda.
  RC488.5M364 2011
  616.89'1562—dc23
                    2011013615

Special discounts on bulk quantities of our books are available to corporations, professional associations, pharmaceutical companies, health care organizations, and other qualifying groups.

If you are interested in a custom book, including chapters from more than one of our titles, we can provide that service as well.

For details, please contact:
Special Sales Department, Springer Publishing Company, LLC
11 West 42nd Street, 15th Floor, New York, NY 10036-8002
Phone: 877-687-7476 or 212-431-4370; Fax: 212-941-7842
E-mail: sales@springerpub.com

Printed in the United States of America by Bang Printing.

To my family,
and to those who learn and practice
the art of marriage and family therapy.
You hold the key to helping families create
successful future generations.

Contents

Contributors

Corey D. Allan, MD, PhD, LMFT
Private Practice, Allen, Texas
Editor of *Simple Marriages*

Kelly Backhaus, PhD, LMFT, CPC
Adjunct Professor, Western Wyoming
   Community College
Military Family Life Consultant
Rock Springs, Wyoming

Elizabeth M. Goodson Beasley, MS, LMFT
University of North Texas
Department of Education
Denton, Texas

Beena Benny, LPC, LMFT
Elementary School Mental Health Professional
Fort Worth, Texas

Fallon Cluxton-Keller, MA, PhD, LMFT
Postdoctoral Fellow
Baltimore, Maryland

Mary Ann Crossno, MS, LMFT
Private Practice
Dallas, Texas

Katherine A. Goodell, MS, LMFT
Private Practice
Flower Mound, Texas

Beth Hollingsworth, MS
Texas Wesleyan University
Department of Education
Fort Worth, Texas

Linda Lee, BA
Texas Wesleyan University
Fort Worth, Texas

Yueh-Ting (Tim) Lee, PhD
Assistant Professor, National University of Tainan
Taiwan

Carla Atkinson Leslie, MS, LMFT-A
Program Director for Journey of Hope Grief
   Support Center
Plano, Texas

Amanda Martin, LPC, LMFT, PhD-C
Texas Woman's University
Department of Family Sciences
Denton, Texas

Jessica Martinez, BS
Probation Officer, Tarrant County
Texas Wesleyan University
Fort Worth, Texas

Teresa Masdon, PhD, RN, LMFT
Private Practice, Enjoy Your Life Center
Dallas, Texas

Linda Metcalf, PhD, LMFT
Director of the School Counseling Program
Professor, Texas Wesleyan University
Department of Education
Fort Worth, Texas

Billee K. C. Molarte, MS, LPC
Texas Woman's University
Department of Family Sciences
Denton, Texas

Edita Ruzgyte, PhD, LPC
Assistant Professor, Texas Wesleyan University
Department of Education
Fort Worth, Texas

Reva Shephard, MA, LPC-I
Texas Wesleyan University
Fort Worth, Texas

Tiffany Nicole Smith, MS, LPC, LMFT, NCC
Private Practice, Tiffany Smith Counseling, Inc.
Flower Mound, Texas

Donald Spinks, PhD, LPC
Assistant Professor, Texas Wesleyan University
Fort Worth, Texas
(deceased)

Christina Stanley, MFT, CSC
School Counselor, Thelma Jones Elementary
    School
Arlington, Texas

Sean B. Stokes, PhD, LPC-S, LMFT-S
Assistant Professor, Texas Wesleyan University
Fort Worth, Texas

Leslie E. Storms, MS
Yoga Instructor
Assistant in Orthopedic Practice
Dallas, Texas

Britt G. Sudderth, MS, LMFT-A
Texas Woman's University
Department of Family Sciences
Denton, Texas

Kelly M. Taylor, MS, LMFT
Private Practice
Dallas, Texas

Foreword

Poor Cinderella's therapist: he could never seem to get it right. He talked with her about her depressive symptoms: her tearfulness, her loss of appetite, her loss of zest for life. He tried to help her see the errors in her thinking. When that didn't seem to help, he recommended that she be evaluated for medical problems or antidepressants. When she complained about her relationship with her Prince, he worked with them as a couple, focusing on their negative interaction cycle and emotional states related to their yearnings for closeness and the behaviors they used that seemed to push them away from each other. He even asked her to bring her parents and stepsiblings to therapy so that they could work on unresolved issues from past years and generations. He tried to help them all understand how difficult it is to be part of a blended family, trying to meld two different sets of rules and values into one. Nothing seemed to work. Perhaps Cinderella's therapist had not found his own best way of working?

I have been teaching family therapy since I was a doctoral student in the early 1980s, then in an accredited doctoral program, and most recently in an accredited master's program. With each year, I have searched for texts that would help students develop perspectives on their own work, to articulate their beliefs and assumptions about families and about therapy, and to help them find practices that fit their ways of working. Although each text I have used has its own strengths, particularly for beginning students, none has been quite sufficient. My hypothesis is that none were sufficiently clear about the *what* of different therapy approaches within a context of the *why* (background of the approach) and the *how it works* (ways that change occurs within the approach). Some provided this information, yet were too dense to completely understand.

Linda Metcalf is a solution-focused therapist who asks her clients, "When we are finished with therapy, what will be different? How will you know that you have accomplished what you need to do in our work together?" or words to that effect. With the present book, it seems that she asked her students, "When we are finished with your education together, what will you be doing? How will you know that you have learned what you needed to know in order to do therapy with clients?" Then, capturing the strengths and perspectives of these students, she guided them through a process of focusing specifically on couple and family therapy approaches that were most enticing to them, that were most likely to fit their ways of thinking, of viewing the world and systems, and of working with clients to help them reach their goals in therapy or life. She set a model outline as a guide and then the students filled it in, each to his or her own specifications after reading original works, commentaries and edited chapters, and interviewing the progenitors of the approaches whenever possible. Finally, she carefully edited the chapters so that their language is accessible and clear. What better way to learn than to write chapters for others to learn from?

The result of that effort is in your hands. Each chapter will provide you, the reader, with background, assumptions and concepts, typical interventions and practices, and evaluation strategies of a multitude of approaches to therapy. Because the chapters are well edited and follow similar outlines, when you are finished, you will have a better understanding of your own ways of thinking, prompted by the chapters' authors. You will be able to understand the basis for family therapy and to integrate ideas from the founding approaches, melding them into a coherence that will be all your own. You will have read about cultural sensitivity and competency, yourself as a person and therapist, and about ethics in therapy. Cinderella and her family will have no sway with you; you will be able to hypothesize, assess, and develop a way of thinking and acting that will help them reach their goals, just as this book will help you reach yours.

Thorana S. Nelson, PhD
Emeritus Professor
Utah State University
Logan, Utah

Preface

As a graduate student of family therapy, I remember being amazed at the approach of family therapy, which always seemed to work flawlessly for the therapists I read about. I was intrigued with the way families listened, did their homework, and came back better. I was excited to try out questions I read about in case studies and could not wait to watch how the questions impacted my clients. Yet it took more than just reading to learn how to construct and ask questions. While I was a graduate student, I packed my bags and went to a week-long workshop with Jay Haley and Cloe Madanes in Maryland to see if that would make a difference (which it did). But I still found I had to attend many workshops, read many more case studies, consult with my teachers, and watch videotapes for hours to get a grasp on how to do family therapy.

So it was no surprise that after getting my PhD in marriage and family therapy (MFT) and becoming an MFT instructor, my students began to approach me with the same dilemma. They learned the theories, they read the case studies, they did role plays, and they practiced using the questions, yet they were still confused and frustrated at how to "do it." As a professor, I found myself consulting with my students for hours, giving them a few tips I had learned and then outlining how each of the family therapy models worked. The students seemed to appreciate the step-by-step ideas and went on to practice and then, eventually, excel at their models.

It was "old hat" for me to put together step-by-step ideas for my students. I had done the same for myself a few years earlier when I was learning the solution-focused approach. Although the steps I developed would not be applied "to" a family because families are unique as we know, they did help me get a grasp on how the model worked. When I was then asked by an editor 4 years ago to do the same for each family therapy model, I thought, "Yes, this could be quite helpful." Then I realized what an overwhelming task it would be. I enlisted the help of the contributors who authored the pages of this book and together, we developed templates to guide MFT students through learning how each family therapy model works.

Therefore, this book is a gift to you, the instructor of MFT, and to you, the student who wishes to learn how systems thinking is employed in every family therapy model currently used today in our field. In this book, you will find brief overviews of every model, including history, views of change, views of the family, and the role of the therapist. The models covered here include the following:

Bowen Family Systems Theory
Contextual Family Therapy
Cognitive Behavioral Family Therapy Models
Rational Emotive Behavior Therapy
Symbolic-Experiential Family Therapy
Satir Human Validation Process Model
Milan Systemic Family Therapy
Structural Family Therapy
Strategic Family Therapy
Solution-Focused Brief Therapy With Families

Narrative Therapy With Families
Emotionally Focused Therapy
Medical Family Therapy
Family Psychoeducation

Each model is covered in a consistent way, so that you can better understand the underlying theories and practical distinctions between them. For example, you will learn how the cognitive behavioral therapist (CBT) differs from the solution-focused therapist (SFT) in the way of being direct and prescriptive with clients (CBT) rather than letting the client decide the direction of therapy (SFT). You will learn how other models compare, contrast, and focus on goal setting, task setting, and providing homework, if any. Throughout each chapter, realistic examples of family problems—many drawn from actual practice—will show you how that particular model addresses issues that are commonly faced by practicing marriage and family therapists.

You will also learn how to choose the model that most appeals to you in Chapter 2, "The Self of the Therapist." Who you are as a person is an integral part of the process of becoming a marriage and family therapist. If you choose the right model for you that fits your personality and beliefs about people, you will not have to worry about questions to ask—they will come naturally.

You will also learn some basics about choosing a supervisor (Chapter 17), doing research (Chapter 18), facing ethical issues (Chapter 19), and working effectively with multicultural families (Chapter 20). And there is more.

Each chapter in Part II contains templates for *every* MFT model currently used as a guide to learning the process of working with couples and families in the model's unique way. These templates will walk you through the process of joining and building rapport, understanding the presenting issue, assessing family dynamics, setting goals with the family, amplifying change, and finally terminating when appropriate.

To encourage you further, there are extensive interviews with many of the gurus responsible for creating and honing the theories you will read about in this book. They shared their ideas on how change occurs, how they set goals, and how they actually do therapy. Additionally, a case study is presented to each master therapist within these pages. You can see how very differently therapists from the various models will approach the exact same case. There is also an Instructor's Manual to help you utilize this textbook in your classroom. Contact textbook@springerpub.com to receive it.

This book, therefore, is a resource for any student learning MFT and any seasoned marriage and family therapist who needs a check-up on what he or she is licensed to do. Use it often. I hope it encourages you to try out models that intrigue and delight you. Use it to review for your exams because there are many references in each chapter that will accelerate your learning curve. But most of all, find in this one volume an opportunity to view the models that have developed and furthered the field of MFT and then read with your own eyes how each model works.

Acknowledgments

Four years have passed since this book was conceptualized by myself and 18 MFT graduate students from Texas Woman's University. As in any family, the authors of this book have grown, graduated, gotten licenses to practice MFT, and established themselves in various communities and practices. We even had some new additions to our family as this project grew—student authors from Texas Wesleyan University, where I now teach, who researched and gathered material on Virginia Satir's work to make this volume complete. Each of these amazing authors has made contributions to the field of MFT education that will forever be read in these pages. As their professor, I will never forget the stars in their eyes as they wrote their words and conversed with the master therapists. They taught me that real teaching comes more easily when I let them show me the way.

But a book needs an editor to get published, and without our editor, Jennifer Perillo, it would not have come to such fruition. I personally appreciate Jennifer's wisdom, sharp eye for detail, and fantastic guidance in this project, taking it from a manuscript to a professional publication that we all can be proud of. It has been a joy to work with you. Thank you very much.

During the time that the book was written, we lost an author whose initial leadership on this project inspired us all. Donald Spinks, PhD, will always be remembered for his early musings about what students needed in a book like this. We each valued his kindness and professionalism throughout the time we spent with him and appreciated the chance to know him. These pages make sure he is never forgotten.

To the students that created this work, I have many words of thanks to express. To Kate, Britt, and Corey, thank you for a marvelous chapter on how to become a therapist and keep track of our sanity thereafter! To Mary Ann, your passion for Murray Bowen's work is so contagious, many of us nearly converted to the model just by listening to you. To Edita, thank you for your work on the contextual theory and in helping to polish Don's chapter on emotionally focused therapy. I know he would have appreciated it. You gave his voice more words that we can remember forever. Fallon, three chapters and you just kept going, with an energy and love of what you do that speaks volumes. To Amanda, your wit and wisdom fit so well with experiential therapy. Thank you for your earnest work in contacting those whose work you admired. To Leslie, thank you for seeking out the Milan therapists—it was not easy, but you did it! To Tiffany, thanks for your strategic candor, creativity, and love of therapy that shines in your chapter. Your assistance with the diversity chapter clearly shows your talent in understanding the intricate strategies that make a difference. To Carla, your admiration of Michael White and your brief interview with him during his last workshop was special to us both. Thank you, Kelly, for constructing a chapter on diversity that is useful and informative. Thanks, Teresa, for your work in medical family therapy and in composing a chapter that students can use to link together the usefulness of combining the two worlds. Thanks, Billee, for your contributions to the supervision chapter by interviewing two top supervisors. Elizabeth, your work on the research chapter is such a gift to students who desire to learn not only about MFT but also about researching MFT. Thank you for your earnest work in interviewing Dr. Chenail. Beena, thank you for including forms in the ethics chapter to assist the readers as they begin practicing. Your ethical way of meeting deadlines was impressive! Thank you to Beth for your excitement and fruitful conversation with a real Satir colleague. It is delightful to read the conversation that you created. To Christina, your work on the Satir chapter was thorough and helpful. You write well and express your thoughts gracefully. To Linda, I appreciate your additions to the Satir chapter, which make it realistic and diverse. Reva, your ability to compose a template so smoothly was remarkable. The template is a great example of Satir's work. And finally, Jessica, I appreciated your quick and nimble ability to add words to the terms that made them understandable. Thank you to my Wesleyan colleague, Sean Stokes, for coauthoring the supervision chapter, updating and making it a stellar addition in the end. Thank you to Dr. Jon Crook for his helpfulness on the multicultural chapter template.

On behalf of the authors, we would also like to acknowledge other professionals whom we interviewed for this project who passed away during its process: Insoo Berg, Albert Ellis, and Michael White, your words are within these pages and live on forever. Thank you for your contributions to our work and to each of us who knew you.

Finally, thank you to my husband, Roger, for his constant support and belief that I can "edit one more chapter tonight." When it was over, and the idea of publishing the work of my students was done, it was you who celebrated with me.

The Practice of Marriage and Family Therapy

1

Linda Metcalf

The happiest moments of my life have been the few which I have passed at home in the bosom of my family.

—Thomas Jefferson

INTRODUCTION

The young woman came to the family therapy office in tattered clothing, with handkerchief in hand, and sat down and started crying before she even spoke. When she finally composed herself, she began to tell her tale to the professional opposite her. She spoke about her mother, who had passed away several years ago and continued on sadly, about how her father had remarried in desperation. His chosen wife had promised both the young woman and her father that she could give them the emotional stability that they needed. The father, who soon became unhappy with his controlling new wife, was depressed and had taken to working long hours away from home. Prior to the marriage, the young woman had finished her schooling, yet had no direction for her life. She had taken up the role of the wife and tended the house. So, when the new woman in her father's life came around, the young woman was pleased, at least, at first. Perhaps now, she thought, her father would be happier and she could move on with her own life.

However, as the next few years passed by, the young woman became depressed, particularly when the new stepmother and her two daughters "took over" the home and demeaned the young woman constantly. At one point, she was banished to sleep in the basement with mice. She readily took on that fate as a means of escape from the family that seemed to never appreciate her even though she toiled day and night to please them.

On this day, the young woman, Cinderella, came to therapy as a last resort, looking for relief from the chaotic life she was living. According to the notes taken by the family therapist in the individual session, Cinderella presented to therapy with symptoms of insomnia, depressed mood, a poor appetite, a need to isolate, and tearfulness. Although she stated that she was not suicidal, the family therapist was cautious, and checked out her sense of hopelessness and helplessness, as well as any kind of plans for hurting herself in the future. The family therapist learned that she planned on attending college, eventually, when she was satisfied that her father was happier, but not until then. With that information, the family therapist suggested that Cinderella's entire family come to the next session. Cinderella was slightly taken aback by the idea, stating that her family would probably refuse to come. She was also worried that they might begin to see her as more of a problem. That might surely make things worse. The family therapist assured her that it would be his job to make sure they felt comfortable and respected in the session. The family therapist also offered to call the family and invite them himself. Cinderella took it upon herself to ask her family to come to therapy, as she was used to such duties.

To her surprise, later that evening at home, when she asked her family to attend the next session, they each agreed to come to therapy, at least once. After all, the stepsisters told her, the family therapist surely needed to learn how awful Cinderella really was at home.

THE INSIDER'S VIEW OF THE CASTLE

The fairy tale of Cinderella is a story that takes only one view of the life of the future princess. An individual therapist might concentrate on the symptoms of depression, check out Cinderella's beliefs and thoughts about herself, and encourage her to find a support system. Maybe there was a group for depressed young women in her community. Maybe medication would help. However, a family therapist sees things differently. What could a family therapist do, systemically, to aid in helping Cinderella's depression? And, is it depression at all, or just a simple malfunction in family relationships? Let's see what happens next as the family system reveals its way of functioning.

When the family arrived the following week, the therapist found the stepmother and father to be distant, sitting far apart from each other across the room. They were cordial to everyone, but both kept looking at their timepieces. The family therapist found the two stepsisters to be angry at Cinderella. They deliberately sat together across from her and claimed that she was rude to them and rarely spoke to them. They said Cinderella was "stuck-up," yet, later in the session, one stepsister, Anastasia, admitted to being jealous of how pretty Cinderella was. She said she wanted a relationship with Cinderella, but felt constantly rejected by her. "She's always working and never takes time to be friendly," Anastasia said.

The other stepsister, Drizella, remained loyal to Anastasia and wanted to "get even" by torturing Cinderella with more laundry and more dishes to clean. She too, however, admitted to wanting to be more sisterly with Cinderella. Cinderella was taken aback and began to cry. She had no idea that her stepsisters wanted a relationship with her.

"Why," Cinderella asked, were her stepsisters so cruel to her instead of being honest about how they really felt? The family therapist encouraged the stepsisters to tell Cinderella why—and they did. They described how pretty Cinderella was and how she could snatch any prince that came along. They also saw her as talented, and they seemed to only see themselves as bookworms. The family therapist was comforted by the fact that the stepsisters were willing to speak their opinions, and complimented them on the courage it took to open up. The stepsisters smiled. The family therapist asked Cinderella if she wanted to move closer to her stepsisters in the room. She said, "yes." He then asked her if she wanted to tell her stepsisters how she felt. She began to tell them that she, being an only child, had always wanted siblings to play with, even as a grown-up. They had no idea that she desired a better relationship with them. The parents were surprised, yet pleased to see their children talk so personally.

Turning to the parents, the family therapist encouraged the stepmother to speak about what was happening in the room. The stepmother acknowledged that she was also defensive to Cinderella because her two daughters were not pursued by Prince Charming or any other suitor as often as Cinderella was. As their mother admitted feeling badly for her daughter's poor social lives, both Anastasia and Drizella sat up and reassured their mother that they were actually more interested in going to college than getting married. The father was surprised at his stepdaughters' aspirations, because he often saw them as lazy and unmotivated. When he learned that they both had high SAT scores despite their lack of study, and were in line for full scholarships to Yale because of their community service at the castle, he was overjoyed. When Cinderella saw her father smile for the first time in years, she relaxed and admitted sneaking out to a ball, where she once met Prince Charming. When her father heard that Prince Charming had asked her to marry him, he smiled again. Cinderella was relieved to see him smile. She had feared that her responsibilities to her father would last forever.

The father then told the family therapist that this new information was very helpful. Now he would have less to worry about financially and could slow down his work schedule at the castle. He might even think about retirement and take his wife on the cruise they had talked about. At that statement, his wife looked at him for the first time in the session and said she didn't think he wanted her to be part of his life, because he always worked such long hours. She told him she had felt ignored for several years. He told her he had felt overwhelmed with responsibility and wanted to give her and her daughters a good life. The rest of the family, Cinderella, Anastasia, and Drizella, looked at each other and smiled. The stepmother began to smile and cry at the same time. The father walked over to her and took her hand.

Things began to change.

A NEW VERSION OF AN OLD STORY

Although this is obviously a new version of the classic Cinderella story, it provides a traditional example of the family therapy field's systemic underpinnings. Notice the "ripple effect" that happened as new versions of beliefs, thoughts, and interactions emerged. Notice how the *affect* (the emotional reactions expressed) of the father, stepmother, and stepsisters changed as their goals and desires were expressed. And, for the *symptom bearer* (the person in the family who develops personal symptoms to call attention to the fact that a problem exists), Cinderella, she was finally able to come clean about the ball and, literally, live happily ever after with Prince Charming. After all, now her father could be happy because he and her stepmother had reconciled. Cinderella also recognized that she wasn't the outcast that her stepsisters had claimed. They had simply felt rejected as much as she had. Now, she felt freer to express her needs to them, without fear of being ridiculed.

This chapter will use the tale of Cinderella to explain some basic tenets of family therapy that will be helpful to the new family therapist who desires to understand the process of thinking and acting systemically. Throughout the chapter, more excerpts from Cinderella's family therapy session will be provided to explain the tenets of family therapy in the most understandable manner.

A HISTORY OF FAMILY THERAPY: ORIGINS AND CONCEPTS

Before 1950, seeing the family as part of psychotherapy was not common. When Murray Bowen began noticing that treating individuals often did not lead to long-lasting change, he began studying relationships of his patients in the hospital instead. He found that unless family dynamics changed, rarely did the individual. He also noticed that, generationally, certain traits left unchanged in a family often surfaced as traits of the next generation. Thus, family therapy evolved out of psychoanalysis and the medical psychiatric model when treatment with an individual meant involving the family in treatment.

As family therapy continued to evolve, so did discoveries about why and how individuals developed as they did. New answers were discovered about how emotional distress occurred, and those answers led to strategies designed to mend interpersonal relationships.

Concepts from the field of psychology, such as small group dynamics, where individuals collaborated, confronted, or negotiated issues, became tools of the family therapist. When the child guidance movement found that treating only the child did not lead to long-lasting change, the invitation to the family to join therapy led to more success. In social work practices, where the practitioner often visited the family in its home context, problems were more understood. New family therapists were often former social workers, so using such conversational techniques resulted in richer dialogue around an individual's problem.

When Gregory Bateson and his colleagues (1972/1956) began studying the causes of schizophrenia, they found that the families they studied had a strong impact on the course of therapy and on the schizophrenia. The group found that schizophrenia could be recognized as a method by an individual to maintain a homeostatic balance in their family. Therefore, the symptom was the result of interactions of family members around the individual. That discovery led to a belief that, by changing the individual reactions, the symptoms lessened.

The discovery by family therapists who began noticing that to change a system meant that patterns had to be disrupted was the prompt that led to various ways of working with families, developing into the many models presented in this book. How such disruptions occurred took on many forms. Some models focused on interpersonal communications, challenging family members with paradox, circular questions, and directives. Other models focused on generational trends, offering insight and discovery to family members. Still others took the approach of understanding systemically how the organization operated and tried changing thought patterns, which led to new actions. The field began to burst with ideas, claims of success, and strategies for intervention with families dealing with various individual issues, which, when brought to the surface in a family therapy session, finally saw relief.

FAMILY THERAPISTS ARE INFLUENCED BY THE MODELS THEY USE

"Family therapists . . . believe that the dominant forces in our lives are located externally in the family. Therapy based on this framework is directed at changing the organization of the family" (Minuchin, Nichols, & Lee, 2006). If Cinderella had moved away prior to her father's remarriage, the chances are her story would appear quite different than the fairy tale. Instead, it was the tie of her family and worries about her father, particularly, that dominated her thinking and her choices. When the family therapist gave Cinderella's family a safe place to talk to each other, they responded with new information that changed the organization of the family. In this retelling of the Cinderella story, the family therapist, who was using a *structural* approach (see Chapter 10), helped the stepsisters to realign with Cinderella and begin a better relationship. By physically moving the sisters together, the parents became more hierarchically in charge and, in turn, allowed the children to act like children.

In contrast, a *Bowen family systems therapist* (see Chapter 3) might have explored how Cinderella's mother's death affected her life and caused her to be so dependent on her father's happiness. The *cognitive behavioral family therapist* (see Chapter 5) might have asked both stepsisters to talk more about their thoughts and beliefs that Cinderella was constantly rejecting them. Family therapists trained in other models might have taken yet other approaches.

But how do novice family therapists know where to begin? How do they know which family therapy model best fits their personality and their client's needs? And how, after learning the theories behind a model, does the beginning family therapist formulate how a session will be conducted? This is the purpose of this book: to provide beginning family therapists with information, practical applications, and steps that will help them understand the impact that family therapy can have on couples and families. However, to skillfully develop that understanding, the new family therapist must first begin to understand how a family therapist thinks.

FAMILY THERAPISTS THINK IN CIRCLES, NOT LINES

"Reality is made up of circles, but we see straight lines" (Senge, 2006, p. 73). In linear models of psychotherapy, A causes B. This is helpful in many situations where there is a simple explanation. If a mother yells at her 13-year-old daughter for her untidy bedroom, and the daughter starts to cry because she is hurt that her mother didn't notice that she had cleaned the living room, it is not hard to understand how A causes B. If, however, the daughter never tells her mother that her feelings are hurt, and the mother continues to yell, and the daughter eventually becomes lazy, resentful, and rebellious, the mother may become frustrated and may decide to think that her daughter hates her, when in fact, her daughter desires her acknowledgment. This type of thinking takes on a more "circular" flavor because A, the yelling, causes B, the resentment; then, A, more yelling, causes B, more resentment. A family therapist intervening in such a situation can disrupt the *circular causality*. This dynamic is referred to as circular causality in that it consists of reciprocal actions that occur within interacting loops.

Cinderella told the family therapist that she worried about her father's unhappiness. In fact, she was even willing to put her life on hold with the prince until her father became happier. In Chapter 3 on Bowen family systems theory, you will read about *differentiation*, a process in which family therapists encourage their clients to partake, so that the choices they make are more rational and thought driven, rather than emotion driven.

In Cinderella's case, she was trying to keep things the same at home. Of course, when she put aside her needs, she also became resentful, which caused her to be rejecting of her stepsisters and caused them to feel rejected, which led to familial chaos. Cinderella's desire to keep things the same is explained by the Bowenian concept of *homeostasis*, meaning that members of the family system seek to maintain their customary organization and functioning of the family over time. The mother of the teenage daughter, who may be worried that her rebellious daughter will be further punished by her strict father, may cover up for her daughter when she comes home drunk. By doing this, she, too, maintains homeostasis. Unfortunately, she also maintains the problem drinking of her daughter.

FAMILY THERAPISTS WATCH FOR COMMUNICATION PATTERNS AND MATCHING BEHAVIORS

As family therapists, we make sense of what we do through *systems theory*. Systems theory focuses on the relationship between parts. For example, our body is more than separate organs. It functions because the organs work together as a system. The way the body is organized and works together determines our level of health. Ludwig von Bertalanffy, a biologist, coined the term "systems theory" in 1936.

> *He felt the need for a theory to guide research in several disciplines because he saw striking parallels among them. His hunch was that if multiple disciplines focused their research and theory development efforts, they would be able to identify laws and principles which would apply to many systems. This would allow scholars and scientists to make sense of system characteristics such as wholeness, differentiation, order, equifinality, progression and others. (Gillies, 1982, p. 56)*

Today, there are many systems, such as health care systems, banking systems, and family systems. Forming individual entities into systems is one way of making sense of the information we receive each day. Families are the same in that they need to organize their family members to stay on track and focused. They do that through generating roles, communication patterns, and behaviors that materialize as a result of how the family system organizes itself.

In all families, whether they are a single mother with a child, a heterosexual family with children, a homosexual family with an adopted child or biological child, or a family with foster children, each family member is part of the family system, sending out and receiving communication. Family therapists have long known that roles in such a family system are taken on by individuals when allowed, often leading either to successful systemic interactions or unsuccessful ones. For example, an only child who "rules" the house with his every whim can often cause dysfunction on how the family interacts on a daily basis. The parents of the child ruler put aside their own needs, personally and intimately, to do as the child wishes. The child, too young to take on such responsibility for two adults' choices, often becomes symptomatic with tantrums, anger, and so forth. A family therapist viewing the dynamics would conclude that, to regain a functional home, the parents would need to hierarchically take on the roles of parents in an authoritative manner.

The need for such boundaries, often created in a family therapy session, would provide the structure needed to disrupt the family system and help it rejoin in a healthier manner. Structural family therapy does this well, often rearranging family members' seating while in therapy. The assumption is that the manner in which the family comes to therapy, sits and interacts, holds clues of how the family interacts at home. By rearranging the system in the therapy room, roles change, which leads to changed interactions at home.

Cinderella's family system consisted of her father, stepmother, two stepsisters, and a few mice that she spoke with when she felt particularly lonely. One might venture to say that Cinderella communicated more effectively with the mice than with her own family. Perhaps it was because the mice listened, supported Cinderella, and listened again. Unfortunately, because Cinderella told the mice how she felt, and not her family, she created a *triangle*, by bringing in a third party to bounce things off of and gain support.

In family therapy, triangles develop when tension between two people is too much for them to handle, so they "triangle in" a third person to relieve the pressure. This often happens in couples with children. Perhaps the mother travels a lot and the father becomes lonely. He may complain to his wife that he is lonely, and she may reply that her paycheck keeps the family going so she can't do a lot at the moment. The hurt feelings lead to the father triangling in a child, such as his 10-year-old son, to whom he becomes like a good friend. The father and son do everything together and the mother is soon frustrated that there is little intimacy between her and her husband when she is at home. Detriangulation during therapy would mean that the therapist would remove the son from between the mother and father (if he indeed sat between them, which often happens) and ask him to play in the reception area while his parents talked to each other. Salvador Minuchin became famous for his confrontation to, in this case, the father, by saying, "When did you divorce your wife and marry your son?" Such strategies often led to insight on the part of the parents, who were then guided by the family therapist to reclaim their couplehood.

Because of the triangle, Cinderella kept to herself some important feelings and needs, and the communication patterns in her family system became dysfunctional as a result. How her family organized and communicated as a result needs further explanation, as do the relationships of most families. We will explore some basic concepts in the following pages.

CYBERNETICS: THE AESTHETICS OF CHANGE

Cybernetics was defined by Norbert Wiener, a child prodigy and mathematician, as the study of control and communication in the animal and the machine (Wiener, 1948). The ideas of cybernetics, as defined by Wiener, have been adopted by clinicians who see it as a homeostatic mechanism whereby communication patterns develop, mostly because of feedback loops, which will be defined later. Many of the family therapy models in this book are based on the theory of cybernetics. How the family therapist observes the family and its interactions has much to do with the therapist's hand at helping the family to achieve change.

W. Ross Ashby was an English psychiatrist and a pioneer in cybernetics. He viewed systems as living, able to respond to variations within the system as simply as one's body responds to a range of temperatures in its environment. The home thermostat works similarly, in that it adjusts itself to keep the temperature the same (Ashby, 1956).

This *first-order change* is often seen in families where alcohol or other destructive habits resonate and family members scamper around trying to pretend that the problem isn't as serious as it seems, often hiding bottles of alcohol or promising to supervise the alcoholic person. First-order change is achieved only through the work of the family members, who must maintain their new roles. It is not a long-lasting change, or second-order change, which occurs when the alcoholic makes the decision to stop drinking and asks her family to help through support. Without second-order change, this homeostatic process will continue, sacrificing not only the identified client's need to change but also that of other family members, who put their own lives on hold to preserve homeostasis. In Cinderella's case, she saw the depression in her father and altered her life, putting her plans on hold and taking on the maternal role in the hope of keeping her father happy. Of course this plan failed, as it enabled her father to do less about his marriage and work more. The plan was also hierarchically unsound because it put Cinderella on the same level as her father, an uncomfortable and inappropriate place for a daughter.

In family therapy, the therapist often sees a family's attempt at change when the first session happens. It is often that very attempt to change their interactions that leads to chaos. By simply asking the family "what have you tried so far," a multitude of *first-order change* strategies are explained, most of which have led to short-term change. In most families, when there is a *symmetrical escalation*, whereby two people escalate simultaneously, there is also a *complementary escalation*, whereby one person escalates to overcompensate for the other, such as that in the previously mentioned alcoholic family. Again, this keeps change at the first-order level. That level of change doesn't always last because the system doesn't change.

Second-order change (Watzlawick, Weakland, & Fisch, 1974) is a longer lasting change, because it requires a purposeful, systemic change. The lowly household thermostat, if broken, requires a physical manipulation or mechanical replacement to set a new temperature. Because it is a new thermostat, a new *system*, it will react differently, maybe more efficiently. By resetting the temperature, things are altered in a different manner, intentionally. Just telling Cinderella to stop being maternal and move on with her life will probably not have much of a chance in helping her to change cognitively and emotionally. That would be an attempt at *first-order change*. But if her father begins to see how his behavior "causes" Cinderella to take on the role, and he resets his behavior by working less, inviting his wife to travel with him, and take on more emotional changes, *second-order change* occurs. That's what happened when Cinderella's father looked up in the session and shared that he would not have to worry about finances any more . . . so he would spend more time at home with his wife. This pleased Cinderella enough that she felt her father could handle information about her sneaking out of the house to meet Prince Charming. The system evolved into a more operational one.

Morphostasis and Morphogenesis

The survival of families depends on two important processes. One is *morphogenesis* and the other is *morphostasis*. When an adolescent, such as Cinderella, grows up, plans to move out, and begin her own life, her family has two options:

1. Support and encourage her, because she is growing up, becoming independent, and needing to launch her academic career. Her family knows it is time to let go.
2. Discourage her from applying to college, as she is not ready to venture out on her own because she may not have the tools necessary to survive . . . she may fail. She must stay close to the nest until she is ready, if ever, to leave. After all, what will the parents, who have an unhappy marriage, do if there is no child to distract them from their sadness?

The first reaction is an example of *morphogenesis* (also referred to as *positive feedback*). In this case, the family is able to be flexible enough, despite their fond feelings for Cinderella, to let go and wish her well. Although not always happy that their offspring is launching, the family puts its own needs aside and sees the individual leaving the nest as an independent person who needs to continue growing. Even though it is a strain on the system, it is still considered "positive feedback" because in the end, positive occurrences result for the family in the form of flexibility and growth. At home, the family will then reorganize the chores, roles, and activities to accommodate this natural evolution of their family. As Cinderella leaves home, goes to college, and marries her prince, the chances are that her role will be given back to her stepmother, who then may desire to be closer to her husband.

The second reaction is that of a family where *morphostasis* (also referred to as *negative feedback*) occurs. Such families often have relational difficulties that keep them from launching their adolescent. Perhaps the marriage has been in shambles for years, with the father and the mother barely speaking except at dinnertime. If the adolescent leaves, the triangle that was created between her and her parents will be disconnected, meaning that the parents may have to face their marital dilemma. Thus, the family overprotects the daughter, which causes her to feel less confident in her own vision of the future, and she remains at home to keep her parents' relationship somewhat alive. The daughter may become depressed, because she is foregoing a normal life stage of launching into an adult. She may go to therapy as an individual and may be treated with antidepressants and complain about her life. Her parents "support" her in going to therapy, but are unable to let go. With the help of a family therapist, the daughter might be able to voice her need to leave to her parents in a session, with the therapist later suggesting that the couple come to therapy.

Morphogenesis and morphostasis occur throughout the family life cycle, such as when a family loses a loved one or must move to a new city. Both concepts happen, too, when a senior adult retires from a job where he worked for 50 years. The desire to finally retire may soon be met with resentment by a wife or partner who has enjoyed her solitude at home as a homemaker for 50 years. Suddenly, she is not alone and arguments abound about boundaries, chores, money, and so forth. Her desire to keep things the same and his desire to finally retire are met with conflict. What is helpful in cases such as this one is for a family therapist to see the couple and offer them an opportunity to negotiate "Chapter 2" in their lives, providing time for them to talk about what each of them wants individually and together. This renewed sense of purpose and vision does much for the elderly couple, who could easily get stuck in a rut and risk health problems later.

The Mechanics of How Families Process Their Lives

Although many families in distress may call a family meeting, some will go to therapy, as Cinderella did, and some may even have a shouting match in therapy. These are routes that aim to accomplish the same thing, although not always . . . to get the relationships back on track so that the family becomes a place of serenity, peacefulness, and comfort. This phenomenon is called *equifinality*, and the premise behind it is that there are many ways to achieve the same result. When the Mental Research Institute began in Palo Alto, its founders believed that problems were simply the results of the family trying to fix itself. Members tried many different avenues to make things better, but were unsuccessful. Thus, this change caused conflict. Equifinality is helpful, however, as it gives the family therapist a reason to believe that families can try different ways to solve their own problem and reach their goal. Some families, for example, may enforce rigid routines and curfews for their teenage children, hoping to teach them self- discipline and to follow rules for being responsible. Other families may be more lenient, asking the teenagers to negotiate a curfew that would be favorable for both parents who work and on the teenager's school responsibilities. Both seek to teach responsibility, yet both try different avenues to do so. Both may be successful.

Additionally, the concept of *equifinality* helps the family therapist by enabling him or her to be flexible in the strategies used during sessions. The communications therapists found that however they approached the family, in whatever manner, change occurred. In Cinderella's case, the therapist could have begun therapy by asking the father what he wanted for his family. That would have allowed the therapist to learn how sad he was because he felt he carried the burden of supporting his two stepdaughters and Cinderella forever. The therapist could have also begun with Cinderella, and helped her to voice her concerns for her father and also her personal concerns of feeling downtrodden by her stepmother and stepsisters. There were many ways to approach the family, but the end product would have led to change in the system and, when that occurs, roles change and behaviors follow suit.

Metacommunication: What Did You Say?

Gregory Bateson was a British anthropologist, social scientist, linguist, visual anthropologist, semiotician, and cybernetician who studied communications on all levels. He wrote about two different levels or functions: *report* and *command* (Bateson, 2000). A mother desiring that her 10-year-old son become more spontaneous, in the hope that he will initiate friendships at school, may scold him by saying, "Good grief, go be spontaneous." She means well, but her command negates what she is trying to instill in him. This is a *metacommunication*. It is a covert message and often is not noticed because it is attached to the first message. How the message is presented through the tone of voice, body language, or action has everything to do with how well it is received and then put into action.

In Cinderella's family, the tone of the stepmother toward Cinderella often "put Cinderella in her place" as a lowly servant. However, a closer observation into the family dynamics showed us that the stepmother was simply jealous of Cinderella's popularity. Rather than talk directly about her jealousy, she sent a metamessage each time she spoke to Cinderella that hurt Cinderella's feelings and made her feel worse about herself. Her metamessage not only kept Cinderella "in her place," but also kept her stuck.

In families, metacommunication can be handed down through generations, creating havoc unless stopped. A young daughter's mother may tell her to grow up and ignore her violent alcoholic father's behaviors. This suggestion of not talking about what was happening keeps the daughter unsure of her real feelings, and makes her question what she thinks. Later in life, the mother may continue their relationship with similar messages of "I love you, you are wonderful," but "You are wrong about this situation, do it this way." The grown daughter may later come to therapy describing how she was reared, with little clue that her mother kept her stuck with metacommunication. A family therapist can then ask the daughter to describe how she would like to live her life as an adult, by opening doors for the daughter to see the metacommunication patterns and learn how to respond so that the mother stops sending the messages.

It is a wise family therapist who can observe metacommunication during sessions, as it teaches the therapist how the system operates. Then, when the metacommunication patterns materialize again, the therapist can intervene, asking the person spoken to what the message meant to him. This examination of interactions will allow family members to identify how they are communicating and what to try that would be more successful.

The Double Bind

A mother brings her 7-year-old daughter to a therapist because the girl is refusing to stay at school when the mother takes her each day. During therapy, the girl sits on her mother's lap and sucks her thumb, clinging to her mother with her other arm. The mother laments how hard a recent move has been for her family, particularly for her, the mother, who left her job and good friends. Although the mother talks about her concern for her daughter, the mother consistently comes back to her own hardship. When the therapist asks the mother what she desires for her daughter, the mother replies that she wants her daughter to be more independent again, like how she was in the town they lived in before. But the more the mother tries to remove her daughter from her lap, the more she clings. The therapist talks to the child later, and learns that she is worried about her mother. The child says that her mother is lonely without her at home. When the mother comes into the therapy room, the therapist asks the child to tell her mother that she is worried about her. The mother is surprised and tells the daughter that she needn't worry. The therapist encourages more dialogue from the mother about her plans for making new friends, finding a job, and so forth. The therapist also encourages the mother to talk about her plans for the day each morning when she drives her daughter to school. The daughter soon attends school without complaint and makes new friends.

The previous scenario is a classic example of a *double bind*, a situation in which a person gets two conflicting demands and can't seem to win by pursuing either demand. The double bind is often seen in families, where one family member is told to do one thing but the interactions and behaviors of other family members tell him or her otherwise. Identifying times when a double bind is occurring helps the family therapist to dissect the communication and behavior behind the double bind, so that the family can begin sending out clearer communications. This is done by a family therapist asking a member who is trapped by the double bind to explain how he or she reacts to and feels about such messages. Once out in the open, the therapist can then help the member discuss how trapped he or she feels and then discuss what needs to happen so that he or she can respond and behave.

In Cinderella's family, if the stepmother wanted a good relationship with Cinderella's father, she might have encouraged him to be open and honest about his work schedule (he often stopped off at the local pub on the way home from work to avoid her) so that she could trust him and thus rekindle their relationship. When the father tried to begin telling her that he stopped by for a drink with the other local artisans, she criticized him for associating with such downtrodden folk that were below her. She thought that such criticism would discourage his involvement at the pub, but it worked the opposite by convincing him he needed to stay away. If he came home to her, it would be giving in to her convictions and not honoring his needs. He was already feeling like less of a man. He was in a double bind.

Emotional Strategies of Families

One of Lyman Wynne's contributions to the field of family therapy was that of his observation of schizophrenic families and their attempts to deal with emotions. As an American psychiatrist and psychologist, he found that they often dealt with emotions in positive and negative, hostile, and unreal way. These patterns were called *pseudomutu.* Wynne was famous for his coined phrase "rubber fence," which described how families would encourage their members to move forward, but keep the rubber fence as a guardian that the members did not move too far out of the family's control. He created the term *pseudomutuality*, describing how a couple may keep up a front of being a loving couple, yet at home are distant. Another term used by Wynne to describe how families keep symptoms developing was *pseudohostility*, a technique whereby bickering keeps a couple from being close, often resulting in their going outside the relationship for intimacy.

If Cinderella was told repeatedly that she should venture out, have her own life, and be productive, she might have done so. But if, in addition to these positive affirmations, she was also told that without her, the household would probably fall into disaster, which would probably also cause her father to be depressed again, she might have felt guilty and never left home. Other comments might also influence her decision. The townspeople might have remarked how "loyal" Cinderella was to stay with her family. Her parents might even say that it was her decision to stay on until she found just the right castle apartment, although they constantly told her that she could save so much more money by living at home.

By these interactions, Cinderella's parents would have been experiencing a double bind. When Cinderella eventually became depressed as a result of feeling stifled in her life, the parents would have wondered why she felt sad. After all, they simply wanted the best for her but, apparently, she simply wasn't ready to move out on her own. Cinderella would begin to feel guilty, say that she wanted to do right by her father and everyone would pretend that things were fine. This is pseudomutuality at its finest. And it cripples people from growing and, in this case, launching.

Then there were the stepsisters. Each of them had sought affection and love from their stepfather for years. They tried to get it through normal means, but with the stepfather working until all hours of the night; their only recourse was to become angry, hostile, and constantly critical of everyone. Their constant sniping and arguing masked their deeper need for longing, affection, and closeness. Unfortunately, when families have patterns of *pseudohostility,* they often produce offspring who know no other way of communicating. The stepsisters' chances of having healthy, loving, and understanding relationships with partners were slim. Their needs were never met, so they would pursue them being met by others, at all costs.

GENOGRAMS: MAPPING FAMILY LIFE

Monica McGoldrick, a groundbreaking family therapist, and her colleagues (McGoldrick, Gerson, & Petry, 2008) at the Multicultural Family Institute of New Jersey, created *genograms* as a diagnostic tool to help families see patterns within their past and present. Genograms display not only family relationships (mother, father, brother, sister, son, daughter, etc.) but

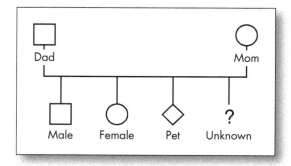

FIGURE 1.1 ■ Gender symbols used in genograms.
Source: GenoPro® http://www.genopro.com

also the emotional issues between family members. Genograms assist the family therapist in understanding the relationships, symptoms, and presenting problem's function. Families are often intrigued by genograms, and it is suggested that the family therapist show the family how their genogram is constructed. This transparent approach continues to build the *therapeutic relationship* (see Chapter 2) and assists the family to identify patterns on their own.

> *Over the past few decades use of the genogram as a practical tool for mapping family patterns has become more and more widespread among health-care professionals. As genograms have become widely used in the fields of medicine, psychology, social work, and the other health care, human service, and even legal fields, I wrote, originally with Randy Gerson,* Genograms: Assessment and Intervention, *a practical guide to genograms, now in its second edition and published by W. W. Norton, to illustrate more fully the growing diversity of family forms and patterns in our society and the applications of genograms in clinical practice. The genogram is still a tool in progress. (McGoldrick, 2010)*

Below are some basic ideas of how to construct a genogram, from GenoPro, a genogram software package (http://www.genopro.com/genogram). Note that other software packages may use slightly different symbols, but the underlying principles are the same.

Figure 1.1 shows the symbols used to identify gender. Male individuals are noted with a square shape, females with a circle.

Figures 1.2 and 1.3 show various symbols for children, pregnancy, and miscarriage, including multiple births. The children are placed below the parental line from the oldest

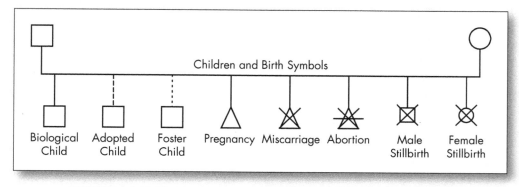

FIGURE 1.2 ■ Various genogram symbols for children and pregnancy.
Source: GenoPro® http://www.genopro.com

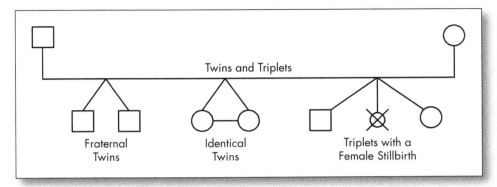

FIGURE 1.3 ▩ Genogram symbols for multiple births.
Source: GenoPro® http://www.genopro.com

to the youngest, left to right. Although this may sound obvious, it will be very important to remember these rules when the situation becomes a bit more complex.

Example: Figure 1.4 shows a husband with three spouses. The husband had three children with the first wife, and then divorced. The husband married the second wife, had one child and separated. The husband currently lives with another woman. As you can see, the oldest child is at the left, and the youngest child, the *half sister*, is at the right of her family, as she is the only child of the husband and the second wife.

Reversing this scenario to depict the wife having had multiple husbands, we get the genogram shown in Figure 1.5, which depicts a female with three husbands. She had three children with her first husband and divorced. She remarried, had one child with her second husband, and now lives with someone else. Please notice that the oldest child is always at the left-most position of the family of his parents. In this scenario, the "oldest brother" is older than the twins and the half sister; however, the half sister must be placed under the family of her biological parents. Because the second marriage is after the first marriage, it follows that the half sister is younger than the children from the first marriage. The half sister, therefore, appears to the left, although she is not the oldest child.

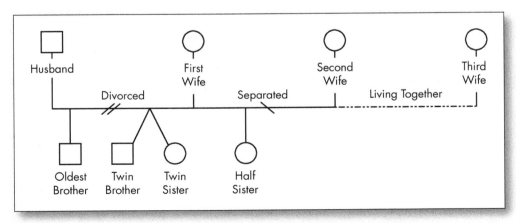

FIGURE 1.4 ▩ Genogram of a husband with multiple wives.
Source: GenoPro® http://www.genopro.com

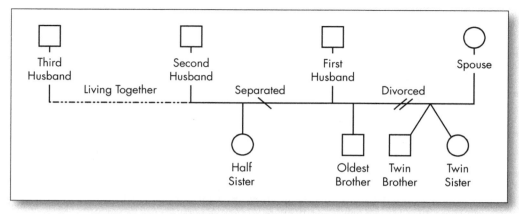

FIGURE 1.5 ■ Genogram of a wife with multiple husbands.
Source: GenoPro® http://www.genopro.com

In summary, here are the three rules to build a genogram:

1. The male parent is always at the left of the family, and the female parent is always at the right of the family.

2. Always assume male–female relationships when drawing the genogram until the client specifies a same-sex relationship. This is done as a protection, because early generations did not always acknowledge same-sex relationships. It is also helpful to ask a client who seems ambiguous whether the relationship is with a male or female, for clarity.

3. A spouse must always be closer to his or her first partner, then the second partner (if any), the third partner, and so on . . . The oldest child is always at the left of his family; the youngest child is always at the right.

As family therapists begin drawing genograms with their family clients, it is important to ask about the relationships between family members, particularly if the family therapist uses a Bowen family systems theory, structural, strategic, contextual, or a cognitive behavioral model of family therapy. By soliciting from the family client how the relationships developed and evolved to present day, the family therapist will learn about patterns of interactions.

Many family therapists use the genogram when working with a client dealing with a dangerous situation such as substance abuse. By drawing the genogram with the family's assistance, other addictive habits are identified. Additionally, if a couple comes for marriage counseling and, after assisting the family therapist in drawing the genogram, notices the pattern of divorce and infidelity in both of their family genograms, or even one of their genograms, the family therapist will learn how previous generations dealt with marital issues. Also, identifying trends in a family toward religion, cultural beliefs, and activities that influenced interactions and choices is valuable for the family therapist to identify with the families. This rich history explains not only to the family therapist how the family arrived at the current dilemma, but also provides an opportunity for the family to explain to the therapist who they are. This dialogue is essential, especially with families of different ethnicities and cultures. A family therapist should always be ready to ask these families, "Would you teach me who you are and how I may work with you best?"

Emotional cutoffs and dyads will be discussed in later chapters in this book, and are also identifiable through drawing genograms. For example, Cinderella and her stepsisters were emotionally cut off at the insistence of the stepsisters, who were jealous of Cinderella. However, when asked about what they desired, they mentioned that they really wanted a relationship with Cinderella. By examining the genogram with the family, the family therapist may find that the stepmother also distanced herself from her siblings as a young girl, leading to loneliness and, later, a tendency to try and control her environment in an unhealthy manner. The wise family therapist who notices such patterns and asks the family to discuss them may find that the family begins healing on its own, recognizing that past cutoffs and strategies did not work.

Family therapists using a solution-focused or narrative family therapy approach may also find the use of genograms helpful in identifying "exceptions" or "unique outcomes" in a family's history. For example, a family coming to therapy with a substance-abuser family member may work with a solution-focused family therapist to identify family members who did not use drugs or alcohol, but did deal with problems in a healthy manner. This identification of healthy family members becomes a resource for the client and an opportunity for the family therapist to explore with the family what the healthy person might say to the substance abuser.

Narrative family therapists may look at the genogram as the family's story, and encourage the family to keep looking closer for "unique outcomes" of times when the family went through challenging times. As a solution-focused and narrative family therapist, I often use exceptions and unique outcomes to empower the client family and the identified client, and invite them to create the next generation genogram. For example, using a current genogram, I may ask a young adult client dealing with substance abuse, "Suppose we were to fantasize and draw in the next generation, a product of your future relationship with someone. How do you want your children to develop as young adults? What behaviors do you think you need to begin taking on so that such development is possible in the future? And who can you use in your family now to help guide you there?"

These are just a few of the applications of the genogram in family therapy. Families enjoy the process of developing a genogram with their family therapist and often ask for a copy to take home.

In addition to the genogram used by family therapists, the *culturagram* may be a great addition to the family therapy toolbox. The culturagram was created by Dr. Elaine Congress, a professor and associate dean at Fordham University Graduate School of Social Service. She writes:

> *The Culturagram is a family assessment tool I developed to help social workers and others under-stand better families from different cultural backgrounds. It basically consists of a diagram with 10 different aspects. I think of culture as not being a singular concept, a singular term. Under cul-ture I feel is subsumed race, ethnicity, national origin, and religion, as well as values and beliefs. So I feel as social workers it's very important for us to understand completely the cultural back-ground of families we work with. I've decided that one way to really do this would be to develop a tool to help social workers really better assess the families they work with. (Congress & Kim, 2007)*

Figure 1.6 is an example of a culturagram, which is included to provide an additional tool for family therapists who work with diverse families.

USING DOCUMENTATION TO RECORD YOUR UNDERSTANDING OF FAMILIES

One just has to go to the local shopping mall, sit for awhile, and watch families interact to understand the various roles, cultures, rules, and interactions that govern who they are and who they will become. Imagine sitting in an office with five other people; some adults, some adolescents. One can only listen to so many messages, metamessages, actions, perceptions, observations, and comments at once. It means that you, the new family therapist, may, at

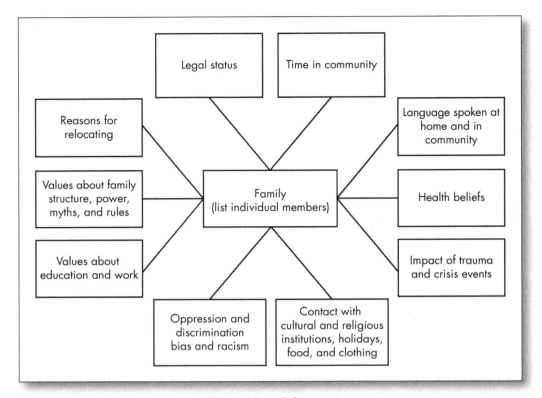

FIGURE 1.6 ▨ Culturagram.

Source: Singer, J. B. (Host). (2008, December 1). Visual assessment tools: The Culturagram—Interview with Dr. Elaine Congress [Episode 46]. Social Work Podcast. Podcast retrieved February 22, 2011, from http://socialworkpodcast.com/2008/12/visual-assessment-tools-culturagram.html

times, find yourself as more than a therapist . . . you may find yourself to be a mediator, a coach, a confidant, and a professional friend. You may be the only one in the family system (because you will become part of the system) who can clearly see the dynamics that keep the problem alive. The way that you share your observations, which then turn into interventions, is what the rest of this book is all about.

To begin, however, you will need to keep notes, both during and after the session is over. Notes serve many purposes. For you, the family therapist, they will keep you grounded as you record interactions that you hear about other family members onto the genogram.

Besides the genogram, you should keep notes of every session. Figure 1.7 displays a sample format that I share with practicum students for them to use during their sessions.

The last question on the Therapy Notes sheet is helpful because it reassures the family therapist that he or she is on track and relays a sense of respect to the family for their opinion about the session. The question also helps keep everyone involved in the process and helps you, the therapist, to know what works best during therapy sessions.

The Therapy Notes sheet can be altered to your family therapy model's specifications. For example, if you use a solution-focused approach (see Chapter 12), you may add a line for The Miracle Question, which is a marvelous goal-setting question. If you use an experiential approach (see Chapter 7), you may add a line for your impressions of the family for later review. If you use a narrative approach (see Chapter 13), leave some blanks for language used by the client that you can use in your conversation with the client.

Therapy Notes

Date: _____

Client name: _____ Age: _____ Sex: _____ Race: _____

Marital status: _____ Family members present: _____

Therapist name: _____

Family therapy model used by therapist: _____

Presenting problem (reason for seeking therapy according to the client):

_____

_____

_____

_____

Draw a genogram on the back of this form.

Goal of therapy:

_____

_____

_____

Strategies developed during the session:

_____

_____

_____

Strengths/Assets of the family:

_____

_____

_____

Task for client:

_____

_____

What client found useful from the session today:

_____

_____

FIGURE 1.7 ▧ Sample therapy note.
Source: ©Linda Metcalf, 2009

CONCLUSION

Becoming a family therapist involves more than reading and understanding theory. It involves practice. It takes drawing a genogram, listening intently for client language and goals, and stepping into a system that will teach you how it operates. Tread softly into this new territory, and do so with curiosity and understanding. Families will welcome the family therapist who empathizes and shares their concern, then gently guides them toward change. The rest of this book will provide insight into those strategies that will give both, you, the family therapist, and your families, direction.

KEY TERMS

Affect   A facial, vocal, or other behavior that serves to indicate a person's emotional status.

Circular causality   The multiple transactions between family members and how each interaction affects other interactions.

Complementary escalation   One spouse or a family member's attempt to give in to another family member to stop a behavior, but results in an escalation of the behavior.

Cybernetics   The interdisciplinary study that describes the vast interplay of networks involved with communication within a system.

Differentiation   The capacity of a person to manage his or her emotions while thinking rationally regarding his or her individuality and his or her connections to others.

Double bind   A dilemma in communication in which an individual or group of individuals receives two or more conflicting messages, where one message negates the other, prohibiting either response from being favorable.

Equifinality   The principle stating that an attempt to achieve a certain end can be approached and reached by many potential means.

First-order change   The idea that doing more or less of something we are already doing, such as raising the temperature on a thermostat, can be reversed and thus is not significantly different enough to create long-lasting change.

Genogram   A pictorial display of a person's family relationships and medical history that goes beyond a traditional family tree by including hereditary traits, patterns, and relationships.

Homeostasis   A tendency for systems to maintain stability, balance, or equilibrium at all times.

Metacommunication   Communication that supports or contradicts verbal communication, often sending a message that is in direct conflict with the words used because of the physical traits exhibited when the communication occurs.

Morphogenesis   The evolutionary development of the structure of an organism or part that creates new organizational forms. The change can occur when environments change, thereby being adaptive or change can occur as a result of positive feedback, which may be destructive.

Morphostasis   The process of retaining a structure, organization, or form in a system.

Negative feedback   Interactions that allow the family to respond superficially by adopting first-order changes that serve only to temporarily alleviate any threat to homeostasis, yet does not result in long-lasting change.

Positive feedback   Interactions that allow the family system to acquire a new level of homeostasis by adopting more long-term and permanent solutions, such as adapting to an adolescent's need for independence and growth.

Pseudohostility   Constant but superficial bickering that is used as a way of avoiding intimacy.

Pseudomutuality   A facade of togetherness, but little affection or real intimacy occurs.

Second-order change   A major transition that occurs within a system (or within an individual person) that leads to long-lasting change.

Symmetrical escalation   When a standoff occurs, leading to escalation between persons.

Symptom bearer   In families, the person acting out to get attention to the system's dysfunction.

Systems theory   An interdisciplinary theory that studies the complex nature of systems and the interactions within the systems.

Triangle   A dynamic created when tension arises between two people, and a third person is engaged to relieve the tension between the original two people, who then focus on the third person, rather than dealing with the tension.

REFERENCES

Ashby, W. R. (1956). *An introduction to cybernetics.* London, England: Chapman & Hall.

Bateson, G. (2000). *Steps to an ecology of mind: Collected essays in anthropology, psychiatry, evolution, and epistemology.* Chicago, IL: University of Chicago Press.

Bateson, G., Jackson, D. D., Haley, J., & Weakland, J. (1972/1956). Toward a theory of schizophrenia. In G. Bateson, *Steps to an ecology of the mind* (pp. 201–227). New York, NY: Ballantine. (Reprinted from *Behavioral Science, 1,* 251–264.)

Congress, E., & Kim, W. (2007). A comparative study on social work ethical codes in Korea and the United States: Focused on confidentiality, dual relationships, cultural diversity and impaired colleagues. *Korean Journal of Clinical Social Work, 4* (2).

Gillies, D. A. (1982). *Nursing management as a systems approach* (pp. 56–74). Philadelphia, PA: W. B. Saunders.

McGoldrick, M., Carter, B., & Garcia-Preto, N. (2010). *The expanded family life cycle: Individual, family, and social perspectives* (4th ed.). Upper Saddle River, NJ: Prentice-Hall.

McGoldrick, M., Gerson, R., & Petry, S. (2008). *Genograms: Assessment and intervention, third edition.* W. W. Norton. Retrieved from http://www.multiculturalfamily.org/genograms/

Minuchin, S., Nichols, M., & Lee, W. (2006). *Assessing families and couples: From symptom to system.* Boston, MA: Allyn & Bacon.

Senge, P. (2006). *The fifth discipline.* Strawberry Hills, Australia: Currency Press.

Watzlawick, P., Weakland, J., & Fisch, R. (1974). *Change: Principles of problem formation and problem resolution.* New York, NY: W. W. Norton.

Wiener, N. (1948). *Cybernetics or control and communication in the animal and the machine.* Paris, France: Hermann et Cie, and Cambridge, MA: MIT Press.

RECOMMENDED READING LIST

Books

Hoffman, L. (1981). *Foundations of family therapy*. New York, NY: Basic Books.

Hoffman, L. (2001). *Family therapy: An intimate history*. New York, NY: W. W. Norton & Company.

McGoldrick, M., & Hardy, K. (Eds.). (2008). *Re-Visioning family therapy: Race, culture, and gender in clinical practice* (2nd ed.). New York, NY: The Guilford Press.

Nelson, T., Trepper, T., & Thomas, F. (1998). *Tales from family therapy: Life-changing clinical experiences*. Binghamton, NY: The Haworth Press, Inc.

von Bertalanffy, L. (1976). *General system theory: Foundations, development, applications*. New York, NY: George Braziller, Inc.

Websites

GenoPro
http://www.genopro.com/genogram

Multicultural Family Institute
http://www.multiculturalfamily.org/

The Self of the Therapist

2

—

—

—

—

—

—

—

—

—

—

—

—

—

—

—

—

—

—

—

—

—

—

—

—

—

—

—

—

—

—

The Self of the Therapist

2

The Self of the Therapist   2

Katherine A. Goodell, Britt G. Sudderth,
and Corey D. Allan

Before you can find that theory that meets you halfway, that underscores what you already know, you need to know what you know, you need to name the values and core beliefs that run your life.

—Robert Taibbi

INTRODUCTION

As you embark on the journey into the world of family therapy, you may reflect on the question, "What is it that draws me to this profession?" Although there is probably no one answer, it is important to be aware of the experiences in your life thus far that have aided in your personal and professional growth. One's self-awareness is a critical component of skilled clinical practice. Being aware of your own experiences will not only assist you in becoming an effective family therapist, but it will also sustain you as you mature in this profession. This chapter aims to help you use who you are in the therapy room, yet also maintain an effective boundary between your professional and personal lives.

PARADIGMS AND THEORIES MAKE THE FAMILY THERAPIST UNIQUE

Throughout the development of any field of study, research, or practice, a certain amount of reflection on the field's key issues and one's role within that field must take place (Boss, Doherty, LaRossa, Schumm, & Steinmetz, 1993). To put it another way, seeking to answer these questions for one's self is vital:

Why am I drawn to this profession?

What is my personal view of the theories and techniques within my profession?

Which theory of practice is most closely in line with my own beliefs?

When the field of study is family therapy, there are many theories and foundational tenets to consider. Any field of science operates under its own *theory*—the framework, assumptions, and prevailing views within that field—and any new practitioner will study these paradigms (Kuhn, 1962). A theory is essential to a field of study in that "no natural history can be interpreted in the absence of at least some implicit body of intertwined theoretical and methodological belief that permits selection, evaluation, and criticism" (Kuhn, 1962, pp. 16–17). The importance of a theory comes into play throughout one's professional career. However, a theory is a lot more than the way a therapist conceptualizes what he or she does (Schnarch, 2000). Within family therapy, a theory will guide and influence your work with families, and the direction therapy will travel. Inevitably, there will come a time when a therapist will be unsure about which path to take with a family. At that time, it should be the therapist's theory that will determine the next step.

Another important fact is that new theories will only emerge because of anomalies that cannot be explained or solved by existing theories (Kuhn, 1962). Kuhn further posits that theories are competitive and, as such, new theories can only develop by replacing rather than incorporating rivals. In the field of family theory, however, Jetse Sprey (1988) proposes that "most current approaches are not necessarily unique in the sense that their underlying theoretical and methodological assumptions contradict those of all others. Nor are they necessarily competitive with each other" (p. 881).

As you begin your journey in the field of family therapy, it is best to become a follower of a theory or paradigm and its community. It is, however, equally important that you retain your own identity and self throughout the process. The idea of *bias-free psychotherapy* came in large part from the psychoanalytic view that analysts should be blank screens to amplify transference reactions and intensify the projections of clients (Patterson, 1989). Carl Rogers was an influential American psychologist and is listed among the founders of the humanistic approach to psychology. He further advanced this idea with his concept of therapist neutrality, although he himself admitted that a therapist could not practice without supplying evidence of personal values and views of human nature (Rogers, 1957):

> *The guru instructs by metaphor and parable, but the pilgrim learns through the telling of his own tale. Each man's identity is an emergent of myths, rituals, and corporate legends of his culture, compounded with the epic of his own personal history . . . The paradoxical interstice of power and vulnerability, which makes a man most human, rests on his knowing who he is right now, because he can remember who he has been, and because he knows who he hopes to become. (Kopp, 1972, p. 14)*

CHOOSING YOUR THEORY

Family therapy offers various models for professional students to learn and practice. As you enter this profession, there will be many opportunities for personal growth and challenge. One of those areas is choosing which model of family therapy best suits your beliefs and personality. This challenge can be exciting and overwhelming. This chapter aims to help you learn from two master therapists who, like you, once started as students. The goal is to initiate a *self-inventory*, which will guide you in understanding why a model fits your personality and belief system. Furthermore, it is our hope that this chapter will aid you in understanding how valuable you are as an individual to therapy and to give you a guideline of different ideas on how to grow as a therapist.

According to Robert Taibbi (1996), theories are "tools for organizing. They are the peg board upon which we hang what we see and hear; they show us where to look and what to listen for" (p. 134). Theories provide us with a lens to view the world. When deciding on a theory that fits your belief system and personality, the first step is taking a personal inventory. To further explore your philosophy, Taibbi (1996) provides a suggested list of questions that can supplement your self-inventory. After the inventory is completed, the next step is to select a theory. The following is a personal inventory questionnaire created by the authors of this chapter, which may help you identify the family therapy model that fits you best.

Personal Inventory Questionnaire

Review the following statements and rate your degree of agreement regarding how it fits your personality and beliefs as a family therapist.

1 = strongly disagree

2 = disagree

3 = neither agree nor disagree

4 = agree

5 = strongly agree

1. I believe change happens over time.	1 2 3 4 5
2. I believe I am a coauthor with my client.	1 2 3 4 5
3. I believe my experiences can aid my clients.	1 2 3 4 5
4. I believe in letting my client lead the session.	1 2 3 4 5
5. I believe in prescribing intervention techniques designed to make the client change.	1 2 3 4 5
6. I believe the client's past experiences can create different meanings through new perspectives.	1 2 3 4 5
7. I believe past generations directly play a significant part in understanding family roles.	1 2 3 4 5
8. I believe that understanding family roles can help clients to change their current roles.	1 2 3 4 5
9. I believe that a hierarchy exists within each system.	1 2 3 4 5
10. I am a direct person.	1 2 3 4 5
11. I am a problem solver.	1 2 3 4 5
12. I am a team player.	1 2 3 4 5
13. I am a storyteller.	1 2 3 4 5
14. I am a quiet observer.	1 2 3 4 5
15. I am an empathetic listener.	1 2 3 4 5
16. I am an explorer.	1 2 3 4 5
17. I am a curious person.	1 2 3 4 5
18. I am a jokester.	1 2 3 4 5
19. I am a change agent.	1 2 3 4 5
20. I am a risk taker.	1 2 3 4 5

From this inventory, examine the items you marked as a 4 or 5 and begin identifying, more specifically, the traits that you possess that will assist you well as a family therapist. Remember, choosing a theory affords therapists the opportunity to explore who they are as a person, what their fundamental beliefs are, and what assumptions they hold about the world. Selecting a theory is similar to walking into a hat store and trying on hats from different generations, different parts of the world, and with different functions.

As you try on these hats (theories), remember the self-inventory and take notice of which theory aligns with you the best. If the hat doesn't fit your personality, or feel right, take this opportunity to try a different one. There may be moments when a particular hat looks and possibly feels good; however, at further glance, you may find that the hat was made for someone else. It might take trying on a couple of different styles before your fit is found.

For some, your hats will change depending on the clients you see, or how your vision of families changes. Remember, it is not important how many hats you try or buy; rather, it is the process of choosing which hat or hats fit best. Piercy and Sprenkle (1988) stated this idea best with "regardless of format, the goal is to challenge students to challenge themselves to link theory and practice. Through the process, students become explorers rather than passive passengers on a guided tour" (pp. 307–309). From the information you gain by doing this self-inventory, summarize what you have learned about yourself and keep that in mind as you go further in your practice.

This Theory Might Be for You If . . .

Read the following list of theories and corresponding beliefs. From the personal inventory, check out the theories that fit the answers you checked with a 4 or 5. Use this to determine which theories might be a match for you.

Bowen family systems theory (see Chapter 3) may be for YOU if:

- You believe human potential is shaped by human interaction.
- You think of family functioning as a natural process rooted in biology and evolution.
- You observe relationship patterns repeating across generations.
- You are committed to "growing yourself up."

Rational emotive behavior therapy (see Chapter 6) may be for YOU if:

- You prefer a direct and active therapeutic approach that is used to assist clients in overcoming their destructive beliefs, feelings, and behaviors.
- You believe clients will change their behavior in relationships by assisting clients to identify new beliefs.

Cognitive behavioral therapy (see Chapter 5) may be for YOU if:

- You prefer a direct therapeutic approach in assisting clients with changing the way they feel and, therefore, act by changing the way they think about things.
- You like being in charge and directing clients to do homework assignments.
- You like organizing a session and keeping track of the therapeutic process.

Family psychoeducation (see Chapter 16) may be for YOU if:

- You prefer an active approach, with an educational emphasis, for helping individuals and their families.
- You like gathering information in manuals, books, and pamphlets and going over such information with families in an attempt to educate them.
- You believe that by educating people, they will use the information effectively.

Strategic family therapy (see Chapter 11) may be for YOU if:

- You think that problems serve a purpose in the lives of your clients.
- You think that clients are in need of a direct approach to reaching change in their lives.
- You see your role as that of setting goals for your clients and designing creative interventions that solve the presenting problem.

Structural family therapy (see Chapter 10) may be for YOU if:

- You believe that by changing the structure of a family, you change the interactions and, thus, the behaviors.
- You enjoy being directive, humorous, and suggestible to clients so that they see their roles differently.
- You like taking an active role in "restructuring" a family, sometimes rearranging them in a session, to illustrate patterns.

Medical family therapy (see Chapter 15) may be for YOU if:

- You can think systemically and can speak in linear terms.
- You enjoy collaboration with health professionals.
- You have a working knowledge of many diseases.
- You think that people with medical issues can benefit from family involvement and effective relationships.

Contextual family therapy (see Chapter 4) may be for YOU if:

- You have a strong commitment to fairness.
- You believe that motivations for present behavior are found in past interactions.
- Words such as justice, trustworthiness, balance of merit and obligation, and fairness attract your attention.
- You believe in loyalty and entitlement in relationships.
- You agree that trustworthiness is essential for individuals to conduct healthy relationships.

Symbolic-experiential family therapy (see Chapter 7) may be for YOU if:

- You believe life's lessons are learned through craziness, humor, failure, and spontaneity.
- You like the idea of stirring up issues in a family and then watching how the family dissects and reinvents itself.
- You like spontaneous and creative interventions that provoke conversations that otherwise would not have occurred.

Milan systemic family therapy (see Chapter 9) may be for YOU if:

- You like thinking outside of the box.
- You enjoy working in teams.
- You are full of questions and more questions.
- You are curious about families.
- You see your role as a therapist as helping the family to view the problem within a more systemic context.

Narrative therapy (see Chapter 13) may be for YOU if:

- You are concerned about promoting social justice.
- You would rather let your client be the expert rather than yourself.
- You really do believe that people make themselves up in stories as they live their lives.
- You are creative and like the idea that constructing new realities with clients can lead to new actions and beliefs.

Solution-focused brief therapy (see Chapter 12) may be for YOU if:

- You tend to notice the strengths and resources within others.
- You like to look at exceptions when a problem happens.
- You tend to focus more on the present than the past.
- You view your clients as experts on their own lives and see yourself as a facilitator of that discovery.

Emotionally focused therapy (see Chapter 14) may be for YOU if:

- You believe your earliest childhood experiences influence your adult behavior.
- You believe in attachment theory's (see Chapter 14) understanding of human relationships.
- You agree that feeling "secure" in your adult relationship is most important.
- You see your role as creating a collaborative alliance with your clients.

UNDERSTANDING YOURSELF IN THERAPY

The decision as to which model(s) are best suited for a particular therapist often is based on a goodness of fit between the therapist and the model as well as the therapist's opinion that the model is effective.

—M. Snider

"Young therapists may need support to see their experiences as a resource" (Roberts, 2005, p. 61). As a student, you can find this support through your professors, mentors, literature, and practical experience. As you journey through this process, it is helpful to identify your beliefs about people and the lifestyles and challenges they partake of in relationships.

Acknowledge Your Beliefs About People

How do you think about people and what they bring to therapy? As therapists, the unexpected gift we receive from our clients is their knowledge. The therapeutic relationship is at times cyclical. In healthy working therapeutic environments, we initiate change for our clients; our hope would be for our clients to initiate change in themselves. When occasions present for the therapists to change it is essential that the therapists have the training to be aware of the influence the client is having on them. "The therapist requires sufficient self-awareness to be conscious of the impact that the client is having on them and the skill to deal with that impact" (Smith, 2002, p. 121).

As you evolve as a therapist, it is hoped that you will explore your biases, because they can impede your work as a therapist. A *bias* is a belief that one holds regarding a particular topic. If you acknowledge your biases, both you and your clients have the opportunity for growth. When we do not acknowledge our biases, we rob our clients and ourselves of the potential for change. Satir, Banmen, Gerber, and Gomori (1981) understood the perception that one holds about the world colors his or her interactions with others.

> *As I perceive my picture of what the world is all about and how I am in it, it's going to be the basis for how I proceed in the world. So that whatever I am doing represents the way I'm seeing. (Satir et al., 1981, p. 24)*

Understanding our biases, which often come from our life experiences, enables us to acknowledge that other realities exist. Our biases develop as a result of our authentic self, the composite of all our skills, talents and wisdom, the things that are uniquely ours—rather than what we think we are supposed to be and do. Recognizing our authentic selves and biases safeguards us from having an unconscious agenda. Once you gain insight into your authentic self and your biases, you will most likely realize some that have the possibility of hindering effective therapy with particular clients. In such situations, it is your ethical obligation to refer those clients to another therapist.

For example, a female therapist who was sexually abused by her stepfather as a young adolescent, yet never legally reported the incident nor received therapy to work through her trauma, may experience "transference" when initially visiting with an adolescent girl with the same experience. The girl may come to the therapist at the encouragement of her mother, whom the girl told about the incident, to discuss whether she should press charges against her stepfather. The therapist may be biased that the girl should report the incident, since she did not report her own abuse. This will be unfair to the client, who needs to make her own decision.

The following list is meant to challenge you to be aware of what biases you hold or could potentially develop. Constant monitoring of your biases throughout your professional career as a therapist is essential to maintaining an ethical practice. Consider the following questions:

1. What are my personal beliefs about religion, if any?
2. Do I have biases toward a gender different than mine?
3. Do I hold biases toward clients of a different race than I?
4. How do I view someone with a different ethnicity than mine?
5. Does a client's age influence how I work in therapy, particularly elderly clients?
6. How do I perceive different cultures and their role in therapy?
7. How do I perceive politics and its place in therapy?
8. How do I perceive a person's educational background and its influence on how I conduct therapy?
9. What are my values about money?
10. What is my view of sex and how it should be discussed?
11. What is my view of clients with a different sexual orientation than mine?

Monitoring yourself and your biases is one method of staying aware of changes that might take place within the therapy process.

Beyond Transference

As you evolve as a family therapist, there will be many times when you will be seated across from clients who are facing similar struggles and concerns as you. This is called *transference*. The struggles may be current ones, or struggles that you experienced growing up. At these times, it is imperative that you remain focused on the client. It is also during these times when your theory will assist you and distract you the most. The following are some suggestions for dealing with the issue of transference:

1. Seek out a colleague or supervisor and discuss what is happening in the session with the client. Often, simply discussing the situation and then taking steps to seeing differences between you and the client can assist you in being more objective.

2. If transference is being felt by the client onto you, the therapist, ask if you remind the client of someone, discussing it directly.

3. Discuss with a colleague or supervisor how working with the client affects you as a therapist. Then, consider devising new thoughts that you can consider prior to each therapy session to help you stay focused and unbiased.

4. Consider seeking counseling to take care of your own issues that try to interfere in the therapy room. Or, seek peer supervision to assist you in helping the client most effectively.

5. Ultimately, if the transference you feel as a therapist, or that the client places on you in therapy, impedes you from doing your best work, talk to the client and explain that you feel a referral is in his or her best interest.

SELF-DISCLOSURE IN THERAPY

What is indisputable is that both therapists and clients struggle to traverse the unique relationship possibilities that therapy offers.

—Janine Roberts

Self-disclosure—the discussion of personal information by the therapist—has the potential to be both helpful and harmful to our clients depending on our motivation to disclose. To use self-disclosure in therapy as a tool is a choice each therapist has to make for himself or herself. The verdict is still out on whether or not disclosure produces desired change in therapy. Sigmund Freud warned other psychoanalysts against self-disclosure. He said that the analyst should remain anonymous, a blank slate on which people could project their unconscious fantasies, conflicts, and desires (Goode, 2002). Although many professional therapists disagree on the effectiveness of self-disclosure, ethically, all family therapists must abide by the The American Association for Marriage and Family Therapy Code of Ethics, and if such a disclosure will hurt or harm their client, the disclosure is unwarranted.

In thinking about a deliberate self-disclosure, it can be important to scan and identify why you think it might be useful to share that story. Will it provide new information for clients? Might it shift your relationship to them? Could it open the therapy and contribute to a healthy sense of shared vulnerability? Will who you are as a therapist and a person perhaps be more available to family members? (Roberts, 2005, p. 57)

Roberts (2005) created the following guideline and questionnaire, which can be helpful when deciding to use disclosure:

1. Check to make sure that your desire to share theoretical beliefs and values that you have is likely to be of interest, support, and use to your clients.

2. Be transparent tentatively and briefly, and look for feedback from clients.

3. After any type of disclosure, keep turning the conversation back to the clients' concerns and their story.

4. Scan and make sure that you are in emotional control of what you are going to share.

5. Make sure that you are not expecting a particular reaction from clients after you disclose something.

6. Offer information in a framework that emphasizes challenges you have faced and issues in process, rather than what the outcome was.

7. Be cognizant of what levels of disclosure are comfortable for you.

8. Think about how presenting information from your life or about your theoretical beliefs or values will affect joining, alliances, and coalitions.

9. Be attentive to what transparency can mean in your particular work setting.

10. Create, share, and write treatment plans and case reports with clients.

11. Overall, keep thinking about your intent whenever you disclose.

Those who believe self-disclosure produces effective change assert that several different positive results can follow a disclosure. Behavioral, cognitive, and cognitive behavioral therapies have emphasized the importance of modeling, reinforcement, and normalizing in therapy and view self-disclosure as an effective vehicle to enhance these techniques (Freeman, Fleming, & Pretzer, 1990; Goldfried, Burckell, & Eubanks-Carter, 2003). Such results can be normalizing struggles, aligning with clients, joining and the opportunity to model for your clients, humanizing the therapist, and introducing new perspective. Those who believe self-disclosure should be avoided or used minimally contest disclosure can lead to discrediting the therapist, unbalancing the therapeutic relationship, distrust of the therapist, agendas, produce undesired changes in the therapeutic environment, and has the potential to harm the client. "I have heard a lot of stories from clients about therapists telling them at length about their own problems," says Candace Coker Smith. "They find it unprofessional." But she often finds herself using the skills she teaches her clients, and she'll bring in those real-life examples. In summation, ". . . there are still many different positions regarding the appropriateness and timing of self disclosure and how these potentially powerful messages to clients should be managed" (Mills & Sprenkle, 1995, p. 373). The master therapist interviews at the end of this chapter also provide some interesting insights about self-disclosure.

SELF-CARE OF THERAPIST

We're talking about doing for yourself what you want your families to learn to do for themselves.

—Robert Taibbi

If there is one fundamental truth in being an effective therapist, it is that you must take care of yourself. *Self-care* includes taking care of your own emotional, physical, intellectual, and spiritual well-being. Self-care allows the therapist to continue to grow as a person. Furthermore, self-care provides the therapist an ability to be more present with clients. When a therapist does not take care of himself or herself, illness can happen, burnout can take place, and boredom in our profession can occur.

Part of self-care is self-monitoring, which enables the therapist to reconnect with his or her belief system, personal goals, theory, and authentic self on a regular basis. Taibbi (1996) illustrated an important aspect of self-care as self-supervision:

In between the dangers of being too easy and too hard on ourselves is the view that self-supervision can be a means of reflecting, of stepping back in a way from your work in order not to scold but to discover; to follow the path of your anxiety and emotions; to cast new light on your assumptions; to look at the patterns of your practice in much the same way we encourage families to look at the patterns in their own lives; to recognize in them the themes that run our living and our work." (p. 197)

In order to care for yourself as a therapist, it is vital to pay attention to *all* the components that make up who you are and how you function. The following list, adapted from the American Counseling Association (n.d.), offers many suggestions:

Wellness Activities: Cognitive

Meditation
Write journals
Read for pleasure
Hobbies
Volunteer at something *not* counseling related
Go to the movies, theater, symphony, museum, and county fair

Wellness Activities: Emotional

Talk to friends
Laugh
Keep in touch with important people
Participate in an encouragement exchange with a colleague
See a counselor
Give yourself permission to cry

Wellness Activities: Physical

Drink plenty of water
Eat regular meals
Exercise regularly
Get enough sleep
Turn off the computer/cell phone
Go for a walk during lunch
Get a massage
Yoga, acupuncture, and meditation

Wellness Activities: Spiritual

Take time for reflection

Learn to garden

Spend time outdoors

Find or connect with a spiritual community

MASTER THERAPIST INTERVIEW

DIANE R. GEHART

Diane R. Gehart, PhD, LMFT, is an associate professor of marriage and family therapy at California State University, Northridge. She coauthored with Amy Tuttle, PhD, Theory-Based Treatment Planning for Marriage and Family Therapists (Thomson/ Brooks/Cole, 1993), and completed a coedited volume with Harlene Anderson, PhD, Collaborative Therapy: Relationships and Conversations that Make a Difference (Routledge, 2007). She has practiced psychotherapy for 15 years and presently maintains a private practice in Thousand Oaks, California.

How did you pick a family therapy model?
When I heard folks from the Houston Galveston Institute describe what they did, I knew immediately that this theory fit for me. I had tried several others up to that point, none of which really fit. But I heard collaborative therapy described during a conference presentation, and I knew I had finally found my approach. I believe the connection was my prior training in Asian philosophy. Both Buddhism and social constructionism are founded on the idea that we construct our realities.

What advice would you give a new student who is picking a family therapy model?
Start with what feels like a good fit—what makes sense to you—and then work with your supervisor to try putting it into practice. I also think it is helpful to think of theory as a tool the therapist uses to be helpful to the client rather than the theory holding the "answer" for the client.

How did you refine the model to fit who you are and what you believe in?
Collaborative therapy is more of a philosophy of therapy than a model, so it fits with what I believe on most levels. I probably have added many more practical elements that are in the description of the theory, but all of my adaptations are consistent with the theory itself.

What role do you believe your personal history, experiences, relationships, views, and biases play in your work as a therapist?
Collaborative therapists believe that our personal histories create a set of norms and biases that color how we see clients. I try to be mindful of this with clients to minimize their affect on clients. I believe that my own personal work and journey are one of my greatest resources in being helpful to clients.

What are your goals as a therapist for your clients?
To be helpful to them in resolving their issues. I try to work with clients to find goals that are meaningful to them and work at a pace that is comfortable for them.

How do you continue to grow as a therapist?
My growth as a therapist happens primarily in two ways. First, I attend numerous conferences and trainings around the world and enjoy trainings in models other than my preferred approach. Along with this, I read books and journals to stay on top of the latest developments in the field. Second, I consciously develop myself, especially in the area of spirituality. I meditate, do yoga, and read from various traditions. My growth spiritually has deepened my work as a therapist.

How do you stay curious about your clients, your theory, and family systems?
Well, my theory is all about curiosity. It has become a habit. My practice of mindfulness meditation reinforces this habit. I think, if you really "get" the ideas of social constructionism and systems, it is impossible to not be curious—each client is always an adventure because each constructs the world in a different way.

What is your philosophy on self-disclosure?
I generally recommend that my trainees avoid it for the first couple of years because it is a double-edge sword that cuts quite deep. If it goes well, then it can be very meaningful. If it goes poorly, then the therapeutic relationship generally cannot be repaired. So I am very careful with how I use it and with whom. In general, I use it minimally. Self-disclosure has been most helpful when people are in crisis and need reassurance a little or when they feel as though they are the only ones on the planet who have experienced something. I find it is most harmful if the therapist [is] using their experience to set a norm, example, or goal for the client rather than allowing the client to find their own way to evaluate their situation and where to go. It also goes quite badly when the therapist unknowingly reveals something that somehow links to the client's life in a way the therapist does not predict—and the client is insulted, angered, or ashamed.

As a therapist, what self-care techniques do you find helpful?
Meditation, yoga, having good friends, journaling, spiritual practice, taking time when I need it, turning off my mobile phone when I [don't] need it, screening calls when I need to.

   Most new students have a lot of personal growth work to do before they can really be effective therapists. So it is important that new therapists find a way to explore who they are, why they respond to life as they do, and how to create a more balanced, productive, and peaceful life. My spiritual practice and faith is very important in my self-care. It gives me a way to make sense of all of the suffering I am seeing, helps me to keep my heart open, and provides guidance for how I can serve others while still taking care of myself. Life feels chaotic; I stop enjoying my work; I laugh less with my students and clients.

Alasdair MacDonald

A leading figure in solution-focused brief therapy (see Chapter 12), Alasdair MacDonald, MD, has greatly contributed to the field of family therapy. Alasdair maintains a private practice as a psychiatrist and supervises therapists in Dorchester, United Kingdom. He has written or edited more than 40 publications and numerous other texts.

How did you pick a family therapy model?
Systemic therapy and network therapy were newly popular during my postgraduate training and so training was available to me. While I was accumulating systemic experience, my supervisor moved to strategic therapy. I found this to be an effective model and so I followed him. My early trainers encouraged respect and attention towards clients. In my opinion, family work fits these values and is time efficient for clients. CBT [cognitive behavioral therapy] requires an expert and didactic attitude to clients, which I find uncongenial.

I had individual psychodynamic training including personal group therapy and a personal analysis. I did not find the insights gained from my personal analysis to be of direct relevance to family work. As a researcher, I review psychotherapy models for effectiveness, but none has been proven to be better than another. When solution-focused therapy became known, our team decided to try it for 6 months instead of our strategic/MRI style. We found it easier and more respectful to clients as well as requiring fewer sessions, and so we have never changed back. Integration is only helpful if one model is not sufficient. I now use solution-focused approaches first in almost every area of my professional work, including consultancy. Because psychotherapies have about 70% effectiveness, I believe that all therapists need skills in at least two models or treatments. Personally, I use medication or strategic approaches if solution-focused work is not effective, as well as referral for specialist input if it fits the client's goals. For example, I will use colleagues who specialize in teaching parenting skills or drug withdrawal.

What advice would you give a new student who is picking a family therapy model?
Study at least three different models. Read, observe sessions, talk to good practitioners, ask clients about their experience, and do this for all three models before deciding. If your trainers do not encourage this, make friends at conferences and visit them during your holidays. Your professional comfort and success depend on being content with the work that you do.

What have you as a person (with all your past experiences, family of origin, personal history, etc.) brought to the family therapy model that you use?
Respect for the resources and skills used by clients in leading their lives to the best of their ability. My training in individual therapy revealed the astonishing complexity of the lives led by the "easy" cases that were passed to the trainees.

My systemic training showed me the importance of teamwork and of context. I believe that these concepts influence my approach to therapy and to life in general.

How did you refine the model to fit who you are and what you believe in?

The move to solution-focused practice led to more enjoyment of my work and more confidence in my clients. So I believe that the model changed me rather than I refining the model. An interest in Zen Buddhism was a parallel development in my life. I see many similarities between the Buddhist teachings known to me and to solution-focused thinking and methods, but this may be a lack of understanding on my part. I was taught in my family that counseling was valuable to humanity. I try to focus on my client's values and not my own in therapy, beyond the necessary ethical and professional boundaries.

What are your personal goals as a therapist?

To assist my clients in moving forward so that their lives become more fulfilling and less painful. To publicize the value of solution-focused therapy, which I believe to be a significant advance in the field of psychotherapy.

How do you continue to grow as a therapist?

Every clinical session brings some new point of learning. I work as a trainer and supervisor, and receive regular interesting inputs from my supervision group and other colleagues. I am a researcher in psychotherapy, and I take part in national and international research and political action about the psychotherapies.

How do you stay curious about your clients, your theory, and family systems?

Curiosity is a healthy human trait. If I find myself uninterested in a session, then I assume that I have missed something important, which is distracting me in the session or in my own context. There is never enough time to explore all the interesting byways that are revealed in conversation with clients. At the same time, it is my task to do what is needed, not to pursue every interesting comment.

What is your philosophy on self-disclosure?

Rarely useful or appropriate. You are there about the client, not to say what you enjoy or what helps you. I occasionally use a generalized form of "self-disclosure" to introduce an idea as a possibility to a client. For example, I may say, "I saw someone recently who found _____ helpful" as a way of introducing _____ from a nonexpert position. "I once lived in a farming community" may assure a farmer that I know something about his troubles, even though I come from the city. If I do have specific advice for a client, I may disclose something about past contact with similar problems. "I have worked with a lot of alcoholics in my career" may reassure a drinker that my advice to reduce his intake is based on professional knowledge rather than moral outrage. Such comments should be kept general and should not be enlarged on; how will it be helpful to the client to know about your life? It is their life that you are paid to talk about.

There is more risk of crossing professional boundaries inappropriately if self-disclosure becomes extensive. You also become vulnerable to disqualifications by clients (e.g., "You said you had never been divorced so you don't know what it is like for me.") You do not need to have experienced something personally in order to provide therapy for it, but saying that to a client is unlikely to be productive. "Tell me more about it" will be a more useful response.

What are your thoughts on self-care of therapist?

There is an ethical duty on therapists, like other professionals, to be able to function competently. If you are tired, jet-lagged, drunk, or preoccupied, then you cannot give your client the attention they deserve. Self-care means not working when in such states and taking action to recover yourself from such states.

I aim to keep physically healthy, take medication when prescribed it, listen to (and sometimes take) advice from family and colleagues even if I don't like it. I seek to keep my workload within tolerable levels and I refuse to attempt tasks which are beyond my capabilities at a given moment. I maintain variety in my work and social life because I know that this helps me to function well. I have interests and relationships outside work, which give me additional satisfactions.

It is important for new students to recognize that they are human and have their own needs. They cannot help everybody and will initially feel dislike for about 10% of the people that they meet in their lives. If necessary, they need to arrange for someone else to treat these people. Time off and sleep are two things that you can never regain if you lose them. You can catch up later, but you cannot repair the work that you did while overtired or overloaded. My contact with spiritual values and my meditation practice help me to maintain my equanimity in difficult times. Many other people achieve similar benefits from nonreligious activities. It is the attention to your self and your needs that matters, not religion/faith as a concept. Outside therapy, my skills benefit from contact with colleagues. I value intellectual study within and outside the field of therapy (e.g., learning another language at evening class extends my knowledge of language as a means of communication as well as being fun). History, drama, and political information from TV and theater remind me of the huge variety possible within the human condition. Play with children shows the talents inherent in them, which we can hope to nurture and support. Every baby might be Shakespeare or Hitler or your best friend.

CONCLUSION

Now that you have reviewed some very important components to help you choose a model, your authentic self can start the dance of therapy. Just as dancers learn positions and steps for a performance, a therapist learns techniques and interventions from his or her models. The recital is ready once the dancers have not only learned the steps, but also, more importantly, have brought themselves to the stage. Like the dancer, the therapist who brings himself or herself to the process of therapy brings life not only to the model but also to the relationship with the client, and that becomes a duet. The life you bring to therapy includes your personality, life experiences, views, biases, and beliefs. As a new therapist, it can be easy to think that you have little to share with your clients. However, the reality is that the life you have lived thus far is filled with truth, wisdom, and knowledge. When all of these parts of yourself are acknowledged, your authentic self becomes invaluable to therapy.

Bias   A belief that one holds regarding a particular topic.

Client   A person who seeks a therapeutic relationship.

Family therapy   An approach to working on individual issues that occur in relationships in a therapy setting with significant others involved in the person's life.

Family therapy model   A specific, unique set of theoretical beliefs and strategies that assists a family therapist to help a family reconstruct healthy interactions.

Paradigm   A framework, assumption, and set of prevailing views.

Self-care   Taking care of your own emotional, physical, intellectual, and spiritual well-being.

Self-disclosure   A therapeutic technique that involves using personal information in an effort to build rapport, join with a client, and/or highlight a belief system.

Self-inventory   A questionnaire that provides feedback for one's awareness of his or her belief system.

Theory   An organization of thoughts and beliefs about the process of change.

Transference   A phenomenon that occurs when a client or therapist "transfers" a relationship from the past to a person in the present therapeutic relationship.

REFERENCES

American Counseling Association. (n.d.). Wellness strategies. Retrieved from http://www.counseling.org/wellness_taskforce/tf_wellness_strategies.htm

Boss, P. G., Doherty, W. J., LaRossa, R., Schumm, W. R., & Steinmetz, S. K. (Eds.). (1993). *Sourcebook of family theories and methods: A contextual approach*. New York, NY: Plenum Press.

Freeman, A., Fleming, B., & Pretzer, J. (1990). *Clinical applications of cognitive therapy*. New York, NY: Plenum Press.

Goldfried, M. R., Burckell, L. A., & Eubanks-Carter, C. (2003). Therapist self-disclosure in cognitive-behavior therapy. *Journal of Clinical Psychology, 59*, 555–568.

Goode, E. (2002, January 1). Therapists redraw line on self-disclosure. *New York Times*.

Kopp, S. B. (1972). *If you meet the Buddha on the road, kill him! The pilgrimage of psychotherapy patients*. Palo Alto, CA: Science and Behavior Books.

Kuhn, T. S. (1962). *The structure of scientific revolutions*. Chicago, IL: The University of Chicago Press.

Mills, S. D., & Sprenkle, D. H. (1995). Family therapy in the postmodern era. *Family Relations, 44*, 368–376.

Patterson, C. H. (1989). Values in counseling and psychotherapy. *Counseling and Values, 13*, 164–176.

Piercy, F. P., & Sprenkle, D. H. (1988). Family therapy theory-building questions. *Journal of Marital and Family Therapy, 14*, 307–309.

Roberts, J. (2005). Transparency and self-disclosure in family therapy: Dangers and possibilities. *Family Process, 44*, 45–63.

Rogers, C. (1957). A note on the nature of man. *Journal of Counseling Psychology, 4*, 199–203.

Satir, V., Banmen, J., Gerber, J., & Gomori, M. (1991). *The Satir model: Family therapy and beyond*. Palo Alto, CA: Science and Behavior Books.

Schnarch, D. M. (2000). Sexual desire: A systemic perspective. In S. R. Leiblum & R. C. Rosen (Eds.), *Principles and practices of sex therapy* (3rd ed.). New York, NY: The Guildford Press.

Smith, S. (2002). Transformations in therapeutic practice. *Contemporary Family Therapy, 24*, 111–128.

Sprey, J. (1988). Current theorizing on the family: An appraisal. *Journal of Marriage and the Family*, *50*, 875–890.

Taibbi, R. (1996). *Doing family therapy: Craft and creativity in clinical practice*. New York, NY: The Guilford Press.

RECOMMENDED READING LIST

Books

Carter, B., & McGoldrick, M. (Eds.). (1989). *The family cycle: A framework for family therapy*. Needham Heights, MA: Allyn & Bacon.

Hanna, S. M., & Brown, J. H. (2004). *The practice of family therapy: Key elements across models*. Belmont, CA: Brooks/Cole.

Hoffman, L. (1981). *Foundations of family therapy*. New York, NY: Basic Books.

Jourard, S. (1964). *The transparent self*. New York, NY: Van Nostrand Reinhold.

Kerr, M. (1981). Family systems theory and therapy. In A. S. Gurman & D. Kniskern (Eds.), *Handbook of family therapy* (pp. 226–264). New York, NY: Brunner/Mazel.

Odell, M., & Campbell, C. (1998). *The practical practice of marriage and family therapy*. Binghamton, NY: The Haworth Press.

Paolino, T. J., & McCrady, B. (1978). *Marriage and marital therapy: Psychoanalytic, behavioral, and systems theory perspectives*. New York, NY: Brunner/Mazel.

Polanyi, M. (1967). *The tacit dimension*. Garden City, NY: Doubleday.

Taibbi, R. (1996). *Doing family therapy: Craft and creativity in clinical practice*. New York, NY: The Guilford Press.

Articles

Beutler, L., Pollack, S., & Jobe, A. (1978). "Acceptance," values, and therapeutic change. *Journal of Consulting and Clinical Psychology*, *46*, 198–199.

Comfort, L. K. (1994). Initiating change: A dialogue between theory and practice. *Journal of Public Administration Research and Theory*, *4*, 323–325.

Demitt, A. D. (1999). Integrating theory: A process of construction, deconstruction, and reconstruction. *The Family Journal: Counseling and Therapy for Couples and Families*, *7*, 287–291.

Eberlein, L. (1987). Introducing ethics to beginning psychologists: A problem-solving approach. *Professional Psychology: Research and Practice*, *18*, 353–359.

Friedman, E. (1987). How to succeed in therapy without really trying. *Networker*, *27*, 31–35, 68.

Haber, R. (1994). Response-ability: Therapist's "I" and role. *Journal of Family Therapy*, *16*, 269–284.

Knox, S., Hess, S. A., Petersen, D. A., & Hill, C. E. (1997). A qualitative analysis of client perceptions of the effects of helpful therapist self-disclosure in long-term therapy. *Journal of Counseling Psychology*, *44*, 274–283.

Liddle, H., & Saba, G. (1982). Teaching family therapy at the introductory level: A conceptual model emphasizing a pattern which connects training and therapy. *Journal of Marital and Family Therapy*, *8*, 63–72.

Maaske, J. W. (1988). Empathetic intervention in self-psychology. *The Journal of Counseling and Development*, *67*, 82.

Mathews, B. (1988). The role of therapist self-disclosure in psychotherapy: A survey of therapists. *American Journal of Psychotherapy*, *42*(4), 521–531.

Miller, S., Duncan, B., & Hubble, N. (1997). *Escape from Babel: Toward a unifying language for psychotherapy practice*. New York, NY: Norton.

Nelson, T. S., & Prior, D. (2003). Theory of change projects in M.F.T. programs. *Contemporary Family Therapy*, *25*, 133–151.

Nielson, E., & Kaslow, F. (1980). Consultation in family therapy. *American Journal of Family Therapy*, *8*, 35–42.

Nilsson, D. E., Strassberg, D. S., & Bannon, J. (1979). Perceptions of counselor self-disclosure: An analogue study. *Journal of Counseling Pschology, 26,* 399–404.

Odell, M., & Stewart, S. P. (1993). Ethical issues associated with client values conversion and therapist value agendas in family therapy. *Family Relations, 42,* 128–133.

Piercy, F. P., & Sprenkle, D. H. (1988). Family therapy theory-building questions. *Journal of Marital and Family Therapy, 14,* 307–309.

Pipher, M. (2003). Advice to young therapists: Learning to trust the wisdom of the family. *Psychotherapy Networker,* 58–61.

Watkins, C. E., Jr. (1990). The effects of counselor self-disclosure: A research review. *The Counseling Psychologist, 18,* 477–500.

Websites

The American Association for Marriage and Family Therapy
http://www.aamft.org

The American Counseling Association
http://www.counseling.org

The International Association of Marriage and Family Counselors
http://www.iamfconline.com

Bowen Family Systems Theory

3

Mary Ann Crossno

Theory defines the thinking about the nature and origin of the problem.

—Murray Bowen (1978, p. 393)

INTRODUCTION

Murray Bowen and his family systems theory are considered the starting point for any study of the human family or family therapy (Papero, 1990). One of the founding fathers of the family movement, Bowen developed a theory of human functioning that conceptualizes the inherent potential of humans for growth and change (Guerin, 1973–1978; Kerr & Bowen, 1988). Bowen's contributions permanently altered our way of thinking about humans in the same way Darwin altered the landscape of evolution. His theory has been described as elegant, complete, radical, comprehensive, thoughtful, pioneering, influential, and a bold conceptual leap (Becvar & Becvar, 2003; Gilbert, 1992; Guerin & Chabot, 1992; Kerr, 1986; Kerr & Bowen, 1988). He is considered the major theoretician in the family therapy field and a founding father of family therapy.

HISTORY AND LEADING FIGURES

Murray Bowen, MD (1913–1990)

Murray Bowen's interest in psychiatry began during his service as a medical officer in World War II (Kerr & Bowen, 1988). He was intrigued by the psychiatrists' uncertainty of how to treat war casualties. Bowen then served at the Menninger Clinic in Houston, Texas, a premier training facility for psychiatrists, where he became an avid admirer and student of Freud's revolutionary psychoanalytic theory.

At Menninger, Bowen's clinical work focused on mother–child symbiosis in families with a schizophrenic member. He saw a connection between the intense emotional functioning in his patients' families and his extensive readings in biology and evolutionary theory (Bowen, 1978).

Observations that mother and child seemed to be two people thinking and feeling as one individual led Bowen to develop the concept of *differentiation of self*, which is the ability to separate intellectual and emotional functioning (Bowen, 1978). The biological term *differentiation* came from its description of the cellular specialization process (Kerr & Bowen, 1988; Papero, 1990), and reflected Bowen's idea of the human need for individuation. His choice of biological terminology was part of his determined effort to ground his theoretical development in solid science and to facilitate future research (Kerr & Bowen, 1988).

In 1954, Bowen moved to the National Institute of Mental Health to study *families* with a schizophrenic member, instead of focusing on the schizophrenic *individual*. The families' intense *emotional process* revealed *patterns of reciprocal functioning* in which members seemed to borrow strength at the expense of another member's functioning (Kerr & Bowen, 1988). Predictable patterns of overfunctioning/underfunctioning, decisive/indecisive, hysterical/obsessive, and dominant/submissive occurred with such precision that the presence of one trait in one family member predicted the presence of its partner in another family member. Alternating between distance and closeness, individual functioning faded from prominence, as the movement of the family unit seemed to be in control. Furthermore, Bowen noticed that *anxiety* within families was transferred to staff as the power of the family unit pulled staff into their *emotional systems* and *triangles* (Bowen, 1978).

Bowen could see the same processes present in all families, with differences a matter of quantitative degree that could be conceptualized on a continuum (Bowen, 1976; Kerr, 1984). This observation was the basis for the *scale of differentiation* in which Bowen described his theoretical range of human functioning (Kerr, 1995). Psychotic and neurotic symptoms merely represented a degree of impairment at the lowest end of the scale (Papero, 1990).

As a clinical professor of psychiatry at Georgetown Medical Center in 1959, Bowen refined and extended his theory (Kerr & Bowen, 1988). He also worked on integrating his theory with a clinical methodology for psychiatric residents in training. Bowen believed that a therapist has a responsibility to *define his or her self* (i.e., differentiate in his or her own family as a prerequisite for professional functioning; Bowen, 1978). Modeling his belief, he experimented with modifying his functioning in his family-of-origin system in an effort to aid future psychotherapists in their own differentiation (Guerin & Chabot, 1992). His 12-year effort, presented at a 1967 conference, electrified the audience for the bold and imaginative step of clinically applying his own theory to his family of origin. He described his differentiation breakthrough as a significant turning point in his personal and professional life. Dr. Murray Bowen died on October 9, 1990.

The Georgetown Family Center

The Georgetown Family Center in Washington, DC (now known as the Bowen Center for the Study of the Family) was founded in 1975 by Bowen. He served as director until his death. The Center is dedicated to the development of Bowen theory into a science of human behavior (Bowen Center for the Study of the Family, 2005).

Training at the Bowen Center emphasizes "self-learning" in a discovery process that focuses on expanding knowledge about the science of human behavior and the communication of ideas. The training process is guided by insights from Bowen family systems theory as teacher and learner take on mutual responsibility for learning in a systemic, interactive environment.

Bowen Theory Descendants

Bowen's descendants include many influential scholars and leaders in the study of families and family therapy.

Michael Kerr, director of The Bowen Center, wrote the most in-depth examination of Bowen theory in *Family Evaluation* (Kerr & Bowen, 1988). Other prominent descendants of Bowen theory include Roberta Gilbert and Kathleen K. Wiseman (Bowen Center for the Study of the Family, 2005).

Dr. Philip Guerin was a second-year psychiatric resident at Georgetown Medical School when he met Bowen in the summer of 1967, and they began a 23-year relationship (Guerin, 1991). In clinical supervision with Bowen, Guerin was motivated to find ways of expanding Bowen's ideas into pragmatic clinical applications.

Guerin developed a therapeutic approach based on modified concepts of Bowen theory that he called "Bowenian" therapy (Guerin & Guerin, 2002). Guerin noted that he chose to call his clinical application of Bowen theory "Bowenian" both in deference to Bowen and to honor Bowen's work.

Guerin and his colleague, Thomas Fogarty, trained many students of Bowen theory, including Betty Carter, Monica McGoldrick, Ed Gordon, Eileen Pendagast, and Katherine Guerin. Guerin and Guerin (2002) defined their work and the work of their colleagues as focused on clarifying and elaborating Bowen theory:

> We adhere to a model of Bowenian therapy that has been strongly influenced by, and is, in fact, based on, the concepts of Bowen theory. However, our model has attempted to develop some of the concepts in a clinically practical way and, from the modified concepts, to develop unique models of intervention for working with individuals, couples, and families. (p. 127)

Although the work of Guerin and his colleagues is grounded in Bowen theory, their work reflects one of the many individual and diverse products of thinking spawned by Bowen theory.

INTRODUCTION TO BOWEN THEORY

Bowen theory is a generalization of human behavior that attempts to define an order to relationships (Kerr, 1988a) based on more than 10,000 hours of family psychotherapy covering a period of more than 12 years. The relationship systems that Bowen observed in families have much in common with relationship systems observed in the natural world.

In a final interview just prior to his death, Bowen stated his belief in the importance of theory in all of life (American Association for Marriage and Family Therapy Annual Conference, 1990):

> An understanding of theory can change your life more than anything else in your life . . . because how we think about a situation creates our reality. Theory is important for thinking because it creates a framework. Everybody is equipped for the ability to think theory, but we will not do it.

Kerr (1999) noted that Bowen theory has been applied to nonfamily groups such as business organizations, communities, and large societies, and potentially explains emotional functioning in nonhuman species. "Family therapy is but one application of Bowen theory" (p. 7). A student interested in becoming a therapist without learning theory would do well to choose something other than Bowen theory to study, because *theory determines every move in this method of therapy* (Kerr & Bowen, 1988).

Systems and Systems Thinking

One cannot understand Bowen theory without understanding systems (Papero, 1990). Systems thinking defines a process of interdependent functioning from one system to a larger system that encompasses it (i.e., a cell to an organ, an organ to a human, a human to a planet, a planet to a solar system, and a solar system to a galaxy; Kerr, 1988a). Bowen's observations led him to define the family as a complex unit of systems and subsystems (Papero, 1990) operating under the same order, and as scientific laws and evolutionary processes that shaped the natural world (Kerr, 1986). "The term *systems* was spontaneously used to refer to the automatic predictable behavior between family members" (Bowen, 1978, p. 417)

Systems thinking is a challenge to rigid cause-and-effect thinking when trying to understand the ways self and society function (Kerr, 1988a). Systems thinking focuses on verifiable information, directing attention to the *how*, *what*, *when*, and *where* of what humans do—not the subjective reasoning of *why* they do it. The inability to see our influence on the functioning of others blocks our ability to observe human behavior (Kerr & Bowen, 1988). Throughout history, the cause of mental illness and emotional distress have been attributed to flaws residing within a person, typically in mystical, religious, organic, or psychological terms. Systems thinking suggests that emotional distress may be part of natural processes instead of personal flaws (Kerr, 2004).

The interrelationship of multiple systems is always in play in Bowen theory, and three of these are as follows: (a) the emotional system—evolutionary and instinctual functioning; (b) the intellectual system—humans' ability to think, reason, and reflect; and (c) the feeling system—the bridge between the emotional and intellectual systems that attaches meanings to emotional reactions (Bowen, 1978). Emotional systems explain what drives the process *within* systems, and relationship systems describe interactions *between* systems (Kerr & Bowen, 1988).

It is important to note that feelings and emotions are *not* used interchangeably in Bowen theory. "The feeling system is postulated as a link between the emotional and intellectual systems through which certain emotional states are represented in conscious awareness" (Bowen, 1978, p. 356). Bowen used emotion to mean the *automatic*, *instinctive*, and *reactive life force* that guides functioning in all living things from the cellular to the societal (Papero, 1990). Emotions rule the "dance of life" as they drive an organism to preserve its species, protect its social unit, and procreate (Papero, 1990). This emotional process is directed by the limbic system, which is the most primitive part of the human brain, and shapes human behavior within family and social systems (Comella, 1995). Emotions are constantly activated by reactions to internal and external sensory inputs, so that reality becomes the interaction of what goes on *inside* humans and *between* humans (Kerr & Bowen, 1988). The emotional system incorporates all guidance systems that direct life, including instinct, reproduction, subjective emotional and feeling states, and the interaction with relationship systems (Bowen, 1978). Bowen theory differs from general systems theory in that it is built on *facts* gained through direct *observation* of the family (Papero, 1990); general systems theory attempts to apply mathematical models to behavioral, social, and physical sciences (Bowen, 1978; Kerr & Bowen, 1988). Bowen (1976) repeatedly sought to dispel the misconception that the emergence of general systems theory in others' work with families was connected to the beginnings of his theory.

EIGHT INTERLOCKING CONCEPTS OF BOWEN FAMILY SYSTEMS THEORY

The core of my theory has to do with the degree to which people are able to distinguish between the feeling process and the intellectual process.

—Murray Bowen (1978, p. 355)

Concept One: Differentiation of Self

Differentiation of self describes the level at which an individual is able to integrate the opposing and basic drives between thinking and feeling, and separateness and togetherness

(Bowen, 1978). This concept reflects the *internal* process of being able to integrate and freely choose functioning between intellectual and emotional systems (Bowen, 1978) and the *external* process of being able to remain a separate self while staying connected with significant others (Bowen, 1961; Kerr, 1985). It also reflects the degree to which one is able to avoid having his or her behavior automatically driven by emotion and/or being determined by relationship processes.

One's basic level of differentiation of self is developed and established early in life by the degree of emotional separation from parents achieved in growing up (Bowen, 1978). This level is passed down from generation to generation and, apart from a determined effort to change it, the level remains fixed throughout life (Kerr & Bowen, 1988; Papero, 1990). Complete differentiation (i.e., total resolution of emotional attachment to family) exists only as a theoretical concept (Kerr & Bowen, 1988).

Fusion describes a relationship in which people's emotions and intellect are so fused that they operate as "emotional hostages" of the relationship (Kerr, 2003). Fusion also defines the emotional (automatic and instinctive) togetherness pull in relationships, the human need for connectedness to *survive* (Hall, 1981). Fusion in families demands and produces pseudo-selves, people who give up or rearrange their authentic self for the sake of togetherness (Kerr & Bowen, 1988).

Differentiation in families encourages and produces solid selves, people who understand and accept the limitations of relationships (Bowen, 1978). Differentiation of self *cannot* occur outside of relationships (Bowen, 1978). Differentiation of self in relationships is a lifelong process; thus, it is not an achievable goal (Bowen, 1978). Differentiation can be measured on a *theoretical scale* depicting human functioning as a range between 0 (representing the lowest functioning) and 100 (representing an imagined level of evolved perfection). On Bowen's (1978) theoretical scale, there is no "normal." The scale applies to all humans and transcends categories such as genius, social class, or cultural–ethnic differences. Table 3.1 lists some characteristics of lower differentiation versus higher differentiation. Table 3.2 explains the differences between the pseudo-self and the solid self.

TABLE 3.1 ▥ Levels of Differentiation

Lower Differentiated People	Higher Differentiated People
Unable to separate feeling from thinking	Able to access thinking, even when in high anxiety
Reactive—emotionally driven	Responsive—capable of thoughtful consideration
Stuck with or cut off from families and significant others	Connected with significant others while maintaining separate self
Conform to a situation or rebel	Self-defined, self-validating
Need to control functioning of others	Focused on control of self-functioning
Less flexible, less adaptable, more emotionally dependent	More flexible, more adaptable, more emotionally independent
Easily stressed into dysfunction, has difficulty recovering from dysfunction	Can cope with life stresses and recover rapidly from stress-induced dysfunction
Inherit a high percentage of all human problems	Remarkably free of human problems, life is more orderly and successful
Life course determined by what feels right	Life course based on principled beliefs

Source: Bowen, 1978

TABLE 3.2 ■ Differences Between the Pseudo-Self and the Solid Self

Pseudo-Self	Solid Self
"Tell me who and how to be, and I will change myself for a relationship with you."	Defines reasonable expectations of what to get from self and what to get from others
Defines self in terms of others; defines others in terms of self	"This is who I am, what I believe, what I stand for, what I will do or what I will not do" (p. 365).
Will alter or adopt principles and beliefs without thought for sake of relationships	Will act on principles and beliefs, even in high anxiety or under duress
Principles and beliefs are created and/or modified by emotional pressure	Clearly defined beliefs, convictions, and life principles based on thoughtful choices
Blames others for consequences of personal choices	Assumes responsibility for self and consequences of choices
Relationship determines words and actions	"I say what I will do; I do what I say."
Principles and beliefs are inconsistent, and inconsistency is out of awareness	Principles and beliefs are consistent with one another, and consistency is pursued
Unstable; *attached* to external self	Stable; *incorporated* into being core
Pseudo-self much larger than most realize	Solid self much smaller than most realize

Source: Bowen, 1978

Concept Two: Triangles

The triangle structure is a three-person emotional configuration that is the basic building block of any emotional system. According to Bowen, the triangle is the smallest stable relationship system because a two-person relationship operates under the constant push–pull forces of differing togetherness and separateness and needs, and has a low tolerance for anxiety. Triangling describes the *process* of the predictable patterned moves of emotional forces between any three people (Bowen, 1978).

In Bowenian terms, *anxiety* is emotional tension, much of which occurs outside of our awareness, and which drives us toward intense emotional closeness. Its impact varies with intensity, duration, and type. Anxiety can be *chronic* (long term), *infectious* (rapidly spreading), or *acute* (intense, but short-lived). Most organisms, including humans, tolerate acute anxiety well and are relatively symptom free in low-anxiety circumstances. However, extended chronic anxiety produces symptoms, illness, and dysfunction in relationships and individuals (Bowen, 1978). Triangling is one way that humans deal with anxiety.

As the *emotional flow* and *counterflow* in an anxious twosome increase, it *naturally* triangles the most vulnerable other person into the twosome, either by *pulling in* the third person, by *overflowing* onto the third person, or by *attracting* a third person to initiate the involvement (Bowen, 1978). Entrance of a third vulnerable person to diffuse anxiety stabilizes the twosome, increasing their tolerance for stress (Kerr & Bowen, 1988). Bowen described two comfortably close people functioning as insiders working to preserve their connection, with an outsider at a less comfortable distance working to move into a closer inside position with one of the twosome. Within the twosome, one person is typically comfortably unaware of tensions, whereas the other is typically uncomfortably aware and seeks a change in the level of togetherness (Bowen, 1978). Initially, the creation of a triangle calms an anxious twosome, allowing them to maintain an optimum level of closeness and distance while permitting the greatest freedom from anxiety (Papero, 1990).

During calm times, the inside position is the most comfortable, desirable, and sought after; during stressful times, the outside position is the most comfortable, desirable, and sought after (Bowen, 1978). As anxiety within a triangle increases, one insider triangle in a fourth and emotional pattern is repeated in the new interlocking triangle. Triangles live on in families, embedded in emotional patterns that continue across generations, with new family members taking the place of ancestors' functioning positions in triangles (Kerr & Bowen, 1988). Triangle patterns are dynamic, fluid, predictable, and accurately reflect functioning levels of families (Hall, 1981).

Kerr and Bowen (1988) summarizes the basic nature of triangles as follows:

1. A stable twosome can be *destabilized* by the *addition* of a third person

2. A stable twosome can be *destabilized* by the *removal* of a third person

3. An unstable twosome can be *stabilized* by the *addition* of a third person

4. An unstable twosome can be *stabilized* by the *removal* of a third person

In some families, a common triangle pattern is mother and child in the overly close insider position, with the father in the distant outside position (Hall, 1981). A couple in which one partner is having an affair is another example of a common triangle pattern (Papero, 1990). Bowen (1978) considered these fixed patterns of interaction to be observable, knowable, and predictable and present in all human interactions—family systems, work environments, or social systems. Triangles can be modified by a knowledgeable third person's ability to engage a twosome without repeating the predictable patterns, or by one member of a triangle modifying his or her emotional reactivity within the family.

Concept Three: Nuclear Family Emotional System

This concept describes the emotional functioning in a single generation and symptomatic patterns produced by intense fusion between partners, reflecting their lack of differentiation (Bowen, 1978). Each of these patterns of emotional functioning occurs in triangles, and symptoms serve the purpose of "binding" the anxiety in a system (Kerr & Bowen, 1988). When symptoms appear in only one pattern, the result is more severe symptoms in one relationship or person, leaving other family members freer from symptoms. When symptoms appear in multiple patterns, anxiety is diffused across patterns, and functioning levels of all family members are less affected.

1. *Emotional distance* is a universal reaction present in all marriages in varying degrees (Bowen, 1978) that occurs automatically and often out of awareness (Papero, 1990). Expressions of distance include external moves away from one another and internal processes that maintain emotional separation. Distancing is a means of avoiding the discomfort of one's own reactivity to other, typically while blaming the other's reactivity for the distance (Papero, 1990).

2. *Marital conflict*, often overt, chronic, and unresolved, cycles through periods of emotional distance and closeness, with intense negative feelings during conflict and intense positive feelings during closeness in roller-coaster fashion (Goldenberg & Goldenberg, 2000). Partners absorb family anxiety as each focuses on the other's need to change (Kerr & Bowen, 1988). In conflictual marriages, neither gives in to the other nor adapts (Bowen, 1961).

3. *Dysfunction in one spouse* occurs as an adaptive mechanism when one spouse absorbs a disproportionate amount of the anxiety generated by the undifferentiated functioning of the twosome (Bowen, 1978). One spouse overfunctions, whereas the adaptive spouse underfunctions until he or she becomes vulnerable to physical or emotional dysfunction. Physical illness, social ineptness and irresponsibility, work inefficiency, and emotional illness are manifestations of the dysfunctional disequilibrium (Bowen, 1961).

4. *Emotional impairment in a child* results when anxiety and sensitivities collected across generations are projected onto one or more children through the parents (Bowen, 1978). Bowen considered this mechanism so important to understanding human interaction that he elaborated it in the fourth of his eight interlocking theoretical concepts.

Concept Four: Family Projection Process

This concept describes the primary manner by which parental undifferentiation is projected onto one or more children, resulting in impaired functioning (Kerr, 2003). Parents *scan* a child for potential problems, *diagnose* the child's behavior as confirmation that the problem exists, and then *treat* the child as though the diagnosis is accurate, shaping the child's development through the parents' undifferentiated projection lens. Inherited problems that affect children most include (a) excessive need for attention and approval, (b) difficulty dealing with expectations, (c) blaming self or others for problems, (d) assuming responsibility for others' happiness or subjugating personal happiness to others, and (e) relieving anxiety by acting impulsively rather than tolerating anxiety while acting thoughtfully (Kerr, 2003).

Some projection occurs in all families, focusing first on one child and shifting to other children when the emotional process is too great for one child (Bowen, 1978). The process is activated by the degree of connection or disconnection between a mother and child, with the father typically in an outsider position supporting the mother's anxious interaction with the child (Kerr, 2003). Symptoms develop from the need to absorb excess undifferentiation in spouses, and symptoms are intensified with increasing anxiety, particularly events such as a death of a close family member occurring near the birth of the child (Hall, 1981). The child most emotionally attached to the parental unit is the most vulnerable to the projection process, commonly seen in only children, an oldest child, a single-sex child among several of the other sex, or a child with a physical or mental disability (Bowen, 1978).

Concept Five: Multigenerational Transmission Process

This concept is a continuation of the family projection process *across generations* (Bowen, 1978) and is easiest to observe when it is moderately intense (Papero, 1990). The most impaired child of the family projection process leaves home with the lowest level of differentiation among siblings and a lower level of differentiation than his or her parents (Papero, 1990). Bowen theory suggests that individuals marry at or about the same level of differentiation, so that the target child's marriage begins a lower level of differentiation than his or her parents' marriage (Kerr, 2003). The family projection process continues to produce individuals in that line of descent with progressively poorer differentiation resulting in dysfunctional impairment such as schizophrenia, chronic alcoholism, and so forth (Bowen, 1978).

Other siblings within the same family unit emerge with similar or better levels of differentiation than the parental unit (Kerr, 2003). As they marry at or near their level of differentiation, higher functioning flows into the lineage. The flow is bidirectional—a low differentiated family can produce a child moving up the scale and a high differentiated family can produce a child moving down the scale (Bowen, 1978). This concept depicts the path accounting for the most chaotic and the most stable lives and explains the great disparity of functioning, success, and failure often seen in one family across generations (Kerr, 2003).

Concept Six: Sibling Position

This concept looks at how interactive patterns between marital partners relate to the sibling position of each partner in his or her family of origin. Bowen found psychologist Walter Toman's work on sibling position so thorough and consistent with his ideas that he included it in his theory. Bowen (1978) was particularly intrigued with Toman's work concerning how sibling position might affect marriage or lead to divorce. Toman (1993) found that "if an older brother of a younger sister marries a younger sister of an older brother, less chance of a divorce exists than if an older brother of a brother marries an older sister of a sister."

Bowen (1978) believed that knowledge of sibling position in past and present generations pointed to active differentiation level, projection process, and triangulated positions. He saw this information as a vital tool for understanding past generations in the absence of verifiable facts and as a predictive tool for understanding how spouses will react in marriage and in therapy.

Concept Seven: Emotional Cutoff

This concept is an instinctive biological process that acts like an emotional safety valve in relationships (Papero, 1990). Bowen called cutoff "a description of immature separation of people from each other" (Kerr & Bowen, 1988, p. 346), reflecting unresolved emotional attachment to parents. Cutoff can be seen as the other side of the fusion coin, expressing an allergic reactivity to emotional closeness so that the runaway is as emotionally dependent as the one who lives next door to the parental unit (Bowen, 1978). Emotional cutoff is expressed in internal process by denying the attachment, in external process by physical separation, or by some combination of the two (Papero, 1990). Kerr stated that emotional cutoff *reflects* a problem of generational fusion, *solves* a problem by reducing anxiety that comes with uncomfortable contact, and *creates* a problem by separating people from important relationships and intensifying fusion in remaining relationships (Goldenberg & Goldenberg, 2000).

Concept Eight: Societal Emotional Process

This concept addresses ways that families shape society and society shapes families (Bowen, 1978). The emotional system drives functioning at all levels— families, society, work, social organizations, and other nonfamily groups—reflecting the systemic consistency of Bowen theory (Kerr, 2003). The triangling process observed in families is played out in society with the same variables in the process:

1. Emotional tension (i.e., anxiety) grows between two groups.
2. Emotionally vulnerable others are involved, and the anxiety spreads.
3. Emotional reactiveness, defensiveness, and counterattacks feed the anxiety.
4. Emotional energy is spent, and the system calms.

Bowen (1978) considered societal problems to cycle through alternating periods of *progression* and *regression* fed by environmental issues such as population growth, depletion of natural resources, and vanishing frontiers. *Societal regression* is Bowen's term that describes "a gradual downward decrease in differentiation of self" (p. 448). An example of societal regression can be seen when poorly differentiated families develop delinquency and other antisocial symptoms that activate societal process (Bowen, 1979). The lifestyle of low differentiated families spills over into societal agencies, as people make choices based on immediate anxiety relief instead of principles and well-thought-out beliefs (Kerr, 2003). Responsibility for the delinquency is then transferred from the family, where the problem developed, to society.

Bowen's (1978) thesis is that the growing discord between man and nature, left unchecked, may lead to human extinction. Alternatively, Bowen's theory of human functioning suggests that overriding emotionality with the thinking process is the *progressive* path for human evolution (Kerr & Bowen, 1988). Self-management (i.e., differentiation of self) is the challenge humans must undertake to maintain a stable society built on solid relationships (Papero, 1996).

THEORETICAL ASSUMPTIONS

> *The theoretical assumption considers emotional illness to be a disorder of the emotional system . . . Emotional illness is considered a deep process involving the basic life process of the organism.*
>
> —Murray Bowen (1978, p. 356)

Theory is considered inseparable from Bowen's approach to therapy, both the *anchor* that grounds therapy and the *map* that guides therapy (Kerr, 1992). Each of the eight interlocking concepts in Bowen theory describes observable, knowable, and predictable variables constantly interacting within a family emotional system, shaping variation in biology, behavior, and the whole range of human functioning (Harrison, 1999). Therapy is guided by theoretical concepts and principles derived from theory, by knowledge from the natural sciences, by facts about the family, and by self-knowledge based on personal work on self and one's own family and life (Harrison, 1999, 2004).

View of the Family and Client

Bowen (1978) defined the family as follows:

> *The family is a system in that a change in one part of the system is followed by compensatory change in other parts of the system. I prefer to think of the family as a variety of systems and subsystems . . . I think of the family as a combination of "emotional" and "relationship" systems. The term "emotional" refers to the force that motivates the system and "relationship" to the ways it is expressed. (pp. 155, 158)*

He noted that all symptoms—emotional, physical, conflictual, or social—reflect adaptation of the family system functioning to change and challenge (Harrison, 2006). Symptoms are produced by changes in relationship patterns between family members that trigger reactivity (Harrison, 1999). Kerr (1992) outlined events that stir reactions associated with symptom development:

> *An individual's ability to adapt to life is most strained by events that (1) threaten his emotional connections with others; (2) increase the anxious focus of others on himself; (3) increase his*

dependence on others; (4) increase the dependence of others on him; (5) threaten the function-
ing of others upon whom he is dependent; or (6) increase his level of responsibility. (p. 105)

Each emotional family system presents as a series of interlocking triangles created in a natural reaction to these stressors as an anxiety reliever between any two family members (Bowen, 1978).

View on How Change Occurs

In Bowen theory, therapeutic change occurs when one person focuses on accepting responsibility for self within the family and in life, developing awareness of the differences between emotional and intellectual functioning and creating problem-solving options based on those differences (Bowen, 1978; Harrison, 1999; Papero, 1992). Bowen theory–based therapy aims to enlighten and inform clients of knowable, observable, and predictable patterns of human functioning. Armed with this knowledge, change occurs as the client does the difficult work of altering those patterns in his or her day-to-day living (Kerr, 1991a). Bowen (1978) described a key application of theory to therapy:

The most important therapeutic principle, which is repeatable in an orderly predictable way, says that when the triangular emotional pattern is modified in a single important tri-angle in the family, and the members of the triangle remain in emotional contact with the rest of the family, other triangles will automatically change in relation to the first. (p. 480)

Therapist's Role

The Bowen family systems therapist functions as a coach or consultant, knowledgeable of human functioning patterns, who shares that knowledge with family members to equip them in becoming experts on their particular family system (Bowen, 1978). The therapist *defines self* to the client family by accepting responsibility for his or her decisions while allowing each family member to be responsible for his or her choices (Papero, 1992). Bowen worked to keep the emotional system engaged but manageable so that spouses or parents could deal with it objectively by directing questions to each partner and inquiring about reactions of one to what the other said to him. Keeping himself emotionally detriangled, he established "I positions"—action stands in relation to the clients—modeling how they could do likewise with one another. Throughout the process, he taught clients about emotional systems and coached them on what it would mean for them to work toward differentiation of self in family-of-origin relationships.

Bowen believed that the therapist's ability to be thoughtful and neutral while emotionally connected with his or her own family of origin directly influenced his or her ability to do so with clients and also affected the client's ability to do so in his or her relationships (Bowen, 1978). Understanding the theory and applying it in the therapist's own family of origin are integral to the role of the Bowen family systems therapist.

Interventions

The following are basic strategies for creating change using a Bowen family systems therapy approach:

- The therapist stays detriangled from the family emotional system at all times.
- The therapist asks questions designed to reveal family functioning, patterns, and history.

- The therapist chooses to work with the most motivated, highest differentiated person in the family.
- The therapist asks questions designed to replace *other-focus* with *self-focus*.
- The therapist keeps the conversation between the therapist and each family member, then asking other family members about their reaction to what they heard.
- The therapist establishes and models "I positions," and encourages family members to do the same.
- The therapist teaches family members how emotional systems work.
- The therapist may use humor to lighten intense reactivity.

Bowen theory is particularly helpful for clients whose family members have anxious relationships within their families on various issues. For example, a single mother whose ex-husband has recently announced he was gay may come to therapy seeking advice on what to tell their teenage children. Her family kept secrets to the point that no one in her family talked about things that raised their anxiety the most. This caused emotional cutoffs within her family and left her with few ways of coping in such a stressful time. Because of such secrecy, the mother has preconceived ideas about homosexuality and needs assistance concerning helping her teenage children adapt to their father's new partner. Bowen family systems theory will be helpful to the mother and her teenage children in that they will explore how to deal with each other when anxiety is rampant in their household. Additionally, Bowen family systems theory will help the single mother to find different, comfortable ways to relay information to her children, allowing them to deal with the information and ask questions. This will improve the chances for both the mother and her children to grow and differentiate.

The purpose of Bowen family systems theory in therapy is to help individuals and families to understand and accept the individual contributions to emotional functioning, both individually and within the family. Because of this purpose, Bowen family systems theory can be helpful when dealing with marital issues, anxiety, anger, depression, sexual abuse, and many more areas of conflict. By learning to recognize the emotional relationship patterns through insight and recognizing how anxiety occurred and was dealt with in a family, individual family members can use the insight to construct new behaviors.

Clients who do not wish to look back into a painful past to understand from whence they came, or clients who want therapy to progress quickly, without explanations, may not find Bowen family systems helpful. In addition, clients who tend to blame their family for their current dilemma may not progress well when the therapist uses Bowen family systems theory, because the answers may fuel more blame.

Bowen theory has been studied for its validity during the last 15 years through a substantial number of studies. A review of this basic research provided empirical support for the relationship between differentiation and chronic anxiety, marital satisfaction, and psychological distress, but not in Bowen's claim that siblings are likely to marry siblings in other families according to birth order (Titelman, 1998).

BOWEN FAMILY SYSTEMS WORKING TEMPLATE

The *Bowen family systems template* is meant to be used as a guideline to learning the process of Bowen family systems therapy. The template provides the beginning therapist with a review of tools for change unique to the model and steps to take and questions to ask that promote collaboration between the therapist and client. There are suggested questions under each heading to help start the process. After using the initial questions, guide the client through each process and ask questions that occur to you, as you stay within the family therapy theory. Although there is no one "script" for any therapy session, it is the hope of the author that the template serves as an impetus to learning this family therapy model.

Tools for Change

In Bowen theory, the therapist is responsible for working on differentiation of self in his or her own family as the basis for the ability to engage and transmit differentiation in clinical practice. The therapist recognizes his or her place as an important triangle in relation to the family. He or she uses his or her knowledge and experience from his or her own family work to establish a neutral position from which he or she can be interested in how all family members function to play a part. He or she can recognize when he or she loses neutrality and will exercise the ability to define self more clearly and effectively over time. Thus, the therapist allows emotional process to filter through himself or herself without being caught in a "therapy triangle" or system of fixing anyone.

The therapist works to get clients to lower anxiety by reducing emotional reactivity so that the client can access his or her thinking process. The therapist must help the family understand family patterns and be able to stay connected without bringing reactivity into play and without being determined by relationships.

The therapist helps identify predictable reactions (avoidance, going along, conflict, overfunctioning) and coaches the clients to define alternative ways based more on their best thinking and on principles or efforts to be a more mature person in their family.

Throughout therapy, the therapist should ask process questions to increase the client's awareness of family emotional process and the client's role in them. The therapist should also encourage "I positions": asking the client to define what he or she thinks and believes based on solid, well-thought-out principles.

Phase 1: Joining and Building Rapport

The therapist's goal as therapy begins is to engage the client's best thinking and establish a collaboration in which each is responsible for self. The therapist should develop a focus on facts and thinking without distancing from the feelings and emotions.

The therapist establishes collaboration with the family by identifying each person as playing his or her part in the system to keep the system functioning. The therapist should help clients get to lower anxiety levels by reducing emotional reactivity so they can access their thinking process. During this phase, the therapist should engage the clients without being reactive and should stimulate the clients without attempting to "rescue" them. Finally, the therapist builds a genogram (see Chapter 1) while collecting data about the family. (Bowen theory–guided therapists typically have a board to draw on in their office for this purpose.)

Here are some comments or questions that a therapist might use during this phase:

- *"As we begin talking today, I will be drawing a genogram, which is a map showing your family members and relationships that will help me begin to understand your present family and your extended family, a few generations before you. While you talk, I may draw items on the genogram. Let's begin.*
- *"What is it that you want to accomplish here?"*
- *"What is your best thinking about?"*

- *"What made you decide to come to therapy now?"*
- *"Who are the most important people in your life?"*
- *"Tell me a little about yourself and the family you grew up in."*
- *"Who are you most like in your family?"*
- *"What does it mean to be a Jones, or Smith, or Williams? [Use paternal and maternal surnames.]*

Phase 2: Understanding the Presenting Issue

In Bowen theory, symptoms are a by-product of acute or chronic emotional anxiety, a natural human state that can be overcome by disciplined, purposeful effort to use thinking to control anxiety. Behavior disorders result from emotional fusion transmitted from one generation to the next. Emotional fusion is a part of all symptoms. The therapist aims to guide the client's thinking to place symptoms in the context of multigenerational family system by inquiring about time, place, and significant events surrounding the onset of symptoms.

Here are some comments or questions that a therapist might use during this phase:

- *"When did you notice [the symptom]?"*
- *"When does this symptom first occurred? Who did you turn to first for help?"*
- *"What was their response? Was that a typical response?"*
- *"What was your explanation for their response?"*
- *"Tell me other ways that this symptom has occurred in your family and with whom."*

Over time, the therapist and family member(s) develop a broader, more factual, and objective perspective on the presenting issue, on factors driving the anxiety, and on his or her own reactivity and that of others.

As this happens, here are some comments or questions that a therapist might use:

- *"What are the sources of anxiety at this time?"*
- *"How does the anxiety affect you? How are you reacting?"*
- *"Who is most anxious? Who reacts to you the most?"*

Phase 3: Assessment of Family Dynamics

The genogram (see Chapter 1) is the primary assessment tool in Bowen therapy. While assessing the family and listening to their descriptions of the presenting problem, refer to the family diagram and begin identifying patterns such as divorces; deaths; and serious problems such as alcoholism, drug abuse, sexual abuse, or emotional cutoffs. Especially identify patterns of emotional reactivity, distancing, fusion, and triangles and how different family members have calmed themselves over the generations, whether it be with drugs, distancing, addictions, workaholism, religion, illnesses, and so forth.

To aid in the assessment, questions such as those that follow are helpful:

- *"How do you understand the feelings that you have now?"*
- *"Who in your family can get you upset, resulting in the symptoms happening?"*
- *"What gets stirred up in you when that happens?"*

- *"As a child, how did you understand _____ interactions in your family?"*
- *"How much responsibility did you take on for making [family member] less angry, drink less, being less sad, and so forth?"*
- *"What relationship in the family do you have the most regrets about?"*
- *"Tell me what you do or think about when things are difficult in relationships."*
- *"When you get anxious, what do you do or who do you think about first?"*
- *"How does the anxiety affect you and your decisions?"*
- *"How do you calm your anxiety, if at all?"*
- *"Who else in the family has/had this problem?"*
- *"At what age did this problem appear for them?"*
- *"What help did the family seek at that time? What was the outcome?"*

Phase 4: Goals

The goals of Bowen therapy include placing the presenting problem in multigenerational context/system, decreasing anxiety within the family members, detriangling three-person systems, and increasing basic differentiation of self among family members.

Here are some comments or questions that a therapist might use during this phase:

For spousal or marital issues:

- *"How is your relationship with your spouse or partner the same or different from your relationship with your mother or father?"*
- *"How did becoming your mother's or father's confidante or ally or distant child affect your relationship with your dad?"*

For family issues:

- *"When _____ died, what changed?"*
- *"What did you learn about how your family operated when_____ occurred?"*
- *"What family rules were handed down to your family from your family or your spouse's or partner's family?"*
- *"What responsibility do you want to take on now as you are older?"*
- *"From our conversations today, what have you realized about the patterns that have developed in your family?"*
- *"From our conversation today, what patterns are you interested in changing?"*
- *"For future generations in your family, what do you hope they achieve?"*

Phase 5: Amplifying Change

According to Bowen theory, change occurs when each client achieves a reasonable level of understanding about his or her family history, his or her roles, and the roles of others. It is hoped that the client will then begin to change and differentiate as he or she becomes aware of his or her patterns of relating in family systems. Progress is measured by how quickly clients recover from emotional reactivity and their ability to create a workable plan to maintain self in the midst of predictable patterns. Change brings about a decrease in anxiety related to the triangle with the therapist and leaves the client with a calmness and direction based on an understanding of the past. There is also a decrease in the symptom of focus and in distress. When that occurs, the client may stop therapy, pleased with the experience. It is important to notice that throughout, the questions used to accomplish change are not confrontational, nor are they directive, with goal setting very vague. Bowen theory relies on the client's intuition and understanding to discover the past patterns and influences and then deduce why he or she has grown as he or she has.

Therefore, in this phase, the therapist should establish a broader perspective on family functioning so that family members are more naturally motivated to continue beyond the symptom focus. As someone begins to work on being a less reactive and more responsible family member, basic change will be accompanied by predictable reactions:

1. Anxious reactions to real change occur in self and are transformed into healthy actions.
2. Change-back reaction or demands from others are met with confidence by the client that the current self is competent.
3. Threats made by others are processed as irrational and, therefore, not harmful when not allowed to be, leaving the client confident that he or she is right to hold an opinion or belief.

It is at this point that other people often *do* react back to the client, leaving the client mad, disappointed, ready to give up, ready to distance himself or herself, and so forth. A therapist who has his or her own experience with this process will be able to anticipate and plan ahead and will be able to coach the client to stay on course and become more independent without blaming the others or reacting back, doing so by helping the client see that such reactions are normal for his or her family functioning.

Progress is also observed through the beneficial effects on the functioning of the family over time. There may be a reduction in symptoms and in improvement in the ability to cope with stress factors. Bowen therapy also takes a factual view of improvement and functioning over time, explaining how such improvement and functioning will affect future generations.

Phase 6: Termination

Differentiation is a lifelong process, not an achievable destination. Clients decide when they have worked enough on self around the presenting issue in Bowen therapy. Coaching is an ongoing process of the approach in which clients check in when in need of guidance and think about how to "hold onto self" in the face of new and/or greater challenges.

MASTER THERAPIST INTERVIEW

ROBERTA GILBERT

Dr. Roberta Gilbert has been a psychiatrist and faculty member at The Bowen Center since 1988 (Center for the Study of Human Systems, 2005). She is the author of Extraordinary Relationships *(1992),* Connecting With Our Children *(1999),* The Eight Concepts of Bowen Theory *(2004), and* Extraordinary Leadership *(2006). She began the Center for the Study of Human Systems (2005) to disseminate information about Bowen family systems theory in 1998.*

What attracted you to the theory behind Bowen family systems theory?
In the beginning, it was difficult to understand what Bowen was saying. He was talking about a new theory. We already had a theory—Freudian theory. When I finally could "hear" what Bowen was saying, I could see that here was a way of thinking that was far superior to anything I had received in my prior training. Bowen theory accounted for more of the facts than I had been looking at, and it made more sense. When I started using it in my own life and practice, I got results of a higher order. That really got my attention and was, as your question indicates, very attractive.

How do you formulate your view of a family when they enter therapy?
When they enter therapy, a family brings a specific problem. So, in the beginning, as they explain the problem, theory being my guide, I will be listening for at least a few of the following:

- *What are the relationship patterns at work here, such as conflict, distance, cutoff, over/underfunctioning, triangling?*
- *How do the triangles work? Who is on the inside, who on the outside?*
- *Have there been any "nodal events" (someone leaving or entering the system) in the last 2 years? Did these events stress the system?*
- *How in touch or cut off are people with their families of origin? Where might other cutoffs be?*
- *How has this family replicated patterns from its family of origin or other generations?*

Of course, my major tool for all of this is assisting the family/individual construct a family diagram, on which are placed all the players they know about (and those they learn about later). It will include facts such as dates of birth, dates of death, important diagnoses, health issues, vocation, location, and educational attainment.

The first task in therapy is to assist the family in lowering anxiety to a level where it can begin to think clearly about its situation. That may take awhile, but when people calm down and begin to think, they can usually get some resolution. It may not be what I or a therapist would "prescribe," but it is their way of going, which may be much better than what I could come up with.

What kinds of families do you think benefit most from Bowen theory?
Any individual or family who applies the theory to self and seeks to work on self will benefit. Of course, some people want to do the work and some don't.

What issues do you think this model works best with?
Since "issues" that we have any control over are either created or contributed to by oneself out of old patterns or anxiety, I can't think of any issues that won't yield in some degree to a thorough understanding and application of Bowen theory in one's life.

Sometimes, symptoms will not completely disappear, because of years of establishment in the body/brain. And sometimes, symptoms will need specific treatments as they take on a life of their own (as with an ulcer or detoxification from substance abuse, for example), but Bowen theory can be relied upon to assist in the improvement or arresting of symptoms, as the relationship system goes on to a better level of functioning. Of course, sometimes, symptoms drop off altogether as people do their relationship work.

In your opinion, what are the necessary characteristics that a therapist should possess to be effective with this model?

The best paradigm for the Bowen family systems theory–directed therapist may be that of "coach." The coach having been involved with the game (thinking systems) longer than the players is a resource to them. The coach may be able to think of plays, on the basis of experience, that the players do not. The coach can see the bigger picture—the whole field—better than the players themselves. By not taking sides, by maintaining the intellectual curiosity of the scientific researcher, the coach is able to ask questions and make a few points to the family that it can use "in the field."

In contrast to other methods of therapy, in Bowen theory–directed therapy, the work of change is actually not done in the consulting room. It is done rather in the emotional field of the family itself. Bowen thought that "what developed in the relationship system can be changed in it." If one takes one's patterns back to the emotional field where they originally developed (in one's family of origin), I have found the results to be strikingly different and much better than when the major work was done in the consulting room.

Bowen theory–guided coaching is anything but passive, though it is rarely actively directive. Rather, questions and considerations, from a knowledge of theory, are given for people to think about. It is only one's own thinking, not that of the therapist, after all, that is life changing.

Characteristics of an ideal Bowen theory–oriented coach would include:

- *Thorough knowledge of theory gained through didactic training over several years, reading, and his or her own personal coaching experience.*
- *A relationship stance that is equal to the person(s) in the room, with openness in communication and separate self-boundaries—an ability to stay out of the anxiety generated in the room.*
- *The ability to be and stay neutral.*
- *The ability to "stay out" of the problem—not taking it on as one's own.*
- *Not knowing the answers and instead, bringing some ideas to the table that might be useful to the family.*
- *Not trying to "fix" anyone. Letting the family take on that task.*
- *An ability to continue to think when the anxiety gets intense.*

How often does the client see you and for how long a period of time?

In the beginning of coaching, I usually recommend weekly sessions, and each session is 45 minutes to 1 hour. Once the anxiety subsides appreciably (usually after two to four sessions), I reduce the frequency to every 2 to 4 weeks. I have no set period of time. People are welcome to continue as long as the work is useful. The door is never closed. After people gain some facility with theory, however, they often attend only when life's intensities indicate the need for a calmer outside angle of a triangle with whom to reflect.

What are you looking for when you are in the session?

I'm looking for patterns (conflict, distance, cutoff, over/underfunctioning, and triangles). I'm also observing the level of anxiety to see functioning level of differentiation and how people will manage their anxiety. Getting the anxiety down is, after all, the first-phase task of therapy.

What is the assessment process of this model?

Perhaps the most in-depth writing on the subject has been done by Dr. Michael Kerr in *Family Evaluation*. My own assessment process, in addition to the questions (above), would feature a listening ear and a curiosity guided by theory and some of the following questions:

- *How open is this family to "a new way of thinking"?*
- *What can I learn from this family?*
- *Are they in a "regression" that will yield to their usual higher functioning level in time? Or are they a chronically anxious and low-functioning group as a rule?*
- *How does their functioning compare to that of their generations?*
- *What specific thoughts can I bring to bear that may be of use?*
- *What traps or land mines do I need to watch out for? (Do they have unrealistic "quick-fix" expectations, or do they want me to fix their offspring, while they are unwilling to do the needed work of becoming a better functioning parent, for example?)*

Who sets the goals, the client or the therapist?

Goals become apparent from understanding the scale of differentiation of self—roughly equivalent to "emotional maturity." The answer to "What would be my/the person's/the family's next step up?" is usually fairly obvious when one stops to think about levels of functioning on a hypothetical scale. I, as a coach or therapist, may have an idea of what I think the next step up would be for someone. However, the only goals that will be actually pursued in the end will be those of the person. Questions like "What would be the next step up for you?" can be most useful in the process, though.

What are some commonly used interventions with this model?

Since Bowen theory is a "bootstraps operation," therapists don't make interventions as are commonly understood. The closest one might be that of making a recommendation for increased or more meaningful contact with family members.

What role do homework assignments have in this model?

Homework assignments imply to me that I know something that will help that you don't. Other than theory, I don't know anything like that. It would be up to the person to take the theory he or she learns and see how to put it into practice. That is the only kind of assignment most responsible people will carry out anyway. Sometimes, people ask for assignments, when they have had prior "training" in other traditions. I ask them to figure out their assignments for themselves.

How do you know when your client is ready to terminate?

I don't terminate with people, but occasionally have suggested less frequent sessions. Change is slow for all of us and, in many ways, it is not intuitive. Therefore, as Bowen said, time on the calendar is needed more than time in the therapist's office.

What have you found to be the limitations of this approach?

The limitations are set only by the people themselves. If they are willing to work, theory is there to assist them to a better level. If they are not, or are looking for a quick fix or easy approach, Bowen theory is not for them. It is not easy to pull up on the scale of differentiation of self. But it is the most worthwhile venture I know of.

What suggestions do you have for students?

After their "basic" training in college and grad school, I would recommend getting into a good solid Bowen theory training program that includes didactic lectures, discussion, and group and individual coaching. Then stay there for several years—preferably until you aren't learning anything anymore. Then get into an advanced program of research, writing, and discussion. In addition, read, read, read. After a few years, when one is able to begin to write one's own papers, do so. Nothing makes for clarity like writing.

Is there anything you would like to add?

Two things come to mind.

1. *The number of people in the room does not determine whether I am doing family therapy. I am always thinking systems and, thus, doing family therapy even when one person is present with me. In fact, that is the more likely scenario.*

2. *One of the concepts of Bowen theory is that of "societal emotional process." It states that all the emotional patterns we see in a family, including how a family can slip into a regression, we can see in society itself. Beginning in the 1960s, Bowen believed that we were heading into a societal regression. Since that time, the regression (with increasing anxiety, increasing irresponsibility, and societal dysfunction) has only increased.*

It may be that in a time of societal regression, it is characteristic for people to unrealistically demand a quick fix, and they don't want to have to think about taking responsibility for increasing their own functioning. It may be that anxiety has reached a point today that only a few can sit still long enough and do the hard work necessary to become trained to be a Bowen theory–oriented therapist or the work on self required of a person in coaching. For those few, the rewards are great.

Case Study

A mother calls and makes an appointment for her family to come to therapy. The family consists of a husband and wife, both in their 40s; their 15-year-old son; a college-aged daughter; and the woman's father, age 82. Three years after the woman's mother died, her father developed Alzheimer's disease. He moved in with the family 6 months ago. When his health began to deteriorate, the woman spent more time caring for him than for other members of the family. Three months ago, the 15-year-old son, who has been treated for attention deficit hyperactivity disorder since age 7, began to refuse to take his medication and is now being truant from school.

During the session, the wife cries and the husband reports their relationship is strained, while occasionally rolling his eyes as his wife becomes tearful. He reports that he has had to take on more work because his wife had to quit her job to attend to her father's needs. The daughter is away at college and the wife smiles as she describes her as a straight-A student. The daughter was asked to attend the session but refused because she has a hard time with her grandfather's illness and dislikes the conflict that has developed at home.

Dr. Roberta Gilbert's Response to the Case Study

I would invite only the parents to the sessions. They are the leaders of the family and, as such, the emotional climate is pretty much determined by their anxiety level. It would be easier for me to assist them with that when just the two of them are present.

- *I would ask them to take turns speaking, to speak only to me and not to each other. As they do that, they will have an opportunity, sometimes for the first time, to "hear" each other. I will work on my own reactivity, trying to stay emotionally calm, not take sides, and think theory.*

- *The initial goal will be for the family or individual to get its anxiety to a level where thinking will start to take place. Thinking, after all, is how problems are solved, even emotional ones.*

- *I would get a family diagram started, and that will give me lots of clues as to what is going on in the relationship system. For example, the parents' sibling positions may reveal how some of their relationship patterns got established. The sibling positions of the parents' parents, in turn, will also often be revealing.*

- *I would draw figures of the relationship patterns I see taking place and see if they agree with what I noticed.*

- *In the first session, I would explain how I work—frequency of sessions, length of sessions, etc. I also explain why I did not see the children. Parents are the leaders of the family and also the best coaches for their children. If I can coach them in stepping up to a better level of functioning and in their relationships with each other and their children, the children's functioning will automatically improve over time. I will also ask them to work only on self and not to try to change the other.*

- *In subsequent sessions, I would work according to the same format, with the family diagram posted somewhere in the room so it can be referred to as needed.*

- *Once the anxiety has subsided and they are beginning to think toward solutions, I would reduce the weekly frequency of sessions to every 2 weeks, schedules permitting.*

- *My goal to always bring theory to bear on whatever is brought in would stay the same. And I would try to manage myself toward emotional calm (not taking on the anxiety of the family) and neutrality (not taking sides).*

- *If one of the two drops out, as often happens, I would continue with whoever comes. Since the family is an emotional unit, if one person in the relationship system works on self and goes up to a higher level of functioning, the whole unit will do the same in time. All the people in an emotional unit (the family) benefit by the work of one.*

Acknowledgment: I gratefully acknowledge Mary Ann Crossno, MS, for inviting me to take part in this effort. Special thanks go to Victoria Harrison, MA, and Joseph D. Douglass, PhD, for their thoughtful reading of and constructive comments about the manuscript.

KEY TERMS

Anxiety   An organism's response to a threat, real or imagined.

Basic self   The ability of one not to change because of coercion or pressure, to gain approval, or to enhance one's stand with others.

Cutoff   A situation that occurs when related people separate from each other because of disagreements or unresolved situations, resulting in little to no communication or recognition of being related.

Defining self   A process of gaining control over one's emotional reactivity to one's family, thereby developing the ability to become a more objective observer in one's own family.

Detriangling   A dynamic that occurs when one is involved in an emotional issue involving two other people and desires not to take sides, counterattack, or defend oneself to have a neutral response.

Differentiation of self   A process of managing one's individuality and togetherness within a relationship system that involves having the ability to distinguish between *feeling* and *intellectual* processes.

Differentiation-of-self scale   A scale that measures a person's current level of differentiation of self on a continuum from 0 to 100.

Emotion   The automatic processes that govern the life forces in all living things; synonymous with instinct but not synonymous with feelings.

Emotional closeness   The built-in life force that draws persons toward intense togetherness.

Emotional functioning   The biological, automatic activity controlled by the automatic nervous system, subjective emotional and feeling states, and the forces that govern relationship systems.

Emotional reactivity   The emotional reflex that occurs automatically and out of awareness, most observable in moderate levels of tension.

Emotional system   The intimate part of human's evolutionary past, which the human shares with all lower forms of life.

Family   A group of people or animals affiliated by kinship, affinity, or coresidence. It is composed of various systems and subsystems, and a change in one part of the system is followed by a compensatory change in other parts of the system.

Family emotional system   The triangular emotional patterns that operate in all close relationships.

Feeling   A subjective awareness; derivative of deeper emotional state registered on a screen within the intellectual system of a person.

Feeling system   The link between emotional and intellectual systems through which certain emotional states are represented in conscious awareness.

Fusion   The ways that people borrow or lend self to another person in such a state that neither person appears to function independent of the other.

Individuality   The ability to maintain growth toward a separate self.

Instinctive biological process   Instinctive biological process refers to the process where behaviors are performed without being based upon prior experience.

Intellectual system   The ability of a person to think, reason, reflect, and govern his or her life in certain areas, according to logic, intellect, and reason.

Interlocking triangles   When a triangle occurs between three people, it is often *interlocking*—meaning that each person in the initial triangle is part of other triangles.

"I position"   The ability of a person to calmly state and own a concern and act on convictions and beliefs, without criticizing others' beliefs and without becoming involved in emotional debate.

Irresponsible "I"   That part of the self that makes demands on others with, "I want or I deserve, or this is my right or my privilege."

Nodal events   The events that lead to major alterations or turning points in the functioning of the family.

No-self   A functioning in a person that occurs as a reaction to others' anxiety and subjectivity where that person functions in a manner borrowed from others.

Parental we-ness   The psychological principle that parents should "present a united front to their children"; presents the child with a locked-in "two against one" position with no emotional flexibility.

Person-to-person relationship   An ideal situation in which two people communicate freely about the full range of personal issues between them.

Projection process   A process whereby parents transmit their own emotional problems to their child in the form of relationship sensitivities, such as heightened needs for attention and approval, difficulty dealing with expectations in life, the tendency to blame oneself or others, and feeling responsible for the happiness of others.

Pseudo-self   The principles, beliefs, and philosophies that are created and influenced by emotional pressure.

Responsible "I"   An ability to assume responsibility for one's own happiness and comfort; avoiding thinking that blames others.

Reversal   The ability to see the other side of the issue, to interject a bit of humor, to change the pace, and to remain casual in the face of family seriousness.

Self   A psychological identity of a person that is composed of constitutional, physical, physiological, biological, genetic, and cellular reactivity factors whereby a pseudo-self is fused with emotional process, resulting in lower levels of differentiation.

Sibling position   Sibling position refers to the placement of siblings in a family in the order of their birth.

Solid self   Has clearly defined beliefs, opinions, convictions, and life principles, incorporated into self from one's own life experiences by a process of intellectual reasoning and careful consideration of alternatives involved in the choices.

Systems thinking   The process of understanding how, what, when, and where an event happened influences one another within a whole.

Togetherness amalgam   The tendency to think about another before self, living for others, sacrificing for others, loving, being devoted and compassionate to others, and feeling responsible for the comfort and well-being of others.

Triangle   A three-person emotional configuration in which two persons out of three bring in a third party to ease the anxiety between the initial two.

Undifferentiated   Undifferentiated refers to people who live in a "feeling-controlled" world, in which their emotions and subjectivity dominate objective-reasoning most of the time.

REFERENCES

American Association for Marriage and Family Therapy Annual Conference, 1990.

Becvar, D. S., & Becvar, R. J. (2003). *Family therapy: A systemic integration* (5th ed.) Boston, MA: Allyn and Bacon.

Bowen Center for the Study of the Family. (2005, July 13). *Murray Bowen, MD*. Retrieved July 20, 2005, from http://www.thebowencenter.org/pages/murraybowen.html

Bowen, M. (1961). Family psychotherapy in office practice. *Family Systems, 7*(1), 30–44.

Bowen, M. (1976). Theory in the practice of psychotherapy. In P. J. Guerin (Ed.), *Family therapy: Theory and practice* (pp. 42–90). New York, NY: Gardner Press.

Bowen, M. (1978). *Family therapy in clinical practice.* Northvale, NJ: Jason Aronson.

Bowen, M. (1979). On emotional process in society. In R. R. Sagar (Ed.), *Bowen: Theory & practice* (pp. 211–217). Washington, DC: Georgetown Family Center.

Center for the Study of Human Systems. (2005). Retrieved from http://www.hsystems.org/

Comella, P. A. (1995). Natural selection, technology, and anxiety. *Family Systems, 4*(1), 19–33.

Gilbert, R. M. (1992). *Extraordinary relationships: A new way of thinking about human interactions.* New York, NY: John Wiley & Sons.

Goldenberg, I., & Goldenberg, H. (2000). *Family therapy: An overview* (5th ed.). Belmont, CA: Wadsworth.

Guerin, P. J. (1978). System, system, who's got the system? In E. G. Pendagast (Ed.), *The family: Compendium I: The best of the family, 1973–1978* (pp. 9–16). Rye Brook, NY: Center for Family Learning.

Guerin, P. J. (1991). The man who never explained himself. In E. G. Pendagast (Ed.), *The family: Compendium III* (p. 24). Rye Brook, NY: Center for Family Learning.

Guerin, P. J., & Chabot, D. R. (1992). Development of family systems theory. In E. G. Pendagast (Ed.), *The family: Compendium III* (pp. 3–21). Rye Brook, NY: Center for Family Learning.

Guerin, P. J., & Guerin, K. (2002). Bowenian family therapy. In J. Carlson & D. Kjos (Eds.), *Theories and strategies of family therapy* (pp. 126–157). Boston, MA: Allyn and Bacon.

Hall, C. M. (1981). *The Bowen family theory and its uses.* New York, NY: Jason Aronson.

Harrison, V. (1999). Psychotherapy, science and Bowen theory. *Family Systems Forum, 1*(4), 1–4.

Harrison, V. (2004). An example of systems therapy. *Family Systems Forum, 6*(3), 3–8.

Kerr, M. E. (1984). The borderline family. In R. R. Sagar (Ed.), *Bowen: Theory & practice* (pp. 91–103). Washington, DC: Georgetown Family Center.

Kerr, M. E. (1985). Obstacles to differentiation of self. In A. S. Gurman (Ed.), *Casebook of marital therapy* (pp. 111–153). New York, NY: The Guilford Press.

Kerr, M. E. (1986). Significance of Murray Bowen's scientific contributions. In R. R. Sagar (Ed.), *Bowen: Theory & practice* (pp. 3–13). Washington, DC: Georgetown Family Center.

Kerr, M. E. (1988a, September). Chronic anxiety and defining a self: An introduction to Murray Bowen's theory of human emotional functioning. *The Atlantic*, 35–57.

Kerr, M. E. (1988b, Spring). Darwin to Freud to Bowen: Toward a natural systems theory of human behavior. *Georgetown Magazine.*

Kerr, M. E. (1988c). Some aspects of systems thinking. In R. R. Sagar (Ed.), *Bowen: Theory & practice* (pp. 23–32). Washington, DC: Georgetown Family Center.

Kerr, M. E. (1991a). Anecdotes and memories of Murray Bowen. *Family Systems Forum, 2*(3), 6–7.

Kerr, M. E. (1991b). Living the theory. *Family Systems Forum, 2*(3), 5.

Kerr, M. E. (1992). Physical illness and the family emotional system: Psoriasis as a model. *Behavioral Medicine, 18*(3), 101–113.

Kerr, M. E. (1995). Theory and therapy. In R. R. Sagar (Ed.), *Bowen: Theory & practice* (pp. 102–103). Washington, DC: Georgetown Family Center.

Kerr, M. E. (1999). Murray Bowen, Bowen theory, and the family movement. *Family Systems Forum, 1*(2), 5–7.

Kerr, M. E. (2003). *One family's story: A primer on Bowen theory.* Washington, DC: Georgetown Family Center.

Kerr, M. E., & Bowen, M. (1988). *Family evaluation.* New York, NY: W. W. Norton.

Papero, D. V. (1990). *Bowen family systems theory.* Boston, MA: Allyn and Bacon.

Papero, D. V. (1992). Responsibility for self. In R. R. Sagar (Ed.), *Bowen: Theory & practice* (pp. 123–132). Washington, DC: Georgetown Family Center.

Papero, D. V. (1996). Stress, society, and the individual. In R. R. Sagar (Ed.), *Bowen: Theory & practice* (pp. 219–229). Washington, DC: Georgetown Family Center.

Titelman, P. (Ed.). (1998). Clinical applications of Bowen family systems theory. Binghamton, NY: The Haworth Press.

Toman, W. (1993). *Family constellation: Its effects on personality and social behavior.* (4th ed.). New York, NY: Springer Publishing.

RECOMMENDED READING LIST

Books

Bowen, M. (1966). Clinical view of the family. In M. E. Kerr (Ed.), *Family systems: A journal of natural systems thinking in psychiatry and the sciences* (pp. 154–156). Washington, DC: Georgetown Family Center.

Bowen, M. (1978). *Family therapy in clinical practice.* Northvale, NJ: Jason Aronson.

Bowen, M. (1980). Clinical addendum. In R. R. Sagar (Ed.), *Bowen: Theory & practice* (pp. 183–190). Washington, DC: Georgetown Family Center.

Bowen, M. (1982a). Mental health and science. *Family Systems Forum, 2*(3), 2–4.

Bowen, M. (1982b). Subjectivity, Homo sapiens and science. In R. R. Sagar (Ed.), *Bowen: Theory & practice* (pp. 15–21). Washington, DC: Georgetown Family Center.

Carlson, J., & Kjos, D. (Producers). (1998). *Bowenian therapy with Dr. Philip Guerin* [Videotape]. Boston, MA: Allyn and Bacon.

Comella, P. A. (2001). Triangles: The "glue" of Bowen family systems theory. *Family Systems, 6*(1), 64–76.

Fogarty, T. F. (1973–1978). Triangles. In E. G. Pendagast (Ed.), *The family: Compendium I* (pp. 41–49). Rye Brook, NY: Center for Family Learning.

The Georgetown Family Center. (Producer). (1970). *The basic series tape two—Nuclear family emotional system and family projection process* [Motion picture]. (Available from Bowen Center for the Study of the Family, 4400 MacArthur Boulevard, NW, Washington, DC 20007–2521)

Gilbert, R. M. (1992). *Extraordinary relationships: A new way of thinking about human interactions.* New York, NY: John Wiley & Sons.

Gilbert, R. M. (1999). *Connecting with our children: Guiding principles for parents in a troubled world.* New York, NY: John Wiley & Sons.

Gilbert, R. M. (2004). *The eight concepts of Bowen theory: A new way of thinking about the individual and the group.* Falls Church, VA: Leading Systems Press.

Guerin, P. J. (1976). Family therapy: The first twenty-five years. In P. J. Guerin (Ed.), *Family therapy: Theory and practice* (pp. 2–22). New York, NY: Gardner Press.

Guerin, P. J., Fay, L. F., Burden, S. L., & Kautto, J. G. (1987). *The evaluation and treatment of marital conflict: A four-stage approach.* New York, NY: Basic Books.

Guerin, P. J., Fogarty, T. F., Fay, L. F., Burden, S. L., & Kautto, J. G. (1996). *Working with relationship triangles: The one-two-three of psychotherapy.* New York, NY: The Guilford Press.

Kerr, M. E., & Bowen, M. (1988). *Family evaluation.* New York, NY: W. W. Norton.

Nichols, M. P., & Schwartz, R. C. (1995). *Family therapy: Concepts and methods* (3rd ed.). Boston, MA: Allyn and Bacon.

Papero, D. V. (1990). *Bowen family systems theory.* Boston, MA: Allyn and Bacon.

Titelman, P. (Ed.). (1998). *Clinical applications of Bowen family systems theory.* Binghamton, NY: The Haworth Press.

Websites

Bowen Center for the Study of the Family
http://www.thebowencenter.org

Center for the Study of Human Systems
http://www.hsystems.org

Center for the Study of Natural Systems and the Family
http://www.csnsf.org

Ideas to Action
http://ideastoaction.wordpress.com/

The Prairie Center for Family Studies
http://www.theprairiecenter.com/

Contextual Family Therapy 4

Edita Ruzgyte

Consider the following. We humans are social beings. We come into the world as the result of others' actions. We survive here in dependence on others. Whether we like it or not, there is hardly a moment of our lives when we do not benefit from others' activities. For this reason, it is hardly surprising that most of our happiness arises in the context of our relationships with others.

—Dalai Lama

INTRODUCTION

Contextual therapy originated from the work of Ivan Boszormenyi-Nagy, who was one of the pioneers in family therapy movement. This therapy approach is about understanding and intervening in relationships (Hargrave & Pfitzer, 2003). It is an integrative, intergenerational, and multilateral family therapy approach. According to Boszormenyi-Nagy, it is integrative because it embraces biology, psychology, transactional patterns, and responsibility (Boszormenyi-Nagy & Krasner, 1986). It is intergenerational because it seeks the understanding of the individual and family context of at least three generations (Goldenthal, 1993). Finally, its multilateral aspect is apparent in the contextual therapist's attempt to understand and be partial to all people who are affected by the discussions in therapy session (Boszormenyi-Nagy, 1987).

IVAN BOSZORMENYI-NAGY, MD

Ivan Boszormenyi-Nagy was born in Hungary, the son of a Supreme Court judge in the lineage of three generations of high judges (Ducommun-Nagy, 2002). The teachings of his father sparked Nagy's interest in loyalty and justice. The entire ancestry undoubtedly influenced much of his thinking considering the ontological (the standpoint of *being* rather than *knowing*) character of contextual theory (Boszormenyi-Nagy, 1987). He grew up in an extended family, which may have influenced his ability to feel comfortable inviting several generations of family members into one session. Boszormenyi-Nagy graduated from medical school in Budapest in 1944 and, a year later, started biochemical studies in his second year of psychiatric residency at the University of Budapest. During this time, Hungary, a comparatively small country but very rich in culture and heritage, was caught in the battle of two oppressive powers: Hitler (Germany) and Stalin (Russia; Boszormenyi-Nagy, 1987).

In 1948, Boszormenyi-Nagy was forced to leave Hungary because he refused to submit to the Stalin regime, which limited his research and creative opportunities (Ducommun-Nagy, 2002). He spent 2 years in Austria as a refugee, where he worked as a neurologist and psychiatrist for the International Refugee Organization. In the early 1950s, he reached the United States and remained there until his death.

Leaving his homeland and accepting the role of immigrant brought him close "to the issues of migration and dual loyalties to a hurt homeland and an accepting host country" (Ducommun-Nagy, 2002, p. 466). At the time he entered the United States, he found the U.S. psychiatrists searching for the cure for schizophrenia. Boszormenyi-Nagy joined those efforts, and his interest turned toward behavioral and psychological issues related to schizophrenia. With the inspiration of Kalman Gyarfas, director of Chicago State Hospital, Boszormenyi-Nagy started to explore the significance of the relationship. His work that later became known as the contextual therapy model was an attempt to look at two core levels of motivation and relationship while tying together "individual insight and transactional patterning of behavior" (Boszormenyi-Nagy, 1987).

In 1957, Boszormenyi-Nagy became a psychiatric research director at the newly created Eastern Pennsylvania Psychiatric Institute (EPPI) in Philadelphia, Pennsylvania. Here, in 1958, Nagy and associates started to see inpatient clients with their families instead of treating them individually, a move that marks the beginning of family therapy. This institute sponsored several family therapy conferences, and by 1967, Nagy helped to create the American Family Therapy Association. Later, the EPPI became the Department of Family Psychiatry, which is known as one of the earliest and largest training centers for family therapy (Ducommun-Nagy, 2002). Later still, it became the Family Institute of Philadelphia, which is one of the earliest freestanding institutes in the country. In the mid-1960s, the Family Institute of Philadelphia became a training facility that reached not only American therapists, but also European therapists as well. Several groups around the world that originally stemmed from the Family Therapy Institute in Pennsylvania are continuing the work and legacy of Boszormenyi-Nagy.

INTRODUCTION TO CONTEXTUAL FAMILY THERAPY

When asked about relationship-based treatment, Boszormenyi-Nagy (1987) replied, "I consider it 'scientifically' the most rational treatment for the 'patient' as well as for all others involved in his important relationships" (p. 119). According to Boszormenyi-Nagy (1986), contextual therapy is not just a school of family therapy, but it also "represents a search for the common denominator of therapy as a whole" (p. 196). It is a therapeutic versus theoretical approach in which all the theoretical facets originated and were validated by Boszormenyi-Nagy's observations of individual, family, or couples therapy (Goldenthal, 1993).

The contextual therapy model links together the individual and his or her needs with the relational aspect of his or her being. People do not live in isolation, and their lives are affected and shaped based on the present as well as past relationships and encounters (Goldenthal, 1996). In some instances, a person can behave in a certain way without realizing what effects the behavior has on a present relationship, and without knowing the origins and the reasoning of that particular behavior. Contextual therapy looks at the patterns of people's relationships and the meaning people place on those patterns.

Contextual family therapy is an intergenerational therapy model that embraces at least three generations in the family session. Issues such as trustworthiness, loyalties, fairness, and entitlement are addressed during the sessions. It is important to note that strategies used in contextual therapy are not meant to delete or discount the impact of a past relationship; instead, they are intended to recognize the patterns that will lead to repair and enrichment of the present and future relationship (Boszormenyi-Nagy, 1987). It can be summarized as remembering a different past to create a free and secure future.

Concepts of Contextual Family Therapy

Entitlement

A fundamental concept of contextual therapy is that of *entitlement*. According to Boszormenyi-Nagy (1987), entitlement in the family is the foundation of "freedom to enjoy life, creativity and courage of commitment" (p. 238). This phenomenon belongs to the individual and is achieved by each family member striving to care about the interests and well-being of others.

Entitlement can be constructive or destructive. *Constructive entitlement* is developed when family members receive a fair return from their giving (acknowledgment, praise, etc.). Boszormenyi-Nagy noted that constructive entitlement allows the individual to maintain freedom and security in his or her life:

> The person capable of earning entitlement through relationships is more able to claim his due in relationships, to enjoy life, including sexuality, to undertake the risks of new relationships, and to be free of either psychosomatic illness or self-destructive patterns of behavior. (Boszormenyi-Nagy, 1987, p. 244)

Destructive entitlement (Boszormenyi-Nagy, 1993) refers to old hurts being revenged in a new present and future. For example, if a child is abused in his or her home, he or she may be hurt and seek both justice and revenge. However, when there is no compensation afforded in the family of origin, this revenge is often taken out on new relationships. The child, later as an adult, believes he or she is entitled to act or behave in this manner because of his or her own history (Boszormenyi-Nagy, 1993). The consequence of this destructive reality can be lack of remorse in the destructive marital or parental behavior (Boszormenyi-Nagy, 1987). In many instances, people who have experienced destructive entitlement from their parents or spouses refuse to blame them and, instead, they continue to earn destructive entitlement through "remaining invisible loyal, captive victims of the past" (Boszormenyi-Nagy, 1987, p. 245).

Loyalty

Loyalty is an ethical concept of obligation to another person in a close relationship. Feelings of loyalty are a psychological domain, and being loyal involves accepting obligations in relatedness and sharing power (Goldenthal, 1993). Loyalty often transcends current imbalances in the ledger of give-and-take because of the human need to be loyal (Brown-Standridge & Floyd, 2000). This can be seen in accepting parents' religion; spouse's profession; or the child's mimicking of parental values, attitudes, and beliefs. Loyalty can also be invisible in some cases where one behavior is substituted for another behavior. An example can be the nonmonogamous parent who has a child who is loyal to his or her spouse but has an "affair" with work, golf, or other nonsexual experiences.

Split loyalty occurs when a person is forced to be more loyal or more disloyal to significant people in his or her life. Usually, it signifies a conflict, where to be loyal to one person, he or she has to be disloyal to another. This situation is very commonly experienced by children whose parents have mistrustful and hostile relationships. Sadly, this phenomenon often occurs in the situation of divorces, especially highly conflictual divorces in which there is a battle for custody or visitation. This is very damaging to children as they mature and can create many relational problems (Goldenthal, 1993).

Parentification

Parentification refers to the misuse of parental authority by engaging in asymmetrical relationships between parent and child. Common examples include children who are forced to "take care" of their parents, and children who are infantilized to maintain the parents' identity (Boszormenyi-Nagy & Krasner, 1986).

Revolving Slate

This concept refers to a multigenerational transmission of injustice and destructive entitlement. When parents are damaged and have unresolved issues with their family of origin, they seek their entitlement from their child. By doing so, they rob the child of his or her own just entitlement. This creates the repetition of the same injustices and distrust experienced by the parents in their family in the child's experience of his or her family (Boszormenyi-Nagy & Spark, 1984).

Ledger of Merits

Ledger of merits is used to describe the balance between give and take within a relationship. Each individual is obligated to give and entitled to receive from the relationship (Hargrave, Jennings, & Anderson, 1991). When this ledger is in balance, the sense of fairness in the individual is satisfied. If this phenomenon continues for a period, people experience a sense of trustworthiness in the relationship (Boszormenyi-Nagy & Krasner, 1980).

Boszormenyi-Nagy (1987) made a clear distinction between symmetrical and asymmetrical relationships. A parent–child relationship is *asymmetrical* in that a child cannot give back to a parent all that he or she receives from the parent. Thus, what is expected here is equitable but not equal between parent and child. However, in adult relationships, one person owes the other person essentially the same due consideration (Boszormenyi-Nagy & Krasner, 1986).

The contextual therapy approach allows the therapist to pay attention to the balance of the ledger in the family relationships. The imbalance in the system is the foundation for pain, unfairness, and loss of trust (Goldenthal, 1996). This imbalance is created if a person continues to give and does not receive back from the relationship. At the same time, the imbalance occurs if a person is blocked from giving to others (Ducommun-Nagy, 2003).

Four Dimensions of Reality

Contextual therapy assumes that the key dynamic of any relationship is trustworthiness, which is achieved by all family members having mutual consideration of each other (Boszormenyi-Nagy & Krasner, 1980). It also assumes that accountability and fairness are the essential connecting powers in the relational association (Soyez, Tatrai, Broekaert, & Bracke, 2004). The term *contextual* refers to a therapeutic model that includes the ethical dimension as its guideline (Boszormenyi-Nagy, 1987) and is connected to other dimensions of facts,

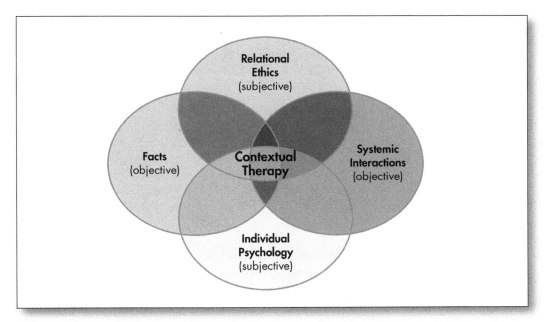

FIGURE 4.1 ▪ Dimensions in the contextual therapy approach.

individual psychology, and systemic interactions. According to Boszormenyi-Nagy (1987), contextual therapy "makes use of the resource of trust inherent in hidden relational invest-ments, instead of focusing on an effort to fight pathology or to impose 'change' in the service of social conformity" (p. 210).

The contextual therapy approach is historically an integrative process of four dimensions of reality: facts, individual psychology, systemic interactions, and relational ethics. Boszormenyi-Nagy wrote that these four dimensions "make up the relational context and dynamics of family functioning" (Boszormenyi-Nagy & Krasner, 1986, p. 44). See Figure 4.1.

Factual (Destiny)

This dimension represents the facts about life and relationships that are difficult to change. It may include biological facts (e.g., age, sex), medical conditions, historical facts (e.g., moth-er's death at childbirth), racial and cultural facts, and personal information (e.g., divorces, adoptions, financial conflicts; Boszormenyi-Nagy, 1987). Knowledge of the facts allows for the investigation of the comprehensive balance of merits (Boszormenyi-Nagy, 1987). Not all clients will recognize or be willing to admit that specific facts of their personal history have had any effect on their lives (Hargrave & Pfitzer, 2003). For example, a client may say that his or her parents' divorce had no effect on him or her even though that may not be the case. It is up to the therapist to recognize and ascertain the facts of the client's life.

Individual Psychology (Needs)

This dimension describes how people transform information from their external environ-ment into cognitive information, experiences, emotions, feelings, motivations, and memories (Hargrave & Pfitzer, 2003). During this process, a person develops a view of self, others, and the world, as well as the relationship between them, which, according to contextual therapy, becomes his or her *personality*. Different from the factual dimension, individual psychology is subjective, meaning that two people can come from identical backgrounds and have similar experiences but may construct very different individual personalities (Hargrave & Pfitzer, 2003).

Systemic Interactions (Power Alignments)

This dimension deals with communication patterns in relationships. This dimension is considered to be objective because of the fact that systemic interactions can be witnessed. The family rules, which constitute homeostasis, and appropriate role formation are communicated through different patterns of systemic interactions (Hargrave & Pfitzer, 2003).

Relational Ethics (The Balance of Fairness)

Relational ethics distinguishes contextual therapy from any other therapeutic approach. It deals with the balance of what people give and what they are entitled to receive from others. Boszormenyi-Nagy (1987) described this process as follows:

> To the extent that I benefit from your contribution, I become indebted to you and you obtain entitlement on the merit side of your "ledger." Then when I contribute to you or at least acknowledge your credit, I begin to restore the merit balance. (p. 207)

Unlike the more common usages of the word, in contextual family therapy, the word *ethics* does not refer to moral perceptions or any criteria of right and wrong (Boszormenyi-Nagy, Grunebaum, & Ulrich, 1991). Hargrave et al. (1991) wrote that this dimension is based on the idea that "without the experience of relating, giving, and receiving from another person, [the] individual has an insufficient basis to experience emotions and thoughts" (p. 146). Relational ethics deals with human beings achieving an acceptable balance of healthy relating among themselves, which in contextual therapy is called the balance between give and take.

The fairness in relationships has two dimensions: vertical (parental relationships) and horizontal (current relationships). These relational patterns of balance and trustworthiness, or imbalance and destructive entitlement, are passed from one generation to another. If a child does not receive adequate care from his or her parents, he or she experiences injustice. According to relational ethics, this child is entitled to some form of compensation. Typically, a child cannot claim it back from the parents, so he or she may attempt to receive it in his or her current relationships—which may turn into unfair treatment of his or her spouse or offspring (Ducommun-Nagy, 2002). In Boszormenyi-Nagy's theory, compensation must be repaid by the original person or entity (in this case, the parents); no substitutions are allowed (Boszormenyi-Nagy et al., 1991).

THEORETICAL ASSUMPTIONS

View of the Family and Client

Looking at an individual or a family through the prism of the contextual therapy model, the therapist assumes that "between people there exists a relational reality, an interlocking of their respective spontaneous motivations" (Boszormenyi-Nagy, 1987, p. xvii). Boszormenyi-Nagy encouraged therapists to limit their judgments toward clients. Instead, he asks that we remember that people are who they are. They are doing the best they can in the situation they are in using the tools that they have learned in their family of origin (Becvar & Becvar, 2003).

View on How Change Occurs

One of the main concepts in the contextual therapy model is the sense of entitlement that each person has in the family (Boszormenyi-Nagy & Krasner, 1986). Even if only one person comes to the session, the therapist has an "invisible contact" (Boszormenyi-Nagy, 1987, p. 246) with all family members who may be affected by the outcome of the therapeutic process. The change occurs when clients are able to earn constructive entitlement, which eventually brings trust that giving can be receiving. "Responsibility for the consequences for the self and others is a more relevant contextual therapeutic goal than mere production of 'change'" (Boszormenyi-Nagy, 1987, p. 246).

In later work (see, e.g., Boszormenyi-Nagy et al., 1991), Boszormenyi-Nagy talked about the purpose of the therapy as "to provide healing for an individual's pain or symptoms, as well as to address relational problems" (p. 201). Despite the number of family members who are present in the session, the goal is to "achieve a responsible orientation to intermember issues of trust and fairness" (Boszormenyi-Nagy et al., 1991, p. 202). It is important to note, however, that even though the contextual therapy model is based on the idea of trust and justice, the model does not provide the therapist with the power to restore and prevent injustice among members in the family (Boszormenyi-Nagy, 1997). In the session, contextual therapists have to limit their goal to family members' own definitions of their individual needs and claims to fairness and to avoid asserting a knowledge of what is "the good in the family life" (p. 192).

Therapist's Role

Within the contextual therapy model, the therapist does not take a neutral stance. The therapist's obligation is to be committed to side sequentially and continuously with every member of relationship who is affected by the therapeutic process (Soyez et al., 2004) even if they are not actively present in the session. Through this process of multidirected partiality, the therapist empathizes and gives credit to each family member, even if the credits may not be obvious at the beginning. This particular stance allows the therapist to open the dialogue among family members, which is based on responsibility, and encourages the family members to reinvest in trustworthiness (Boszormenyi-Nagy & Krasner, 1986). One of the main goals for the contextual family therapist is to encourage clients to talk about their justified relational position in the family as well as listen to the response of other family members. Boszormenyi-Nagy (1987) emphasized the importance of therapists' ability to involve all the family members in the session:

> This is an extremely significant, often overlooked point. The therapist's offer of simultaneous concern for the balance of fairness in relationships is thus a priori and not dependent on diagnostic criteria, the family's awareness of shared problems, or the particularities of feelings and hidden motivations in family members. The essential definition of family or relational therapy lies, therefore in the therapist's capacity for transcending the ethical limitations of the traditional individual psychotherapeutic contract. (p. 163)

According to Boszormenyi-Nagy, in the contextual therapy session, the therapist needs to be concerned with the issues of fairness among all members who are part of the relationship, their integrity, indebtedness, entitlement, and exploitation of each other. The role of the therapist is to "elicit and facilitate the self-reinforcing process of mutually merited trust between closely related people" (Boszormenyi-Nagy, 1987, p. 196). This can be achieved by the therapist modeling relational fairness through multidirected partiality, encouraging mutual care, consideration, and commitment among the members of the family.

Boszormenyi-Nagy (1987) made a distinction between the ability to "therapeutically utilize this deep dimension of relationships" (p. 166) versus "merely follow the 'technical' rule of 'seeing family members together'" (p. 166). One of the main challenges of a contextual therapist is not to avoid dramatic, complicated, and usually painful stories that clients bring to the session. The role of the therapist is to listen for family legacies, the state of the merit ledger, as well as rules of loyalties and entitlement among the members of the family. To achieve this depth in the session, the therapist has to use multidirectional partiality, which helps the therapist to be sensitive to each alternative aspect of each family member on the continuum of merit account of relationships.

Interventions

Boszormenyi-Nagy (1986) wrote that a therapist's insistence on seeing the whole family, or as many people as possible who are involved in the relationship, in itself constitutes the intervention of the contextual therapy model.

Multidirective partiality is one of the most important therapeutic tools as well as the main theoretical concept of the therapy process itself (Hargrave & Pfitzer, 2003). It is a therapeutic attitude that prevents therapists from siding with one particular person in the room. It is the aim of this attitude to "replace the dehumanizing attitude of therapeutic 'neutrality' and at the same time avoid the trap of becoming a judge of what is right and what is wrong" (Boszormenyi-Nagy, 1997, p. 172). Each family member learns that, once one is heard, it is easier to hear others and start building mutual trust and trustworthiness (Boszormenyi-Nagy, 1987).

The specific techniques of multidirective partiality are as follows:

1. *Empathy*—The therapist's ability to create emotional connectedness with clients' loss, pain, and grief (Goldenthal, 1996).

2. *Crediting*—The therapist acknowledges unfairness, violations, and imbalance that the client is experiencing (Goldenthal, 1996), at the same time, crediting the love and trustworthiness that can be separated from the "harm that was perpetuated" (Hargrave & Pfitzer, 2003, p. 100).

3. *Acknowledgment*—This emphasizes the attempts and contributions that the client has made in the relationship.

4. *Accountability*—Is holding clients responsible for their behaviors in the relationship. After emphasizing the feelings, crediting, and acknowledging the efforts, the therapist holds the client as well as other members of the family responsible for each of their actions that caused pain or violations of love and trustworthiness (Goldenthal, 1996).

During the process of *rejunction*, the therapist helps clients to explore their ability to re-create the balance among the family members, look at how each family member is available for each other, and look at how they use each other for their own needs. By discovering his or her own and other family members' part in the imbalance of the system, each member of the relational unit will gain sense of inner entitlement to autonomy and growth (Boszormenyi-Nagy, 1987).

The goal of contextual therapy is the restoration of trustworthiness in the relationship. In order for clients to reach this goal, the therapist has to assess the issues of mistrust and trust among the family members. It is important to note that the concept of trust as it is used in contextual family therapy cannot be forced or imposed by the sense of guilt or manipulation among the family members. Trust has to be earned through the actions of giving and earning merits (Boszormenyi-Nagy, 1987).

This model works best with families that deal with such intergenerational issues as grandparents raising grandchildren, abuse in the family, lack of parental presence, and others. Numerous articles (Brown-Standridge & Floyd, 2000) suggest that therapists using this model help clients to look at their families from a different perspective, develop new understanding for the motives of people's behaviors, and distinguish which aspects of relational ethics belong to them and which aspects belong to other family members. This new understanding can help clients develop compassion for each other and create an environment that nurtures emotional connections.

Literature also documents the success of therapists who use this model while working in the community of substance abusers (Soyez et al., 2004). More empirical data are needed to support the effectiveness of contextual family therapy while working with other populations.

Contextual family therapy is a multigenerational approach that works very well with families whose members are stuck in the past, troubled by the hurt that they experienced from their parents, and cannot move forward. According to Snyder, Wills, and Grady-Fletcher (1991), insight-based therapies such as contextual family therapy decrease the chances of divorce to 3%, whereas clients who experience behavioral therapies have a 38% chance of divorcing (Snyder et al., 1991, p. 1). Therefore, couples in need of marital therapy whose genogram is marked with several divorces, family members who have difficulties giving love and affection to another person, and people who have trust issues and feel that others have been unfair to them in their lives are excellent candidates for contextual family therapy.

For example, a 14-year-old girl was brought to a session by her parents to work on her troublesome behavior at school, drug use, and explicit sexual behavior. After doing the genogram and listening to family members' descriptions of interactions at home, the therapist learned that the daughter is the third and youngest child. A year ago, the parents told the first two children that they had to choose between using drugs and staying at home. They both chose to use drugs and left the house. As the parents were describing the situation, the youngest daughter made a statement: "They (parents) are doing exactly the same things as they did with my older siblings. When my siblings got older, they became in charge of the house. Every time something happened, my mom would cry, dad would be silent and never say anything and we (the kids) got to do whatever we wanted to do."

The therapist who worked on this case using the contextual family therapy approach started to talk to the parents about their childhood experiences. The therapist learned that both maternal grandparents abused alcohol and became physically disabled when the client's mother was 13 years old. At that time, the client's mother took over the parents' role. During the therapy sessions, the client's mother discovered how much pain, hurt, and grief she was experiencing over her parents' bad choices and the fact that she had to grow up and take charge of her and their lives. Because of this parentification process, she did not receive the love and support that she deserved from her parents.

The therapist helped the mother to understand that she became loyal to her parents and maintained the patterns alive not by becoming alcoholic but by working three jobs at a time, emotionally eliminating herself from her husband, and expecting the children to learn to be independent at an early age in the same way she did. She felt that she was entitled to receive it, but she wanted her children to pay the debt that her parents created. This was the beginning of several sessions during which each family member learned about each other from a different perspective. They understood the path that had led each of them to be where they are and make the choices that they did. This helped the family to create a more open communication and adopt healthier family roles whereby the parents were in charge of the family and did not expect their children to resolve the hurts and unfairness that the parents experienced in their past.

CONTEXTUAL FAMILY THERAPY MODEL WORKING TEMPLATE

The *contextual family therapy model template* is meant to be used as a guideline to learning the process of contextual family therapy. The template provides the beginning therapist a review of the tools for change in contextual therapy, followed by steps to take and questions to ask that promote collaboration between the therapist and client. There are suggested questions under each heading to help start the process. After using the initial questions, guide the client through each process and ask questions that occur to you, as you stay within the contextual therapy theory. Although there is no one "script" for any therapy session, it is the hope of the author that the template serves as an impetus to learning this family therapy model.

Tools for Change

Contextual family therapy is a psychodynamic and insight-based theoretical model. The main conceptualization is that there is a dynamic that is happening in the family. This dynamic is not an isolated, present event but the continuation of past loyalties, injustices, and entitlements from the family members. How the client conceptualizes what happened in his or her family continually results in dysfunction in current relationships.

Multidirected partiality is one of the most important tools used in the process of assessment and intervention. The therapist has to attempt to see the situation from the perspective of each individual who will be affected by the therapy. To help clients begin to work on the unbalanced ledger of merits, the therapist may ask them about their childhood, which can be especially helpful if their children are also in the session.

To maintain multidirected partiality and continue to be fair to each individual in the session, the therapist can use past situations of concern. For example, if one person is currently abusing his or her spouse, the therapist can refer to a past injustice and hurt, which that person has experienced another time. However, the therapist does not have an authority to make a distinction of what is right and what is wrong.

The therapist will design a plan that will help to form a valid base for trustworthiness between the members of the relational unit, thereby increasing client satisfaction and opportunities for change.

Phase 1: Joining and Building Rapport

This is the period for the therapist to build trustworthiness with the client. The therapist has to listen to the situation and assess the appropriateness of this psychodynamic, multigenerational model. At the same time, the client is assessing his or her interest in working with a specific therapist.

Here are some comments or questions that a therapist might use during this phase:

- *"What concerns brought you to this session?"*
- *"Please tell me about the family that you grew up in."*
- *"What was it like growing up in your family?"*
- *"What would you like to be different in your family after this session?"*

Phase 2: Understanding the Presenting Issue

When listening and forming therapeutic strategies, the therapist is making an assessment regarding all four dimensions: existential facts, individual psychology, family transactions and power, and relationship ethics.

Here are some comments or questions that a therapist might use during this phase:

- *"I would like to hear your side of the story about what happened."*
- *"What meanings have you chosen to give these events?"*
- *"How would things be different if your family was more trustworthy?"*

Using multidirected partiality questions also helps the therapist and family to understand the presenting issue:

- *"I am beginning to understand how the way your father treated you as a child causes you pain when your husband criticizes you. Can you tell me how you wish your father had treated you?"*
- *"I am beginning to sense that in your family, your father was head of the household and you saw that it troubled your mother. Can you tell me what your view is today of what might have been fairer in a marriage, such as with your parents?"*

Phase 3: Assessment of Family Dynamics

The contextual therapist's role is to listen to the client and family and invite them to think about the issues of fairness and trustworthiness. It is important that clients themselves discover and assess the fairness of their actions instead of the therapist identifying what is fair and what is not. The therapist's role is not to pose as a judge. The therapist should be very directive in asking questions, which allows the client to assess the basic ethical balances and learn the fundamentals of all the relationships in the family. The therapist uses the process of assessment to identify the intervention strategy based on the accessibility of trustworthiness reserves.

Here are some comments or questions that a therapist might use during this phase:

- *"How did you know that you were loved in your family?"*
- *"When was a time you felt especially valued by your family?"*
- *"How did you think about what your parents did as your caretakers?"*
- *"Did it ever make sense to you that the things your parent(s) did were their way of showing you_____?"*
- *"Can you see ways in which your family member tried to be helpful to you?"*
- *"Have you noticed other ways that the particular family member was making an attempt to give you more fairness (balanced ledger)?"*

Phase 4: Goals

The therapist encourages the clients to aim toward increased trust and exoneration, as well as accountable personal stance, which is directed toward clients acquiring inner entitlement for growth and personal freedom within the relationship.

Here are some comments or questions that a therapist might use during this phase:

- *"What would you like to see different in the relationship with your parents as a result of our meetings together?"*
- *"How will you begin to show your parents that you want things to be different in a way they will understand?"*
- *"What would it take for there to be more fairness in this marriage?"*
- *"Now that you are realizing that your family member was attempting to be fair to you, how might you have reacted to her differently?"*
- *"Now that you recognize that your adolescents are experiencing unfairness such as that which you experienced in your family, how might you change your interactions with them?"*
- *"Now that you understand what your parents did not do for you as a child to help you feel loved, how might you begin showing your own children your love for them so they feel differently than you did?"*

Phase 5: Amplifying Change

When the family members begin to recognize the change that they want in themselves and start doing things differently, it can be said that the goal has been met.

Here are some comments or questions that a therapist might use during this phase:

- *"I have noticed that you have made great progress in recognizing how your past relates to your current behavior. Can you summarize it for me?"*
- *"I have noticed that you are now asking your children to verbalize their concerns in therapy today. Can you help me understand how it is that you have encouraged this experience?"*
- *"Mom, the changes that you have apparently made with your adolescent daughter seem to have dramatically changed your relationship with her. Can you explain how you did this?"*
- *"Jack, I notice that your wife seems to be enjoying times to be close to you at home. Can you summarize how this is different from how things were before you came to therapy?"*

Phase 6: Termination

In the contextual therapy model, the termination of the therapy is a mutual decision between the therapist and the client. This decision can be made when the client can solve the situation at home, without needing the therapist. However, in the event further help is needed, the therapist should let clients know that they can call and make an appointment if necessary.

CATHERINE DUCOMMUN-NAGY

Catherine Ducommun-Nagy, MD, is a licensed family therapist and an approved supervisor of the American Association of Marriage and Family Therapy. She is an assistant professor in the graduate program in couples and family therapy at Drexel University in Philadelphia, Pennsylvania. She is the current director of the Institute for Contextual Growth, Inc., in Glenside, Pennsylvania, and she teaches contextual therapy internationally. She is the author of several articles and book chapters on the application of contextual therapy. Catherine Ducommun-Nagy was married to Ivan Boszormenyi-Nagy.

What attracted you to the theory behind contextual family therapy?

There are several elements that attracted me to contextual therapy. The first was my early interest for family therapy in general. This came from my clinical interest: Early on during my training as a psychiatrist in Switzerland, I worked for a state psychiatry program that provides services for a large population in a mostly rural area. Clients were grouped not according to similar diagnosis or similar treatment needs but according to postal codes. All people coming from a same location had to be treated by the same team. So if two members of a family needed help at the same time, they had to be referred to the same team. This obviously forced us to think about family dynamics and to become interested in family therapy. From my clinical experience, I gained a specific interest for multigenerational determinants of relationships. I was also very interested in the issue of family loyalties based on the complexity of my own family background. In my family of origin, people had very diverse interests, from a grandfather who was a dairy farmer to people interested in medicine, history, and arts. So for me, it was important to find a way to balance these very diverse influences. This led me to read.

How do you formulate your view of a family when they enter therapy?

You need to make a distinction between the family system described by classical family therapists and the relational context defined by the contextual therapists. The notion of relational context is bigger than the notion of family system because it encompasses relationships outside of the family transactional system. Therefore, it includes deceased relatives, absent family members, as well as members of the future generations. For instance, from the vantage point of a structural family therapist, one would like to know who is present and what place do family members occupy in the family power hierarchy. For example, if one observes a family formed by the wife, the wife's child, the husband, the husband's child, and the couple's common child at a dinner table, one could discuss their interaction in terms of power hierarchy without knowing anything more about the family. On the other end, if one wanted to discuss giving and receiving responsibilities, one would need to take into consideration the ex-husband as a father of one of the children or the ex-wife as a mother of the other child and both would be part of the relational context, even if one of the parents has moved to Australia or if the other had died.

What kind of families do you think benefit most from this model?

There is a large spectrum of families who can benefit from contextual therapy, because exploring relationships from the point of view of responsibilities is never something that could be detrimental. So in that sense, any family can benefit from contextual therapy because anyone can benefit from giving and anyone can benefit from receiving. From that vantage point, there is no contraindication to contextual therapy. People who are unable to care about others, who are blind to their needs and exploit them, may not look [like] good candidates for contextual therapy but, in fact, are the one who could benefit the most of it.

What issues do you think this model works best with?

It's my clinical conviction that, for instance, young people with conduct disorders are people who can be definitively helped with contextual therapy. By definition, people who present with conduct disorder infringe on the rights of others, but I believe that it is not because they are unable to care about others but because they have become discouraged to give to others based on their own experience of injustices. So in acknowledging the injustices in their lives, there is a chance to help them to take the risk of giving again.

In your opinion, what are the necessary characteristics that a therapist should possess to be effective with this model?

The role of the contextual therapist is not prescriptive or directive. As a contextual therapist, I am in a very different role than the psychiatrist who would tell a client, "This is your prescription. Until next week, take two pills a day and don't forget any." We do not prescribe tasks, we do not prescribe rituals. What we want is to help our clients bring up their points or their needs so that other family members can hear them and decide for themselves how to respond to them. So the therapist is responsible for the dialogue between family member and for helping each of them explore the consequences of their choices. The client is the one to decide then what to do and face the consequences for his or her decisions. As an experienced therapist, you might know which is the best move to bring the family to the place when one family member could start to give and the other to receive, which is the healing moment in therapy; but once you have made your move, you have to wait for the reaction of the family. You cannot control their moves. So you're always very active and very precise—No one wants to play chess sloppily—but your responsibility stops with your own moves, and the rest is the responsibility of the family members.

How often does the client see you and for how long a period of time?

Generally speaking, contextual therapists tend to be available to the families they treat for the long haul. I know that my husband (Ivan Boszormenyi-Nagy) worked with a woman first when she had her first psychotic episode as a young woman, later when she was struggling to raise her children, and much later when she asked to see him again as she was dying of cancer in her 50s. On the opposite side, he did an enormous amount of demonstration interviews in many different countries. The format was always the same: two interviews on 2 consecutive days. What he really wanted to accomplish was to give a chance to the family to react to the first interview by asking questions like "What are the things you regretted to have said? What has been helpful for you?" His purpose was simply to demonstrate to his student how to use the family reactions to a first session to plan for the next one, not specifically to help the family because it did not seem a realistic goal. Nonetheless, many families reported a significant improvement after those two meetings.

What are you looking for when you are in the session?

What interests me in the session is, of course, the interaction between family members, but also I am interested in understanding what people see in me: Do they see me as supportive, as critical? How do they use me? Do they see me as a good parent or as a frustrating parent? This is important to me because it can give me an idea of their relational needs. For that reason, I also often ask people about the very first reaction to their children. Whom did their child reminded them of? What was their first reaction to their child? For instance, a mother told me, "I saw my daughter as somebody who would never leave me." So, in this situation, the need of the mother to have someone who is close to her will clash with the right of the child to grow. Of course, I am interested in communication patterns in the family, but what interests me the most is to see if clients can hear each other's needs or if they [are] blatantly unfair to them. Some clients have the mental equivalent of a blind spot. As they have been wronged, they turn to others for compensation and in doing so, they do not realize that they are unfair themselves.

What is the assessment process of this model?

The first step in meeting with a new family is to assess the presenting problem as viewed by each family member, and to assess not only how it affects each of them but what each of them can see as a path towards a solution. Then, I try to assess all the factors that could contribute to the problem. While I am engaged in that process, I also gather a picture not only of the family transactions patterns and communication, but on the giving and receiving between family members during the session. I use a genogram to record information about family members and about family relationships. For me, it is much easier to recall information if it is organized this way than in the form of written notes. It also serves me as a tool to remember important family information. It is always very important to date genograms because they contain only the information that the family is willing to give you on a given date. At a later date, the family might change the story that was given to you or add new facts.

Who sets the goals, the client or the therapist?

One of the big questions in family therapy is to come to an agreement about treatment goals. In individual therapy, the goals are set by the individual clients. In family therapy, things are very different because each person has his or her own goals that might not match with the goals of others. So, already, the setting of treatment goals becomes part of the therapeutic process. The therapist has therefore to be able to help people deal with their conflict of interests in reference to their goals for therapy. A mother would like to help her daughter to recognize that she is not ready to leave home, the daughter might want the help of the therapist to gain more independence, and the father may mostly want the two women to stop arguing. There is no surprise that one of the goals of parents is to postpone the separation from the child because it is always a loss and the goal of the child is to be able to leave home. So, from the point of view of the contextual therapist, treatment goals are set through a dialogue between the family members, and the role of the therapist is not to set the goals for the family but to foster that dialogue. In many ways, therapy starts at the minute when the therapist offers his support to each family member to stand for their own goals while respecting goals of others.

What are some commonly used interventions with this model?
The main tool of the contextual therapist is multidirected partiality. The therapist offers to each person a chance to bring up his or her side of a claim, and the therapist offers his willingness to try to understand this persons' predicament. The therapist, then, does the same with each person in the family. One important intervention is to tell a person, for instance a wife, "Now I am going to listen to you." If the husband wants to interrupt, you will say, "I'm going to ask you to wait, but I will come back to you and give you the same chance to talk. But for now, I would like your wife to have a chance to finish with her points." In general, you never gratify the person who interrupts, but you gratify the person who is willing to make a responsible statement. This helps structuring the session because people will learn that you will listen to the ones who are willing make a positive contribution to the session, not the ones who just want to capture your attention out of their own neediness.

This brings me back to a question that was raised once to my husband. He was asked why he never worked with chaotic families. He answered, "Simply because they stop being chaotic when I see them." If you focus on stopping the chaos in sessions like a fireman who tries to stop a fire, family members will act in a very disruptive fashion to catch your attention. If you don't focus on the chaos, and focus only on rewarding people who attempt to make responsible statements, the others will quickly try to do the same because they want your attention, too. So, instead of competing with each other to become the most disruptive ones, they will start to compete for being the most cooperative ones. Another intervention is to listen patiently and not to interrupt clients with your own hypothesis or comments before you are sure that they have been given enough time.

What role does a homework assignment have in this model?
I never assign homework to families because my role is not to prescribe tasks but to be an agent who promotes the dialogue between family members. Occasionally, I recommend considering a specific subject, but if the family is not ready, I suggest a moratorium: "Okay, this is an important subject, but if you are not ready to discuss now, this is okay." On the other end, I will allow myself to come back to it at a later time. So I do not push the family further, but I do not give up either. What is important for me is to understand how family members have reacted to my session, so I do not give any tasks between sessions but ask family members to discuss their reactions to the last session. Did anyone regret to have said something, or did anyone realize that something more should have been said? These answers give you very useful information about the response of the family to the therapy process. So it helps you in designing your next interventions. On the other end, you never give family members the task to talk about the session during the week or conversely the task of avoiding any discussion.

How do you know when your client is ready to terminate?
Again, there are no fixed criteria. We also need to make a distinction between family therapy and individual therapy because criteria for termination are quite different. So, I will discuss the end of a treatment involving an entire family. As for the discussion of treatment goals, the discussion of termination needs to include the point of view of each family member. One person might be ready to terminate treatment while another family member might not be ready. But in general, clients who are ready to terminate therapy are clients who do not need the help of a therapist to maintain a productive dialogue with each other.

Since many of my clients used to go to a nearby pizza place either before or after their sessions, I used to tell them, "If you can handle talking to each other while eating your pizza as well as you do in session now, then you don't need me anymore." And again, whether or not people are ready for termination depends a lot on the goals set in therapy.

What have you found to be the limitations of this approach?

I see more limitations in the capacities of therapists to be good contextual therapists than in the approach itself. I believe that contextual therapy is a very effective form of therapy. What is difficult with contextual therapy is for the therapist to always keep in mind the complexity of the determinants that affect humans. So it is tempting for therapists to try to avoid this complexity by seeking simpler models of human relationships and simpler models of therapy, even if this simplification has a cost in terms of clinical effectiveness.

What are your suggestions that you have for students learning this model?

Young therapists need to learn that they have a right to feel comfortable and safe when they work so that they can give full attention to their clients. In that area, I can be rather demanding myself. I want to work in a quiet environment. If there is any noise that bothers me, I make sure to address this problem before starting the session. I want to be fully available for the family, so if something distracts me, I want to find a solution. I would rather take 2 minutes to address the problem of, for instance, a squeaky chair, rather than being distracted by that noise during the session. If someone plays with something dangerous like a paper cutter or a heavy object, I say, "Look, let's make things safe," and I take the object out of the room. Therapists have a right to feel safe and comfortable so that they can relax and devote all their attention to the session. I also strongly believe that when you indicate to your clients that you care about the setting so that they get the best out of the session, you can also demand more of them and expect that they, too, will try to do the best they can.

MASTER THERAPIST INTERVIEW

TERRY HARGRAVE

Terry Hargrave, PhD, is nationally and internationally recognized for his work with inter-generational families. Dr. Hargrave has authored numerous articles and books, including Loving Your Parents When They Can No Longer Love You *(Zondervan, 2005),* The New Contextual Therapy: Guiding the Power of Give and Take *(coauthored with Franz Pfitzer, MD, Brunner-Routledge, 2003),* Forgiving the Devil: Coming to Terms With Damaged Relationships *(Zeig, Tucker & Theisen, 2001), and* Families and Forgiveness: Healing Wounds in the Intergenerational Family *(Brunner/Mazel, 1994). Dr. Hargrave has studied with Boszormenyi-Nagy and is currently practicing and promoting the contextual therapy model. He is a professor of counseling at West Texas A&M University in Canyon, Texas, and is the president of the Amarillo Family Institute, Inc.*

What attracted you to the theory behind contextual family therapy?

My idea is that theory doesn't drive technique as much as theory orients the therapist on how to conceptualize problems and how to assess problems. So, that's I think what theory does for you. I don't think there's any particular magic. Whatever theory you're attracted to is usually representative of something that came along in your family. It helps you contextualize what happened to you. I come from a very physically abusive family. I lived in a very, very unhappy family of origin. So, basically, this theory helped me to contextualize what was going on my own family.

When I read the original chapter from Ulrich and Nagy, that they wrote in the early 80s, I thought, "This is great, there's something that's going on here that makes sense to me." And I think primarily what I was picking up is the second-ordered issue that exists with families, that existed in my family. The sense of entitlement that people carry from one generation to the next. Particularly, an emotional ledger that's going on, that they feel entitled to get something that they didn't ever receive. And they take that out destructively on innocent parties, mainly spouses and children. That made sense to me, and I did not understand that part growing up. So, that's why I took off to Philadelphia to Dr. Nagy and spent a week there, trying to understand a little bit more.

How do you formulate your view of a family when they enter therapy?

Whoever passes your genetic heritage along to you, that's who it is. The biological parents cannot excuse themselves from a ledger in other words. Even if I'm a child of a biological parent, and I'm adopted into a wonderful family, I'm not excused. I still inherit the ledger from this biological group. Because I have all sorts of questions—why you left me, why didn't you take care of me, was I not adequate enough, why were you irresponsible? And I'm going to carry that into the adoptive family. So, you can say, certainly there's value, you can say that the group is together as a family.

What kind of families do you think benefit most from this model?

Two kinds of situations I think benefit highly from it. First of all, people that are very, very destructive, that have no idea why they are. In other words, they have very little understanding of why they do what they do. A person hates themselves because they beat up their children or hate themselves because they're always critical of their spouse. But they can't stop themselves. It just comes out of their mouths. This model is very helpful in articulating to them, this is why that's happening. This is a basic program in you that you're fighting against. The next is fairly chaotic families that have very little history of trustworthiness. When they have the therapist initiate trustworthiness among them, even with just slight changes, they recognize the dramatic difference. And so, they usually respond to them.

What issues do you think this model works best with?

It is THE model in long-standing family-of-origin issues, where problems of the past show up in present relationships. There isn't any other model that articulates that nearly as well. If I had past issues with my parents, then I will carry those issues over into the relationships with my children and my spouse.

Different models of therapy require the therapist to be directive or nondirective. In your opinion, what are the necessary characteristics that a therapist should possess to be effective with this model?

The therapist must be able to articulate some of the things that actually happen in the process of the operation of the ledger. I'm very aware that this is very different than what a traditional contextual therapist would say. The articulation of that is the insight of a client saying, "Ah, I understand how I work" and, "Finally, somebody's been able to put words around that feeling, that emotion that I've had." And so, that's a key element I think is in contextual change. Then the therapist can move in and explain things for the client. "Well, of course you did that, you know, that's the multidirective partiality. Of course, that's what happened to you. You were doing what you had to do to be able to survive in that situation." That is the initial invitation to trustworthiness. Trustworthiness, very simply, gives a person the ability to give. If they feel like they trust you, then they'll give. Giving is the way out of family dysfunction. But to be able to do that, you have to build this ground level of trustworthiness. And you do it through insight and understanding of what is actually happening. You do some of it by emotionally connecting what contextual therapists would call multidirective partiality.

How often does the client see you and for how long a period of time?
It depends on what kind of therapy it is. In marital therapy, I have to have four sessions to figure out what's going on. Nine out of ten times, I'll know the essential dynamics in the relationship by the fourth session. Now, if I'm able to do that, then therapy will usually last around 6 to 8 months. In individual therapy, depending on the situation, if it's depression or something of that nature, it could last in the neighborhood of 4 to 8 weeks. In family therapy, where you have really long-standing issues, it depends on the age of the family. If it's an impacted family with children, we're going to move very quickly on that. Usually about 6 weeks. If it's adult children, parents, usually that's going to unfold a little longer. Probably about 12 to 16 weeks, because it's much more disengaged.

What are you looking for when you are in the session?
It depends on what the problem is. I want to find out what the problem is from the client's perspective. But what I'm listening for is if they have questions on how they conceptualize things. Do they understand things clearly? Within the first two sessions, I'm always going to do a complete genogram on the person. But I'm going to do it fairly economically. What I'm looking for are basically two issues. I'm going to ask a lot of questions around the issue of "How did you know you were loved?" And "How did you know your family was trustworthy?" "How did you learn about trustworthiness?" Those are the two elements that I'm going to focus on most in doing an intake. Those are the elements that are going to tell me most about the individual's psychology and tell me most about their relational ethics structure.

What is the assessment process of this model?
A lot of the things that I've adopted, as I think through those four dimensions, are what's going on physically, what's going on in the interior emotion of the individual, what's going on systemically around them, and what's going on with them in relational ethics. Then I get an emotional feel of the relationship that this person is involved in.

Who sets the goals, the client or the therapist?
The goal, for me, is always defined by the client. They say, "I'm depressed, I want my marriage to be better, I want my relationship with my children to be better . . ." To me, that's the goal. You have to keep that in focus. It's the therapist's job to find the mechanisms that are connected to that goal that have to change. If a client said, "I want my relationship with my children to be better," I know some things that will do that. They can stop yelling at them, or be supportive of them, or be cooperative. The question is, "Why can't those things happen right now?" That's where contextual therapists basically say, "These are the elements that have to happen emotionally before you can behaviorally make the change."

What are some commonly used interventions with this model?

Well again, there are interventions that belong to the contextual model, and there are interventions that belong to my own version of the contextual model. For me, the most effective, overall contextual intervention, which I really think is the only intervention that they actually use, is multidirective partiality. I'm not neutral and can subsequently go from person to person, even people that are not in the room. Maybe someone has been dead for years, and I make identification with their ledger issues, their loyalty issues, the things that they do, what they felt. I think that that's very effective.

I do a lot of techniques that help people start in the giving process. For instance, I have one technique that's called "Working Up, Working Down." Basically, when a person holds a ledger issue that, if you take it on directly with them, saying, "You know, you're not giving to your son. You need to do something different." The person becomes very defensive with that. If I move that up one generation, working up, I can say, "What would you have liked to have had from your father?" And they articulate that very quickly. Then say, "Can you give those things to your son?" Well, now they're not defensive, because they make the connection. Working down is the same thing. You're trying to say, "What is it that you missed out from your father?" Perhaps they can't answer. Then I'll say, "What do you think the kids are missing out from you?" They are able to articulate that much easier. And then, "Isn't that the same thing you missed out from your father and mother?" And they are much more able to do process that. It's just not the generation that's there, you think in terms of increased flow, up the generational scale, and down the generational scale, depending on what's more effective. I have particular diagrams that I use in articulating love and trust. Particularly, the rage, shame, controlled chaos framework that's very, very helpful to people to conceptualize why they're taking the destructive action that they're taking right now.

What role does a homework assignment have in this model? Do you assign homework?

I think that it's important that you give directives to families so that they know something to watch for, in terms of change. If a husband is dominated by shame, and he's afraid to take leadership because he's basically expecting his wife to build him up, what he needs to do is take some initiative into the relationship. It's very important to articulate that and tell the husband, I want you to do three things: A, B, and C. See if you can initiate this. And then tell the wife to watch for this. By the husband doing these things, he would build trustworthiness. I think it's really important to pick our directives, no matter what framework we're dealing with. Whether it's giving directives that are relational or forgiveness issues, they give people something to work on during the time in between sessions.

How do you know when your client is ready to terminate?

I think that when the goal is met, or the symptom's alleviated, that's a good way to know. I always bring up termination when I think that the client can do the therapy themselves. In other words, they're not going to get a whole lot more from me. That they're able to articulate and understand their problems from a perspective, and be their own therapist, that's when I bring up termination. Some people want to keep coming at that point, because it helps them stay on track. I think that's a reasonable goal, a reason to come back to therapy and stay with the therapist, so I let them stay on, if that's the case. But at that point, I'm not doing therapy, I'm doing accountability.

What have you found to be the limitations of this approach?

I think that it's heavily psychodynamic. Lots of people that come in and hear this [mumbo jumbo] about the entitlement and destructive entitlement and things like that, don't want to hear that. So, people that don't want a lot of insight may not fit well with this model. People that don't have any education at all and have a little trouble understanding some of the dynamics that go on in their family may have a tough time with the model. Then there's some people that want to understand. It works for them. It doesn't work with people that just want to change.

What are your suggestions for students learning this model?

I think the most important thing if you're going to be a contextual therapist is that you have to listen to your intuition and your gut. And you've got to hold that tentatively, but you've go to listen to the intuition and what that's telling you. Because the emotional feel is there, not in your head. You have to pay attention to what the family's doing to you. How does their relationships feel around you? A lot of people say, "I've got to make sense of this and then say something brilliant." I think if you take the pressure off and you listen to your intuition and feel the things in the family, then that will enlighten much more. And then you can make sense of it. Pay more attention to your own intuition.

Case Study

A mother calls and makes an appointment for her family to come to therapy. The family consists of the wife and her husband, both in their 40s; their 15-year-old son; a college-aged daughter; and the woman's father, age 82. Three years after the woman's mother died, her father developed Alzheimer's disease. He moved in with the family 6 months ago. When his health began to deteriorate, the woman spent more time caring for him than for other members of the family. Three months ago, the 15-year-old son, who has been treated for attention deficit hyperactivity disorder since age 7, began to refuse to take his medication and is now being truant from school.

During the session, the wife cries and the husband reports that their relationship is strained, occasionally rolling his eyes as his wife becomes tearful. He reports that he has had to take on more work because his wife had to quit her job to attend to her father's needs. The daughter is away at college and the wife smiles as she describes her as a straight-A student. The daughter was asked to attend the session but refused because she has a hard time with her grandfather's illness and dislikes the conflict that has developed at home.

Dr. Terry Hargrave's Response to the Case Study

First of all, I would do an assessment based on all dimensions. From a factual dimension, you have a situation that's going to create an enormous amount of stress. So from a factual dimension, we do not have enough time to be dedicated to just taking care of self and family. With the father having Alzheimer's and the family having a caregiving duty, it's going to be very difficult. The idea is to give the caregiver some support. We try to create a situation where the husband will head up the support team to specifically give the wife respite away from this, so that she does have time to not be with the father.

Secondly, in the dimension of individual psychology, the question would be "Why did this woman feel more loyalty to her father than she feels toward her husband?" Is that out of destructive needs? Did that come because she's destructively entitled toward her father, where she feels like she's still trying to get something from him? Or does it go the other way—the father's been nurturing and the husband has been destructive to her, and she, naturally, is not close to her husband at all. Particularly, you see that with the husband rolling his eyes—this classic thing that we conceptualize about bad marriages, criticism, and contempt, where contempt is rolling the eyes, defensiveness, and stonewalling.

Systemically, we look and ask who is driving this family. There's a belief system that's driving the family. The wife has this belief system: "I shouldn't have to take care of my father." Everybody else has a belief system that they are the most important thing in the nuclear family system. There is a systemic value system that is in conflict. Those would be all the traditional things to look at.

The fourth dimension is the dimension of relational ethics. A question is, "How do we initiate some kind of trust building in the family?" The most overt thing that you see taking place is the husband rolling his eyes and being disgusted with the wife's efforts and the daughter separating herself out. Those are the most suspicious of being destructive; the most suspicious of being constructive is the son's truancy. I try to build all of that toward a positive framework saying, "These people are trying to save you. They see that you are giving more than what you can afford to give. And all these people are trying to save you: your daughter by staying away, your husband by being disgusted and critical with your work, and your child trying to create other problems for you. Is there a better way that you all can try to help her, besides these types of activities?" In that way, you can balance some giving, that is actually a trustworthy effort. At the same time, mother exclusively giving to the father is not a trustworthy item either, but it's probably the only thing that she knows how to do, trying to understand the loyalty issue between her and the father, and spreading that out to unrealistic things. It is not a problem that can be solved, so you have to start the process of letting go, looking at terms of strengthening the future generations versus trying to problem solve with this generation. Your father's dying. Let's grieve that, let's connect over that, and let's give the younger generation a chance.

If the father were in moderate stages of Alzheimer's, I would try to pick up the emotional feel of what he wanted for his daughter. If there was a constructive relationship where the father wants his daughter to be happy, I would try to work that into some kind of release for her. Then she could say, "OK, there are some problems that I'm not going to be able to solve. One of them is that I'm not going to be able to stave off Alzheimer's. One of them is that I may have to put my father in an Alzheimer's unit." Those are the types of things that may, or may not, be necessary for her to start entering into an equal exchange with the family, in rebalancing the emotional ledger. But the issue has to be connected to the idea that intergenerational exchange or transitions saying, "I have got to take the strength that happened between me and my father, and I've got to move it into my marital situation and the coming generation."

Accountability   A situation in which the therapist holds the client and all other family members who are involved in a particular relationship responsible for their actions that caused damage and violation of trust in the relationship.

Acknowledgment of efforts   This occurs when the therapist asks questions that invite other family members to notice the contributions or injustices that the clients have made in the relationship. This applies to positive (refraining from argument) and negative (harmful actions) efforts. This action of acknowledgment allows family members to be heard.

Asymmetrical relationship   A type of relationship in which one party is obligated to give more and receive less from the other (e.g., parents are obligated to give more than to expect to receive from their children).

Constructive entitlement   This develops when family members receive a fair return from that which they give in the relationship.

Crediting   A technique used in the session when the therapist role models the acknowledgment and acceptance of the unfairness, insults, and violations that the client has experienced in his or her life.

Destructive entitlement   Destructive actions or emotions that individuals demonstrate as a way to claim a self-justified compensation for the pain and injustice that they have experienced in their lives.

Dimensions   In contextual therapy, these are the dilemmas that the therapist evaluates during a session: facts, individual psychology, systemic interactions, and relational ethics.

Empathy   One part of the multidirected partiality techniques during which the therapist recognizes the pain and injustice that clients have experienced in their lives and helps them to distinguish the specific actions or events that created unfairness.

Entitlement   An ethically valid claim for the compensation in return for the contribution that a person has made in a relationship.

Facts dimension   One of the four information-gathering dimensions in the contextual therapy model concerned with the facts about life and relationships of a client that are true and difficult to change (gender, birthplace, illness, parents' divorce, etc.).

Fairness   The preservation of long-term, oscillating balance among family members that leads to benefits on both sides of the relationship.

Give-and-take   The polarity of an emotional exchange in the relationship that allows people to maintain balance in the relationship.

Horizontal relationship   A relationship between people from the same generation (e.g., spouses, siblings, or friends).

Individual psychology dimension   The second of four interconnected dimensions that evaluates different aspects of a client's life. This dimension encompasses the individual's mental and emotional characteristics, such as thinking style, cognitive abilities, and defense mechanisms.

Invisible loyalty   Indirect actions through which people who have experienced pain and injustice in the relationship attempt to gain love and respect by repeating the same patterns that caused them pain.

Ledger   A balance that is achieved in the relationship between two members of a family by using the method of giving and receiving.

Legacy   The patterns and characteristic behaviors that are consciously or unconsciously carried from one generation to the next.

Loyalty   In the contextual therapy model, *feeling* loyal refers to an obligation to another person in the relationship.

Merit   A leverage that maintains the balance in relationships. When a person invests in the relationship, he or she creates merit and trusts that another party will bring his or her contributions to the relationship to bring balance.

Multidirected partiality   An attitude that the therapist must exhibit of being fair and giving credit where it is due in the session. It is a principle that allows the therapist to be aware of each individual in the session, give each individual respect, consideration, and credit.

Parentification (destructive parentification)   A concept that was created by Boszormenyi-Nagy and refers to the relationship in which one or more children assume the parental role.

Rejunction   An intervention during which the therapist invites clients to evaluate and realize their capacity to restore balance between their obligation to give and their entitlement to receive in the relationship.

Relational ethics   A criterion that establishes the balance between fair giving and receiving among the members of relational unit.

Relational ethics dimension   The fourth and most important dimension in contextual therapy that evaluates the balance in the relationship of what people give and what are they obligated to receive from other people.

Revolving slate   The patterns of injustice that repeat from one generation to another, creating a new victim in the family.

Right to give   A relationship between children and parents that is asymmetrical, which means that children are not required to be obligated to return to their parents as much as they have received from them.

Split loyalty   The phenomenon that occurs when a person can be loyal to one individual at the cost of being disloyal to another person in a deserving relationship.

Symmetrical relationship   The relationship between partners who have equal position within the generation and have mutual obligations and expectations of each other.

Systemic interactions dimension   The third dimension that deals with such systemic aspects as communication patterns, boundaries, roles, and so forth.

Therapy   The interaction between the client and the therapist that includes all interventions that aim at bringing out the healthiest possible performance in the client.

Trustworthiness   The relational resource that collects from a reliable and responsible partner who justly gives what he or she is obligated to give in the relationship to maintain the balanced ledger.

Vertical relationship   The relationship that exists between generations, such as grandparents, parents, and children.

REFERENCES

Becvar, D. S., & Becvar, R. J. (2003). *Family therapy: A systemic integration* (5th ed.). Boston, MA: Allyn & Bacon.

Boszormenyi-Nagy, I. (1986). Transgenerational solidarity: The expanding context of therapy and prevention. *The American Journal of Family Therapy*, 14(3), 195–212.

Boszormenyi-Nagy, I. (1987). *Foundations of contextual therapy: Collected papers of Ivan Boszormenyi-Nagy*. New York, NY: Brunner/Mazel.

Boszormenyi-Nagy, I. (1993). From here to eternity. *Psychology Today*, 26(2), 12–13.

Boszormenyi-Nagy, I. (1997). Response to "Are trustworthiness and fairness enough? Contextual family therapy and the good family." *Journal of Marital and Family Therapy*, 23, 171–173.

Boszormenyi-Nagy, I., Grunebaum, J., & Ulrich, D. (1991). Contextual therapy. In A. Gurman & D. P. Kniskern (Eds.), *Handbook of family therapy* (Vol. 2, pp. 200–238). New York, NY: Brunner/Mazel.

Boszormenyi-Nagy, I., & Krasner, B. (1980). Trust-based therapy: A contextual approach. *American Journal of Psychiatry*, 137(7), 767–775.

Boszormenyi-Nagy, I., & Krasner, B. (1986). *Between give and take: A clinical guide to contextual therapy*. New York, NY: Brunner/Mazel.

Boszormenyi-Nagy, I., & Spark, G. (1984). *Invisible loyalties*. New York, NY: Brunner/Mazel. (Original work published 1973)

Brown-Standridge, M. D., & Floyd, C. W. (2000). Healing bittersweet legacies: Revisiting contextual family therapy for grandparents raising grandchildren in crisis. *Journal of Marital and Family Therapy*, 26(2), 185–197.

Ducommun-Nagy, C. (2002). Contextual therapy. In F. W. Kaslow, R. F. Massey, & S. Massey (Eds.), *Comprehensive handbook of psychotherapy: Vol. 3. Interpersonal/ humanistic/existential* (pp. 463–488). New York, NY: John Wiley & Sons.

Ducommun-Nagy, C. (2003). Can giving heal? Contextual therapy and biological psychiatry. In P. S. Prosky & D. V. Keith (Eds.), *Family therapy as an alternative to medication: An appraisal for pharmland* (pp. 111–137). New York, NY: Brunner-Routledge.

Goldenthal, P. (1993). *Contextual family therapy: Assessment and intervention procedures*. Sarasota, FL: Professional Resource Press.

Goldenthal, P. (1996). *Doing contextual therapy. An integrated model for working with individuals, couples, and families*. New York, NY: W. W. Norton & Company.

Hargrave, T. D., Jennings, G., & Anderson, W. (1991). The development of a relational ethics scale. *Journal of Marital and Family Therapy*, 2, 145–158.

Hargrave, T. D., & Pfitzer, F. (2003). *The new contextual therapy. Guiding the power of give and take*. New York, NY: Taylor & Francis.

Snyder, D. R., Wills, R. M., & Grady-Fletcher, A. (1991). Long-term effectiveness of behavioral versus insight-oriented marital therapy. A 4-year follow-up study. *Journal of Consulting and Clinical Psychology*, 59, 138–141.

Soyez, V., Tatrai, H., Broekaert, E., & Bracke, R. (2004). The implementation of contextual therapy in the therapeutic community for substance abusers: A case study. *Journal of Family Therapy*, 26, 286–305.

RECOMMENDED READING LIST

Books

Boszormenyi-Nagy, I., & Krasner, B. (1986). *Between give and take: A clinical guide to contextual therapy*. New York, NY: Brunner/Mazel.

Boszormenyi-Nagy, I., & Spark, G. (1984). *Invisible loyalties: Reciprocity in intergenerational family therapy*. New York, NY: Brunner/Mazel. (Original work published 1973)

Buber, M. (1958). *I and thou*. New York, NY: Charles Scribner & Sons.

Ducommun-Nagy, C. (1998). Contextual therapy. In D. Lawson & F. Prevatt (Eds.), *Casebook in family therapy* (pp. 1–26). New York, NY: Brooks/Cole & Wadsworth.

Fairbairn, W. R. (1952). *An object-relatedness theory of the personality.* New York, NY: Basic Books.

Giat-Roberto, L. (1992). *Transgenerational family therapies.* New York, NY: The Guilford Press.

Goldenthal, P. (1996). *Doing contextual therapy: An integrated model for working with individuals, couples, and families.* New York, NY: W. W. Norton & Company.

Hargrave, T. D. (1994). *Families and forgiveness: Healing wounds in the intergenerational family.* New York, NY: Brunner/Mazel.

Hargrave, T. D. (2001). *Forgiving the devil: Coming to terms with damaged relationships.* Phoenix, AZ: Zeig, Tucker & Theisen.

Hargrave, T. D., & Anderson, W. T. (1997). *Finishing well: A contextual family therapy approach to the aging family.* New York, NY: Brunner/Mazel.

Hargrave, T. D., & Pfitzer, F. (2003). *The new contextual therapy: Guiding the power of give and take.* New York, NY: Taylor & Francis.

Roberto-Forman, L. (2002). Transgenerational marital therapy. In A. S. Gurman & N. S. Jacobson (Eds.), *Clinical handbook of couple therapy* (pp. 118–147). New York, NY: The Guilford Press.

Van Heusden, A. (1987). *Balance in motion: Ivan Boszormenyi-Nagy and his vision of individual and family therapy.* New York, NY: Brunner/Mazel.

Articles

Boszormenyi-Nagy, I. (1978). Contextual therapy: Therapeutic leverages in mobilizing trust. *The American Family.* Report No. 2. New York, NY: Smith Kline and French Laboratories.

Boszormenyi-Nagy, I. (1986). Transgenerational solidarity: The expanding context of therapy and prevention. *The American Journal of Family Therapy, 14*(3), 195–212.

Boszormenyi-Nagy, I., & Krasner, B. (1980). Trust-based therapy: A contextual approach. *American Journal of Psychiatry, 137*(7), 767–775.

Hargrave, T., & Anderson, W. (1990). Contextual therapy and older people: Building trust in the intergenerational family. *Journal of Family Therapy, 12*(4), 311–320.

Hargrave, T. D., Jennings, G., & Anderson, W. (1991). The development of a relational ethics scale. *Journal of Marital and Family Therapy, 2*, 145–158.

Websites

Contextual Family Services
http://www.contextualfamilyservices.org/contextualtherapy.asp

Center for Contextual Family Therapy and Allied Studies
http://www.livestrong.com/business-center-for-contextual-family-therapy-and-allied-studies_610-341-9230/

Cognitive Behavioral Models of Family Therapy

5

Fallon Cluxton-Keller

Men are disturbed not by things, but by the view which they take of them.

—Epictetus

INTRODUCTION

The cognitive behavioral models of family therapy were established when cognitive therapy and behavior therapy were combined. Both of these models are primarily based on the theoretical assumptions of learning theory and social learning theory. This chapter describes the origins of behavior therapy and cognitive behavioral models of therapy. Although there are many different types of cognitive behavioral models of family therapy, this chapter includes the commonly used empirically supported treatments. Specifically, this chapter provides descriptions of dialectical behavior therapy (DBT), behavioral parent training, behavioral marital/couple therapy, conjoint sex therapy, and functional family therapy (FFT).

HISTORY AND LEADING FIGURES

Historical Origins of Behavior Therapy

Behavior therapy evolved from *behaviorism*, which was mostly rooted in the works of Ivan P. Pavlov, John Watson, Joseph Wolpe, Hans Eysenck, M. B. Shapiro, and Burrhus Frederic Skinner. Behavior therapy was derived from three types of learning, which included classical conditioning, operant conditioning, and learning theory. Ivan P. Pavlov (1849–1936), a Russian physiologist, was recognized for his study of conditioned reflexes, which progressed to classical conditioning. In his famous experiment, Pavlov conditioned dogs to salivate when they heard a bell ring. In his study, every time the bell rang (conditioned stimulus), the dogs were given food (unconditioned stimulus). Eventually, the sound of the bell led the dogs to salivate (unconditioned response) because they assumed that food would be brought to them (Pavlov, 1932, 1934).

John B. Watson (1878–1958) and his colleague Rosalie Rayner (1899–1935) demonstrated the use of classically conditioned emotional responses in the case of "Little Albert." They discovered that Albert, who was 9 months old, exhibited no fears to various objects, such as a white rat, a dog, a monkey, and other common objects. Eventually, Watson and Rayner (1920) were able to condition Albert to fear a white rat through a loud, frightening noise that they created when the rat appeared. They then transferred the fear to a white rabbit, a dog, a Santa Claus mask, and a fur coat. Eventually, little Albert developed a conditioned fear response every time he looked at anything white and furry. Watson and Rayner concluded that many phobias are probably true conditioned emotional reactions either of the direct or transferred type.

The psychologist Burrhus Frederic Skinner (1904–1990) developed *operant conditioning*. Operant conditioning uses *reinforcers*, which can be positive or negative. *Positive reinforcement* is the strengthening of a tendency to behave in a certain situation by presenting a desired reward following the desired behavior. For example, a child may learn that making good grades in school is an effective way to get praise from his parents. Thus, the praise will lead the child to continue to strive for good grades. *Negative reinforcement* is a process by which there is an increase in the preferred behavior because of an avoidance of an aversive situation that is not pleasant. For example, a child may take his clothes to the laundry room instead of leaving them on his bedroom floor to avoid being denied a privilege later that day.

In behavioral family therapy, the therapist focuses on increasing desired healthy behaviors and eliminating problematic behaviors through accessing the strengths of the family. The approach does not focus on changing the family's cultural belief system; rather, it focuses on alleviating the problematic behavior(s) by altering consequences to the undesirable behavior(s).

For example, the Brown family is composed of a mother, who is an executive assistant for a CEO, and a father, who is a salesman. Their 10-year-old child began throwing temper tantrums recently, which prompted the father to take the child to therapy at his wife's request. The father was inconsistent with the suggestions made by the therapist to provide negative reinforcement whenever the tantrum occurred. The therapist then asked whether the mother could attend therapy. The therapist noticed that the child behaved very well in the session when the mother was present. The mother was consistent in her requests to the child, and when the child rebelled and cried, the mother ignored the negative behavior, whereas the father tried to comfort him. The therapist noticed this difference in interactive patterns and tapped into the mother's skills as an executive assistant, which involved planning, following up on requests, and consistently monitoring college interns. The therapist asked the mother to develop a behavior plan with rewards and consequences and then share it with the father. The child soon experienced his parents' alignment together in support of the plan, and later gave up the tantrums.

Historical Origins of Cognitive Behavioral Therapy

The basis of the cognitive approach to emotion can be traced as far back as Aristotle (384–322 B.C.) and Epictetus (ca. 50–138). The cognitive paradigm is the root of cognitive theory. The paradigm focuses on how people structure their experiences, assign meanings to these experiences, and how they relate their current experiences to past experiences (Davison & Neale, 1998, p. 46). "When did modern cognitive behavior therapy (CBT) start? Probably in 1953, when I abandoned psychoanalysis and started to develop REBT" (Ellis, 2001, p. 248). Albert Ellis was a pioneer of cognitive behavioral therapy (CBT). More information is provided in Chapter 6. Other contributors to the development of CBT are Albert Bandura, John W. Thibaut, Harold H. Kelley, and Aaron Beck.

Early behavioral therapists believed that cognitive factors, such as one's attitudes, thoughts, beliefs, attributions, and expectations, all influenced behavior. They also saw experiences as influential in a person's life, as such experiences "labeled" a person and caused schemas to develop. These schemas, or beliefs about oneself, kept maladaptive behaviors in check because the thoughts and beliefs surrounding the schema trapped the individual into only one way of reacting in the world. The behavioral therapists adapting the ideas to families made even bigger discoveries—that interactions, developed through individual schemas, perpetrated into the family system and created behaviors as a result. Seeing children, for example, for misbehaviors or depression, individually, rarely worked. However, once the family appeared in therapy and the child could be seen interacting with his/her family, therapists were able to understand how the behaviors were maintained.

The "cognitive revolution" in psychology occurred during the 1950s. In this approach, judgments about events in one's environment influence emotions because emotions are generated by judgments about the world. The two main figures associated with the creation of cognitive therapy are Dr. Albert Ellis and Dr. Aaron Beck. Ellis (1962) asserted that disturbed feelings and maladaptive behaviors are a result of *irrational beliefs*. Ellis developed rational emotive therapy (see Chapter 6) to help clients to challenge these irrational beliefs. Rational emotive therapy has many behavioral components; this ultimately led Ellis to change the name to rational emotive behavior therapy (REBT) in 1993.

Dr. Aaron Beck, a psychiatrist, developed cognitive therapy in the 1960s. Unlike Ellis, Beck posited that each mental disorder is characterized by a set of unique faulty cognitions, whereas Ellis suggested that all mental disorders are characterized by the same set of irrational beliefs. Beck asserted that a person's *automatic thoughts* trigger feelings, not events. Automatic thoughts are thoughts or images that occur to a person simultaneously and are usually associated with negative affect (Dattilio, 2004). An example of a negative thought by a depressed person might be to think "I'm no good"; "I'm unlovable, no one likes me"; and/or "I'm worthless, nothing ever works out for me, why even try anymore?" A person with this thinking would be challenged by a cognitive behavioral therapist who might inquire who does love him/her or like him/her a little, and begin to help the person see that he/she is not worthless. A cognitive behavioral family therapist would ask other family members to discuss their view of the person's thinking. This systemic effect is particularly helpful when several family members begin to contradict the automatic thoughts. The therapist would then try to help the person to construct new thoughts to "argue" with the automatic thoughts when they simultaneously occur.

Automatic thoughts can lead to *maladaptive assumptions* and *cognitive distortions*. Maladaptive assumptions are defined as rules that a person follows to guide and evaluate his/her own behavior and others' behavior (Dattilio, 2004). An example of a maladaptive assumption is "I should never show my vulnerability, it's too risky." Cognitive distortions are exaggerated and irrational thoughts, which perpetuate certain psychological disorders. The theory of cognitive distortions was first proposed by Beck in 1961. The following are examples of cognitive distortions:

- *"I will never fall in love again."*
- *"Who will ever love me again if I leave my wife?"*
- *"Yes, I got a new job, but I will probably lose it because no one will like me."*
- *"There is no reason to think positively. Things never work out for me anyway."*
- *"He should know when he upsets me because we have been married for 20 years!"*
- *"Yes, I passed the last test with a 98, but that does not mean I will pass the next one. No way!"*
- *"She made me beat her. She provoked me on purpose."*

Beck (1976) suggested that automatic thoughts are a reflection of a person's *schema*—a core belief he/she holds about himself/herself, the world, and the future. Therefore, the person fits new information into an organized network of already-accumulated knowledge. The person may seek information to fit the schema or reorganize the schema to fit the new information. A person's underlying schemata (plural for schema) can produce cognitive distortions or irrational thoughts. Here is an example of automatic thoughts, maladaptive assumptions, and the underlying schema:

Scenario: Joe and Margaret had a fun time on their first date on Friday night. Joe promised to call Margaret on Saturday afternoon, and he did. During their conversation, Joe said he would call Margaret on Monday. Now it is Tuesday night, and Margaret has not received a call from Joe.

Automatic thought: *"Joe didn't call me, which means he does not like me."*

Maladaptive assumption: *"He will never speak to me again."*

Underlying schema: People lie to avoid hurting other people's feelings.

Figure 5.1 shows a list of common cognitive distortions in couples (Dattilio, 2004). When therapists assist clients with modifying their thoughts to eliminate the cognitive distortions, a person's mood often improves and the person is able to ascertain a more objective reality. This process is referred to as *cognitive restructuring*. From an evidence-based perspective, cognitive behavioral therapy is currently the treatment of choice for anxiety and depressive disorders in children and adolescents. Future research in this area will need to focus on comparing cognitive behavioral psychotherapy with other treatments, component analyses, and the application of exportable protocol-driven treatments to divergent settings and patient populations (Compton et al., 2004). Some examples for which cognitive behavioral therapy has been clinically demonstrated through randomized controlled trials to be an effective treatment include the following (Butler, Chapman, Forman, & Beck, 2006):

- Depression
- Anxiety
- Bipolar disorder
- Eating disorders
- Some substance abuse disorders
- Gambling (in combination with medication)
- Marital discord
- Anger
- Borderline personality disorder
- Erectile dysfunction (CBT is effective for reducing anxiety associated with sexual performance)

INTRODUCTION TO COGNITIVE BEHAVIORAL MODELS OF FAMILY THERAPY

Cognitive behavioral models of family therapy are based on Albert Bandura's social learning theory (1969), which blends cognitive and behavioral components of learning and emphasizes vicarious learning and symbolic/cognitive processes in addition to self-regulation. Bandura, Ross, and Ross (1961) asserted that vicarious learning occurs as a person is observing, retaining, and replicating unique behavior that is executed by others. Symbolic/cognitive processes occur as the person takes in information and processes it in his/her own unique, individual way, based on past experiences and present psychological state of mind.

Arbitrary Inference. Conclusions are made in the absence of supporting/substantiating evidence. For example, a man whose wife arrives home a half-hour late from work concludes, "*She must be having an affair.*"

Selective Abstractions. Information is taken out of context and certain details are highlighted, while other important information is ignored. For example, a woman whose husband fails to answer her greeting the first thing in the morning concludes, "*He must be angry at me again.*"

Overgeneralization. An isolated incident or two is allowed to serve as a representation of similar situations everywhere, related or unrelated. For example, after being turned down for an initial date, a young man concludes, "*All women are alike, I'll always be rejected.*"

Magnification and Minimization. A case or circumstance is perceived in greater or lesser light than is appropriate. For example, an angry husband "*blows his top*" upon discovering that the checkbook is unreconciled and states to his wife, "*We're financially doomed.*"

Personalization. External events are attributed to oneself when insufficient evidence exists to render such a conclusion. For example, a woman finds her husband re-ironing an already-pressed shirt and assumes, "*He is dissatisfied with my preparation of his clothing.*"

Dichotomous Thinking. Experiences are codified as either black or white, a complete success or total failure. This is otherwise known as "*polarized thinking.*" For example, upon soliciting his wife's opinion on a paperhanging job underway in the recreation room, the wife questions the seams, and the husband thinks to himself, "*I can't do anything right.*"

Labeling and Mislabeling. One's identity is portrayed on the basis of imperfections and mistakes made in the past, and these are allowed to define oneself. For example, subsequent to continual meal preparation mistakes, a spouse states, "*I am worthless,*" as opposed to recognizing her errors as being human.

Tunnel Vision. Sometimes spouses see only what they want to see or what fits their current state of mind. A husband who believes that his wife "*does whatever she wants anyway*" may accuse her of making a choice based purely on selfish reasons.

Biased Explanations. This is almost a suspicious type of thinking that partners develop during times of distress when they automatically assume that their spouse holds a negative alternative motive behind their intent. For example, a woman states to herself, "*He's acting real 'lovey-dovey' because he'll probably want me to do something that he knows I hate to do.*"

Mind Reader. This is the magical gift of being able to know what the other is thinking without the aid of verbal communication. Spouses end up ascribing unworthy intentions onto each other. For example, a husband thinks to himself, "*I know what is going through her mind, she thinks that I am naïve to her 'shenanigans'.*"

FIGURE 5.1 ■ Common cognitive distortions with couples.
Source: Dattilio, 2004.

According to Bandura (1969), social learning theory is composed of classical and operant models of learning in addition to interactions between the person and the environment that emphasizes the importance of awareness of rules as well as contingencies associated with the consequences of behavior. In social learning theory, Bandura proposed that cognitive processes are acknowledged and that these processes are related to learning and *modeling*. Social learning and modeling are the key components in behavioral parent training and other skills training interventions.

Cognitive behavioral models of family therapy are also rooted in the theory of social exchange. The theory of social exchange (Thibaut & Kelley, 1959) encompasses family interactions, which are analyzed in terms of the relative amounts of supposed rewards and costs to people in relationships. According to Thibaut and Kelley (1959), people tend to maximize rewards and minimize costs, and reciprocity is created and equilibrium is established. Negative behaviors elicit negative behaviors in return, and negative forces elicit negative forces in return so that an imbalance is created. The theory of social exchange is also the basis of problem solving, which is used in CBT in addition to cognitive behavioral family therapy.

Cognitive behavioral family therapy involves assisting clients with changing their self-defeating or irrational beliefs to change their feelings and behaviors. It assumes that family relationships, cognitions, behaviors, and emotions have a mutual influence on one another; cognitive inference evokes emotion and behavior; and emotion and behavior can influence cognition (Becvar & Becvar, 2003, pp. 242–243). When this cycle occurs among family members, dysfunctional cognitions, behaviors, or emotions can result in conflict (Becvar & Becvar, 2003, p. 243). Cognitive behavioral family therapy does not necessarily include every family member; this form of therapy includes family members who are needed to help bring about change in the family.

Cognitive behavioral family therapists attempt to pinpoint the specific problem(s; called *problem analysis*) in order to work toward resolving problems and increase positive interaction between family members. The therapist does so by identifying and suggesting changes to the interactions that occur within the family. The clients are then trained to maintain their newly acquired, more positive way of interacting with each other. One way the therapist helps the family to eliminate the problematic behaviors is through helping clients to think in ways that are more constructive, which will then motivate them to stop engaging in the problematic behaviors. The cognitive behavioral family therapist also educates the family on ways to maintain the positive changes that are made in therapy. The therapist is directive and prescriptive, often assigning homework exercises in which the family practices new ways of interacting.

There are many cognitive behavioral therapeutic approaches. The remainder of this chapter focuses on the following models: DBT, behavioral parent training, behavioral marital/couple therapy, conjoint sex therapy, and FFT.

Dialectical Behavior Therapy

DBT was developed by Marsha Linehan, PhD, a psychologist at the University of Washington, during the 1980s to 1990s. This approach was originally based on her work with individuals diagnosed with borderline personality disorder, but it has additional uses for individuals with other problems (e.g., depression, posttraumatic stress disorder, binge eating disorder). Fruzzetti, Iverson, Buteau, and Hoffman have applied this approach to discordant couples and families.

According to Linehan's model, a person's behavior/functioning and the environment are continuously impacting and influencing one another (Hoffman, Fruzzetti, & Swenson, 1999, p. 401). One important environmental element has to do with the importance of validation from one's environment (in this case, the family). A scale entitled the "Validating and Invalidating Behavior Coding Scale" (Fruzzetti, 2001) was developed to help clinicians assess these behaviors. Linehan (1993a) defined an *invalidating environment* as one in which the communication of private experiences is met by erratic, inappropriate, and extreme responses. The two main characteristics of an invalidating environment include the following:

1. A person is told by others that he/she is wrong in his/her description and analyses of his/her own experiences, particularly in his/her views of what is causing his/her own emotions, beliefs, and actions.

2. An environment in which the people in the person's environment insist that the person feel what he/she does not feel, or say that the person has done something that he/she did not do.

According to Linehan (1993a), growing up in an invalidating environment can have one or more of the following consequences:

1. Failure to validate emotional expression does not teach a person to label his/her own private experiences, including emotions, in a socially appropriate manner (Linehan, 1993a, p. 51). For example, it would be useless to tell a child to control his/her emotions when he/she never learned how to do so.

2. By oversimplifying the problems in life, a child is not taught to tolerate distress or to form realistic expectations and goals (Linehan, 1993a, p. 51). Therefore, the child has a tendency to set unattainable goals and will experience distress (without knowing how to handle distress in a healthy way) when these goals are not accomplished.

3. In an invalidating environment, extreme emotional displays and/or extreme problems are necessary to incite a helpful response (Linehan, 1993a, p. 51). If a child learns that he/she needs to create a crisis to generate support or attention, he/she will most likely carry these behaviors into adulthood and transmit the patterns transgenerationally to his/her own children if he/she does not learn to respond in a healthy and adaptive way.

4. An invalidating environment does not teach a child when to trust his/her own emotional and cognitive responses as reflections of valid interpretations of events (Linehan, 1993a, p. 51). As an adult, this person may frequently invalidate himself/herself and not express his/her true feelings in hopes of satisfying others.

Linehan (1993a, pp. 56–57) described three common types of invalidating families:

1. Chaotic families—These families tend to include members with substance abuse problems, financial problems, or parents who are out of the home so much that little time is devoted to the children.

2. Perfect families—In these families, the parents cannot tolerate negative displays of emotions from their children.

3. Typical families—These families exhibit Western cultural tendencies for individuals to maintain cognitive control of their emotions and to focus on achievement and mastery as criteria of success. In these families, if a person tries to define himself/herself differently, he/she may be labeled immature, pathological, or in an unfavorable light.

DBT promotes the clients' acceptance of self and their family members as well as increasing their skills to accurately express themselves and effectively manage problems (Fruzzetti & Linehan, 2006, p. xi). DBT requires that each client have an individual therapist and a separate skills trainer. DBT usually includes weekly individual therapy sessions, weekly group skills training, therapist consultation meetings, and brief telephone coaching between sessions (Hoffman et al., 1999, p. 401).

Behavioral Parent Training

Behavioral parent training teaches parents to encourage desired behaviors in their children and not to reinforce problematic behaviors. Gerald Patterson and John Reid, psychologists at the Oregon Social Learning Center, pioneered this therapy. Patterson and Reid posited that faulty parent–child interaction patterns are developed and maintained through *reciprocity* (a child responding negatively to negative parental input) and *coercion* (parents influencing behavior through use of punishment). According to Windell and Windell (1977), behavioral parent training aims to change the mutually destructive pattern of interaction by training parents to observe as well as measure the child's problematic behavior(s) in addition to applying social learning techniques to increase desirable behavior(s), decrease problematic behavior(s), and maintain the cognitive and behavioral changes.

Patterson and Reid (1970) emphasized the importance of assessment in behavioral parent training. First, a therapist is required to do a baseline assessment to identify and measure the child's specific problematic behavior. The parents are usually required to observe and graph their own behavior in addition to developing a contingency contract with the child. A contingency contract specifies who is to do what for whom, under which circumstances, times, and places. In a contingency contract, each participant knows what is expected of him/her and what may be gained in return. Additionally, the contract also states the consequences if the guidelines of the contract are not followed (Dimeff & Koerner, 2007, p. 169). A typical example of a contingency contract may be made between a child and a parent, describing the types of grades that the parent expects the child to make in school. The contract would state the reward, such as free time or a token, which is awarded when the grades are achieved, and a consequence, such as less television time or play time, if the grades are below expectations.

Behavioral Marital/Couples Therapy

Robert Stuart and Neil Jacobson are the founders of *behavioral marital/couples therapy*. Their approach is based on social exchange theory (described earlier in the chapter), and it emphasizes the importance of reciprocity in the marital/couple relationship. The goal of this therapy is to help couples to achieve and maintain reciprocity and positive reinforcement through communicating effectively and improving their problem-solving skills.

Conjoint Sex Therapy

Conjoint sex therapy, a cognitive behavioral approach, was originally developed by Masters and Johnson but has been expanded by Helen Singer Kaplan. The focus of this approach is to alleviate sexual dysfunction. Masters and Johnson (1970) assumed that sexual inadequacy is a relationship problem. Helen Singer Kaplan (1974) expanded the approach by distinguishing personal and interpersonal factors (sexual ignorance, fear of failure, demand for performance, excessive need to please one's partner, and failure to communicate openly about sexual feelings and experiences) of sexual dysfunction.

Functional Family Therapy

FFT is a nationally recognized evidence-based practice for at-risk youth, ages 10 to 18, whose problems range from acting out to conduct disorders to alcohol and/or substance abuse. Therapists must be formally trained in this model to implement it, and a link for the training information is provided in the recommended websites section at the end of this chapter. The overview provided in this chapter does not substitute for formal FFT training.

The FFT model, founded by Dr. James Alexander in 1972, posits that clients need help in understanding the function that the behavior plays in regulating relationships. To accomplish this task, functional family therapists use a mixture of education, skills building, strategic, and other cognitive behavioral therapeutic interventions. According to Alexander, FFT is a strength-based, short-term, high-quality intervention program with an average of 12 sessions over a 3- to 4-month period. Alexander asserted that assessment of risk and protective factors that affect the adolescent, his/her environment, intrafamilial and extrafamilial factors, and how the adolescent presents within and influences the therapeutic process are emphasized in this model.

THEORETICAL ASSUMPTIONS

According to Dattilio (2004), some of the main assumptions of CBT, as it relates to working with individuals, couples, and families, include the following:

1. It is a problem-solving model that focuses on how the problem develops, continues, and expands.
2. There is an emphasis on the present rather than on the past experiences of the client.
3. A person's thoughts are seen to trigger his/her feeling(s), which cause the person to behave in a certain way with his/her family.
4. If problematic thinking processes are changed, then a person's feelings and behavior will change as a result.
5. Personal functioning is determined by reciprocal interaction between behavior and its controlling social conditions.
6. A person's maladaptive behavior is maintained by current reinforcements from others.
7. Assessments are continuously used throughout therapy to determine whether the treatment is effective, whether the clients are benefiting from treatment, and whether the problematic behaviors have decreased.

View of the Family and Client

Cognitive behavioral approaches to family therapy emphasize the cognitive and behavioral aspects of family interactions (Epstein, Schlesinger, & Dryden, 1988; Leslie, 1988). Family relationships, cognitions, emotions, and behaviors are viewed as exerting mutual influence on one another in that cognitive inferences evoke emotion and behavior, and emotion in addition to behavior can influence cognition. Because of this dependence on others, a family member's behavior triggers cognitions, emotions, and behaviors in other family members, which in turn elicit reactive cognitions, behavior, and emotions in the original family member. Frank Dattilio (2004) asserted that individuals have two separate sets of schemata about families. The first is related to the parents' family of origin and the second is related to families in general. Figure 5.2 illustrates the family schema (Dattilio, 2004).

When a family has a set of schemata that impairs their functioning and leads to unsatisfying relationships, those schemata need to be changed. The therapist helps family members to identify distorted cognitions that reflect the underlying set of dysfunctional schemata. Through challenging these distorted cognitions, family members feel better and are able to behave in beneficial ways that improve the quality of their relationships. Figure 5.3 illustrates an example of how family members rework their schemata (Dattilio, 2004).

In DBT, all dysfunctional behaviors that occur inside and outside of therapy are viewed as problems to be solved or faulty solutions to problems in living (Linehan, 1993a, p. 250). Key DBT assumptions about clients and therapy are shown in Table 5.1.

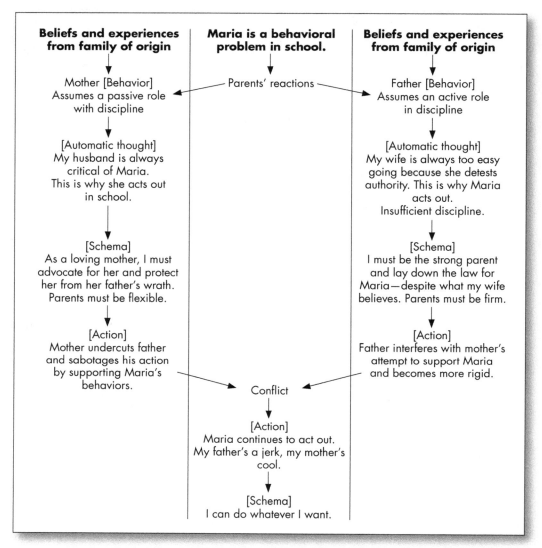

FIGURE 5.2 ■ Family schema.
Source: Dattilio, 2004.

View on How Change Occurs

Cognitive behavioral therapeutic models' emphasis on the importance of challenging faulty thoughts to improve mood and promote healthy behavior changes is vital. This process, along with identification of interactive patterns that result in dysfunction in a person and his/her family, provide the therapist with assessment information that can be renegotiated and provided back to the family. Change, therefore, occurs when new thinking and interactions occur, therefore leading to a different outcome. Cognitive behavioral therapists assign homework exercises that the client family can practice with each other to monitor their progress and make adjustments to the treatment plan if needed.

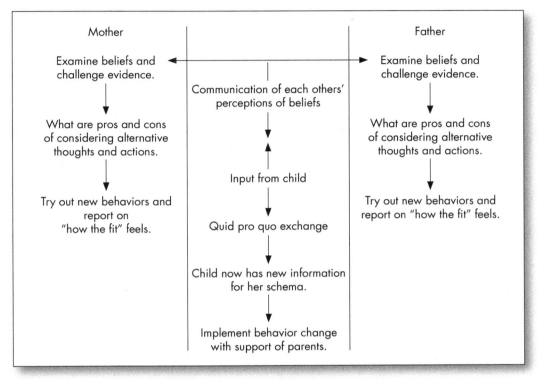

FIGURE 5.3 ▒ Reworking family schemata.
Source: Dattilio, 2004.

TABLE 5.1 ▒ Dialectical Behavior Therapy (DBT) Assumptions About Clients and Therapy

Assumptions About Clients	Assumptions About Therapy
1. Clients are doing the best they can.	1. Therapists need to assist clients' changes in ways that bring them closer to their own goals.
2. Clients want to improve.	2. The therapist must display clarity, precision, and compassion.
3. Clients must learn new behaviors in all relevant contexts.	3. The therapeutic relationship is between equals.
4. Clients may not have caused all of their own problems, but they have to solve these problems.	4. Principles of behavior are universal, which affect therapists and clients.
5. Clients cannot fail DBT.	5. The DBT therapist can fail.
6. Clients need to do better, try harder, and/or be motivated to change.	6. DBT can fail even when therapists do not fail.
7. The lives of suicidal individuals diagnosed with borderline personality disorder are unbearable as they are currently being lived.	7. Therapists treating clients diagnosed with borderline personality disorder need support.

Source: Rizvi & Swenson, 2006, p. 10.

Therapist's Role

The cognitive behavioral therapist tends to be direct and active in therapy with his/her clients. The therapist assesses clients' thoughts, feelings, and behaviors throughout therapy. A baseline is determined at the beginning of therapy to measure the changes made in therapy sessions and determine whether the therapy is beneficial for the clients. These models involve ongoing assessments to determine whether clients are benefiting from treatment. The therapist's role in traditional CBT is to assist clients with changing their thoughts to improve the way they feel and eliminate problematic behaviors. Dialectical behavior therapists may employ more coaching and skill building than other therapists who rely more on changing interactional patterns through teaching new communication techniques. The dialectical behavior therapist assumes some additional role responsibilities that are not included in more traditional cognitive and behavioral therapeutic models.

Many cognitive behavioral family therapists assign homework to measure changes in the clients' behaviors toward others and other areas. An example of a homework assignment in a family in which a 10-year-old boy is having temper tantrums, at home after dinner, wanting to watch television, might call for the mother to validate the child's feelings while maintaining her boundary and remove herself from the scene of the tantrum. After the child stopped the tantrum, the mother would give him a choice of what to do prior to bedtime that did not involve watching television. Cognitive behavioral therapists observe and evaluate the clients' interactions as well as each person's thoughts and behaviors in the family. This dynamic allows the cognitive behavioral family therapist to monitor the family interactions.

The DBT therapist works with various cognitive and behavioral therapeutic strategies. According to Linehan (1993a), there is an emphasis on assessment, data collection on current behaviors, precise operational definition of treatment targets, a collaborative working relationship between the therapist and the client that includes attention to and orienting the client to the treatment in addition to a mutual commitment to treatment goals, and the application of standard cognitive behavioral therapeutic techniques.

Generalizations from the client's relationship with the therapist to the client's other relationships are not an assumption of DBT (Linehan, 1993a, p. 519). However, the therapist is encouraged to use the therapeutic relationship difficulties to explore similarities with the client's other relationships and suggest analogous approaches that may be productive in producing more satisfying relationships (Linehan, 1993a, p. 519). The therapist is also encouraged to acknowledge when the therapeutic relationship is going well and compare it to the client's other relationships because these comparisons can highlight what the client wants from a relationship and what is missing from his/her relationships (Linehan, 1993a, p. 519).

In DBT, goals are referred to as targets, and this term is used to describe the measurable increases or decreases in behavior(s). Linehan (1993a) asserted that the main target of DBT is to increase dialectical behavior patterns through enhancing dialectical thought patterns. Dialectical thinking requires the ability to view reality as complex and multifaceted, to entertain contradictory views, and to unite and integrate these views in addition to being comfortable with flux and inconsistency (Linehan, 1993a, p. 121). When a person is stuck in a problem, the dialectical approach would enable him/her to see what has been left out or how he/she has established rigid boundaries or oversimplified a problem (Linehan, 1993a, p. 121). Linehan (1993a) highlighted the importance of the dialectical behavior therapist helping clients with identifying the influences over time on their worldviews and examining the worldviews of others with whom they interact.

Fruzzetti and Iverson (2004) outlined the following core dialectics that need to be resolved in successful treatment with couples and families:

1. Closeness versus conflict
2. Partner acceptance versus partner change
3. One partner's needs and desires versus another partner's needs and desires
4. Intimacy versus autonomy

Linehan (1993a) warned against interfering behaviors by the therapist, which can create a therapeutic imbalance or show a lack of respect for clients. A therapist who is overfunctioning during therapy sessions may maintain clients' underfunctioning roles, thus causing a therapeutic imbalance. For example, a therapist who announces a fee increase to a family at the end of a session and demands the money at that time is demonstrating a lack of respect.

Behavioral parent training therapists serve as observers, educators, and skill-building specialists. They teach parents various skills (communication, problem-solving, etc.) that they can use to alter or extinguish their child's problematic behavior(s). Most often, behavioral parent training therapists provide psychoeducation on the child/adolescent's stage of development and training on how to talk to children and adolescents so that they listen. This may involve taking the child/adolescent to a quiet place; sitting level with each other; and speaking in a calm voice, even though the child is screaming. The steps are specific and structured, and are presented to parents as a set of skills.

The role of the therapists in behavioral marital/couples therapy is to teach the couple social learning educational tools that they can use in the relationship. They also highlight relationship strengths throughout the educational process. The therapist assists partners in negotiating agreements, especially while developing contingency contracts. The behavioral marital/couple therapist empowers partners to view themselves as agents of change, rather than victims.

Cognitive behavioral marital/couples therapists acknowledge the role that cognitions play in affecting feelings and behaviors of each partner. It is essential for the therapist to assess cognitions, emotions, and behaviors in this approach. The goal of cognitive behavioral marital/couples therapy is to help partners to challenge their irrational/dysfunctional thoughts in order to elicit feelings and evoke more appropriate behaviors that create a more satisfying relationship. Often, one partner will have some deeply held dysfunctional belief about himself/herself or his/her partner. The dysfunctional belief creates tension and relationship dissatisfaction. One partner's distorted belief influences the other partner's behavior, which ultimately creates tension in addition to relationship dissatisfaction. It is abundantly clear that the partner with the distorted belief wants to be heard by the other partner; however, this partner's behavior is affected by the distorted belief and can drive the other partner to react in ways contrary to what he/she wants. Thus, the partner with the distorted belief may have a tendency to sabotage the very thing that he/she wants in this relationship. Therefore, the therapist helps clients to identify and challenge cognitive distortions to change the way that they feel and behave to create more satisfying relationships.

Cognitive behavioral therapists working on sexual issues plan specific exercises for each partner that are aimed at overcoming negative, self-defeating feelings and images regarding sexual experiences (Maxwell, 2009). Marital therapy and sex therapy are integrated in some cases to provide the maximum therapeutic benefit for the couple. Sometimes, medication is also needed to help alleviate a sexual problem; thus, clients are usually required to go to a physician for a thorough medical exam before beginning treatment. The therapist provides education about the role of anxiety regarding the sexual dysfunction, how it develops, and how it is maintained (Nichols & Schwartz, 2004, p. 275). The therapist also provides education about irrational beliefs that are impeding sexual performance and sexual satisfaction.

FFT posits that clients need help in understanding the function that the behavior plays in regulating relationships. To accomplish this task, functional family therapists use a mixture of education, skills building, strategic, and other cognitive behavioral therapeutic interventions.

Interventions

Cognitive behavioral family therapists employ several different strategies to promote change within the family system. They often provide various forms of skills training in areas such as communication, problem solving, and time management. They also help some families to develop behavioral contracts to select reinforcements for problematic and desired behaviors. Cognitive behavioral family therapists also frequently assign homework to determine what interventions will be most effective and beneficial for the family in meeting their therapeutic goals. Family members are encouraged to complete the homework assignments on an as needed basis.

Dialectical Behavior Therapy

Some basic DBT treatment strategies are highlighted in this section; it is important to remember that this is only a brief overview and not a substitute for training in DBT with individuals, groups, couples, and/or families. The basic DBT treatment strategies include dialectic strategies, core strategies, stylistic strategies, and case management strategies (Linehan, 1993a, p. 199). Each set of strategies serves as a cornerstone of the treatment.

The *dialectical strategies* stress creative tensions generated by contradictory emotions and oppositional thought patterns, values, and behavioral strategies both within a client as well as in his/her system(s; Linehan, 1993a, p. 201). The main therapy dialectic consists of change in the context of accepting reality as it is (Linehan, 1993a, p. 201). The therapist must be alert to the dialectical tensions occurring in the therapeutic relationship and must teach and model appropriate dialectical behavior patterns (Linehan, 1993a, p. 201). The former involves the therapist focusing on the dialectics of the therapeutic relationship by combining change and acceptance strategies and maintaining the collaborative working relationship (Linehan, 1993a, p. 201). The latter requires the therapist to focus on the clients, independent from their interactions with the therapist (Linehan, 1993a, p. 201). Some dialectical strategies described by Linehan (1993a) include the following:

1. The therapist can use metaphors and storytelling to teach clients dialectical thinking and explore possibilities of new behaviors.

2. The therapist allows change, development, and inconsistency inherent in any healthy environment to proceed naturally.

3. The therapist uses dialectical assessments to examine each client and his/her broader social context to obtain a better understanding of the client and his/her system(s).

Validation strategies and problem-solving strategies comprise the *core strategies* and serve as a cornerstone of the treatment along with the dialectical strategies. Linehan (1993a) referred to these strategies as the core because all of the other treatment strategies are built around them. The first set of strategies within the core is the validation strategies. Linehan describes the validation strategies as the most obvious and direct acceptance strategies because the therapist clearly communicates that clients' behaviors make sense within the current context and the therapist engages the clients in trying to understand their actions, emotions, and thoughts. An example of a validation strategy offered by Linehan (1993a) is the therapist providing the clients with opportunities for emotional expression and teaching the clients how to observe, describe, and label emotions.

The *change strategies* are integrated throughout the therapeutic process and include contingency procedures, behavioral skills training, cognitive modification, and exposure-based procedures (Linehan, 1993a, p. 292). *Stylistic strategies* specify interpersonal and communication styles compatible with the therapy (Linehan, 1993a, p. 199). The stylistic strategies are strategies that the therapist uses to communicate with clients. They emphasize process rather than content.

> *Style has to do with tone (warm vs. cool or confrontational), with edge (soft and flowing vs. hard and abrupt), with intensity (light or humorous vs. very serious), with speed (fast, quick-moving, or interruptive vs. slow, thoughtful, and reflective), and with responsiveness (vulnerable vs. impervious). (Linehan, 1993a, p. 371)*

There are two styles of communication within DBT. A *reciprocal communication style* is defined by responsiveness, self-disclosure, warmth, and genuineness (Linehan, 1993a). An example of the first style might be appropriate therapist self-disclosure to model healthy responses to situations or demonstrate ways to handle difficult situations (Linehan, 1993a, p. 381). The second style is the *irreverent communication style*, which Linehan described as unhallowed, impertinent, incongruous, and confrontational. An example might be a therapist challenging a client's thought by asking, "Are you getting irrational on me again?" Both of these communication styles balance each other and must be synthesized through the therapist rapidly moving back and forth between the two styles in such a way that the blending itself constitutes a stylistic strategy (Linehan, 1993a, p. 371).

Case management strategies have to do with how the therapist interacts with and responds to the social network in which the patient is enmeshed (Linehan, 1993a, p. 199). Case management strategies are used to facilitate interaction between the clients and their social networks or systems outside of therapy. They include environmental intervention, consultation to the client, and therapist supervision/consultation. The environmental strategies include the therapist intervening in systems that inhibit or prevent clients from engaging in healthy and adaptive behaviors. Linehan (1993a) highlighted one central rule for the environmental strategies, which is that direct or unilateral interventions by the therapist should be kept to a minimum consistent with the well-being of clients. Therefore, the therapist intervenes only when the harm to clients of not intervening outweighs the harm of intervening on behalf of clients (Linehan, 1993a, p. 401). The basis of the consultation-to-the-client strategies is to get clients to actively solve their own life problems (Linehan, 1993a, p. 400).

For example, the therapist may consult with a client about ways in which he/she can effectively manage his/her relationship with an unruly colleague at work. The therapist's supervision/consultation strategies assist the therapists with self-care while aiding them in providing clients with the maximum therapeutic benefit. According to Linehan, therapeutic behavior requires a context that reinforces it, and the supervisor/consultation team provides a dialectical balance for therapists in their interactions with clients.

Dialectical Behavior Theory Skills

In DBT, the word *skills* is used synonymously with abilities and includes a wide array of cognitive, behavioral, and emotional response repertoires that are integrated to produce effective performance that is gauged by direct and indirect consequences of behaviors (Linehan, 1993a, p. 329). Linehan (1993a) defined effective performance as those behaviors that lead to a maximum number of positive outcomes and a minimum number of negative outcomes. According to Linehan (1993b), there are four skills training modules that clients are taught throughout therapy:

1. *Mindfulness skills* are considered to be the core skills because these skills are practiced throughout the other modules and they are reviewed at the beginning of the other skills modules. According to Linehan (1993b), the mindfulness skills are psychological and behavioral versions of meditation practices from Eastern spiritual training. However, one does not have to subscribe to Eastern spiritual training to practice mindfulness skills. Linehan (1993b) described three states of mind in DBT that include the following:

   a. Reasonable mind—A person in this state of mind is focused, thinks rationally, does not act impulsively, approaches knowledge from an intellectual stance, and logically approaches problems.

   b. Emotion mind—A person in this state of mind is controlled by his/her emotions, exaggerates facts to suit the current emotional state, has irrational thoughts, and has a tendency to be unreasonable, and the energy of the behavior reflects his/her current emotional state.

   c. Wise mind—A person in this state of mind has integrated the reasonable mind and emotion mind. This state of mind adds intuitive knowing to emotional experience and logical analysis.

   Linehan (1993b) categorized the mindfulness skills into two sets of skills that include what skills and how skills. These are summarized in Table 5.2.

TABLE 5.2 ■ What Skills and How Skills

What Skills	How Skills
1. Observing by attending to events, emotions, and other behavioral responses, even the distressing ones.	1. Take a nonjudgmental stance, which means not judging something as good or bad but rather focusing on consequences of behaviors and events and maybe suggesting the possibility of changing the event or behavior but not necessarily labeling it as bad.
2. Describing events and personal responses in words.	2. Because mindfulness primarily has to do with the quality of awareness that an individual brings to activities, another goal is to learn to focus the mind and awareness on the moments in current activities.
3. The ability to participate without self-consciousness, which involves entering into activities of the current moment without separating oneself from ongoing events and interactions.	3. Being effective is directed at reducing the clients' tendencies to be more concerned with what is "right" at times than with doing what is actually needed or called for in a particular situation.

2. *Distress tolerance skills.* These skills emphasize an ability to accept, in a non-judgmental way, both oneself and one's current situation, which includes the ability to perceive one's own environment without demanding it to be different and to experience one's own current emotional state without attempting to change it (Linehan, 1993a, p. 147). These skills also focus on observing one's own thoughts and action patterns without attempting to stop or control them (Linehan, 1993a, p. 147).

3. *Emotion regulation skills.* Like the other skills modules, this module requires the application of the mindfulness skills, in particular, a nonjudgmental observation in addition to describing one's own emotional response (Linehan, 1993a, p. 149). Fruzzetti and Iverson (2004) posited that two of the biggest problems that the couples therapist faces are one partner's emotional reactivity toward the other in addition to the partner's general distress and psychopathology. Fruzzetti and Iverson further conceptualized that a way to tie these two problems together is to consider the role of emotional dysregulation in both individual distress and couple distress. Fruzzetti and Iverson posited that the DBT model for emotion regulation may offer opportunities to synthesize individual skills as well as relationship skills to improve treatment outcomes for couples with distressed or emotionally dysregulated partners. Linehan (1993a) outlined some of the following emotion regulation skills:

   a. Identifying and labeling affect
   b. Identifying obstacles to changing emotions
   c. Reducing vulnerability to an emotion mind
   d. Increasing positive emotional events
   e. Increasing mindfulness to current emotion
   f. Taking opposite action, which is defined by changing the behavioral and expressive component of the emotion by acting in a way that opposes it or is inconsistent with the emotion (i.e., approaching something one is afraid of).
   g. Application of the distress tolerance techniques

4. *Interpersonal effectiveness skills.* These skills include asking for what one needs, saying no, and coping with interpersonal conflict (Linehan, 1993a, p. 151). Linehan (1993a) defined the word *effectiveness* as obtaining the changes one wants, keeping relationships, and keeping one's self-respect.

Linehan (1993a, p. 339) summarized three types of skills training procedures:

- Skill acquisition (e.g., directions, modeling)
- Skill strengthening (e.g., behavior rehearsal)
- Skill generalization (e.g., homework assignments)

The therapist needs to encourage the client to experiment with as many different skills as possible in various situations in addition to duplicating, in the therapeutic relationship, important characteristics of the client's interpersonal relationships outside of therapy through genuinely highlighting similarities between situations and the problems outside of therapy as well as the interactions that occur within therapy (Linehan, 1993a, p. 339).

Table 5.3 summarizes some of the key features in this section as well as the research on DBT.

Behavioral Parent Training

Table 5.4 illustrates the therapist's role, assessments, common interventions, and research that supports the efficacy of behavioral parent training.

Behavioral Marital/Couples Therapy

The therapist's role, assessments, common interventions, and research that supports the efficacy of behavioral marital/couples therapy are illustrated in Table 5.5.

Conjoint Sex Therapy

Table 5.6 illustrates the therapist's role, assessments, common interventions, and research that supports the efficacy of conjoint sex therapy. (Readers should check state laws to determine whether a separate sex therapist license is required.)

Functional Family Therapy

Table 5.7 illustrates the therapist's role, assessments, common interventions, and research that supports the efficacy of FFT. The information in Table 5.7 was retrieved from the FFT, Inc. website (http:www.fftinc.com/about_model.html).

COGNITIVE BEHAVIORAL THERAPY WORKING TEMPLATE

The *cognitive behavioral family therapy template* is meant to be used as a guideline to learning the process of CBT with families. CBT was chosen for this template in this chapter because it provides a basic framework for most behavioral models. The template provides the beginning therapist with steps to take and questions to ask that promote collaboration between the therapist and the client. There are suggested questions under each heading to help start the process. After using the initial questions, guide the client through each process, asking questions that occur to you, as you stay within the family therapy theory. Although there is no one "script" for any therapy session, it is the hope of the author that the template serves as an impetus to learning this family therapy model.

Tools for Change

Cognitive behavioral therapists shift the focus from the family member with the problematic behavior to the family system to help the family engage in shared responsibility. Therapists use various interventions, such as cognitive restructuring, contingency contracts, and skills-building exercises. Additionally, the following specific techniques are used:

Cognitive rehearsal: The client recalls a problem from the past, and the therapist and the client work together to develop strategies to the problem so that if it occurs in the future, the client has a plan.

Validity testing: The therapist tests the validity of the client's beliefs or thoughts, giving the client time to defend his/her viewpoint. If the client cannot defend the beliefs or thoughts, they are said to be invalid.

TABLE 5.3 ■ Summary of Dialectical Behavior Therapy

Role of the Therapist	Commonly Used Assessments	Commonly Used Interventions	Empirically Supported Research
Reciprocal communication styles and irreverent communication styles are used as catalysts for implementing acceptance strategies and change strategies. Elimination of therapy-interfering behaviors	Dialectical assessment Chain analysis	Validation Use of metaphors Problem-solving strategies Allowing natural change Behavioral skills training Cognitive modification Contingency procedures	Shearin, E. N. & Linehan, M. M. (1993). Dialectical behavior therapy for borderline personality disorder: Treatment goals, strategies and empirical support. In J. Paris (Ed.), *Borderline personality disorder: Etiology and treatment* (pp. 285–318). Washington, DC: American Psychiatric Press. Shearin, E. N., & Linehan, M. M. (1994). Dialectical behavior therapy for borderline personality disorder: Theoretical and empirical foundations. *Acta Psychiatrica Scandinavica, 379*(Suppl.), 61–68. Linehan, M. M. (2000). The empirical basis of dialectical behavior therapy: Development of new treatments vs. evaluation of existing treatments. *Clinical Psychology: Science and Practice, 7,* 113–119. Fruzzetti, A. E., Lowry, K., Mosco, E., & Shenk, C. (2003). Emotion regulation skills training. In W. T. O'Donohue, J. E. Fisher, & S. C. Hayes (Eds.), *Empirically supported techniques of cognitive behavior therapy: A step-by-step guide for clinicians.* New York, NY: John Wiley and Sons. Lynch, T. R., Chapman, A. L., Rosenthal, M. Z., Kuo, J. R., & Linehan, M. M. (2006). Mechanisms of change in dialectical behavior therapy: Theoretical and empirical observations. *Journal of Clinical Psychology, 62*(4), 459–480.

TABLE 5.4 ■ Behavioral Parent Training

Therapist's Role	Assessments	Interventions	Behavioral Parent Training Effectiveness Research
1. Do the initial interview with at least one of the child's primary caregivers to determine the problematic behaviors, the antecedents, the frequency and duration of the problematic behavior in addition to the reinforcements.	• A baseline assessment is required to obtain a stable, reliable performance level, against which behavioral changes can be compared (Goldenberg & Goldenberg, 2000, p. 434).	• Apply the *Premack Principle* (Premack, 1965), which is the high probability behavior, specifically the pleasant activities chosen to reinforce behavior with a low probability of occurrence (Nichols & Schwartz, 2004, p. 264).	• Behavioral parent training is part of the Strengthening Families Program, a drug abuse prevention program that received recognition from the Substance Abuse and Mental Health Services Administration, U.S. Department of Health and Human Services.
2. Perform a baseline assessment in addition to ongoing assessments.	• *Behavior analysis*		
3. Decide what behaviors need to be decreased or eliminated and what behaviors need to be increased.	• Use the *SORKC model of behavior* (Kanfer & Phillips, 1970; as cited in Nichols & Schwartz, 2004, p. 263): S (stimulus), O (state of the organism), R (target response), and KC (nature and contingency of consequences).	• *Operational conditioning* techniques such as *shaping, token economy, time-out, contingency contracting,* and *contingency management.*	
4. Observe antecedents, frequency, duration, and consequences of problematic behavior in addition to teaching parents how to make and record these observations.		• Communication skills training	
5. Provide education about triggers for problematic behavior(s).			
6. Teach parent(s) operant conditioning principles.			
7. Provide support and encouragement for parent(s).			

TABLE 5.5 ▇ Behavioral Marital Couples Therapy

Therapist's Role	Assessments	Interventions	Effectiveness-Based Research Studies
1. Fulfill obligations in assessment process. 2. Teach social learning education tools to assist couples in analyzing their relationship. 3. Highlight relationship strengths throughout education process. 4. Assist partners in negotiating agreements (especially when developing contingency contracts). 5. Empower partners to view themselves as agents of change, rather than victims. 6. Therapy can be provided with multiple couples or a single couple, depending on the partners' level of comfort and need for support from other couples.	• Thorough clinical interview required to identify target behavior(s); this can include a historical analysis. • Direct observation of couple interactions • Marital assessment questionnaires • Marital self-report instruments	• Provide *communication skills training*; this involves instruction, modeling, role-playing, structured exercises, behavior rehearsal, and feedback (Nichols & Schwartz, 2004, p. 271). • Provide *problem-solving skills training*. • Provide *assertiveness training*. • *Behavior exchange techniques*, such as *"caring days"* • Contracts, such as *"quid pro quo contracts"* and *"good faith contracts"*	• Drug abusers and their spouses/partners (Epstein & McCrady, 1998; Fals-Stewart, Birchler, O'Farrell, 1996; Fals-Stewart, O'Farrell, & Birchler, 1997; O'Farrell & Fals-Stewart, 1999) • Partner violence and alcoholism (Fals-Stewart, Kashdan, O'Farrell, & Birchler, 2002; O'Farrell & Murphy, 1995; O'Farrell, Murphy, Hoover, Fals-Stewart, & Murphy, 2002; O'Farrell, Van Hutton, & Murphy, 1999) • Marital discord and depression (Beach & O'Leary, 1992; Emmanuels-Zuurveen & Emmelkamp, 1996; Jacobson, Dobson, Fruzzette, Schmaling, & Salusky, 1991)

TABLE 5.6 ■ Conjoint Sex Therapy

Therapist's Role	Assessments	Interventions	Effectiveness-Based Research Studies
• Therapist needs to require the client with the sexual dysfunction to get a thorough medical exam before beginning treatment. • Provide education about the role of anxiety regarding the sexual dysfunction how it develops, and how it is maintained (Nichols & Schwartz, 2004, p. 275). • Provide education about irrational beliefs that are impeding sexual performance and sexual satisfaction.	• Conduct extensive interviews to identify the specific problem and to determine antecedents, frequency, duration, and consequences of the sexual dysfunction to establish the treatment goals. • Explore the etiology of the sexual dysfunction. • Assess the psychological, physical, and interpersonal factors involved in the sexual dysfunction. • Assessment is ongoing to determine whether the degree of sexual dysfunction is decreasing and if so, what is eliciting the desired sexual behavior.	• *Sensate focus* • *In vivo desensitization* • *Systematic desensitization* • Encourage a series of progressively intimate encounters while avoiding thoughts about erection and orgasm (Nichols & Schwartz, 2004, pp. 274–275). • *Squeeze technique* • *Teasing technique* • Communication skills training • Assertiveness skills training in order for clients to learn how to accept and express their desires and feeling • Teach clients how to challenge irrational beliefs.	• Conjoint sex therapy has been shown to be an effective treatment for orgasmic dysfunction (Heiman, LoPiccolo, & LoPiccolo, 1981); and premature ejaculation (Masters & Johnson, 1970).

TABLE 5.7 ■ Functional Family Therapy

Therapist's Role	Assessments	Interventions	Empirically Based Research Findings
• Proceed in therapy that includes the following components: pretreatment activities, engagement in change, motivation to change, relational/interpersonal assessment and planning for behavior change, behavior change, and generalization across behavioral domains and multiple systems.	• Identify problematic behavior. • Identify interpersonal states. • Assess how the problem behavior is serving interpersonal functions. • *Assessment stage:* • Determine the interpersonal functions supplied by the behavior sequences of family members.	• Use strategic therapeutic techniques in addition to cognitive behavioral therapeutic techniques. • Alter family members' assumptions, attitudes, expectations, and emotions. • Shift focus from the individual with the problematic behavior to the family system; emphasize shared responsibility. • *Relabel* the problematic behavior(s). • Provide education and necessary skills training to maintain benefits in therapy (communication skills training, assertiveness training, etc.). • Contingency contracting may be necessary, especially with adolescents who exhibit problematic behaviors.	• Functional family therapy has been used for approximately 30 years for youth conduct problems (Alexander & Parsons, 1973; Barton, Alexander, Waldron, Turner, & Warburton, 1985; Gordon, Arbuthnot, Gustafson, & McGreen, 1988; Gordon, Graves, & Arbuthnot, 1995; Klein, Alexander, & Parsons, 1977). • Functional family therapy is incorporated in the national model Parenting Wisely Program, which is recognized by the Substance Abuse and Mental Health Services Administration. • A nationally recognized Blueprints program • High rates of effectiveness have been recognized by the Centers for Disease Control and Prevention, American Youth Policy Forum, and U.S. Department of Justice. • Functional family therapy is one of four model programs named by the U.S. Surgeon General as a model program for seriously delinquent youth. • Deinstitutionalization of Status Offenders best practice because outcome findings of the research conducted over the past 30 years show that functional family therapy can reduce adolescent rearrests by up to 60%.

Writing in a journal: The client may be asked to journal thoughts and situations that occur daily. The therapist and the client then review the journal to figure out any maladaptive thought patterns that could affect the client's behavior.

Guided discovery: The therapist guides the client through a scenario, enabling the client to understand any cognitive distortions.

Modeling: This involves role-playing exercises by the therapist so that the client may learn new ways of responding to certain situation.

Homework: The therapist commonly gives assignments to clients to help them learn new ways of dealing with current dilemmas.

Systematic positive reinforcement: This technique involves the client performing a desirable behavior and then being provided with a pleasant reinforcement or reward.

Phase 1: Joining and Building Rapport

Therapists should be genuine, empathic, and active listeners and convey understanding by asking clarifying questions and validating all family members. Assessment begins in the first session and is an ongoing process throughout therapy. To prepare clients for the assessment, Cormier and Cormier (1998) recommended communicating the purpose, such as the following:

Today I would like to focus on the concerns that have been bothering you the most. In order for me to find out exactly what you are concerned about, I will be asking you for some specific information. This information will help us identify exactly what you would like to work on in our sessions. How does this sound to you?

After the clients agree, some of the following questions can be used as a guide:

- *"How did you make the decision to come to therapy?"*
- *"What are your present concerns in your life?"*
- *"What situations are not going as well as you would like?"*

Phase 2: Understanding the Presenting Issue

The following questions could be asked to identify the presenting issues:

- *"Which of the problems that you have described are you the most consumed with today?"*
- *"What feelings are you experiencing when you think of these situations?"*
- *"What do these situations prevent you from doing?"*
- *"What thoughts make you feel worse?"*
- *"How would you feel if you did not have these thoughts?"*
- *"Where is the proof that what you are telling yourself is true?"*

Phase 3: Assessment of Family Dynamics

Therapists identify family schemata through identifying automatic thoughts and maladaptive assumptions. Therapists may use a problem analysis, functional analysis, and a behavior analysis.

- *"When you have these thoughts and experience those feelings as a result of the concerns, how do you respond to others?"*
- *"How do others respond to you when this happens?"*
- *To the family: "What do each of you think when your (family member) has these experiences? How do these thoughts affect your interactions?"*
- *"What do you each think about when these experiences happen to your family member? Does anyone work harder than others to help the family member?"* If so, then proceed with the following question: *"What happens to that family member when he/she works so hard to help?"*

Phase 4: Goals

In CBT, the clients decide the therapeutic goals. The therapist helps the clients to change problematic thinking so that feelings and behaviors will change.

Here are some comments or questions that a therapist might use during this phase:

- *"What would you each like to be doing that you are not doing at this time in your life?"*
- *"Who in your family do you think would be most relieved when (family member) is no longer having these problems?"*
- *"If you (identified person) did not have these problems, how would your relationships be different in your family?"*
- *"What would you like to change in your relationship with your family so that the problem is less of a burden?"*
- *"What are you needing, wanting, and expecting of each other?"*

Phase 5: Amplifying Change

The therapist continues to assess and evaluate the family's progress throughout treatment. Homework is given to amplify new behaviors that are defined and discussed in therapy. The therapist continuously recognizes change when clients first report improvements in their moods in addition to other improvements in functioning. The therapist notes changes in activities and inquires about the thoughts and beliefs that contribute to the client's mood and behaviors.

- *"I am noticing that you are each getting along better today in our session. Can each of you tell me what you are thinking about and feeling to help this happen?"*
- *"It seems that you have each had a better week. Can you each tell me how your thoughts contributed to what you did that helped things to be better?"*
- *"What were you each thinking about that helped you to do things better?"*
- *"In your opinion, what have other people in your family been doing recently that has helped your behavior to change?"*

Phase 6: Termination

Clients terminate when they achieve their therapeutic goals. Most therapists allow clients to schedule follow-up sessions to aid in maintaining progress.

ALAN FRUZZETTI

Alan Fruzzetti, PhD, is a psychologist and an associate professor in Clinical Psychology at the University of Nevada. He is widely published in the area of borderline personality disorder, depression, and suicidality. He is a research advisor and a member of the board of directors of the National Education Alliance for Borderline Personality Disorder (NEA-BPD). He is a well-known practitioner and researcher of dialectical behavior therapy (DBT).

What attracted you to the theory behind your model?

I think the model itself is an integrative model, and I was attracted to the fact that it integrated different things that are important to me and that I already liked. For example, the dual emphasis on both acceptance and change are particularly attractive to me. The idea that we can be both validating—accepting and understanding of our clients and their experiences—and at the same time, we can be very dedicated to change in helping them do things differently to improve their lives. Dialectics has a long history. Basically in this case, it refers to the idea that we can synthesize or integrate two things that seem to be, at first glance, opposite. They seem to be incompatible, like acceptance and change. Or when you work with families, one person's perspective and another's might be quite different and, actually, often seem completely incompatible. So, dialectics really undergirds the whole thing, but it allows us to integrate a lot of other models. Systems theory, for example, is quite a big piece of it, although I think that this approach transcends, goes beyond, systems theory as well.

How do you formulate your view of the family when they enter therapy?

There's a certain structure in DBT with families that allows us to organize targets from more severe to less severe. So, one dimension of formulation is trying to assess the severe targets, and figure out, "What are the really out-of-control things?" Is there violence, is there severe coercion, is there suicidality, child neglect, aggression? Those types of things that would be considered life threatening in one way or another. Those would be the most severe, continuing from there to less severe targets down a continuum. One thing I do is look for things I would call primary targets, like family violence, or if somebody is very depressed, or lots of substance abuse, or aggression, or whatever it might be.

Then at another level of analysis, I try to determine what are both the internal emotional determinants of those primary targets and the interpersonal or systemic determinants of those same targets. And that second level I would call secondary targets, not being secondary in importance but second level of analysis. So as I go along and ask for people's experiences, I try to get them to be descriptive and put very specific incidents on the table and try to understand the context of those behaviors in those situations. It is rather a more inductive approach to case formulation, taking specific incidents of various problems and trying to build a formulation out of specific incidents.

Then the idea would be to think about a different dimension. Are there things people are doing that are reinforcing certain types of dysfunction? For example, how is it working that somebody is suicidal? You can understand that from both an internal standpoint that suicidality helps them to regulate their own emotions on one hand, but on the other hand, it also might function to get somebody to back off from their demands in certain situations or to become more affiliative or nurturing. And so I constantly would be looking for both emotional regulation function on any given problem, as well as a social or systemic function in the family. That doesn't mean that there would always be both, but I would look for both to see if that's likely.

What kinds of families do you think would benefit most with this model?
It's certainly true that this came out of our work with suicidal and self-injurious families with members with suicidal and self-injurious tendencies. We have actually done a couple of interesting studies with ordinary couples seeking work on their relationship and ordinary families with adolescents with more ordinary and sometimes more severe adolescent problems. It is not limited to suicidality and borderline personality disorder. I think this model is more general than just for [borderline personality disorder].

Different models of therapy require the therapist to be directive or nondirective. In your opinion, what are the necessary characteristics a therapist should possess to be effective with this model?
I think the therapist, to be the most effective with this model, has to have absolutely great skills in both of them (directive and nondirective repertoires). That's part of the hallmark of the approach: There are times when it's very important within the model to be nondirective, extremely supportive, accepting, and validating. And in other times, it's extremely important to be quite the opposite, very pushy, very irreverent, very change oriented, very directive. Sometimes you can go back and forth in the same minute between the two.

How often does the family usually see you and for how long a period of time?
It varies, as you could imagine. Anywhere from 45 minutes to 90 minutes per session. When we do groups, we sometimes have couples groups or parent groups, they can be longer, 2 hours. We certainly do a lot of standard family therapy, 50 to 60 minutes, an hour, as well as 80 or 90 minutes. It varies a lot depending on context. If it's a severe case, where someone in the family is very suicidal, self-injuring, we may see the family, and they may be in individual therapy as well, a few weeks in a row, and then see them every 2, 3 weeks, or once a month for a long time or even for a year. In other cases, we might see a person or family every other week, for six or eight sessions. We've done a couple research projects with groups, couples, or groups of parents where we just have them for six or eight visits and have shown pretty substantial results. So, I think it's not clear what length of treatment is optimal. Sometimes it's short and sometimes it's longer. I've never seen a family every week for 3 years, I can't imagine that. I might see the family once a month for the first year of that or maybe longer. It's hard to get families to come in for that many visits.

What are you looking for when you are in the session?
I'm looking for whether people seem to expressing their emotions accurately. Expressing their wants, desires accurately. Or whether they seem to be coming out inaccurately. I'm looking for the cycle of people (generally) accurately disclosing and other people validating them. Are people disclosing accurately, making validation difficult, or are they invalidating, punishing people in terms of disclosure? I am looking to assess that cycle. I am also looking for patterns. With couples, there's the same pattern you will also find in literature: engage/distance patterns, which shows up in the literature with the names demand/withdraw, rejection/intrusion, those kinds of things. And with parents, the various dialectical dilemmas, the things the parents grapple with, in terms of too much autonomy versus too much dependence. We attempt to find the synthesis.

What is the assessment process of this model?

The assessment process has a couple of different facets. One is to orient people to what we are doing constantly. There's a short orientation just leading to the assessment. We always give people some self-reports to complete separately. For example, we give them assessments about aggression and violence in their relationship. There are different rooms so that they're able to do that independently. We also ask them questions of their views of their relationship quality and their individual well-being, including depression, anxiety, emotion regulation, substance use, etc. Then we conduct one, sometimes two, interviews with them trying to get at things you and I have talked about. And we always also get a videotape sample of the family interacting. And depending how chaotic it is, if it's a lot of people, we might break them down into pairs and get separate interactions, videotapes between the parents themselves, mom and dad, each parent with the child, and/or with the whole family together. In that videotape assessment, we typically ask people to specifically talk about how satisfied they are with their family life, discuss any changes they would like to see. We do video feedback with couples. We also do that with parents. Although we don't usually show the child something: We are usually focusing on how the parent can do something different. Parent–child relationships are different in the responsibility for change.

Who sets the goals, the client or the therapist?

We map targets out for families and we're very explicit while also being collaborative. We tell them, "This is what we are working on here." We want to work on things that are more dangerous first. Families are usually willing to do that, and if not, we try hard to convince them. It's very hard to do much of anything else if the consequence is going to possibly be something that is aggressive or violent. So, we get them onboard with the hierarchy of targets and/or goals, if you prefer. Then of course, when we get with others, we talk to them about various priorities. It's very collaborative from the beginning about what the goals are, and we are very explicit about it. We give them diary cards so they're tracking their goals, hopefully on a daily basis and are able to track information we want them to become more aware of, like "I was feeling sad, I was feeling angry."

What are some commonly used interventions with the model?

There are so many. I start with the ones that are most structured, like skills training. One of the most common things we'll do is teach skills. We can do that formally by having a family skills group, or we can also just do it in the moment. We're looking at a chain of a given transaction between, say, partners, or between a parent and a child or something. We say, okay, what can you do differently there? They don't know, so we may actually teach one or two or three different things they could do right there. We might do that in 2 minutes, and we might actually stop and do that for quite a long time for the rest of the session.

We also do chain analysis. We do these pretty, but complicated, multiperson chains where we look at each person's chain and how it intersects with another person. With families, you know, they're complicated, so we overlap when it's something that's public, like one person criticizes another person. That's a common link, that's one place where chains cross, we draw these things out. Families love this, to my utter surprise. They really like it because they can really understand the context for each other's behavior and see where it's coming out of and see how if either of them did something different, the whole thing would go differently. So chain analysis is a big piece.

And, of course, loads of validation, which both soothes them and helps them to continue to participate. It also models that these things do make sense. People's reactions do make sense even when they're self-sabotaging or sabotaging of others. So lots of acceptance-oriented interventions, lots of validation, some mindfulness, and lots of change-oriented ones like chain analysis, problem solving, skill training. And what lots of family therapists do, call it reenactment or rechoreographing, is to try to change the dance. We do a lot of that as well. So they have this particular transaction, they start at the beginning and try to do it differently this time. In particular, we help them regulate their emotions and stay descriptive—not make too many inferences or interpretations—along the way.

What role does a homework assignment have in this model?
Homework assignments are really a central piece of the model. We don't always call them homework because some people don't like that term. We try to call it practice, but the idea is that we're trying to get people to do many different things differently and be more aware of their own internal experiences and their family members' behavior. We want them to be more aware and less judgmental. Those are both part of mindfulness. We also want people to be more accurate in their expressions and more validating when they express themselves. We want people to have better negotiation skills. When it comes to couples, we want to look at their intimacy skills on many, many different dimensions.

How do you know when your client is ready to terminate?
There are a couple of ways to do that. Sometimes, people without severe problems will set a goal at the beginning that they want to work on for a certain length of time. At the end of that length of time, they say we've made enough progress and just want to be done, at least for now. Sometimes it comes out of a best guess, best collaborative guess from the beginning of treatment. At other times, it's because the goals are so explicit, the goals get accomplished. And once the goals are accomplished, we have a collaborative meeting where we talk about whether we are done or are there new targets? Or do we just want to say we want to refer you to somebody else because we've given this our best shot. So, it's either a failure to get better, or it's getting better.

Have you found any limitations of this approach?
Well, there are different kinds of limitations. One is that it's a tough population that DBT typically works with. There are lots of therapists, who, when you ask them if they would like to work with a family that's got a suicidal member, they say that's not their first choice on a Monday morning. So one of the limitations are that DBT has a reputation, and appropriately so, of being a treatment with people with pretty severe problems. Even though I think family approaches with DBT are much more generally logical beyond that. The other is that DBT is a relatively new approach, so its applications to families and couples and parents are not widely taught. For clients, I think the limitation is its ambiguity. This dialectical "both/and" thing can be frustrating for some people. Some people find it extremely valuable because nobody's wrong in the family, they have different experiences. Sometimes, some people in some families do have a hard time with the dialectic. In some ways, it's pretty different than what's in the larger mainstream culture, this idea in DBT that things are not right or wrong. They are matters of preference, or whether they work, so forth and so on, that's tough for some people.

What are your suggestions for students learning this model?
Any DBT resources are going to be helpful, including Marsha Linehan's books, which are terrific, in addition to training manuals. There is a recent book by Alec Miller, Jill H. Rathus, Marsha M. Linehan, and Charles R. Swenson, *DBT With Suicidal Adolescents*. This book incorporates, very nicely, some parent work and family therapy that is useful for working with adolescents exhibiting suicidal behavior. Also, my book for couples, *The High-Conflict Couple: A Dialectical Behavior Therapy Guide to Finding Peace, Intimacy, and Validation* (2006). There are different trainings around and resources are available. Get on a team with at least one other person who wants to do this model. Learn to recognize that any kind of practicing any piece of the therapy, such as being nonjudgmental and teaching any client a skill in family therapy, can be helpful. Begin trying to help someone accurately disclose or learn how to validate more. As the pieces accumulate, they are more and more able to do this spontaneously, then it's really fun. It's harder at first, but it can become quite fun.

Case Study

A mother calls and makes an appointment for her family to come to therapy. The family consists of the wife and her husband, both in their 40s; their 15-year-old son; a college-aged daughter; and the woman's father, age 82. Three years after the woman's mother died, her father developed Alzheimer's disease. He moved in with the family 6 months ago. When his health began to deteriorate, the woman spent more time caring for him than for other members of the family. Three months ago, the 15-year-old son, who has been treated for attention deficit hyperactivity disorder since age 7, began to refuse to take his medication and is now being truant from school.

During the session, the wife cries and the husband reports that their relationship is strained, occasionally rolling his eyes as his wife becomes tearful. He reports that he has had to take on more work because his wife had to quit her job to attend to her father's needs. The daughter is away at college and the wife smiles as she describes her as a straight-A student. The daughter was asked to attend the session but refused because she has a hard time with her grandfather's illness and dislikes the conflict that has developed at home.

Dr. Fallon Cluxton-Keller's Response to the Case Study

I would ask each family member for his/her perspective of their current circumstances. I would ask questions to assess how their thoughts affect their feelings and their behaviors while assessing for cognitive distortions in each family member. The family schemata would also be assessed to determine if there were dysfunctional beliefs about family roles and/or family life that influence the ways they respond to each other and cope with their circumstances. Assessments of the strengths and weaknesses in the marriage as well as in the family as a whole would be beneficial in determining a baseline for areas such as decision-making skills, problem-solving skills, boundaries, and their communication skills. Their major complaints would be elicited, and I would assess how these complaints are expressed through their specific behaviors and the ways in which these behaviors are reinforced.

I would assess for the severity of the behavioral disturbances in the family to determine which behaviors are most problematic. For example, the parents may be asked to do a functional analysis of their son's behavior in which they would observe and record the target behavior in addition to the antecedents and consequences of the target behavior, which would most likely reveal strengths and weaknesses in their parenting skills. I would ask each family member to talk about what he/she wants, needs, and expects from therapy to assess whether their wants, needs, and expectations were realistic. I would ask the family members to talk about changes they would like to see happen in the family so they can begin to formalize their family's therapeutic goals.

Specifically, I would ask questions about desired behaviors or desired behavioral changes in order to assist them with reinforcement skills. Cognitive behavioral family therapeutic interventions would be performed, such as communication skills training, teaching them to identify cognitive distortions and challenge these distortions. Any additional skills training would be provided to assist this family with accomplishing their therapeutic goals. I would also request to see the couple for several marital therapy sessions to determine their level of commitment to their marriage and whether they demonstrate a willingness to make changes to improve their relationship. If they want to pursue marital therapy, then cognitive behavioral marital therapeutic techniques (cognitive restructuring, communication skills training, interventions to increase positive behavioral exchanges and decrease negative behavioral exchanges, etc.) would be used to assist them with developing specific skills to increase their relational satisfaction, depending on their marital therapeutic goals. Assessments would continue throughout the marital and/or family therapeutic process to measure their progress in accomplishing their therapeutic goals. The interventions would be tailored to assist them with accomplishing their goals. I would recommend weekly family therapy sessions and marital therapy sessions and, depending on their progress, I would recommend doing biweekly sessions and monthly sessions. Follow-up sessions would most likely take place to assist them in maintaining their progress.

KEY TERMS

Behavior analysis   An assessment procedure conducted by the therapist to identify the target behaviors, determine factors maintaining these behaviors, and construct a treatment plan with specific criteria to measure change efforts.

Behavior therapy   Therapy influenced by Wolpe, Eysenck, Shapiro, and Skinner that is representative of principles of learning theory and is used to treat psychopathology through techniques designed to reinforce desired behaviors and extinguish problematic behaviors.

Behavioral regulation   The ability of humans and animals to use adaptive behaviors that achieve a balance in a system that keeps things the same.

Behaviorism   Theory in which the environment, rather than genes, is the primary determinant of both human and nonhuman animal behavior (Barker, 2002, p. 646). John B. Watson was the father of behaviorism, and he focused on overt behavior influenced by environmental factors.

Classical conditioning   According to Pavlov (1927), this is the pairing of a neutral (conditioned) stimulus with one that evokes a response (unconditioned stimulus), such that the neutral stimulus comes to evoke the response when events occur closely together in time.

Cognitive behavioral therapy   A model of therapy that emphasizes the importance of identifying and challenging distorted thoughts to produce changes in mood and reduce or eliminate problematic behaviors.

Cognitive rehearsal   A technique in which the client recalls a past problem and the therapist and the client rehearse new, more desired responses to the past problem.

Cognitive restructuring   An intervention in which the therapist attempts to modify the client's thoughts, perceptions, and attributions about an event (Cormier & Cormier, 1998).

Cognitive therapy   A time-limited, present-focused, problem-solving therapeutic approach, usually associated with Aaron Beck, in which clients learn how to identify distorted thoughts and challenge those thoughts to improve their moods (Beck, Rush, Shaw, & Emery, 1979).

Contingency contract   A contract in which participants specify who is to do what for whom, under which circumstances, times, and places.

Functional analysis   According to Falloon (1991), a behavioral assessment of family functioning typically occurs at two levels, and the second level is a functional analysis, which is geared toward revealing the interrelationships between behavioral deficits and the interpersonal environment where they are functionally relevant.

Guided discovery   An opportunity for the client to revisit a past or current issue with therapist assistance, so that the client can discover cognitive distortions and later begin cognitive restructuring.

Irrational beliefs   Beliefs that are rigid, dogmatic, cannot be fully supported by social reality, and tend to hinder goal achievement (Ellis & MacLaren, 2005, p. 59).

Modeling   According to Bandura, this is a process in which a person vicariously learns through observing and imitating other people.

Negative reinforcement   According to Skinner, a reinforcement that occurs when a response that leads to the removal of an aversive event is increased.

Operant conditioning   A procedure developed by Skinner (1938) that consists of the creation of an operant contingency and the recording of its effect on a target behavior. This process involves acquiring or eliminating a response as a function of the environmental contingencies of reward and punishment.

Positive reinforcement   According to Skinner, this is the strengthening of a tendency to behave in a certain situation by presenting a desired reward following previous responses in that situation.

Problem analysis   According to Falloon (1991), a behavioral assessment of family functioning occurs at two levels, and the first level is the problem analysis, which is directed at identifying the specific behavioral deficits that underlie problems and modifications that could lead to problem resolution.

Rational belief   Flexible, adaptive beliefs that help people reach their goals and are consistent with social reality (Ellis & MacLaren, 2005, p. 59).

Reinforcement   In operant conditioning, increasing the probability that a response will recur by presenting a contingent positive event or by removing a negative event.

Reinforcers   According to Skinner (1938), a reinforcer is anything that maintains a response or increases its strength.

Schema   According to Beck (1976), a core belief a person has that guides his/her thinking and actions.

Skills building   Procedures in which the therapist teaches his/her clients skills to resolve the presenting problem(s).

Systematic desensitization   A behavioral therapeutic technique developed by Joseph Wolpe based on counterconditioning in which a fearful person, while deeply relaxed, imagines a series of progressively more fearsome situations in which the two responses of relaxation and fear are incompatible, and thus the fear is dispelled (Davison & Neale, 1998, p. G-24).

Systematic positive reinforcement   This technique involves the client performing a desirable behavior and then receiving a positive, pleasant reward or stimulus.

Therapeutic contract   A written negotiated agreement between two people, typically the therapist and the client or family members, that specifies behavior changes and consequences.

Validity testing   A technique in which the therapist "tests" or questions the validity of a client's thoughts, allowing the client to defend his/her thinking. If the client cannot defend the thoughts, they are said to be invalid.

REFERENCES

Alexander, J. F., & Parsons, B. V. (1973). Short-term behavioral intervention with delinquent families: Impact on family process and recidivism. *Journal of Abnormal Psychology, 81*(3), 219–225.

Bandura, A. (1969). *Principles of behavior modification*. New York, NY: Holt, Rinehart & Winston.

Bandura, A., Ross, D., & Ross, S. A. (1961). Transmission of aggression through imitation of aggressive models. *Journal of Abnormal and Social Psychology, 63*, 575–582.

Barker, L. (2002). *Psychology*. Upper Saddle River, NJ: Pearson Education.

Barton, C., Alexander, J. F., Waldron, H., Turner, C. W., & Warburton, J. (1985). Generalizing treatment effects of functional family therapy: Three replications. *The American Journal of Family Therapy, 13*(3), 16–26.

Beach, S. R., & O'Leary, K. D. (1992). Treating depression in the context of marital discord: Outcome and predictors for response for marital therapy versus cognitive therapy. *Behavior Therapy, 23*, 507–528.

Beck, A. T. (1976). *Cognitive therapy and the emotional disorders*. New York, NY: International University Press.

Beck, A. T., Rush, J. A., Shaw, B. F., & Emery, G. (1979). *Cognitive therapy of depression*. New York, NY: The Guilford Press.

Becvar, D. S., & Becvar, R. J. (2003). *Family therapy: A systemic integration* (5th ed.). Boston, MA: Pearson Education.

Butler, A. C., Chapman, J. E., Forman, E. M., & Beck, A. T. (2006). The empirical status of cognitive-behavioral therapy: A review of meta-analyses. *Clinical Psychology Review, 26*(1), 17–31.

Compton, S. N., March, J. S., Brent, D., Albano, A. M., V, Weersing, R., & Curry, J. (2004). Cognitive-behavioral psychotherapy for anxiety and depressive disorders in children and adolescents: An evidence-based medicine review. *Journal of the American Academy of Child and Adolescent Psychiatry, 43*(8), 930–959.

Cormier, B., & Cormier, S. (1998). *Interviewing strategies for helpers: Fundamental skills and cognitive behavioral interventions*. New York, NY: Brooks/Cole Publishing Company.

Dattilio, F. M. (2004). *Cognitive-behavioral strategies with couples and families*. Philadelphia, PA: University of Pennsylvania School of Medicine. Retrieved from http://www.dattilio.com/handouts.ppt

Davison, G. C., & Neale, J. M. (1998). *Abnormal psychology* (7th ed.). New York, NY: John Wiley and Sons.

Dimeff, L., & Koerner, K. (Eds.). (2007). *Dialectical behavior therapy in clinical practice applications across disorders and settings*. New York, NY: The Guilford Press.

Ellis, A. (1962). *Reason and emotion in psychotherapy*. Secaucus, NJ: Citadel Press.

Ellis, A. (2001). *Overcoming destructive beliefs, feelings, and behaviors: New directions for rational emotive behavior therapy*. Amherst, NY: Prometheus Books.

Ellis, A., & MacLaren, C. (2005). *Rational emotive behavior therapy: A therapist's guide* (2nd ed.). Atascadero, CA: Impact Publishers.

Emanuels-Zuurveen, L., & Emmelkamp, P. M. G. (1996). Individual behavioural-cognitive therapy versus marital therapy for depression in maritally distressed couples. *The British Journal of Psychiatry, 169*(2), 181–188.

Epstein, E. E., & McCrady, B. S. (1998). Behavioral couples treatment of alcohol and drug use disorders: Current status and innovations. *Clinical Psychology Review, 18*(6), 689–711.

Epstein, N., Schlesinger, S. E., & Dryden, W. (Eds.). (1988). *Cognitive-behavioral therapy with families*. New York, NY: Brunner/Mazel.

Falloon, I. R. H. (1991). Behavioral family therapy. In A. S. Gurman & D. P. Kniskern (Eds.), *Handbook of family therapy* (Vol. 2, pp. 65–95). New York, NY: Brunner/Mazel.

Fals-Stewart, W., Birchler, G. R., & O'Farrell, T. J. (1996). Behavioral couples therapy for male substance-abusing patients: Effects on relationship adjustment and drug-using behavior. *Journal of Consulting and Clinical Psychology, 64*(5), 959–972.

Fals-Stewart, W., Kashdan, T., O'Farrel, T., & Birchler, G. (2002). Behavioral couples therapy for drug-abusing patients: Effects on partner violence. *Journal of Substance Abuse Treatment, 22*(2), 87–96.

Fals-Stewart, W., O'Farrell, T. J., & Birchler, G. R. (1997). Behavioral couples therapy for male substance-abusing patients: A cost outcomes analysis. *Journal of Consulting and Clinical Psychology, 65*(5), 789–802.

Fruzzetti, A. E. (2001). *Validating and Invalidating Behavior Coding Scale manual* (Version 3.1). Reno, NV: University of Nevada.

Fruzzetti, A. E., & Iverson, K. M. (2004, Spring/Summer). Couples dialectical behavior therapy: An approach to both individual and relational distress. *AABT Couples SIG Newsletter*. Retrieved from http://www.aabtcouples.org/

Fruzzetti, A. E., & Linehan, M. (2006). *The high-conflict couple: A dialectical behavior therapy guide to finding peace, intimacy, and validation*. Oakland, CA: New Harbinger Publications.

Fruzzetti, A. E., Lowry, K., Mosco, E., & Shenk, C. (2003). Emotion regulation skills training. In W. T. O'Donohue, J. E. Fisher, & S. C. Hayes (Eds.), *Empirically supported techniques of cognitive behavior therapy: A step-by-step guide for clinicians*. New York, NY: John Wiley and Sons.

Goldenberg, H., & Goldenberg, I. (2000). *Family therapy: An overview* (5th ed.). Belmont, CA: Wadsworth/Thomson Learning.

Gordon, D. A., Arbuthnot, J., Gustafson, K. E., & McGreen, P. (1988). Home-based behavioral-systems family therapy with disadvantaged juvenile delinquents. *The American Journal of Family Therapy, 16*(3), 243–255.

Gordon, D. A., Graves, K., & Arbuthnot, J. (1995). The effect of functional family therapy for delinquents on adult criminal behavior. *Criminal Justice and Behavior, 22*(1), 60–73.

Heiman, J., LoPiccolo, L., & LoPiccolo, J. (1981). The treatment of sexual dysfunction. In A. Gurman & D. Kniskern (Eds.), *Handbook of family therapy* (pp. 592–627). New York, NY: Brunner & Mazel.

Hoffman, P. D., Fruzzetti, A. E., & Swenson, C. R. (1999). Dialectical behavior therapy—Family skills training. *Family Process, 38*(4), 399–414.

Jacobson, N. S., Dobson, K., Fruzzetti, A. E., Schmaling, K. B., & Salusky, S. (1991). Marital therapy as a treatment for depression. *Journal of Consulting and Clinical Psychology, 59*(4), 547–557.

Kanfer, F. H., & Phillips, J. (1970). *Learning foundations of behavior therapy*. New York, NY: Wiley.

Kaplan, H. (1974). *New sex therapy: Active treatment of sexual dysfunctions* (Vol. 1). New York, NY: Routledge.

Klein, N. C., Alexander, J. F., & Parsons, B. V. (1977). Impact of family systems intervention on recidivism and sibling delinquency: A model of primary prevention and program evaluation. *Journal of Consulting and Clinical Psychology, 45*(3), 469–474.

Leslie, L. A. (1988). Cognitive-behavioral and systems models of family therapy: How compatible are they? In N. Epstein, S. E. Schlesinger, & W. Dryden (Eds.), *Cognitive-behavioral therapy with families*. New York, NY: Brunner/Mazel.

Linehan, M. (1993a). *Cognitive-behavioral treatment of borderline personality disorder*. New York, NY: The Guilford Press.

Linehan, M. (1993b). *Skills training manual for treating borderline personality disorder*. New York, NY: The Guilford Press.

Linehan, M. M. (2000). The empirical basis of dialectical behavior therapy: Development of new treatments versus evaluation of existing treatments. *Clinical Psychology: Science and Practice, 7*, 113–119.

Lynch, T. R., Chapman, A. L., Rosenthal, M. Z., Kuo, J. R., & Linehan, M. M. (2006). Mechanisms of change in dialectical behavior therapy: Theoretical and empirical observations. *Journal of Clinical Psychology, 62*(4), 459–480.

Masters, W. H., & Johnson, V. E. (1970). *Human sexual inadequacy*. New York, NY: Bantam Books.

Maxwell, S. (2009). Resolving relationship difficulties with CBT. *Sexual and Relationship Therapy, 24*(3–4), 378–379.

Nichols, M. P., & Schwartz, R. C. (2004). *Family therapy concepts and methods* (6th ed.). Boston, MA: Pearson Education.

O'Farrell, T. J., & Fals-Stewart, W. (1999). Treatment models and methods: Family models. In B. S. McCrady & E. E. Epstein (Eds.), *Addictions: A comprehensive guidebook*. Boston, NY: Oxford University Press.

O'Farrell, T. J., & Murphy, C. M. (1995). Marital violence before and after alcoholism treatment. *Journal of Consulting and Clinical Psychology, 63*(2), 256–262.

O'Farrell, T. J., Murphy, C. M., Hoover, S., Fals-Stewart, W., & Murphy, M. (2002). *Domestic violence before and after couples-based alcoholism treatment: The role of treatment involvement and abstinence*. Unpublished manuscript.

O'Farrell, T. J., Van Hutton, V., & Murphy, C. M. (1999). Domestic violence before and after alcoholism treatment: A two-year longitudinal study. *Journal of Studies on Alcohol, 60*(3), 317–321.

Patterson, G. R., & Reid, J. B. (1970). Reciprocity and coercion: Two facets of social systems. In C. Neuringer & J. L. Michael (Eds.), *Behavior modification in clinical psychology* (pp. 133–177). New York, NY: Appleton-Century-Crofts.

Pavlov, I. P. (1927). *Conditioned reflexes*. New York, NY: Oxford University Press.

Pavlov, I. P. (1932). Neuroses in man and animals. *Journal of the American Medical Association, 99*, 1012–1013.

Pavlov, I. P. (1934). An attempt at a physiological interpretation of obsessional neurosis and paranoia. *Journal of Mental Science, 80*, 187–197.

Rizvi, S., & Swenson, C. R. (2006). *Chaos to freedom: DBT for the multiply-disordered client* (Workshop presented at the Houston Marriott Medical Center, Houston, TX). Seattle, WA: Behavioral Tech, LLC.

Shearin, E. N., & Linehan, M. M. (1993). Dialectical behavior therapy for borderline personality disorder: Treatment goals, strategies and empirical support. In J. Paris (Ed.), *Borderline personality disorder: Etiology and treatment* (pp. 285–318). Washington, DC: American Psychiatric Press.

Shearin, E. N., & Linehan, M. M. (1994). Dialectical behavior therapy for borderline personality disorder: Theoretical and empirical foundations. *Acta Psychiatrica Scandinavica, 379*(Suppl.), 61–68.

Skinner, B. F. (1938). *The behavior of organisms*. New York, NY: Appleton Century Croft.

Thibaut, J., & Kelley, H. H. (1959). *The social psychology of groups*. New York, NY: John Wiley and Sons.

Watson, J. B., & Rayner, R. (1920). Conditioned emotional reactions. *Journal of Experimental Psychology*, 3, 1–14. Reprinted in *American Psychologist*, 55(3), 313–317.

Windell, J., & Windell, E. (1977). Parent group training programs in juvenile courts: A national survey. *The Family Coordinator/The Family and The Law*, 26(4), 459–463.

RECOMMENDED READING LIST

Books

American Psychiatric Association. (2000). *Diagnostic and statistical manual of mental disorders* (4th ed., text rev.). Washington, DC: Author.

Beck, A. T. (1988). *Love is never enough*. New York, NY: Harper & Row.

Beck, A. T., Rush, J. A., Shaw, B. F., & Emery, G. (1979). *Cognitive therapy of depression*. New York, NY: The Guilford Press.

Cornelius, R. R. (1996). *The science of emotion: Research and tradition in the psychology of emotion*. Upper Saddle River, NJ: Prentice Hall.

Ellis, A., & MacLaren, C. (2005). *Rational emotive behavior therapy: A therapist's guide* (2nd ed.). Atascadero, CA: Impact Publishers.

Fruzzetti, A. E., & Linehan, M. (2006). *The high-conflict couple: A dialectical behavior therapy guide to finding peace, intimacy, and validation*. Oakland, CA: New Harbinger Publications.

Fruzzetti, A. E., Santisteban, D., & Hoffman, P. D. (2007). Dialectical behavior therapy with families. In L. A. Dimeff & K. Koerner (Eds.), *Dialectical behavior therapy in clinical practice: Applications across disorders and settings* (pp. 222–244). New York, NY: The Guilford Press.

Hazelden Foundation (Producer). (1992). *Understanding: Discover your personal power to change* [Motion picture]. Center City, MN: Hazelden Foundation.

Linehan, M. (1993). *Cognitive-behavioral treatment of borderline personality disorder*. New York, NY: The Guilford Press.

Linehan, M. (1993). *Skills training manual for treating borderline personality disorder*. New York, NY: The Guilford Press.

Morris, S. B., Alexander, J. F., & Waldron, H. (1988). Functional family therapy. In I. R. Falloon (Ed.), *Handbook of behavioral family therapy*. New York, NY: The Guilford Press.

Sadock, B. J., & Sadock, V. A. (2003). *Synopsis of psychiatry* (9th ed.). Philadelphia, PA: Lippincott Williams & Wilkins.

Wolpe, J. (1948). *An approach to the problem of neurosis bases on the conditioned response*. Unpublished MD thesis, University of Witwatersand, Johannesburg, South Africa.

Wolpe, J. (1958). *Psychotherapy by reciprocal inhibition*. Stanford, CA: Stanford University Press.

Articles

Baucom, D. H., Shoham, V., Mueser, K. T., Daiuto, A. D., & Stickle, T. R. (1998). Empirically supported couple and family interventions for marital distress and adult mental health problems. *Journal of Consulting and Clinical Psychology*, 66, 53–88.

Beck, A. T., Ward, C. H., Mendelson, M., Mock, J., & Erbaugh, J. (1961). An inventory for measuring depression. *Archives of General Psychiatry*, 4, 561–571.

Beck, H. P., Levinson, S., & Irons, G. (2009). Finding little Albert: A journey to John B. Watson's infant laboratory. *The American Psychologist*, 64(7), 605–614.

Butler, A., Chapman, J., Forman, E. M., & Beck, A. (2006). The empirical status of cognitive-behavioral therapy: A review of meta-analyses. *Clinical Psychology Review*, 26(1), 17–31.

Butler, D. L., & Winne, P. H. (1995). Feedback and self-regulated learning: A theoretical synthesis. *Review of Educational Research*, 65, 245–281.

Carrère, S., & Gottman, J. M. (1999). Predicting divorce among newlyweds from the first three minutes of a marital conflict discussion. *Family Process, 38*(3), 293–301.

Ellis, A. (1993). Changing rational-emotive therapy (RET) to rational emotive behavior therapy (REBT). *Behavior Therapist, 16*, 257–258.

Ellis, A. (1993). The rational-emotive therapy (RET) approach to marriage and family therapy. *Family Journal: Counseling and Therapy for Couples and Families, 1*, 292–307.

Freeman, J. B., Choate-Summers, M. L., Moore, P. S., Garcia, A. M., Sapyta, J. J., Leonard, H. L., & Franklin, M. E. (2007). Cognitive behavioral treatment for young children with obsessive-compulsive disorder. *Biological Psychiatry, 61*(3), 337–343.

Fruzzetti, A. E., & Iverson, K. M. (2004). Couples dialectical behavior therapy: An approach to both individual and relational distress. *Couples Research and Therapy, 10*, 8–13.

Fruzzetti, A. E., & Iverson, K. M. (2004, Spring/Summer). Couples dialectical behavior therapy: An approach to both individual and relational distress. *AABT Couples SIG Newsletter*. Retrieved from http://www.aabtcouples.org/

Fruzzetti, A. E., & Shenk, C. (2008). Fostering validating responses in families. *Social Work in Mental Health, 6*, 215–227.

Hoffman, P. D., Fruzzetti, A. E., & Buteau, E. (2007). Understanding and engaging families: An education, skills and support program for relatives impacted by borderline personality disorder. *Journal of Mental Health, 16*, 69–82.

Hoffman, P. D., Fruzzetti, A. E., & Swenson, C. R. (1999). Dialectical behavior therapy—Family skills training. *Family Process, 38*(4), 399–414.

Karver, M., Handelsman, J., Fields, S., & Bickman, L. (2006). Meta-analysis of therapeutic relationship variables in youth and family therapy: The evidence for different relationship variables in the child and adolescent treatment outcome literature. *Clinical Psychology Review, 26*(1), 50–65.

Schmidt, U., Lee, S., Beecham, J., Perkins, S., Treasure, J., Yi, I., . . . Eisler, I. (2007). A randomized controlled trial of family therapy and cognitive behavior therapy guided self-care for adolescents with bulimia nervosa and related disorders. *The American Journal of Psychiatry, 164*, 591–598.

Young, K. M., Northern, J. J., Lister, K. M., Drummond, J. A., & O'Brien, W. H. (2007). A meta-analysis of family-behavioral weight-loss treatments for children. *Clinical Psychology Review, 27*(2), 240–249.

Websites

Academy of Cognitive Therapy
http://www.academyofct.org

Association for Behavioral and Cognitive Therapies
http://www.aabt.org/

Beck Institute
http://www.beckinstitute.org

Behavioral Tech, LLC
http://www.behavioraltech.org

Blueprints for Violence Prevention (FFT is a Blueprint program)
http://www.colorado.edu/cspv/blueprints/

Evidence-Based Behavioral Practice (website is sponsored by National Institutes of Health)
http://www.ebbp.org

Functional Family Therapy, Inc.
http://www.fftinc.com/index.html

Functional Family Therapy Training Link
http://www.fftinc.com/implement_new.html

National Association for Cognitive-Behavioral Therapists
http://www.nacbt.org

National Institutes of Health Office of Behavioral and Social Sciences Research
http://obssr.od.nih.gov

Office of Juvenile Justice and Delinquency Prevention Deinstitutionalization of Status Offenders Best Practices Database (overview of functional family therapy as an evidence-based practice)
http://www2.dsgonline.com/dso2/dso_program_detail.aspx?ID=29&title=Functional%20Family%20 Therapy

The Albert Ellis Institute
http://www.rebt.org

Rational Emotive Behavior Therapy

Fallon Cluxton-Keller

When we feel, we think, and act; when we act, we feel and think;
and when we think, we feel and act.

—Albert Ellis

INTRODUCTION

This chapter explores the usefulness of rational emotive behavior therapy (REBT) in working with couples and families. The developer of REBT, psychologist Albert Ellis, PhD, is considered one of the most prolific psychologists of the 21st century. He was the pioneer of cognitive behavioral therapy.*

HISTORY AND LEADING FIGURES

Albert Ellis, PhD

Albert Ellis received his MA and PhD in clinical psychology from Columbia University. He practiced psychotherapy, marriage and family therapy, and sex therapy for more than 60 years. He is the founder of REBT, which was the first of the cognitive behavioral therapies (Ellis, 2005, p. 331). He was the president of Albert Ellis Institute in New York City (Ellis, 2005, p. 331). During his career, he was ranked as one of the "most influential psychologists" by both American and Canadian psychologists and counselors (Ellis, 2005, p. 332). He served as a consulting or associate editor of several scientific journals; published more than 800 scientific papers, and more than 200 audiocassettes, in addition to videos; and he authored or edited more than 75 books, as well as monographs, that included several best-selling popular and professional volumes (Ellis, 2005, p. 332). Dr. Ellis served as president of the Division of Consulting Psychology of the American Psychological Association and president of the Society for the Scientific Study of Sexuality (Ellis, 2005, p. 331). He served as an officer of the American Association of Marriage and Family Therapists; the American Academy of Psychotherapists; and the American Association of Sex Educators, Counselors, and Therapists (Ellis, 2005, p. 331). He also served as a diplomate in clinical psychology of the American Board of Professional Psychology and several other professional organizations (Ellis, 2005, p. 332). He was 93 years old at the time of his death on July 24, 2007.

---

*This chapter is based on the innovative therapeutic approach of Albert Ellis, PhD. I would like to express my gratitude to Debbie Joffe Ellis, MDAM, for her integrity in reviewing this chapter dedicated to her late husband's work.

He created his therapeutic model in the early 1950s. Ellis was originally trained in psychoanalysis, like most psychologists were at the time, and he practiced classical psychoanalysis in addition to analytically oriented therapy. Ellis decided to stop practicing psychoanalysis in 1953, in part because he discovered that the amount of insight the clients gained, especially about their early childhoods, did not reduce their tendencies to create new symptoms. As a result, Ellis realized that these clients were indoctrinated with self-defeating ideas in addition to actively inventing, accepting, and continuing to reindoctrine themselves with dysfunctional beliefs (Ellis, 2001, p. 154). Ellis found that these clients had a tendency to resist changing their irrational beliefs (IBs) and that they placed unrealistic demands on themselves and others.

Ellis also found that these clients had a tendency to turn their healthy preferences for love, approval, success, and pleasure into needs, especially in intimate relationships, and that their IBs spilled over into their current relationships (Ellis, 2001, p. 154). As a result, he decided to use prepsychoanalytic techniques, specifically those that he learned in sex and marital therapy. In addition, he started giving the clients homework assignments and providing skills training (Ellis & MacLaren, 2005, p. 8). Ellis discovered that his clients improved in a matter of weeks when he integrated these behavioral techniques with analytical therapy (Ellis & MacLaren, 2005, p. 8).

Ellis performed a few experiments on himself to test his new theories and techniques. In one notable experiment, highlighted in his autobiography *All Out*, he attempted to overcome his shyness about interacting with women.

> *I made verbal overtures to 100 different women sitting on park benches in the Bronx Botanical Gardens, [and] got rejected for dating by all of them (one woman kissed me in the park, and made a date for later that evening, but never showed up!). (Ellis, 1996, p. 109)*

Although he did not get a date that night, he did realize that his methods helped him overcome his shyness.

INTRODUCTION TO RATIONAL EMOTIVE BEHAVIOR THERAPY

Key aspects from several other therapeutic models are incorporated into REBT. There are humanistic aspects similar to Carl Rogers's theory of unconditional positive regard, especially in dealing with problems of self-worth; in particular, Ellis's concept of unconditional self-acceptance (which will be discussed later in the chapter) is based on the constructionist and existentialist positions of Martin Heidegger, Paul Tillich, and Carl Rogers, which assert that humans can choose to define themselves as good and worthy (Ellis, 2001, p. 39). Ellis fully addressed his views on self-esteem in his 2005 book *The Myth of Self-Esteem*. Ellis also preached the importance of full unconditional acceptance in addition to encouraging clients to change, a technique based on existential therapy (D. Joffe Ellis, personal communication, May 2010).

Therapists who use REBT are actively directive and use behavioral therapeutic techniques, such as in vivo desensitization and operant conditioning, and they give clients homework assignments. In vivo desensitization is used in REBT to encourage clients to expose themselves to past or current traumatic scenes to work through their emotions in thinking about traumas in their lives (Ellis, 2001, p. 180). Ellis (2001) asserted that REBT also encompasses the experiential, encounter, and feeling methods, in addition to exposing clients' unconscious motives and defense mechanisms, as in psychoanalysis. Occasionally, although rarely, REBT uses some of the paradoxical techniques that are based in strategic therapy when clients are too sensitive to the rational techniques. For example, Ellis would occasionally prescribe a symptom, and he designed a handout entitled *"How To Be A Better Procrastinator."*

Ellis is known for the *ABCDE* model, in which he states that an activating event (A) is not responsible for a person's feelings, it is the person's beliefs or thoughts (B) about that event that lead to the consequences or his/her feelings (C). The goal is to dispute the IBs (D) to arrive at an effective new philosophy (E).

Rational Emotive Behavior Therapy in Couples and Family Therapy

Ellis (2001) asserted that rational emotive behavior family therapy follows the same principles and practice of individual REBT because it exposes the fundamental premises that underlie family members' disillusionment with themselves and family arrangements in addition to using cognitive, emotive, and behavioral methods of teaching them communication, intimacy, relationship, and other skills that will help them to improve their relationships.

Ellis's ABC theory can be effectively applied in couple and family relationships. Ellis (2001) posited that family members feel upset or engage in dysfunctional behavior at point C (emotional or behavioral consequence), and C is usually preceded by A (an activating event or adversity), such as a family member failing at an important task, which is triggered by B (the family member's belief about what happened at point A). Ellis noted that one person's (C) may easily be used to interpret another person's (A) and that, in family therapy, it is important to help reduce the emotional and behavioral distress of all of the interrelated individuals:

> . . . a husband feels upset about almost anything at point C (Consequence), he has both Rational Beliefs (RBs) and Irrational Beliefs (IBs) about what the family members are doing (or supposedly doing) to frustrate or bother him at point A (Activating Experience). His Rational Beliefs at B take the form of wishes, wants, and preferences—for example, "I would like to be a good husband and have my wife love me. I don't like failing as a father or mate and having her despise me." These Rational Beliefs (RBs) almost invariably lead him to feel healthy negative emotional Consequences, such as sorrow, regret, or annoyance, when he fails and gets rejected at A. If this husband stayed rigorously with Rational Beliefs, REBT contends he wouldn't feel and act in a disturbed manner when Adversities (As) occurred . . . however, this husband often adds to his Rational Beliefs (RBs) a set of Irrational Beliefs (IBs) along these lines: "I must be a good husband and have my wife love me! How awful it is I don't succeed in these respects! I can't stand family and being rejected by my family! What a rotten person I am for doing so badly!" As a result of these Irrational Beliefs (IBs) and not merely as a result of his failing and being rejected at point A, this husband tends to feel the Consequences (C) of horror, low frustration tolerance, and self-downing, and he thereby becomes what we often call "emotionally disturbed." Also, at C, he may resort to dysfunctional behavior, such as abusing his wife and children, alcoholism, staying away from home, or a hasty divorce. (Ellis, 2001, p. 156)

Ellis suggested that people have demands consisting of "shoulds" or "shoulding," "musts" or "musturbating," and "awfulizing," which create tension in their relationships when they do not accept themselves or their mates and family members. The "shoulds" are unrealistic expectations or demands people impose on themselves or others. "Shoulds" can be directed inward, as when people blame themselves for events they have little control over, or directed outward, as when people put unrealistic expectations and self-centered demands on other people (Horney, 1950).

TABLE 6.1 ▦ Unpleasant and Disturbed Emotions

Unpleasant Emotions	Disturbed Emotions
Sadness	Depression
Irritation	Despair
Annoyance	Anxiety
Remorse	Panic
Frustration	Horror
Regret	Terror
Sorrow	Resentment
Grief	Fury
	Rage
	Self-hatred
	Hostility

Source: Perlman, A. (1992). *Understanding: Discover your personal power to change* [Videocassette]. Center City, MN: Hazelden Foundation.

Ellis (2001) defined the "musts" or "musturbating" as people turning their healthy, strong desires, goals, and values into absolutistic "musts" because their preferences become demands or necessities. REBT asserts that clients' "musts" are not merely learned from their parents and culture, but are also generated by deep cognitive structures about themselves and the world that may be unconscious (Ellis, 2001, p. 39).

"Awfulizing" occurs when people exaggerate an unpleasant situation to make it much worse than it actually is; people can awfulize about past, present, or future events (Ellis, 2001). When people engage in shoulding, musturbating, and awfulizing, they devalue themselves and their value to others. This leads to what Ellis defined as *self-defeating behavior*, which is the behavior that involves acting against one's healthy goals and stems from the state of disturbed emotions (D. Joffe Ellis, personal communication, May 2010). *Disturbed emotions* are defined as emotions that are inappropriate, destructive, and serve few useful functions. *Unpleasant emotions* can be appropriate and healthy responses to certain situations. Disturbed emotions arise when people insist that they should not have these unpleasant emotions. Table 6.1 offers a list of disturbed emotions and unpleasant emotions (Perlman, 1992).

REBT prepares individuals for difficulties they are likely to encounter in marriage and family relationships by encouraging clients to experience unconditional self-cceptance (*USA*), unconditional other acceptance (*UOA*), unconditional life acceptance (*ULA*), and high frustration tolerance (D. Joffe Ellis, personal communication, May 2010). Ellis (2001) defined these four major concepts in the following ways:

- *Unconditional self-acceptance* encourages clients to accept themselves even if they think they have committed bad acts or made mistakes. REBT therapists are also encouraged to have *USA*. This does not imply that bad acts are okay but, simply that, as fallible humans, we can accept ourselves unconditionally, whether we act well or badly (D. Joffe Ellis, personal communication, May 2010).

- *Unconditional other acceptance* encourages clients to accept other people no matter how inadequate or wrong they think their behavior is (D. Joffe Ellis, personal communication, May 2010). In the case of couples or families, it encourages family members to fully accept each other, even when they misbehave. The therapist also had better demonstrate *UOA* (D. Joffe Ellis, personal communication, May 2010).

- *Unconditional life acceptance* encourages clients to accept their lives, even in difficult circumstances.
- *High frustration tolerance* is taught and encouraged in clients, to help them tolerate and, at times, possibly even enjoy some of the hassles of intimate relationships (D. Joffe Ellis, personal communication, May 2010).

Rational Emotive Behavior Therapy and Other Types of Family Therapy

REBT both complements and differs from other types of family therapy. For example, Ellis noted that Murray Bowen's family therapy (see Chapter 3) and Jay Haley's family therapy significantly overlap with REBT and can be integrated with it. In the following sections, I compare REBT with systems theory–oriented family therapy, psychoanalytic family therapy, and behavior-oriented family therapy.

Rational Emotive Behavior Therapy and Systems Theory–Oriented Family Therapy

According to Ellis (2005), REBT agrees with some aspects of family systems therapy in that manipulation of the family can be an effective way to help family member(s), and individuals are affected by the family system, which is emphasized in the treatment of individuals. However, Ellis asserted that a diversion is that REBT includes the element of treating family members for their own individual disturbances, as well as treating them with systemic methods.

Ellis (2001) agreed with the basic views of systems theory–oriented family therapy. However, he offered the following caveats (Ellis, 2001):

1. Families become disturbed not merely because of their organization or disorganization but because of the serious personal problems of individual family members. Those problems need to be dealt with in addition to creating change within the family system.

2. REBT helps show family members how they basically create their own personal and family problems and their own disturbed emotions (D. Joffe Ellis, personal communication, May 2010).

3. REBT focuses on identifying family members' "shoulds" and "musts" in addition to their own and their family members' behaviors, and on disputing them to come up with healthy new beliefs (D. Joffe Ellis, personal communication, May 2010).

Similarities and Differences With Psychoanalytic Family Therapy

REBT is similar to psychoanalytic family therapies in that it may reveal family members' unconscious thoughts (especially their unconscious demands), but Ellis (2001) proposed that most of these hidden demands are barely below the surface of awareness and are only occasionally repressed. Ellis asserted that REBT differs from psychoanalytically oriented family therapies because it is more present centered, philosophically oriented, realistic, and takes a more problem-solving oriented approach.

Similarities and Differences With Behavioral Family Therapy

REBT encompasses many behavioral theories and methods, such as operant conditioning and in vivo desensitization procedures. REBT emphasizes the use of behavioral techniques to assist families with changing their basic philosophic assumptions, as well as their thoughts, feelings, and actions. Ellis (2001) also asserted that REBT teaches family members effective relationship skills, USA and UOA.

THEORETICAL ASSUMPTIONS

View of the Family and Client

Ellis (1987a, 1987b, 1992, 1993, 1994, 1996; Yankura & Dryden, 1994) identified several assumptions of REBT that involve views of the family/client. Corey (2000) outlined the following assumptions for REBT:

1. A client's thoughts, feelings, and behaviors continually interact with and influence one another.

2. Emotional disturbances are caused or contributed to by a complex of biological and environmental factors. Frequently, therapy is best when taking a present-centered approach; exploring the past and reliving early childhood emotional trauma is not necessary to understand and work with human problems (D. Joffe Ellis, personal communication, May 2010).

3. Humans can be affected by the people and the things around them, and they can intentionally affect the people around them. People choose to disturb themselves or undisturb themselves in response to the influences of the system in which they live.

4. People disturb themselves cognitively, emotionally, and behaviorally, and they often may think in self-defeating ways in addition to ways that defeat those in their social groups.

5. When unfortunate events occur, people tend to create irrational beliefs about these events that are characterized by absolutist and rigid thinking. The focus of these IBs is usually on competence and success, love and approval, being treated fairly, and safety and comfort.

6. It is not the events that cause emotional disturbances; it is the IBs that often lead to personality problems.

7. Most humans have a tendency to make and keep themselves emotionally disturbed, and therefore they find it difficult to maintain good mental health. They need to clearly and tough-mindedly acknowledge reality to prevent themselves from sabotaging their best efforts at changing.

8. When people behave in self-defeating ways, they do have the ability to become aware of ways in which their beliefs are negatively affecting them. With this awareness, they also have the capacity to dispute their IBs and change them into RBs. Through

changing these IBs, they can also change their unhealthy feelings and self-defeating behaviors.

9. Once discovered, IBs can be counteracted by using REBT techniques to prevent self-sabotaging thoughts, feelings, and behaviors and to create healthy ones (D. Joffe Ellis, personal communication, May 2010).

10. First, clients had better be willing to first acknowledge that they are mainly responsible for their own disturbed thoughts, emotions, and behaviors; second, to look at how they are thinking, feeling, and behaving when they are disturbing themselves; and third, to commit themselves to the hard work and practice it will take to change.

View on How Change Occurs

Ellis asserted that disturbed thinking and emotions often lead people to behave in counter-productive ways that usually have negative consequences (D. Joffe Ellis, personal communication, May 2010). For example, Kevin was laid off from work, and he awfulized about this circumstance as he thought, "I was laid off and this is really awful!" When people awfulize, they imagine that their circumstances could not be worse. In Kevin's case, his awfulizing made him feel depressed and withdrawn from his friends, as well as his family, in addition to draining his energy to go on job interviews. As a result, the awfulizing prevented Kevin from finding a new job, which fueled even more irrational thoughts and led him to feel more depressed and engage in more isolation. Ellis described this type of pattern as the *vicious circle of self-defeat* (Perlman, 1992).

Thus, people experience disturbed emotions and attempt to get away from them through engaging in self-defeating behaviors, such as isolating or withdrawing from others. The self-defeating behaviors usually lead to self-defeating consequences, such as destroying important relationships or financial problems. The way to break this vicious circle of defeat is through challenging the irrational beliefs.

According to Ellis (2001), some of the main goals for rational emotive behavior family therapy include the following:

1. Assist family members with recognizing that they largely disturb themselves, and they can choose to not upset themselves about other persons' misbehavior (no matter how other family members behave).

2. Assist family members with maintaining their wishes, desires, and preferences while developing the ability to recognize and revise their musts (demands and commands that other family members act the way they would prefer them to act).

3. Encourage parents and children to feel their healthy negative feelings; encourage them to change things when they are not getting what they want, in and out of the family setting. Teach them to clearly differentiate their healthy negative feelings from their unhealthy feelings.

4. Teach family members cognitive, emotive, and behavioral techniques that will reduce their self-defeating behaviors and family-defeating behaviors and encourage them to think, feel, and behave more sensibly.

5. While family members' challenge their IBs, they can also work on changing the As (adversities) that contribute to these Bs (beliefs) in addition to the Cs (dysfunctional consequences) of the beliefs.

Therapist's Role

The REBT therapist does his/her best to accept clients (despite their shortcomings and their sometimes poor behavior to the therapist and/or others) and emphasizes his or her UOA, as described earlier in this chapter (Ellis & MacLaren, 2005, p. 116). The therapist takes a direct and active approach in helping clients, which includes educating them about their responsibility for creating emotions and the principles of REBT (D. Joffe Ellis, personal communication, May 2010). The therapist finds out the clients' goals, values, ideals, and disturbances. The therapist examines clients' relationships with others through their relationship with the therapist (Ellis & MacLaren, 2005, p. 116).

Both clients and therapists preferably work in a highly active–directive and persistent manner to help bring about profound behavioral changes (Ellis, 2001, p. 39). When clients are able to identify their dysfunctional core philosophies, they can constructively change their thinking (Ellis, 2001, p. 39). Ellis (2001) asserted that a therapist using this approach discovers the client's preferences and goals and identifies how the client escalates these preferences and goals into needs and demands. The therapist shows the client how to change his/her demands back to preferences. The therapist also does a lot of teaching; psychoeducation is important in this model. Ellis asserted that the therapist teaches clients that they usually upset themselves and, that although they can change, they need to work at disputing their IBs. They teach the clients to find workable goals.

The therapist focuses on interpersonal relationships with others and sometimes gives clients skills training in social relating. Group therapy may be recommended for some clients to provide them with further opportunities to examine and practice their social skills (Ellis & MacLaren, 2005, p. 116). The therapist may also recommend workshops, books, lectures, and/or audiovisual materials to help clients be more socially effective (Ellis & MacLaren, 2005, p. 116). Therapists also frequently assign homework so that clients can continue progress outside of the therapy sessions.

Interventions

Some common REBT techniques are listed subsequently; however, many additional techniques can be found in the books listed in the Recommended Reading list at the end of this chapter. Ellis and MacLaren (2005) identified and defined the following therapeutic techniques used in REBT:

Disputing. This active approach is used to help clients determine the efficacy of their belief systems, and it is among the most well-known interventions. After clients are aware of the ABCs of REBT, disputing allows them to identify, debate, and ultimately replace their irrational beliefs. The therapist can take either a *didactic* or a *Socratic* approach to disputing.

Didactic approach. An informational portion of the session in which the therapist provides an explanation of different terms; he/she may explain the difference between irrational beliefs and rational beliefs.

Socratic questioning. The therapist asks a series of leading questions so he/she can specifically identify how and where the client's thinking, feeling, and behaving is becoming problematic. The therapist may ask the client a question such as "How is this belief affecting your life?"

Philosophical disputes. This approach may be used to address a life-satisfaction issue and is useful for clients who have lost their perspective because they have been so focused on the identified problem. An example might be to ask the client, "Despite the fact that things will probably not go the way you want in this area, can you still derive some satisfaction from your life?"

Functional disputes. This approach is used to question the practical applications of some clients' beliefs, emotions, and behaviors. For example, clients may be asked the following questions (Ellis & MacLaren, 2005, p. 60):

- *"How is continuing to think this way affecting your life?"*
- *"Is the anger (or another emotion) helping you?"*
- *"Are there other ways to get the positive consequences without getting yourself so upset?"*

Empirical disputes. These questions focus on factual components of the client's beliefs. Some examples include the following:

- *"What factual evidence supports this belief?"*
- *"Where is the proof that what you are telling yourself is true?"*
- *"What evidence supports your belief?"*
- *"What is the evidence against your belief?"* (Ellis & MacLaren 2005, p. 63)

Psychoeducation. The therapist can supplement therapy with psychoeducational assignments to further reinforce the work that is being done in therapy. For example, the therapist could assign helpful videos, pamphlets, or workshops that contribute to the client's understanding of the problem and progress in changing inappropriate and unhelpful reactions. It is important for the therapist to review any assignment that he or she gives to the client to assess its helpfulness and prepare himself/herself to answer any questions or concerns that the client may have about the assignment.

Rational coping statements. This is a self-statement that is a factual, encouraging phrase that clients are encouraged to consistently repeat to themselves, to reinforce ideas, for example, "I don't have to get upset in these situations." Statements that reflect a deeper philosophical acceptance are preferable, for example, "I don't have to like that my partner keeps behaving in this way, but I had better deal with it without demanding that he change."

Reframing. This is a technique widely used in several different therapeutic approaches (not just REBT) that assists clients in gaining perspective on their problems. Therapists can encourage clients to find positive aspects in their problems. For example, the client may be asked to view an adversity as an opportunity to practice the tools he or she has learned in therapy.

Role playing. The therapist and the client identify a previously upsetting or potentially upsetting interaction with another person that the client would like to handle more effectively. The therapist and the client converse in their assigned roles. After the role play is finished, the therapist asks the client how he or she thinks it went, what he or she thought and felt during the role play, and if there is anything he or she would have liked to have done differently. The therapist can also provide the client with feedback about how he or she came across during the interaction. Therapists can also use role-playing in couples therapy. In this case, each partner plays himself/herself and can switch roles (D. Joffe Ellis, personal communication, May 2010). The feedback process is the same as in individual therapy.

RATIONAL EMOTIVE BEHAVIOR THERAPY WORKING TEMPLATE

Unlike other templates within this volume, this template does not include examples of therapeutic questions. The template is based on conversations with Dr. Albert Ellis in 2005, and Dr. Debbie Joffe Ellis (D. Joffe Ellis, the wife of Dr. Albert Ellis). Therapeutic questions are included in the "Interventions" section of this chapter.

Tools for Change

Phase 1: Joining and Building Rapport

In the first session, the therapist focuses on intake information, such as general biographical data, prior therapeutic experiences, and past and current diagnoses. In addition, the *Millon Clinical Multiaxial Inventory* may be used (D. Joffe Ellis, personal communication, May 2007). The *Millon Clinical Multiaxial Inventory* is used to assess for personality disorders and clinical syndromes. Therapeutic needs assessment and therapeutic goals are also established early in therapy. Therapists can assess each client's level of disturbance and identify ways that each client consciously and unconsciously interferes with his/her own pleasure and happiness through irrational thinking and self-defeating behaviors.

Rapport building is important during this phase. Toward this end, the therapist may demonstrate UOA by completely accepting the client as a fallible human even though the therapist may not like some aspects of the client (D. Joffe Ellis, personal communication, May 2007). It is also important for the therapist to demonstrate USA.

Phase 2: Understanding the Presenting Issue

According to Ellis and MacLaren (1998), it is important for therapists to first identify the client's problematic consequences (Cs) because these usually represent the presenting issue. Therapists should ask clients what really bothers them in addition to asking about their anxiety, depression, and/or anger. It is important for the therapist to identify very specific triggers; this can be accomplished by asking clients to describe what they tell themselves when they are with others and/or in certain situations.

Phase 3: Assessment of Family Dynamics

The therapist should recall Ellis's *ABCDE model* as he/she identifies what the clients' main problems are and how they disturb themselves. Then, together, the therapist and clients can explore how the clients keep themselves from being happy by themselves and with others, including their family (D. Joffe Ellis, personal communication, May 2007).

The therapist assesses the presenting issue through asking the following questions (Ellis & MacLaren, 1998, pp. 49–50):

1. What are clients' specific cognitive, emotional, behavioral disturbances, and lack of skills (Cs)?
2. What activating events or adversities (As) commonly accompany their undesirable consequences?

3. What rational beliefs and irrational beliefs tend to evaluate As and lead to dysfunctional Cs?

4. What cognitive disputes (Ds), as well as emotive and behavioral methods, are likely to help clients retain their RBs and change their IBs, so they strongly and persistently arrive at effective new philosophies of life (Es)?

5. What thoughts, feelings, and actions will best maintain each client's progress and preferably help him or her to actualize and enjoy himself or herself more?

Phase 4: Goals

Ask clients open-ended questions about their personal goals, values, ideals, and disturbances. When discussing goals, the therapist works to help the clients identify their preferences (rational) versus their demands (irrational) to correct the beliefs, which create disturbances (D. Joffe Ellis, personal communication, May 2010). Note that goals may be discussed repeatedly throughout therapy to determine whether clients' goals have changed.

Phase 5: Amplifying Change

The REBT therapist gives clients tools to help them identify and change their harmful thinking, behavior, and emotions (D. Joffe Ellis, personal communication, May 2007). Clients can be taught to identify when they are changing their preferences to demands, which can strongly interfere with their happiness (D. Joffe Ellis, personal communication, May 2010). This can be accomplished from the first session onward. Therapists may reinforce clients' rational statements, which are those statements about their beliefs that are healthy, productive, adaptive, and consistent with social reality (Ellis & MacLaren, 2005, p. 52). These beliefs generally consist of preferences, desires, and wants (Ellis & MacLaren, 2005, p. 52). Other techniques may include humor, Socratic questioning, didactic approach, reframing, psychoeducation, disputing, rational coping statements, and role playing, which have been discussed earlier in this chapter.

Change is recognized when clients experience improvements in their feelings, behaviors, thinking, and/or relationships (D. Joffe Ellis, personal communication, May 2007). Ellis and MacLaren (1998) recommended for therapists at the Albert Ellis Institute to give clients a "satisfaction of life" assessment every 4 to 6 weeks to aid in charting progress. Ellis believed that if clients did not see good results from REBT practice after some time, then the therapist could propose alternative REBT techniques to the ones originally given (D. Joffe Ellis, personal communication, May 2010).

Phase 6: Termination

Ellis believed that when clients truly work in therapy, they are less anxious, less depressed, and experience less anger. When clients are less disturbed, they may have less to talk about in therapy sessions. At that point, it may be appropriate to ask clients about other issues that have not yet been discussed in the sessions to determine whether anything else needs to be addressed in therapy. Follow-up sessions can be scheduled to assist clients with maintaining progress.

ALBERT ELLIS

Albert Ellis (September 27, 1913–July 24, 2007), PhD, is considered the originator of the cognitive revolutionary paradigm shift in psychotherapy and the grandfather of cognitive behavioral therapies, as well as the founder of REBT (D. Joffe Ellis, personal communication, May 2010). He is routinely regaled as one of the most influential psychotherapists in history. This volume is fortunate to include the transcript of a telephone interview conducted with Dr. Ellis on July 14, 2005.

What attracted you to the theory behind REBT?

I became an expert on philosophy at the age of 15, and used it on myself and on other people, and I was more philosophic than most therapists are. I found it fascinating that by finding out what the person's preferences and goals are, and how they normally escalate them into needs and demands, it shows them the vast difference between their preferences and their demands. It also assumes that all humans, as the Buddha said 2,500 years ago, are out of their goddamn minds. They are all pretty crazy; they are born that way and they are also raised that way, so it is both heredit[ar]y and environmental.

How do you formulate your view of a family when they enter therapy?

I find out very, very quickly in the first session, the first two sessions, what their problems are, and then I show them how they are creating their problems. I go back to the philosopher Epictetus: "It's never the things that happen to you that upset you, it's your view, your philosophy about them." So I find the things that upset them today and in the past, but particularly today, and what their philosophy is and how to change that.

What kinds of families do you think benefit most from this model?

The so-called Yavis kind, Y-A-V-I-S, who are young, who are active, who are verbal, who are intelligent, and who are sensitive. Those kind benefit most by all kinds of therapy, including our therapy.

In your opinion, what are the necessary characteristics that a therapist should possess to be effective with this model? I know you mentioned that they need to able to teach and to be direct. Are there any other characteristics?

The therapist had better not be too disturbed himself or herself, not prejudiced, and be very directive, very active, very teaching. I do the main things that rational emotive behavior therapy teaches. First, USA: unconditional self-acceptance. I always, always accept myself no matter how I screw up and do stupid and unhealthy things. Second, unconditional other acceptance, I do my best to always accept other people no matter how stupid[ly] or inadequate[ly] they behave. I accept them, their whole person, and then I have ULA, unconditional life acceptance, I accept my life with all my disabilities; I have diabetes and arthritis and lots of other disabilities, and it's too damn bad that I do, but I don't awfulize. I accept what I can change, have the serenity to accept what I cannot change, and the wisdom, I hope, to know the difference, as Reinhold Niebuhr, a protestant minister, said in 1915.

How often does the client see you and for how long a period of time?

Usually, people, when they come individually, can have 30 minutes or 60 minutes; but if they come in couples or more, I usually have 60 minutes and, sometimes, 2 hours. Usually, I see people once a week, but sometimes twice a week; and most people, including marriage and family clients, come for about 12 sessions, and more disturbed people with severe personality disorders come for more.

What are you looking for when you are in the session?

I'm looking for how disturbed clients are and how they consciously and unconsciously interfere with their own pleasure and happiness. I ask myself: What are their main problems? What bothers them? What keeps them from being happy by themselves and with their mate and with their family, and I also ask myself how disturbed they are. Are they normal nice neurotics, which practically everybody in the world is, or are they severe personality disorders, which about 30% of my own clients, 30% to 40% are, or in a few cases, are they psychotic, brain injured, etc.?

What is the assessment process of this model?

Well, at the Albert Ellis Institute, we give everybody the Millon Clinical Multiaxial Inventory. Everybody gets that. But we don't stress that it has to be done. It's preferable to do it, but you can find out most of the relevant information by asking some direct questions.

Who sets the goals, the client or the therapist?

The client mainly sets them all, not the therapist. I ask all the clients, individually and married, what their main goals are, and I try to get them to see what their preferences are and what their demands are, in order to correct the things that make them disturbed. I ask open questions. What do you really want to do? What do you don't want to do? And I find out their goals and values, and ideals and disturbances. And I keep doing this in other sessions to see if they changed their goals.

What are some commonly used interventions with this model?

Mainly to find out, again, their shoulds, oughts, musts, absolutistic thinking and feeling, and behavior; and to try to find out if they do not have unconditional self-acceptance, unconditional other acceptance, and unconditional life acceptance. How I do this varies widely depending on how the client answers the questions first. But I get them to talk about their problems at home, at work, at school, in sports, and any major things that they do in their life. Whenever they tell me their goals and values and what they do, I show them that they have both preferences, "I would like to succeed with my mate and other people, and I'd like to be loved by significant others"; and then I show them how they are not getting what they want because they are raising their preferences to shoulds and musts, and interfering with their own happiness; and I do that from the first session onward.

Psychoeducation is also very significant, much more than in other models, because people not only forget and repress their bad acts but they [also] don't know what they have to do to improve. So we teach, teach, teach that they make up unrealistic and illogical and unpragmatic desires, goals, and values, and then we show them that they won't work no matter what they do. And we teach them that they had better find, with our cooperation, other workable goals and values. Then, as I said before, they have to work their butts off to do the homework implementing those goals and values.

What role does a homework assignment have in this model?

Homework is very, very important in REBT; because we show that even though people usually upset themselves in order to change, they have to desire to change, know that they can change, and keep working at it—working, working, working, and working. Work and practice! Just knowing it and doing nothing about it won't get them very far, so they had better do their homework over and over again and change their thoughts, feelings, and behaviors. Also, do other homework when the homework works or doesn't work. If they don't do their homework, then we show them what bad results they get and keep getting and sometimes we reinforce them for doing it. Or sometimes, though not that often, we give them, with their consent, penalties or self-penalties for not doing the homework. If they don't do the homework, then they are not allowed to do something they enjoy most, such as TV or socializing or having sex or something like that. If they don't do it, they agree not to do their most enjoyable acts. So in the long run, we get most of the people, most of the time, to do their important homework.

How do you know when your client is ready to terminate?

I get to see what results they achieve. If they really work at the therapy, they become less anxious, less depressed, and especially in couples therapy and family therapy, less angry. So, as they become less disturbed, they therefore have less to talk about. Finally, I ask them if there are any other things that they haven't brought up yet, and see if there is anything that we haven't tackled. But usually, it's a matter of their doing or not doing the rational emotive behavior therapy and getting good or bad results; and if they get bad results, of course, then we change its methods.

What have you found to be the limitations of this approach?

Well, most people have low frustration tolerances, and they want to change, but they don't want to do the work of changing and, therefore, they resist doing the work. REBT is quite revolutionary because it doesn't emphasize people's early childhood disturbances but how they make themselves disturbed today. It shows them that early traumas may have been a factor, and we go through it and show them how not to be disturbed today about their early experiences. But we mainly stay in the present and get people over their present disturbances. So, some of them don't like to do that and would rather waste time and talk about the past.

What are your suggestions for students learning this model?

I think they first better try it out on themselves admit that they have disturbances and that they can use REBT to undo and minimize those disturbances. Then when they work with others, experiment, experiment, experiment, and try REBT and other therapies and see which works. They also need to know that therapists will always be scientists. Don't take anything just on faith but on faith founded on fact. Experiment, experiment, experiment cautiously but definitely. Try various aspects of [REBT], and any other kind of therapy that therapists think will work. See how it actually turns out and then perhaps change. Each individual, and especially each family, is different from other individuals and families. So try a wide variety of methods and see which is more effective, and then keep changing it to make it more effective.

Case Study

A mother calls and makes an appointment for her family to come to therapy. The family consists of the wife and her husband, both in their 40s; their 15-year-old son; a college-aged daughter; and the woman's father, age 82. Three years after the woman's mother died, her father developed Alzheimer's disease and moved in with the family 6 months ago. When his health began to deteriorate, the woman spent more time caring for him than for other members of the family. Three months ago, the 15-year-old son, who has been treated for attention deficit hyperactivity disorder since age 7, began to refuse to take his medication and is now being truant from school.

During the session, the wife cries and the husband reports that their relationship is strained, occasionally rolling his eyes as his wife becomes tearful. He reports that he has had to take on more work because his wife had to quit her job to attend to her father's needs. The daughter is away at college and the wife smiles as she describes her as a straight-A student. The daughter was asked to attend the session but refused because she has a hard time with her grandfather's illness and dislikes the conflict that has developed at home.

Dr. Albert Ellis's Response to the Case Study

I would mainly, at first, ascertain how angry the wife, husband, and daughter are, as well as how anxious or panicked they are about the family situation, and how depressed about it each of them is. If they are angry, anxious, or depressed, I would show each of them, preferably in the presence of each other, how the bad family conditions that seem to upset them, upset them, but largely involve their attitudes toward these conditions. I would show all of them, using several REBT methods, how to feel healthily sorry and disappointed instead of feeling unhealthily angry, anxious, and depressed. I would also teach each of them how to relate healthily to each other (and to other people), assertively but still lovingly and cooperatively, using several REBT methods. In addition to seeing family members together, I might sometimes see one or more of them separately to see that they can understand more clearly the REBT points and methods. Then, I would see them together again to check their new thinking, feeling, and behaving.

KEY TERMS

ABCDE model   Albert Ellis's model in which an activating event (A) is not responsible for a person's feelings; it is the person's beliefs or thoughts (B) about that event that lead to the consequences or his/her feelings (C). The goal of REBT is to dispute the irrational belief(s) (D) to arrive at an effective new philosophy (E).

Awfulizing   According to Ellis, this form of generalizing occurs when people see something that has unfortunate qualities as entirely bad.

Disturbed emotions   Inappropriate, destructive emotions that do not serve useful functions and often lead to self-defeating behavior (D. Joffe Ellis, personal communication, May 2010).

Irrational beliefs   According to Ellis, these beliefs, which are rigid and dogmatic, cannot be fully supported by reality and, by and large, get in the way of goal achievement.

Musts   Turning healthy desires, goals, and values into unrealistic demands. This behavior can be problematic when clients demand that they and/or other people must perform a certain way at all times and under all conditions; Ellis referred to this as *musturbation*.

Rational beliefs   Flexible, adaptive beliefs that can help people reach their goals that are consistent with reality (D. Joffe Ellis, personal communication, May 2010).

Self-defeating behavior   Behavior that acts against healthy goals. It usually follows from disturbed emotions (D. Joffe Ellis, personal communicaton, May 2010).

Shoulds   Unrealistic demands that a person places on himself/herself and/or others; Ellis referred to this as "shoulding."

Unpleasant emotions   Appropriate and healthy responses to certain situations.

REFERENCES

Corey, G. (2000). *Theory and practice of group counseling* (5th ed.). Belmont, CA: Wadsworth/Thomson Learning.

Ellis, A. (1987a). The evolution of rational-emotive therapy (RET) and cognitive behavior therapy (CBT). In J. K. Zeig (Ed.), *The evolution of psychotherapy* (pp. 107–132). New York, NY: Brunner/Mazel.

Ellis, A. (1987b). The impossibility of achieving consistently good mental health. *American Psychologist*, *42*(4), 364–375.

Ellis, A. (1992). Group rational-emotive and cognitive-behavioral therapy. *International Journal of Group Psychotherapy*, *42*(1), 63–80.

Ellis, A. (1993). Fundamentals of rational-emotive therapy. In W. Dryden & L. K. Hill (Eds.), *Innovations in rational-emotive therapy* (pp. 1–32). Newbury Park, CA: Sage.

Ellis, A. (1994). *Reason and emotion in psychotherapy* (Rev. ed.). Secaucus, NJ: Birch Lane Press.

Ellis, A. (1996). *Better, deeper, and more enduring brief therapy: The rational emotive behavior therapy approach.* New York, NY: Brunner/Mazel.

Ellis, A. (2001). *New directions for rational emotive behavior therapy: Overcoming destructive beliefs, feelings, and behaviors.* New York, NY: Prometheus Books.

Ellis, A., & MacLaren, C. (1998). *Rational emotive behavior therapy: A therapist's guide.* San Luis Obispo, CA: Impact.

Ellis, A., & MacLaren, C. (2005). *Rational emotive behavior therapy: A therapist's guide* (2nd ed.). Atascadero, CA: Impact.

Horney, K. (1950). *Neurosis and human growth: The struggle toward self-realization.* New York, NY: W. W. Norton.

Perlman, A. (1992). *Understanding: Discover your personal power to change* [Videocassette]. Center City, MN: Hazelden Foundation.

Yankura, J., & Dryden, W. (1994). *Albert Ellis.* New York, NY: Sage Publications.

RECOMMENDED READING LIST

Books

Ellis, A. (1988). *How to stubbornly refuse to make yourself miserable about anything yes, anything!* Secaucus, NJ: Lyle Stuart.

Ellis, A. (1993). Fundamentals of rational-emotive therapy. In W. Dryden & L. K. Hill (Eds.), *Innovations in rational-emotive therapy* (pp. 1–32). Newbury Park, CA: Sage.

Ellis, A. (1994). *Reason and emotion in psychotherapy* (Rev. ed.). Secaucus, NJ: Birch Lane Press.

Ellis, A. (1996). *Better, deeper, and more enduring brief therapy: The rational emotive behavior therapy approach*. New York, NY: Brunner/Mazel.

Ellis, A. (2007a). *Overcoming resistance: A rational emotive behavior therapy integrated approach* (2nd ed.). New York, NY: Springer Publishing Company, LLC.

Ellis, A. (2007b). *The practice of rational emotive behavior therapy* (2nd ed.). New York, NY: Springer Publishing Company, LLC.

Ellis, A. (2010). *All out: An autobiography*. Amherst, NY: Prometheus Books.

Ellis, A. (2011). Rational emotive behavior therapy. In D. Wedding & R. J. Corsini (Eds.), *Current psychotherapies* (9th ed., pp. 196–234). Belmont, CA: Brooks/Cole, Cengage Learning.

Ellis, A., Gordon, J., Neenan, M., & Palmer, S. (1997). *Stress counseling: A rational emotive behavior approach*. London, England: Cassell and New York, NY: Springer Publishing Company, LLC.

Ellis, A., & Harper, R. A. (1997). *A guide to rational living* (3rd rev. ed.). North Hollywood, CA: Melvin Powers.

Ellis, A., & MacLaren, C. (2005). *Rational emotive behavior therapy: A therapist's guide* (2nd ed.). Atascadero, CA: Impact Publishers.

Ellis, A., Sichel, J. L., Yeager, R. J., DiMattia, D. J., & DiGiuseppe, R. A. (1989). *Rational-emotive couples therapy*. Needham, MA: Allyn & Bacon.

Ellis, A., & Wilde, J. (2001). *Casebook of rational emotive behavior therapy*. Columbus, OH: Merrill.

Articles

Ellis, A. (1957). Outcome of employing three techniques of psychotherapy. *Journal of Clinical Psychology*, *13*, 344–350.

Ellis, A. (1958). Rational psychotherapy. *Journal of General Psychology*, *59*, 35–49. Reprinted: New York, NY: Institute for Rational Emotive Therapy.

Ellis, A. (1987). The impossibility of achieving consistently good mental health. *American Psychologist*, *42*(4), 364–375.

Ellis, A. (1992). Group rational-emotive and cognitive-behavioral therapy. *International Journal of Group Psychotherapy*, *42*(1), 63–80.

Ellis, A. (1993a). Changing rational-emotive therapy (RET) to rational emotive behavior therapy (REBT). *Behavior Therapist*, 16, 257–258.

Ellis, A. (1993b). The rational-emotive therapy (RET) approach to marriage and family therapy. *Family Journal: Counseling and Therapy for Couples and Families*, 1, 292–307.

Ellis, A. (1994a). Post-traumatic stress disorder (PTSD) in rape victims: A rational emotive behavioral theory. *Journal of Rational-Emotive and Cognitive-Behavior Therapy*, *12*, 3–25.

Ellis, A. (1994b). The sport of avoiding sports and exercise: A rational emotive behavior therapy perspective. *Sport Psychologist*, 8, 240–261.

Ellis, A. (1994c). The treatment of borderline personalities with rational emotive behavior therapy. *Journal of Rational-Emotive and Cognitive Behavior Therapy*, *12*, 101–119.

West, G. F., & Reynolds, J. (1997). The applicability of selected rational-emotive therapy principles for pastoral counseling. *The Journal of Pastoral Care*, 187–194.

Websites

REBT Network
http://www.rebtnetwork.org

Dr. Debbie Joffe Ellis's website
http://www.debbiejoffeellis.com

Note. Dr. Ellis did not recommend the Albert Ellis Institute website http://www.rebt.org from 2005 onward (D. Joffe Ellis, personal communication, May 2010).

Symbolic-Experiential Family Therapy

7

Amanda Martin

My theory is that all theories are bad except for preliminary game playing with ourselves until we get the courage to give up theories and just live.

—Carl Whitaker

INTRODUCTION

Symbolic-experiential family therapy focuses on here-and-now experiences, playfulness, humor, intuition, craziness, spontaneity, and personal growth. It is a pragmatic, atheoretical method for treating families. The approach incorporates growth of the therapist and clients as the ultimate motivation, and focuses on circular, recursive patterns in a family that lead to mutual benefit and interpersonal context. The main goal of the theory is not to provide insight, but to focus on *experiencing* the process of therapy to produce change in the family.

HISTORY AND LEADING FIGURES

Carl A. Whitaker described the development of the symbolic-experiential model as a personal pattern of growth (Whitaker & Keith, 1981). Born in 1912 in Raymondville, New York, on a dairy farm (Neill & Kniskern, 1982), and educated in psychology, Whitaker was trained in play therapy during a child psychiatry internship in Louisville, Kentucky (Whitaker & Keith, 1981). Play became a key aspect in Whitaker's approach to treating families. This experience also led Whitaker to understand the importance of nonverbal communication and the power of symbols.

Whitaker worked at Ormsby Village with delinquent adolescents from 1941 to 1944 (Connell, Mitten, & Bumberry, 1999). This experience taught him that the therapeutic relationship was more important than the content discussed in therapy.

During World War II, Whitaker worked at Oak Ridge Hospital in Tennessee (Whitaker & Keith, 1981). He and a colleague, Dr. John Warkentin, began seeing clients conjointly. Their mixed backgrounds helped them learn from each other and their clients. Out of this partnership, the use of cotherapy emerged. Whitaker moved to Emory University in 1946 and was later joined by Dr. Thomas Malone, who was trained in psychoanalytic psychology (Whitaker & Keith, 1981). Together they published *The Roots of Psychotherapy* to explain a core process of individual therapy (Whitaker & Malone, 1953).

Whitaker left Emory University in 1956 and formed a private practice, the Atlantic Psychiatric Clinic (Connell et al., 1999). The Atlantic Psychiatric Clinic provided Whitaker with a "professional cuddle group" that he felt all therapists needed to prevent burnout and provide more personal and professional growth. Whitaker viewed family therapy as system to system versus individual therapy, which is person to person (Whitaker, 1989). Whitaker began a faculty position in the Department of Psychiatry at the University of Wisconsin in 1965 (Connell et al., 1999), where he introduced himself as a family therapist using the symbolic-experiential approach (Whitaker & Keith, 1991). Whitaker remained at the University of Wisconsin until 1982, when he retired. After retirement, Whitaker began hosting professional workshops all over the world. The approach has waned in popularity because of its difficulty in learning. It has been claimed to be more a way of being effective with families rather than a proven model.

Whitaker wrote about his style of therapy reluctantly, often saying that writing it down would make it something too permanent. Instead, he wrote about case studies and examples from his practice. Later in life, he took more time to explain about what he was thinking and doing in therapy, yet remained cautious that he did not develop a structured approach. Doing that, he often stated, would put him at a risk of becoming less systemically consistent, as he would observe the family less, concentrating on an approach.

To date, students learning symbolic-experiential therapy often ask questions about process and structure of sessions because of little literature about the approach. Instructors would be wise to advise such inquisitive students to study case studies written by Whitaker and attempt to understand on their own what direction Whitaker found himself being led to by the family.

Although Whitaker is considered the founder of this theory, many other therapists contributed to its development. David Keith, MD; Gary Connell, PhD; Augustus Napier, PhD (co-author with Whitaker of *Family Crucible*, 1978); and William Bumberry, PhD, are among the family therapists who have helped evolve and refine the symbolic-experiential approach.

INTRODUCTION TO SYMBOLIC-EXPERIENTIAL FAMILY THERAPY

Symbolic-experiential family therapy uses personal growth and symbolic experiences. This approach views craziness and pathology as healthy, allowing a therapist to create an atmosphere in which pathology is less threatening and, instead, the family feels free to be themselves, no matter what the diagnosis. Although not all experiences may be symbolic, if the therapist can get into the family's symbolic world and stay active in the session, there will be more success.

For example, a single mother and her two adult sons came to therapy after the husband/father suddenly died. The family was very distraught, and the single mother had become so depressed that her two adult sons moved home to care for her. Therapy began with the therapist listening to the family's story of how losing their husband and father had denied them all his vision of a truly happy life. Formerly, the husband had saved for their future and desired to travel with his wife and give money to his sons for homes when they married. Instead, after his death, the mother and sons could see no future.

In an attempt to get into *their* symbolic world, which was currently dictating how they lived (i.e., without Dad's vision), the therapist remarked, "So you let the vision die when your father died. I wonder what your dad would say about that?" The family was startled to realize that they were denying their father's vision to come true. At first, there was blame on each other, then on the death, but eventually the family began talking with the therapist about rekindling the father's vision. This helped the family to see that their role was to go on, rather than become stagnant. The sons soon moved out on their own and their mother took a new job, recalling her husband's belief in her as a career woman.

There are four stages to treatment, and treatment begins with the initial phone call. The stages are not meant to flow in a linear direction throughout therapy, and it is common for clients to move back and forth between stages in the course of treatment. The therapy is present focused and all interventions discussed later in the chapter can be used in any stage of therapy. A novice therapist must remember to maintain the present-focused interactional pattern in session and trust personal intuition.

Stage 1: Battle for Structure

The first stage of therapy is the Battle for structure (Connell & Mitten, in press). This stage begins with the first phone call for an appointment. The therapist is an active agent during this phase and responsible for establishing the tone of therapy. The therapist must set the structure of the therapy while joining with the family. Therefore, the therapist becomes a "foster mother" who is attentive to the family's morale. In addition, the therapist needs to be aware of his/her own personal experience during the session. During this stage, the therapist acts as an investigator to learn about the family's problems and expand the problem from one person to an entire family and past generations.

Stage 2: Battle for Initiative

During the Battle for Initiative (Connell & Mitten, in press), the therapist must begin to shift the responsibility of therapy to the family. This encourages the family to begin to take charge of their own experiences. Therapists may use several techniques to aid this shift in responsibility, like play and humor. For example, a therapist talking to a car salesman who was distant from his family might remark that the salesman was having an affair with an automobile rather than his wife, by working so much. This lighthearted talk is extreme but serves the purpose to brighten a session with laughter and create an atmosphere where "anything goes." The therapist must be able to tolerate pain and anxiety in order for the family to experience the therapist's tolerance. This helps build the therapeutic alliance and maintains the therapist's role as a strong foster parent. In this stage, the therapist is still joined with the family, but begins to disconnect to allow them to begin taking on their own reality.

Stage 3: Trial of Labor

In this stage, the therapist must be able to push the family to discuss the "pain behind their pain." What does the pain mean, and what does it represent for each family member? This is when the therapist uses double meanings and confusion to aid the family in taking the therapist to that painful experience. For example, the family whose father died suddenly only saw the pain of his death and their loss. In therapy, going deeper revealed a pain of not following through with the father's vision for his family. Once the family regressed to the old pain, the therapist was able to reshape the meanings and symbols associated with that pain and anxiety, giving a new way of thinking about the father's vision. This can be the hardest stage for a novice therapist, because the pain must be exposed without protection. The caring must be present in the therapeutic alliance for regression and reshaping to take place.

Stage 4: Termination

During the termination phase, the therapist begins to disengage with the family and use experience to aid the family in looking inward. The therapist wants the family to begin asking questions of their system and themselves. Often, a therapist may use play, humor, irony, and deviation amplification (spontaneity and absurdity) to help the family in this process.

Once, Carl Whitaker asked an amputee when he was going to go dancing again. The client, who previously had talked little about the amputation of his leg, was shocked, yet began to laugh with Whitaker. By talking about what no one else talked about, the elephant in the room disappeared and in place was a topic that the husband and wife really wanted to talk about—intimacy and companionship. This helps the family become more flexible and adaptable to change. The family must find a way to become comfortable with ambiguity: Nothing is certain in life or in therapy.

THEORETICAL ASSUMPTIONS

The main focus of symbolic-experiential family therapy is on the power of experiencing emotions, feelings, and the symbolic world in which we all live. This experience allows for personal growth of the clients and the therapist. Following are the three basic principles of this approach:

1. Working within the symbolic framework of the family is necessary.

2. Examining the nature of new experiences in therapy sessions is necessary.

3. The therapist must provide full participation in the group to achieve goals. (Kempler, 1981)

View of the Family and Client

This form of therapy is seen as a symbolic project that focuses on unique family symbols that hinder personal and familial growth (Connell et al., 1999). A novice therapist must work within these principles and understand that the meanings behind them may be ever changing, as growth occurs.

Symbolic-experiential theory has many assumptions about human beings, marriage, life, and growth. Following are some of these assumptions: (Malone, Whitaker, Warkentin, & Felder, 1961)

- Pathology is a symptom of growth. Pathology or dysfunction by a member of a family is considered healthy. The identified patient is often the one who is willing to admit being "stuck" in the growth process. Therefore, he or she is often the healthiest member of the family.

- Every person and family is capable of growth. Every family has the potential for growth, but may not be desperate enough to pursue it.

- Humans are healthy in that they exercise their freedom of choices in living their lives. All people are capable of making choices on how to live their lives, but many of these decisions are rooted in experiences from their family of origin.

- All humans have the potential for growth. Whitaker believed that "people are just fragments of families" (Connell et al., 1999). People develop and redevelop their values, beliefs, cultural identity, and sense of self through relationships. This leads to the assumptions that people are more similar than different, and everyone seeks growth.

- It is important for the family members to preserve, protect, and maintain a sense of self, or, "I-ness," while belonging to a family. While the model does not emphasize nor attempt to discover the origin of a person's personality, it does consider the influences of the family on a family member's I-ness and assists each member in protecting that

I-ness, so that the person grows intrinsically, yet does not direct his/her growth to the needs of the family, but rather to himself/herself. The therapist then assists the person in pursuing such personal growth by encouraging and enticing the family to see the person as an extension of the family, even as the person moves outside the realm of the family unit. Then, once a person has a sense of I-ness, moments of "we-ness" become richer and more fulfilling, as individual families see their family unit as supportive of who they are, yet still valuing their time together.

Whitaker (1989) believed that universally, matches between partners are absolutely accurate. He believed that people chose partners on a conscious and unconscious level. One often hears, "you married your mother." Such statements can be accurate if a shy, dependent young man, whose mother controlled his every move, marries someone similar to his mother, who takes on the responsible role in the couple's life. Following are several assumptions about marriage that need to be addressed (Whitaker, Greenberg, & Greenberg, 1979):

- Marriage is a third entity. In therapy, the clients are the husband, wife, and the marriage.
- Marriage is greater than its parts. This is a systemic belief that parts can never be greater than the sum of the whole. An example is to think of marriage as a cake. Can you take the eggs out of a baked cake?
- People choose partners on the basis of set core values and beliefs. This is not a random process. The process of choosing a partner may be unconscious, conscious, or both.
- Marriage is both legally and emotionally binding. A marriage attempts to constrain two persons from getting emotionally involved with other people outside the marriage, in the same way that it constrains them legally to be faithful.
- Marriages must learn to grow and resolve unexpected and predictable impasses that occur during the course of the marriage. Learning to be adaptive and flexible in their roles is essential for marital partners' continual growth.

Symbolic-experiential therapy also includes some presuppositions about life and growth (Kaye, Dichter, & Keith, 1986):

- Life is confusing, complex, paradoxical, and painful.
- People's initiative is sacred; growth is most likely to occur when a person is closed to his/her own gestalt, or his/her own wholeness.
- Activation is what occurs through gestalt and drives development and change as perceptions deepen.
- Facts don't change, but one's interpretations, attitudes, explanations, and feelings about them can. Experiences are internal and external.
- Failure is one's only teacher; success allows one the courage to fail.

View on How Change Occurs

Symbolic-experiential therapy has several goals for the families and the therapist. They are as follows (Whitaker & Malone, 1953):

- Personal growth
- Symptom relief and depathologization
- Character development

- Resolution of dependencies based on fear of solitude
- Ability to experience a wide range of emotions and levels of anxiety
- Increased spontaneity and creativity

The therapist plays a key role in instigating these changes, which will be discussed in the following section.

Therapist's Role

The role and characteristics of the therapist are pivotal in this approach. The theory comes alive only when it is filtered through the *personhood* (the internal characteristics and strengths) of the therapist. Whitaker believed that the process of therapy is based on relationships, and the therapist must be a human being first (Whitaker & Bumberry, 1988). Therefore, a therapist must find a personal meaning for what a human being is and what makes people act the way they do. Whitaker believed that people don't exist, but are just fragments of their family of origin (Whitaker & Bumberry, 1988). Basically, a therapist must be able to deal with anxiety, pain, and ambiguity in their own life to deal with therapeutic relationships. The personhood and humanness of the therapist is a core ingredient of this approach (Connell & Mitten, in press).

With symbolic-experiential family therapy, knowledge of the theory and interventions are necessary, but they come alive only when filtered through the therapist. Most of these skills can be fully developed only through experience and self-discipline. However, the following are some basic skills a novice therapist needs to begin using this approach:

- Ability to deal with pain, ambiguity, and anxiety, both personally and professionally
- Understructure of caring
- Ability to listen to personal intuition
- Self-discipline
- Ability to become the family's foster parent and balance between nurturing–toughness duality (Whitaker & Bumberry, 1988)
- Belief in continuous personal growth
- Ability to interweave beliefs, assumptions, and biases into therapy (Connell & Mitten, in press)

The role of the therapist tends to change throughout the stages of therapy (as described earlier in the chapter). As a therapist, you fill the role of a foster parent. Therefore, the family is in *your* house and must follow *your* rules, or find another place to live.

Interventions

Whitaker believed that in many cases, an indirect approach can be more beneficial than directive methods in helping families, and this belief underlies many of the techniques used in this therapy, such as symbols, intuition, craziness, spontaneity, confusion, fantasies, and growth. Underlying these concepts is the use of play, humor, and care.

Symbols. Symbolic language helps the therapist join with the family's symbolic world. The therapist needs to view the family from inside "looking out" (Connell, Mitten, & Whitaker,

1993). With this perspective, the therapist can then reshape the family's symbols from within the system. This right brain approach uses three typologies of languages: (a) language of pain and impotence, (b) language of inference, and (c) language of options (Connell, Mitten, & Whitaker, 1993). For example, if a family comes in talking about their pain (language of pain and impotence), the therapist would respond in a way that challenges the family's irrationality (language of inference). When the two adult sons moved home to care for their mother after their father passed away, the therapist addressed the pain of the family and shocked them by accusing them of killing their father's vision. Such language may seem inappropriate, but the symbolic-experiential therapist listens for words like "vision," and uses it to ambush the family's current plan. This shift, away from the current way of living, gave the family options for dealing with their father's and husband's death more effectively.

This method exposes the family's world without a commitment to the process of change. Symbolic language offers the family creative suggestions that may allow them to think outside of their reality.

Intuition. Intuition is based on the unconscious. Play therapy often helps enhance intuition because it is a nonlogical approach to communication, and uses symbols for communicating. A therapist's intuition will help increase a family's stress and expand the symptom. Although this may sound counterintuitive, in this therapy, heightened anxiety is beneficial; it helps the family be more willing to regress and, ultimately, experience a more creative and flexible reality. A therapist using this model may ask himself how he feels at that moment in therapy with the client family. Then the therapist would disclose that "I feel uncomfortable with the way that your husband speaks for you and wonder if you ever feel that way too." Such intuition expressed by a therapist offers families the opportunity to disclose how they feel or to experience things in a safer manner.

Craziness. Craziness allows a person to not be constrained by rigid, socially accepted realities. The use of craziness in therapy allows the therapist to be more spontaneous and symbolic. A therapist may suggest to a family that the fact that their 15-year-old depressed daughter is not going to school certainly helps the mother by keeping her focused on the girl, rather than her marriage. The therapist might even openly thank the daughter, telling her that she is obviously wise to keep Mom from talking to Dad and, that she, the daughter, should continue to be depressed, because it is the only way the mother gets closeness. This absurd and crazy reflection of the therapist to the clients gives them a new experience.

Whitaker believed that there are three types of craziness: driven crazy, going crazy, and acting crazy. The three types of craziness have three different motivations: seeking intimacy, experiencing intimacy, and fleeing (Neill & Kniskern, 1982). The person who is driven crazy has been driven out of the world of intimacy. The person who is going crazy wants to experience intimacy. Finally, the person who is acting crazy is using craziness as a way of fleeing the relationship. Craziness is not pathology but a mere symptom of someone seeking a way to further the growth process.

Spontaneity. Spontaneity is rooted in intuition and the use of craziness. Spontaneity is a right brain function and considered to be an unconscious process. The therapist must feel alive in the session. Therefore, he has the freedom to intervene or share an experience or fantasy at any given moment, if it may be symbolically useful. Spontaneity is an antidote to aloneness and helps keep the therapeutic relationship alive and intimate (Connell & Mitten, in press). Spontaneity is usually used more by the mature therapist, but may also be used by the novice therapist. Spontaneity is a key aspect for personal interaction in therapy. A therapist may glance at an adult daughter suddenly in the session and exclaim that it is quite nice of her to give up her life professionally and become an old maid, taking care of her parents. Such provocation might ignite parents to look at their daughter and tell her it is time for her to leave.

Confusion. Confusion is a symbolic way to open up the infrastructure of the family (Whitaker & Bumberry, 1988). Confusion is a way of disrupting family patterns and reshaping symbols. It helps individuals and families unlearn old patterns and learn new ways to adapt and live with anxiety. For example, a therapist may make confusing statements about the roles the family members take on to encourage more creative thinking (Whitaker & Bumberry, 1988). An adolescent son may be acknowledged for having school problems so that his mother has something to worry about, because the father works too much and she feels neglected. The father may be acknowledged as being married to his job and divorced from his family. Such outlandish and seemingly inappropriate words spontaneously change the environment, and thus the experience, so that real feelings emerge in defense or recognition that perhaps some of the words are true.

The therapist may offer absurd solutions to challenge the family to rely on their own strengths. A couple whose marriage was compromised because of a mother-in-law's interference may be cautioned not to try and work out too much in between sessions. What else would the mother-in-law have to do if she didn't interfere? They must be thoughtful of her needs to feel important. Such words to a couple working on a relationship may be a wake-up call that perhaps they were listening to others rather than to each other.

Finally, a therapist may use metaphorical language or double entendre, double messages, or innuendo, suggesting an explicit remark without saying it. This is a technique often used by comedians. Saying to a wife that her husband's need to seek her affection may mean she has to open up more to him could have many implications. Therapists must be careful to be sure that confusion is used constructively and symbolically to help produce change and be effective.

Fantasy. The therapist may encourage the family to share fantasies about how they handle life (anger, rage, sex, etc.) to gain access to the family's symbolic world (Mitten & Piercy, 1993). Fantasy is a form of play that allows the therapist and family to address their separate symbolic worlds and meanings. By sharing fantasies, families can experience the intensity of their emotions and decrease their anxiety (Neill & Kniskern, 1982). Fantasies provide a way for the therapist to challenge the idealistic nature of a fantasy, such as happily-ever-after-endings. Finally, fantasies allow the therapist to teach the family to be more creative and not be constrained by social stereotypes.

Growth. Growth is the ultimate motivation of this approach to family therapy. John Warkentin used the term "the growing edge" to describe events that occur out of nowhere in therapy (Haley & Hoffman, 1967). Therefore, therapy can take on its own course of growth unconsciously.

Growth is often learned through play. People learn the basics about family structure as infants through the use of play. Whitaker used the concept of playing beside a child, or parallel play (Zeig, 1992). Therefore, in therapy, the therapist plays alongside the family. The therapist does this by becoming a member of the family, leveling the field so that he/she is not seen as the expert. He/she will joke, cajole, talk candidly, and take a stance of just observing how the family interacts, pointing out observations along the way.

Like most family therapy models, little empirical research has been conducted on symbolic-experiential therapy, as family therapists agree that there are too many variables that occur within the family system to determine whether therapy itself was responsible for outcome. The symbolic-experiential family therapy model is suited to families with many relational and traumatic situations, because it allows each family member to reveal deep emotions and indulge in deep conversations that otherwise may not occur. The context created by the symbolic experiential therapist is that "anything goes" in therapy and is coupled by the therapist's stance of instigation of "the unsaid," often bringing into view hidden secrets and forbidden topics that cripple the family's functioning and need to be discussed. Because the model is spontaneous and the therapist does not sit back and just observe, making polite comments at times, some families may find the process uncomfortable at first, but eventually they may find that the *discomfort* was merely a symbol of the family's stress that needed addressing.

SYMBOLIC-EXPERIENTIAL THEORY WORKING TEMPLATE

The *symbolic-experiential family therapy model template* is meant to be used as a guideline to learning the process of symbolic-experiential family therapy. The template provides the beginning therapist with steps to take and questions to ask that promote collaboration between the therapist and client. There are suggested questions under each heading to help start the process. After using the initial questions, guide the client through each process, asking questions that occur to you, as you stay within the family therapy theory. Although there is no one "script" for any therapy session, it is the hope of the author that the template serves as an impetus to learning this family therapy model.

Tools for Change

The symbolic-experiential therapist uses the symbols and language used by the family in the therapy process to help the family have a "corrective experience" by hearing from an outside person what their problem is like. Once inside the family's symbolic world, the therapist find ways to help them experience different meanings associated with the pain. The therapist responds to metaphors and symbolic language and asks about the metaphors such as "Dad's vision" and what it means to the family. The therapist tries to get the family to open up about the meaning their world has for them in a safe place. The therapist is directive, playful, absurd, and spontaneous to accomplish helping a family to relax and share with each other. Being provocative is also a tool, in that it surprises the family and causes reactions.

The therapist:

- Reshapes or creates new symbols using absurdity (amplification deviation), craziness, fantasies, or humor.
- Verbally defines the roles and power structure of the family.
- Helps each family member gain more access to his/her emotional self and promotes growth by asking directly how they feel about certain issues.
- Forms a relationship with each member so each member feels cared for and will take risks in therapy.
- Helps the family deal with the unknown and ambiguity in life. Promotes more flexibility to help them embrace the unknown by being flexible as a therapist.
- Changes the historic "facts" into a symbolic historic experience for the family, providing a new view of themselves as people.

Phase 1: Joining and Building Rapport

During this phase, the therapist's role is to be like a "foster parent": caring and understanding but directive and clear about the therapeutic structure.

- Make introductions and explain your role as a family therapist.
- Explain the guidelines of your practice or center and begin to define the problem that has brought the family to see you.
- Start questioning the family member who is the one most on the periphery of the family system first, then the youngest siblings, then the scapegoat or the family member who seems to absorb the family's discomfort and acts out, often identified as the "patient." The mother is interviewed last.
- Start by constructing a genogram three generations back, four, if possible. (For more on genograms, see Chapter 1.)
- Relate to the family as a peer, remembering that you are not the expert in knowing how their family system works, but they are.

Here are some comments or questions that a therapist might use during this phase:

"My name is _____, and I am here to _____."

"During the course of our conversations, I will be drawing a genogram, and if you would like to see it at any time, just ask."

"I want to begin by asking what has brought you into the office today and what you would like me to do to help? I would like to start with Dad."

"Tell me how your family works. How do you guys relate to each other?"

Phase 2: Understanding the Presenting Issue

During this phase, the therapist should interview only one person at a time and not allow interruptions. Begin with the father, then siblings, identified patient, and finally the mother.

- Refuse to talk about the identified patient in an effort to delabel him/her and refocus on the entire family system. This will serve to expand the symptom past the identified patient to include the whole family as well as to past generations (the genogram will help).
- Then attempt to increase the anxiety within the family system, which will help the family be more willing to regress.
- The therapist takes this radical move of raising anxiety to see how the family reacts, providing a demonstration of family life with the issue.

Here are some comments or questions that a therapist might use during this phase:

"Dad, what do you think is the problem that has brought you in today?"

"How do you see your role in the family and in the problem?"

"How do you think I can help you with dealing with this problem?"

"Mom, do I get the feeling that your children belong to you while your husband is married to his business?"

"I don't hear that your husband is depressed . . . I think he is frustrated that the dog gets more attention than he does. What do you think?"

Phase 3: Assessment of Family Dynamics

The symbolic-experiential therapist looks to increase anxiety and gauge desperation in the family to instigate change and personal growth. Therefore, assessing the presenting issue correctly is vital. The therapist observes where the pain is in the family and observes how he/she, the therapist, feels while being with the family.

The therapist helps the family trace the pain back to the root of the past symbolic experience that has created this meaning and colored their world. For example, *"When your husband/father died, how did you let his vision for you die with him?"*

The following questions will assist in assessing the problem:

"Who does the problem bother the most in your family? How do you know? Who does it bother second? Third?"

"What does this problem mean to each of you? How do you each contribute?"

"What good will it do [to] any of you if this problem goes away? What will it do for Mom, Dad, sister, etc.?"

"Is there anyone who is happy that your family is having this problem?"

"How will it change things if the problem goes away? Who will benefit most?"

Phase 4: Goals

Some healthy goals for therapy are to help families:

- embrace personal ambivalence,
- find more flexibility in their roles,
- feel free to be silly and play, and
- develop tolerance for ambiguity and complexity in life.

"So, you all have told me what you don't like; tell me what you want."

"Who needs to begin doing things differently in this family, so that life gets better?"

"So I'm guessing that when your older sister finally gets sober, and maybe even finds a husband, you, her brother, can finally leave home, is that right?"

"I'm not sure what anyone wants . . . who can tell me?"

"So when you start getting as much attention as the dog, how will that make your marriage better?"

Phase 5: Amplifying Change

Whitaker remarked that his role was to get into a family and then get out as soon as possible, leaving no remnants around. Such actions are suggested to therapists who engage in the symbolic-experiential model. Are some strategies worth the try when change is evolving into a positive outcome?

"You seem to be in better spirits; what went wrong or right?"

"So, what do you think: Should you do more or less of that?"

"Now that _____ is better, where would you like to go next? I don't think I need to be here anymore. It's your turn. What do you think? Should we stop?"

Phase 6: Termination

If a client or family feels it is time to terminate, wish them luck and inform them that the door is always open for them to return. Acknowledge the change and growth that have occurred. Move out of the family system by distancing or saying less and less during sessions and summarizing their progress. Relate on an egalitarian status, as if you appreciated being invited into their lives and are now ready to exit because of their expertise in solving their own problems.

Here are some comments or questions that a therapist might use during this phase:

"It looks like things are going okay for each of you. How did that happen?"

"I wish you the most success, and drop me a line in a few years to let me know how you're doing."

MASTER THERAPIST INTERVIEW

DAVID V. KEITH

David V. Keith, MD, is a professor of psychiatry and behavioral sciences at Upstate Medical University in Syracuse, New York. He has published Family Therapy as an Alternative to Medication *(2003), with Phoebe S. Prosky, and* Defiance in the Family: Finding Hope in Therapy *(2001), with Gary Connell; and worked closely with Carl A. Whitaker in evolving symbolic-experiential theory. Dr. Keith is a wonderful psychiatrist, professor, and blues harmonica player.*

What attracted you to the symbolic-experiential model of family therapy?

Well, I'm a psychiatrist, so I had to work at solving problems that come into a psychiatrist's door. I was trained and oddly remain licensed to practice medicine and surgery. In the days when I was involved with the diagnosis and treatment of more clearly medical problems, I was puzzled by patients who had symptoms, but no signs of disease. My intuition suggested that the family, the intimate relationships, and how they talk about themselves had something to do with the ambiguous illness. Medicine encouraged us to talk with the families, but the talk was superficial and not likely to add much. I met Carl Whitaker in 1971 when I was beginning my psychiatry residency. Dr. Whitaker was working with families, and his language in and about therapy was remarkably dynamic and engaging. I became fascinated because those ambiguous illnesses looked different when we interviewed the families in the way he did. I was hooked and never got over it.

How do you formulate your view of a family when they enter therapy?

I usually interview the family briefly on the phone before I see them. That gives me some sense what the problems are going to be about. I guess I think about who's doing what to whom, who's disappointed and how? I always assume that if the parents are worried about the children, then the children are worried about the parents the same amount, plus ten percent. I think that I assume that women in the family tend to have a higher investment in the relationship. The women are more likely to embody the relationship. I think men have an easier time backing away or walking away, whereas, even when women leave the marriage, they oftentimes become more symptomatic as the relationship breaks down. I formulate my view metaphorically. Metaphors can handle dynamic relationships better. Sometimes if I'm supervising someone, I like to ask them if the family reminds them of a movie they've seen or a novel they've read, more of a multidimensional pattern. That leads to another idea about this whole way of working, in that I feel a great freedom to invent words for what I do or to adapt other languages to what I'm doing rather than create a separate language to describe this stuff.

A family is a multigenerational group, made up of living and ghostly presences, mostly biologically related, and interacts in nonrandom ways. The first one, it's a multigenerational group for me says that the family is not just the husband and wife in my office; it also includes the grandparents and the grandparents' parents. The family that I'm thinking of goes back multiple generations. It's made up of living and ghostly presences, means that all the important family members don't have to be alive and present. Then, it's mostly biologically related says that the biological relationships tend to have the most voltage and power, despite the geographical abrasion or time separation. Families are people who live in a close and intimate way. The last one is that they interact in nonrandom ways, and I'm overstating this to make a point; and that is, that inside our families, inside these groups with long histories, we don't have complete freedom. The group and history of the group shape the behavior.

What kinds of families do you think benefit most from this model?
It's hard to tell ahead of time. I think that families that are somehow cornered by the system are helped by this model. This pattern is good at giving the family back its power. I think families that are amused by me and like my humor can get something out of it; if they don't, then they probably won't. It's hard to tell in advance and it requires a trial, an interview or two, to get an idea. I think there are lots of families that I don't get attached to and they don't get that attached to me, and they do well because it's not contaminated by the dynamics of transference. Whereas there are a lot of families that I work with for long periods of time, and feel not much has happened. I don't always know who benefits unless they refer another family. Sometimes a family will refer another family and it's startling to me because I didn't think it went that well.

What issues do you think this model works best with?
It works best with families that are defeated by the medical system or social services system. I do well with families where psychosis is an issue and families where there is a physical illness that is an issue. Physical illness might include anorexia nervosa and its variations. I think it works well with power issues in families like big money families. We're good at making fun of anyone, especially men. I think it doesn't work well with families with a political agenda.

In your opinion, what are the necessary characteristics that a therapist should possess to be effective with this model?
Like most therapists, I attempt to join with them when I'm first seeing them, but I think we're somewhat different in our also being sure that we disconnect from them. That we have both capacities to join and disconnect is important to mention. I think that my involvement tends to evolve. I've been doing this for 30 years and, in my early years, if I didn't get an instant connection, I would feel disappointed. Now I'm not so eager. They need to prove themselves to me. I'm not available to everyone just because they show up. I would say that I'm fairly double-binding, a combination of seriousness and playful[ness], encouraging and pessimistic. For a number of years, and I stole this one from Carl Whitaker, he

use[d] to say that he was going to get a sign and hang it over his door, "All hope abandon, ye who enter here." That would be a model of a double-binding statement. I allow myself the freedom to push them or bump them a little bit. It's particularly important with male patients. If you are too nice to male patients, whether the therapist is male or female, the male patient feels like he's being seduced and that tends to scare him. Generally the mother's sins tend to be sins of coalition, where she's the most involved with the kids or most involved in trying to save the marriage. Therefore, it's easier to figure out what she's doing wrong. The father's sins tend to be sins of omission. They're not doing anything; therefore, what they're not doing is oftentimes not so palatable, so I go out of my way to accuse them.

It's useful for the therapist to think of their involvement in a metaphorical way. I like Carl's way, as the foster mother. Clients come to live in my house and I want them to do well. If they don't, it won't alter my life much, but if they're going to live in my house, they must follow my rules. If they don't, they can go live somewhere else. That also builds in the hierarchy in the therapist–family relationship. I'm not a collaborator with the family; I'm like a parent. But they have to agree to that arrangement. If they don't, I don't feel that we'll get anywhere. At the end of the therapy, we can go back to being peers again. The problems belong to the family, not the therapist. I probably appear nondirective, but I believe that I point people in different directions or make suggestions. I think what's required is a certain maturity and restraint. The people who do best with me have done something else in their life, where they've failed, but didn't lose their idealism. Necessary agents are people who know how to take on responsibility . . . it's not an egalitarian role. All practitioners have a responsibility for being a therapist. You have to be able to tolerate people being mad at you and you must tolerate a parental role.

How often does your client see you and for how long a period of time?
There's a group of patients that come one to three times. There's a group of patients that come 8 to 12 times. Usually I see them for 60 minutes. Then there are some that I work with for years in a small group. It's variable. There's some that come mostly for a consultation. It would be interesting to follow up on those to see what's come of it. There's a suicidal adolescent that has taken an overdose and may come 8 to 12 times. Anorexic families come for a longer period of time. A lot of families leave a lot earlier than I think they should or when I think we're just getting started.

What are you looking for when you are in session?
Where's the door, which way is north, and what time is it? What's the family spirit like? Is there a generation gap? Are the parents a team? Are the kids all in the second generation or is one a parental assistant? Can they talk about their background families with richness, or do they avoid talking about it because they believe it's not important? I suppose that's the map. The map as a metaphor doesn't fit me very well. It's more like a situation and a general awareness that I have. It's like an athletic model. What's my body like? What do I feel from them? What's the group morale? Who's doing what to whom? Can they talk about their history? What's the problem and what do they want me to do about it?

What is the assessment process of this model?
The assessment process is what I call the interview process, but it can last 3 to 5 interviews with some families. That's the part of the therapy that has to do with defining the problem, teaching them how to be patient. I don't think that when you work with families there is ever a clear and clean assessment. The assessment part is really a collection of

stories and perspectives of their lives. It's not aimed at collecting concrete data, but impressions. I always start off by asking the family member with the most rank and most emotional distance to begin. Then I interview the kids. How does the family work? Sometimes that can be structured by family members' talk about relationships they're not involved in. The mother often gives the family emotional meaning to a situation. If the mother starts, the family is likely to follow her definition. Emotionally, she tends to have the most power in the family. The father is often regarded as irrelevant if he speaks after the mother. If someone says they don't have an opinion, I say, "I don't believe you; I think you are being over careful, but if you are over careful, you won't get anything out of this." That puts the pressure on them versus me trying to rephrase the question. I don't acknowledge the importance of them coming to see a schmuck like me, rather, I turn it around that they have a lot more to live up to if they're going to be mental patients.

Who sets the goals, the client or the therapist?

In terms of experiential therapy, I don't see it being important to me. I ask them what they want when I begin the interview. I ask them what they want and let that color be the tone of therapy. It's a color in the back of my mind during therapy as it evolves.

This interferes with the fantasy that I know what they need. Goals are a part of conscious purpose and I don't feel that conscious purpose is important in doing this type of therapy. I'm looking for the goals behind the goals. What cannot be clearly articulated? I may ask what they want 3 to 4 times in the first interview. The idea of goals is valuable, but the specific goals aren't particularly valuable. I do have goals, and I'll outline them for you. There are general goals that apply to all cases.

1. Augment the administrative capacity of the family. So they can deal more effective with their problems. Whether those problems have to do with the relationship of the family, to the community, or one of the family's members.

2. To help each family member gain more access to himself or herself. To help them grow.

3. For the therapist to form a relationship with each member so each feels sufficiently cared for, and they take risks required to expand their consciousness of what goes on in their family and the world.

4. To figure out the mystery of not knowing and to embrace the unknown. The therapeutic possibilities for this are much greater in family therapy than other therapies because change happens more quickly and is more enduring.

5. To change the family time/face history into a symbolic history. A symbolic history blends a subjective experience with the facts or blends meaning with the facts. A symbolic history includes pattern and not just time sequences.

What are some commonly used interventions with this model?

The most common one is to add more people, on either side of the therapeutic relationship. At the end of the first interview, I tell them not to talk about the first interview for at least 24 hours. That's not a paradoxical instruction. I believe that the therapeutic experience is different from life and there should be a boundary established between the therapeutic experience and the lived experience because, hopefully, people will be more honest in therapy. If they are, they shouldn't have to pay for it when they get out, or if during the course of the interview, I say something that makes the husband anxious, I don't want someone else stating what they thought I meant. It neutralizes the therapeutic experience because it puts it back into their language. The advantage of not talking about it leaves it ambiguous and open for each person to try and figure out what it means to them. A good interview is when a family leaves confused. It's better to relish the confusion for 24 hours before trying to put it into their language. Another intervention is no fighting between interviews. Save it for therapy; if it's too hot, call for an emergency interview.

I've outlined a pattern for how I interview a family. The father goes first, then second sibling, then the oldest sibling, then the third sibling, scapegoat, and finally the mother. When I'm interviewing a person, I interfere with interruptions. If I'm interviewing the father and the mother interrupts, I tell her to sit back and relax. I want him to talk about what he sees and not what she sees. Then to the kids I say, "What do you think of the family," and if the mother interrupts, I tell her to butt out. Then I tell her, "I think he understands me okay and we can work it out without your help." I have other kinds of questions that I ask, such as "What's the family like?" I pay attention to any kind of change. Like if the father quit smoking or the mother decided to drop out of school or someone found religion. Why did it happen then, and how did it affect the family? How has death affected the family? Pay attention to all metaphorical language because those words give clues as to what the problem is behind the problem.

What role does a homework assignment have in this model?
I don't really use homework very much. Part of it has to do with the fact that I'm trying to keep the therapeutic experience separate from the lived experience. So I don't really give much homework. Unless it's something paradoxical, like I don't think you should do anything, but keep things the same. I don't really use homework.

How do you know when your client is ready to terminate?
When they start missing appointments or only part of the family shows up. I really don't work on termination with families, but I might with individuals. I could say that I treat every interview as the last interview. I don't expect to see them again, so I'm operating to get something to happen that will be valuable.

What have you found to be the limitations of this approach?
One of the limitations is in the way life is that I don't think insurance companies like. They like concrete things to happen. One of the problems with family therapy is that it challenges the institutions in which it engages. In other words, each person is as responsible as the institution. Institutions don't like that idea. I think this keeps a family in therapy without the family taking responsibility for the choice of staying in therapy. It's a pattern of therapy that's organized around the choice of change than support. I think that I also pay attention to the limitations of psychotherapy. Psychotherapy doesn't represent a new way of living, or it's something a family uses to either help themselves survive or enrich their living. It's a pattern that doesn't work as well when there's a need to divide the family. An example of that is where there's some kind of abuse going on. It doesn't work so well when there's built in divisions or factions.

What are your suggestions that you have for students learning this model?
You can't be an expert as a therapist, because if you become an expert, it suggests a loss of openness. Don't try to do it alone. Develop a group that you can work with and share your experiences. Don't get too isolated.

GARY CONNELL

Dr. Gary Connell is an associate professor in the Professional Studies Department at Edinboro University, Edinboro, Pennsylvania. He has a PhD in counseling and human development; an MEd Counselor Personnel, is a National Certified Counselor, Licensed Professional Counselor; and has his Secondary School Counselor certification. Dr. Connell worked with Carl A. Whitaker for more than 12 years and is widely published and known in the family therapy field. He is the coauthor of Reshaping Family Relationships: The Symbolic Therapy of Carl Whitaker *(1999) and* Defiance in the Family: Finding Hope in Therapy *(2001).*

What attracted you to the symbolic-experiential model of family therapy?

I think it fits with my personality and view of life. During my training in family therapy, I was drawn to experiential models of therapy, in part, because it allows me to operate from a systems perspective and be congruent with families that I work with. I think there's a lot of synchronicity in how I view the world and how the model of symbolic-experiential therapy functions. I became interested in symbolic-experiential therapy and began supervision with Gus Napier during my doctoral training. Several years later, I was at Auburn University, where I co-led a supervision class with John Warkentin, so I was exposed to his view on symbolic-experiential therapy. Later I connected with Carl Whitaker and for 12 years, we did phone consultations, writing, and presenting. Currently, I enjoy working with Dave Keith, who is a strong proponent of the model. We have our own language, which makes it kind of difficult for outsiders to understand. I would look at the approach as being grounded in more of a phenomenological existential approach to human nature. Carl often said, "The brain is a secondary organ, the heart is a primary organ, trust your heart more than your brain." And, he said, "Anything worth knowing can't be taught." In the book I wrote with Tammy Mitten and Bill Bumberry, *Reshaping Family Relationships*, we're certainly trying to break the language down to show that it is both learnable and teachable. This is not a goal-directed theory; it is process, not progress, that we stress. The therapeutic relationship with the family is the impetus for change. My goal is for families to become more intimate and alive during the therapy process. They are ultimately responsible for the direction of therapy. I think our generation of symbolic-experiential therapists is trying to challenge the extreme privacy of the model and bring it into mainstream therapy. Dr. Mitten has been a major impetus in the effort to clarify and expand the therapeutic techniques use in this symbolic-experiential model.

My whole world is symbolic. It's interesting, after I agreed to do this with you, that night, I had a dream that I was talking to Carl and he was cold and very wobbly. We talked a lot about the importance of keeping his beliefs alive and we talked a lot about also, which is very weird, his concern that his daughter is depressed. He wanted me to help keep his orientation alive and to talk with his daughter. The weird thing is, the next morning, I got an e-mail from one of his daughters thanking me for keeping Carl's approach alive. It's that kind of synchronicity around symbols that we attend to.

How do you formulate your view of a family when they enter therapy?

A family is a three-generational system. We very much believe in systems principles and thinking. Carl always said he believed in families and he didn't believe in individuals. The individual is just an extension of the family sent out to do the family's bidding. I think a lot of the system's principles fit very neatly into our definition. We always like to remember its in a continuing evolution, a state of growth that exists over generations; probably as far back as you could track. I do think families are organized with specific ways of interacting and ways of being, values and idiosyncrasies that are passed down through generations. Carl's article on family, the four-generational model that he wrote in *Defiance in the Family: Finding Hope in Therapy* (2001), would give you a representation of Carl's best definition of family. I think families can be either biological or relational. For example, I think of Dave Keith as much of a brother as my biological brothers. It's important in our orientation to try to expand the system as much as possible in the first encounter. Actually we look at pathology as developing over 3 to 4 generations, so initially we really like to get everybody that's involved to the session. I ask the caller to bring in all family members who are living together for the first session. This is the ideal situation, but at times it doesn't happen that way. I want to see how the family is organized and whether the caller has significant influence to bring the family to discuss how they see themselves individually and collectively. I want to get to know them a bit before I explore their reasons for seeking therapy. I like to expand their initial explanation of problems to include the pain behind their pain and get a sense of who they are for several generations. Rather than trying to blame the identified patient, if you can scapegoat the family 2 to 3 generations back, it's easier to embrace the pathology, and then work with it.

What kinds of families do you think benefit most from this model?

I like working with a lot of at-risk families. High-functioning families work well with the model, provided they can tolerate regression. I enjoy working with mood disorders. I am currently involved with a grant to work in the school system from a family-based intervention model where we're really trying to operationalize experiential components and see if we can have a positive impact on school performance and behavior change with high-risk students. We want to teach them behavioral coping skills like better self-regulation and see how this impacts their academic performance.

What issues do you think this model works best with?

I think this model works well with at-risk families, defiance, mood disorders, and [attention deficit hyperactivity disorder]. It really varies [with] the family.

Different models of therapy require the therapist to be directive or nondirective. In your opinion, what are the necessary characteristics that a therapist should possess to be effective with this model?

I'm willing to be both. Carl used to say, "If I thought they'd do it, I'd tell them to do it, but hell, most of the time they don't." I have an interesting story with that one. I'm working with a couple where the husband is a very successful businessman and they have not been sexual in over a year. We went through sensate focus (an intervention often used in sex therapy where the person is to focus on felt senses and arousal), and I talked with them about it and they were going to try it. Several sessions later, they still hadn't tried it. I said I wasn't sure how I could be helpful if they weren't interested in trying my suggestions; perhaps this wasn't really a problem. They came into the next session and the husband said, "Well, we had sex twice this week." I said, "Well what's going on, you didn't even try sensate focus?" He just laughed and said, "Oh Gary, I'd try anything for you." It's that understructure of caring, the intervention which was more directive, I think that it followed protocol even though they didn't do it. They did and have changed significantly, and I think it's because of the relationship we've developed and the freedom to experiment in the therapeutic relationship. The pressure is off.

I see myself as a collaborative spirit within the therapeutic process. One of the things that attracted me to the approach is the recognition of personal growth through professional endeavor. I think that's a key phrase; while therapy is always for the client, I think that both sides grow and develop in an honest collaborative endeavor. I think that as long as there is an understructure of caring, that it's a powerful approach and that it will affect all parties involved, if there is intimacy and vulnerability. Technical skill is needed, but quality therapy is dependent on an understructure of caring and the art of the therapist. The core ingredient of therapy is the therapist's humanness. Interventions come alive and are necessary, but they come alive when filtered through the personhood of the therapist. There is an honest attempt to connect emotionally with all parties in the therapeutic endeavor.

How often does the client see you and for how long a period of time?
This can vary depending on what the client thinks they need and if I feel I can be helpful. I like to see the first session for a couple of hours so I don't feel rushed, then, after that, usually an hour. Although if people come from far away, I'll try to see them like Carl used to do, 2 hours in the morning, 2 hours in the afternoon for 3 consecutive days.

I saw one guy that wanted me to see him practically every day for however long it took to work on his anxiety. I told him that I didn't think that would be helpful. I'm usually pretty honest about whether I feel I can be helpful or not with clients. Sometimes there is a no-fault failure to relate, in which case I am glad to refer them to someone who is better suited for them. Some clients come to therapy with a rigid idea of what they need from their therapist; if this is inconsistent with my personality, or the model I operate from, I don't see how I can be helpful.

What are you looking for when you are in the session?
The overall goal of the therapy is to restore group spirit, to translate history into symbolic history, to help families develop affect, and deepen their own affective investment with one another. Carl likened therapy to a chess match. This fits for me so I try to have a fairly consistent structure of saving the queen for last because she has the most power, and you don't want to use her unnecessarily. If you use the mother too quickly, it will set the tone, so I tend to move in and out. I make sure I touch bases with everyone. There's a very consistent way for joining and disengaging with families that Dave Keith wrote about, the battle for structure, battle of initiative, trial of labor, and termination. In this, I think, that we're very structured. In the first session, the therapist needs to be attentive and skillful and provide an unanxious presence. I try to be aware verbally and nonverbally of each family member's presence, to feel what the family is feeling experientially. After years of therapy, I am guided by my intuition.

I am also guided by Augustus Napier, director of The Family Workshop in Atlanta, Georgia, who wrote *The Family Crucible* (1978) with Whitaker. He would try to make an initial interpretation in the first session that the family agrees to. If this was unsuccessful, he felt the prognosis was bad. If there is no connection early on in the therapy process, I am less hopeful I can be helpful.

I want to develop a therapeutic relationship with each family member and the family as a group. All psychopathology is interpersonal. Dave Keith always likes to say, "Where there's caring and sharing, there will be repairing."

What is the assessment process of this model?
I want to see if there is flexibility in the roles, whether the family can negotiate between being individuals and part of the group, and whether there is freedom to regress. Can they tolerate ambiguity? The system needs to be able to question its motives in depth. I want to know whether I can push them to behave differently. A healthy family system can be skeptical about themselves; there is flexibility and an ability to entertain new ways of being. One of the goals is to induce a regression in the system, to figure out what therapeutic techniques might facilitate that regression. It's during the regressed state that reorganization on an interpersonal level is possible. You want to achieve a primary process of relating. This is where the defenses are lowered and the system is on automatic pilot. You can do it with laughter and confusion, and storytelling.

Who sets the goals, the client or the therapist?
I think that it is necessary for the client and the therapist to come to a realistic negotiation on goals. I think it's important to figure out what the family wants to achieve from the therapy experience. We need to be able to talk about goals, but the goals are the family's goals, not mine. These need to be negotiated between the therapist and [the] family. What I cringe at are vague goals like, "I just want to be happy." I think happiness is a by-product of experience. You need to work on quality life experience, and then happiness is a byproduct. So if someone just wants to be happy, I think that the goal is not a very achievable one. Dave Keith use[d] to say he's happy about 40% of the time and considers himself lucky; is that going to be enough for them or do they need to be happy 100% of the time? It's a realistic negotiation. I am okay with renegotiating goals as therapy progresses, and the family has a more realistic idea of what is possible from the therapeutic journey.

What are some commonly used interventions with this model?
I think that the article Dr. Mitten and I published in JAMFT (2004) on the core ingredients of symbolic-experiential therapy provides a good overview of techniques we think are useful. The techniques used in therapy are often idiosyncratic to the therapist. I mainly use metaphors, storytelling, and deviation amplification. I really like deviation amplification, the use of metaphors, and storytelling. I tend to use these techniques a lot. Dr. Mitten and I have some idea that there are differences in terms of the gender of the therapist that defines who's more comfortable with particular techniques. I think storytelling and the use of metaphors lowers the defenses of the listener so that they are able to take in information in a new way. An example would be telling a story about a family with a similar issue and [how] they're struggling to make changes. My wife uses the metaphor of sand in a bathing suit for my type of therapy. The sand is irritating but you know you had a good time.

Interventions are about getting the family to open itself up to you in the initial sessions, with some of the questions I've mentioned before. As the sessions continue to become more symbolic, as the underlying structure deepens and deepens, I think you enter in the second stage, a more parallel process and storytelling so you don't invade their world but move along beside it. In the trial of labor, it becomes more intrusive and direct. It can become more confrontational and deliberate. Dr. Mitten did a video of me working with a destructive family. One of the adolescent sons was selling drugs to kids, but he was taking money and not delivering the drugs. I was worried that he was going to get killed. We had it all on tape where I confronted him because I was sick of what he was doing. He joined the Marines and was used to fighting and taking on two or three people. He stood up, and I stood up and we were ready to get into it because I was sick of it. He was acting out totally and I was sick of it, but he backed down and we ended up giving each other a hug. I think that was a crucial stage in therapy. In termination, we're careful not to invade and to compliment the system on its growth. That is not a time you want to make sure the T's are crossed and I's are dotted. You want them to know you have every belief in their ability to live life, it's very disengaged and you want to wish them well. There's always the option of coming back, but you trust they don't need to.

What role does a homework assignment have in this model?
I think we like to encourage families to have adventures. John Warkentin used to begin every session asking "So what kinds of adventures have you had since our last session?" or "Did you think about me over the past few weeks?" Any homework I assign is intended to increase the interpersonal focus between therapy sessions. I see a lot of families with extreme depression and I might say, "Can you do something that might give you pleasure over the next week? Try and remember what you do so you can share it with me next week." This plants the seed that change is possible, but it will be at their pace and with their initiative. I am only a guide.

How do you know when a client is ready to terminate?
If the client starts looking at their watch a lot early on in the session, I discuss termination. If they [are a] no show, that's a clear sign. If they start talking about difficulty scheduling, that's another good sign. Again, termination is a good thing; I respect the family's opinion. I am always willing to discuss termination or referral if things do not seem to be progressing.

What have you found to be the limitations of this approach?
If someone wants to be told what to do, this is not a good approach for him or her. I see a lot of VIP families for some reason, but I was seeing a businessman that owns a couple of big industries. He had gotten his girlfriend pregnant and his wife pregnant at the same time and, he said, "Tell me what to do" and I said, "I don't know what to do, I can't figure that out at all, I'm not telling you what to do." He stood up and said, "Well what the hell am I paying you for?" and left. I wasn't very helpful to his needs.

I'm thinking of another patient that will call at the last minute and cancel because something important has come up, but then he'll call at night because his world is falling apart and his wife has left on a date with another man. He's demanding that I see him the next day so I can talk his wife out of leaving. I am not willing to enter into this type of therapy contract.

What are your suggestions that you have for students learning this model?
I suggest that students take advantage of meetings like the national AAMFT yearly conference. Dr. Mitten and I have presented several workshops on our writings and research to understand the experiential model. We have been making a consistent effort to demonstrate that this model is teachable; that there are techniques [for which] to use this model. Certainly reading the book we wrote is a good way to get organized. Dave Keith has written extensively on this model, as have other influential practitioners. Finally, group supervision is a key component to learning this model.

Case Study

A mother calls and makes an appointment for her family to come to therapy. The family consists of a husband and wife, both in their 40s; their 15-year-old son; a college-aged daughter; and the woman's father, age 82. Three years after the woman's mother died, her father developed Alzheimer's disease. He moved in with the family 6 months ago. When his health began to deteriorate, the woman spent more time caring for him than for the other members of the family. Three months ago, the 15-year-old son, who has been treated for attention deficit hyperactivity disorder since age 7, began refusing to take his medication and is now being truant from school.

During the session, the wife cries and the husband reports their relationship is strained, while occasionally rolling his eyes as his wife becomes tearful. He reports that he has to take on more work because his wife had to quit her job to attend to her father's needs. The daughter is away at college and the wife smiles as she describes her as a straight-A student. The daughter was asked to attend the session but refused because she has a hard time with her grandfather's illness and dislikes the conflict that has developed at home.

Dr. David Keith's Response to the Case Study

It's a family that's in what I call in a "triple layer identity crisis," in that there are three generations and they are all unstable. The mother's mother died and the grandfather's health is failing, and he's dealing with death. The kids are in identity struggle and the parents are as well. The distress is augmented by the distress in any other generation. My question is, "What does the kid's refusal in taking medications have to do with the grandfather's illness?"

The way I would approach the family is, I would want everyone to come. The daughter is away at college and I don't know the circumstances about that. If anyone is against the therapy, I would suggest they follow their plan and, if it doesn't work, they can always come back. I would want everyone there for the first interview. I would propose that they bring the grandfather, even though he has Alzheimer's. The more people you get in the first interview, the farther you tend to get and see the problem.

I have a fairly standard way of structuring the first interview. I would interview the father first about what the problem is and what they want to get out of it. How does the family work? Then I would interview the son about the family. In the course of that, I'd probably ask him how he decided to stop taking his medications. What's he trying to get at or what's the problem with it? Then I'd interview the mother. After I finish with the mother, I'd ask the husband about her crying and his rolling eyes. "Do you have any idea about what you're trying to tell me? It occurs to me that you think her tears are for show." Then I could push on that one for awhile. What do tears mean in his family? I would want the grandfather to come to the next visit because he needs to have a sense of what's going on with the family. He needs communication, even emotional communication.

The daughter is away at college, so I'd probably talk a lot about her. I tend to talk a lot about people who don't show up and try and induce some paranoia in them. One of the questions of someone who chooses not to come is, "What do they think you should do as opposed to therapy?" I would really want to get the daughter to come in. I might say, "I don't think you'll get anywhere if the daughter doesn't come in, she sounds too important."

The kid's got ADHD and that's another ambiguous diagnosis. I'd probably play around with that. It's a little hard to tell what they think the problem is, and [how] they are defining the problem. I would need to ask them what they want. What are they looking for? It's hard to predict what will happen, I never really know.

I do think that it's always important to find out about background families. I think of that part of the history taking as a psychological projection test. Whatever they talk about is being colored by their concerns with the present. I don't think my strategies change much with different families. My goals are to help the family deal with this problem.

The family is like a basketball team, but there's dissention on the team. Dad never gets the ball. The daughter wants to play somewhere else. The son is pissed off because no one pays attention to him unless he's pissed off. Usually about 20 minutes into the interview I say, "It sounds like you're leaving something out." It would be tempting to work on the marriage, but usually the marriage is the most delicate part of the therapy. Marriage is sometimes best addressed indirectly. Beginning therapists would need to start tough. This team has fired an old coach and is hiring you as a coach. Everyone needs to come to practice and learn to play together again.

Dr. Gary Connell's Response to the Case Study

I very much believe that it's better to fail initially then to begin and fail. If the daughter's in the family, they need to have enough power to bring the daughter with them. So during the phone conversation, that would be one of the things that I would deal with. The daughter would need to come, she wouldn't have to talk, but she would have to be there. If they didn't have enough power to get everyone into the session, I would probably not see them. I would suggest they would do better seeing someone else, and fail right from there. It's not my desperation to see people, but their desperation to see me. I've got more people that are willing to see me on my terms than I need. So if we can't work it out, it's a no-fault failure to relate.

During the first session, I usually blueprint how the session will go so the family has some idea what to expect. If the family does arrive for therapy, it would be important for me to expand the initial complaint about the son not taking his medication to include the family system as well. My assumption is, the initial complaint is the ticket for admission, but is rarely the underlying problem. I would explore relationships within the family and how things have changed since the grandfather moved in and the mother quit her job.

During therapy, I am alert to not only what is said, but the obvious things that are spoken. I focus on both verbal and nonverbal interaction, which family members defend each other, who are the dominant personalities in the group, and how do family members engage each other to get their needs met. I would want to know how the family has functioned historically, how decisions are made, what the emotional tone of the family is, and why they think they are having problems now. My goal is for each person to talk during the session, although if someone refuses I don't make that an issue; it is important for me to see if I can connect with people individually as well as with the family as a whole. I ask what they see as a good outcome for therapy. I do a brief recap of the session to make sure I got things straight. At the end of the session, I ask if they would like to reschedule or think about it. If they hesitate about rescheduling, I ask them to discuss it at home and let me know.

KEY TERMS

Assessment   An evaluation of the client's current emotional state.

Atheoretical   A descriptive term for a theory without strict guidelines and assumptions for methods of treatment.

Battle for initiative   A stage in the therapeutic process in which the responsibility of the sessions shifts to the family.

Battle for structure   A stage in therapy, usually in the beginning, in which the therapist actively interviews the family and sets the rules for the sessions.

Confusion   A concept used to disrupt existing patterns and open an infrastructure to respond and adapt in new ways to a situation.

Congruence   A clear, direct form of communication that acknowledges the needs of the individual and others. Congruent communication is considered the healthiest form of communication.

Craziness   The concept that non sequitur, irrelevant, and paradoxical thoughts can be used as an intervention in therapy.

Deviation amplification   A therapeutic intervention that takes an issue of a client and pushes it to an unrealistic realm so that the client can begin to lose fear through confusion.

Dialect   A concept in different types of language and pattern of linguistics.

Dichotomy   A division usually with a clear boundary.

Double entendre   A therapeutic intervention that gives a word or group of words a double meaning with a covert message.

Dysfunction   When a person is stuck in the growth process and acting outside of society's norms.

Fantasy   A concept that allows people to communicate symbolically and explore meanings without being distracted by factual occurrences that inhibit growth.

Fusion   A concept describing a relationship that is enmeshed to the point of unclear boundaries between "I" and "We."

Growth   A concept that is assumed to motivate a person to be both independent and yet joined in a relationship with others in the daily process of life and existence.

Infrastructure   The underlying framework of a family or system.

Intervention   A therapeutic tool used to initiate change in a system.

Interview   The process in which the therapist asks questions of the family to gain knowledge of their values, relationships, and descriptions of the problem.

Intuition   The unconscious ability of people to perceive insight to truth, through an illogical process, without using practical reasoning skills.

Irrelevant stance   A form of communication in which a person avoids addressing the topic through random statements, humor, or other methods.

Metalearning   Learning through linguistics and symbols.

Metaphorical   Using metaphors as a therapeutic intervention to address underlying issues without confronting the family.

Multigenerational   Describes the theory that families develop through generations and that past unresolved problems and traumatic experiences transition to the next generation, affecting development and functioning.

Parallel play   A therapeutic intervention where the therapist plays alongside a family to view the system until invited to play with the family.

Pathology   A deviation from healthy and normal development.

Personhood   The internal characteristics and strengths of a therapist that help create individualistic styles and presentation in treatment.

Placating stance   A form of communication where the person disregards personal needs and feelings to give power of decisions to the other.

Polysemantics   The effects of language on a person's interpretation and placed meanings.

Polysemy   Multiple meanings in language.

Psychoeducation   The process of providing educational materials and information on mental/physical health and illness.

Psychotropic medication   Medication used to alter brain functioning and aid in balancing the emotional state.

Semiotics   The study of signs and symbols in the communication process.

Spontaneity   A concept that is rooted in the unconsciousness that allows quick natural impulses to be expressed that are inspired by insight to help instigate change in a therapeutic relationship.

Storytelling   An intervention that is used to address an issue with a client without seeming confrontational. The process allows the client to choose to discuss the issue or disregard the story.

Super-reasonable stance   A communication pattern of a person using a pure objective stance without regarding personal feelings and feelings of others.

Symbol   The most basic form of learning and expressing personal impulses.

Symbolic-experiential family therapy   A theory that is present and growth oriented with emphasis on symbols and experiences in therapeutic treatment.

Therapeutic psychosis   The concept that therapy induces a sense of confusion in clients and is surrounded by the caring of the therapist to help produce change.

Trial of labor   A stage in the therapeutic process in which the underlying pain of the family is exposed and discussed.

Unconscious   A part of a person's psyche that the person lacks awareness of, but can influence a person's reactions and behaviors.

Understructure   The foundation of the therapist-client relationship.

REFERENCES

Connell, G. M., & Mitten, T. J. (in press). Symbolic-experiential family therapy. *Journal of Marital and Family Therapy*.

Connell, G. M., Mitten, T. J., & Bumberry, W. B. (1999). *Reshaping family relationships: The symbolic therapy of Carl Whitaker*. Philadelphia, PA: Brunner/Mazel.

Connell, G. M., Mitten, T. J., & Whitaker, C. A. (1993). Reshaping family symbols: A symbolic-experiential perspective. *Journal of Marital and Family Therapy, 19*(3), 243–251.

Haley, J., & Hoffman, L. (1967). The growing edge: An interview with Carl A. Whitaker. In *Techniques of family therapy* (pp. 265–360). New York, NY: Basic Books, Inc.

Kaye, D., Dichter, H., & Keith, D. V. (1986). Symbolic-experiential family therapy. *Individual Psychology: Journal of Adlerian Theory, Research, & Practice, 42*(4), 521–536.

Kempler, W. (1981). *Experiential psychotherapy within families*. New York, NY: Brunner/Mazel.

Malone, T. P., Whitaker, C. A., Warkentin, J., & Felder, R. E. (1961). Rational and nonrational psychotherapy: A reply. *American Journal of Psychotherapy, 15*, 212–220.

Mitten, T. J., & Piercy, F. P. (1993). Learning symbolic-experiential therapy: One approach. *Contemporary Family Therapy, 15*(2), 149–168.

Napier, A. Y., & Whitaker, C. (1978). *The family crucible: The intense experience of family therapy*, New York, NY: HarperCollins Publishers, Inc.

Neill, J. R., & Kniskern, D. P. (Eds.). (1982). *From psyche to system: The evolving therapy of Carl Whitaker*. New York, NY: The Guilford Press.

Whitaker, C. A. (1989). *Midnight musing of a family therapist*. New York, NY: Norton.

Whitaker, C. A., & Bumberry, W. M. (1988). *Dancing with the family*. New York, NY: Brunner/Mazel.

Whitaker, C. A., Greenberg, A., & Greenberg, M. L. (1979). Existential marital therapy. A synthesis-A subsystem of existential family therapy. *Interaction, 2*, 169–200.

Whitaker, C. A., & Keith, D. V. (1981). Symbolic-experiential family therapy. In A. Gurman & D. Kniskern (Eds.), *The handbook of family therapy* (pp. 187–225). New York, NY: Brunner/Mazel.

Whitaker, C. A., & Keith, D. V. (1991). Experiential/symbolic family therapy. In A. M. Horne & J. L. Passmore (Eds.), *Family counseling and therapy* (pp. 107–140). Itasca, IL: F. E. Peacock.

Whitaker, C. A., & Malone, T. P. (1953). *The roots of psychotherapy*. New York, NY: Blakiston.

Zeig, J. K. (1992). Symbolic-experiential family therapy: Model and methodology. In *The evolution of psychotherapy: Second conference* (pp. 13–20). New York, NY: Brunner/Mazel.

RECOMMENDED READING LIST

Books

Connell, G. M., & Connell, L. C. (2001). *Defiance in the family: Finding hope in therapy*. New York, NY: Psychology Press.

Duhl, F. J., Kantor, D., & Duhl, B. S. (1973). Learning, space, and action in family therapy: A primer of sculpture. In D. A. Bloch (Ed.), *Techniques of family psychotherapy: A primer*. New York, NY: Grune & Stratton.

Goldenberg, I., & Goldenberg, H. (2004). Experiential models. *Family therapy: An overview* (6th ed.). Belmont, CA: Thomson Brooks/Cole.

Keith, D. V., Connell, G. M., & Connell, L. C. (2001). *Defiance in the family: Finding hope in therapy*. Philadelphia, PA: Brunner-Routledge.

Prosky, P. S., & Keith, D. V. (Eds.). (2003). *Family therapy as an alternative to medication: An appraisal of pharmland*. New York, NY: Brunner-Routledge.

Satir, V. M. (1964). *Conjoint family therapy*. Palo Alto, CA: Science and Behavior Books, Inc.

Satir, V. M. (1988). *The new peoplemaking*. Mountain View, CA: Science and Behavior Books, Inc.

Satir, V. M., Banmen, J., Gerber, J., & Gomori, M. (1991). *The Satir model: Family therapy and beyond*. Palo Alto, CA: Science and Behavior Books, Inc.

Satir, V. M., & Bitter, J. R. (2000). The therapist and family therapy: Satir's human validation model. In A. M. Horne & J. L. Passmore (Eds.), *Family counseling and therapy* (3rd ed.). Itasca, IL: F. E. Peacock.

Thomas, V. (2003). Experiential approaches to family therapy. In L. Hecker & J. Wetchler (Eds.). *An introduction to marriage and family therapy* (pp. 173–187). New York, NY: Haworth Press, Inc.

Articles

Connell, G. M., & Mitten, T. J. (2004). Core variables of symbolic-experiential therapy: A qualitative study. *Journal of Marital and Family Therapy, 30*(4), 467–478.

Connell, G. M., & Russell, L. A. (1987). Interventions for the trial of labor in symbolic-experiential family therapy. *Journal of Marital and Family Therapy, 13*(1), 85–94.

Keith, D. V. (1987). Intuition in family therapy: A short manual on post-modern witchcraft. *Contemporary Family Therapy, 9*(1–2), 11–22.

Napier, A. Y. (1987). Early stages in experiential marital therapy. *Contemporary Family Therapy, 9*(1–2), 23–41.

Napier, A. Y. (1987). Later stages in experiential marital therapy. *Contemporary Family Therapy, 9*(1–2), 43–57.

Websites

depression-guide.com
http://www.depression-guide.com/experiential-family-therapy.htm

Nathen's Miraculous Escape
http://www.nathensmiraculousescape.wordpress.com/category/experiential-family-therapy

Satir Human Validation Process Model

8

Jessica Martinez, Beth Hollingsworth, Christina Stanley,
Reva Shephard, and Linda Lee

INTRODUCTION

Virginia Satir developed an experiential family therapy theory that has several similarities with the symbolic-experiential model (see Chapter 7). The Satir human validation process model focuses on the communication patterns, self-esteem, and self-worth of each individual member and family and the innate internal strengths in every human (Satir & Bitter, 2000). The model is experiential in design and growth oriented. The family's experiences in therapy lead to change, and then they develop insight. Although there are similarities between the theoretical construct and assumptions of Satir's theory and symbolic–experiential theory, there are significant differences in the methods of working with families, interventions, and role of the therapist.

HISTORY AND LEADING FIGURES

Virginia Satir was a curious child, teaching herself to read by age 3, and by age 9 she had read all the books in the library of her small one-room school. When she was 5 years of age, Satir decided that she would grow up to be "a children's detective on parents" (Satir, 1976). She began seeing clients in 1951 and quickly noticed differences in relationship patterns when treating individuals versus families. Her experience seeing a young woman with schizophrenia and her family in the same session led to the publication of *Conjoint Family Therapy* (1983), her first major publication. The book covers her treatment of families based on a systemic theoretical framework and family relationship communication styles. This was the first of many books she authored over her model of treatment.

She became prolific in her work and her beliefs that her model could help change families everywhere. She said, "The family is a microcosm of the world. By knowing how to heal the family, I know how to heal the world" (Satir, 1988). With this belief, she established professional training groups in the Middle East, Asia, Western and Eastern Europe, Central and Latin America, and Russia. The Institute for International Connections, Avanta Network, and the International Human Learning Resources Network are concrete examples of organizations teaching people how to connect with one another and then extend the connections. Her world impact could be summed up in her universal mantra: Peace within, peace between, and peace among. Throughout Satir's career, she continued to evolve her model and inspire other individuals on this approach until her death in 1988.

INTRODUCTION TO THE SATIR HUMAN VALIDATION MODEL (THE SATIR MODEL)

The Satir model is a strength-based approach that focuses on empowering human growth. There are several assumptions in this model: (a) all humans have the ability to change, (b) all humans have internal resources to allow growth throughout life, (c) humans are innately good, (d) coping is related to a person's level of self-worth, (e) change occurs from experiences and leads to insight, and (f) healthy relationships are based on equality (Satir, Banmen, Gerber, & Gomori, 1991). These core assumptions are the foundation for Satir's model of family therapy. The treatment is present focused and addresses the following components in human interactions: human internal resources, communication, and the stages of change.

The human validation process includes the germination of Satir's "seeds" for family healing. She believed that by healing the family, we could help heal the world, resulting in peace within, between, and, therefore, among us all. This leads to a process of connection in which we link with one another and thus extend the connections. Regardless of our own or our client's sexual orientation, the therapeutic relationship can include Satir's values of compassion and genuine warmth to help clients face their fears.

The Satir model works well with individuals and families of all ethnicities, culture, and backgrounds. Despite its potential use with gay and lesbian families, Satir's approach may not be a perfect fit. Some researchers (LaSala, 2007; Spitalnick & McNair, 2005) believe that family models are not designed for work with gay or lesbian couples and their special issues, such as societal pressures, a history of nonmonogamous relationships (gay men), and a lack of legally sanctioned marriage (for the most part). Perhaps a more flexible, experiential model such as Satir's would be a better fit because nontraditional relationships might best be viewed from a nontraditional therapeutic viewpoint.

One development is Satir transformational systemic therapy, which focuses on congruence, connection, and becoming more human (Banmen, 2009). This shift in application of Satir's principles indicates promising directions for future use of the human validation process model and further evolution of communication theory.

Satir's ideas about self-concept and congruence include the mind–body–feeling triad. Integrating these components for a more genuine self can aid us in making contact with one another.

THEORETICAL ASSUMPTIONS

This theory assumes that every human has eight universal internal resources. The resources start with a core and expand out with added layers on a circle. The following are the universal internal resources, starting with the core (Satir et al., 1991):

1. Physical – This represents the body and all its physical parts. It is the house of the "I."

2. Intellectual – This includes the brain's ability to be logical, creative, and emotional.

3. Emotional – This represents a person's feelings and emotions.

4. Sensual – This includes the body's senses and responses to sensations.

5. Interactional – This refers to the interactional pattern of humans and connectedness felt in relationships.

6. Nutritional – This includes what people put into their bodies and how they care for themselves.

7. Contextual – This refers to feeling of things, sight, sound, environment, temperature, and presence in the "now."

8. Spirituality – This accounts for a person's spiritual connectedness and life energy.

Based on these eight internal resources, Satir found seven levels of experiences within the self: yearning, expectations, perceptions, feelings, feelings about feelings, coping, and behavior. A person's experiences and level of self-worth create an explanation of the driving forces in his or her interactions in relationships and development of communication patterns. The communication patterns in relationships provide information on the family system and roles of each member.

Satir labeled four dysfunctional communication styles of placater, blamer, super-reasonable, and irrelevant stances, which keep people from expressing their true feelings, being themselves, building self-esteem, and connecting with each other. For example, because the issue of internalized homophobia is so great (Derlega, Griffin, Krowinski, & Lewis, 2003) for many gays and lesbians, this emphasis on authentic self can be useful. The placater will try to avoid and cover up uncomfortable truths, which is an accurate way to describe a gay or lesbian who has not disclosed his or her sexuality and is battling self-acceptance. The blamer feels isolated (a very common state for closeted gays and lesbians) and may then attribute the fault for stressful feelings to others. The super-reasonable computer uses logic to deny or discount stressful emotions, thus denying core emotional feelings (e.g., sexual orientation issues). The irrelevant distracter may attempt to deflect stress and may flounder between the first three types. The leveler, however, is comfortable with uncertainty and ambiguity and can meet and accept stress in a head-on, matter-of-fact manner.

View of the Family and Client

Satir characterized family systems as open or closed based on the system members' self-esteem level, communication, rules, and outcome. A closed system represents a troubled family dynamic, and an open system represents a nurturing family dynamic (Satir, 1988). A closed system has low self-esteem and indirect communication and is unclear and incongruent with internal feelings. The closed system uses blaming, placating, super reasoning, and irrelevant communication styles. The rules in a closed system are inflexible, covert, and growth impeding. Therefore, the outcome of a closed system is chaotic and dysfunctional (destructive). An open system is defined as having a high self-esteem and a direct and congruent communication. The rules are overt, flexible, and can be changed as needed for the growth of the family. The outcome of an open system is constructive and realistic. Most families who enter therapy may start as a closed system, but it is hoped that by the end of the treatment, change has occurred in order to move to an open system.

Facing and owning one's own biases, fears, and assumptions about clients is an important quality for any therapist. Despite our training in multiculturalism, many of us may have developed a heterosexist partiality (Telford, 2004) from living in a heterosexual majority society. However, not all agree in the applicability of the Satir's model to culturally diverse populations because they assume it focuses on the individual versus the collective.

Satir's work led the way for new developments in family therapy. Feminist theory, which holds that most family theories are biased in favor of a patriarchal family unit and lead to less restricted views on gender roles, has been suggested as one approach that recognizes some of the problems unique to same-sex parented families (McKinney & Negy, 2006). The definition of the American family has evolved from a small nuclear group, defined by marriage and genetics, to a model that expanded to encompass changes resulting from the country's new counterculture youth, gay liberation, and women's movements. Does the Satir model address differential factors (e.g., conflict resolution styles [Metz, Rosser, & Strapko, 1994]) for gay or lesbian versus heterosexual couples? Most therapy models address most of the family systems, but models that adapt to the alternative family systems (e.g., gay and lesbian couples with biological and/or adopted children and the special circumstances of donor children) are needed. Perhaps the experiential models, with their emphasis on wholeness and the here-and-now, are a good choice for these families. Of these experiential models, Virginia Satir's human validation process model is a good fit for gay and lesbian families because it emphasizes greater access to one's self and the history of innovations in family therapy. However, we need to continue asking ourselves whether our typical systemic approaches work for a typical families (Carr, 2010).

Satir's emphasis on congruence and the whole person supports the idea that a gay man or lesbian who has "come out" (i.e., publicly disclosed his or her sexual orientation) feels more "whole" in the synchronicity between inner person and outer world. The research on sexual identity and stressors for this population also supports a link between disclosure, moderators, and perceived stress (Fingerhut, Gable, & Peplau, 2010; Rowen & Malcolm, 2002).

Virginia Satir believed we all possess the resources needed to nourish ourselves for positive growth. Family therapy models, such as the Satir model, should foster the growth that these resources can provide for all clients.

Satir's universal and human ideals have been spread worldwide via her training and conferences. Perhaps we can ultimately use these concepts to foster exponential connection and harmony among all kinds of people and families, whether heterosexual or homosexual. Satir's ideas about self-concept and congruence include the mind–body–feeling triad. Integrating these components for a more genuine self can aid us in making contact with one another. That contact between partners in a relationship or between counselor and client(s) can carry over into a more sincere contact with families of origin, with neighbors, with community, and on and on in a ripple effect.

View on How Change Occurs

The stages of change are usually in motion when a client begins voluntary treatment. The process of change in the Satir model is a six-stage model focusing on the belief that all humans are capable of change and can seek it. It is assumed that all people go through the six stages of change (Satir et al., 1991):

1. Status quo – Awareness for the need to change.

2. Introduction of a foreign element – The person or family acknowledges the need to change and has verbalized it to an outside agent (a friend, a therapist, or someone not involved in the situation).

3. Chaos – The person begins to make different choices from past routine. Chaos is unpredictable, involves moving into the unknown, and creates anxiety and fear.

4. Integration – The person evolves from new experiences and begins learning new concepts.

5. Practice – As the person continues to use the new skills, change is furthered and comfort is found in the new personal state.

6. New status quo – The person is able to feel confident in the new growth and functions at a higher level.

The Satir model is based on the premise that to achieve change in one's life, everyone has to have basic needs or yearnings that strive to be fulfilled and must be fulfilled to accomplish inner peace (Satir et al., 1991). Satir looked at the client's inner world and conceptualized it into a metaphor of an iceberg that has eight phases or layers: "Like icebergs, we show only parts of ourselves. Much of our experience lies beneath the surface. We also show only parts of what we know" (Satir et al.,1991, p. 34). At the tip of the iceberg is the behavior that one sees and hears. Baldwin and Satir (1987) went on to write the following:

> When I am in touch with myself, my feelings, my thoughts, with what I see and hear; I am growing toward becoming a more integrated self. I am more congruent. I am more "whole," and I am able to make greater contact with the other person." (Baldwin & Satir, 1987, p. 23)

Virginia Satir used the *iceberg* metaphor to describe people's inner experience during the steps: "Like icebergs, we show only parts of ourselves. Much of us lies below the surface" (Satir et al., 1991, p. 34). The iceberg metaphor describes what experiential therapists do when they explore and deconstruct internal emotional baggage in clients. The therapeutic exploration of how people are below the surface leads to an exploration of perceptions, feelings, feelings about feelings, expectations, yearnings, and a feeling of satisfaction for a client.

In the Satir model, the therapist explores rules for the family. For example, one may be taught as a child to keep secrets within the family. As an adult, the same person may keep secrets as a method to achieve happiness and harmony within his or her family. If the family comes to therapy and has kept secrets about a member with an alcohol problem, for example, the therapist using the Satir model would talk about the feelings of loneliness, anger, shame, and worthlessness, enabling the client to reexamine the rule of keeping secrets in childhood and adult life. Once the client makes the switch to stop keeping the secrets, change can then occur. Loneliness and self-doubt become less dominant, and the client becomes more accepting of the childhood experiences he or she had and can move to a more positive pathway. Once the client realizes that the problem does not define who he or she is, he or she begins to see that he or she no longer needs to be in conflict with each other and can see himself or herself as separate from other members.

The feeling about the feeling is a thought, a reaction to the acceptability of the feeling we experience. For example, feeling anger or jealousy can produce a thought or a rule that it is not acceptable to feel that way. If we have been taught that being angry is bad, this can produce a feeling of shame or guilt. Incongruent communication is a strategy one might use to protect the self.

During the phase of perceptions, the therapist talks about how the client learned or believed life to be. For the family of the alcoholic, for instance, the client may believe that not talking about the issue keeps the problem away. If the client were to talk about the issue of shame, loneliness, and sadness, he or she would be drawn out. The new mind-sets that he or she has as an adult are then talked about and moved into the next stage.

The next iceberg phase is expectations. Explorations of how a mother, a father, and other family members should act are examined. Unmet expectations of others, from others, and of oneself are talked about in the model. Satir continued to look at rules traced back to the family of origin that still tell the client how to behave and what to do, such as keeping secrets. Many of these rules no longer apply to the adult world, but still have deep roots within the person. Rules and expectations can be reframed and changed into new guidelines for a more positive self-concept. The client from the alcohol-abusive background can learn that it is okay to talk about the secrets and create a new way to express loneliness and shame.

Yearnings to be heard, understood, accepted, and loved are universal feelings that build self-worth. During this phase, the therapist attempts to find out when the person has felt heard and understood. The person who grew up in an alcoholic home may want to speak up for himself or herself and not feel ashamed. This process attempts to build the self-worth and nurture the person to live in the present. The last goal of yearning may be to no longer hold responsibility for keeping the secrets or for making the family happy.

Lastly, in the model, a new sense of self is created. New defined rules and discovering self-empowerment and worth are parts of creating a new self. In addition, choosing what to share becomes a choice within the person and is not associated with a shameful meaning. Moreover, a client can remove the blame, learn to deal with his or her past, and move forward with a more complete wholeness. Clients can start to see themselves as lovable, worthy, and apart from childhood experiences. They see themselves as not defined by the experiences and education from their past. People can experience intense feelings toward family members and transform them into acceptance and apply the feelings in other areas relevant to their lives in the present and future. Allowing clients to see icebergs from new perspectives allows for compassion and inner peace. In turn, this allows clients to feel connected within their own comfort level. Satir believed that every person is a growing human being, capable of making responsible choices, of achieving self-worth, and of accomplishing inner and outer congruence (Satir, 1983).

Therapist's Role

The process of change is further helped with the therapist's role as an encouraging resource tool for the family. The stages of change are usually set in motion when client(s) begins voluntary treatment.

Satir used to say, "The job of a therapist is to help people have stars in their eyes—to truly feel their own value" (Loeschen, 2002). She achieved this by sharing her view that people are a manifestation of the life force, which is sacred. Her belief was people are miracles and all are worthy of love, which led her to look beyond people's behavior and to connect to their pure spirit. People have inner resources to be tapped into to enable them to enhance their self-worth. She believed they had the capacity to imagine, to create, to explore, to perceive accurately, to feel, to express, to choose, to be courageous, and to be wise.

Therapists using this model connect with their clients and educate, support, and encourage them to make changes for themselves.

In most models, this is referred to as building rapport and relationships. While talking to clients, Satir built trust, made connections and observations, and processed with her clients. Without these elements, Satir felt that no change could occur. Satir said, "We need 4 hugs a day for survival. We need 8 hugs a day for maintenance. We need 12 hugs a day for growth" (BrainyQuote.com, n.d.). Satir went against the rule that hugging is intrusive and politically incorrect. For her, the goal was to create a new experience.

When people come to therapy, they want to talk with someone they can trust. In the Satir model, the therapist is kind and understanding, talking in a calm voice with a warm tone that creates trust. The environment is relaxed, with direct eye contact and humor being traits incorporated into a session.

Interventions

The following interventions are used in the Satir model, incorporating the genuineness of the therapist and the willingness of the family to find change within themselves.

Parts party: The parts party is an intervention that helps clients to identify, recognize, use, and transform their inner resources into a new and integrated self-worth (Satir et al., 1991).

Integration and self-acceptance are the goals. Parts refer to a person's different roles and resources in life (daughter, parent, teacher, wife, fear of criticism, desire, playfulness, etc.). The focus is on identifying all the parts of a person's resources, the present views of the parts (family rules, labels, and acceptance or disregard), and finding alternative ways of viewing the parts as strengths. The parts party is a five-step exercise in which the parts are identified and personified, and therapist and client work through a conflict through an integration ritual.

Family sculpting: This intervention involves each member of the family, positioning the family in a live portrait of how the family's dynamics and relationships are felt and perceived.

Each member of the family will present his or her perception at a time (Satir et al., 1991). For example, emotionally close members may be positioned standing close together with arms linked, and an emotionally distant member is placed across the room. A person who is perceived as powerful is represented standing on a chair. The communication stances in the sculptures demonstrates the sculptors' perception about how he or she experiences the others' communication. After the family is sculpted, each member shares his or her feelings and perceptions about the experience. The goal is to work toward congruent communication.

Family reconstruction: The family reconstruction is a larger and lengthy process that uses family sculpting. It usually includes 15 to 20 people playing various roles (roles of family members, resources, feelings, etc.). The process uses a detailed three-generational family map (Satir et al., 1991). Originally, family reconstruction followed a four-stage process, which included the following: (a) sculpting the family of origin, (b) sculpting the identified patient's parents' families of origin, (c) sculpting the relationship of the identified patient's parents, and (d) resculpting the identified patients' family of origin. The process promotes acceptance and validation of the self in the context of the three-generational family, helping the person to take responsibility for his or her life and choices. It helps clients perceive family members as real people, not simply as figures in stereotyped roles. Letting go of what no longer fits provides the freedom to make new choices and conclusions about the self and family (Gomori & Adaskin, 2008).

The family reconstruction process allows the person to identify, transform, and integrate strengths and resources.

Metaphors: Metaphors are a useful therapeutic tool that help engage the creative side of a person's thinking (Satir et al., 1991). They can be used throughout the process of therapy to address deeper issues without directly confronting a painful or stressful situation. By addressing an issue through a metaphor, the client tends to be more open to discussion and creative when identifying strengths.

Self-mandala: The self-mandala intervention requires at least eight other participants to represent the eight universal resources of the client (Satir et al., 1991). The client is in the center and he or she represents the "I." The client is asked to choose role players to play each resource. These role players are introduced to illustrate that we are born with them. To demonstrate this harmony at birth, each is connected with ropes to each other and to the star in a circle format. The next step is to make a sculpture based on the star's family-of-origin experiences, showing which resources will shine to the world, and which will be covered up, neglected, or hidden. To dramatize the intent further, those in hiding are covered up with a blanket, and those that are more recognized will walk clockwise and then counterclockwise. The covered-up resources are instructed to create as much chaos as possible under their cover. The purpose is to give the client a message that he or she wants to be seen and heard.

The constant movement and the tangled ropes create a situation in which everybody experiences some physical discomfort.

The client is asked to discuss his or her reactions, feelings, and observations throughout the process of things moving in harmony.

Through chaos, the ultimate purpose of this process is to get all the resources into the original harmonious situation. In the process, the client becomes aware, accepting and taking charge of each resource in the present.

The Satir model continues to flourish today, with a cyberspace community of followers and trainers who provide opportunities to learn the model all over the world. A recent evolution of the model is its possible association with emotionally focused therapy. In "Integrating Emotion-Focused Therapy With the Satir Model," author Lorri Bruebacher (2006) wrote of the helpfulness in combining the two models to give empirical credibility to Satir's model. The two models match in theory and in the passionate way they are delivered.

SATIR HUMAN VALIDATION PROCESS MODEL TEMPLATE

The *Satir model template* is meant to be used as a guideline to learning the process of Satir's human validation model of family therapy. The template provides the beginning therapist with steps to take and questions to ask that promote collaboration between the therapist and client. There are suggested questions under each heading to help start the process. After using the initial questions, guide the client through each process and ask questions that occur to you, as you stay within the parameters of the Satir model. Although there is no one "script" for any therapy session, it is the hope of the authors that the template serves as an impetus to learning this family therapy model.

Tools for Change

In the Satir model, the primary goal is to address a person's or family's self-worth, which is the most effective factor in changing behavior. The purpose of therapy is to help the person realize that these capacities of family and societal rules have often blocked resources and that adhering to these rules has lessened his or her self-worth (Loeschen, 2002).

The tools for the model have been discussed in this chapter in the "Interventions" section and include the following: family sculpture, family reconstruction, parts party, metaphors, and self- mandala. However, perhaps out of all the interventions, the most important tool is the relationship that the therapist builds with the family members by "being present" with the family and by connecting with them. The goal of therapy is for the client to become congruent (a state of internal and external harmony); the therapist must show this from the beginning.

Phase 1: Joining and Building Rapport

The manner in which the therapist makes the initial contact with the client is most important. Creating a safe, nurturing environment conveys respect and reverence for people, which emphasizes each person's uniqueness in the therapy room. The therapist will want to "establish an atmosphere that encourages hopefulness and goodwill" (Satir, 1983).

Reaching out: One way the therapist accomplishes this is by reaching out and offering to shake hands. Touch is a basic human need and was used extensively by Satir as a way of connecting.

Attending: In addition, the therapist should take time to learn each client's name as a unique person who has value.

Mirroring: The therapist reaches out with his or her attitude, touch, and proximity to the client. He or she mirrors the body language of the client, leaning in when the client leans in, and so forth. He or she meets each client or member of the family face to face, and gives each his or her full attention. Through his or her whole being, his or her eyes, voice, and touch, he or she expresses his or her belief in the client's value.

Observing: The therapist can closely observe the client for any body cues, which reflect the client's feelings and interactional pattern (Loeschen, 2002).

Questions that might be asked of each person as part of the therapeutic process are as follows (Satir, 1983):

- *"What brings you here today?"*
- *"What would you like to look at today?"*
- *"What are we going to work on today?"*
- *"What do you expect will happen here?"*
- *"I would like to hear from each of you, what do you hope to have happen here today?"*

Most clients want to share what is wrong with them or with some other members of the family. It is important that the client be allowed to express his or her story. "What the Satir model encourages is to keep the story short and use it as part of the context within which to do therapy" (Banmen, 2002).

Phase 2: Understanding the Presenting Issue

In the Satir model, *the problem is not the problem, but coping is the problem.* The therapist seeks to emphasize the process of coping rather than trying to solve specific problems. The task is to help the client learn effective ways of coping in order to decide to do the things that work for him or her in a more creative way with the other members of his or her family. The therapist will not seek to eradicate the symptoms. Instead, the therapist searches for ways to develop health in the client. The addition of developing healthy ways of coping in the client(s) will cause symptoms to disintegrate.

Most of the following questions Satir used in sessions were taken from Loeschen (2002):

- *"I can really appreciate the way the two of you have tried to resolve this."*
- *"I can really appreciate the many different ways this family has tried to cope."*
- *"Making mistakes is wonderful because we can look at them and learn and grow."*
- *"Everyone in this family has been doing their very best."*
- *"Did you know that you could have that much impact on someone?"*
- *"You both had the best of intentions for your marriage."*
- *"You are each wonderful, unique people with different perspectives. I'm wondering how you see the situation."*
- *"I see lots of new possibilities for this family as you learn how to be with each other in different way."*
- *"What right at this moment would make life better for you if it could happen, living in this family?"* (Andreas, 1991)
- *"I see that each of you has inside pain that is coming out in the relationship in hurtful ways."* (Loeschen, 2002)

Phase 3: Assessment of Family Dynamics

When assessing family dynamics, the therapist does not focus on behaviors; instead, the therapist will pay attention to clients' perceptions, feelings, expectations, and yearnings. It is during this phase that a therapist may use family sculpture.

The therapist assesses the family by using the three-generational perspective that reveals to the client(s) how family learning took place with their parents and grandparents. This helps them to appreciate their childhood learning, not pass judgment on themselves and their families, and to use this to perspective as a system of coping (Satir et al., 1991).

The therapist takes a thorough history of the three generations, called "mapping," which is a type of genogram (see Chapter 1). The history will include not only factual data and experiential data, but also perceptional data about the past and the present family members.

The therapist will ask questions that stimulate hope and communicate to the client, "*I know what to ask. I take responsibility for understanding you. We are going to go somewhere.*" The therapist is the leader of the therapy session. Some questions and comments Satir used to communicate to the client, taken from Loeschen (2002), are as follows:

- *"Give me some adjectives that would describe your grandmother's personality. How do you feel about these characteristics, positively or negatively?"*
- *"What would your mother have said about money?"*
- *"Were there others outside of your family who were influential in your growing up?"*
- *"How did your parents have fun? How do you have fun?"*
- *"We learn to deal with conflict from our models, let's take a look back at your models, and see what we can learn."*
- *"There are always choices, so let's look at yours in this situation."*
- *"Joey, can you give me a picture of how you see your brother and dad getting along?"*
- *"How are you talking to yourself right now that is making you feel bad about yourself?"*
- *"Are you aware that you really don't have this to say to your mother, but to your image of your mother?"*
- *"Is it true that you must always be nice? Are there times when it would be okay to be other than nice?"*
- *"Do you really think that if you tell your wife what's going on for you, she will disintegrate?"*

Phase 4: Goals

The goals of the Satir model are for the client family to learn to find acceptance of self and cope in the best way possible. Therapists using the Satir model have the role of educator, teaching clients how to perceive, respond, and act more effectively when communicating and behaving in their relationships. The therapist will ask himself or herself, "What can I add to this person's life so he won't want to do the problem behaviors anymore?" (Andreas, 1991). The therapist will therefore set goals addressing the whole person and the family. The goals will include working with feelings, perceptions, expectations, yearnings, and goals for coping. The following are some questions and/or comments that could be used by the therapist:

- *"Are you willing to work on achieving that goal?"* (Banmen, 2002)
- *"Now that you are an adult and have other resources, are you willing to let go of the expectation that your mother be supportive of you, since she has not been able to do that? Who would be able to be there for you?"* (Loeschen, 2002)
- *"Who in your current life is capable of nurturing you?"* (Loeschen, 2002)
- *"Use 'I' instead of 'we,' speak for yourself."* (Loeschen, 2002)
- *"You are saying that you want more involvement from your husband. What does more involvement mean to you?"* (Loeschen, 2002)

Phase 5: Amplifying Change

After the clients begin to experience some of the meta-goals of higher self-esteem, such as becoming better choice makers and being more responsible and congruent, the therapist will reinforce these changes by using, among other techniques, anchoring and imagery. The therapist will give homework that is designed to practice the changes that were worked on during the counseling session. This homework is internally focused rather than behavioral, for example, monitoring one's feelings or tracking one's expectations. The therapist could use some of the following comments or questions by Satir, taken from Loeschen (2002), that demonstrate ways to reinforce:

- *"How wonderful that you two can now be with each other in this new way."*
- *"It's marvelous that you could say this to your parents. Now they have new information for understanding you."*
- *"How do you feel at this moment, seeing new possibilities for your family?"*
- *"I'm wondering if the two of you would be willing to close your eyes and see yourself being this new way with each other the next time you encounter a difference?"*
- *"You look like you have been having strong feelings while your wife was talking. Can you put words to them?"*
- *"What would you like to say to your mother as you see her position in this sculpt?"*

Phase 6: Termination

Therapists using the Satir model will understand that each session is unique, and the work is never totally finished because people will always continue growing. The following are some of the criteria a therapist can use for terminating treatment using the Satir model (Banmen, 2002):

- *When family members can complete transactions, check, and ask them:*
- *Can they interpret hostility, see how others see them and how they see themselves?*
- *Can they share hopes, fears, and expectations from another member?*
- *Can they disagree, make choices, and learn through practice?*
- *Can they free themselves from harmful effects of past models?*
- *Can they be congruent?*

MARIA GOMORI

Maria Gomori, BA, MSW, DipC, PhD, was born in Budapest, Hungary, in 1920. She is a survivor of the Nazi Holocaust and the succeeding occupation by the Red Army. She immigrated to Canada in 1957 and shortly began her advanced academic growth and has never stopped learning since.

She is a retired associate professor of the University of Manitoba and a tireless advocate of the Satir method in family therapy. In 1991, she founded the Satir Institute in Winnipeg, Canada, and is recognized as the foremost living proponent of the Satir method for family therapy in the world.

She is an approved supervisor with the American Association of Marriage and Family Therapy. In her long career, she has participated in workshops and interacted with some of the premier names in the field, such as Milton Erickson, C. Whitaker, S. Minuchin, Elisabeth Kübler-Ross, and Yetta Bernhard, to name a few.

Gomori, now a nonagenarian, first met Virginia Satir in 1969. She worked with Satir for more than 20 years and has been an advanced trainer in Satir's Avanta International Training Organization since 1981. After Satir's death in 1988, Gomori continued to expand the influence of the Satir method all over the globe. She has established an international reputation as a workshop leader—teaching, demonstrating, and applying her interpretation of the Satir model. She has conducted workshops throughout Canada, the United States, Europe, South America, Thailand, and Australia. Currently, she continues her work in China, Hong Kong, Taiwan, and annually at The Haven on Gabriola Island, British Columbia, as she has for the past 27 years.

She coauthored with Satir The Satir Approach to Communication *and* The Satir Model Family Therapy and Beyond. *Her autobiography,* Passion for Freedom, *was published in 2002. Her recent book,* Personal Alchemy, The Art of Family Reconstruction, *with Eleanor Adaskin, was published in 2008.*

Having been not only a colleague of Satir's and a gifted practitioner in the field, but also a trusted, close friend for 20 years, Gomori is uniquely prepared to "speak" for the Satir method.

What attracted you to the Satir method for family therapy?

I just finished my master's degree in social work and I never ever heard anything like what I was reading in this book, working with more than one person and working with a family. I didn't understand it, but I got the feeling that I wanted to know more about this. That was my first encounter. I wanted to learn more. Then I met Virginia in a 5-day workshop 1 year later. After this workshop, I worshiped Satir. All was magic, and the magic was that these people have changed in front of my eyes and it was experiential, which is very typical of this model. I never saw sculpting. All kinds of things happened experientially to people so that they could make some new choices. At first, I did not understand what was happening, and for me it was magic. I told Virginia, at the end of the fifth day, "I feel this is magic, and only you can do it." She said, "Oh, I hope not because I'm teaching it, and my hope is that people find their own magic. The magic is in everybody and that is my work. To help people find their magic." I really got passionate about this concept, and I wanted to learn more. I followed Virginia until she died because I wanted to learn her process. Now I know the magic can be learned. But really, what attracted me, most importantly, was the humanness of this approach, the belief system on which it is based, which is very, very human, and loving and caring, and full of hope. The universality of the model means that I can teach it to everybody in the world, and it relates to people in a universal way, regardless of culture, race, color, or religion. It is experiential. I am very visual, and I had many experiences myself in my life. I felt very much connected in many ways to this model. Maybe that gives you an idea about what attracted me. Most importantly, I am and I was attracted to the person, Virginia, who she was as a human being.

She was not only teaching this model, she was living it. I never experienced anything like that from any of my teachers before.

How do you formulate your view of a family when they enter therapy?

Your second question, "How do you formulate your view of a family when they enter therapy?", is why I sent you copies of the handout pages that I give to my students. It is an outline of how I am teaching people. It is about the transformation process. You get an outline of the basic elements in the Satir model. When I make an assessment of a family, I keep in mind many elements of the process.

First of all, I make contact with every person. I observe each person's communication, level of self-esteem, their communication with each other, the family rules, each person's yearnings, feelings, and expectation. As soon as possible, I encourage them to talk to each other. When I feel a level of trust developed, I move into sculpting, sharing with them my picture and observation about the dynamics in the family.

- *Communication*

It is my goal to change incongruent communication to congruent communication in the family system. It is communication that holds the system together and holds relationships together. There is a whole model of communication that Virginia developed of how people communicate under stress. She noticed that when people are under stress that they protect themselves in four major ways: by placating, blaming, super reasonable, or irrelevant. She also added the body position that shows how people feel when using these ways of communication. You can read details about this in Virginia's book, *The New Peoplemaking*, or in the *The Satir Model*. The purpose is to teach and encourage congruent communication in a family system. Congruent communication is connecting and an opportunity for intimacy. I do not have to protect myself, I can share myself with the other person, and I can share my vulnerabilities. If people can relate to people in this way, they will not have any problems in the family system. We try to help people to change their communication, to have them more connected, to feel freer and whole with high self-esteem.

- *Self-esteem*

Low self-esteem leads to incongruent communication. If I feel I'm not of value, I'm going to protect myself and blame you or control you or placate you. Therefore, if I can help people to go from low self-esteem to high self-esteem, their communication will also change.

- *The family is a system*

If we look at the family system and it is closed, it is reluctant to change—it is very much defining the environment as a dangerous place. We hope to change a dysfunctional, chaotic family life to a more functional and harmonious family life.

- *Changing rigid and inhuman rules into guidelines and boundaries*

This is a very short summary of what we look for when I see a family and how I assess a family. I do not ask what the problem is. It is a basic principle in the Satir model not to ask, "What is the problem?" Never ask what the problem is. You can look at any DVD or video [t]hat Satir did, and she would never ask what the problem is. She would ask what they want to change. People already know what the problem is and what they want to change . . . This also indicates that the therapist believes that change is possible, creates hope.

It is accurately experiential. We believe that people need the experience in the present, in their bodies, to really understand what they are doing, how they are protecting themselves, and how they would like to be different. Your body tells you, and the experience is very important. Therefore, we create experiences. When I change internally, it will affect my interactions and relationships. If my relationship changes, that has an affect on me internally.

- *We look for intrapsychic change as well as interactive change*

Now, what is really important is that we focus on the positive health. We do not focus on the pathology. We do not focus on the problem or the traumatic event. The problem is not the problem. The coping is the problem. We help to access the resources that people have. The basic belief is that everybody has the same resources and life energy. The therapist who believes it, will have this energy shine from her. If you don't believe it, don't say it. It is not a technique, it is the energy between the therapist and the clients that creates that magic healing connection.

- *The congruence of the therapist*

We can help people to find their own resources and to make choices for themselves. A most important ingredient is the congruent self of the therapist. The therapist is the most important tool in the therapeutic process.

Before we go on to question number three, I will give you an example about coping. Five couples may have the same problem. The first-born child has, let us say, [Down syndrome]. The problem is the same, so the coping will be related to each couple's values, ideas about themselves, about the child, beliefs, and all that. So some keep [such children] at home, some send them away, some don't even want to feed them. So it's not the problem, it's the coping. The coping has to do with the whole internal process. How I cope is the important thing because we never live without our problems. The coping has to do with how we are using our resources. So a lot of family therapy is education. Satir believed that this is an educational process—teaching people how to live differently and give them hope and the tools that they can do it. We provide them experience, a process to change. I show them my picture, using the communication stances, and then I got each person to show me their picture in sculpting: like how far or how close they are, how they are seen by each person. They learn how each person perceives the other person. Then I say, okay let's talk to each other about it, and they learn a lot about each other's perception—about each other. Of course, every family who comes in for help, they want to change things, and they want to be congruent, and they want to be connected. This is such a basic idea and it is true. I helped many, many families in many countries. I ask them what they want. What the desired outcome would be, and they all stand up and create a circle and look at each other and feel connected. They all want to be connected. But they carry all the learnings and rules from their family of origin, how and what to do or not to do, how to communicate or how not to communicate, and how to protect themselves. To be connected is the yearning. So we give them an experience on how to connect differently, but we don't tell them what to do or how it should look. They have to figure it out. I don't tell them what to do. I just tell them what I see. They tell me what they see and then they decide what they want. I truly don't give advice. It is not the traditional approach that I learned in the school of social work. I should know better what their life should be. I should assess and set their goals for them because I know better what their life should be. That is how I learned it. I have to make an assessment and set the goal for their life.

What kinds of families do you think benefit most from the experiential approach?
Well, I think all kinds of families. The model is not problem or symptom focused. Therefore, we are not saying, "Do this in families with alcohol problems, or do this with mental health problems, or this for anorexia, or this for violence," etc. The symptom is only a message that the energy is blocked in all those five or six areas. So we are not treating the symptom, we are treating what is behind the symptom. Therefore, it works with all families. "What kinds of families" is irrelevant to our approach. It works in all families and in all cultures. It is universal.

What issues do you think this model works best with?
We work with all issues because the issue is not the focus of our attention. The issue is on the surface, the signal of the inner energy block. If you tell me a problem that we cannot work with, I will be willing to take it back. I have done family therapy in many countries, and it was only my limitation if it did not work. It was not the process. I absolutely believe in the process because the process works. Treat it as your magic. I always tell my students to know that the process is magic. It is my belief that the energy between the family and me is that works.

In your opinion, what are the necessary characteristics that a therapist should possess to be effective with this model?
That is a very important question. Who can be a therapist? A therapist has to, first of all, clear their own "stuff." We have to do our own family reconstruction—as much as we can, because we can never clear our own "stuff" totally. This is a process Satir developed—a transformational, mutigenerational process for change. As much as I can, I have to know about my family of origin, my limitations, my feelings, my biases, my relationship to my parents, and my level of caring for other people. In every family situation in front of you, you will meet your own parents and your own issues.

Satir believed that the therapist is the center of the whole process. The family is like an orchestra. We are asked to be the conductor, but the family is really the conductor of this whole symphony that we have in front of ourselves. So we are together with the family, conducting this symphony and playing the music. The therapist is just holding the hands of the people there to help them to figure out a different way of living. In a metaphor, they are learning to play different music, and they can do it, too. They can change. It's important for me, first of all, to hear their music, and then for them to change their music. I tell them what I believe. I tell them what I see. I am not just nice.

I can also be very tough. If I believe in the possibility of change and they believe in it, then they can change. I know that my congruence is modeling for the family what I am trying to teach them.

The therapist can only be helpful if she believes in herself. Therapy is a teaching and healing process between therapist and the patient. Building a relationship is the first step. Traditionally, and even now, many therapists use power and control. In this model, I feel that I have a lot of power, but it is my congruence that is my power. I model what I teach. I do say what I see and what I think. I don't say that you <u>have</u> to change. This is what I see—the reality of it. You can destroy your child's future, that is up to you. The meeting becomes really a joint process. I think a lot of empowering goes on when I show respect for the other person. I can empower them to believe in themselves. I learned that from Satir. She demonstrated empowerment and congruence all times.

At first, I was thinking that Satir had a magical gift. There would be 800 people in a room, and somebody would come up and share an issue that was almost shocking, and in 10 minutes, that person would change. I said, "Well, what was going on? What was the magic you performed?" She said, "Nothing. I just looked at that person and connected and said what I wanted to say and that person felt my energy." We all have that magic in us; we can share ourselves with another person. The most important thing is congruence. This was one of the cornerstones of Virginia's teachings. To be congruent meant I don't play games. To give you an example of her definition of congruence, she might say: "I feel down or I feel depressed. I feel it. I am aware of it. I acknowledge it. I accept, I look and sound like it. I own it, and if I decide to share it with you, I will tell you." That is high self-esteem. I don't pretend, or hide, or cover up when I am aware of what is going on with me.

How often does the client see you and for how long a period of time?

Well, we have an idea that this is an educational process and they, the family, have to do the work, not me or not us, not the therapist. We have a contract. I will see you four times. After four times, we will evaluate where you are and I will give you homework. I will see how it goes. That gives them an idea that change is possible and that they have to work on it. We do evaluate after four times and, maybe, we will have a few more sessions, but if nothing has changed, then we will deal with that. Maybe we are the wrong people to work with you. If nothing has changed, there is some other reason, and usually, that is reluctance for change. Usually, then we say, "Okay, this is the end of our relationship unless you tell us what really goes on." Resistance is always related to some fear, self-protection. We do not use the concept of resistance. It is a protection—self-protection. They do not want to change. They are afraid of it, or there is something more than we know about. I usually don't see people more often than two or three times. They have learned a lot. Then I say, "Let me know if there is a new issue." Some people may phone 6 months later, something is happening in their life, and they need to talk more. It is an ongoing process, but it's not like, "I'm going to see you every week for the next 6 months."

What are you looking for when you are in the session?

I'm looking for those things that we mentioned—communication, self-esteem, family rules change, system, and productivity. So, I'm not looking for the problem.

What is the assessment process of this model?

I'm looking to develop trust and safety when making contact by connecting with each person and by connecting the family members with each other. I use self-disclosure when appropriate. I don't take sides and give equal time to each person. I'm curious and nonjudgmental. Then I find out what each person wants by using the iceberg. Satir used the iceberg metaphor to describe people's inner experience: "Like icebergs we show only parts of ourselves. Much of us lies below the surface" (Satir et al., 1991, p. 34). Some of the process tools used in assessment is family origin background when it fits the circumstance, and I look for the positive resources in the family. (The previous is scripted from Maria's workshop document titled tools.) A very useful tool in assessment is sculpting, you see that sculpting not only helps the family, it helps the therapist a lot. In sculpting, we actually make body pictures of how close people are, so we put them in distance from each other. If somebody is very powerful, we put them on a chair. In sculpting, we use communication stances in expressing or showing whenever somebody is placating or blaming. So sculpting shows everything: power, distance, relationships, and communication. In the sculpting, I see everything, and they see everything.

Who sets the goals, the client or the therapist?

We can only talk about meta-goals, and we have already discussed them. All the rest is to work on these with the particular family system. They will make the choices. Who sets the goals? We are not talking about goals, but the nature of the process sets the goals together. They set the goals. They decide. So let's imagine that a family comes in where the relationship issue between the husband and wife and one says, "I want to divorce." They will have to decide what they are going to do. I cannot decide. Usually, they want me to be the judge. I say, "I'm not the judge; I'm not here [to] tell you what to do. You discuss it." I ask the wife to show (sculpt) me how she feels with him, [and] through the sculpt[ure] she shows the picture. She feels very small, makes herself very small physically, makes him very big and tall, and puts him on the chair. There is a powerful distance between them in this sculpt. He suddenly sees something that he has never seen before, and then he shows his picture and his picture is almost the same. He thinks that he is nothing and she is everything. It's amazing. Then I ask him how it was between him and his father, and her and her father and mother, and it goes back, back, back— old learnings. They decide what they want to do with their own life. I don't think anybody else can tell them. I think that is wrong.

The meta-goal is to help them to go inside, to learn to know themselves first, then to share and connect on a deeper level. To learn to be responsible to make their choices and to value the self and the other person. They even can separate in this way of being open, honest, and vulnerable way. And even if they separate, they can do it in a peaceful way. They may find out that they never really connected.

What are some of the commonly used interventions with this model?

As outlined in the family therapy Satir model of healthy interventions, we strive for people to be congruent and constructive in communication, develop high self-validating self-esteem, [have] flexible human boundaries and guidelines in the family rules, [be] open to and welcoming change, have or maintain an open and flexible family system, and remain stable and grounded.

What role does a homework assignment have in this model?
Homework is very important. Usually, there is a communication issue, so we give them homework. Homework is always something that they are already learning in the session. Never give homework that they do not know how to do. We don't want them to fail; we want them to fully engage in a certain way, maybe for 20 minutes a day, or whatever they can do. We give them homework every time so that they go away with some things that they already learned and they can practice.

How do you know when your client is ready to terminate?
Well, I don't know—they know. I do not have to talk about termination because right at the beginning, we decided that we would reevaluate after four times. There is never a termination because we have a relationship and they think at any time [they] want to come back, [they can] let us know. So it's a process. We never terminate. You see the idea is that their growth is ongoing, so there is never termination in this process.

What have you found to be the limitations of this approach?
Only myself. I can be a limitation if I am not open enough, congruent enough, knowing enough, sharing enough. Limitation can be if I don't feel good, then I better cancel my session. This [is] not a job to do. This is being with these people. This model has to be lived and demonstrated.

What suggestions do you have for students?
This is my suggestion. Learn who you are, who you want to be, and sharing your being with your clients. Learn as much as you can and develop your own style of therapy that fits you.

Is there anything you would like to add?
You need to read Virginia's (1988) book, *The New Peoplemaking*.

Case Study

A mother calls and makes an appointment for her family to come to therapy. The family consists of the wife and her husband, both in their 40s; their 15-year-old son; a college-aged daughter; and the woman's father, age 82. Three years after the woman's mother died, her father developed Alzheimer's disease. He moved in with the family 6 months ago. When his health began to deteriorate, the woman spent more time caring for him than for other members of the family. Three months ago, the 15-year-old son, who has been treated for attention deficit hyperactivity disorder since age 7, began to refuse to take his medication and is now being truant from school.

During the session, the wife cries and the husband reports that their relationship is strained, occasionally rolling his eyes as his wife becomes tearful. He reports that he has had to take on more work because his wife had to quit her job to attend to her father's needs. The daughter is away at college and the wife smiles as she describes her as a straight-A student. The daughter was asked to attend the session but refused because she has a hard time with her grandfather's illness and dislikes the conflict that has developed at home.

Dr. Maria Gomori's Response to the Case Study

Now, because of all I have told you and the need to be with a family first, it is very hard for me to talk about your case. I have no preconceived idea about what is going to happen. It's a very interesting case, and I can have assumptions. One of the assumptions is that Papa [is] moving into the family system and that can cause anxiety, chaos, problems, and probably not communicating enough. They probably did not communicate about this change, and they did not share their feelings to begin with. The wife spends too much time with Papa and so everything falls apart. Of course, there is definitely tension in the air, but probably this family system was functioning already before Papa's arrival in a dysfunctional way when he was well, then his moving in wouldn't cause all these problems, they only intensified the situation. In a healthy family system of four people, where people can talk openly with each other and they know each other and are not afraid to say what they want to say, this issue would be handled with less stress, more loving and caring, some discomfort, and different coping. They say Papa needs help, but probably the husband was reluctant to say [that] this might be too much for the family to handle. If they had a rule that they have to live with him under these circumstances, then they could have looked at the rule and how it fits to their life now. I don't know how they discussed it. My first question would be how did it happen? How did they get into this situation? How was life before in this family?

In this system, there was already an identified patient in the system. The young man had [attention deficit hyperactivity disorder] and was probably just another symptom. This was a signal early on that something was not okay in this whole system. So I would like to know how did it happen. How do things happen? It sounds also like the girl is the perfect one. So there is one child that is perfect and one child who is less than perfect. I have lot of questions in mind as I read this, and it would be very interesting to figure it out. So, I would insist that everyone comes in, including the Alzheimer's patient. Because I want to see who sits where and how the mama will look after him and what her body messages are. In communication, we not only observe what people say, but what the nonverbal says is more important. What are the relationships in this family? It is very interesting that the girl does not want to come in. With her absence, she had a lot of control. That's my assessment. I would be very curious about it. I would try to set it up so that she has to come in. If she cannot, or if she will not, then that shows something. That she has all the power in this family. Mama and Papa cannot tell her what to do. Anyway, she's the perfect one. She doesn't like the conflict, but she doesn't want to help the conflict. I might even phone her and say, "If you don't like the conflict, you better come in and help it."

One thing is that we usually insist that the whole family should be there. If someone doesn't want to, then that's already a symptom. We look at family system as energy. So you look at the symptom as a signal that something is stuck in the system. The "stuckness" is, should [Papa] live there and how to deal with the Alzheimer's, which is a very difficult illness to deal with. So he does need perfect and total attention. It is at the price of the whole family system so these are the issues to discuss. How does everybody feel? What does the father have to do to accept that? What does the mother have to do to somehow share her time equally with the family? Why is [Papa] with the family? Why is he not in a nursing home situation? There is the whole other issue about family values and family origin learnings. Maybe she feels obliged that she has to take care of her father at the expense of herself. But if she can put words to it and talk with her husband, then it puts a whole different human value to it, rather than just neglecting him. Situations can change on the level of feelings and understanding. So I would talk to her or them—about everything. About how it affected everybody so that everybody could share their feelings and perception. So the first thing in a family interview, we ask everybody equally, giving equal time to everybody, making contact with everybody. The therapist has to make contact with every single member in the family, not just one or two. This is something we have to work a lot to teach our students. Because usually moving from individual therapy to family therapy, it's very easy just to focus on the individuals in the family. Maybe I would ask, first of all, the father, because it seems to me that he's the loser here, what he wants to change. And I don't know if he would change, maybe he would change and wants Papa to move out. Maybe he would say he would like more attention. Whatever he says, I would ask the wife whether she knew this is what he wants. I would give them time to discuss this together. Then I would ask the wife what she wants. Ask the boy what he wants. Ask the Papa, if he can talk. But I would include him because I want to know in what condition he is. So I find out what everybody wants and, hopefully, I can ask the questions in a way that everybody else finds out what everybody else wants in the family and their conflicts to[o]. There are possible conflicts. Maybe the husband wants him out and Mama wants him in. That is a difficult situation. But getting Papa out of the house is not the issue. The issue is how they cope with Papa in the house. I would focus on that first. If they can see that they need, instead of focusing on the conflict, to focus on the resources they have. They have resources. They can have external resources if they have money. So I cannot tell you what I would do because it is a process I would start so that the family starts dealing and coping differently. This is a whole approach that I'm talking about, which is different from some other approaches and somewhat similar. It is experiential and human. We focus really on self-esteem, on congruence, on connections, and helping everybody to be a grown-up, to be choice makers, and be responsible. So these are the goals for everybody to obtain when you are a family or a group. The rest is falling into their place because they have to decide. The contents are unique in every family but the process is the same.

KEY TERMS

Battle for initiative   A stage in the therapeutic process where the responsibility of the sessions shifts to the family.

Battle for structure   A stage in therapy, usually in the beginning, where the therapists actively interview the family and set the rules for the sessions.

Blamer   A person who blames others for everything that goes wrong. This person never takes responsibility for his or her choices. A blamer respects the context and himself or herself but disrespects others.

Blaming stance   A form of communication whereby the person discredits others' feelings and focuses only on expressing his or her own needs. This is one of the communication patterns in the Satir model.

Closed system   Described by Satir's model as having poor communication patterns, inflexible rules, and growth-inhibiting patterns.

Communication   The internal and external change of interactions between people.

Confusion   A concept used to disrupt existing patterns and open an infrastructure to respond and adapt in new ways to a situation.

Congruence   This is a form of communication that is clear, direct, and uses awareness of personal and others' needs. Congruent communication is considered the healthiest form of communication.

Craziness   A concept that uses non sequitur, irrelevant, and paradoxical thoughts that can be used as an intervention in therapy.

Deviation amplification   A therapeutic intervention that takes a client's issue and pushes it to an unrealistic realm where the client can begin to lose fear through confusion.

Dialect   A concept in different types of language and pattern of linguistics.

Dichotomy   A division usually with a clear boundary.

Distracter   A person who pretends not to understand, changes the subject, and may be seen as a clown. This person does not respect himself or herself, others, or the context.

Double entendre   A therapeutic intervention that gives a word or group of words sending a double message with a covert message.

Dysfunction   A term used to describe a person that is stuck in the growth process and acting outside of society's standard norms.

Family sculpting   An action-oriented intervention using body postures and spacing as a demonstration of the family's patterns of communication, especially when the family is under stress. By making the covert patterns overt and visible, and the abstract concrete, it is a powerful kinesthetic and visual process for illustrating family dynamics to family members and learners of family therapy.

Fantasy   A concept that allows people to communicate symbolically and explore meanings without being distracted by factual occurrences that inhibit growth.

Fusion   A concept that a relationship is enmeshed to the point of unclear or no boundaries between the I-ness and we-ness.

Growth   The process of moving from the stage of comfort through the fear of change by becoming self-aware and challenged.

Infrastructure   The underlying framework of a family or system.

Intervention   A therapeutic tool used to initiate change in a system.

Interview   The process of the therapist asking questions of the family to gain knowledge into values, relationships, and descriptions of the problem as presented by the family.

Intuition   The unconscious ability of people to perceive insight to truth through an illogical process without using practical reasoning skills.

Irrelevant stance   A form of communication where the person is in constant movement in the conversation to avoid addressing the topic. Often identified as the class clown or person that makes random statements to get people off topic.

Metalearning   A deeper level of learning often through types of linguistics and symbols.

Metaphorical   A concept of incorporating metaphors in session that can be used as a therapeutic intervention to address underlying issues without confronting the family.

Nurturing triad   A family unit that consists of two parents and child in which every member is nurtured.

Open system   A family system described by the Satir model as having high self-esteem, flexible rules, nurturing qualities, and growth-seeking interactions.

Parallel play   A therapeutic intervention where the therapist plays alongside a family to view the system until invited to play with the family.

Parts party   A therapeutic intervention used with the Satir model to help identify, transform, and integrate the eight internal resources.

Pathology   A deviation from a healthy and normal development throughout life.

Personhood   The internal characteristics and strengths of a therapist that help create individualistic and human styles and presentation in treatment.

Placator   A person who accepts responsibility for anything that goes wrong, even if it was not his or her fault to make everyone happy, ignoring his or her own feelings. This person respects context and others, but disrespects and discounts himself or herself.

Satir human validation process model   A growth-oriented experiential model of therapy that is present focused and addresses helping people to identify the eight universal internal resources, improve communication patterns, increase self-worth, and growth oriented.

Self-esteem   The ability to connect and experience validating oneself, which includes a sense of self-confidence, self-acceptance, and empowerment.

Self-mandala   An intervention used in the Satir model to help a client integrate all eight internal resources and use them in a harmonious way.

Self-mandala   The wholeness of a person, which includes the person's physical, sensual, nutritional, intellectual, emotional, interactional, contextual, and spiritual resources in order to create and maintain harmony within one's self and with others.

Semiotics   The study of signs and symbols in the communication process.

Spontaneity   A concept that is rooted in the unconscious that allows quick natural impulses to be expressed that are inspired by insight to help instigate change in a therapeutic relationship.

Storytelling   An intervention that is used to address an issue with a client without seeming confrontational. The process allows the client to choose to discuss the issue or disregard the story.

Super-reasonable stance   A communication pattern of a person using a pure objective stance without regarding personal feelings and feelings of others.

Survival stance   The way we protect ourselves from the nonverbal and verbal threats that are real and perceived.

Symbolic experience   An experience that occurred when a person did not fully understand or see what was happening but influences his or her way of life today.

Therapeutic psychosis   The concept that therapy induces a sense of confusion in clients and is surrounded by the caring of the therapist to help produce change.

Three-generational family reconstruction process   Developed by Virginia Satir, this process is one of her major vehicles for change. It is a transformational process, leading to a shift inside a person that provides freedom to make new choices. It offers an opportunity for the reintegration of a person into the family of origin as an adult, and a way to find out who he or she can be (Gomori & Adaskin, 2008).

Trial of labor   A stage in the therapeutic process where the underlying pain of the family is exposed and discussed.

Unconscious   A part of a person's psyche that the person lacks awareness of, but can influence a person's reactions and behaviors.

Understructure   The foundation of the therapist and client relationship.

REFERENCES

Andreas, S. (1991). *Virginia Satir: The patterns of her magic*. Palo Alto, CA: Science and Behavior Books.

Baldwin, M., & Satir, V. (Eds.). (1987). *The use of self in therapy*. New York, NY: Haworth Press.

Banmen, J. (2002). The Satir model: Yesterday and today. *Contemporary Family Therapy: An International Journal, 24*(1), 7–22.

Banmen, J. (2009). Satir model developmental phases. *Satir Journal, 3*(1), 14–19.

BrainyQuote.com. (n.d.). Virginia Satir quotes. Retrieved from http://www.brainyquote.com/quotes/quotes/v/virginiasa175185.html

Bruebacher, L. (2006). Integrating emotion-focused therapy with the Satir model. *Journal of Marital and Family Therapy, 32*, 141–153.

Carr, A. (2010). Ten research questions for family therapy. *Australian & New Zealand Journal of Family Therapy, 31*(2),119–132.

Derlega, V. J., Griffin, J. L., Krowinski, A. C., & Lewis, R. J. (2003). Stressors for gay men and lesbians: Life stress, gay-related stress, stigma consciousness, and depressive symptoms. *Journal of Social & Clinical Psychology, 22*(6), 716–729.

Fingerhut, A. W., Gable, S. L., & Peplau, L. A. (2010). Identity, minority stress and psychological well-being among gay men and lesbians. *Psychology & Sexuality, 1*(2), 101–114.

Gomori, M., & Adaskin, E. (2008). *Personal alchemy: The art of Satir family reconstruction* (T. Macklin, Ed.). Hong Kong: The Hong Kong Satir Center for Human Development.

LaSala, M. C. (2007). Old maps, new territory: Family therapy theory and gay and lesbian couples. *Journal of GLBT Family Studies, 3*(1), 1–14.

Loeschen, S. (2002). *The Satir process practical skills for therapists*. Fountain Valley, CA: Halcyon Publishing Design.

McKinney, C., & Negy, C. (2006). Application of feminist therapy: Promoting resiliency among lesbian and gay families. *Journal of Feminist Family Therapy, 18*(1/2), 67–83.

Metz, M. E., Rosser, B. R., & Strapko, N. (1994). Differences in conflict-resolution styles among heterosexual, gay, and lesbian couples. *Journal of Sex Research, 31*(4), 293–308.

Rowen, C. J., & Malcolm, J. P. (2002). Correlates of internalized homophobia and homosexual identity formation in a sample of gay men. *Journal of Homosexuality, 43*(2), 77–92.

Satir, V. (1976). *Making contact*. Berkeley, CA: Celestial Arts.

Satir, V. (1983). *Conjoint family therapy*. Palo Alto, CA: Science and Behavior Books.

Satir, V. (1988). *The new peoplemaking*. Palo Alto, CA: Science and Behavior Books.

Satir, V., Banmen, J., Gerber, J., & Gomori, M. (1991). *The Satir model: Family therapy and beyond*. Palo Alto, CA: Science and Behavior Books.

Satir, V. M., & Bitter, J. R. (2000). The therapist and family therapy: Satir's human validation process model. In A. M. Horne (Ed.), *Family therapy and counseling* (3rd ed., pp. 62–101). Itasca, IL: F. E. Peacock.

Spitalnick, J., & McNair, L. (2005). Couples therapy with gay and lesbian clients: An analysis of important clinical issues. *Journal of Sex & Marital Therapy, 31*(1), 43–56.

Telford, L. (2004). Therapy with lesbian couples. *Australian & New Zealand Journal of Family Therapy, 25*(3), 141–147.

RECOMMENDED READING LIST

Books

Banmen, J. (1986). Virginia Satir's family therapy model. *Individual Psychology: The Journal of Adlerian Theory, Research & Practice, 42*(4), 480–492.

Banmen, J. (2002). The Satir model: Yesterday and today. *Contemporary Family Therapy: An International Journal, 24*(1), 7–22.

Beaudry, G. (2002). The family reconstruction process and its evolution to date: Virginia Satir's transformational process. *Contemporary Family Therapy: An International Journal, 24*(1), 79–91.

Gomori, M. (2002). *Passion for freedom: Maria's story*. Palo Alto, CA: Science and Behavior.

Gomori, M., & Adaskin, E. (2006). A learner's guide to family sculpturing. In V. Satir & J. Banmen (Eds.), *Applications of the Satir growth model* (pp. 113–125). Palo Alto, CA: Science and Behavior Books.

Gomori, M., & Adaskin, E. (2008). *Personal alchemy: The art of Satir family reconstruction* (T. Macklin, Ed.). Hong Kong: The Hong Kong Satir Center for Human Development.

Satir, V. (1990). *Peoplemaking*. London, United Kingdom: Souvenir Press. (Original work published 1972)

Satir, V. (1976). *Making contact*. Berkeley, CA: Celestial Arts.

Satir, V. (1978). *Your many faces*. Berkeley, CA: Celestial Arts.

Satir, V. (1983). *Conjoint family therapy*. Palo Alto, CA: Science and Behavior Books.

Satir, V. (1988). *The new peoplemaking*. Palo Alto, CA: Science and Behavior Books.

Satir, V. (2001). *Self-esteem*. Berkeley, CA: Celestial Arts.

Satir, V., & Baldwin, M. (1983). *Satir step by step: A guide to creating change in families*. Palo Alto, CA: Science and Behavior Books.

Satir, V., & Baldwin, M. (1983). *Satir: Step and step*. Palo Alto, CA: Science and Behavior Books.

Satir, V., Bandler, R., & Grinder, J. (1976). *Changing with families: A book about further education for being human*. Palo Alto, CA: Science and Behavior Books.

Satir, V., Banmen, J., Gerber, J., & Gomori, M. (1991). *The Satir model: Family therapy and beyond*. Palo Alto, CA: Science and Behavior Books.

Satir, V., Stachowiak, J., & Taschman, H. A. (1994). *Helping families to change*. Northvale, NJ: Jason Aronson.

Schwab, J., Baldwin, M., Gerber, J., Gomori, M., & Satir, V. (1989). *The Satir approach to communication: A workshop manual*. Palo Alto, CA: Science and Behavior Books.

Suhd, M., Dodson, L., & Gomori, M. (Eds.). (2000). *Virginia Satir: Her life and circle of influence*. Palo Alto, CA: Science and Behavior Books.

Articles

Arpana, G., & Szymanski, D. M. (2009). Examining the relationship between multiple internalized oppressions and African American lesbian, gay, bisexual, and questioning persons' self-esteem and psychological distress. *Journal of Counseling Psychology, 56*(1), 110–118.

Berndt, A., Derlega, V. J., Lewis, R. J., Morris, L. M., & Rose, S. (2001). An empirical analysis of stressors for gay men and lesbians. *Journal of Homosexuality, 42*(1), 63–88.

Blumer, M., Green, M. S., Murphy, M. J., & Palmateer, D. (2009). Marriage and family therapists' comfort level working with gay and lesbian individuals, couples, and families. *American Journal of Family Therapy, 37*(2), 159–168.

Caston, C. (2009). Using the Satir family tools to reduce burnout in family caregivers. *Satir Journal, 3*(2), 39–72.

Gomori, M., & Adaskin, E. (1993, March). Desperately seeking french fries: A case example of Satir's family sculpting. *Anchor Point*, 11–16.

Haber, R. (2002). Virginia Satir: An integrated, humanistic approach. *Contemporary Family Therapy: An International Journal, 24*(1), 23–34.

Innes, M. (2002). Satir's therapeutically oriented educational process: A critical appreciation. *Contemporary Family Therapy: An International Journal, 24*(1), 35–56.

Lum, W. (2002). The use of self of the therapist. *Contemporary Family Therapy: An International Journal, 24*(1), 181–197.

Morrison, A., & Ferris, J. (2009). The Satir model with female adult survivors of childhood sexual abuse. *Satir Journal, 3*(2), 73–100.

Tam, E. (2006). Satir model of family therapy and spiritual direction. *Pastoral Psychology, 54*(3), 275–287. doi:10.1007/s11089-006-6327-6

Taylor, G. (2002). Family reconstruction. *Contemporary Family Therapy: An International Journal, 24*(1), 129–138.

Websites

Company is Satir Institute of the Pacific
http://www.satirpacific.org/membership/membership_info.htm

Satir Centre of Australia for the Family
http://www.satiraustralia.com/satir_model.asp

Satir Institute of the Rockies
http://satirtraining.org/

Virginia Satir Global Network
http://www.avanta.net/

Milan Systemic Family Therapy · 9

Leslie E. Storms

The essence of life is the progression of such changes as growth, self-duplication, and
synthesis of complex relationships.

—Eugene Pleasants Odum

INTRODUCTION

It has been more than 30 years ago since Mara Selvini Palazzoli and her team introduced the Milan model to the world of family therapy. Their insights were dramatic and profound. They interacted as a team, typically treated families over long periods (generally, a 10-month period), and had an elaborate interviewing process, which consisted of five parts. The Milan model has been promoted as helpful even with the most difficult and severely disturbed families (e.g., those whose members include individuals with anorexia or schizophrenia). In this chapter, I examine the unique aspects of this therapy.

HISTORY AND LEADING FIGURES

While working with a group of eight Italian psychiatrists in Milan, Italy, Mara Selvini Palazzoli, also a psychiatrist, began to grow dissatisfied with the slowness and lack of results experienced during individual psychotherapy. Her discontentment eventually led her to create a dramatically different way of practicing therapy (Selvini Palazzoli, 1988). This new approach began in 1967, when Luigi Boscolo and Gianfranco Cecchin joined the group of eight in the first agency setting, attempting to work with couples and families in Italy. The four psychiatrists were interested in treating the entire family but struggled in applying their psychoanalytic concepts to the family. They formed a study group to more fully understand strategic theories and techniques. While they were meeting, the group was oblivious to the pivotal impact their systemic way of thinking would have on the future of family therapy.

Finally, in 1971, Selvini Palazzoli, Boscolo, Cecchin, and Prata opened the Milan Center for the Study of the Family. By this time, their systemic and innovative methods of treating families were incompatible with their previous psychoanalytic work. They began to experiment with conjoint family therapy (having more than one family member in the session at the same time), while contemplating the interactive communication and relationship patterns established within families (Boscolo, Cecchin, Hoffman, & Penn, 1987).

In 1972, the Milan team discovered Gregory Bateson's research on circular epistemology. Bateson saw families as systems composed of individuals, who are also systems that incorporate feedback and process information. This shift in focus from traditional linear thinking with individuals to circular systems thinking led to a better way of understanding the mind of an individual in a family. Thus, Bateson's way of thinking became the foundation and essence of the Milan model to such an extent that the team has been referred to as cybernetic Batesonian family therapists (Anderson, 1999).

In addition, Selvini Palazzoli and her team were greatly influenced by the works of the Mental Research Institute (MRI) in Palo Alto, California, which assisted Selvini Palazzoli in shifting from psychoanalytic therapy to a systemic approach. More specifically, they studied *Pragmatics of Human Communication*, authored by Bateson's coworkers Watzlawick, Beavin, and Jackson (1967). The Milan model began to spread across Europe (and eventually, North America), with the publication of *Paradox and Counterparadox* (Selvini Palazzoli, Boscolo, Cecchin, & Prata, 1978). A few years later, another publication, "Hypothesizing-Circularity-Neutrality" (Selvini Palazzoli, Boscolo, Cecchin, & Prata, 1980), expanded the model even further.

The Milan model offered a new way of looking at the family. It thoroughly and systematically emphasized understanding the family over time and trying to determine how the family came to "need" the problem they were attempting to resolve (Nichols & Schwartz, 1991). In addition, the concept of therapist neutrality was a new and welcome addition for those family therapists who were uncomfortable with the directive nature of strategic family therapy (see Chapter 11) or structural therapy. Additionally, the Milan group emphasized searching for the "pathological nodal point" (Tomm, 1984, p. 115) which, if changed, would help the family evolve itself into a different form. The original *team* approach designed by the Milan group continues to be a useful model today.

In 1980, the foursome split. Selvini Palazzoli and Prata began to delve into research, whereas Boscolo and Cecchin continued to build on the original Milan approach, eventually creating what is known today as the post-Milan approach.

The Milan model has been criticized for its beliefs on neutrality, specifically, its propensity to overlook the emotional connectedness between the therapist and family. This approach has also been accused of lacking cultural sensitivity, particularly with regard to gender, race, and/or sexual orientation. However, rather than judging families and providing details of problems to families, leading to feelings of hopelessness, the group was recognized for its ability to give positive connotations to families, engendering trust and respect for everyone involved in the therapy process. Despite the relatively recent deaths of Mara Selvini Palazzoli in 1999 and Gianfranco Cecchin in 2004, their ideas continue to influence therapists today. This chapter will elaborate on the strengths and limitations of the Milan model.

INTRODUCTION TO MILAN SYSTEMIC FAMILY THERAPY

I am always a bit disappointed that Americans, when compared to Europeans, don't like the Milan method much because it's not prescriptive enough. It's pretty neutral and leaves the direction of change to be negotiated and so on. I think it is a shame that this model gets thrown out (maybe gets thrown out like bathwater). I think that people should see it as a very important skill to learn as one of many skills. Let people play with this and try out the skills that are here and then decide whether they want to use it or not, but not feel it has to be taught as a model that you have to take on and you have to be that kind of therapist.

—David Campbell (2005)

The Milan model was among the first to teach therapists to think systemically, even conceptualizing the therapist as part of the evolving system (Campbell, 2003). Additionally, the Milan model included unique features such as a reliance on the team behind the mirror, positive connotation, the use of prescription or ritual at the end of the session, and the timing of sessions (usually 1 month would elapse between sessions; Boscolo, Cecchin, Hoffman, & Penn, 1987). These elements will be discussed in more detail later in the chapter.

The Milan model begins with an intensive, five-part interview, which consists of the presession, the session, the intersession, intervention, and the postsession. During the presession, a team of four therapists formulates an initial hypothesis about the family's presenting problem. Two members of the team meet with the family; the other two observe the session through a one-way mirror. The two members meeting with the family begin to modify, validate, or change their initial hypothesis through questioning. Following a roughly 40-minute session, the entire team meets to create the appropriate intervention, often by positively connoting the problem or prescribing a ritual with the intent of introducing change. Then the two therapists return to the therapy room and deliver the intervention. The intervention may simply instruct the family to do nothing, or it may take the form of a letter. The team has some choices about how to implement the prescription. They may read the letter to the family, or mail the letter out to the individuals or the whole family. Many times, they tell the family to take the letter home and instruct them to continue reading it at home until their next appointment.

Finally, the team meets for the postsession discussion to examine the family's reactions and to prepare for the next session. Later on, the Milan team decided to have only one therapist to meet with the family while the remaining group members observed behind the mirror (Boscolo, Cecchin, Hoffman, & Penn, 1987).

THEORETICAL ASSUMPTIONS

The principal assumption of the Milan approach is that the presenting symptom served a function, helping to maintain the family system's homeostasis. Early on, the Milan team theorized the family as "a self-regulating system which controls itself according to the rules formed over a period of time through a process of trial and error" (Selvini Palazzoli, Boscolo, Cecchin, & Prata, 1978, p. 3).

To test this theory, the Milan therapist gathers information surrounding the symptom by questioning the family. The feedback provided to the therapist helps the therapist begin to construct a positive connotation of the negative symptom, so that the family relaxes and begins to consider a new context concerning their presenting symptom. A ritual is often constructed from the positive connotation, resulting in a prescription that enables the family to see itself differently. For example, a case of a young boy who developed headaches may be hypothesized by the team as "helpful" to his unemployed father, providing a distraction to his lack of a job. The ritual may consist of the therapist instructing the boy to have more headaches more often, particularly during times when the boy would rather be out playing with friends. This may result in the father changing his focus from unemployment to taking care of his son's worries by getting out to seek a job in a more rigorous manner.

At the same time, the therapist's questions offer the family an opportunity to hear each individual family member's point of view, which could help to soften family rules. For example, a troubled adolescent who chooses to remain silent when situations at school bother her may reveal that in her family, unless she has something good to say, she is criticized for always being negative. Thus, desiring more positive interactions, she has little to say when feeling depressed, because saying anything may leave her more depressed. By encouraging the adolescent to speak about how the sequence occurs, the mother may learn how she interacts with her daughter from her daughter's perception and change her responses so that the girl communicates more often. The team may make the positive connotation that the girl is trying to keep the mother from getting depressed, too, by talking only about positive things, which opens the door for the mother to correct her actions and invite her daughter to talk about whatever bothers her. This renegotiation of interaction in the session paves the way for the mother to appropriately take sides with her daughter, allowing the girl an outlet, through her mother, to discuss what bothers her.

There were times when the group engaged in an intervention referred to as a counterparadox, in which the therapist would prescribe *no change*. The no-change intervention supported the Milan group's early beliefs that families are self-correcting. They also wanted the family to think that they were competent and, by commending the family on their past efforts, helped the family feel less pathological and more open to new strategies. Later, the group modified this notion and began to conceive that families were "stuck" in ideas that were no longer suitable for their current reality. Hence, the Milan group lessened the use of paradoxes, which consisted of prescribing more of the problem, such as "clean more," "argue more," or "sleep less," and began to move through hypothesizing, circularity, and neutrality—techniques that are discussed in the "Interventions" section of this chapter. This led to a more respectful stance on the therapist's part rather than a condescending one, which was often criticized by therapists using other models.

View of the Family and Client

The original Milan theorists described the family as "a self-regulating system, which controls itself according to the rules formed over a period of time through a process of trial and error" (Selvini Palazzoli, Boscolo, Cecchin, & Prata, 1978, p. 3). They assumed that the entire system is caught up in "family games" whose purpose is to control individual family members' behavior in response to flaws within the family hierarchy (Kalinyak & Jones, 1999). The games are played through unacknowledged alliances and coalitions. Family members become symptomatic in an attempt to either deal with isolation or retaliate against family members for the hurt they are experiencing (Campbell, 1999). The symptom or problem that developed within the family was not viewed as coincidental. It can be said that the symptomatic family member has taken his or her attempt to control too far and the result is a symptom or diagnosis!

View on How Change Occurs

In the Milan approach, change occurs when the family is able to see their problems in a more systemic and healthy way (i.e., recognize that their problem may be serving a purpose). Through the use of relationship-centered questions, the Milan therapist helps reveal new ways of thinking and even embracing the problem. As the family members begin to share their responses to the questions, the family must face the reality of the relationships experienced by each individual family member. As therapy progresses, the therapist will begin to notice a shift in how the family views their problems. They will no longer ascribe blame to an individual family member—rather, they will see their problems as family problems. In Milan therapy, every family member must change, as opposed to only the symptomatic family member, resulting in second-order change, which involves a family purposefully changing the rules of their system. This kind of change is long lasting compared to first-order change, which involves a single behavioral change, such as receiving a token for a good deed. Second-order change is more likely to continue because the interactions associated with the change benefit family members' interactions, which are then carried on in family members' interactions with others outside the system.

Therapist's Role

The therapist's role, simply stated, is to be curious and creative. The Milan model offers the therapist a way of observing the patterns of family interactions and techniques for making therapeutic interventions (Bateson, 1972; Watzlawick, Weakland, & Fisch, 1974). Consciously searching for patterns of interactions between family members is an important and facilitating role of the therapist that helps lead to change. The therapist needs to assess the family member who is most willing to accept new ways of viewing his or her problems. In sum, the therapist uses curiosity to help navigate the questions, which allows the therapist to be observant for openings. The opening, coupled with the most motivated family member, conceives a space for the therapist to help the family to see their problems in a new way. The Milan model offers the therapist a way of observing the patterns of family interactions and techniques for making therapeutic interventions (Bateson, 1972; Watzlawick et al., 1974).

Interventions

There are several innovative intervention techniques developed by the Milan group. Those that will be discussed here include positive connotation, which was an early innovation; circular questioning; and hypothesizing. As the Milan team continued to develop their theories, hypothesizing, circularity, and neutrality became their focus. All three of these terms are deeply rooted in family therapy's history and can be found embedded in other family therapy models.

I also briefly discuss newer developments that are part of the "post-Milan" approach.

Positive Connotation

The Milan approach introduced the term positive connotation. Positive connotation is very similar to positive reframing; however, it includes a systemic component. The Milan foursome believed that when a therapist reframes a situation, it helps establish a "good" and "bad" element to the family, hence the importance of reframing for the family system.

A good example is the case of a family in which a little 8-year-old boy had been brought in for treatment by his parents. Since his grandfather's death, the boy had stopped doing well in school and was talking and acting like a caricature of a little old man. He insisted he saw his grandfather following him when he took walks with his father. The message the therapists gave to the boy went as follows:

> *MALE THERAPIST: We are closing this first session with a message to you, Ernesto. You're doing a good thing. We understand that you considered your grandfather to be the central pillar of your family [the hand of the therapist moved in a vertical direction as if tracing*

an imaginary pillar]; he kept it together, maintaining a certain balance [the therapist extended both hands in front of him, palms down, both at the same level]. Without your grandfather's presence, you were afraid something would change, so you thought of assuming his role, perhaps because of this fear that the balance in the family would change [the therapist slowly lowered his right hand, which corresponded to the side where the father was seated]. For now you should continue in this role that you've assumed spontaneously. You shouldn't change anything until the next session, which will be January 21, five weeks from now. (Selvini Palazzoli, Boscolo, Cecchin, & Prata, 1978, p. 81)

Note that in the example, the positive connotation given to the boy's actions is not tied to a particular person, but more concerned with maintaining homeostasis within the system (Boscolo, Cecchin, Hoffman, & Penn, 1987, p. 8). By reframing all of the family's symptomatic behaviors in a positive way, the therapist can help the family begin to realize the homeostatic need for the behaviors. The symptomatic family member is suddenly seen in a more favorable light, and the symptom may actually be welcomed.

For example, the Milan therapist might say to a family, "The reason your child continues to complain daily of a stomach ache is because she wants to stay home in order to ensure that [M]ommy is happy during the day" (Goldenberg & Goldenberg, 2004, p. 273). The family becomes more open and willing to change when the symptomatic behavior is seen as "good." At this point, the therapist assigns "no change" (because the family now sees the symptom as "good"), which strengthens the intervention even more. Therefore, "the family is left to resolve the paradoxical absurdities on its own."

Circular Questioning

Circular questioning is an interviewing method used to gain descriptive assessments and deliver interventions through questioning of the family members (Boscolo, Cecchin, Hoffman, & Penn, 1987; Penn, 1982, 1985; Tomm, 1985, 1987a, 1987b). The Milan team's innovative interviewing technique used the client's feedback as a means for the therapist to generate a new question that helped the family to see their ideas and behaviors in a different context (Campbell, 2003). The Milan therapist's mission through circular questioning is to expand the family's beliefs beyond the meanings that they currently hold. This is often done by asking questions to individuals that probe how others view the situation.

Meaning formulation is an important component of this approach, which helps to develop context. "Without context, there is no meaning" (Campbell, 2003, p. 19). The Milan group strived to help families and their members to examine their belief systems and the *meanings* that they attached to their behaviors. When a family member became more aware of the patterns in which he or she was caught, by hearing from other family members in therapy, the individual family members had a better perception of what was occurring. By hearing new views, a new meaning was formulated and put the family member in a better position to consider solutions.

Formulation of questions in this search for meaning must be based on inquiries about the differences within the relationships of family members and their perceptions, as well as the therapist's systemic hypothesis of the family dynamics (Scheel & Conoley, 1998). Any therapist applying the Milan approach must be able to use detective-like characteristics. The therapist must continually search for patterns, feedback loops, differences in beliefs among family members (called openings), and the covert rules that support family interactions. Openings allow a place during the session to begin questioning, exploring differences, and understanding how a family has come to form and need labels and a diagnosis. An example of an opening would be a parent saying that her mother never supported a teenage girl calling a teenage boy. In the case of an overprotective single mother with an acting-out adolescent daughter, this "opening" would serve the therapist with a way of exploring meanings in the family rules.

Hypothesizing

Systemic hypothesizing is the Milan therapist's way of confirming or disconfirming necessary information regarding how the family functions and how the therapist conceptualizes their functioning. Hypothesizing begins with the initial telephone call from the family. Prior to the first session, the Milan team exhausts all possible hypotheses about the family's symptoms and functioning based on the telephone conversation. During the session, the therapist is often summoned by reflecting team members who are observing the session behind a one-way mirror. Once behind the mirror, the therapist listens to the hypotheses developed by his or her colleagues. Then, a new therapeutic direction may develop based on the consensus of the reflecting team. The reflecting team members are equal, and thus each member's hypotheses are seen as important. As the session comes to a close, the brainstorming team arrives at a final neutral hypothesis (believed to be the most systemic and powerful hypothesis) for the family. It is important that the final hypothesis not ascribe blame to any single family member. Instead, it often results in a prescription or ritual developed by the reflecting team. Later, after the family leaves, the reflecting team and therapist discuss how the family reacted to the intervention and plan for the next session. In some cases, a therapeutic letter is written, such as the sample letter that follows:

Dear Sue and Edward,

I was very impressed with the conflict and hurt between the two of you in our last session. I am glad you were both able to talk about the conflict so readily. It is important to share your feelings about the conflict between you two. Couples who can share feelings about conflict are couples who really love one another.

However, I am concerned that you both may share too much too soon with each other, so I would like to ask that you distract yourself from sharing feelings too often. Perhaps you could even quarrel at least two times during the next week to avoid sharing any intimate feelings too quickly. I suspect a quarrel is coming anyway, as you have been silent with each other for a long time.

Good luck! See you in 2 weeks.

Dr. Feelingood

Neutrality

"Cecchin once said that his definition of neutrality was that if every family member were asked at the end of a session, 'Whose side was the therapist on during the session?' they would all say, 'My side'" (Campbell, 2003, p. 17). Neutrality is an attempt for the therapist to see each person's point of view. The Milan model stressed the importance of the prescription or intervention remaining as systemic and neutral as the team could postulate. However, since the introduction of the term, neutrality has been misunderstood and challenged as implying cold or aloof (Cecchin, 1987). In 2003, Cecchin stated, "It is impossible to be neutral. It is impossible not to have prejudices" (Bertrando, 2004, p. 215). However, Cecchin also suggested that what the Milan refer to as neutral is really "curious." A curious therapist allows all family members a voice, which is essential when practicing systemically. Therefore, adhering to neutrality, the curious therapist is more likely to be open to numerous hypotheses about the system and invite the family members to explore those hypotheses, increasing the number of options for change.

Post-Milan

When Boscolo and Cecchin separated from Selvini Palazzoli and Prata, they decided to continue to refine the Milan approach. The twosome devoted time to training other therapists as well as introducing new ideas and patterns of thinking to family members (Pirrotta, 1984). Questioning techniques became their primary focus; they used questions to help each family member understand the other's perspective. They tossed their original view that the therapist is not part of the family system and replaced it with what is called "second-order cybernetics" (von Foerster, 1974). In second-order cybernetics, the therapist becomes part of the system being observed rather than being an outsider observing a family system.

Post-Milan therapists also moved away from desiring particular outcomes from therapy and instead saw their role as merely to "poke the system" (jar the system, perturb the system), which left families responsible for the outcome. *Post-Milan* is the term used to denote the range of ideas and techniques that therapists currently use to contrast with the earlier, perhaps more coherent, Milan approach (Campbell, 1999).

A review of publications revealed that Milan family therapy has been shown to be effective with families dealing with various childhood disorders, including oppositional defiant disorder, attention deficit disorder, autism, childhood depression, and anxiety. Additionally, couples with marital/relational issues find benefits, as do families with a member involved in drugs or alcohol. The model has evolved from interventions of paradox and counterparadox, which were criticized as being too directive, to circular questions, which resulted in more respectful dialogue. Hence, the model is suitable for any family or couple wanting change quickly, assisted by a team of therapists who work together to compose interventions based on a hypothesis. Families desiring communication improvement will benefit greatly from a Milan family therapist, who steers the therapy sessions by encouraging interactions from family members so that everyone has a chance to be understood.

Couples or families seeking answers to the past or desiring an analysis of why their problems have developed will not benefit as much because the Milan family therapist does not pathologize. Instead, the Milan therapist attaches positive connotations to symptoms and strives to help families understand meaning on situations and beliefs from each other.

Early in this chapter, I mentioned that Milan family therapy might not be as culturally sensitive as necessary. Perhaps this perception is due to the neutrality taken by the Milan family therapist, who hypothesizes on how "a normal" family should interact. Applying the needed diversity sensitivity to various families today means taking the hypothesizing a step further, incorporating cultural differences into a hypothesis prior to designing an intervention. For example, a therapist recently worked with a Hispanic male who had engaged in risky behavior with drugs and alcohol. Because he was 15, he was sent to a rehabilitation agency for 6 months for psychoeducation while completing his school year. Upon completion, his probation officer instructed him to get family therapy. Although the entire family was invited, only the mother and the son attended the session; the father refused to attend. A Milan family therapist may hypothesize that the son was acting out to engage the father more in the family's life and would continue until the father began to interact more with the mother, who was feeling neglected. However, when asked, the father simply stated that he did not believe in counseling and that his wife was better suited to hearing "feeling talk," which he did not appreciate. With this in mind, a family therapist would work with the mother and son without the father, constructing a hypothesis with the system that presented itself to therapy.

To conclude, all family therapists should be culturally sensitive to cultural, racial, and sexual orientation entities and incorporate such sensitivity into all family therapy models. It is important for students of family therapy and practitioners of family therapy who meet families of diverse cultures to ask the family to "teach" them about themselves. This is the ultimate respect to diverse families who are asking a stranger to enter their lives, week by week, and assist them toward a more functional way of living. By inviting such information gathering, families feel heard and the direction of family therapy takes on a better direction, which can ultimately lead to better interventions that suit each family.

MILAN SYSTEMIC FAMILY THERAPY WORKING TEMPLATE

The *Milan systemic family therapy template* is meant to be used as a guideline to learning the process of Milan systemic family therapy. The template provides the beginning therapist with steps to take and questions to ask that promote collaboration between the therapist and the client. There are suggested questions under each heading to help start the process. After using the initial questions, guide the client through each process, asking questions that occur to you, as you stay within the boundaries of the theory. Although there is no one "script" for any therapy session, it is the hope of the author that the template serves as an impetus to learning this family therapy model. *Note: The Milan family therapy model involves a reflecting team throughout the therapeutic process.*

Tools for Change

The primary tools that the therapist uses will be asking circular questions, stating positive connotations, and including interventions such as a presentation or a letter. Throughout the therapy, hypothesizing with the team during the session and afterward will serve for developing future questions and positive connotations because the model theorizes that by helping the family see itself within a different context, change will occur.

Phase 1: Joining and Building Rapport

At the first session, the therapist introduces himself or herself and the team behind the mirror. It is crucial for each therapist to be curious, wondering what is behind the *individual* family member's stories. It is important for the therapist to ask many questions to understand the family system. The therapist should stay neutral and join with everyone in the room. During this phase, the therapeutic team behind the one-way mirror will begin to formulate theories about the family's functioning, which should include any presession hypothesizing. The team will then formulate ideas about why the symptom is occurring and how it is a function for the family.

Here are some comments or questions that a therapist might use during this initial phase:

- *"Hello, I am _____ and I will be working with a team. The team will be observing behind the mirror in an effort to more effectively help your family. I will be collaborating with them throughout our session."*
- Ask all family members individually:
  - *"How do you see the problem/symptom?*
  - *"Who do you think the problem has bothered most in the family? "What impact has the problem had on your family?"*

Phase 2: Understanding the Presenting Issue

When discussing the presenting issue, it is important for the therapist and the team to see what benefit the problem is providing to the family. Here, the therapist begins to apply positive connotation—taking what the family construes as problematic or bad and refine it as helpful and good (Tomm, 1984). The therapist helps the family see the presenting problem in a different context—as being more systemically beneficial to all family members. The therapist may suggest that it is "needed" for family functioning. The therapist continues asking questions and even questioning the family's beliefs.

Here are some comments or questions that a therapist might use during this phase with a family member dealing with anger:

- *"How has it been helpful to you to deny being angry?"*
- *"Has your family expressed their appreciation of you for denying that you are angry inside?"*

To the family:

- *"How has dealing with the anger problem helped your family to put aside other pressing issues?"*

Phase 3: Assessment of Family Dynamics

There is not an assessment in the sense of diagnosis, classification, or making an objective judgment about what is going on. But there is a constant testing, discarding, and refining of hypotheses, which is unlikely to be shared with clients more and more as the work goes on. (Jones, 1993)

During this phase, the therapist searches for relational dynamics and patterns of interaction between family members as the questions are asked and answered. The therapist is always searching for the family members who are open to self-exploration and systemic thinking. The therapist may make statements aloud about family behavior that gives the family a plausible and beneficial reason for the problem or symptom.

Here are some comments or questions that a therapist might use during this phase:

- *"It sounds as if the anger issue has brought your family closer. You are here together, whereas you state that you are often scattered at home. You should all be commended for creating a problem that could draw your family together. Have you always been this helpful to each other?"*
- *"I am impressed with the passion that you, Mom, express in regard to your concern about your daughter's anger. Have you always been so dedicated to listening to her and spending time to understand her, even if it means taking time away from the other children?"*
- To identified client: *"How did you decide to be so helpful to your family and attempt to hide anger? Who do you think this strategy has helped the most?"*
- *"What would your dad say happens when you get angry and try to hide it?"*
- *"Who is the most helpful in getting you to deal with your anger?"*

Phase 4: Goals

There are typically no goals set within this model; rather, the Milan therapist will trust the family system to resolve itself. If goals *are* discussed, the family sets them.

Here are some comments or questions that a therapist might use during this phase:

- *"How will we know when to stop therapy?"*
- *"Who will be making changes soon that will tell you that your family life is improving?"*
- *"What will that person be doing that will tell you he or she is on track to helping your family life improve?"*
- *"How will the changes that person makes affect the rest of the family?"*
- *"What will your family be able to do that it has not done in awhile because of the problem?"*

Phase 5: Amplifying Change

During this phase, the family deals with the different, positive connotation and systemic ideas and recognizes the problem or symptom within a different and more systemic context. The family members may smile, laugh, or appear confused. It is this change in thinking and experiential reaction that instigates their seeing themselves and their family unit differently. Such new reactions lead to different actions. The therapist must get a "feel" for whether the family accepts or rejects the positive connotation presented by the team. Either way, their view is changed and the chances of the family doing things differently as a result are increased.

Here are some comments or questions that a therapist might use during this phase:

- *"I am interested in your thoughts, now that the team and I have given you our impression of what is really going on in your family. Who wants to start first?"*
- *"It is our belief that your actions certainly benefit your family, yet you, (example) Dad, have decided to drink less over the past week. Are there other ways that you can be drawn closer without the aid of drinking in case you make this a permanent change?"*

- *"What would that be like for each of you if (example) Dad makes drinking less a permanent change? What would you each be doing as a result?"*
- *"What have you each seen each other do over the last week or so that tells you this family is already changing?"*
- *"Daughter, tell me what your brother would say you are doing differently?"*
- *"Tell me, Daughter, what other actions do you wish other people will continue or discontinue?"*

Phase 6: Termination

The family itself decides when therapy is completed: "When they are satisfied and they have achieved what they wanted to achieve" (Tomm, 1984). The therapist and team commend the family on working through the issues that they brought and choosing the new actions that they developed as a result. The therapist may ask:

- *"Are we near the end of working together?"*
- *"How do you know?"*

MASTER THERAPIST INTERVIEW

LAURA FRUGGERI

Laura Fruggeri is a full professor in social psychology and chair of the Department of Psychology at the University of Parma and a member of the senior faculty at the Milan Center for Family Therapy. She is also a licensed psychologist and family psychotherapist. She consults to mental health services and social services in the application of systemic and social constructionist ideas and has published widely in this area. She has also published several papers on the development of the process of social construction implied in all therapeutic interventions.

What attracted you to the theory behind Milan family therapy?
Several aspects. The relational view; that is, the idea that events, behaviors, episodes have meanings from their reciprocal relationships. The idea of context: Again, behaviors, episodes, events don't have absolute meanings, but flexible ones according to the context. It is a nonjudgmental approach. The focus is in fact on the aesthetics of relationships, on forms and processes, on interdependency, not on individual characteristics or lineal causality.

Before meeting the Milan group, I had been involved in the psychiatric movement that had stressed the social processes connected to mental illness and all the problems related. I have always considered the social responsibility of therapists as central. The Milan approach gave me a new lens for connecting the interpersonal experiences to the broader social process.

The systemic/constructionist theory is rooted in Bateson's thinking. The ideas of interdependency and social construction are central. While interacting, people influence reciprocal experiences, goals, preferences, opinion or behaviors, but they also influence the definition of self, of their relationship, of the episodes they are involved in, and of the broader context they are part of and within which constructs and binds their relationships, identities, and social realities. The process is triadic: Within a complex relational context, the relationship between two partners has an effect on the relationships that each one of them has with others. In other words, the meaning that the relationship has between two people is not dependent only on the interaction between the partners directly involved, but also on the quality of the relationships they have with others. And vice versa, the meanings that two partners negotiate through their direct interaction will have some sort of repercussion on others directly or indirectly involved.

How do you formulate your view of a family when they enter therapy?
It depends on the information I have beforehand: The type of problem presented inevitably makes me think of the families' relational patterns as well as the dynamics described in the literature that I know. I think of a family as a group of persons that are interconnected by tight binds, either strong positive or negative feelings, a high level of interdependence, and significantly linked (one to the other) for the development of their identities. But while talking to the family, I usually don't try to verify the hypothesis that I have. I'd rather aim at falsifying it. It is in fact from the tension between what I know from my experience as therapist and the unexpected presented by the family that is the way new ideas are generated.

What kinds of families do you think benefit most from this model?
I don't see the Milan model as a technical model; I see it as a perspective. It is an epistemological and theoretical approach useful for understanding the complexity of situations and for contributing to the development of a different shared view of such situations. For this reason, I would say that all families benefit from this model and all issues can be dealt with.

What issues do you think this model works best with?
The model works best when a broader view is needed. When different aspects, events, or issues have to be connected and when relationships have to be redefined or rejoined.

Different models of therapy require the therapist to be directive or nondirective. In your opinion, what are the necessary characteristics that a therapist should possess to be effective with this model?
Be curious and enjoy the aesthetic of relationships.

How often does the client see you and for how long a period of time?
Once every month and usually for a year or a year and a half. The sessions are 1 and a half hours or 2 hours.

What are you looking for when you are in the session?
It depends on the information I have beforehand: The type of problem presented inevitably makes me think of the family's relational patterns or dynamics described in literature that I know of, but then, while talking to the family, I usually don't try to verify the hypothesis that I have, rather to falsify it. It is in fact from the tension between what I

know from my experience as a therapist and the unexpected presented by the family that new ideas are generated.

I think that the most important and vital thing for people is to make sense of what they do, of what others do, and of what happens around them. People might suffer terribly, dislike their conditions, hope for better situations, but they don't act in a senseless way (they don't live senseless lives). The sense of what they do might be obscure to others, but there is always a context (a story, a narrative, a relationship, an event, a desire) that makes sense of what people do. So my wonder is: What is there that makes sense of the behaviors in this absurd, crazy, and painful situation? This for me means to reach the clients where they are, from where they can start a new journey to some other "place" where new meanings could give sense to new stories.

What is the assessment process of this model?
Starting from a constructionist perspective, the assessment is not an autonomous process. Since the very beginning of their meeting, therapist and clients are involved in a process that can confirm or change the context within which the problem has been generated.

Who sets the goals, the client or the therapist?
Goals are coconstructed. We could say that all participants in the interaction have their goals, but the goals of therapy are a process of negotiation, so goals do not come first, they emerge from the therapeutic process.

What are some commonly used interventions with this model?
Any intervention can be used within a systemic/constructionist framework.

I know of colleagues who have elaborated on psychoeducation from the systemic point of view. Personally, I think that as long as it doesn't become a way to label someone or objectify processes and relationships, it could be used (just as any other type of intervention). As long as it is evaluated from the perspective of the particular kind of social realities it contributes to the construct.

What have you found to be the limitations of this approach?
The limitations that all approaches have: It can happen that it fits the beliefs, patterns, and processes that created the problem.

What are your suggestions that you have for students learning this model?
The more ideas you have, the more differences you'll see, the more you can choose among them, change them or abandon them. The less ideas, the more you will remain stuck to them.

Practice the interactive analysis, exercises on "the pattern which connects," that is how parts, elements, aspects, events, behaviors, stories, as well as opposite polarities connect.

Develop different points of view or perspectives or stories or narratives on the same situation.

Become aware of how you yourself contribute to the construction of the interactive process.

DAVID CAMPBELL

David Campbell, PhD, trained as a clinical psychologist at Boston University before moving to live and work in London, United Kingdom, in 1972. He currently works at the Tavistock Clinic as a family therapist and course organizer for various family therapy training courses. He also works as a freelance organizational consultant and has written a book about applying systemic ideas to work with organizations, Taking Positions in the Organization *(Campbell & Groenbeck, 2006, Karnac Books, London).*

What attracted you to the theory behind Milan family therapy?

This is a model that has evolved quite a bit. What attracted me to the theory is that it sets up a relationship between theory and practice, which I thought was very exciting. It was a model of doing family therapy, which was very much consistent and congruent with systemic thinking and systemic theory as it was emerging out of Bateson's work and various other pioneers from the early days. So the theory to me was really being brought alive. It kind of built on systemic ideas and took them into the therapeutic field in a way that I thought was very exciting.

It goes back to Bateson's ideas about context, where you're trying to create a new context through your interviewing by identifying new connections. There are all types of different connections that you're trying to make, but by doing that, you help people into seeing things differently— you take them into a new context for seeing family relations, or seeing their beliefs, or seeing the meaning that they attribute to behavior. So I think, fundamentally, it's about shifting context and the way that you do that through the interview itself.

How do you formulate a view of a family when they enter therapy?

My view of the family is based primarily around what they want me to listen to and what they want to say rather than looking at a family structure or family relationships. I might start by asking myself, "Who is sitting in front of me and why are they sitting in front of me and not sitting in front of someone else?" They are sitting in front of me because somewhere, somebody along the line has defined a problem and I am a problem-solving person, so I am on the other side of the room, and so here we are. So I would be defining the family pretty much around whoever wants to be in this room and why do they want to be here and what are they hoping they can get. I might also add that the Milan model teams were famous for working with extended families and three-generational themes and things like that. So, a simpler answer would be to say that an extended family with a belief system about wider relationships is also something that is important.

I also think about entering and about formulating, and I would be interested to say to myself and to them, "What do you really want other people to understand and hear about where you're coming from and what is important to you"—let's start with that. So I would be speculating about what do they really want—to be appreciated and heard and so on—and then start to build a picture of the family relations from that point. So if Dad wants to talk about the son being on Ritalin, then I would be interested to know how that makes a relationship and how people connect to that and what supports it and challenges it. Then I would start to build a more complex, or systemic, picture once I had identified some things people really want to be understood and appreciated about.

What kinds of families do you think benefit most from this model?

I think the families that are bound pretty tightly together and the families that are interested in each other and interested in how they are connected—those are the ones that take to this model very well. Now, having said that, I think part of the task of the therapist is to try to create that environment, so that people do get interested in each other and then they become interested in how they are connected through their belief systems, through their interactions, and so on. I think also families that are more at the verbal end of the spectrum, who like words, who like to talk, and who are responsive to language probably do better with this model.

What issues do you think this model works best with?

I think it works best with issues that people feel distressed about but can also appreciate that the distress has a relational component to it.

Different models of therapy require the therapist to be directive or nondirective. In your opinion, what are the necessary characteristics that a therapist should possess to be effective with this model?

The main characteristic that a therapist needs is to be able to change their responses in relation to the family that is sitting with them. Some families will like a more directive approach and some a nondirective approach, and I think that the therapist should be free and happy to move in one direction or another. You can see these on a continuum in the way that you put your questions, and I would say that some families will position themselves more at one end and some at the other. What I would train people to do is to be able to engage a family in the style the family would want to be engaged in and not in the style that the therapist has fallen in love with. I think it was Paul Ricoeur who said he wanted to amend the golden rule. It is not "Do unto others as you would have them do unto you," but "Do unto others as they would want to be done unto." I like that.

How often does a client see you and for how long a period of time?

I tend to see families every 2 or 3 weeks. I see them for about an hour and a quarter. The length of treatment varies for each case, but I think, generally, on average, I would see families for 6 months to a year.

What are you looking for when you are in a session?

I like to make hypotheses—I like, either on my own or with somebody else, to generate as many ideas as I can and then I like to put them aside and try to be open-minded. I think the advantage of that is that if you put them aside, then you can listen better. On the other hand, when they start speaking and making some points, then you have the possibility of making some more connections yourself because you've done some prethinking, so you can follow certain lines of thinking rather than getting completely down the track that the family wants to take you on.

What is the assessment process of this model?

Again, that is not a strong pillar of this model because assessment is a part of the therapeutic process. We are always thinking about what do they need to talk about and what do they want to bring into the session. That is part of an ongoing assessment we are doing. If you ask someone to stop and formulate something and write some notes and put them in a file, then you are in a different place, then you're having to do an assessment for a different context.

Who sets the goals, the client or the therapist?
It is a process of negotiating with the clients about the process of change and how it is going and how they want to influence it and what they want me to think about, rather than having preset goals that people are working towards, and that is one of the things in particular about the Milan model, it's not a very goal-oriented model.

What are some commonly used interventions with this model?
I think the most commonly used interventions would be the circular questioning, the use of positive refraining, exploring connections. The hypothesizing is not really an intervention—it is more a position that the therapist takes to prepare themselves, as well as the neutrality that the Milan people wrote about. I ask people to observe each other a lot. Sometimes, I give them homework to observe various things at home. I talk to people about acknowledging differences and getting really interested in differences. I often find myself slowing down, the pace of change, on the basis that family are often coming to you because things are changing too quickly and they want to slow things down, so I go with that in a big way.

What role does a homework assignment have in this model?
A pretty big role. I often give people things to think about or some particular task. It was part of the original model and is something I do quite a bit of.

How do you know when your client is ready to terminate?
You need to discuss it with them. Clients' views have always got to come first, and you also have to pay attention to the context that you are working in. If you are in a context where there is some legal framework around the work, then you have to factor that into the decision to terminate. For example, a child protection case: Are the authorities happy if the work should terminate? That is something that has to be discussed.

What have you found to be the limitations of this approach?
I think that people that like a lot of structure and hierarchy, guidance and education—I think, would find that there is a limitation here, and we would have to work in a more eclectic way with those families. I think that the people with very strongly fixed ideas about how things should be are harder to work with, and those are the people I would call difficult. If people are open to taking on some new information, then it becomes easier.

What are your suggestions that you have for students learning this model?
Supervision in a group is what I would recommend. When you've got a group working together over several years and they are observing therapy behind the screen while their colleagues are working and then they are getting a lot of "indirect" supervision as they observe their colleagues being supervised by the supervisor.

I think that I would give them a lot of exercises in how to listen to people. For example, I might put them in 2s and 3s and get people to tell a story and then ask what did they listen to and what do they think people really want to say, what are the things that are most important and less important and get them used to listening. The second thing would be practice asking, linking, or connecting questions or circular questions. I think it is very good to do those exercises in student groups and then turn them loose on a family.

I would like to say something else about students and about learning this model. I've lived in Britain for 30 years, but I grew up in Chicago and then I moved to London, aged 27, after I did one training in clinical psychology in Boston. I am always a little bit disappointed when Americans discuss this model compared to Europeans—they (Americans) do not like the Milan method much because it is not prescriptive enough, it is pretty neutral and leaves the direction of change to be negotiated and so on. I think it is a shame if the model is cast aside for this reason. I would prefer to think that this model offers trainees some very important skills to learn as one of many skills they should have in their repertoire rather than a religion that you have to be loyal to. Let people play with these ideas and techniques and try out what's on offer and then decide whether they want to use them or not, but not to feel that it has to be taught as a model that you have to take on and that you've got to be that kind of therapist. That is what I would like to say to students.

MASTER THERAPIST INTERVIEW

KARL TOMM

Karl Tomm, MD, LMCC, FRCP(C), CRCP(C), is a professor in the Department of Psychiatry at the University of Calgary, where he founded the Family Therapy Program in 1973. He is well known in the field of family therapy for his work in clarifying and elaborating new developments in systems theory and clinical practice. For many years, he was at the forefront of a new approach to therapy that emerged from systemic, constructivist, and social constructionist ideas. This approach is collaborative rather than hierarchical and emphasizes therapeutic conversations to deconstruct problems and to coconstruct healing and wellness. Dr. Tomm has organized many workshops, conferences, and seminars at the University of Calgary. He has also conducted numerous workshops throughout North America, Europe, Australia, Asia, and South America. His articles have been published extensively in the international family therapy literature and he has been on the editorial boards of several family therapy journals.

What attracted you to Milan family therapy?

As I see it, the Milan approach was extremely important in facilitating a shift in the field, a shift from first-order perspective to a second-order perspective. Are you familiar with that distinction? The first order is more looking at observed systems, where the observer is separate from that which he/she is observing. The second-order perspective is to see their own patterns of observation as part of the process, and also to attend to how looking at ways in which people look at themselves and their relationships influences them and organizes them in their patterns of relating. The Milan approach was quite instrumental in facilitating that shift, because it was the first approach that focused mainly on belief systems (what family members believed rather than on the actual interaction and relationships per se). So the structural approach or strategic approach would be more first order. The Milan [approach] and more recent developments like narrative therapy and solution-focused therapy would be more second-order perspective. I think, historically, it was extremely important and inferential, but whether people actually practice it the way it was originally developed, I don't know. I doubt it very much—they have been influenced by other developments recently.

What attracted me to the model at first was the notion of *positive connotation*, being able to take what the family construed as problematic or bad and refine it as helpful and good. That possibility resonated with me as having significant potential and that was what captured my imagination in the beginning. At the time, I didn't realize the significance of what they were doing in reframing and redefining. In retrospect, I can see how they were coming from a social constructivist point of view rather than an imperial point of view. Where the therapist is contributing to the construction of realities and, hopefully, their contribution would be to a more therapeutic reality than a pathologizing one. The original theory also revolved around the notion that the symptom served some kind of function for the whole family system. Because it did serve that function, it could be seen in a positive light and so that was a core issue called functional hypothesizing. That's how they viewed the family.

How do you formulate your view of a family when they enter therapy?
Usually, it is a particular family member that is in enormous distress. They take an issue to seek help and so that person is the person who is usually has the most interest in trying to effect change. So, attending to that person's view of the situation and their impulse or desire for change is a very important process of joining. If you don't pay attention to that person, then it is going to be hard to engage the family. I like the definition of problems that the Swedish team developed. Problems are unfulfilled desires for which a solution cannot be seen. When people have a desire for something but they don't know how to fulfill that desire, they can't figure out how to solve it; then that constitutes the problem. Unfulfilled desire that I can't see a solution to then [is] the focus of reaching outside the family in order to get some help.

What kinds of families do you think benefit most from this model?
I would say families that are highly connected to one another. Some people describe it as enmeshed families or David Reece's model calls them environment-sensitive families. Family members are really tuned into each other and are very reactive to one another. Those kinds of family systems, I think, respond well to the Milan approach. Disengaged families, where people are not that connected, probably wouldn't respond as well.

What issues do you think this model works best with?
Probably, the life transition issues; those would be useful. Additionally, conflicts that are quite entangled like couple conflict. Couple conflicts that are characterized by a lot of turmoil, shame, guilt, and fear. Relationships where there are efforts to regulate and control one another.

Different models of therapy require the therapist to be directive or nondirective. In your opinion, what are the necessary characteristics that a therapist should possess to be effective with this model?
The Milan therapist is not directive. One of the things that was important in the later years [was when] Gianfranco and Cecchin developed the notion of irreverence. What

[it] meant was promoting a stance for a therapist to adopt, where they don't overvalue things and they are prepared to question everything, like values that people hold. They are to be challenged and questioned and that immobilizes more possibilities. I would say that the Irish team has extended that a bit in their notion of questioning at the extreme. They actually, through their questions, pushed the limits and boundaries of meanings that the family is accustomed to, so when you ask questions that are often considered outside the scope of an ordinary conversation, you increase the possibilities for the family to think more creatively. If therapist has the capacity for a lot of creative and lateral thinking (being able to think outside the box), then that would be a very desirable characteristic or quality for the Milan therapist to have.

How often does the client see you and for how long a period of time?
Well, with the classical Milan approach, there was that long time interval—4 weeks. Selvini wrote about it. Part of the reason for that was, the team didn't want to have interaction with the family to (which might) disqualify the intervention that they delivered at the end of the session. So by giving it a longer period of time, the family had to make sense of it or keep working on it or chewing on it. This maintained the process of change. Now, when I use the Milan approach, I don't follow that so rigidly. I sometimes did [long time intervals]. I see most families for an hour and a half. My practice at the moment is to set up an appointment, it could be a week to 2 weeks, it could be 4 weeks, it depends on the clinical situation.

What are you looking for when you are in the session?
Well, I am looking for those relational dynamics and patterns of interactions between family members that is my primary focus. The Milan team used to talk about *presession hypothesizing*—where they would formulate some ideas about why the symptom could be serving a function for the family. With beginning therapists, I think that is useful. But I don't do that and I don't need to do that anymore. I've done lots of hypothesizing and I've got lots of hypotheses available to me. I can respond on the basis of what the family presents to me very quickly with [based on] past experiences. But generally speaking, I don't come to the first session with a map. I've got a general map with respect to systematic process. How family members interact with each other to create meaning and relationships, and that binds with me, of course, to notice interaction patterns.

What is the assessment process of this model?
The invariant prescription was a very interesting way of working with families. It's where Selvini would begin by seeing the whole family and she would try and understand how the children were involved in interaction with the parents—and vice versa. She would then dismiss the children and continue working with the parents. She would enter into an agreement with the parents whereby she would ask them to enact disappearances. That is, they were to leave a note on the table for the kids to find when they came home from school and the note would say something like, "Your father and I are out and we'll be back at 7:30." She then says to the parents that it is very important that you can't be found or reached by the children during this time. She would tell them you can go anywhere you want; you don't even have to go together, but don't go with friends or extended family where the kids could track you down. She told them it was very important that they show up at the time that they had specified and that they show up together. Lastly, when the children ask you questions like, "Where did you go?" "Why

didn't you tell us where you went?" Then you answer by saying, "Well, that's between your father and me." Selvini used that intervention as assessment tool. She used it as a way to understand how families operate. Their response to that prescription was different. It would disrupt some of the connections between a generation and that would give her a lot of information. Sometimes, one parent could do it easily and one parent couldn't and so on . . . So that became part of their assessment process.

Who sets the goals, the client or the therapist?
Goals are not a big issue in the Milan systemic therapy, except to free the family to find their own path and that's not a specific goal (it's sort of a general goal). The goal is to enable a direction of greater freedom and ability to problem solve with each other. We don't set a particular goal, such as get the child back to school or things like that.

What are some commonly used interventions with this model?
Well, in the early years, *positive connotation* was really a complex intervention, but my thinking changed and I went on to narrative therapy. My main intervention is questions, reflexive questioning. One important intervention in the first session is establishing neutrality with respect to person. You're not neutral with respect to the problem necessarily, but you are neutral with respect to person. At the end of the last session, you would probably (really more narrative) ask the family how they achieved the changes that they have achieved. You want them to own the changes, to inform you, and help you in learning about the nature of change. You do take the position of being one down. Hierarchy changes where you become a learner and the family then teaches you about how they achieved the changes that made it possible for them [to] move on.

Other typical interventions for the Milan approach were ritual prescriptions and invariant prescription with the classic *positive connotation*. There are four elements, possibly five:

1. The first element is to redefine what is presented as the problem. In order for the family to accept this in any way, you have to connect that redefinition to a relationship. You have to give a plausible reason (such as, it's good because . . .).

2. The second component [is when] you connect that redefined behavior to a pattern of interaction, and because you've connected the pattern of interaction you imply that other people are involved in maintaining the pattern. You then imply that if people don't want the problem that the other person is the cause. You have to positively connote the behavior of the other people.

3. You have to redefine their behavior as good, too, and that's the third component.

4. The fourth component is to connect the whole pattern to a deeper underlying problem that the surface pattern protects the family from.

5. The fifth component, which is optional, is to prescribe no change, say, "Because this is helping the family, you should continue the work that you're doing by having acceptance."

[As] a concrete example, a person dealing with anorexia and bulimia (this is actually a case that I worked with), where you would come back from the team discussion, you say, "The team thinks that by refusing to eat or vomiting when you do, it is a good thing." And, of course, that's quite a shock, and you say, "It's good because it helps your parents worry." That's connecting it to a pattern of interaction. Say and, "It's good that you worry because if you didn't worry about your daughter, she'd be able to move out now because she's a young adult. Her eating behaviors mean she's not ready for that. We all know that many years ago, the father was depressed and if she left home, he might get depressed again—so we think you should continue in this work that you're doing for your family in refusing to eat or vomiting." That would be a fully developed five-part positive connotation intervention that could be used at the end of the session.

How do you know when your client is ready to terminate?
When they are satisfied and they have achieved what they wanted to achieve.

What have you found to be the limitations of this approach?
It certainly has a problem when you need immediate action. When there are threats of violence or suicide, you have to take action and be directive. You have to step out of the model to do that. And, of course, if the family wants clear direction (to be told what to do), that's not compatible with the model. Like some people respond to that by giving direction, but then the family comes back to say the directions didn't work and this becomes the basis for therapy, basically to use a more typical Milan style of working. I think it's probably not that useful for disengaged families [where there's] not much connection between family members. Obviously, there is a limitation with respect to dealing with organic problems (aging, Alzheimer's, brain injury, etc.). In general, obviously, people who are very rigid in their belief systems—that would make it very difficult. The approach is based on posturing change in belief systems. Another difficulty is if the family or a member of the family is caught in another system, a larger system context (the legal system, hospital system) where certain patterns are serving a function; those larger system issues could be a significant problem that makes things difficult, and this model does not address those larger issues usually.

What are your suggestions that you have for students learning this model?
Probably one of the most important things is to be in a context in which other people practice the model. To have an opportunity to observe the model in application.

People who have an empirical way of thinking find that Milan systemic therapy just blows their mind because everything goes. One of the exercises the Milan team did from time to time was to go through a process of systematically saying, "Let's take the mother and say that the mother's behavior is the cause of all the problems in the family." Then after hypothesizing on that, they would say, "Okay now, let's take the father; the father's behavior is the cause of all the problems within the family." Then they would say, "Let's take the oldest child; the oldest child is the cause of all the problems in the family." If you do this systematically for all the family members, after awhile, your head is spinning because there are so many possibilities. That loosens you up from a single view about objective reality. Then you can play with these different possibilities. You can see which one might be more enabling of change for this particular family system, in terms of the way in which they are construing the situation.

Be a member of a team (a therapeutic team). The Milan approach, I think, partly became quite popular because of their systematic teamwork and doing a five-part session. Now, there has been a very significant modification of that, which is due to Tom Anderson's work where it is no longer used a closet team (although the Milan team in Italy still uses more of a closet team). The term closet team means that the family is not aware of what's going on in the team discussion. The therapist comes back (from the team discussion) to deliver the message. The message is very cleverly crafted. On the other hand, the reflecting team process—the family gets to hear the team's ideas and their exchanges with one another. And, of course, it is that approach that has been modified and extended by other people like Michael White. Being part of that team is very important part of training.

Place yourself within the context where people are practicing it and participate with other people in team as much as you can. Get people to watch your work and form a team with you. Remember (according to Gianfranco and Cecchin) to never marry your hypotheses and just flirt with them. Never get stuck in a particular belief about what's happening in a family. That way, you have irreverence to yourself, as well as in relation to what the family presents to you. You have to question your own assumptions, presuppositions, and values as well.

Case Study

A mother calls and makes an appointment for her family to come to therapy. The family consists of a husband and wife, both in their 40s; their 15-year-old son; a college-aged daughter; and the woman's father, age 82. Three years after the woman's mother died, her father developed Alzheimer's disease and moved in with the family 6 months ago. When his health began to deteriorate, the woman spent more time caring for him than for other members of the family. Three months ago, the 15-year-old son, who has been treated for attention deficit hyperactivity disorder since age 7, began refusing to take his medication. The school is now calling home to report truancy by the 15-year-old boy.

During the session, the wife cries and the husband reports that their relationship is strained, while occasionally rolling his eyes as his wife becomes tearful. He reports that he has had to take on more work because his wife had to quit her job to attend to her father's needs. The daughter is away at college and the wife smiles as she describes her as a straight-A student. The daughter was asked to attend the session but refused because she has a hard time with her grandfather's illness and dislikes the conflict that has developed at home.

Dr. David Campbell's Response to the Case Study

This assignment reminds me of the joke about the traveler who stops in the middle of remote countryside to ask the local farmer standing by the fence how to get to a certain town. The farmer scratches his head, and after a long thoughtful pause, replies, "I sure wouldn't have started from here."

As I look at the case vignette, I would want to wind the tape back to the point where the mother telephoned to make the referral. At that point, I would ask her if she had thought about a family meeting, and what her thoughts had been. Had she spoken to others in the family and [if so] what were their ideas? I might say that there are different ways that families like to start out (i.e., parents coming on their own, or the whole group living together at home). On the basis of this discussion, I would be arranging the first appointment and also gathering information to help me make hypotheses about the family.

Hypotheses are aimed at the question, "What meaning do the presenting problem and the referral have for various relationships in the family?" I always assume that various relationships are changing at the time of referral and some family members are not happy with the way things are changing. Thinking about the role of hypothesis making [has] evolved over the years, so that it is no longer seen as a divining rod for a hidden pattern that needs to be exposed or explored, but it is rather a way for the therapists to organize their own thoughts to enable them to engage with the family and the issues on their minds.

So, on the basis of what I have heard so far from the mother, I would be wondering, or hypothesizing, about the changes brought about by the grandmother's death, the onset of grandfather's Alzheimer's, his arrival in the family, the daughter's departure to college, and the stopping of medication. These all seem like important events loaded with meaning. I would like to learn whether these events have had major impacts on the marital relationship and the son's relationships in the family. Yet having said this, it is also important for me not to overorganize my own thinking, but to follow the family and discuss the things they want to discuss—to let them tell their story. The hypothesis sits in the back of my mind to help me make some connections and some meanings out of what the family tells me.

And that is how the session would progress. I would be asking about the changing network of relationships and what that means, and I would gather everyone's view through circular questioning, regardless of whether they were present in the session or not. I might explore past events that make the meaning of the present so difficult, and gradually, as we all shared a picture of the situation together, I would explore how they want to move forward from the current situation they are in. This would combine the resources in the family and help them develop their own strategies for changing their pattern of behavior. The particular mix of understanding past patterns and planning future strategies depends on the way the therapist and family work together. Each family has a different way of relating to therapy.

KEY TERMS

Circular questions   A questioning technique based on the idea that in any relationship, all parties concerned must coevolve. The questions aim to transform families' ways of thinking from linear, causal chains of thought into reciprocal, interdependent worldviews, allowing each family member to experience other family members' worldview.

Conjoint   A therapy session that includes at least two family members at the same time.

Counterparadox   A therapeutic double-bind strategy used by systemic therapists aimed at stopping the family's unhealthy paradoxical patterns by encouraging the family to continue doing them, even though the patterns are an ordeal.

Cybernetics   A scientific discipline concerned with the communication within an observer and between the observer and his or her environment.

Epistemology   The science of "knowing"; the study of how we know what we know.

First-order change   Change that occurs when only a specific behavior within a system changes.

Homeostasis   In systems thinking, a term used to describe the action of maintaining balance and equilibrium within a family system.

Hypothesizing   A technique used by systemic therapists to theorize how and why a family problem or symptom has developed and endures. Hypothesizing can be done individually or with a team of colleagues.

Neutral hypothesizing   A theoretical mindset adopted by the Milan therapists, in which the therapist takes a neutral position with a family, hypothesizing that his or her solutions up to now were appropriate, yet now seek a different direction.

Neutrality   An attempt for the therapist to see each person's point of view.

Openings   Term for the therapeutic "space" that is created when the systemic therapist notices a difference in beliefs among family members.

Positive connotation   A method of reframing the problem, but in a way that the family members are not blamed or labeled as bad.

Second-order change   Change that occurs as a result of new rules and premises, which leads to a permanent change in patterns.

Second-order cybernetics   A theory that suggests that the therapist, in observing a system (e.g., a family), becomes part of the system as opposed to an outsider observing a system.

Systemic family therapy   A family therapy approach used by the Milan team in which the family is seen as a system.

REFERENCES

Anderson, C. (1999). In memoriam: Mara Selvini Palazzoli, M.D. (1916–1999). *Family Process, 38*(4), 391–398.

Bateson, G. (1972). *Steps to an ecology of mind.* New York, NY: Ballantine Books.

Bertrando, P. (2004). Systems in evolution: Luigi Boscolo and Gianfranco Cecchin in conversation with Paolo Bertrando and Marco Bianciardi [Editorial—Farewell to Gianfranco]. *Journal of Family Therapy, 26*, 213–223.

Boscolo, L., Cecchin, G. F., Hoffmann, L., & Penn, P. (1987). *Milan systemic family therapy: Conversations in theory and practice.* New York, NY: Basic Books.

Campbell, D. (1999). Family therapy and beyond: Where is the Milan systemic approach today? *Child Psychology & Psychiatry Review, 4*(2), 76–84.

Campbell, D. (2003). The mutiny and the bounty: The place of Milan ideas today. *Australian & New Zealand Journal of Family Therapy, 24*(1), 15–25.

Cecchin, G. (1987). Hypothesizing, circularity, and neutrality revisited: An invitation to curiosity. *Family Process, 26*, 405–413.

Goldenberg, I., & Goldenberg, H. (2004). *Family therapy: An overview* (6th ed.). Pacific Grove, CA: Brooks/Cole.

Jones, E. (1993). *Family systems therapy: Developments in the Milan-systemic therapies.* New York, NY: Wiley.

Kalinyak, C. M., & Jones, S. L. (1999). Appropriately timed interventions with the family and the adolescent: The role of the therapist. *Mental Health Nursing*, 459–472.

Nichols, M. P., & Schwartz, R. C. (1991). *Family therapy: Concepts and methods* (2nd ed.). Needham Heights, MA: Allyn & Bacon.

Penn, P. (1982). Circular questioning. *Family Process, 21*(3), 267–280.

Penn, P. (1985). Feed-forward: Future questions, future maps. *Family Process, 24*(3), 299–310.

Pirrotta, S. (1984). Milan revisited: A comparison of the two Milan schools. *Journal of Strategic and Systemic Therapies, 3*, 3–15.

Scheel, M. J., & Conoley, C. W. (1998). Circular questioning and neutrality: An investigation of the process relationship. *Contemporary Family Therapy, 20*(2), 221–235.

Selvini Palazzoli, M. (Ed.). (1988). *The work of Mara Selvini Palazzoli*. Northvale, NJ: Jason Aronson.

Selvini Palazzoli, M., Boscolo, L., Cecchin, G., & Prata, G. (1978). *Paradox and counterparadox*. New York, NY: Jason Aronson.

Selvini Palazzoli, M., Boscolo, L., Cecchin, G., & Prata, G. (1980). Hypothesizing–circularity–neutrality. *Family Process, 19*, 73–85.

Tomm, K. (1984). One perspective on the Milan systemic approach: Part I. Overview of development, theory and practice. *Journal of Marital and Family Therapy, 10*(2), 113–125.

Tomm, K. (1984). One perspective on the Milan systemic approach: Part II. Description of session format, interviewing style, and interventions. *Journal of Marital and Family Therapy, 10*(3), 253–271.

Tomm, K. (1985). Circular interviewing: A multifaceted clinical tool. In D. Campbell & R. Draper (Eds.). *Applications of systemic family therapy: The Milan approach method* (pp. 33–45). New York, NY: Norton.

Tomm, K. (1987a). Interventive interviewing: Part I. Strategizing as a fourth guideline for the therapist. *Family Process, 26*(1), 3–13.

Tomm, K. (1987b). Interventive interviewing: Part II. Reflexive questioning as a means to enable self-healing. *Family Process, 26*(2), 167–183.

von Foerster, H. (1974). Cybernetic of cybernetics (physiology of revolution). *The Cybernetician, 3*, 30–32.

Watzlawick, P., Beavin, J., & Jackson, D. (1967). *Pragmatics of human communication: A study of interactional patterns, pathologies, and paradoxes*. New York, NY: Norton.

Watzlawick, P., Weakland, J. H., & Fisch, R. (1974). *Change: Principles of problem formation and problem resolution*. New York, NY: Norton.

RECOMMENDED READING LIST

Books

Bateson, G. (1999). *Steps to an ecology of mind*. Chicago, IL: University of Chicago Press.

Bergman, J. (1985). *Fishing for barracuda: Pragmatics of brief systemic therapy*. New York, NY: Norton.

Boscolo, L., & Bertrando, P. (1993). *The time of time: A new perspective in systemic therapy and consultation*. New York, NY: Norton.

Boscolo, L., & Bertrando, P. (1996). *Systemic therapy with individuals*. London, United Kingdom: Karnac Books.

Cade, B., & O'Hanlon, W. (1993). *A brief guide to brief therapy*. New York, NY: Norton.

Campbell, D., & Draper, R. (Eds.). (1985). *Applications of systemic family therapy: The Milan approach* (Vol. 3). Orlando, FL: Grune & Stratton.

Gelcer, E., McCabe, A., & Smith-Resnick, C. (1990). *Milan family therapy: Variant and invariant methods*. Northvale, NJ: Jason Aronson.

Hoffman, L. (1981). *Foundations of family therapy*. New York, NY: Basic Books.

Jones, E. (1993). *Family systems therapy: Developments in the Milan-systemic therapies*. New York, NY: Wiley.

Jones, E., & Asen, E. (2000). *Systemic couple therapy and depression*. London, United Kingdom: Karnac Books.

Manturana, H. R. (1978). Biology of language: The epistemology of reality. In G. A. Miller & E. Lennenberg (Eds.), *Psychology and biology of language and thought*. New York, NY: Academic Press.

Papp, P. (1983). *The process of change.* New York, NY: Guilford Press.

Selvini Palazzoli, M., Boscolo, L., Cecchin, G., & Prata, G. (1978). *Paradox and counterparadox.* New York, NY: Jason Aronson.

Selvini Palazzoli, M., Cirillo, S., Selvini, M., & Sorrentino, A. M. (1989). *Family games: General models of psychotic processes in the family.* New York, NY: Norton.

von Foerster, H. (1982). *Observing systems.* Seaside, CA: Intersystems Publications.

Articles

Bertrando, P. (2002). Narrative, postmodernism, and cybernetics. *Journal of Family Therapy, 22,* 83–103.

Brown, J. E. (1995). Teaching hypothesizing skills from a post-Milan perspective. *Australian & New Zealand Journal of Family Therapy, 16*(3), 133–142.

Brown, J. E. (1997). Circular questioning: An introductory guide. *Australian & New Zealand Journal of Family Therapy, 18*(2), 109–114.

Campbell, D. (2004). Methods in the madness: Re-reading "Paradox and Counterparadox" twenty-five years on. *Clinical Child Psychology and Psychiatry, 9,* 437–442.

Cecchin, G. (1987). Hypothesizing, circularity, and neutrality revisited: An invitation to curiosity. *Family Process, 26,* 405–413.

Jones, E. (2003). Reflections under the lens: Observations of a systemic therapist on the experience of participation and scrutiny in a research project. *Journal of Family Therapy, 25,* 347–356.

Selvini Palazzoli, M. (1986). Towards a general model of psychotic family games. *Journal of Marital and Family Therapy, 12,* 339–349.

Selvini Palazzoli, M., Boscolo, L., Cecchin, G., & Prata, G. (1980). Hypothesizing–circularity–neutrality: Three guidelines for the conductor of the session. *Family Process, 19*(1), 3–12.

Tomm, K. (1987). Interventive interviewing: Part I. Strategizing as a fourth guideline for the therapist. *Family Process, 26*(1), 3–13.

Tomm, K. (1987). Interventive interviewing: Part II. Reflexive questioning as a means to enable self-healing. *Family Process, 26*(2), 167–183.

Tomm, K. (1988). Interventive interviewing: Part III. Intending to ask lineal, circular, strategic, or reflexive questions? *Family Process, 27*(1), 1–15.

Websites

Priory Medical Journals
http://www.priory.com/psych/milan.htm

Structural Family Therapy

10

Yueh-Ting (Tim) Lee

In all cultures, the family imprints its members with selfhood. Human experience of identity has two elements; a sense of belonging and a sense of being separate. The laboratory in which these ingredients are mixed and dispensed is the family, the matrix of identity.

—Salvador Minuchin

INTRODUCTION

Structural family therapy (SFT) was developed by Salvador Minuchin, a psychiatrist, and his colleagues in the 1960s. Based on a systemic point of view, this approach conceptualized how the struggles of families, human problems, and relationship difficulties developed as a result of interactional dysfunction. This chapter will focus on the period when the approach was beginning to mature, around the mid-1970s. More information about the continuing evolution of SFT is provided in the interviews at the end of this chapter. This chapter was designed to provide some of the basic concepts of SFT as well as resources where a reader can gain more knowledge of SFT, such as reading materials, training centers, and programs to train to be a structural family therapist.

HISTORY AND LEADING FIGURES

The originating concepts of SFT were first developed and practiced in the early 1960s at Wiltwyck School for Boys, populated by boys from a New York slum. Salvador Minuchin and his colleagues taught themselves to do family therapy, inventing it as they went along. They built a one-way mirror and took turns observing each other in an effort to perfect the model. Minuchin and his colleagues noticed that most people seeking mental health treatment at Wiltwyck were not able to afford the money and time for mental health services (Jenkins, 1990). They also found that many families in this population were not structured and they had no rules or regulations. For example, a son could yell at his parents without any consequences, or the family never established a regular time to eat, bringing the family together on a regular basis.

Minuchin led a program at the school, which tried to improve family functioning. This marked the formation of SFT. Minuchin provides more detail in his book, *Families of the Slums: An Exploration of Their Structure and Treatment* (Minuchin, Montalvo, Guerney, Rosman, & Schumer, 1967). This humble beginning with disadvantaged persons was a landmark in the field of family therapy and led to the creation of one of the largest and most prestigious child guidance clinics in the world, the Philadelphia Child Guidance Clinic (PCGC), now called the Philadelphia Child and Family Therapy Training Center, Inc., a leading center of training and research in family therapy. Minuchin's SFT approach was initially described in his 1974 book *Families and Family Therapy*. By the mid-1970s, SFT had become one of the most influential and widely practiced of all models of family therapy. Later, he invited Jay Haley, one of the developers of strategic family therapy (see Chapter 11), to collaborate with him and Braulio Montalvo at the clinic. The Philadelphia Child and Family Therapy Training Center, Inc., is now a nonprofit center that continues to serve families in Philadelphia as well as training professional structural family therapists (Minuchin, 1974).

In 1981, Minuchin stepped down as director and moved to New York and opened Family Studies, Inc., a nonprofit center, which was renamed the Minuchin Center for the Family in 1995. Minuchin shifted his interest to treating families with psychosomatic illnesses until he retired in 1996 (Nichols & Schwartz, 1998). The Minuchin Center for the Family continues to provide SFT training programs and serves people who are marginalized because of their race, socioeconomic status, or sexual orientation.

INTRODUCTION TO STRUCTURAL FAMILY THERAPY

SFT looks at family members' relationships and interactions (Aponte, 2003) through a systems theory lens. The structural approach defines how a family should organize their relationships and functioning. Intervening in the pattern of interaction and the structure of the family brings about changes and resolves dysfunction in the family. Therefore, the structural family therapist spends time understanding and tracking family interactional patterns, boundaries, and subsystems so that he or she may intervene and alter the current structural patterns. The structural family therapist does this by actively changing the sequence of events or changing the structure in the family through directions or even moving family members physically in the room so that the family can experience itself differently.

An example of a change in sequence may involve instructing a mother and father to discuss a child's behavior together, separately from the child's presence, rather than the father giving in to a child's wish after the mother refuses. An example of a physical move might be to remove a child who is sitting between his parents in a therapy session to demonstrate the importance of the parental hierarchy to the child and the parents. The child would then be placed in a nearby chair or even on the floor to symbolize a proper hierarchy. The purpose of SFT is thus to reorganize how a family functions so that change to a more healthy function is inevitable.

Family Structure

"Family structure is the invisible set of functional demands that organize the ways in which family members interact" (Minuchin, 1974, p. 51). Family structure represents the power, patterns, and the organization in the family. Each family has its own rules of interacting (or not interacting) with each member. Family structure is formed on the basis of interaction patterns and dynamics. Each family member has roles and functions in varied positions within different family subsystems, and each member has his or her own boundary with other individuals. Individual functioning, visible or invisible, is based on family rules, spoken or unspoken, and such functioning shapes family structure.

The way a family is structured defines how the family deals with a problem from inside or outside the family. It also determines how a member responds or does not respond. The structural family therapist seeks to understand the structure in a family so that he or she can understand how the family gains balance, misbalance or maintains balance of the family system. For example, in families, roles evolve without any conscious awareness as a method of keeping the family functioning. Sometimes, the roles that evolve are dysfunctional, such as one parent being domineering and controlling because of the other parent being inconsistent and irresponsible. The structural family therapist pays attention to the evolution of roles in the family and introduces interventions that change the roles of family members and thus the structure of the family.

Power and Hierarchy

In a family, the person with the most power makes all of the final decisions and takes responsibility for the outcome of the family dynamics. Appropriate persons to have power in families are the parents. For example, when a father tells his child not to play video games, the child obeys because the father has consistently shown the child through and through that he expects compliance in his child. This interaction defines the relationship between them as well as creates the appropriate hierarchy. The father is in control. The father has the power and the child gives the father power, respecting the father's request. However, in dysfunctional families, if the relationship between parents is not healthy, children may be given more attention than the couple gives each other, and the child is therefore given control. Such situations leave the child insecure because he or she is not mature enough to have such power and cause parents to continue their conflict over the child rather than deal with their own issues. Those children grow up needing to be more mature than they are capable of and often act out. The structural family therapist strives to place parents in their proper hierarchical role above the children, helping the children feel safe and secure and creating a natural boundary between parents and children.

Family Subsystems

A large system contains smaller subsystems. For example, a family system might contain several subsystems, as mentioned previously, mostly the spousal, parental, and sibling subsystems. The subsystems include different family members, and a member may be involved in one or more subsystems in the family. Subsystems may be hierarchically arranged, with power in subsystems and/or between subsystems. The subsystems can also be divided by genders, functions, generations, or interests. The family has developmental tasks, which it must carry out as it grows, such as helping children grow up into adolescents and later launching them into young adults. These tasks are processed within bounded subsystems and, if healthy, the subsystems allow the family members to encourage growth and independence, resulting in an adolescent feeling confident enough to leave home.

For example, an adolescent reaches her senior year in high school and begins looking for a college to attend. If she feels her parents are in a healthy place and she is not part of a triangle between them, keeping them from quarreling, she will more likely seek a college out of town and feel comfortable leaving home. But if she feels that her parents still need her to mediate, illustrated by her mother telling the daughter that she will be unhappy and lonely when she leaves, the daughter may put college off and stay at home. Healthy families recognize that growth and independence are important and do not put pressure on a member to mediate. Instead, they encourage that person to seek his or her own unique future and assure the person that the rest of the family will function.

Boundaries

Boundaries may be established by spoken or unspoken rules. They are psychological, not physical. The degree of boundary permeability represents how much the subsystems allow interaction among each other, or with external systems. Rigid boundaries are those that basically disengage members from each other, either in communities or at home. There is a very limited access; they do not engage with other systems, and they cannot negotiate or accommodate developmental challenges or problems.

An example would be the very strict parent who is unable to hear his child's request because of rigidity in his own childhood or a desire for complete control, leaving the child feeling unheard and rejected. Clear boundaries are those that are negotiable. For example, new parents may need to construct a clear boundary with grandparents who try to instruct them on how to rear their new baby and insist on visiting them constantly, giving the new parents no room to grow. Such clear boundaries involve setting limits on visits in a polite but friendly manner, yet rearing their child in the manner they feel is appropriate. Diffuse boundaries refer to enmeshment among subsystems or individuals in relationships, such as a father being so enmeshed with his younger daughter that he confides in her about his poor relationship with her mother so that the daughter alters her relationship with her mother. Eventually, the enmeshment with her father keeps her from stepping out of her family as a young adult and cultivating a relationship with a future partner. When boundaries are diffuse, adaptability is low and change rarely occurs. Without clear boundaries, the roles in a family are confusing, the hierarchy is difficult to discern, and the family structure is threatened.

Alignments, Coalitions, and Triangulations

Alignment indicates that a certain group of family members (typically two or more) share reciprocal benefits, interests, or values and thus team up with each other against another person (Wynne, 1961). It usually refers to a positive bond between family members. An example of a positive alignment is two parents working together, providing a secure life for their children. Children may also align with each other in an effort to make it through a rough time, such as a parental divorce. There are benefits to both parties to be in such an alignment. Sometimes, however, alignments that seem to have benefits can undermine families. A grandmother may align with a grandchild who has behavioral issues, taking up for the grandchild and allowing the child to stay over when the misbehavior becomes chaotic. The grandmother sends a message that the child is fine, and it is his parents who have the problem, making things very difficult for the family to resolve. The alignment serves the grandmother, who is lonely, and the grandchild, who feels misjudged and treated unfairly.

Coalitions refer to an alliance of some family members against other family members. A *stable coalition* unites two members of a system in a rigid way against a third member (Minuchin, Rosman, & Baker, 1978). For example, a mother whose marriage is in turmoil may complain to her 16-year-old son about her husband, his father, and gain the son's support, which results in an alignment against the father. This results in the son responding to the father in a disrespectful manner and disobeying him. Further, such actions result in the father and mother quarreling over how the mother turned the son against the father. This breakdown of hierarchy between the two parents elevates the son to practically the same level hierarchically, leaving no one in proper control. A structural family therapist would see the alignment and try to disengage it, forcing the mother and father to talk about marital issues rather than confide in their son, leaving him to grow appropriately. Other families may attempt to decrease the tension in a family by designating a *scapegoat* (also called the identified patient [IP]) as the focused person or issue between the two members. A common IP is the acting-out adolescent, trying to grow up but not feeling the support to do so. Rebellion is often an alternative to continuously seeking appropriate support, resulting in everyone forming a coalition against the IP.

Triangulation occurs when one member of a two-member system who are against one another attempts to distract from the conflict by bringing in a third person to focus on. A common example might be two parents who are fighting; one member may attempt to win the child over to his or her "side." This situation puts the child in a no-win position. If the child allies with one parent, the child may experience betrayal of the other parent, and the original conflict is never resolved.

THEORETICAL ASSUMPTIONS

Minuchin (1974) found that when families are faced with a stressful situation or crisis, the rigidity of their transactional patterns and boundaries may prevent any further exploration of alternatives. After that, symptomatic behavior is seen as a maladaptive reaction to changing environmental and developmental requirements (Minuchin, 1974, p. 9). When family rules that govern family transactions become inappropriate or rigid, the family is dysfunctional (Vetere, 2001). According to this approach, a dysfunctional family has failed to fulfill its purpose of nurturing growth and dealing with a crisis of its members.

A family system is therefore stabilized by each individual member's contribution. During critical times, family tasks are carried out within bounded subsystems, and members play different roles in varying subsystems. Moreover, the subsystems are organized hierarchically in a way that power is distributed appropriately within individuals and between subsystems, making reliance on some members more expected than on others. Because all family systems desire homeostasis, each individual member desires to stabilize the system and will contribute his or her part to balance the system so that he or she can continue to be satisfied by the system (Minuchin, 1974). Normal families adapt to life's inevitable stresses, problems, or crises by remaining flexible enough to permit family restructuring.

View of the Family and Client

The health of the family and client depends on the abilities of the system to adapt alternative patterns when internal and/or external conditions demand the system to change. Although SFT focuses on the present and deals with the problem in the present, Minuchin (2007) suggested that a person's past leads to his or her distorted view of the present and that people are all prisoners of their past. This means that how the family interacts can reveal or determine the structure of the family (New Developments in Structural Family Therapy Conference, 2007). For example, if family members deal with stress in a rigid way, as their parents did, the pattern and their system stay the same (Vetere, 2001). This way, they may not be able to handle stress or problems originating from inside or outside the family. It is the structural family therapist's role to understand how, for example, a family deals with stress through sequential interactions, and suggest different methods and strategies so that the outcome is different. By changing how the system operates, each family member will develop new roles. This is often done in an actual session through enactments, so that the therapist can help the family to work through their typical way of responding to a situation differently.

View on How Change Occurs

Structural family therapists believe that when the structure of the family changes, the positions of members in the group change, and vice versa. The structural family therapist believes that there must be a proper hierarchy in place, with the caretakers or parents in charge, in a healthy coalition. In terms of healthy and unhealthy functioning, symptoms in an individual are rooted in the context of family transaction patterns, and family restructuring must occur before an individual's symptoms are relieved (Minuchin, 1974). Structural changes must first occur within the family because how a family functions has a direct effect on how an individual functions within. Only then will individual symptoms be limited, reduced, or resolved. If each member's experience changes as the family functions differently, then symptomatic distress will decrease. Therefore, the therapist focuses on changing the experience of family members.

For example, an acting-out adolescent might be seen by the therapist to be in a triangle with his parents, whose marriage is unhappy. The therapist may acknowledge to the son that it is nice of him to keep his parents occupied with his problems, but would he rather not see his parents having a night out together so he could finally get some peace? The therapist may say to the son, "Would you be willing to give up your misbehaviors for 1 week so that your parents have less to worry about and go out on Friday night, leaving you alone with the television?" The son may agree that having a break from his parents would be a real treat and abide by some rules so that his parents would go out the next week. This indirectly and discreetly puts the proper hierarchy back in place (rules are expected to be followed) so that the adolescent can relax and the parents be placed in a situation where they are together, forming a clear boundary between them and their son.

"Structural family therapy is a therapy of action" (Minuchin, 1974, p. 14). Structural therapeutic efforts are based on the principle that action leads to new experiences and insight (Vetere, 2001). Change begins when an individual's experience of certainty (his or her role) starts to become uncertainty or confusion, which helps the family become more fluid (New Developments in Structural Family Therapy Conference, 2007). By helping the family member to step out of his or her current role into an unknown role, family dynamics shift and everyone resettles into different roles. In the previous example of the son who was willing to behave so that his parents would go out, he shifted his thinking from "I am the problem" to "I have the solution." By directing the family to take new actions without actually understanding it (they do later), change is likely to occur spontaneously and the system gets the credit for the changes. Moreover, family changes in structure result in changes in the family styles or patterns of interaction.

Therapist's Role

The goals for this approach are to restructure how a family has organized itself, alter dysfunctional transactional patterns, and thereby reducing symptoms in identified patients. A structural family therapist is commonly described as a stage therapist, because he or she directs who should talk to whom, who should not talk, or who should sit where. The therapist tries to help the family create permeable boundaries and subsystems. Minuchin suggested (New Developments in Structural Family Therapy Conference, 2007) that the family therapist's task is to break the certainty of the family of what the problem is or who the "problem" is. This confusion helps family members to rethink their roles and try out new ones.

Based on the therapist's theoretical blueprint of proper hierarchies and boundaries, the therapist's task is to modify the family's present situation, not to explore or interpret its past.

Although the past formed the issue or rigid pattern, the goal for the structural family therapist is to intervene in the present and bring about change in the family (Minuchin, 1974). The therapist therefore intervenes with the family actively during sessions by assuming a leadership position, understanding the family's underlying structure, and transforming the structure with direct requests of the family designed to change how the members interact with each other (Minuchin, 1974). When the family has restructured itself and thus freed its members to relate to one another in a nonpathological pattern, then the therapeutic goal is reached (Prochaska & Norcross, 1999).

Interventions

SFT interventions focus more on current interactions than past experiences. The model greatly emphasizes changes and patterns that can take place in the present, which will have outcomes for the future.

Initially, the interventions begin with the therapist joining with the family, a task in which the therapist tries to make a connection with the family members by demonstrating concern and understanding. In joining, the therapist encourages each person and acknowledges his or her pain and stress. "Joining is letting the family know that the therapist understands them and is working with and for them by using the right frequencies to communicate with family members" (Minuchin & Fishman, 1981, p. 31). "*Mimesis* refers to the process of joining the family by imitating manner, style, affective range, or content of its communications in order to solidify the therapeutic alliance with the family" (Minuchin & Fishman, 1981, p. 133). In this sense, the therapist acts like a long-distance relative or a member in the family. If the family sits back in their chair, so will the therapist. If the family sits rigidly, so will the therapist.

Structural therapists next perform an assessment by exploring the family's structure and patterns. In this phase, the therapist tries to identify areas of strength, resilience, possible flexibility, and change of the family as well as enmeshment of the family system. The therapist needs to evaluate the subsystems, rigid systems, and balance of the family. In SFT, assessment is an ongoing process.

Structural family therapists may create a map of the family's structure. This is similar to the genogram (described in Chapter 1). The map designates who is in what position with what kind of power. The map is also a reference for diagnosing the dysfunction in the family. It gives a therapist a clear picture of where and/or when he or she should intervene. For more detail on family mapping, please refer to Becvar and Becvar's (2000) book, *Family Therapy: A Systemic Integration*.

The following is an example of a functional two-parent family with an adolescent child and other children. The dotted lines represent clear boundaries:

Tracking is the term Minuchin used to refer to gathering members' communication contents and using them in conversation with the family. Thus, the therapist uses the same level of vocabulary as the family. For example, a parent may describe her young daughter as "a real pain." The therapist may take on this language literally by saying back, "So tell me about your daughter, the pain," in a playful attempt to help the mother see how silly the description is and to join with her. A wife may describe her husband as a television junkie, unable to drag himself away from the television for dinner with his family. The therapist may ask her to tell him what she loves about the television junkie in an attempt to assure her that he is listening.

After an initial assessment, the therapist may suggest an *enactment* in which the family performs a conflict scenario, which happens at home during the therapeutic session. Sharf (2004) suggested that enactment offers the therapist an opportunity to observe the family rather than simply listening to the family story. It also helps the family to act out a situation of conflict; for example, purposely forcing a conflict is not easy and often results in family members recognizing how useless it is. In this phase, the therapist may not only observe, but also offer alternative transactions for the family. It will be difficult to perform an enactment if the therapist does not feel comfortable with the unpredictable responses of engaging people, such as a possible shouting match (Minuchin & Fishman, 1981). Therefore, doing an enactment should be done with care.

Reframing is also a tool to use at this stage of restructuring that serves to offer an alternative and more positive meaning or explanation of an event or situation happening in the family. Reframing offers the family members a different perspective and, as a result, may bring constructive change in the family. Again, the previous example of the acting-out adolescent boy was given the reframe that it was "nice of him to keep his parents occupied with his problems," providing the rebellious adolescent with a perception that did not match what he was actually trying to do, which was to seek freedom. He received it, however, by doing the opposite, and that is by behaving.

Much empirical evidence has proven the efficacy of SFT, particularly with difficult families. "Thus, families with a juvenile delinquent, families with an anorectic family member, families with a chemically addicted member, families of low socioeconomic status, and alcoholic families" (Aponte & Van Deusen, 1981) have all benefited from the SFT approach.

The direct and sometimes intrusive strategies have drawn critiques from feminists, yet Minuchin's claim to become a distant relative in the session is often seen as compatible with feminism. However, early in his work, Minuchin did not write or address gender roles. In 1981, he remarked that his model would work with any family, traditional or nontraditional, because his focus was on how the problem could help him help the family, no matter who the members were (Minuchin & Fishman, 1981, p. 51). SFT continues to evolve in response to challenges mounted from within and out of the systemic field, and as part of integrative practice and multisystemic approaches. It has been shown to be effective with large families, single-parent families, blended families, and three-generational families because of the helpfulness of generating proper hierarchies that assist parents and children in understanding their roles and boundaries as family members (Vetere, 2001).

STRUCTURAL FAMILY THERAPY WORKING TEMPLATE

The *structural family therapy template* is meant to be used as a guideline to learning the process of SFT. The template provides the beginning therapist with steps to take and questions to ask that promote collaboration between the therapist and client. There are suggested questions under each heading to help start the process. After using the initial questions, guide the client through each process, asking questions that occur to you, as you stay focused on the structure of the family. Although there is no one "script" for any therapy session, it is the hope of the author that the template serves as an impetus to learning this family therapy model.

Tools for Change

The structural family therapist may use various tools to effect change in families, most of which are extrinsic and require the family to take on new actions.

One of the tools to effect change includes the use of providing direct assignments to the family to carry out tasks, such as the following:

"I want you to not worry about sleep this week . . . not sleeping is good too. Use the time to catch up on work."

"After the session, I want _____ to talk to_____ an hour once in this week."

"This week, I want you to stop talking for your son and let him have his voice."

The therapist may rearrange the family members' seating arrangements to help new interactions to happen:

"I would like Mom to sit near Dad, away from the children, so the children see you as a team."

The therapist may use tracking, enactments, or other tools mentioned in this chapter to effect change:

"Mom, show me what it's like when your younger son has a temper tantrum and you give in."

Phase 1: Joining and Building Rapport

During this phase, the therapist is active in the therapeutic process, getting to know the family members and observing the interaction of the family members. The therapist may map the family's power structure, role, boundaries, alliance, and subsystems during this phase to help him or her understand the family's culture and the context. It is important to remember to focus on the here and now.

Here are some comments or questions that a therapist might use during this phase:

- *"Hello, my name is _____. Can someone start introducing themselves by using his or her name and relationship in this family?"*
- *"Tell me what it is like to be part of your family."*
- *The therapist also inquires about:*
  - *The culture, religious beliefs, or gender of family members and how that influences their actions*
  - *The family's socioeconomic status*

Phase 2: Understanding the Presenting Issue

During this phase, the therapist tries to understand how the family members are organized and how the problem is conceptualized by the members.

Here are some comments or questions that a therapist might use during this phase:

- *"I want to know why you are here. Who wants to tell me?"*
- *"Can some of you begin to tell me what the issues are that you have at this point?"*
- *"Who is the most worried about the problem?"*
- *"Who tries hardest to fix the problem?"*
- *"Do you _____ (identified client) think that you are the problem?"*

Phase 3: Assessment of Family Dynamics

Assessment is an ongoing process in SFT. During assessment, the therapist observes:

- *Who speaks most of the time?*
- *Who speaks for whom?*
- *When _____ (the problem) happens, where are the other family members?*
- *What did they say they were doing when _____ (the problem) happened?*
- *How have the (family members) tried to solve the problem?*
- *What are the verbal and nonverbal signals used in the family?*
- *Are the family members inconsistent in the session or in enactment?*
- *Is there a flexibility point where the therapist can begin working within the family? (Where does the family see a need for change?)*

Phase 4: Goals

The goal of SFT is for the therapist to restructure the family systems and change the transactional patterns so that there is a proper hierarchy in place where the parents are in charge. If there is enmeshment, the therapist will seek to separate subsystems. If there is disengagement, the therapist will seek to increase interaction between family members. To accomplish this, the therapist is directive, active, and leads the family.

- *"How do you want things to be in your family?"*
- *"Who do you think needs to be doing things differently?"*
- *"What do you think _____ (the discussion, communication, interaction in the family) should be like? Make it happen here, now. Whose help do you need?"*
- *"Talk to _____ (the person who is involved in the issue) about _____ (the problem)."*
- *"I would like you to let your mother speak first, so your father can hear her."*

Phase 5: Amplifying Change

The therapist notices changes as they occur in therapy and compliments the family. When the family returns from a week during which interactions were different, the therapist asks what happened specifically. The therapist may also warn the family that change is not easy and that slipping back into old habits is easy. He or she may predict that they may relapse, a strategy to keep the family focused on their changes. The therapist is constantly highlighting the interactions that are working well and give the credit to the family.

Here are some comments or questions that a therapist might use during this phase:

- *"You just made your daughter sit still. Sometimes she needs to hear a strong voice. She needs both strong and soft voices from you. That is good."*
- *"Last week you and your husband were a team again when you discussed Sally's behavior together in private. Your kids saw you as they should see you as people they could depend on to be consistent and reliable. That is good."*
- *"It looks like you have recovered your role as son in the family by sitting back and letting your father take your mother on a date. You got to stay home and have some freedom from your parents. That is great for you."*

Phase 6: Termination

When the family changes their pathological structure and transactional patterns, termination occurs. The family and the structural family therapist determine when therapy should end based on the changes in the structure and hierarchy of the family. As this occurs, most symptoms disappear, leaving the family to believe that therapy has been successful.

MASTER THERAPIST INTERVIEW

HARRY J. APONTE

Harry J. Aponte, LCSW, LMFT, is a professor of the couple and family therapy program at Drexel University. He worked with Minuchin in the PCGC in 1968 and was the director of the PCGC from 1975 to 1979. Mr. Aponte is a family therapist with a special interest in the treatment of the poor and many of the problems associated with poverty, including the single-parent family, sexual and physical abuse in families, school failure, and crime. His ecostructural approach combines family therapy with a community perspective.

What attracted you to the theory behind structural family therapy?
I went to a conference many years ago and Braulio Montalvo was presenting with Satir and Bowen ... what Braulio was saying I could relate to immediately. I could see the relationship between the theory and the practice. It was transparent, the connection between the two.

How do you formulate your view of a family when they enter therapy?
There has to be some pain that would motivate a person to get over that threshold of where they have been to where they want to go. I get a real picture of the family by observing the interaction within a family. These concepts provide a way of articulating what is actually taking place there and how the family members organize themselves around [the] issue. The type of family is not a factor of the model. It's really a question of how the therapist is employing the model.

What kinds of families do you think benefit most from this model?
The model was born out of work with underprivileged families. It was later applied to work with "psychosomatic" families. I do not believe there are any limits to what kind of family SFT is relevant.

What issues do you think this model works best with?

I don't believe there is any model of therapy that can claim that it can solve all human problems. I think every model of therapy has something to contribute, but if you're going to be a complete therapist, I believe you need to learn from the various models. SFT offers a particular insight into the organization of a family, and it focuses on the here-and-now interaction among family members. It is particularly strong in bringing the experience of the family into the therapeutic context so that the therapist has access to the family in action around their issue.

In your opinion, what are the necessary characteristics that a therapist should possess to be effective with this model?

The therapist can be viewed as observer and commentator, or as a director, and when needed, as a participant actor. Minuchin often used the metaphor of a theater where the therapist is the director and (he) invites one person to talk to another or one person to change seats with another person, creating an enactment and testing the viability of different family relationship configurations. To stay within the same metaphor of the theater, the structural family therapist may also step onto the stage as needed and become one of the actors in the family in order to help bring about the desired outcome in a family interaction. What you're seeing in both of these images is that the therapist is working through experience. The therapist is trying to generate an interaction and/or work with a spontaneous interaction in the present moment. The therapist may suggest, may direct, [and] may just get into the action within the family to be supportive of this person, to try to quiet down this other person or to get between these other two people who are in conflict. It's a work that is done through the energy of the human interaction within the system.

In systemic therapies, therapists are active agents in relative contrast to the psychoanalytic models where the therapist assumes a more passive and anonymous role. Obviously relatively speaking, SFT demands the therapist be particularly active. The therapist will work with the momentum the family's pain generates for change. The structural therapist may also act as the agent who activates the family in such a way that the underlying pain is brought out into the open so that the therapist has access to the family in their struggle.

Therapists need to be able to join the system, that is, to engage at a human level with the family members. Within this human relationship, I need to relate to the family members in a way that is going to be helpful to them. The therapeutic context is a personal human relationship within professional boundaries. Therapists need to know how to use their humanity in therapeutically effective ways.

How often does the client see you and for how long a period of time?

A number of clients come for a double session, and I see them for an hour and [a] half because we don't accomplish a great deal in 45 minutes. Some people I see once a week and others I see once every other week. Others I see once a month, or simply as needed. I don't determine that by myself. That is a decision that we make together, and we make it together in light of what [we are] trying to accomplish and where we are in the journey of our work.

What are you looking for when you are in the session?

What I'm looking for is the pain because that's what drives the therapy. They are not here to make friends with me. They may not be clear about what the pain is. When I first see people, I just totally open myself to listening, to reading them, to getting a sense of them so that I have a feeling for what is disturbing this person. What is really bringing them in here? I can't just say, "Oh, tell me what your problem is," and expect they'll be able to articulate it, have it analyzed for me, and save me months of work. I need to make a connection with this human being where they feel I understand and care. I'm always looking for what's broken, but also what I can build on. As I'm listening to them, one of the very key factors is I want to know where they have freedom in relation to this wound. Where they have personal freedom to make choices, there is the key to change. I'm looking for where/what this person or family has control over in relation to the issues they are presenting.

I also watch for who influences whom so that I can see who has the power to determine the outcome of the interaction. I conceptualize who is aligning with whom during that interaction and the interplay between that and who has the power . . . then I can think of boundaries and who is within the system in which the interaction is taking place. I have to stand outside of the system and observe what is going on. I've put a great deal of emphasis on therapists understanding themselves, not only understanding their history, but understanding themselves in action. Being in touch with what is it that I'm doing, what is it that I'm feeling, and why am I doing this. That way, we become experts on ourselves, so that when we stand outside the therapeutic interaction and observe, we are also observing what's going on inside of ourselves as well as what's going on between ourselves and our clients.

What is the assessment process of this model?

Our assessment of a family or of an individual client is largely going to come out of our experience of the person, not just listening to their words. It depends on what stages you're in because the assessment never ends. You're always looking for trying to understand more. So, even if you have gone over this threshold, there's always another threshold to have to go over. You learn to pay attention, to ask, to develop new hypothesis, or to elaborate on other ones. The most effective way to understand the person is through helping the person to make an effort to change. In SFT, you are trying to make the assessment of the person in action through the experience, not just through what they tell you . . . It's always a process of gathering data, forming and assessment, making an intervention, getting the outcome of the intervention, using that as the basis of new data, then, which will then affect my hypothesis, and form the basis of my next intervention. Until the end of therapy, you should always be learning more about your client till the very last moment that you see them. You should always be looking at them and relating to them in an inquisitive manner that says I want to understand them further. The day you assume that you know is the day your mind stops working. In SFT, you are making your assessment as well as your intervention through the enactment, through the experience—what happens in session as well as out of session.

Who sets the goals, the client or the therapist?

Setting the therapeutic goal has to come out of human interaction between the client and the therapist. I don't come in with preconceived goals. I come in with preconceived ideas about what I think is healthy and appropriate, but I also need to hear what they think is healthy and appropriate because we will work that out together. The determination of goals [is] driven by the pain people feel, but [is] ultimately shaped by the values and ideals that shape how they wish to live their lives.

With every intervention in SFT, you have a goal. It's an evolving goal within the session. I have a building that I'm going to build with bricks. When I put the brick down, I have to know how this brick relates to the entire structure and any time I open my mouth, or decide to keep my mouth shut, in therapy, and that's an intervention. Looking away from somebody instead of looking at them, or looking at this person instead of that person, that's another brick. I need to know if that brick fits. If it doesn't fit, then I need to redo it and do it again. But right now, the goal is to get this brick lined up with the next brick. The goal of this intervention needs to fit with the goal of the session that needs to fit with the overall goal of the therapy. In SFT, every intervention is driven by what you are trying to achieve at the moment, which is based on your hypothesis of the moment—all of which needs to align with your general hypotheses about the sources of the clients' issues along with your hypotheses about the sources of their strengths. In SFT, you build on strength.

What are some commonly used interventions with this model?

There are lists of interventions and techniques that are specifically related to addressing the structure of a relationship, but that's only a piece of the therapy. Working through the enactment is a technique which is working through the experience that is taking place here and now, or I will try to create an experience, stimulate an experience if people are only offering words to picture their issue. The structural family therapist is looking for experience, either natural experience that comes spontaneously or is trying to create a situation that will stimulate an action or interaction that carries within it the dynamics of their struggle. The therapist can then intervene in that interaction so that, in SFT, the work is being done through actual human experience of people with each other.

What role does a homework assignment have in this model?

The homework assignment is to take the experience that we are engaging in during the session and extend it into life outside of the session. It is a sense of continuity. You can also use the homework assignment as a way of their consolidating what they just accomplished in session. Because they did something in the session, you don't want it to be diluted by time. You try and construct something that they succeed at while at home, and make it more of their own rather than something that belongs only to the therapy session.

How do you know when your client is ready to terminate?

My goal is always that when they walk out of the office, they know that they don't need me. I'm always working in the direction that fosters the person taking ownership of the process of change so that they experience the therapy as their journey. People need to experience their insights as their own, their decisions to change as their own, [and] their actions to change as their own. They are ready to end therapy when the changes they have made belong to them. We can affirm and celebrate the changes, but the changes are theirs.

What have you found to be the limitations of this approach?

The only limitation of the approach is if I try to stay within this model and not learn from others, so I'm always anxious to learn from other models because they all have insights that this approach doesn't have. I always consider myself as a learner.

What are your suggestions that you have for students learning this model?

The training has to reflect the therapy. It needs to be experiential. Students need to use role play, videotape, and live supervision.

MARION LINDBLAD-GOLDBERG

Dr. Marion Lindblad-Goldberg, PhD, is the director of the Philadelphia Child and
Family Therapy Training Center, Inc., and a professor of clinical psychology in the
Department of Psychiatry at the University of Pennsylvania School of Medicine.
She was formerly the director of the Family Therapy Training Center of the PCGC.

What attracted you to the theory behind structural family therapy?

My knowledge of psychodynamic and behavioral theories did not prove adequate
when I began working with families. When Dr. Salvador Minuchin encouraged me to
work with him at the Philadelphia Child Guidance Clinic in 1969, there were no books
on family therapy. Dr. Minuchin's use of general systems theory and structural theory
provided a more adequate theoretical basis to assess and treat families. Dr. Minuchin's
theory helped to guide therapists in knowing what to do in a family session as compared to other family therapy theories. The elegant simplicity of his theory originally attracted me. Furthermore, it was a theory that lent itself to clear training and
supervisory methods.

Over time, however, I moved to develop my own biodevelopmental-systemic
model, which is called "ecosystemic structural family therapy" (ESFT; Jones & Lindblad-
Goldberg, 2002; Jones & Lindblad-Goldberg, 2008; Lindblad-Goldberg & Jones, 2005;
Lindblad-Goldberg, et al., 1998; Lindblad-Goldberg, Jones, & Dore, 2004). I thought
that Minuchin's structural family therapy model did not emphasize the individual
family member's historical, biological, cultural, developmental (emotion, cognition,
social), and attachment influences, and that these factors were important in the assessment and treatment of child, adolescent, and adult-focused families.

In ESFT, assumptions about human nature, problem formation, development and
adaptation, and family processes are informed most broadly by a synthesis of general
systems theory; structural family therapy; developmental-contextual theory, currently
embraced in the discipline of developmental psychopathology; and theories of human
ecology. Four interrelated constructs that guide ESFT therapists in their understanding
of clinical problems include family structure, family emotion regulation, individual
differences (historical, biological, cultural, developmental), and family development.

How do you formulate your view of a family when they enter therapy?

I am pleased when a family enters therapy because there are so many more resources
available to me as a therapist than if I only have an individual as a resource. Since
families inevitably have the potential to find solutions to problems, I know that if I can
establish a collaborative relationship with family members, change can happen. When a
family enters therapy, the underlying competence of family members to solve problems
might not be immediately apparent, and I need to work therapeutically to bring these
strengths to the foreground. I always operate with the assumption that the family's
potential for change exists.

What kinds of families and clinical problems do you think benefit most from this model?

While the ESFT model can be used with families at any stage of development, it
has been most frequently used with families having children, adolescents, and young

adults. The ESFT model has addressed a wide range of child and adolescent clinical problems across all levels of severity. For example, in Pennsylvania, the ESFT model is being used as an in-home/community service with children and adolescents having severe emotional and behavioral disturbance that puts them at risk for out-of-home placement in psychiatric inpatient hospitals and/or residential placement settings. This population manifests multiple diagnoses on Axis I and covers the spectrum of disorders in the *DSM- IV [Diagnostic and Statistical Manual of Mental Disorders]*. A 7-year study of in-home ESFT treatment outcomes was conducted on 1,968 families having a child or adolescent with [serious emotional disturbance]. Pre- and posttreatment measures showed significant reductions in presenting symptoms and use of out-of-home placement. Significant positive changes were also found in family functioning and in the child or adolescent's psychosocial functioning that were maintained up to 1 year posttreatment (Lindblad-Goldberg, Jones, & Dore, 2004).

Different models of therapy require the therapist to be directive or nondirective. In your opinion, what are the necessary characteristics that a therapist should possess to be effective with this model?
The most essential characteristic a therapist must possess is the ability to demonstrate a commitment to create safe, caring, collaborative, and trustworthy relationships with family members. Therapists must be able to engage and motivate families through empathic listening, validation, respect, acceptance, partnership, and accommodation [of] the family's needs, preferences, and cultural values. Therapists must also demonstrate adherence to the ESFT model as measured by the Brief ESFT Treatment Scale (Jones & Lindblad-Goldberg, 2008).

The length of a session should vary depending on client needs. At my center, outpatient training program sessions are at least 1 hour. In our home-based treatment, sessions are as short or as long as a family needs. In my adult family therapy marathons, I may meet with families for 6 hours the first day and up to 6 hours the second day.

How often does the client see you and for how long a period of time?
In my outpatient private practice or in-home practice, I always schedule an hour and a half so that if change has begun, I can continue it in the session as long as possible. The length of outpatient treatment depends on what the client needs and wants. For example, it could be 1 session or 15 sessions. In general, the center's average length of outpatient treatment is 6 to 8 sessions. Traumatized families need more sessions. In the mental health home-based treatment for children and adolescents with [serious emotional disturbance] that I helped to develop in Pennsylvania, we specified that length of treatment would be up to 8 months. In the adult family therapy marathons I developed, treatment length was 2 days (up to 12 hours) with follow-up after 6 months.

Let me put in a caveat here. My thinking about length of sessions or treatment is predicated on the fact that my private clinical practice and the center's clinical service are not based on the need for patient income. If my only source of income was my clinical practice or if the center could not financially continue to offer a free clinical service, I would probably have to do things differently.

What are you looking for when you are in the session?
In ESFT practice, there is considerable overlap between the two functions of assessment and intervention. While assessment has a clear data-gathering purpose, it is also

considered interventional because it both sets the stage for change and activates the change process. One objective of assessment is to strengthen the therapeutic alliance and sense of partnership with the family. Assessment allows family members to teach the therapist about the nature of their challenges and how their family operates. While more formal assessments may occur in the initial stages of treatment, ESFT assessment is actually an ongoing process throughout treatment. Assessment is used to develop an understanding of the bio/developmental/systemic context wherein the strengths and difficulties of the identified patient, other family members, and the family as a whole are manifested.

What is the assessment process of this model?

During the assessment phase, information is obtained about the family's formal and informal helpers. Decisions are made with the family regarding which current helpers and/or potential new resource helpers would make good collaborative partners in helping the family to achieve its goal. See the Case Study.

Who sets the goals, the client or the therapist?

Goal setting is used as a way of coevolving a treatment contract that demonstrates a partnership between client and therapist. The client's goals become a road map that helps the therapist to maintain an intentional stance and stay focused within sessions and throughout the stages of therapy.

What are some commonly used interventions with this model?

Creating key growth-promoting interpersonal experiences [is] accomplished through actions the therapist takes with families and through the way the therapist relates with families. The former involves the use of concrete methods or techniques, while the latter involves the emotional posture or stance the therapist assumes with a family.

ESFT incorporates techniques from many different models of psychotherapy to create relational change. It is the relational objective that determines its appropriateness. Techniques that are unique to the model and that are commonly used to reorganize or restructure the way family members relate to one another include boundary making, rebalancing power or clarifying hierarchy, and adjusting emotional proximity. The most common intervention used by ESFT therapists to create change is behavioral enactments. This refers to the spontaneous in-session playing out of a core family interaction pattern. These interactions create rich opportunities for therapists to help family members become more aware of self-defeating patterns as well as to practice "in vivo" relating in an entirely different way with one another, particularly with respect to emotional regulation and expansion of distress tolerance skills. Enactments allow family members to engage in what they most often avoid: interpersonal conflict and negative emotions.

What role does a homework assignment have in this model?

Homework tasks between sessions are used to practice these new patterns of relating. Other commonly used techniques in ESFT address thinking, beliefs, or knowledge in the family such as reframing, constructing growth-producing narratives, psychoeducation, and use of rituals.

How do you know when your client is ready to terminate?

When the goals in a treatment contract have been mutually developed between the therapist and family, then the achievement of these goals can be mutually evaluated. Clients will let you know when the therapy is no longer needed. However, I believe that once a therapeutic relationship has formed with family members, the therapist should remain available if a future need arises. Therefore, for me, the concept of "termination" does not apply. Rather, I say to clients, "Au revoir"—until we see each other again if the need arises.

What have you found to be the limitations of this approach?

The one limitation of the ESFT model when used with children or adolescents is that an optimal requirement is the willingness of at least one caregiver (biological or nonbiological) to work toward the possibility of developing a parenting relationship with a child or adolescent. Without an identifiable caregiver expressing the desire to be involved in the youth's development, the model would not be effective. The model's systemic view of a problem in context can be applied to children or adolescents and their relationships with staff in residential settings. However, there may be less motivation to develop and maintain relational change in these settings.

What are your suggestions for students learning this model?

If a student wants to learn the ESFT model, they should read the references at the end of this chapter and seek training in the form of workshops, courses, or ideally, one of our clinical programs providing cases and one-way mirror supervision (e.g., 3-week summer practicum, 1-year part-time program, COAMFTE-accredited 2-year program) at the Philadelphia Child and Family Therapy Training Center. Since our traveling faculty train agencies, cities, states, and countries nationally and internationally, students can contact us to locate a potential supervisor in their geographic area.

Case Study

A mother calls and makes an appointment for her family to come to therapy. The family consists of a husband and wife, both in their 40s; their 15-year-old son; a college-aged daughter; and the woman's father, age 82. Three years after the woman's mother died, her father developed Alzheimer's disease. He moved in with the family 6 months ago. When his health began to deteriorate, the woman spent more time caring for him than for other members of the family. Three months ago, the 15-year-old son, who has been treated for attention deficit hyperactivity disorder (ADHD) since age 7, began to refuse to take his medication and is now truant from school.

During the session, the wife cries and the husband reports their relationship is strained, while occasionally rolling his eyes as his wife becomes tearful. He reports that he has had to take on more work because his wife had to quit her job to attend to her father's needs. The daughter is away at college and the wife smiles as she describes her as a straight-A student. The daughter was asked to attend the session but refused because she has a hard time with her grandfather's illness and dislikes the conflict that has developed at home.

Harry J. Aponte's Response to the Case Study

The obvious hypothesis is that the mother's diversion of attention from husband and children to attend to her father is creating a crisis at home. If the hypothesis proves valid, my goal would be to help the mother create a caregiving arrangement for him that allows her to shift the main responsibility for his care to others, such as an institutional facility, or even private nursing help if they can afford it. On the other hand, we would have to work to reengage her with her husband and children not only timewise but also emotionally.

Of course, we must first better understand what is operating under the surface. First of all, we cannot simply assume that the 15-year-old is reacting to his mother's involvement with her ailing father. We would have to meet with the parents and son, as well as the son alone, to explore the nature of his problem. We may also have to contact the school for their observations. We would need to meet with the couple to better understand the strain they are experiencing in the marriage, again to see whether indeed it is all related to mother's immersion in her father's care. Finally, preferably in a session or more, we would want to meet with the mother and, hopefully, a supportive husband to better understand why she has given herself over to caring for her father at her family's expense. What is her family history; what is her culture; what has been her relationship with her father?

What then do we do should our original hypothesis be proven true? Even if it were, one would have to assume that we have gathered particular information about why this family is responding to this particular crisis the way it is. We would need to tailor our therapeutic strategy to fit the particular picture that emerges from our explorations. However, we cannot speculate about this, given the synopsis of the family situation we have started working with.

Therefore, we can only outline a broad approach to the family's treatment. From a structural standpoint, we would need to work on both sides of the problem at the same time. We work with the boy's issues and the marital strain on one side, and alternative forms of care for the mother's father on the other. We would want her investing time and energy in her son and husband even as we are promoting, with the husband's support, alternative forms of care for her father. The son needs to experience his mother fully invested in him. The husband needs to reclaim his wife. Just these efforts alone will create some distance for the mother from the care of her father. Hopefully, the family and couple's sessions will help her refocus on her son and husband, which would lead to her reinvesting in self-care.

In a parallel process, we work with the couple on a solution for the mother's desire to provide her father with the best of care. The reframe must be in line with her desires, and not with the wishes of others that she get rid of him. We would be examining what her father needs and what other options exist that may be better than what she is doing, given that she has other responsibilities in her life, as well as personal limits to her own energy. We need to ride her sense of responsibility for her father, and not be opposing what she is currently doing for him simply because other people want her time. Assuming she is feeling guilty about not taking total responsibility for him, she needs to feel from us that we, including her husband, are also invested in securing good care for her father that also allows her to demonstrate her love for him.

Dr. Marion Lindblad-Goldberg's Response to the Case Study

In the ESFT model, the first stage of therapy, "constructing a therapeutic system" (i.e., relationship building), and the second stage, "creating a meaningful focus" (i.e., assessment data collection leading to clinical hypotheses relating clinical problems to assessment information), are combined in clinical practice. Therefore, in this case example, I would want to gather assessment information in a way that facilitates my development of a therapeutic alliance with the husband and wife and, eventually, the son and daughter so that the therapeutic system is a collaborative partnership between me and each family member. The style I would use to gather assessment information would be to demonstrate genuine curiosity and interest in exploring their concerns and ideas. I would want to have a conversation with each individual and not a rigid question–answer style. As each individual gave information, I would want to know the meaning he/she made of an event, his/her emotional experience, and how the partner coped. Continual empathetic validation would be given regarding the difficulties each family member has had to overcome. Competent coping mechanisms would also be validated. I would want each individual to feel that I can be trusted to understand his/her experience and that he/she can expect me to be emotionally in the moment with each of them. Specifically, in this first session, I would express empathy for the real challenges the couple is facing in dealing with maternal grandfather's (MGF's) debilitating progressive illness in addition to addressing the developmental needs of their two children and their own needs as individuals and as a couple.

As each told the story of his/her concerns, I would organize this assessment information in my head in the following ways. First, how does each family member define the problem(s)? Second, what are the observed or described sequences of behaviors that revolve around each problem (i.e., the negative interaction cycles)? What are the patterns of organization in the family related to dealing with stated problem? Third, what is each individual's emotional experience with regard to each problem and what beliefs exist regarding the meaning of a problem(s)? Fourth, what has been this family's history and emotional experience of developmental and external stressors and who have been each family member's key attachment figures to provide crucial emotional support during stressful times? From this family timeline, I would create hypotheses regarding what "birthed" the problem(s) and what have maintained them. I would want to know what the family's organizational patterns were before and after the stressors. Fifth, I would explore any biological and/or developmental explanations for the problems. Sixth, I would pay attention to how each partner demonstrates the ability (or lack of ability) to emotionally regulate negative emotions such as fear, anger, sadness, guilt, anxiety, etc. and how each partner helps to soothe the other partner through empathy, softening responses, etc. Seventh, I would want to know who is in the entire family system and summarize this information in a genogram. Of the individuals named, I would assess who is a part of the problem and who can be counted on for support. Eighth, I would explore the family's ecology to determine the extrafamilial supports and stressors.

The information in this case study is limited to a brief family history, minimal problem information, minimal couple relational process information, and no relational information about parent–child or sibling relationships. In real-life clinical work, the assessment stage of my model involves a comprehensive evaluation. In this case study, only three brief descriptions of problems are given: (1) For the past 3 months, the 15-year-old son has refused to take his medication for ADHD; (2) the son has begun to truant from school; and (3) the husband reports the spousal relationship is strained with conflict in the home since his wife quit her job to attend to her father's needs.

The family's timeline of stressors reveals the following: (1) death of the maternal grandmother (MGM); (2) 3 years later, MGF's diagnosis of Alzheimer's; (3) 6 months ago, MGF began living with the couple and their two children; (4) mother quits job to attend to MGF and father increases his work time; (5) mother begins to spend more time with MGF and less time with other family members; (6) 3 months ago, son begins to refuse to take his medication for ADHD; (7) currently, school has reported the son's truancy; (8) currently, father reports that the spousal relationship is strained.

A first assessment question generally is, "Why is the couple coming for help now?" The couple didn't come when MGM died, when MGF was given an Alzheimer's diagnosis, when MGF moved in 6 months ago, or when son refused to take his ADHD medication 3 months ago. Rather, they came for help when son began to truant school, father began feeling strain in the spousal relationship perhaps due to his work overload, and mother quit her job to attend to MGF's needs.

Since neither the son [n]or college-age daughter came to this session, we only have access to one subsystem in the family. However, a general rule of thumb is that often who does come to a session is whoever is hurting most.

In the session, I would elicit more assessment information such as:

1. What were the grandparent, parent, children, and grandchildren relationships: (a) before MGM died and after MGM died, (b) before MGF developed Alzheimer's, and (c) after MGF moved to his daughter's home? What was the family's organization? What were the roles in the nuclear and the extended family? For example, what were daughter's or son's role vis-à-vis the mother, father, and sibling? Was she/he a helper to mother, father, or sibling? What were the alliances, coalitions, and conflicts between family members? What were the primary emotional attachments for each family member in the nuclear and extended family?

   a. What was the nature of MGM's death? What was the impact of the MGF's diagnosis? How did these events influence mother, father, son, and daughter? What were the emotional experiences of each family member and what meaning did family members make of these events? How did everyone cope?

2. With regard to the 15-year-old adolescent:

   a. Is he also diagnosed with a learning disability, and, if so, what is the nature of the disability? Should he be evaluated for a potential learning disability? Perhaps he truants because he cannot handle senior high school work. When he truants, where does he go, what does he do?

   b. Is his behavior reflective of a developmental issue? Does he not want to take Ritalin because it's not "cool"? Does he truant to hang out with non–pro-social teens?

   c. Is the rearrangement of the family pattern related to the boy's truancy? Has the frequency of involvement changed between son and mother, father, or sister who is now in college? Since the mother is spending more time with MGF and less time with her husband and son, is there less parental monitoring and/or does the boy feel less connected? Did the boy's relationship with his sister change when she left for college? Does the boy feel his mother and father are metaphorically "truanting" from the family?

   d. Is son allied with father and does the son's truancy reflect the father's unspoken feeling that his wife is metaphorically truanting from him?

3. What does the family know about the impact of an Alzheimer's diagnosis on a family and the course of this disease?

The onset of the disease is gradual with a progressive course of deterioration. The MGF's behavior is going to fluctuate from day to day, but in a progressive manner. He's not going to be better. He's not going to become perfect and then relapse. The outcome, eventually, is going to be fatal. What is the nature of MGF's incapacitation? What he can he do now? How incapacitated is he? Can he dress himself? Can he eat by himself? Can he toilet himself?

How has the family reorganized in response to the challenge of MGF's illness? What is the task load on this family? By reading the case study, the family's current organization appears to be that mother has primary day-to-day responsibility for MGF. Father is contributing financially by working extra hours since mother had to quit her job. The daughter is contributing by not worrying her parents since she is receiving As in college. Son has begun to rebel.

Does mother feel she is getting enough emotional and concrete support to take on this new role as "caretaker of MGF"? From the case study, it seems that she is on overload and receives minimal support. Assessment inquiries should also focus on what possible concrete and emotional support is available to the family, particularly to the mother.

4. What ecological influences have helped or hindered family members' ability to master challenges, particularly MGF's illness?

I would look at the family's extended network. Does mother have friends? Does she have other extended family members (uncles, aunts, siblings) who could share responsibility for MGF? Is there anybody in her family of origin that could be enlisted to help with this care situation? Are there any Alzheimer's agencies in her community that can provide some support or concrete services to her family?

5. What is the couple's relational process and what are the family's relational processes? What are the strengths of each family member?

A very critical assessment area is whether the husband and wife are emotionally supportive of each other and whether they appreciate what each is doing to try to address the challenges. I think it's fine that the couple made the decision to come in by themselves for the first session because they may be indicating "we need help." It's not just our kid who's truant or our daughter who's not getting involved with the illness and doing her own thing, but we need help. It's important to have a session with just the couple where I can really connect with their pain and difficulties, and highlight their resilience in trying to do what needs to be done.

Obviously, as an ecosystemic structural family therapist, I wouldn't feel that the assessment was complete until I saw the parents with their children. I probably would not push initially to have the college-student daughter come to the office session. I would have the parents ask her if she would like to attend some sessions in person or by speakerphone. I would understand that she's trying to be academically successful in college, that she has a life there, but I also know that she must have feelings about what's going on. I would validate her for being able to not to worry her parents by getting straight As.

I would ask the parents when they would like their son to attend sessions with them. When the son came, I would explore his concerns while his parents listened. Since he's 15 years old, I would direct many of my assessment and hypothesis questions to him directly in the session. He could help me understand what the atmosphere in the home is like. Does the atmosphere make it hard for him to concentrate? Perhaps he doesn't want to be considered a patient like his MGF. He may not want to have an illness like ADHD, so he's not taking the medicine. After forming a therapeutic alliance with the boy and sister (by speakerphone), I would create enactments between the brother and sister, and between each child and each parent to assess the quality of their relationships at this point in time.

These assessment issues would all be a part of the inquiry during the first and second sessions because I would be exploring the couple's priority in addressing concerns. For example, do the parents want to immediately address this teen's truancy? If mother is overloaded with the care of MGF, she may not have the time or energy to deal with yet another problem.

There's no way I could say how I would treat the case because it really would depend on the answers to a lot of the assessment inquiry questions that I explored and the treatment goals desired by the family.

KEY TERMS

Boundaries   An abstract method of separating parts of a system from each other, such as children from parents or interpersonal boundaries between husband and wife, typically defined by personal rules and roles in a family.

Enactment   In SFT, a facilitating intervention in which the family is asked to enact or play out its relationship patterns spontaneously during a therapeutic session, allowing the therapist to observe and then restructure future transactions.

Enmeshment   The manner in which family members organize themselves so that boundaries between members are blurred and members are overinvolved in each other's lives, limiting individual autonomy.

Family mapping   An assessment technique used to graphically depict a family's organizational structure and determine which subsystem is involved in dysfunctional transactions.

Joining   The therapeutic act of entering a family system, getting to know the family, and developing trust, thereby becoming part of the family system so that the strategic interventions can occur more naturally through the therapist's comments and direction.

Reframing   A method of relabeling behavior with a new perspective, altering the context in which it is perceived, resulting in new responses to old behavior and thus a change in interactional patterns.

Subsystems   Organized, coexisting components consisting of family members within an overall system that have their own autonomous functions as well as a specified role in the operation of the family. There are three types of subsystem: parental, sibling, and spouse. Each subsystem has its own boundary and hierarchy.

Tracking   A therapeutic tactic associated with structural family therapy in which the therapist deliberately attends to the interactions, language, and values of the family in an attempt to understand the sequence of events as they occur interactionally in the family.

Triangulation   This dynamic occurs when one person involved in a conflict with another person invites a third person to a dialogue in an attempt to distract from the original conflict, thereby lessening the chance of resolution.

REFERENCES

Aponte, H. J. (2003). Structural family interventions. In A. C. Kilpatrick & T. P. Holland (Eds.), *Working with families: An integrative model by level of need.* Boston, MA: Allyn & Bacon.

Aponte, H. J., & Van Deusen, J. (1981). Structural family therapy. In A. S. Gurman & D. P. Knistkern (Eds.), *Handbook of family therapy* (pp. 310–360). New York, NY: Brunner/Mazel.

Becvar, D. S., & Becvar, R. J. (2000). *Family therapy: A systemic integration.* Boston, MA: Allyn & Bacon.

Jenkins, H. (1990). Csalad therapia: Family therapy training in Hungary. *Association for Child Psychology and Psychiatry Newsletter, 12*(6), 9–13.

Jones, C. W., & Lindblad-Goldberg, M. (2002). Ecosystemic structural family therapy: Elaborations of theory and practice. In F. Kaslow (Series Ed.) & R. Massey and S. Massey (Vol. Eds.), *Comprehensive handbook of psychotherapy: Vol. III. Interpersonal, humanistic, and existential models* (pp. 3–33). New York, NY: John Wiley & Sons.

Jones, C. W., & Lindblad-Goldberg, M. (2008). *The ecosystemic structural family therapy training manual for families with children and adolescents having severe emotional and behavioral disturbance.*

Lindblad-Goldberg, M., Dore, M., & Stern, L. (1998). *Creating competencies from chaos: A comprehensive guide to home-based services.* New York, NY: Norton.

Lindblad-Goldberg, M., & Jones, C. W. (2005, September–October). Contemporary structural family therapy. *Family Therapy Magazine,* 22–25.

Lindblad-Goldberg, M., Jones, C. W., & Dore, M. (2004). *Effective family-based mental health services for children with serious emotional disturbance in Pennsylvania: The ecosystemic structural family therapy model.* Harrisburg, PA: CASSP Training and Technical Institute.

Minuchin S. (1974). *Families and family therapy.* Cambridge, MA: Harvard University Press.

Minuchin, S. (2007). New developments in structural family therapy conference.

Minuchin, S., & Fishman, H. C. (1981). *Family therapy techniques.* Cambridge, MA: Harvard University Press.

Minuchin, S., Montalvo, B., Guerney, B., Rosman, B., & Schumer, F. (1967). *Families of the slums: An exploration of their structure and treatment.* New York, NY: Basic Books.

Minuchin, S., Rosman, B., & Baker, L. (1978). *Psychosomatic families: Anorexia nervosa in context.* Cambridge, MA: Harvard University Press.

Nichols, M., & Schwartz, R. (1998). Family therapy: Concepts and methods. Boston, MA: Allyn & Bacon.

Prochaska, J. O., & Norcross, J. C. (1999). *Systems of psychotherapy: A transtheoretical analysis* (4th ed.). Pacific Grove, CA: Brooks/Cole.

Sharf, R. S. (2004). *Theories of psychotherapy and counseling: Concepts and cases* (3rd ed.). Pacific Grove, CA: Brooks/Cole.

Vetere, A. (2001). Structural family therapy. *Child & Adolescent Mental Health, 6*(3), 133–139.

Wynne, L. C. (1961). The study of intrafamilial alignments and splits in exploratory family therapy. In N. W. Ackerman, F. L. Beatman, & S. N. Sherman (Eds.), *Exploring the base for family therapy.* New York, NY: Family Service Association of America.

RECOMMENDED READING LIST

Books

Goldenberg, I., & Goldenberg, H. (2004). *Family therapy: An overview.* Belmont, CA: Brooks/Cole.

Lindblad-Goldberg, M., Dore, M., & Stern, L. (1998) *Creating competence from chaos: A comprehensive guide to home-based services.* New York, NY: Norton.

Minuchin S. (1974). *Families and family therapy.* Cambridge, MA: Harvard University Press.

Minuchin, S., & Fishman, H. C. (1981). *Family therapy techniques.* Cambridge, MA: Harvard University Press.

Minuchin, S., Montalvo, B., Guerney, B., Rosman, B., & Schumer, F. (1967). *Families of the slums: An exploration of their structure and treatment.* New York, NY: Basic Books.

Articles

Aponte, H. J. (1998). Love, the spiritual wellspring of forgiveness: An example of spirituality in therapy. *Journal of Family Therapy, 20*(1), 37–58.

Colapinto, J. (1991). Structural family therapy. In A. S. Gurman & D. P. Kniskern (Eds.), *Handbook of family therapy* (Vol. 2, pp. 417–443). New York, NY: Brunner/Mazel.

Lindblad-Goldberg, M. (1989). Successful minority single-parent families. In L. Combrink-Graham (Ed.), *Children in family contexts*. New York, NY: Guilford.

McLoyd, V. C., Jayaratne, T. E., Ceballo, R., & Borquez, J. (1994). Unemployment and work interruption among African American single mothers: Effects on parenting and adolescent socioemotional functioning. *Child Development, 65*(2), 562–589.

Minuchin, S., & Montalvo, B. (1966). An approach for diagnosis of the low socio-economic family. *Psychiatric Research Reports, 20*, 163–174

Olson, S. L., & Banyard, V. (1993). Stop the world so I can get off for a while: Sources of daily stress in the lives low-income single mothers of young children. *Family Relations, 42*(1), 50–56.

Wylie, M. S. (2005, May/June). Maestro of the consulting room. *Psychotherapy Networker, 29*(3), 41–50.

Websites

The Minuchin Center for the Family
http://www.minuchincenter.org

The Philadelphia Child and Family Therapy Training Center, Inc.
http://www.philafamily.com/

Wikipedia
http://en.wikipedia.org/wiki/Salvador_Minuchin

Conference

New Developments in Structural Family Therapy Conference, 2007, Denver, Colorado

Strategic Family Therapy

11

Tiffany Nicole Smith, Edita Ruzgyte, and Donald Spinks

If you are distressed by anything external, the pain is not due to the thing itself, but to your estimate of it; and this you have the power to revoke at any moment.

—-Marcus Aurelius

INTRODUCTION

There is a natural hierarchy within most families, with parents and primary caregivers as leaders. When the family hierarchy is unbalanced, serious problems arise. It is the strategic family therapist's job to realign the family by teaching parents and primary caregivers how to lead. Once the natural balance and order in the family is achieved, problems dissipate.

Although it is important that strategic family therapists review the current structure of the family when the family presents in therapy, the focus of the therapy is more about the problem. Strategic family therapists focus on discovering the purpose of the problem within the family structure. Once the therapist unveils the purpose of the problem, it is then up to the therapist to convince his or her client to take action. This creates change within the client and the entire family system. Strategic family therapists believe that "action" not "insight" leads to change (Richeport-Haley, 2003).

From these principles come the hallmark of strategic thinking: A problem-centered and pragmatic approach that is more interested in creating change in behavior rather than change in "understanding." This separates strategic therapy from the more "insight-oriented" therapies. In this therapy, insight and understanding are dismissed in favor of tasks and directives (Haley & Richeport-Haley, 2003). Strategic family therapy is also noted for being brief, for not considering clients' pathology, and for asserting that change can happen suddenly and rapidly.

Because the strategic family therapist focuses on how the problem is maintained, rather than specifically on the hierarchy as a structural family therapist does, it is ideal for many different kinds of families, individuals, and couples. The author of this chapter worked with elderly clients for more than 2 years. Many of the clients presented with various issues, including dementia, depression, posttraumatic stress disorder, and anxiety. Focusing on how the client maintained the problem in his or her life gave the therapist opportunities to be creative and very helpful to this population.

Activities included offering an elderly woman an opportunity to divorce her dead husband, gaining satisfaction for his infidelities; celebrating the blossoming of an elderly woman by asking her to visit the rose gardens frequently on the grounds; and challenging a 30-year-old male who was fearful of leaving the facility to not go too far and escape his comfort zone, of which he ventured out on his own shortly thereafter. Additionally, strategic family therapy has been shown to be effective with Hispanic individual adolescent drug abusers (Szapocznik, Kurtines, Foote, Perez-Vidal, & Hervis, 1986). Such work emphasizes the usefulness of strategic family therapy either with families or with individuals because it creates change through various interventions designed to change perceptions and, therefore, actions.

HISTORY AND LEADING FIGURES

Strategic family therapy developed from the strategic therapy of Milton Erickson, the brief therapy model of the Mental Research Institute (MRI), the structural therapy of Minuchin (see Chapter 10), the cybernetic theories of Gregory Bateson, and the communication theory of Don Jackson. Jay Haley combined these elements into strategic problem-solving therapy, which then evolved into a family systems approach that Haley outlined in *An Introduction to Family Therapy* (1974). Over the following sections, we will discuss the important contributors to strategic family therapy.

Milton Erickson, MD

Milton Erickson, a psychiatrist and psychologist, had a major impact on the thinking of strategic therapists. Dr. Erickson is most famous for his hypnosis techniques that were self-taught. Erickson was able to incorporate hypnosis techniques with psychotherapy (Haley, 1967). Erickson's emphasis on a symptom- or problem-focused approach to treatment, along with his belief that people can change quickly and realistically, led him to conclude that therapists are responsible for the success or failure of treatment. "Erickson had made a contribution to psychology parallel to Freud's. Where Freud had made his contribution in terms of theory, Erickson had made an equal impact in terms of intervention" (Saudi, 2005, p. 38).

Haley called Erickson's approach strategic because the therapist took control of the session and dictated how the problem was going to be resolved (Foley, 1986; Haley, 1973). Haley then used Erickson's *paradox directives techniques* and used them to create interventions (Foley, 1986). The paradox technique consisted of the therapist giving a directive to the family in such a manner that the problem behavior was resisted by the client. The directive was usually one that the family or individual viewed as an ordeal, strange, or absurd. By making the choice to either follow or refuse the directive, the problem became something the family was able to control and thus something they could choose to solve (West & Zarski, 1983).

For example, a young woman begins attending therapy and states that she does not have a good relationship with her family. Upon exploration, the therapist learns that the woman dislikes family gatherings because she feels her family never takes her seriously. She states that they are constantly critical and reports that they often laugh at her when she attempts to join in adult conversation. The therapist instructs the woman to go home to a family gathering that weekend. However, when the family begins having serious conversation that she wants to engage in, the woman is to stand on her head while speaking. Because the family never takes her seriously anyway, she might as well speak to them while standing on her head. The young woman views this directive as absurd. This paradoxical directive allows the client to take control of her problem and begin to solve it. If the woman stands on her head, this will open the dialogue for the woman to express her feelings of how she feels when her family does not take her seriously. If she refuses to stand on her head, then she is asserting herself as a person to be taken seriously.

The Mental Research Institute

In the 1960s, at the MRI in Palo Alto, California, Don Jackson, Jay Haley, and Virginia Satir first began teaching their communication model of family therapy. In this model, which grew out of Gregory Bateson's work with people diagnosed with schizophrenia, directives and paradoxical instructions were used to manipulate families into changing their problem-maintaining sequences of behavior.

The MRI's approach to family issues was based in part on cybernetic theory; specifically, its focus on identifying positive feedback loops that surround family issues and creating ways to change those feedback loops through reframing and other methods. The MRI approach is pragmatic and problem-focused, characteristics that were retained in strategic family therapy.

Jay Haley

Jay Haley was born in the Midwest but spent most of his life in California. He served in the U.S. Army and then went on to attend the University of California at Los Angeles, where he received his bachelor's degree in theater arts and, later, a second degree in library science from the University of California at Berkeley. He attended graduate school at Stanford University, where he earned a master's degree in mass communication. During his studies at Stanford, he met and began working with Gregory Bateson, Donald Jackson, and John Weakland on research involving double bind communication in family dynamics with people diagnosed with schizophrenia, also known as the Bateson Project (Bateson, Jackson, Haley, & Weakland, 1956). His work on the Bateson Project also allowed him to begin working with Milton Erickson, whose work became the focus of his book *Uncommon Therapy*. He later joined his colleague, Don Jackson, at the MRI in 1959 as the director of research. During his time there, he was also asked to become the editor of the journal *Family Process*. Haley left MRI to work with Salvador Minuchin and Braulio Montalva at the Philadelphia Child Guidance Center (PCGC) as the director of research. It was during his work with PCGC that he met his second wife, Cloé Madanes, a psychologist from Argentina.

The partners left PCGC and began their own training facility in 1976, known as the Family Therapy Institute of Washington, DC. During the 1990s, Haley returned to California and continued his research and teaching at Alliant International University, where he earned an honorary doctorate. At Alliant, Haley and his third wife, Madeleine Richeport-Haley, produced several psychotherapy films and books until his death in 2007 (*In Tribute: Jay Haley*, http://www.mri.org/memoriam.html). Cloé Madanes worked with Haley to make this transition, and is still influential in strategic therapy and its development. The author of several books, including *Strategic Family Therapy* (1981) and *Sex, Love, and Violence: Strategies for Transformation* (1990), Madanes was known for her playfulness and creativity, leading often to functional paradoxical interventions. Although Madanes adheres to the strategic idea of mapping families, she also believes that issues of love and violence are at the root of all problems.

Madanes continues to practice in California and is currently working with Tony Robbins and has formed the Robbins-Madanes Center for Strategic Intervention (www.cloe-madanes.com).

Minuchin and Structural Family Therapy

Haley left MRI in 1967 to join Salvador Minuchin at the PCGC. It was there that Haley learned the structural concepts of Minuchin and incorporated them into his thinking. (Structural family therapy is discussed in Chapter 10.)

The seminal work *Pragmatics of Human Communication* (Watzlawick, Beavin, & Jackson, 1967) influenced Haley through its study of *semantics* (the clarity of meaning between what is said and what is received), *syntax* (the pattern as well as manner or style in which information is communicated), and *pragmatics* (the effects or consequences of communication). The impact of these ideas will be discussed in more detail later in this chapter.

Structural family therapy had a large impact on Haley as he realized the impact of family structure and hierarchy on the family's functioning. The task of the therapist is to restore the hierarchy and reorganize the family so that the parents are in a superior position and thus the child does not take care of the parents in unfortunate ways. Reorganizing the hierarchy is an important element because it allows the clients to begin to take action toward change by accepting their position within the family system. This also applies to all relationship systems because "When two people get together, there is a communication structure and, so, an issue of power. A strategic approach requires the exploration of hierarchical structures since the communication is in that form" (Haley & Richeport-Haley, 2003, p. 3).

The Creation of Strategic Family Therapy

In 1976, Haley and Cloé Madanes established their own institute in Washington, DC. The Washington School was the birthplace of what came to be known as the Haley-Madanes model, a blend of structural theory and strategic methods.

It was not until the 1980s that strategic family therapy was fully formed. By then, Haley and Madanes had formulated the key characteristic of the approach: The strategic therapist has the responsibility of creating a strategy or strategies to help solve the client's presenting problem (Madanes, 1981). Strategic family therapists are primarily interested in the promotion of change in families, specifically in the areas of family interaction cycles, family structure, power, and control. In strategic therapy, families are assumed to have the psychological capacity for change; but current family behavior, communication patterns, or hierarchical structures enable the problem to persist. Therefore, change in the family system will result in problem resolution. All family behaviors, patterns of interaction, or problematic structures need to be realigned for change to happen in the family. It is small amounts of change in families that are often enough to promote more broad and deep changes in family interactions and structure.

Haley and Madanes both contributed unique aspects to the strategic therapy approach. Haley emphasized the vertical element of the family structure, essentially, who holds the power and who does not. He saw all human interactions as a struggle for control and power. Madanes emphasized the function-of-the-symptom aspect of problems, particularly when children use their symptoms to try to change their parents. She categorized family problems according to four intentions:

1. The desire to dominate and control

2. The desire to be loved

3. The desire to love and protect others

4. The desire to repent and forgive

Strategic family therapy is not a popular model of therapy. It is often criticized for its paradoxical interventions as well as its stance, in that it is vital that the therapist controls the outcome of treatment (Wilner, Breit, & Im, 1988). Others criticize it because feelings are not the focus, causation is not explored, and each case requires a unique individualized approach versus following a specific method for every case (Haley & Richeport-Haley, 2003). Although Jay Haley is deceased, his legacy and teachings continue today. The MRI in Palo Alto, California, offers trainings to clinicians in strategic family therapy. Additionally, Cloé Madanes has teamed up with Tony Robbins to create the Robbins-Madanes Center for Strategic Intervention located in La Jolla, California. Additionally, there are therapists who trained under Jay Haley and Cloé Madanes who offer strategic training to therapists wanting to use the model in their clinical work. The American Association of Brief and Strategic Therapy is promoting and educating therapists who are interested in using strategic therapy techniques in their practice.

INTRODUCTION TO STRATEGIC FAMILY THERAPY

Pragmatics of Human Communication (Watzlawick, Beavin, & Jackson, 1967), which heavily influenced Haley and Madanes, suggests that people are always communicating, even when they are not speaking verbally. Furthermore, all messages have a report function and a command function (Watzlawick, Bavelas, & Jackson, 1967). The report, or content of the message, conveys information. The command function may be implicit or implied. For example, the report, "Our next door neighbor just insulted me!" may convey a command: "Do something about it." The command is not captured by words alone, but also through facial expression, intonation, color, breathing, and body posture.

In families, command messages are patterned as rules, which Jackson termed *family rules* (Jackson, 1965). These rules can be deduced from observing repetitions in behavior and interactions. The rules are not codified and, in fact, most people in the family are generally unaware of the rules. The rules exist to preserve family homeostasis, meaning that people develop routine interaction behavioral patterns among each other. These behaviors bring families back into equilibrium when there has been disruption, and therefore serve as strength against change.

Watzlawick, Bavelas, and Jackson (1967) analyzed patterns of communication that linked together in chains of stimulus and response, known as *feedback loops*. These feedback loops can be positive or negative. A *positive feedback loop* exacerbates the problem, whereas a *negative feedback loop* diminishes the problem. The advantage of this analysis is that it focuses on interactions that perpetuate problems (which can be changed), instead of looking for underlying causes that are not normally subject to change. A positive feedback loop is created when a client attempts to solve problems in the same manner by using his or her same ineffective coping mechanisms (Soo-Hoo, 1999). For example, a woman comes to therapy distressed because she reports that she always took on the job of solving all the problems of her friends and family. She felt others always "imposed" this burden on her but continued to "assist others with unresolvable difficulties" (Riley, 1990, p. 74). Through the course of therapy, it is discovered that the woman's grandmother taught her to always do for others, but the woman was also molested by the grandfather. When the client decided to "bury the grandmother," she would be taking action to "bury" the behavior that kept the "grandmother's belief alive" (Riley, 1990, p.75). This change in approaching how to solve the problem created a negative feedback loop and thus a second-order change. In other words, positive feedback introduces change, whereas negative feedback maintains the status quo.

Strategic therapists took the concept of the positive feedback loop and made it central to their model. The MRI group (Watzlawick, Weakland, & Fisch, 1974) saw that all families experience difficulties throughout their development; whether the difficulty becomes a problem or not depends on how the family responds. The family may attempt to solve the problem through various means; if the problem persists, they tend to do more of the same attempted solution. This escalates the problem, at which point the family will try more of the same "solution," and a cycle is created. For example, a father becomes upset regarding his son's recent behavioral problems in school. The father decides to take away items from the child, such as video games, toys, and so forth, for every day the child gets a bad report from school. He tells the child that he loses the items for a month. The child continues to not respond to the father's discipline tactics and at the end of 2 weeks, the child has an empty room and still continues to have behavioral problems at school. Instead, the strategic family therapist may suggest that when the boy brings home a bad mark, the father must sit with the boy and restrain himself from enjoyment for the evening as well, showing the boy that he is upset, too. The boy may not like seeing his father upset and may begin working on his schoolwork to free them both.

To interrupt this cycle, a totally new solution is required. There are issues that keep the problem maintained and the boy reluctant to change his behavior. The afore-mentioned family rules govern much of the family's behavior (Jackson, 1965) and may restrict which solutions can be tried. In such cases, change is required not only in the problem behavior, but also in the underlying rule. This concept raises the distinction between a first-order change and a second-order change, terms which will be discussed later in this chapter.

One way Haley suggested to bring about second-order change is to prescribe *ordeals* (Haley, 1984). Borrowed from Erickson, the ordeal involves a prescription to maintain the symptom; however, the family soon realizes that the price of maintaining the symptom far exceeds that of giving it up (Haley, 1973). Haley suggested that many people will change just to avoid the ordeals inherent in doing therapy (Haley, 1984). For example, a woman reports that she always wakes up at 3 a.m. and would like to sleep through the night. The woman complains that she is so fatigued that her house is not clean. The therapist asks what household chores she feels need to get done. They make a list of the chores. The therapist then tells the woman to set her alarm for 3 a.m. every night and get up and do things on the chore list until it is time for her to get ready for work. The woman dreads the idea of getting up at 3 a.m.; and after one night of getting up and cleaning, she decides that she would rather sleep and do the chores on the weekends.

The uniqueness of strategic family therapy lies in how the therapist focuses on the problems of families. The goal of strategic family therapy is to motivate the family to change signature behavioral patterns associated with the identified problem (Gardner, Burr, & Weidower, 2006; Thomas, 1992). The strategic therapist views problems and symptoms as a result of how people communicate to one another. "If a man is depressed to the point of neglecting his work, a strategic therapist might hypothesize that he is metaphorically com-municating to his wife his concern that she does not appreciate him or his work" (Nevels & Maar, 1985, p. 349).

Strategic family therapists believe that to change family organizational patterns and therefore alleviate the identified problem, the routine in which the clients communicate with one another must be altered (Riley, 1990). Therefore, the strategic therapist uses the session to experience the interactions of family members with one another in the room to bring the family dynamics into the here and now (Madanes, 1981). The strategic family therapist must immediately begin collecting clues about the identified problem from the family members talking about the problem (Gardner et al., 2006). Once the therapist has observed the family and formulates a hypothesis, he or she then creates a plan of action to provide treatment for the family. Strategic therapists believe that action, not insight, leads to change (Haley & Richeport-Haley, 2003).

For examples, see *Treating the Tough Adolescent: A Family-Based, Step-by-Step Guide* by Scott P. Sells.

THEORETICAL ASSUMPTIONS

Strategic family therapy has been found helpful in working with families who are concerned with childhood and adolescent behavioral problems (Gardner et al., 2006; Nikel, Muehibacher, Kaplan, Love, & Nikel, 2006; Steinberg, Sayger, & Szykula, 1997). Strategic family therapy is also helpful in using with families of various cultures because of the use of its systemic perspective (focusing on how problems occur rather than why they occur) as well as working with the family to reorganize the family hierarchy (Gardner et al., 2006; Soo-Hoo, 1999). The technique of rearranging the sequences in family organizational structures allows strategic family therapy to be used widely with families of various cultures (Richeport-Haley, 1998). However, it is important to note that strategic family therapy should only be used by therapists with proper training and supervision because of the difficulty of the techniques and inappropriateness with clients who act violently and on impulse (Riley, 1990).

Strategic family therapy merges the concepts and theories of the structural family therapy model (see Chapter 10), family systems theory (see Chapter 3), and unique strategies, which were created specifically to help clients (Szapocznik & Williams, 2000).

The structural ideas of maintaining the organization of the family hierarchy are important when using the strategic family therapy model. For example, if a family was to seek therapy for a teenager who was refusing to follow the rules, the strategic therapist would approach treatment of the family from the perspective that the parents were not in charge and therefore the hierarchy was malfunctioning and must be reorganized (Nevels & Maar, 1985; Schiff, 1990). The therapist would become directive and help the family to rearrange how they operate. However, the difference between strategic family therapy and structural family therapy is the goal of the therapy. Strategic family therapists strive to "eliminate a presenting problem," and structural family therapists strive to "change the family structure" (Fish & Piercy, 1987, p. 113).

Concepts from *systems theory* are also part of the foundation of strategic family therapy. Within the family system, members develop behavioral patterns over time, thus creating a delicate balance of interaction within the system known as *homeostasis*. Thus, the behaviors of one family member directly affect the reactions and subsequent behaviors of other family members (Szapocznik & Williams, 2000). According to systems theory, if one part of the system changes, all parts of the system are forced to change as well (Hanson, 1995). Thus, strategic family therapists look to create small change with the family member who appears to be the most willing to change, which then results in dramatic change within the family system—also known as the *butterfly effect* (Gardner et al., 2006; Ward, 1995).

In systems theory, *triangles* occur when tension between two family members exists and a third party is brought in by one of the family members in an attempt to stabilize the unbalanced system (Bell, Bell, & Nakata, 2001; Toker, 1972). An example of triangulation might be when a husband and wife are experiencing tension and one spouse begins to have an extramarital affair to ease the tension. Another example might be when a husband and wife have marital difficulties and either spouse attempts to align closely with one of their children. When working with a family, the strategic therapist must attend to the various triangles within the family; this will help create a strategy so that change can occur (Madanes, 1981; Sells, 1998).

View of the Family and Client

In terms of how the family, client, and their contribution to the presenting problem are conceptualized, there are six dimensions to consider when using strategic family therapy:

1. *Involuntary versus voluntary behavior:* A strategic therapist prefers to think of all symptoms (excluding organic illness) as voluntary and under the control of the individual. Sometimes a problem can be resolved simply by redefining it as the result of voluntary rather than involuntary behavior (Madanes, 1991). This can be the only intervention that is necessary if the client solves the problem once he or she accepts the idea that it is under his or her control.

2. *Helplessness versus power:* The symptom bearer can appear helpless if he or she presents unfortunate and/or involuntary behavior that he or she cannot change even though he or she wants to do so (Madanes, 1991). The helplessness, however, is actually a source of power over the other family members whose lives and actions are restricted and even ruled by the demands, fears, and needs of the symptom bearer. The nonsymptomatic persons in the family are helpless to influence the symptom bearer. The strategic therapist is free to think about the power and helplessness of the various family members (Madanes, 1984). How the therapist conceives power and helplessness determines how the therapist will design a strategy for change, or if one is designed at all (Madanes, 1991).

3. *Metaphorical versus literal sequences:* The idea that a symptom may be a metaphor for the problems of another family member may lead the therapist to focus on resolving those other problems instead of focusing directly on the symptoms. The therapist may also think of the problem as a sequence that is metaphorical for another sequence and may decide to introduce change in one sequence of interaction, believing it will have repercussions in another relationship (Madanes, 1984).

   For example, a woman attends therapy after her foster child was exhibiting violent outbursts and aggressive behaviors. The teen reports anger toward his parents, the Child Protective Services, and his older siblings for not keeping his family together. Upon exploration, the therapist learns that the foster parent does not understand the teen's anger and often becomes anxious and frustrated when he becomes upset. The therapist asks the woman if she has ever been on a camping trip. The therapist explains how camping in the wilderness unprepared can be very dangerous. The woman states she has and the therapist asks her to give examples of all the items she needs to take with her to survive on the trip. The woman names a list of items. The therapist then asks the woman to begin packing a suitcase to go camping with the teen. In the suitcase, they will place items to make the teen successful during this difficult time. The therapist then asks the woman to take the suitcase home with her and the teen and use it. The woman was unable to see that her anxiety and fear of the teen kept her from being in the position of authority. The metaphor of packing a suitcase allowed the woman to feel prepared, shift the hierarchy, and therefore allow the teen to no longer be in charge.

4. *Hierarchy versus equality:* When the family hierarchy is incongruous, problems arise. Strategic therapy addresses this problem by changing the structure to its proper hierarchy (Haley & Richeport-Haley, 2003). For example, "an incongruous hierarchy exists in which the adolescent is in charge and more powerful than the parents" (Sells, 1998, p. 9). In such a case, the goal of the strategic therapist would be

to restore the organization of the hierarchy within the family by assisting the parents to become more powerful, thus the adolescent would lose power and the problems would dissipate (Haley, 1976; Schiff, 1990).

5. *Hostility versus love:* Some therapists see family problems in negative terms, such as hostility, jealousy, power, and fear. Other therapists see people as essentially healthy and compassionate. Once a therapist understands a problem in a certain way, then the therapist has attributed meaning to the motivations of the people involved. This meaning is important when the therapist considers his or her choice of strategy and interventions. Strategic therapists prefer to think of people as being benevolently motivated, rather than motivated by negative characteristics (Madanes, 1991).

6. *Personal gain versus altruism:* According to Madanes (1991), if a person is hostile, he or she is being motivated by personal gain or power. If the person is concerned with helping others or receiving more affection, he or she is being motivated by love. Whatever the motivation, once determined, the strategy for the therapy is formed. The therapist only has to arrange for the same consequences of the problematic symptom to take place without the symptom occurring, and the problem behavior should abate. Issues of personal gain and altruism, which are considered more important in relation to the symptomatic person than to the other members of the family, and a correct understanding of the person's wishes can lead quickly to a strategy for change (Madanes, 1991). For example, a couple enters therapy reporting that they argue daily and are looking for relief from their constant conflict between each other. A strategic therapist would direct the couple to schedule a time to argue from 8 p.m. to 10 p.m., in which they would argue for the entire 2 hours without interruption. The couples will usually not follow through with the directive (Haley & Richeport-Haley, 2003).

View on How Change Occurs

According to strategic family therapy, two types of change can occur within the family system. First-order change occurs when family members attempt to solve a problem repeatedly with the same solution, only by increasing the level of intensity (Coyne, 1984; Fraser, 1982). For example, a teen continues to be tardy to school because he is talking to friends outside, even when the bell rings. The parent reports that she always begins nagging the teen to be on time and "hurry up," but the teen continues to ignore her. As the school continues to report that he is still tardy to class, she begins nagging at him in a much louder tone and reports "yelling" at him. The teen continues to not respond to her.

Strategic family therapists focus on creating second-order change, which allows the system to shift into a new level of homeostasis and allows for permanent rather than temporary change (Foley, 1986). This is achieved by changing the existing rules within the family system to create new behavioral responses to the identified problem (Fraser, 1982).

After hearing the identified problem of the previous family, the therapist instructs the mother, in front of the teen, not to discuss with her son his previous tardiness. Her son is able to read a clock and is aware what time he has to be in his seat. Rather, the mother is to drive the teen to school at 8 a.m. in her pajamas. If the teen is not in his class by the time the bell rings, she is to escort her son to his class in her pajamas and sit with him through the first period (Sells, 1998). The teen becomes horrified by the idea of his mother escorting him to class in her pajamas. By following through with this, a second-order change has occurred because the rules within the family system have been changed. The mother no longer nags the teen and the teen begins to respect the mother's position in the hierarchy because she does have the ability to embarrass him.

Therapist's Role

Haley himself said, "Therapy can be called strategic if the clinician initiates what happens during therapy and designs a particular approach for each problem" (Haley, 1973, p. 7). This statement illustrates the directive and strong role of the therapist in this approach. At the same time, it is important to note that strategic therapists focus on tasks rather than gathering family information. This is because of the belief that the presenting problems in the family are the result of an unbalanced hierarchy; the therapist must explore the communication structure within the hierarchy rather than family patterns (Haley & Richeport-Haley, 2003). Strategic therapists focus on how to solve problems rather than where the problem started. Additionally, strategic therapists do not focus on how clients experience their feelings, because they believe that clients express their emotions through their behavioral patterns, which are more significant than emotions (Klecker, Bland, Frank, Amendt, & duRee, 1992).

The therapist plans a strategy that sets clear goals, which will lead to solving the presenting problem. The therapist designs intervention, which is appropriate for the client's social situation (Madanes, 1981). The therapist uses metaphors, which are created specifically for each client and his or her presenting problem.

Interventions

Milton Erickson viewed each of his clients as unique, with the strength and abilities to deal with their problems. Because of this attitude, Erickson used various techniques that were very specific for each case. According to Haley (1973), to grasp the logical progression of Erickson's therapeutic techniques, it is important to realize that he was treating people in therapy the same way as he was dealing with resistance in hypnosis. The following are some of the techniques used by Milton Erickson, as described by Haley (1973).

Encouraging resistance is one of the most notorious therapeutic interventions that was proposed by Erickson in use with the resistant clients. When clients are not cooperating, the therapist does not engage in a power struggle; rather, he or she accepts and even encourages the resistance. By doing so, the therapist interprets clients' behavior as cooperative and not resistant. This places the client in a double bind, where he or she cooperates no matter what he or she does.

For example, a young man living in a long-term care facility reports that he is a "paranoid schizophrenic" and refuses to leave the facility to attend much needed doctor appointments. He repeatedly tells the therapist that she cannot convince him to leave the facility. The therapist tells the client that he is the expert and because it is not safe for him to leave the facility, the therapist encourages him to stay inside at all times. The therapist begins telling him about how much better off he will be if he stays indoors to protect himself. The client, wanting to resist the therapist's directive, begins going outdoors and to doctor's appointments.

Providing a worse alternative. Even though the strategic therapy approach is very directive, the therapist wants his or her client not only to follow his or her directions, but also eventually to achieve autonomy in making decisions. Providing a worse alternative allows the therapist to help clients make decisions by themselves. This therapeutic intervention makes it harder for a client to maintain the problematic behavior than to give it up. For example, a woman attends therapy because she reports anxiety and insomnia. The woman is resistant to interventions and reports that "nothing helps." The therapist learns that the client dislikes running outdoors. The therapist does not urge the client to stop the symptom of insomnia, but encourages the client to run outdoors at 2 a.m. on the days when the insomnia symptom occurs. Naturally, the client will not want to get up at 2 a.m., dress, and go running and would prefer to give up the symptomatic behavior of insomnia.

Causing change by communication in metaphors was another Ericksonian technique. When clients felt uncomfortable or resistant to talking about their issues, Erickson would use analogies and metaphors without directly mentioning the problem. For example (Haley, 1973), when a couple refused to talk about their sexual life, Erickson talked about their dining habits as an analogy. He was able to talk about appetizers, leisurely dinner, and dessert while never mentioning sexual behavior. Once the clients started to connect the communication about dining experience to a discussion of their sex life, Erickson would change the subject and come back to it later when they were not expecting it.

Encouraging relapse is another technique that allows the therapist to maintain in charge of the session and prevents client's disappointment in the case of relapse. Erickson used this technique because he wanted clients to feel as bad as they did prior to the therapy, so they could see if there was anything they missed or wanted to recover from that time (Haley, 1973).

Encouraging a response by frustrating it helped Erickson to deal with clients who were unwilling to cooperate or participate in the session. This technique involves asking a question and not allowing the client to answer it when he or she is ready to, or by saying something untrue about the client, which would frustrate the client and force him or her to explain himself or herself. This is one more way for Erickson to deal with resistance.

Emphasizing the positive. Erickson believed in the power and abilities of each person. He personally had dealt with several hardships in his life (Erickson & Keeney, 2006) and welcomed his clients with his caring, friendly nature and ability to make each of his clients feel special. This philosophy allowed Erickson to concentrate on the positive experience.

Seeding ideas. With this technique, Erickson would present a client with some information, and then allow the client time to get used to it. Later, Erickson would re-present the information. When the client heard it for the second time (or repeatedly), the information would not seem so new or strange.

Amplifying a deviation. Erickson would take the deviation that is present in the family and amplify it to the point where the family has to reorganize into a new set of patterns because they are no longer able to maintain the old ones (Haley, 1973). For example, a therapist would ask a client, "Can you think of a time last week when you thought (presenting problem) would happen, but then did not happen?" (Rhodes, 2008).

Later, Haley expanded the list of strategic interventions to include the following techniques:

The process of joining is an important part of strategic family therapy because of the impact of the directives on the clients (Nevels & Maar, 1985). Joining involves developing empathy, concern, connectedness, and a trusted relationship with a client. Joining and empathy must occur first so that the client will begin to trust the therapist (Haley & Richeport-Haley, 2003).

Straightforward and *indirect directives* are core interventions in strategic therapy. The purpose of directives is to alter how the family members interact with one another (Nevels & Maar, 1985). There are two types of directives: straightforward and indirect directives. *Straightforward directives* are used when the therapist sets rules, boundaries, and structure within the family (Madanes, 1981). These directives encourage the client to modify his or her existing patterns of interactions, which are causing problems (Gardner et al., 2006), and include "giving advice, coaching, setting up ordeals, and exacting penance" (Haley & Richeport-Haley, 2003, p. 8). *Indirect directives* include restraining, metaphors, ridiculous tasks, and paradox directives (Haley & Richeport-Haley, 2003).

Paradox directives. Strategic family therapy is most famous for its use of paradox directives, so they deserve special mention. Paradox directives are used when the therapist discerns that family members are more likely to follow a directive when they are unaware that the therapist has given them one (Madanes, 1981).

For example, if a therapist notices that the client is not following through on directives given or resistant to him or her, then the therapist does not have the power and an indirect approach is needed (Haley & Richeport-Haley, 2003). A paradox directive such as prescribing the symptom or restraining would be appropriate to use. Paradoxes are used as a catalyst to progress the course of therapy but are not the main element of change (Klecker et al., 1992). Paradoxes create a therapeutic double bind by placing clients in a win-win situation (Riley, 1990). This is because regardless of whether the clients follow the directive, a second-order change will occur (Foley, 1986). This is important because the strategic therapist believes that the client taking action causes change and not insight (Haley & Richeport-Haley, 2003). When placing the client in a therapeutic double bind by using a paradoxical technique, the client is forced to take action. "You get into a posture where, instead of you pulling people to change, they are pulling you to change" (Haley & Richeport-Haley, 2003, p. 9).

When prescribing the symptom, the therapist orders that the behavior the client is complaining of be restricted to a particular time period. For example, if a couple complains of their constant bickering, the therapist might prescribe that the couple only be allowed to argue for 30 minutes per day, from 6:00 p.m. to 6:30 p.m. (Haley & Richeport-Haley, 2003).

Ordeal intervention is similar to prescribing a symptom and encourages the client to undergo significant change in a short amount of time. The therapist must "impose an ordeal appropriate to the problem of the person who wants to change, an ordeal more severe than the problem" (Haley, 1987, p. 6). For example, a man reports that he has insomnia and is fatigued at work. The therapist asks him what he should do more of and the man reports he should read more books. The therapist directs the man to read more books and instructs him to get dressed for bed but not go to sleep, but rather read all night long. To ensure that the man does not fall asleep while reading, the therapist instructs him to stand while reading. He was directed to do this for 3 nights. The man fell asleep each night and slept the whole night (Haley & Richeport-Haley, 2003). The ordeal needs to cause more anxiety and distress than the problem itself; thus, the distress created by the ordeal will result in change within the system.

Restraining is an intervention in which the client is urged not to change because of the complexity of his or her presenting issues (Madanes, 1981; Papp, 1980; Riley, 1990). The purpose of restraining is to address the misconception that change must be immediate and permanent or it is unobtainable. Restraining often encourages clients to rebel against the therapist; they become more concerned with proving the therapist wrong than being concerned about making the change.

Unbalancing is an intervention in which a repetitive pattern is halted through the introduction of a behavior that is drastically different (Riley, 1990). For example, a woman enters therapy stating that she is angry at her husband for criticizing her. She provides an example of an argument that occurred while she was cooking as she states that her husband grabbed her knife and insisted that she was cutting the onions improperly. The strategic therapist states the following to the woman:

> *Each time your husband comes into the kitchen and asks you to change the way you are preparing dinner, stop what you are doing and go over and give him a kiss and a hug. You may then return to preparing the meal in the same way you were doing. Do not change. (Riley, 1990, p. 76)*

Reframing. When a therapist uses the reframing technique, he or she changes the meaning of the presenting problem so that the family changes the way they view the problem (Keeney, 1983). This allows the family to be able to solve a problem they previously were unable to. For example, a family attends therapy reporting that their child is "bad" and is constantly getting into trouble at school and at home. The therapist learns that the parents have trouble within their marriage. The behavior that the parents view as "bad" can be reframed as "self-sacrifice" because the child is behaving in this manner to distract the parents from their unhappy marriage (Riley, 1990, p. 74). What is then changed by the use of reframing is the "meaning attributed to the situation, and therefore its consequences, but not its concrete facts" (Watzlawick, Weakland, & Fisch, 1974, p. 95).

STRATEGIC FAMILY THERAPY WORKING TEMPLATE

The *strategic family therapy template* is meant to be used as a guideline to learning the process of strategic family therapy. The template provides the beginning therapist with steps to take and questions to ask that promote collaboration between the therapist and client. There are suggested questions under each heading to help start the process. After using the initial questions, guide the client through each process, asking questions that occur to you, as you stay within the family therapy theory. Although there is no one "script" for any therapy session, it is the hope of the author that the template serves as an impetus to learning this family therapy model.

Tools for Change

The therapist may use tools that have been described earlier in this chapter: directives, prescribing the symptom, unbalancing, therapeutic double bind, reframing, restraining, and using metaphors throughout the session to assist the family or individual to make changes in their lives. The following phases will address how these tools are used.

Phase 1: Joining and Building Rapport

During this phase, the strategic family therapist meets with the family, greets each member, and begins to point out the strengths or successes of the family. It is helpful to use empathy and humor during the sessions. In particular, it is helpful to emphasize how much the clients care—and that it is their kindness that has brought them to therapy (Nevels & Maar, 1985).

Here are some comments or questions that a therapist might use during this phase:

- *"You seem to have a successful family."*
- *"You must love your mother very much to act out and cause her to bring you here. You take care of her very well."*

Phase 2: Understanding the Presenting Issue

In this phase, the clients need to agree on what the specific problem is (Nevels & Maar, 1985). Toward this end, the therapist can inquire about how the clients wish to resolve the presenting problem (Haley & Richeport-Haley, 2003).

Here are some comments or questions that a therapist might use during this phase:

- *"I'd like for each of you to tell me what you think the problem is."*
- *"How do you want things to be when the problem is resolved?"*
- *"What would that look like, specifically?"*
- *"Who would be doing things differently?"*

Phase 3: Assessment of Family Dynamics

By observing the family and taking a brief history, the therapist is able to assess how the problem is maintained or what purpose the problem has. The focus is on solving the problem, not where it originated (Klecker et al., 1992).

Below are some ideas and questions that are useful for assessing family dynamics:

- A genogram or family map is helpful in gathering this information about the current family system.
- Timelines of when the problem first appeared, intensity, and frequency of it are helpful in the assessment of family dynamics.
- *"How have you tried to solve this problem in the past?"*
- *"What worked? What did not?"*
- *"When you talked, I noticed that your husband looked away."*
- *"When you corrected your son, he didn't seem to hear you. Does this happen at home?"*
- *"So, to get this straight, what happens at home is that when your son acts out, your husband corrects him and then the son comes to you crying. Then you take his side and let him out of his punishment. What are you teaching your son about your husband and yourself?"*
- Questions a therapist should ask of themselves before proceeding: *"What do you want in the ideal situation to solve this problem? How would you like the family to look when you are done with it?"* (Haley & Richeport-Haley, 2003, p. 80).

Phase 4: Goals

The goal of the strategic family therapist is to "solve the presenting problem" (Madanes, 1981, p. 19). If the therapist sets clear goals, the therapeutic progress will be less likely to be influenced by distracting issues (Haley & Richeport-Haley, 2003). The clients and therapist negotiate the goals, gaining a clear vision of what the family wants to accomplish.

Below are two strategies and a question to use to help a family set goals:

- Ask each family member what he or she feels are the top three problems he or she wants to be solved. Find common themes, if any. Then ask them to all agree on which ones they want to tackle first, second, third, and so forth.

- *"Sounds like both you and Betty feel you don't have a close relationship anymore. Is that what you would like to work on first?"*
- Write the problems on a list and give them a copy and keep one in the file. Bring out the list and cross them off as they are solved while you are working with them.

Phase 5: Amplifying Change

Although strategic therapists are directly responsible for the outcome of therapy, they should never take credit for the progress of clients because this could lead to a potential setback for the client. Rather, the therapist should act puzzled by the change and progress the clients have made, because taking credit or even sharing credit creates an environment where the client could relapse (Haley & Richeport-Haley, 2003). The therapist should always remain a neutral party in how change occurs because it promotes long-lasting, second-order change when the clients see themselves as responsible and makes the client less dependent on the therapist.

Here are some comments or questions that a therapist might use during this phase:

- *"You each had a good week. I don't know how this happened. I can't imagine how hard that was. How do you explain this?"*
- *"You have worked so hard this week. I bet this problem really tested you. How were you able to avoid it?"*
- *"In spite of all the obstacles, you were able to have good days at work. How does this happen? Do you have ideas?"*

Phase 6: Termination

Once progress has been made, the therapist should slowly begin to disengage and eventually, the clients will terminate (Haley & Richeport-Haley, 2003, p. 11).

Clients may return to therapy for help with new presenting problems as they arise throughout their life. Most often, the bond developed between the strategic family therapist and clients is so strong that a natural reliance on the therapist for techniques is seen as a resource.

MASTER THERAPIST INTERVIEW

JEROME PRICE

Jerome Price, MA, LMSW, LMFT, is the director and founder of the Michigan Family Institute. He completed a strategic therapy apprenticeship under the supervision of Jay Haley and Cloé Madanes at the Family Therapy Institute of Washington, DC. Jerome Price has been a faculty member at the Family Therapy Institute of Washington, DC, since 1993, where he provides supervision and training in strategic family therapy. He has given numerous workshops and training throughout the United States, Canada, and Europe. He is currently an editorial board member for the Journal of Systemic Therapy.

What attracted you to the theory behind strategic family therapy?
I started out as a behaviorally trained therapist, although there was a fair amount of intrapsychic processing in my training. What I had been taught when I started putting

it into practice led me to not like my clients very much. I had been taught to think of them as sick. So I found myself almost in competition with them to convince them there was something wrong with them. I think the first work I was exposed to was the work of Salvador Minuchin and structural family therapy. And from there, because they are so closely related, I got more interested in strategic because it was basically more practical and hands-on. It assumed better things about the people I was working with, so I liked my clients better—and I found that if I liked them better, they liked me better. Since they liked me better, they more often did what I asked them to do. And if they did what I asked them to, they got better faster. When I first saw Haley and Madanes at a conference, I was thrilled by their warmth and their positive involvement with their clients, despite the totally inaccurate views in the field of strategic being a sort of manipulative or button-pushing therapy.

I think it is important to mention that there are four primary schools of strategic thought; there is Milan strategic (Mara Parazolli's work), Ackerman School strategic, and there is MRI Strategic, and the Washington school, which is Jay Haley and Cloé Madanes. Although they have similarities, they have significant differences. I am going to speak only for the Washington school. It's best defined by something Jay Haley once said: "The great therapist is not someone who can tell people what to do in order to get better, he or she is the one who can get them to do it." So what defines strategic therapy is that everything we learn, teach, and do is organized around what it's going to take to get people to do the things they need to do to get better.

So if Joe is beating his wife, we don't care if Joe understands why he is beating his wife, we just want him to stop beating his wife. And our focus is on how to get him to stop beating his wife. Our assumption is that once Joe stops beating his wife and experiences life no longer being a wife beater, he is going to have some theories and hypothesis of his own about why he beat his wife. So insight comes after the fact rather than before—and it doesn't always come at all. So the purpose of therapy is to get people to change. The ones who do get insight, that insight is always accurate because it's based on exactly what really happened and the person's actual experience; it's not a manufactured insight.

Under the MRI strategic, John Weakland always suggested that people keep doing things for a variety of reasons, but then again, the dilemma is how to get them to stop doing counterproductive things and get them to do productive things. It's a consumer approach in which the clients tell us what they want to change, so the things we are trying to get them to do are always toward the goal they have set for themselves. Therapists in our approach don't tell people what they need to change in their lives. They may come in and tell us that they want their kid to stop swearing at them, and we work on the kid to stop swearing at them. We don't worry about whether their childhood is related to why they are upset that their child is swearing at them. As a result, it's a short-term approach because when their child is no longer swearing at them, we are done, unless they ask us to work on something else at that point.

How do you formulate your view of the family when they enter therapy?
First, I formulate my view based on what they tell me. I consider them the experts on their family and their lives. I agree with Jay Haley in calling strategic family therapy an organizational approach. I would think of family as the nuclear and extended family, but the unit that we're treating as part of the family therapy includes the community,

friends, neighbors, church, synagogue, the authorities, school. The family may be everyone you have to get involved to bring about change—and the tougher the cases, the greater the likelihood is that you are going to have to do that.

The formulation of what's actually going on, who's involved, what things mean, that actually comes from the client and it's very respectful. When I was first starting, I had the assumption that clients didn't understand properly; and now I know they understand a great deal, so they teach me. The other thing that underlies the conceptualization—and this includes structural therapy as well—is that strategic therapists have a hierarchical view. When families are operating well and people are symptom-free, we assume that they have a well-functioning hierarchy, in which parents are in charge and the children follow their guidance. Maybe the parents are advised by grandparents. The law dictates things to parents; the world is set up hierarchically. So we work from the other end. We work on the understanding that when people get in trouble, often the hierarchy is disturbed—children are doing the parent[s]' jobs, parents are acting like children, grandparents may be doing the parenting when parents are still there, parents may be in conflict with each other—all of which upsets the hierarchy. What we know from experience is that when you correct that hierarchy, the symptoms abate and the situation improves. Some things, like schizophrenia, are tougher than others, but regardless of what the symptoms are or whether they have any kind of genetic or organic base, you still get improvement. A useful theory is one that gives you an idea about what to do. That's why the strategic model is helpful, because it gives you some immediate ideas as a therapist about what to do to help solve the problem.

What kinds of families do you think benefit most from this model?
Anyone. It's not a model that is designed for a specific population. It's a model that's designed for whoever walks in the door. One of the unique things about it is that every strategy, every treatment plan, every hypothesis about the purpose of the symptom is fresh and tailor-made for each family. I think one of its unique qualities, as far as effectiveness, is that the educational level of the clients and the socioeconomic level are not significant factors in determining whether it's going to be helpful. When you are doing therapy rather than conducting a talking therapy, it doesn't matter whether someone has an IQ of 50. If you have access to their family, you can change them and their family to whatever extent they are capable of. Sometimes, the more educated and intelligent [they] are, the harder they are to change because they second-guess everything. In our approach, if people do what we are asking them to do, we can almost certainly bring about improvement.

What issues do you think this model works best with?
I would say, in general, the more specific the symptom, the more effective therapy is. We have a problem-solving approach, so if people don't present us a problem, we don't necessarily really know what to do. So people come in and just want to talk—that's a confusing presentation for this approach and we are likely to be ineffective. With our focus, we would then be inclined to pin them down on what exactly it is they want changed. If I can visualize what's happening based on their description, [it] is easier for me to bring about change than if I am dealing at high levels of abstraction.

Different models of therapy require the therapist to be directive or nondirective. In your opinion, what are the necessary characteristics that a therapist should possess to be effective with this model?

Directiveness! If you went to your mechanic and your car was making a funny noise and your mechanic asked you, "What you think the problem was?"; you wouldn't be very encouraged that this mechanic knew what they were doing. We assume that we have the obligation to actually know what to do to help bring about change. We are being hired as an expert, which is something that is very unpopular these days. People are very into collaboration and everything having to be collaborative—and we are very collaborative. Our clients probably come up with 90% of the directives that we wind up giving through our discussion with them and our learning from them. But we still see our job as being an expert. I think this is what makes this approach unique because a lot of other approaches don't want to be seen as experts. I've watched experienced therapists say to people, "What do you think ought to be done about this problem?"; and my internal response to that is, if they knew that, they wouldn't be sitting there. I think it's a horrible question that people get asked that kind of shames them, like they ought to have known what to do. We treat our clients very respectfully, and we are very careful to see that they are also treated as experts of their families.

People with a more directive personality are going to feel more comfortable in this approach. People who take charge, who don't mind giving an opinion, who are willing to take a higher level of responsibility do well in this approach. We tend to want to be liked by our clients and have this kind of cuddly relationship. And in order to be directive, you have to be willing to be unpopular—confrontational if necessary—and you have to be able to be willing to demonstrate a range of affect and a range of approaches, depending on what the particular family needs. One family may need kindness and another may need a good swift kick in the butt and another may need a therapist who seems a little confused and does sort of a Colombo sort of approach. I know Jay Haley always recommended that all therapists take a course in Ericksonian hypnosis because the art of communicating on multiple levels and knowing precisely what your words mean impact those people you're talking to. One of my favorite quotes from Cloé Madanes is "The more complicated the problem, the simpler the solution you want to use"; and most therapies complicate the situation and our approach is to actually simplify it, create the smallest change necessary to bring about the outcome people are asking for.

How often do you see clients and for how long a period of time?

Sessions are scheduled based on the regular clinical hour of 50–60 minutes, but my sessions are more likely 1 hour and 10 minutes or an hour and 15 minutes because I tend to run chronically late. If my sessions are back to back in the evenings, I tell people not to come early. It's actually in my permission form for treatment that we don't actually stick to a clinical hour if something is happening that needs to be finished. We don't send people out the door with something half-done, otherwise it's just a waste of a session. We start out weekly and quickly; as progress begins, we back that off to every second week. Our average case is typically well under 10 or 12 sessions. That's why I don't drive a terribly good car! We move them through fairly quickly. The sessions can cover 6 months to a year because they get spaced out further and further, so we may be involved with people for quite some time.

We want people to come and go freely throughout their lives or throughout their families' lives. A fair amount of my caseload are people who I had years ago and are in a different stage of their lives. They'll have a bigger problem and come in for four or five sessions with their spouse, now that the kids are gone, or they have a sexual problem or retirement issues or whatever is happening and life goes on. So we are sort of like a general practitioner: You have a family doctor, you have a family dentist, you have a family therapist. And when you work briefly, they are comfortable moving in and out. You know, if it takes 2 or 3 years to get rid of your therapist, you are going to think very carefully before walking back in the door.

What are you looking for when you are in the session?
I'm looking for two things: the understanding of why the symptom is occurring and who it's helping. My goal is [to] come out of the session with some understanding—and if I can't, then to have an understanding of the recursive cycles that are going on. That way, I can give a directive that is meant to disrupt that psychosis struggle. But more truthfully, I want to get to know the clients. I remember Cloé Madanes saying, "A therapist going into a session should think of themselves as needing to be both interested and interesting." And most therapists are trained to be interested, but they are also trained to be boring and to not have a personality. My office is set up like a small living room and what people experience is that we are having a chat.

Who sets the goals, the client or the therapist?
When a family comes in, I ask them to tell me what brings them in and what they would like to see better. And if it's a family with children, I will tell them that I am going to ask the parents first what the concerns are and that I would like for the children to listen courteously even if they don't agree. Then I ask each of the children what they agree with and what they don't agree with, so it's a hierarchical interview. Then I will say, "I'm going to tell you all more about me and how I'm going to work and how I approach this sort of thing and what kind of recommendations I'd be making up to this point." So it is more the map of walking through the first session and learning what I really need to understand, and then being able to have a clear enough sense of how I would approach things so that they would know who they are hiring and can decide to stay in therapy.

I don't do anything until people tell me. There is an old Jewish proverb that says, "If you don't know where you are going, any road will get you there." So you have got to know where you are going; otherwise, I don't have a sense of what direction to head in, and if I don't, they don't. What we do in strategic therapy (that has developed into other therapies as well) is ask the question, "How will you know when this problem is solved?" Maybe clients will say, "My husband and I won't be fighting," or, "Our son will be attending school." But that is their call.

They might also say, " I just want my kid back in school and not address my relationship with my husband or wife," and we will respect that, unless the only way to get the kid back in school is to also address their relationship. I would be honest with them and say, "We can't get your kid back in school unless we address the two of you fighting with each other, because I think that is a part of the cause. Would you give me permission to help you guys with that at the same time?" We insist on permission to enter into someone's life, to address it, and to begin to alter it.

What is the assessment process of this model?

Assessing hierarchically what needs to be done to correct the system and seeing if there is an understandable purpose to the symptom that we can use as a guide. When I was working in North Carolina as a young therapist, there was a 13-year-old girl who authorities were ready to take to court because she wasn't going to school and was in a lot of trouble. I asked one question that nobody else had asked: "Where do you go when you are not in school?" It turned out that she went to her 92-year-old grandmother's house, and that her grandmother lived in fear of falling, having no one there to help her. The rest of the family was basically neglecting her and leaving her alone in her own house without sufficient care. The only thing that [the] little girl was guilty of was loving her grandmother. She went to keep her grandmother company and as soon as we made sure that the grandmother was cared for properly, she went back to school. She would take a shift watching her grandmother at other times than during school. I like to think that organizing the hierarchy and then sequences of interaction, which is identifying the sequences of, you can identify the problems. You are always assessing danger and making sure that protection and safety are in place. You are also assessing people's flexibility or rigidity and how rigid their boundaries are, helping you to understand how tough it is going to be to get them to do something different.

What are some commonly used interventions with this model?

Most interventions that the strategist uses are straightforward ones that help clients to take the steps that they need to take. If someone is depressed, they need to get outside and not just sit in the chair—so your directive is to get outside for an hour a day. Most of it is really just the same straightforward stuff that really any good therapist would do. Indirect strategies—like prescribing the symptoms, rate of change, ordeals, things like that—are by far the exception when you are dealing with a high level of resistance. But most people we find really want to change. I think finding hope for them in the first session is critical. If they come out hopeful from the first session, they will usually do something you've asked them to. We believe people want to be happy and they want to change, and when they begin to feel better, they like it and tend to keep doing it that way.

What role does a homework assignment have in this model?

Based on the directive approach, homework is all of it. Most of our therapy happens between sessions. Every session ends with a directive to go home and actually do something. The assumption of this therapy is that people will be going home and taking the steps we agreed on. If they don't do it, then it becomes our job to figure out whether we made an error in the homework we gave them, whether we made an error in how we framed it, or our timing of it. And then after we've assessed these factors, we reassign it in a way that increases the chances that it will be done.

What have you found to be the limitations of this approach?

I remember Cloé Madanes once saying, "That we'll steal from anybody." This is a model that has a framework, but the range of things that you can do within that framework are totally unlimited. I can use a narrative strategy, solution-focused therapy, behaviorism, neo-Freudianism . . . it doesn't matter because anything can be a directive, and that can be a strategy for getting people to do something new. We just make sure to give credit where credit is due.

What are your suggestions that you have for students learning this model?
One of the biggest mistakes they make is trying to teach. They share too much too quickly and they create a constant flow of information back and forth rather than clearly formulating how they are going to approach it. Beginning therapists are like parents . . . they tend to talk too much and all it does is confuse people. We tend to look and think carefully before we put out anything that qualifies as an opinion, a definition, or a hypothesis. So for instance, the hypothesis that we make, we don't share with the family in most cases. I think it is helpful for students to read a lot of cases. Be sure to be live supervised by a good strategist or directive therapist so that you actually get the experience of doing it. You have to read a lot and be very informed to use this approach, and you have to keep expanding your sense of what the possibilities are and keep expanding your cases. See a lot of cases and have fun with it. It's really an entertaining approach in a lot of ways because every session you step into is like a mystery to be solved.

MASTER THERAPIST INTERVIEW

Scott Sells

Scott Sells, PhD, LCSW, LMFT, holds doctorate degrees in both social work and family therapy from Florida State University, and a master's degree in social work. He has previously served as a full professor at Savannah State University, teaching masters students in advanced clinical practice. Dr. Sells wrote Treating the Tough Adolescent: A Family-Based, Step-by-Step Guide *(Guilford, 1998) and* Parenting Your Out-of-Control Teenager: 7 Steps to Reestablish Authority and Reclaim Love *(St. Martin's, 2001). In addition to these two books, Dr. Sells has had more than a dozen major publications in preferred journals, and a book chapter in the* Handbook of Family Therapy Research Methods *(Guilford, 1996). Dr. Sells has extensive experience as a keynote speaker for national professional organizations like the American Association of Marriage and Family Therapy, the National Association of Social Workers, and the Southeastern Psychological Association.*

What attracted you to the theory behind strategic family therapy?
The original readings of Minuchin's work. I did an apprenticeship with Charles Fishman and he led me to really appreciate the idea that if you change the structure in the family, the child's symptoms get better. For example, if the child is really controlling the mood of the household and is in charge hierarchically, and you put the parents back in charge, the kid initially tries to keep things the way they were. But if you can get the parents to hang on and realign the hierarchy, the kid settles down. I was also fascinated by Minuchin's work of enactments, bringing the issues into the room and changing the way people communicate right in front of him, like dancing in his presence.

Strategic is like jet fuel when it gives the parents the interventions or consequences to change the structure. For example, creative interventions for a child that is not going to school and changing the whole family is to get the parents to go to school with the child and keep an eye on him. Strategic gives you the interventions to change the structure. So that's why you frequently find both structural and strategic therapy together, and that's how I see the two models working together.

How do you formulate your view of the family when they enter therapy?
The first thing I do is ask each family member for their hunch or theory about why they think their child is misbehaving, because that belief system tells me how hard I have to work. Their definitions of the problem are critical. If you have a parent that says their child is violent and that they are worried that if they push to[o hard], the child will get more violent or they are threatening that they will kill themselves, that parent may say she is not going to take charge of this problem. Or if the parent says I think it's a chemical imbalance that needs medication and someone else needs to fix the problem because I am not an expert on mental health issues, that too, tells me my role. So when I see a family, I am immediately seeing their point of view and how hard I am going to have to work.

Then I have two choices at that point. First, I can try to convince them almost like a salesman that the way they are looking at the problem is not helping the child change. I do that through video clips of good examples of a better way to communicate. I also show them a contract, because 80% of people learn by what they see and 20% learn by what they hear, and most therap[ies are] all talk therapy. So I try to convince them through maps and visuals that their belief system is helping their child misbehave.

If that doesn't work, I go into "Why don't you try to act your way into my way of thinking?" or "Fake it until you make it." So I ask them to go ahead and make a contract with me, even though their heart isn't in it. For example, I have a parent that said he spent $100,000 on his child and yet he still had a problem. He didn't want to give up the idea that he might have lost $100,000, so he really didn't buy into the fact that he would have to take charge of the problem and get the child to go to school. So I told the father, "Well, would you at least try the experiment with me? I know your heart is not in it, but can we go ahead and try contracting for at least 2 weeks, and if you see progress, maybe your belief system will change." The father agreed to fake it until he made it, and then he saw his daughter go to school and all of [a] sudden, his belief system changed, and he went from "My kid has a problem and I can't fix it because it's a chemical imbalance," to "My kid has a problem and I can fix it with the right set of tools, and my kid is more stubborn than mentally ill!"

I give the concrete micro steps that are from my apprenticeship with Jay Haley and are in my book *Treating the Tough Adolescent* (Gilford Press, 1998). To find out how not only how to tell the parents how to contract but how to button push and how to restore nurturing because these kids usually don't like the parents anymore and the parents don't like these kids anymore and, without that nurturance piece, the kid is going to eventually rebel again if we can't restore that attachment between the parent and child.

What kinds of families do you think benefit most from this model?
Families that benefit most with this model are those that are labeled almost drunk with power, where the child has been in charge for many, many years and basically controls the mood of the household and uses creative symptoms to keep being in charge. For example, that kid may be disrespectful, but if the parents start to get in charge, that kid might all of a sudden start running away or threatening violence as a way to scare the parents and counselors into submission. So this model helps to show the parents and the therapist that it is going to get worse before it is going to get better—but if the

parents maintain authority and change the way they parent and the therapist helps them to catch their kids doing something right, the dance changes between parent and child on a communication level. Then the child's symptoms start to go away.

Different models of therapy require the therapist to be directive or nondirective. In your opinion, what are the necessary characteristics that a therapist should possess to be effective with this model?

The best analogy, I guess, is super nanny. I'm a process therapist and I use content therapy. I'll educate the parents on the tools like how to hug their child again or how to catch their kid doing something right, and then I'll go into super nanny role of being a coach and showing them how to deliver contracts. I think that's a missing piece with therapy today . . . too many therapists are nondirective and give parents advice and say to the parents, "Go home and try this." But the parents have not changed their dance, their style of communication, their voice tone, and so it fails because the person was not a dance instructor, so to speak, who showed them how to use it. So my role as a therapist is very directive, more like a consultant or coach, where I do both education by showing them the tools and application by showing them how to use it through role plays.

How often does the client see you and for how long a period of time?

Freud invented the 50-minute session. But Freud was a therapist who could see clients for 2 or 3 years. We live in [a] society that wants instant results and the symptoms to be alleviated. Because I am asking families to dance differently in my presence and to do role plays and contracts, oftentimes, the first three sessions optimally are 2 hours long. We take a break after the first hour, get some coffee or drinks, relax. In the first hour, you educate the family on what the principles are and work with the family on what their belief systems are. The second hour is about showing them how to use the tools. So it takes about 2 hours.

If a family is in crisis and the managed care setting you work in can't handle more than 1 hour, then you try to see the family back to back Monday and Tuesday or Wednesday and Thursday because they are in crisis. After they get established with a new way of dancing, you can move it down to an hour. Or, if the parents can take the parenting class first, they'll have the tools, so you don't have to spend the first hour going over the different concepts. You can jump right into showing them how to use it like super nanny.

If you are able to do 2-hour sessions as needed, things really get going in about six to eight meetings. Then you try to do it every other week and then about once a month, because you really want to set an atmosphere where the client gets all the credit for the changes and then they see you more as a consultant. If you keep seeing them every week, a phenomenon called "learned helplessness" might take place, where they may learn to be helpless and you may be triangulated into their relationship, which hurts them instead of helping them.

There is some really good research that shows that the biggest changes are going to happen between sessions one and eight and after that, the changes may level off. There is no real reason to change if they know they can come to you week after week and talk about their problems and feel better without having to make really hard changes. So about six to eight to get things going and then after that, wean them off once they get going to once every other week and then to once a month and then see them for tune-ups.

What are you looking for when you are in the session?

I am looking for cotherapists in the session. I am looking for people that are flexible enough or have opportunities for me to work with, to kind of join with me to help the family members that are more resistant. I'm also looking for ways to join with the family on common things. I'm also looking for strengths. You know, I always walk out of session with the ability to name five heroic qualities from each family member. I see so many therapists focus on what the families are doing wrong. The therapist hasn't communicated to them that they see the family as competent or having strengths. For example, many therapists don't even ask the family, "If I got to know you better, what qualities would I come to admire about you?" And just that simple question shocks families because the therapist doesn't ever ask those kinds of questions to look for strengths. I also look for ways to compliment people. Many parents and many kids have deficits in the areas of self-esteem and that makes all the difference in the world when they can see a sincere and honest compliment from the therapist in what they are doing right, not what they are doing wrong.

The research that was done with Haley resulted in a 15-step road map, and I actually show it to the clients. I actually have it on my desk so it actually shows me where the families and the therapist are, using the strategic model. I have it blown up into poster size so we can actually look at where we are at in the model at any time. That is the unique feature of this model. Most models keep the map in the therapist's head.

What is the assessment process of this model?

The first is asking the family how they define the problem. Is their definition of the problem leading them to stay stuck or is it leading them towards change? For example, if they say, "My kid has a problem and I can't fix it," that is not going to lead them to take charge and that definition of the problem is going to keep them stuck. So I always try to learn everybody's theory in the room.

The second assessment is what I call undercurrents—where the problem first began and who feeds that symptom. For example, a kid's symptom of being drunk with power may make me wonder if his being drunk with power is a product of parents who are inconsistent. Is the kid's symptom a product of unhealed wounds or traumas like sexual abuse, unforgiveness, violence, or is it a creative way to get their needs met? A lot of kids need attachment, like foster care kids, and they'll act out to get noticed or get stuck in a developmental life cycle change.

For example, if I assess that the child is acting this way because they are drunk with power and there is a lack of structure, I know that the undercurrent that is feeding that symptom is an inconsistent parent or a parent that doesn't have the same philosophy as the other parent. I fill in what's missing and I give the parents concrete examples of how to work together as a team or how to be consistent. I look for the triangles. I look for the hierarchy and I look for the dysfunctional sequences of communication around two parties and the symptomatic child, and I try to change those communication patterns.

Who sets the goals, the client or the therapist?

The goal is negotiated between the therapist, parent, and child. The therapist asks for their opinions on what the goals are and asks them to actually take their top three problem behaviors that they want to solve. It could be disrespect, it could be running away, it could be drug use. Whichever problem when solved, will give the family the most bangs for their buck. I'll say to the parent, "Which one do you think you have the best chance of solving in the quickest amount of time?" Because the same tools the parent uses to get the child to clean their room are the same tools he can use to get the child to stop running away. So it's a negotiation process of not only which goals, but the therapist's recommendation to the family about which goals they should do first, second, and third.

What are some commonly used interventions in this model?
In the first session, there is joining and finding the strengths, letting them vent their 10,000 defeats, letting them air out how frustrated and hopeless they feel, but then moving them to more solution talk where I ask them, "With everything you've gone through, how come you haven't yet thrown in the towel?" I also ask them to look at their strengths, compliment them, find out what their hunch or theory is about, why they think their kids are having problems, and then in the last session, I consolidate gains throughout therapy.

I especially hold a graduation ceremony where we talk about all their successes and we talk about what could happen in terms of future stressors. Also, enactments, creating intensity, paradox, reframing, joining, restoring nurturance, contracting, role plays . . . those are some common techniques used, which are a part of the strategic camp. I always use reframing, I almost always use role play, I almost always use creating intensity to go above the family's threshold of deafness. Those are the main ones, and I always use education where I kind of educate them using the model in regard to where they are and where they are going.

What role does a homework assignment have in this model?
Very big. I think what they do outside the session really sets the tone for how they are doing change, and the homework is also a litmus test to see if they are buying into the model. It also tells me if there are other issues that I missed. The homework assignment is essential because you want to create a sense of ownership of the process. If they are doing homework, they are co-owners of the therapy and that's exactly what you want to have happen so it doesn't create learned helplessness.

How do you know when your client is ready to terminate?
The kid looks better or there is a different atmosphere in the room where the family feels more at peace. There is less stress. You spend more time talking about what they are doing right than what needs to change.

What are some suggestions that you have for students learning this model?
Often, they try to apply the techniques without understanding process and theory. They don't understand how to do role plays and they don't understand how to troubleshoot or to help the family come up with plan B if plan A doesn't work. They are too rigid in their application of the steps, they don't think on their feet, and they haven't spent the time joining with the family properly, finding out the strengths. They don't let the family vent their frustrations enough so they don't get a chance to teach the therapist about their point of view about the world.

It would be great for them to read the material and talk it out with a friend like we are doing. I think they need to have instructors who are willing to do role plays in class or work with families so they can watch how therapy can be done. That is something very different than watching a videotape of a session and then having the students try it out. The supervisor needs to be gentle and tender in their criticism. The student therapist also needs to have a field placement where the supervisor can use the one-way mirror or just sit in the back of the room while the therapist is working.

Case Study

A mother calls and makes an appointment for her family to come to therapy. The family consists of a husband and wife, both in their 40s; their 15-year-old son; a college-aged daughter; and the woman's father, age 82. Three years after the woman's mother died, her father developed Alzheimer's disease and moved in with the family 6 months ago. When his health began to deteriorate, the woman spent more time caring for him than for the other members of the family. Three months ago, the 15-year-old son, who has been treated for attention deficit hyperactivity disorder since age 7, began to refuse to take his medication and is now being truant from school.

During the session, the wife cries and the husband reports that their relationship is strained, while occasionally rolling his eyes as his wife becomes tearful. He reports that he has to take on more work because his wife had to quit her job to attend to her father's needs. The daughter is away at college and the wife smiles as she describes her as a straight-A student. The daughter was asked to attend the session but refused because she has a hard time with her grandfather's illness and dislikes the conflict that has developed at home.

Jerome Price's Response to the Case Study

This family has got an elderly person who has drawn a huge amount of the mother's attention. This may have caused marital problems, which may or may have not been there to begin with. Looking at it straightforwardly, mom has had to attend at a high level to her father's needs so her marriage is stressed, and her son is becoming more and more symptomatic, which could be from a variety of things. I would focus more on the marital dilemma than the mother's attention to the grandfather. I think the way I would think about the boy's symptoms is he sees his family in distress and he is creating an opportunity for the mother and father to have to get together with each other in order to solve his problem, so then they will be more unified with the grandfather, or whatever the problems are that have to be addressed.

Having an 82-year-old father in the house who has huge needs doesn't require a marital problem and it doesn't require a child who is having behavioral problems in being truant from school. Keep in mind that this is a kid who has been identified at an early age as the symptomatic child anyhow. Anyone who has been on stimulant medication since the age of 7 and is now 15 has something else going on that is not being addressed. So he's obviously got some needs, and I would think that him melting down now is because his family is melting down worse. If he had strong leadership, meaning that the mother and father were doing well with each other and they had an agreement with each other about how both her father and their son would be taken care of properly, and they were being supportive of each other so that they each felt okay despite all of the stressors, which are significant, then he wouldn't be having these symptoms. So I would work under the assumption that first, it's possible that the mother and father could be drawn together to help their 15-year-old son, and in the process of doing that, they would begin to feel better about each other.

We could then talk about now if that solved the problem of the son, then when that's done, we'd be done unless they asked us for something else. We would stop right there because that's what they were asking for. Although we know we may be helping the relationship by helping them to come together to help the son once that got done, there is a reasonable chance that they would then be talking about each other.

Organizing things so that the grandfather is being taken care of well may mean they need to bring somebody else into the house to help with the grandfather to take some stress off the mom. Resources such as the Alzheimer's Association often provide financial assistance to people, and these associations often have stipends to help get aid for people with this particular disease. So we are trying to strengthen the marital unit and the coparental unit because they are the base off of which everything else runs. We start with the simplest thing we can do that will hopefully be like a pebble in a pond and the ripples will spread out because we focused on the place where everything else begins.

Dr. Scott Sells' Response to the Case Study

The first thing I would do is engage them. I would ask them what they would like to see changed, how can I help, and what are some of their frustrations or stressors. I would have to ask the husband, "If I got to know your wife a little better, what qualities would I come to admire about her?" I might ask the wife the same question about her husband. I would ask people why they aren't throwing in the towel and I would start to engender some hope. I would go around the room and ask everybody what their theory was about why the 15-year-old was having truant behavior or refusing to take his medication. I would assume that they were there to work on the 15-year-old and they were not to work on their marital issues in the first session, so out of respect for the family, I would work on their issue, the identified patient. I would get them to give me all kinds of theories and I'd listen closely for one that might perk my interest. I would put up a chart and I would say to the family, "Here are some theories I have from what you have given me. I'd like to tell you what I think might be going on. Here's a multiple-choice test. I would like for each of you to take out a piece of paper and to privately rank where you think the bulk of the reason is as to why Johnny might be having problems right now." I'd say, "Here are the possibilities: Do you think Johnny might be acting this way as a lack of consistent structure and nurturance, as this happens in a lot of families?" I would normalize a lot, saying, "Sometimes, kids need consistent structure and nurturance."

I'd talk about how in some families I work with, grandparents or parents suddenly get ill or somebody dies, like a grandparent or family member or even a pet dog, and there's a trauma and the child and the other families don't heal that trauma because they don't talk about it [and] don't deal with the loss. They go to the funeral, and then everybody goes into their shell. Another possibility is that sometimes children act out as a way to get noticed and get their needs met because the family is experiencing a lot of wounds or traumas and everybody is just shut down emotionally. The child is really saying, "Hey, I'm over here. I'm hurting."

The third possibility is that some people can get stuck in a developmental life when they have kids, and they go from being a couple to a parent and then they launch their kid into adulthood. They don't basically give time for themselves. They don't negotiate their roles as a couple, [therefore] they get stuck. I would give them a handout of the different stages of development. The last option would be that the kid has a chemical imbalance.

So my guess would be:

1. Unhealed trauma

2. Chemical imbalance

3. Lack of structure/drunk with power

I'd try to get the family to achieve consensus and say, "Hmm, all these are good but could you give us examples to show us why you chose the way you did?" Then I would say, "Well, which one do you want to work on first?"

In some families, the wounds are so deep they have to talk about those first. So then I basically put my three cents in and I negotiate, which is called setting the terms of therapy, which is what's called the battle for structure. Carl Whitaker said that "is the most important part of treatment" because they are stuck. If they weren't stuck, they wouldn't be seeing you. I think there has been a lot of loss in this family, so I'd normalize and use what's called reframing and help educate the husband and wife about how their roles have had to change. I'd tell them that it makes perfect sense when you have a father that is ill that you would have to change your roles and, in this case, you have had to stop working and the wife is out a limb, wondering when she is going to get your emotional support, and you are exhausted by the end of the day. I'd help them to negotiate to fill in what's missing.

Structurally, what the kid is probably reacting to is that he's triangulated into the stress between husband and wife, and since the husband and wife are very unstable and they are not able to work on the issues themselves, they are detouring their conflict toward the kid. The kid's acting out is almost like a way of deflecting the stress from the parents, and the daughter is saying, "I don't want to come back at all. I'm happy to be out of this craziness. I don't like the conflict so I'm out of the triangle. I was probably in the triangle before when mom and I were pretty tight." I would add that, based on the mom's smiling that the daughter got all straight As . . .

So, structurally, if you could help the husband and wife renegotiate how they are going to have time together in the face of the father's Alzheimer's getting worse, that would take a lot of stress off of them and the kid would probably get better. I think it would help to draw them closer and be able to have the 15-year-old talk about the loss he's feeling or how scared he might be of the grandfather developing Alzheimer's. So if you could release the tension of the parents, you could get the kid out of the triangle because right now, the kid is serving a function to deflect the conflict of the family.

I would role play with the parents and actually role model for them how to talk to each other, and then I would meet with the kid alone and try to work with both sides of the fence. He might just say, "You know what I like . . . rewards once in a while. I'm only being punished so I think I would do school better if only my parents would reward me some." So I'd write down the kid's ideas on the notepad and show the kid what I'm writing down, and the kid would be pleasantly surprised if he saw some of his ideas in the contract. So I'd use the contract as a way of changing their dance. The mother and father would reward the kid some of the time as part of the contract, so that things go from a negative interaction where the parents catch their kid doing something wrong to catching their kid doing something right. So the husband might say he can pitch in little more, so on Tuesday nights the wife might say she can give the husband a break while she takes care of the father-in-law while he watches TV, or reads a good book. I would help them to understand that this is probably why their kid is acting this way, as a way of protecting the parents from their own stress. I think the whole way of treatment is finding the right piece of Jenga and negotiating with the families where the origins of the symptom came from.

KEY TERMS

Amplifying a deviation   The therapist accepts and enlarges an offering by the client and uses it as an intervention.

Causing change by communication in metaphors   A technique used by Milton Erickson while working with resistant clients; the therapist avoids directly talking about the problem or issue, and uses metaphors or analogies instead.

Directives   Instructions given to the clients that are designed "to change the ways in which people relate to each other and to the therapist" (Madanes, 1991, p. 396).

Emphasizing the positive   Therapist's view that each person has a natural desire to grow.

Encouraging relapse   Technique in which the therapist predicts or encourages the client to relapse.

Encouraging resistance   Technique in which the therapist promotes the resistance expressed by the client.

Encouraging the response by frustrating it   Technique in which the therapist encourages and provokes client to respond and then delays his or her ability to do so.

First-order change   A short-term, superficial change in the system.

Homeostasis   A state of equilibrium that is balanced and stable.

Indirect directives   Tasks that are not obvious to the client; are given to move the family members into specific behavior or interaction pattern.

Ordeal technique   A prescription of behavior that causes more distress than the problem itself.

Paradoxical directives   A technique in which the therapist instructs the client to continue to perform the symptomatic behavior all the time or during the specified times.

Pragmatics   The effects or consequences of communication.

Prescribing the symptom   Paradoxical directive technique in which the therapist asks clients to perform the problematic behavior during restricted periods.

Providing a worse alternative   By giving choices to the client, even those that may be suboptimal, the therapist promotes the client's autonomy.

Reframing   A technique used to change the meaning of a presenting problem.

Retraining   An intervention in which the therapist encourages client not to change because of the complexity of his or her presenting issues (Papp, 1980).

Second-order change   Long-term change that results in creation of a new homeostasis in the system.

Seeding seeds   Technique used in which the therapist suggests ideas in the information-gathering stage, with the intention of building on them later in therapy.

Semantics   The degree of agreement between what is said and what is received.

Straightforward directives   Techniques used by the therapist to set rules, boundaries, and structure in the interaction of family members. They may include advice, coaching, ordeals, and penance.

Syntax   The pattern as well as manner or style in which information is communicated.

Unbalancing   An intervention in which a repetitive pattern is halted because of the introduction of an opposite behavior.

REFERENCES

Bateson, G., Jackson, D. D., Haley, J., & Weakland, J. (1956). Toward a theory of schizophrenia. *Behavioral Science, 1*, 251–264.

Bell, L. G., Bell, D. C., & Nakata, Y. (2001). Triangulation and adolescent development in the U.S. and Japan. *Family Process, 40*(2), 173–186.

Coyne, J. C. (1984). Strategic family therapy with depressed married persons: Initial agenda, themes, and interventions. *Journal of Marital and Family Therapy, 10*, 53–62.

Erickson, B. A., & Keeney, B. P. (Eds.). (2006). *Milton H. Erickson, M.D.: An American healer*. Sedona, AZ: Ringing Rocks Press.

Foley, V. D. (1986). *An introduction to family therapy*. New York, NY: Grune & Stratton.

Gardner, B. C., Burr, B. K., & Weidower, S. E. (2006). Reconceptualizing strategic family therapy: Insights from a dynamic systems perspective. *Contemporary Family Therapy, 28*, 339–352.

Fish, L. S., & Piercy, F. P. (1987). The theory and practice of structural and strategic family therapies: A Delphi study. *Journal of Marital and Family Therapy, 13*, 113–125.

Fraser, J. S. (1982). Structural and strategic family therapy: A basis for marriage, or grounds for divorce? *Journal of Marital and Family Therapy, 8*, 13–22.

Haley, J. (1967) *Advanced techniques of hypnosis and therapy: Selected papers of Milton H. Erickson, M.D.* New York, NY: Grune & Stratton.

Haley, J. (1973). *Uncommon therapy: The psychiatric techniques of Milton H. Erickson*. New York, NY: Norton.

Haley, J. (1976). *Problem solving therapy*. New York, NY: Jossey Bass.

Haley, J. (1984). *Ordeal therapy: Unusual ways to change behavior*. New York, NY: Jossey-Bass.

Haley, J. (1987). *Problem-solving therapy*. San Francisco, CA: Jossey Bass.

Haley, J., & Richeport-Haley, M. (2003). *The art of strategic therapy*. New York, NY: Brunner-Routledge.

Hanson, B. G. (1995). *General systems theory beginning with the wholes*. New York, NY: Taylor & Francis.

Jackson, D. D. (1965). Family rules: Marital quid pro quo. *Archives of General Psychiatry, 12*, 589–594.

Keeney, B. (1983). *Aesthetics of change*. New York, NY: Guilford Press.

Klecker, T., Bland, C., Frank, L., Amendt, J. H., & duRee, B. R. (1992). The myth of the unfeeling strategic therapist. *Journal of Marital and Family Therapy, 18*, 17–24.

Madanes, C. (1981). *Strategic family therapy*. San Francisco, CA: Jossey-Bass.

Madanes, C. (1984). *Behind the one-way mirror*. San Francisco, CA: Jossey-Bass.

Madanes, C. (1991). Strategic family therapy. In A. S. Gurman & D. R. Kniskern (Eds.), *Handbook of family therapy* (Vol. 2, pp. 396–416). New York, NY: Brunner/Mazel.

Nevels, R. M., & Maar, J. E. (1985). A supervision approach for teaching structural/strategic therapy in a limited setting. *The Journal of Psychology, 119*(4), 347–353.

Nikel, M. K., Muehibacher, M., Kaplan, W. K., Love, T. K., & Nikel, C. (2006). Influence of family therapy on bullying behavior, cortisol secretion, anger, and quality of life in bullying making adolescents: A randomized, prospective, controlled study. *Canadian Journal of Psychiatry, 51*, 355–362.

Papp, P. (1980). The Greek chorus and other techniques of family therapy. *Family Process, 19*(1), 45–57.

Rhodes, P. (2008). Amplifying deviations in family interactions: Guidelines for trainees in post-Milan family therapy. *Australian and New Zealand Journal of Family Therapy, 10*, 1375.

Richeport-Haley, M. (1998). Ethnicity in family therapy: A comparison of brief strategic therapy and culture-focused therapy. *American Journal of Family Therapy, 26*(1), 77–90.

Riley, S. (1990). A strategic family systems approach to art therapy with individuals. *American Journal of Art Therapy, 28*, 71–78.

Saudi, F. (2005). A journey through the life and work of Milton Erickson: The world's leading practitioner of medical hypnosis. *European Journal of Clinical Hypnosis, 6*(2), 38–43.

Schiff, N. P. (1990). Strategic therapy for children's school problems. *Guidance & Counseling, 5*(3), 32–38.

Sells, S. P. (1998). *Treating the tough adolescent: A family-based, step-by-step guide*. New York, NY: Guilford Press.

Soo-Hoo, T. (1999). Brief strategic family therapy with Chinese Americans. *American Journal of Family Therapy, 27*(2), 163–179.

Steinberg, E. B., Sayger, T. V., & Szykula, S. A. (1997). The effects of strategic and behavioral family therapy on child behavior and depression. *Contemporary Family Therapy, 19*, 537–551. New York, NY: Springer.

Szapocznik, J., Kurtines, W. M., Foote, F., Perez-Vidal, A., & Hervis, O. (1986). Conjoint versus one-person family therapy: Further evidence for the effectiveness of conducting family therapy through one person with drug-abusing adolescents. *Journal of Consulting and Clinical Psychology, 54*(3), 395–397.

Szapocznik, J., & Williams, R. A. (2000). Brief strategic family therapy: Twenty-five years of interplay among theory, research, and practice in adolescent behavioral problems and drug abuse. *Clinical Child and Family Psychology Review, 3*(2), 117–134.

Thomas, M. B. (1992). *An introduction to marital and family therapy*. New York, NY: MacMillan.

Toker, E. (1972). The scapegoat is an essential group phenomenon. *International Journal of Group Psychotherapy, 22*, 320–332.

Ward, M. (1995). Butterflies and bifurcations: Can chaos theory contribute to our understanding of family systems? *Journal of Marriage and the Family, 57*, 629–638.

Watzlawick, P., Beavin, J., & Jackson, D. (1967). *Pragmatics of human communication: A study of interactional patterns, pathologies, and paradoxes*. New York, NY: W. W. Norton.

Watzlawick, P., Bavelas, J. B., & Jackson, D. D. (1967). *Pragmatics of human communication: A study of interactional patterns, pathologies, and paradoxes*. New York, NY: Norton.

Watzlawick, P., Weakland, J. H., & Fisch, R. (1974). *Change: Principles of problem formation and problem resolution*. New York, NY: Norton.

West, J. D., & Zarski, J. J. (1983). Paradoxical procedure in family therapy. *Personnel & Guidance Journal, 62*, 34–38.

Wilner, R. S., Breit, M., & Im, W.-G. (1988). In defense of strategic therapy. *Contemporary Family Therapy, 10*(3), 169–182.

RECOMMENDED READING LIST

Books

Gaulier, B., Margerum, J., Price, J. A., & Windell, J. (2007). *Defusing the high-conflict divorce: A treatment guide for working with angry couples*. Atascadero, CA: Impact.

Haley, J. (1973). *Uncommon therapy: The psychiatric techniques of Milton H. Erickson*. New York, NY: Norton.

Haley, J., & Richeport-Haley, M. (2003). *The art of strategic therapy*. New York, NY: Brunner-Routledge.

Madanes, C. (1981). *Strategic family therapy*. San Francisco, CA: Jossey-Bass.

Madanes, C. (1984). *Behind the one-way mirror*. San Francisco, CA: Jossey-Bass.

Madanes, C. (1987). Advances in strategic family therapy. In J. K. Zeig (Ed.), *The evolution of psycho-therapy* (pp. 47–55). New York, NY: Brunner/Mazel.

Nichols, M., & Schwartz, R. (2007). *The essentials of family therapy*. Boston, MA: Pearson/Allyn & Bacon.

Price, J. A. (1996). *Power and compassion: Working with difficult adolescents and abused parents*. New York, NY: Guilford Press.

Sauber, R. S., L'Abate, L., & Weeks, G. R. (1985). *Family therapy: Basic concepts and terms*. Rockville, MD: Aspen Systems.

Sells, S. P. (1998). *Treating the tough adolescent: A family-based, step-by-step guide*. New York, NY: Guilford Press.

Sells, S. P. (2001). *Parenting your out-of-control teenager: 7 steps to reestablish authority and reclaim love*. New York, NY: St. Martin's Press.

Articles

Coyne, J. C. (1984). Strategic family therapy with depressed married persons: Initial agenda, themes, and interventions. *Journal of Marital and Family Therapy, 10*, 53–62.

Dammann, C. A., & Jurkovic, G. J. (1986). Strategic family therapy: A problem-focused, systemic approach. *Individual Psychology, 42*(2), 556–567.

Fish, L. S., & Piercy, F. P. (1987). The theory and practice of structural and strategic family therapies: A Delphi study. *Journal of Marital and Family Therapy, 13*, 113–125.

Fraser, J. S. (1982). Structural and strategic family therapy: A basis for marriage, or grounds for divorce? *Journal of Marital and Family Therapy, 8*, 13–22.

Gardner, B. C., Burr, B. K., & Weidower, S. E. (2006). Reconceptualizing strategic family therapy: Insights from a dynamic systems perspective. *Contemporary Family Therapy, 28*, 339–352.

Olson, D. H., Russell, C. S., & Sprenkle, D. H. (1980). Marital and family therapy: A decade review. *Journal of Marriage and the Family, 42*, 973–993.

Richeport-Haley, M. (1998). Ethnicity in family therapy: A comparison of brief strategic therapy and culture-focused therapy. *American Journal of Family Therapy, 26*(1), 77–90.

Websites

Jay Haley on Therapy
http://www.jay-haley-on-therapy.com/html/strategic_therapy.html

Cloe Madanes, Innovator and Teacher
http://www.cloemadanes.com

Michigan Family Institute
http://www.mifamilytherapy.com

Parenting With Love and Limits
http://www.difficult.net

Mental Research Institute
http://www.mri.org

American Association Brief and Strategic Therapists
http://www.aabst.org

Solution-Focused Brief Therapy With Families

12

Kelly Backhaus

The longer we dwell on our misfortunes, the greater is their power to harm us.

—Voltaire

INTRODUCTION

Solution-focused brief therapy (SFBT) is a future-focused, goal-directed approach to brief therapy that uses questions designed to identify exceptions (times when the problem does not occur or could occur less in the client's real life), solutions (a description of what life will be like when the problem is gone or resolved), and scales, which are used both to measure the client's current level of progress toward a solution and reveal the behaviors needed to achieve or maintain further progress (Trepper, Dolan, McCollum, Nelson, 2006). It is one of a family of approaches, known as systems therapies, making it useful for working with families, that have developed over the past 50 years, first in the United States and eventually evolving around the world. This new paradigm challenged family therapists, who had traditionally focused on past experiences, generational patterns, and family legacies, to explore instead what was working in the client's life. Additionally, SFBT suggests that instead of examining and studying their clients' problems, therapists should focus on discovering solutions *with* their clients.

SFBT takes a distinctly *postmodern* approach, whereby therapists dismissed the notion that examining the past was necessary and began to focus on the future. According to the postmodern view, there are no fixed truths or realities. Rather, postmodernists believe that the truth or reality is whatever the client presents. In other words, the postmodern view places the client as the expert, not the therapist.

In addition, *social constructionism* has heavily influenced the solution-focused approach. According to social constructivism, the therapist should take a "not-knowing stance" (de Shazer, 1988). This means that the therapist should enter the therapy session not knowing what the client should do to solve his or her problem. Many SF therapists insist on having very little information before the first session so that they are not biased into thinking what the client should do.

Social constructionists also believe that language shapes and is shaped by relationships. How a person sees another person has much to do with how the relationship develops. For example, if a person meets someone who says she is a sexual abuse victim, perhaps a negative response will be generated in how the person sees the new friend. If, however, the new friend describes herself as a sexual abuse survivor, the person meeting her for the first time may see her as having a proactive and positive outlook on her life, not allowing the incident to trap her. Therefore, language can be a tool for creating change in therapy by conjuring up new descriptions or meanings for the client.

Pragmatism has also played an influential role in the solution-focused approach. William James, the founder of pragmatism, encouraged the mental health field to stop trying to predict the truth and instead begin identifying what works (Visser, 2008). Prior to the introduction of pragmatism, many therapeutic models focused on problems and their causes (Walter & Peller, 2000). Additionally, therapists were seen as experts who could or should lead the client to change. SFBT challenged these assumptions.

Eventually, from these theories, two models developed: the *solution-focused* model and the *solution-oriented* model. The distinctions between these approaches will be discussed later in this chapter.

HISTORY AND LEADING FIGURES

Founders of the solution-focused model include Steve de Shazer, Insoo Kim Berg, and their colleagues at the Brief Therapy Center in Milwaukee (Berg & Dolan, 2001; Cade, 2007).

Both Shazer and Berg and many of their colleagues were greatly influenced by Milton Erickson, a famous American psychiatrist and pragmatist. Erickson believed that everyone possessed the skills and abilities to solve their own problems and that small changes could lead to bigger changes.

In addition to Milton Erickson, Gregory Bateson played an influential role in the development of the solution-focused model. His work at the Bateson Project was the name given to a groundbreaking collaboration organized by Gregory Bateson beginning in 1953. Its members were Gregory Bateson, Don Jackson, Jay Haley, John Weakland, and Bill Fry. Perhaps the most famous and influential publication of the Project was *Towards a Theory of Schizophrenia*, which introduced the concept of the double bind. This project formed what would eventually become the Mental Research Institute (MRI) in Palo Alto, California (Visser, 2008). Founders of the MRI included Don Jackson, Jay Haley, Paul Watzlawick, John Weakland, Richard Fisch, and Janet Beavin (Hoyt, 2002). (See Chapter 11 for more on Jay Haley and his work.)

After several years, Fisch, Weakland, and Watzlawick departed from the MRI and founded the Brief Therapy Center (Cade, 2007). Unlike their predecessors, they allowed clients to direct the therapeutic conversation and they placed more emphasis on what the clients stated rather than what they as therapists thought should be stated. This resulted in a briefer therapeutic process. This ultimately affected the development of SFBT in that the client was seen as the expert on his or her own life and the job of the therapist was to work alongside the client, assisting the client through conversation, to identify times when life was better. These times became known as "exceptions," which also led the therapist to concentrate more on the present and future solutions rather than the past.

Insoo Kim Berg

As the center gained notoriety, more therapists wanted to study there. Insoo Kim Berg happened to be one of them. Berg, a psychotherapist who was raised in Korea and moved to the United States in 1957, was dissatisfied with traditional therapy methods. As a beginning therapist, she found her "failures" with clients perplexing. She noticed that although some families dropped out of therapy prematurely, they still referred their friends and family to her. She became curious about what she might have done right with those families. Gradually, she created an approach for clients who wanted to solve their problems right away, not next month or next year.

Eventually, Berg stumbled on the (then meager) literature on brief therapy, which motivated her to attend postgraduate school at the Family Institute of Chicago and the Menninger Foundation. After graduate school, she arrived at the MRI. She found that the brief therapy model made sense to her, and she was enticed by its pragmatic approach. While there, she met Steve de Shazer, whom she later married, and together they began questioning some tenets of the MRI approach. They became more intrigued by the role of solutions in therapy than the role of problems. Their interest in solutions eventually led to the formation of solution-focused therapy (SFT) and the Brief Family Therapy Center (BFTC) in Milwaukee, Wisconsin.

Insoo Berg wrote on various applications of SFT, including that of social services, substance abuse, school applications, and solution-focused work with children. She was well known for her training, which won the hearts of her participants by her warm smile and enthusiasm about the model. Her work took her around the world to work with clinicians, agencies, and schools. Insoo Kim Berg passed away at the age of 72 in 2007. The Solution-Focused Brief Therapy Association (SFBTA), of which she was a founder, said the following:

> Berg was widely recognized as a profoundly gifted clinician. Her impressive intellect was balanced by an abiding compassion for others and a modest, informal demeanor. Her deeply caring attitude was punctuated by a lively sense of humor, a warm, ready smile, infectious optimism, and enthusiasm. She radiated undeniable respect and absolute confidence in the self-expertise of each individual person. She affected everyone she came into contact with in profound ways both personally and professionally. (SFBTA, 2007)

Among her many works, she was the author of *Interviewing for Solutions* (2007), *Tales of Solutions* (2001), *Family Based Services: A Solution-Focused Approach* (1994), *Solutions Step by Step* (1997), *Children's Solution Work* (2003), *Brief Coaching for Lasting Solutions* (2005), and most recently, *More Than Miracles* (2007).

Steve de Shazer

Steve de Shazer was one of the most prominent figures in the SFBT approach, which he developed with his wife, Insoo Kim Berg. Upon moving from the MRI in California where Berg and de Shazer met, the two set up what they called "the MRI of the Midwest," where with a group of like-minded colleagues they developed the ways of thinking and the practices that became known as the solution-focused approach. This approach was based on the assumption of preexisting abilities, on client strengths and resources, and on the certainty that there have invariably been exceptions already to the behaviors, ideas, feelings, and interactions associated with problems. Therapy would be focused on an amplification of these exceptions and on helping clients through techniques such as the miracle question and scaling questions to build a detailed picture of how their future could be different. It was not seen as necessary to explore problems or their origins unless the client particularly wished to do so.

De Shazer was the author of many chapters and articles and of five books: *Patterns of Brief Therapy* (1982), *Keys to Solutions in Brief Therapy* (1985), *Clues: Investigating Solutions in Brief Therapy* (1988), *Putting Differences to Work* (1991), and *Words Were Originally Magic* (1994). Each book demonstrated a stage in the development of the thinking behind and the practicing of the approach (Cade, 2005).

> Steve de Shazer was a pioneer in the field of family therapy and was in fact often referred to in his later years as the "Grand Old Man of Family Therapy." An iconoclast and creative

genius known for his minimalist philosophy and view of the process of change as an inevitable and dynamic part of everyday life, he was known for reversing the traditional psychotherapy interview process by asking clients to describe a detailed resolution of the problem that brought them into therapy, thereby shifting the focus of treatment from problems to solutions. (Trepper et al., 2006)

Prior to his untimely death in September 2005, de Shazer and his colleagues completed writing the text *More Than Miracles: The State of the Art of Solution-Focused Brief Therapy* (Trepper et al., 2006).

The Brief Family Therapy Center

In 1978, Berg and de Shazer along with Jim Derks, Marilyn LaCourt, Eve Lipchik, Don Norum, and Elam Nunnally formed the Brief Family Therapy Center (BFTC) in Milwaukee. As a team, they sought to discover what worked in therapy. Initially, a great deal of their work used the one-way mirror, which allowed a team of therapists to closely examine a therapeutic session to learn what made therapy effective. As they observed the therapeutic process, they wrote down interventions that clients reported to be helpful. The team eventually became known for the strategy of the therapist "taking a break" midsession to converse with the team behind the mirror. In their journey, they also learned that what worked with one client did not always work with another client. Through these observations, the solution-focused approach eventually emerged (Yalom & Rubin, 2003). The founding members of BFTC and their colleagues trained many new therapists who are still working with a solution focus. The approach is popular in many countries around the world. Currently, some leaders in the field include Chris Iveson, Evan George, and Harvey Ratner and their team at The Brief Therapy Centre in the United Kingdom; Alasdair McDonald of Scotland; Australia's Brian Cade and Michael Durrant; and Scott Miller, Mark Hubble, and Barry Duncan of the Institute for the Study of Therapeutic Change in Chicago. Other current leaders in the United States include Michele Wiener-Davis, Linda Metcalf, Yvonne Dolan, Eve Lipchik, John Walter, and Jane Peller.

Bill O'Hanlon

Bill O'Hanlon's journey to solution-oriented therapy began long before he ever started seeing clients. In his book, *Do One Thing Different* (2000), O'Hanlon describes how his journey began with his desire to commit suicide in 1971, because he no longer saw any possibilities for his future. He described himself as a "hippie poet," afraid to show his writing to others, which led to some of his hopelessness and loneliness. As he began telling his friends of his desire to kill himself, all but one appeared to understand his dilemma and accept his decision. In an effort to convince Bill to continue living, his one *exceptional* friend offered him a place to live rent-free on her aunt's farm. Bill began seeing the possibilities in this offer and decided to focus not on death, but on how to survive in the meantime. O'Hanlon's desire to learn how people become *less* miserable led him to psychology and marital and family therapy. He found traditional psychiatry and psychology "too depressing." He did not like clinical diagnoses that were laden with medical terminology.

Eventually, he encountered the work of Milton Erickson, who inspired him to look at problems differently. Bill eventually landed on the idea of focusing on what was working in a client's life and on building solutions rather than focusing on what was going wrong. He further honed this idea until it became known as *solution-oriented therapy*. To date, Bill has written 23 books, including *Change 101: A Practical Guide to Creating Change in Life or Therapy* (2006), *A Field Guide to Possibility Land* (1996), *In Search of Solutions: A New Direction in Psychotherapy* (with Weiner-Davis, 1989), and *Thriving Through Crisis: Turn Tragedy and Trauma Into Growth and Change* (2004).

His work focuses on such subjects as sexual abuse, solution-oriented therapy, self-help for the layperson, and various professional books that promote and teach the solution-oriented approach.

INTRODUCTION TO SOLUTION-FOCUSED THERAPY

Solution-focused models have a worldwide appeal among practitioners because of their simple and practical ways of working with people. As mentioned earlier, two variants include solution-*focused* therapy with families and solution-*oriented* therapy with families. We will now examine the similarities and differences between the two models.

One of the core similarities is the agreement that a client is never seen as pathological or resistant. Rather, a solution-focused therapist believes that clients possess the necessary skills and tools to change and make their life better, if they decide that their goal is good for them and what they truly want.

In this therapy, what sometimes appears as resistance is really the therapist's inability to open the right door to change for the client. "There is no such thing as a resistant client, only an inflexible therapist" (de Shazer, 1988). If a client does not change after a task is developed between therapist and client, for example, the therapist assumes that he, the therapist, must have not understood what the client was trying to achieve.

Similarly, both models pay a great deal of attention to the clients' motivation level. S. de Shazer (1988) suggested that there are three types of clients—visitors, complainers, and customers—and each provides insight into the client's motivation level.

- In general, *visitors* come to therapy involuntarily and are not looking for help. With these clients, the therapists' role is to demonstrate how the client might benefit from the session.

- A *complainer* is a client who had decided to seek help for a problem; however, complainers lack clarity and are unsure how to work toward a solution. Therapists need to help complainers to construct attainable goals and to view *exceptions* to their problems. (Exceptions is an SFT term that will be explained later in this chapter.)

- *Customers* have constructed clear goals and are actively working toward them. When working with customers, the therapist's role is to provide them with additional support.

Although both solution-focused and solution-oriented models share many of the same beliefs and assumptions, the two are different in part because their founders came from different orientations, personally and professionally.

O'Hanlon has stated that solution-oriented therapy (which he also refers to today as *possibility therapy*) "is different in its emphasis on the importance of validation of felt experience and points of view and a flexible rather than formulaic method" (O'Hanlon, 2010). Solution-oriented therapy focuses more on emotions and the clients' own experience of the problem. However, de Shazer and others have examined the role of emotions in SFT

(Miller & de Shazer, 2000). However, their examination did not lead to adding a focus on emotions to their work. It was O'Hanlon who kept the focus on emotions and their role in resolving issues.

The two models also differ in their attention to structure. O'Hanlon (2010) has said the following:

> Another difficulty I see with the Milwaukee approach is its tendency to be formulaic. One invariably asks certain questions (like "The Miracle Question") and follows certain sequences. There are flow charts providing procedures for various client responses. While this may be a fine way to learn a new approach, the ultimate effect is sometimes one of rigidity and imposition. While the proponents of the Milwaukee approach may protest that this is evidence of the approach being done incorrectly, my experience is that a formulaic approach has this built-in risk.

Therefore, solution-oriented therapy advocates the use of techniques and solution-based interventions, but offers no specific format for their uses.

In the solution-focused approach, the miracle question (which will be discussed in detail later in this chapter) should always be asked during the first session; whereas in the solution-oriented approach, the miracle question is seen as helpful but not always necessary (O'Hanlon, 2010). Despite the differences between the two models, their core assumptions and beliefs remain the same. Clients are the experts on their own lives and, when given a context where they can discover exceptions in their lives, can formulate solutions that work for their own, unique lives.

Unlike problem-focused models, solution-focused models do not suggest that a client's history is necessarily needed to strategize solutions. Instead, the model teaches therapists to believe that the clients need to create and renegotiate their future. A criticism of the solution-focused approach is that the therapist may minimize the client's experience of the problem and be too hasty to identify exceptions of the problem, convincing the client that the exception is significant, even though not as significant to the client (Efran & Schenler, 1993, p. 73).

Bill O'Hanlon responds to this criticism by comparing the philosophy to traveling. In a workshop in Austin, Texas, he once described arriving at an airport and trying to get a taxi to his destination. The taxi driver first asked him, "Where are you coming from?" Bill said, "Well, it doesn't matter, I need to go to this destination." He went on to ask the audience, "What if the taxi cab driver asked again, 'But, where are you coming from?'" The conversation would be pointless; knowing where we come from does not give us directions for where we are trying to go. Our past may explain how we got here, but as for our future plans, those directions start in the present.

Additionally, the solution-focused model asserts that individual constructs are shaped entirely through conversations with others (Lethem, 2002). Therapists using a solution-focused approach pay special attention to the clients' words and phrases because they believe the client is the expert and only the client has a detailed knowledge of his or her own experiences and definitions of the problem (Berg & De Jong, 1996). Unlike the family therapy models associated with a more positivist approach such as cognitive behavioral therapy, which prescribes interventions or strategies matched to the family concern, the solution-focused model contends that reality is constructed by the individual. As a result, change results from the construction of new ideas of what is real (Berg & De Jong, 1996). Clients are more likely to follow through when the strategies they develop are theirs.

In essence, the solution-focused model pays a great deal of attention to language, and how language shapes the conversation between therapist and client. Parting from traditional models in which both clients and therapists converse about the client's problems, solution-focused therapies use conversations to help shape and determine what kind of life the client wants, what the client knows how to do to achieve the desired outcome (referred to as exceptions), and to help the client find ways to do it.

THEORETICAL ASSUMPTIONS

A summary of the basic theoretical assumptions in SFT are listed as follows:

1. Clients have resources and strengths to resolve complaints.
2. Change is constant.
3. The therapist's job is to identify and amplify change.
4. It is usually unnecessary to know a great deal about the complaint in order to resolve it.
5. It is not necessary to know the cause or function of a complaint to resolve it.
6. A small change is all that is necessary; a change in one part of the system can affect change in another part of the system.
7. Clients define the goal.
8. Rapid change or resolution of problems is possible.
9. There is no one "right" way to view things; different views may be just as valid and may fit the facts just as well.
10. Focus on what is possible and changeable, rather than what is impossible and intractable. (O'Hanlon & Weiner-Davis, 1989, pp. 34–50)

View of the Family and Client

Adhering to the theoretical assumptions of the model, solution-focused therapists do not go into the therapy session with any preconceived notions about what a client needs to change; instead, they rely on the client's definition of what the problem is. Although solution-focused therapists do not define problems or families, they do tend to define the context of the problem. According to Miller (1997), solution-focused therapists view clients, couples, and families in the context of being stuck. The therapist then sees it as his or her responsibility to help the clients to try something different, rather than continuing to do what is not working. When the client is a family, the solution-focused therapist asks each family member to identify times when the problem is not occurring as often. This systemic approach allows change to occur more quickly and gives the family a multitude of options that are within their own expertise.

View on How Change Occurs

The first step in guiding a client or family away from being stuck and toward their goal is to change the way that they see the problem. "How we look at things influences what we see and what we see influences what we do" (Hoyt & Berg, 1998, p. 204); therefore, solution-focused therapists need to help their clients to reconstruct new stories. If the therapist continues to let the client play his or her self-defeating story, it may eventually become a self-fulfilling prophecy.

It is also the therapist's job to help clients find exceptions to their complaints. Finding exceptions helps the client begin believing that change can happen. An example might be a 20-year-old male presenting with an anger issue. The therapist would ask the client to think back to a time when the anger was not an issue for him. Then, after identification of the "exceptions" to anger, the therapist would ask the client to describe recent times when the client was also able to refrain from anger, at least briefly. These discoveries provide the client with the recognition that he has indeed not given in to anger issues and promote the chance that he will repeat the "exceptions" again by identifying where he was, what he was doing, and what he was thinking about. Possibilities can also be emphasized by asking clients to describe in detail what their life *would* be like without their presenting complaint. This presuppositional language provokes the client into imagining the possibility that things can change and serves as an actual intervention (O'Hanlon & Weiner-Davis, 1989, p. 80).

Because solution-focused therapists believe that change is ultimately dependent on the client, it is the therapist's job to help tailor the goals to the client, making them specific and visual. Then, if the client is motivated to change, the therapist guides the client toward identifying more frequent, predictable, and controllable exceptions (Kingsbury, 1997). For clients who are not initially motivated to change, the therapist gives suggestions that require little effort and are likely to be completed. Steve de Shazer coined "the first session task," which basically asks the client:

> *Between now and the next time we meet, we (I) would like you to observe so you can describe to us (me) next time, what happens in your (pick one: family, life, marriage, relationship) that you want to continue to have happen. (de Shazer, 1985, p. 137)*

Ultimately, goals should be small, salient to the client, specific and concrete, achievable, and involve the client's own hard work (Hoyt, 2000). In fact, most of the time, the goals and homework in solution-focused therapies are set by the client and only reinforced by the therapist's encouragement.

Therapist's Role

Guided by their assumptions, solution-focused therapists work collaboratively with their clients to construct goals and develop solutions based on exceptions, times when the presenting problem is occurring less frequently or less intensely. In essence, the therapist can be seen as a cocreator (Shilts, Rambo, & Huntley, 2003). While the therapist and client work together, the therapist always operates from the assumption that the client is the expert and is always curious about how the client has coped so far. The therapist has to trust that the client knows what is best for himself or herself and lets him or her take the lead. "Empowerment of the client starts with honoring and following their lead in deciding what is important to them" (Metcalf, Thomas, Duncan, Miller, & Hubble, 1996, p. 343). Usually, the therapists assume a one-down or a "leading from behind" position by asking clients how they can help them to change their situation. It is helpful for beginning therapists who seek to master the solution-focused model to place themselves in the position of needing to be informed by the client, rather than having an assumption of what the client should do. Remaining curious about how clients have functioned so far in their lives will go a long way in learning the solution-focused model. When training supervisees, Metcalf (2010) suggests to supervisees to remain curious—the questions will then follow.

Interventions

Adhering to their roles, therapists rely on the use of techniques or interventions to guide their clients toward change. Solution-focused therapies are composed of two main tools or strategies: questions and interviewing techniques (O'Hanlon & Weiner-Davis, 1989, p. 77). *Questions* are designed to help clients focus on exceptions and make presuppositions (presuppositional questioning) about future actions while building a positive outlook and encouraging achievement. *Interviewing techniques* serve to validate concerns and assist clients in experiencing significant shifts in their thinking about their situation.

Questions

The initial technique used in therapy is questioning. The questions used in solution-based therapies can be categorized into three main types: the miracle question, exception-finding questions, and scaling questions.

Miracle Question. The miracle question is perhaps the single most important intervention in the solution-focused model (de Shazer, 1988). The miracle question asks the client to begin to think about what things would be like if the problem no longer existed and instead, a miracle occurs. In other words, the miracle question seeks to access the clients' preferred future. The miracle question encourages clients to assume that their lives will get better and provides them with interpretive lenses for seeing their lives in new ways (Miller, 1997). When therapists use phrases or talk about the client's problems as if it no longer exists, they are considered to be using "presuppositional language" (O'Hanlon & Weiner-Davis, 1989). Generally, the miracle question is stated in the following manner: "Suppose that one night, while you were asleep, there was a miracle and this problem was solved. How would you know? What would be different?" (de Shazer, 1988, p. 5).

In essence, the miracle question requires the client to focus on the solution versus the problem. In addition to its other uses, the miracle question provides a framework for where therapy should go. The miracle question serves to define the clients' goal and thereby allows the therapist to assist the clients in tracking their progress toward the resolution of their goal.

Exception-Finding Questions. Exception-finding questions ask clients to think about times when their troubles were/are less severe, less frequent, or altogether absent from their lives (Lethem, 2002). The form of the question assumes that there will be an exception to be remembered. Exception-finding questions are designed to open up the door to possibilities. Exception-finding questions can also help to emphasize how clients are already managing their problems and how they might be able to build on their current successes in the future.

Additionally, when examining exceptions and possibilities, the therapist may focus on how clients have achieved what they have so far, given their complaints and troubles. These "how did you do that?" questions emphasize how clients already possess the personal and social resources needed to solve their own issues and competently manage their lives. Examples of exception-finding questions include the following:

- *"Take me back to a time when you and your wife got along slightly better."*
- *"Tell me about a time when things went slightly better for you in school."*
- *"Please tell me how you have been able to cope up to now with this situation."*
- *"Between our last session and today, did you notice any times when the problem was less severe or frequent?"*

In general, exception-finding questions ask clients to think about times when the problem is not present and/or to notice what they are doing differently when things are going well. One of the main purposes for pointing out exceptions or looking for exceptions is to encourage the client to do more of what works. Exception-finding questions bring the client and therapist closer to the resolution of the problem.

Scaling Questions. Scaling questions are often considered the "workhorses" of the solution-focused model (de Shazer, 1988) because they are helpful in moving the client from the definition of the goal to the resolution of the goal (Lethem, 2002). Normally, scaling questions ask clients to rate where they feel they are at on a scale of 1 to 10. On the scale, 1 usually represents the worst that things have been and 10 represents what life would look like after the miracle. Some examples for the use of scaling questions include setting goals, measuring progress, creating a shared vision or understanding, examining past troubles, and identifying the magnitude of the problem on the client's life. Oftentimes, when working with families, differences will emerge among family members' responses to the scaling questions. For example, a mother may be concerned that a divorce has affected her daughter's life in a very negative way. However, after being asked the scaling question, the daughter reveals that she is a "6" on the scale. The mother thought that the daughter's score would be much lower, giving relief to the mother and a chance for the daughter to reveal that she is thankful her parents divorced because the quarreling was very chaotic for her. When differences in ratings or responses emerge, therapists should encourage clients to dialogue about their different views. The therapist should also assist the family in exploring these differences because they often highlight important clues to both increase and maintain progress.

Once a client has initially scaled his or her progress, it is the therapist's responsibility to assist the client in defining how he or she will move up the scale toward resolution of his or her problem. To accomplish this, the therapist may ask the clients to define what it would take between now and their next session for them to be able to move up the scale and closer to their goal. The scaling question should also be frequently used to reassess the clients' progress toward their goals. In doing so, therapists will be able to quickly identify whether the clients have become stuck or whether they are continuing to make progress toward the resolution of their problem.

Interviewing Techniques

In SFT, interviewing the client with curiosity helps to shift the manner in which a client views the current situation.

Ideas, Not Techniques. Solution-focused therapists do not use "techniques" with clients, unlike other models such as cognitive behavioral therapy and structural therapy. Instead, they see SFT as a mind-set, believing that clients have expertise and therapy as a context for discovering such expertise. The solution-focused therapist, therefore, validates the client's experience and promotes the client's suggestions for change, based on what the client desires. The ideas of the model involve discovering what clients want to achieve. One question that therapists use to help define the client's complaint and then the solution might be, "What do we need to talk over today to enable you to feel that this meeting has been worthwhile?" This allows the client to state up front what he or she wishes to discuss. This beginning premise of the solution-focused approaches provides the client with a tool to move quickly to the heart of the issue that is most important to the client. This contributes to the brevity of the model because there is little time wasted in discussing what the therapist thinks needs to be discussed. Instead, the client is immediately placed in charge.

Problem-Free Talk. The idea of problem-free talk is often overlooked but is an integral part of SFT because it is a useful technique for eliciting resources. A solution-focused therapist presented with a client who needs to vent about problems will listen attentively, inserting problem-free words such as "So, you want things to be better, how will that look when it begins to happen?" This helps the client to begin to abandon the problem-focused thinking for solution-focused thinking, catapulting the client into a conversation of what he or she wants versus what he or she does not want. It is also more respectful than jumping too quickly into exception-finding questions and not listening to what the client needs to say. A therapist who can consistently steer his or her client gently and respectfully toward what the client prefers, instead of dwelling on how difficult the concerns are, will find that the client moves more readily toward resolution.

Compliments. Compliments are used in SFT with some degree of restraint, currently, because they have been criticized as putting the therapist in the expert role if given too freely. They usually include validation of concerns, recognition of competencies, and recognition of how a person has coped. Compliments serve to normalize the client's experiences, restructure the meaning of the problem, and highlight the client's own solution-building competencies (Campbell, Elder, Gallagher, Simon, & Taylor, 1999). Compliments are usually constructed using a five-step procedure:

1. The therapist begins by issuing a normalizing statement. (*"It makes sense to me that you are concerned about your children after the divorce. You are commended to be such a thoughtful mother."*)

2. Then the therapist follows with a restructuring statement. (*"I wonder what your kids would say that you have done recently that has been helpful to them during this time?"*)

3. Next, the therapist gives the client an affirmation of competencies. Affirmations draw the client's attention to how personal and social resources can be used to develop solutions. (*"When you think of how you have handled other situations revolving around the divorce, what would you say your strengths have been?"*)

4. The fourth step is the bridging statement. Bridging statements make connections between the suggested next steps and what has been previously discussed. (*"Based on what you have told me so far, that you have taken off early from work to be with your kids, helped them to call their father at night before bedtime and talked to a colleague for support, what would you suggest doing more of just for the next week?"*)

5. The final step is the homework task. Homework tasks are usually given in the form of a suggestion to notice what is already helping to move the client toward a solution, or to carry on and to build on partial successes. Ideally, the homework task should serve to keep the client focusing on exceptions and should only be based on the exceptions. Some examples of homework tasks include asking the client to go home and answer the miracle question, or watching for times when the problem occurs less. (*"I am impressed with your ideas and the strategies that you have suggested. What would you suggest doing for the next week that your kids would recognize as helpful to them?"*)

Evaluating the Process of Constructing Solutions. Although the client is ultimately responsible for change, the therapist constantly evaluates the client's progress. It is not uncommon for the therapist to evaluate the client's progress toward change both at the beginning and at the end of the session. At the beginning of the session, the therapist may ask the client what's gotten better or changed since the previous session. This helps to initially identify any progress the client may have made and help the client to stay on track with solutions. At the end of the session, the therapist may evaluate progress by asking the client what he or she found helpful in the session, as well as whether he or she would like to return for another session. It is also at this point when the therapist may ask the scaling question:

> *"Based on where you were when you first came to therapy, on a scale of 1 to 10, with 10 being the best, where would you say you were then? Where are you now, after meeting for two times? What will it take for you to go one point higher over the next week?"*

Aside from directly asking the client about his or her progress, the therapist can pay attention to the client's thoughts and behaviors. Changes are reflected in what the client pays attention to and his ideas and constructions, as well as his interactions and behaviors (O'Hanlon, 1998).

Effectiveness of SFT. In the last 30 years, the solution-focused model has gained worldwide appeal. More recently, the model has gained popularity outside of the therapy context. The solution-focused approach is now being applied in child protective services (Berg, 1994), business world (Greene & Grant, 2003), education (Metcalf, 1995, 2008; Murphy, 1997), and as a supervision model in various contexts (O'Connell & Jones, 1997, pp. 289–292). In addition, the model is being used as an overall philosophical framework for many organizations.

Research suggests that SFT may be an effective approach with certain populations and issues. Gingerich and Eisengart (2000, 2005) conducted a systematic qualitative review of multiple outcome studies on the solution-focused model. Their results indicated that the SFT model was better than no treatment or comparable to empirically supported interventions. They concluded that there is "preliminary support for the idea that SFBT may be beneficial to clients" (Gingerich & Eisengart, 2000, p. 495).

In a meta-analysis conducted by Kim (2006), the SFBT approach was found to demonstrate positive outcome measures related to both internalizing and externalizing behavior problems and to family and relationship problems.

More specifically, research has shown that the solution-focused model is effective in treating the following: school-age children (Franklin, Moore, & Hopson, 2008; LaFountain & Garner, 1996), parenting skills (Zimmerman, Jacobsen, MacIntyre, & Watson, 1996), rehabilitation of orthopedic patients (Cockburn, Thomas, & Cockburn, 1997), recidivism in prison populations (Lindforss & Magnusson, 1997), antisocial behaviors of adolescent offenders (Seagram, 1997), and hopefulness among depressed clients (Bozeman, 1999).

SOLUTION-FOCUSED THERAPY WORKING TEMPLATE

The *SFT working template* is meant to be used as a guideline to learning the process of SFT. The template provides the beginning therapist with steps to take and questions to ask that promote collaboration between the therapist and client. There are suggested questions under each heading to help start the process. After using the initial questions, guide the client through each process, asking questions that occur to you, staying curious about the client's expertise. Although there is no one "script" for any therapy session, it is the hope of the author that the template serves as an impetus to learning this family therapy model.

Tools for Change

Throughout the sessions, keep the conversation as problem-free as possible. Let the client guide you toward his or her goal and avoid letting your ideas on what needs to change interfere. Use the miracle question as a goal-setting question to assist the client in stepping out of his or her problem-saturated world into a momentary glimpse of what he or she wishes life to be. Use the exceptions identified in the sessions as tools for clients to use in between sessions as tasks. Use presuppositional language to promote change in the future. Assign tasks based on the client's ideas of what could be helpful. Use the scaling question to rate where the client begins and as change occurs.

Phase 1: Joining and Building Rapport

Introduce yourself and greet everyone in the room. Explain your role as a solution-focused family therapist. Be friendly and curious.

Here are some comments or questions that a therapist might use during this phase:

- *"My name is_____. As we begin talking, it would help me to get to know you if you would tell me about yourselves and things you appreciate about each other."*
- *"What could we talk about that would be helpful to you today?"*
- *"What has gotten a little better between the time that you called to make an appointment and today?"*
- *"Would it be alright if we talked about your son's diagnosis differently?"*

Phase 2: Understanding the Presenting Issue

Inquire about what brought the client/family to therapy. Clarify as the client talks. Listen, empathize, and be curious about what the clients expect to accomplish in therapy. Pay attention to the strengths and resources of the clients in their personal and professional lives. Listen for client's descriptions of the presenting issue and "normalize" the issue. Help the client to see himself or herself as competent. Clarify exceptions to the problem with the client as he or she hears them.

Here are some comments or questions that a therapist might use during this phase:

- *"I am amazed that you have been able to_____ (keep a job, stay focused, not drink) while this has been going on. How have you done this?"*
- *"How do you explain your ability to_____ during this time?"*
- *"Tell me about times when this issue occurs less. What is different then?"*
- *"Tell me the last time that you were able to _____ and not allow_____ to occur, even in other situations. How did you do that? What else?"*

Phase 3: Assessment of Family Dynamics

The solution-focused therapist does not assess the presenting issue, as many other therapeutic models do, to learn why the issue exists. The therapist does listen for exceptions, within the family system, that provide possibilities to solutions. In this phase, it is helpful to ask the family to help with exceptions to times when the problem does not occur. By doing so, family members learn from each other what they each do that either keeps the problem present or helps it to occur less.

Here are some comments or questions that a therapist might use during this phase:

- *"Could each of you describe times when the problem occurs less?"*
- *"Daniel, your mom said that you are rarely angry at school, only at home. Can you tell us all what is different at school that helps you be in control of your anger?"*
- *"Helen, you said that the times when Joe listened to you rather than told you how to solve a problem at work were the most helpful to you. What difference did that make to you?"*

Phase 4: Goals

The solution-focused therapist works with the client to set specific goal(s) that will be meaningful and relevant to the client. It is important to help the client to be specific when setting goals. The goal must be a visible goal such as the following: "I will talk to my boss early in the day, before 10:00 a.m., rather than late in the day"; "My son will improve his math grade by 10 points in 3 weeks"; "I will exercise for 15 minutes three times a week to get started on an exercise plan"; and "I will move up the scale 1 point during the next week by being assertive to my daughter when she has a tantrum."

Here are some comments or questions that a therapist might use during this phase:

- The miracle question: *"Suppose tonight while you sleep, a miracle occurs. When you wake up tomorrow, what will be different? Who will be there? What will you be doing?"*
- *"When things get better someday soon, what will you be doing differently?"*
- *"Someday, after this problem is resolved, what will I see you doing that will let us both know that the problem is solved?"*

Phase 5: Amplifying Change

Whenever you hear exceptions, verbalize your discoveries with curiosity and sincerity to the client, even if the exceptions are slight. Consistently ask the client, "How did you do that?" Use scaling questions with the client to get direction and measure successes. Comment on the client's score: "I am surprised the score is not lower. How is it that you have not let things get worse?" Support the client, look for change, and realize that change is constant. Emphasize the clients' successes and improvements toward the goal.

Here are some comments or questions that a therapist might use during this phase:

- *"Tell me what has gone better since we last met."* (This is a useful question for each session after the initial session.)
- *"What has helped you to be able to move forward?"*
- *"What else helped?"* (Ask several times for more exceptions.)
- *"What difference did that make for you?"*
- *"I am not surprised that things were difficult. How did you get through it?"* (Good question for a client who had a tough week.)
- *"On a scale of 1 to 10, with 10 meaning that things are perfect and 1 meaning that there is work to do, where are you today? Where would you like to be next week?"*

Phase 6: Termination

Each week, ask the clients whether they wish to come back, and, if so, when. This puts them in charge of therapy. When clients report that things are better, inquire about whether they think it is time to stop or take a break. If a client decides to terminate, the following question is useful and gives both client and therapist reassurance of the process:

- *"What did we do during our time together that you found helpful, if anything?"*

MASTER THERAPIST INTERVIEW

INSOO KIM BERG

A native of Korea, Insoo Kim Berg balanced her heritage with Western scientific training in her clinical practice and teaching. Until her death in early 2007, she was the executive director of Brief Family Therapy Center in Milwaukee, and a codeveloper of the solution-focused brief therapy model. A prolific writer, she published eight highly acclaimed books in 10 years and coauthored books with other solution-focused therapists, such as Scott Miller, Yvonne Dolan, and Peter De Jong. Her recent books include Tales of Solutions *(2001),* Building Solutions in Child Protective Services *(2000), and* Interviewing for Solutions *(1997 & 2001, 2nd ed.). Internationally, Insoo was a highly sought-after speaker and trainer on the solution-focused model. This interview took place in 2007.*

What attracted you to the theory behind solution-focused therapy?
I became unhappy with the model I was using; I didn't like the outcomes I was receiving. I knew there had to be a better way to work with people and their outcomes. As a result, I helped to codevelop this model.

What kind of families or issues do you think work best with this model?
I don't think of it that way, because all families have some issues and some concerns.

Different models of therapy require the therapist to be directive or nondirective. In your opinion, what are the necessary characteristics that a therapist should possess to be effective with this model?
I don't think it has to do with directive or nondirective; it is how well they can listen. Rather than imposing our models on the family, we listen to the family first and respond to what the family's needs are. I like to emphasize not trying to fit the family into a model, but making the model work for the family. So I would say the most important characteristic is someone's abilities to set aside their own ideas and listen to families' ideas. The families are not there to be lectured; they are there because they are in pain.

What are you looking for when you are in the session?
I start by finding out and learning about the territory, rather than creating my own map, and learning about what kind of a place it is to be in this family. What's the terrain and atmosphere like and where do they want to go and how do they think they are going to get there?

What is the assessment process of this model?
There really isn't one. I begin where the clients are. If they are very determined to hang on to their label, I would say, "So you have been to see Dr._____, and how helpful has that been?" And then they will tell you some amazing amount of information about what they didn't like or what they liked. What I get normally is what they didn't like. They are unhappy with what Dr. So-and-so has done or has not done. So, if a client has been told that he [has] a borderline personality disorder, for example, sometimes, I will say, "What tells you that, what is your understanding of what borderline is? What do you mean, 'I have been depressed all my life'?" Many of them say that. Then I ask them, "So how do you know you can get better? What tells you that you can get better?" Then they say, "Well there are days when I feel better," and there's the exception right there. So, "Tell me about [the] days when you feel a little bit better." I never get into debates about labels or nonlabels, I just leave it alone. Sometimes, if I meet someone who has had a long therapy, many, many, many therapies, then I say, "Well, since you have worked so hard to gain all the insights about yourself, I suppose we don't need to do that here anymore because you have already done that." I let them know that I am not interested in that and that they don't have to go through all that again. Then, I ask what needs to happen here to make this a helpful experience for them.

Who sets the goals, the client or the therapist?
The client sets the goal. The goal is the guidepost. It's like a landmark, and we are always looking for this landmark or this next landmark. I think that might be the most important part of the process. This is a very goal-driven model, and everything we do is defined by what the goal is and what the outcome is that we are looking for.

We use scaling questions from 1 to 10, where 10 means you don't need to come back to see me anymore and 1 means you feel like your life is in a desperate situation. Ten means you are making it and 1 is the worst hell you have experienced recently. So what would a 10 look like? I gather lots of description of what a 10 would look like by asking, "What is your best hope? What would make spending this hour worthwhile for you? How could your best friend and/or your children tell that this has been a good session for you? How could your partner tell?" Certainly, the miracle question would help towards that conversation.

What are some commonly used interventions with this model?
I consider the conversation as the intervention. It's the conversation that changes not just the clients, but their perspective.

What training do you feel is necessary to become an effective therapist with this model?
I think it's more what the therapist brings with them, such as their general view, general attitude toward life, toward work, toward clients and how they see clients. Are they willing to expand their views and learn from clients? Because everything we do, we learn from clients. Clients are the most important teacher. I describe it as having one foot in the client's world and one foot in the professional world. That way, you can go back and forth, balancing between two feet and being able to be flexible enough to move back and forth. You can never just stand on one leg. You have to stand on both legs, both feet.

What have you found to be the limitations of this approach?
It's not like I do a procedure on them, they can take as much or as little as they want, they can change a little or they can change a lot. When you talk like we are in charge of the interventions, meaning that I prescribe certain interventions or I decide whether you can be helped or not, you're using medical language.

What suggestions do you have for students learning this model?

Oh wow! I don't know what I would suggest. I guess you just have to hang in there. We have a saying, "It's very easy to learn the solution-focused approach, but it's very hard to practice, because you get continuously pulled into the problem, so it takes a lot of discipline and lots of hard work to practice." It's also hard to avoid the tendency to not to categorize or classify people, because we are very trained in that. It's a continuously evolving process. I've been at this for 25 to 30 years now, and we are trying to make it simpler and simpler and simpler. We are also taking this model outside of the therapy room into schools, classrooms, prisons, and businesses. I am doing a lot of writing and teaching in application of this to other fields other than therapy itself.

Is there anything you would like to add?

Well, I'll tell you about a common discussion among trainers or supervisors: "Can anyone be trained to be solution-focused or are they just born that way? That's not a new question. Certain people are drawn to this model and find immediate affinity to the model. They say, 'Oh this is what I've been looking for.'"

What people do tell me is that learning to practice this model has changed their lives, because they start to use it in their own personal lives. They tell me, "I like my husband a lot more because I notice the good things about him. I learned the scaling question and went home and practiced it on my kids and it just worked wonders." They even tell me they asked their friends or family the miracle question. The personal application is very appropriate.

MASTER THERAPIST INTERVIEW

BILL O'HANLON

Bill O'Hanlon, MS, LMFT, has authored or coauthored more than 24 books, some of the latest are Pathways to Spirituality *(2005),* Change 101: A Practical Guide to Creating Change *(2006), and* Thriving Through Crisis *(2005). He has published 54 articles or book chapters and appeared on* The Today Show, Oprah, *and other various television and radio programs. Since 1977, he has taught in more than 1,200 seminars around the world.*

Bill O'Hanlon is the developer of solution-oriented therapy and founder of possibility and inclusive therapies. His clinical work is recognized for its collaborative, respectful approach to clients. He is known for his storytelling, irreverent humor, clear and accessible presentation style, and his psychotic enthusiasm for whatever he is doing.

Is there a distinct difference between solution-oriented, solution-focused therapy and solution-oriented and possibility therapy?

I make a pretty sharp distinction, but to tell you the truth, everyone else says, "Oh, Bill is a solution-focused therapist." So I try to stay pure on it, and over the years, people introduce me at workshops and they'll say, "Bill O'Hanlon does solution-focused therapy," and I just roll my eyes and say, "Yep, I do solution-focused therapy." I make this esoteric distinction, yes, I think they are very different, but almost everyone else in the field does not think they are that different. They don't make the same subtle and fine distinctions.

Do you prefer me to call your therapy solution-oriented or possibility therapy?
Well, either way is okay with me. Initially, I started to call it possibility because I started to shift the emphasis and I wanted to distinguish it from solution-focused therapy, so it didn't get confused. However, I think there are a bunch of solution-based therapies. I consider narrative therapy to be solution based, although they don't consider themselves to be solution based. I think they call themselves competency based. I think there are probably a bunch of flavors of solution-based therapies.

What attracted you to the theory behind solution-oriented family therapy?
I thought it didn't involve a great deal of blame and shame. When people come into therapy, I think they are suffering from having been blamed and shamed and invalidated in some way—and to hear somebody ask you about what you do well is sort of a counter to that blaming and shaming. We're oriented toward what's right with people so we are sort of lifting them up. The other thing that attracted me was my personal experiences and work with Milton Erickson.

Additionally, I'm very attracted to therapies that help people relieve themselves from their suffering as quickly as possible. Clients come into therapy and they put themselves in a vulnerable position, in our hands if you will, and to be able to help them relieve or minimize or eliminate their suffering pretty rapidly was very attractive to me. I've seen people go from being so discouraged that they want to kill themselves to smiling and laughing and saying, "I guess it wasn't so bad and I'm not crazy or I'm less stuck than I thought I was." It's really a great joy to me! One of the things that attracted me to the field was that I wanted to make that kind of contribution to people, and what I really loved about this approach was it seemed very rapid.

How do you formulate your view of a family when they enter therapy?
What you focus on expands. What we pay attention to very much influences what we do and how we develop stories about our lives and our situations. So, one part of the theory is if you focus people on what's wrong and how they are messed up, more of that will occur and they will probably be more focused on it. So this idea says, if you shift the focus, people will pay attention to what they are good at, what they are skilled at, and what their resources are and create a cascading effect of competence and positive change.

What kinds of families do you think benefit most from this model?
Any kind. I think it just either works or it doesn't.

Different models of therapy require the therapist to be directive or nondirective. In your opinion, what are the necessary characteristics that a therapist should possess to be effective with this model?
When I look back or listen to my tapes, I notice that I'm constantly joining with people and inviting them into possibilities. Also, in the first session, I ask, "What

brought you here and how will you know when you got what you came for?" That is kind of unique to the first session; and in the last session, I say, "You know, I think we're done—is there anything else?" There aren't any formal or particular techniques that I use in the first and last session. I think I'm a change agent that people have come to for two things: One is understanding and validation of their suffering and current situation, and another is to get help with change. They want to change, but for some reason or another, they don't quite know how to do it or haven't figured it out yet. My job is to create an atmosphere of validation and understanding and compassion, as well as a compelling invitation into change. That's my job entirely.

How often does the client see you and for how long a period of time?
Fourty-five to 50 minutes, typically, unless I run over, I'm notoriously terrible with time. At the end of a 50-minute session, I ask the client, "Did you get what you came for and are we done?" and they'll say yes or no. If they say no, then I'll say, "What's your sense of when you'd like to come back?" They'll say 2 weeks or next week or next month, and I'll say, "Great if that's possible with both of our schedules." But sometimes they'll say, "What's your sense?" and I'll say, "About 2 or 3 weeks." I prefer 2 to 3 weeks because, typically, I'm talking to them about something they are going to go out and do or think about, and I want to give it some time.

What are you looking for when you are in the session?
I'm really curious about this family, this couple, or this person. I just want to know what they are worried about and how they are suffering and what they want. That's the first map. The second map is what can they tell me about what's worked and is working and what's not working or what hasn't worked. Then, how will we know when they've got what they've come for. What's the stopping point? What do they want and how will they know when we get there?

What is the assessment process of this model?
To me, it's an ongoing process. I don't think I ever fully understand my client's situations or my clients; I think I always get closer approximations, as I know more. I have them fill out a brief form, usually at the beginning, so I have some basic information; but most the assessment is done by conversation. It's not a formal assessment; I vaguely assess suicidality, homocidality, drug abuse, and violence or anything like that, which might include emergency or dangerous situations and the rest is all up in the air. It's just what's interesting to them and what's interesting to me. Anything is relevant at that point, and I learn more and more as time goes on.

Who sets the goals, the client or the therapist?
Goals are set by both of us. I help them articulate the goals so it is a mutual process, but they set the direction of their goals. With this question, I'll make a distinction between possibility and solution-oriented therapy. With possibility therapy, there really isn't a goal; it's just a direction that we are going towards. In solution-oriented therapy, the goal is what the client wants and what we talk about in therapy.

I really like a line Steve de Shazer used, "How will we know when we are going to stop meeting like this?" The second one is video talk, which is "What will we be able to see or hear on a videotape when you've reached your goal?" In a typical interaction, a person will say, "Well, I won't be depressed anymore." Then I would continue with "How would we know that . . . what would we see on the video if you are not depressed and what would we hear on the video if you are not depressed?" I think it provides a very clear definition so that we don't pass the goal or miss the goal because we don't know what it looks like and sounds like. It helps us know whether we've gotten there or not.

What are some commonly used interventions with this model?

I feel that joining with people verbally and inviting them to new possibilities, along with changing the viewing, changing the doing, and changing the context, are the most common interventions. Changing the viewing is figuring out how people see things and what they are focused on in their perspective and changing that slightly. It's changing the meaning they are making of it. Changing the doing is changing the actions or interactions or the language. Changing how they're talking about it or around the problem or involved with the problem. Changing the context involves things like timing, location, and who else is involved in both the therapy and in the situation since the problem has occurred. Additionally, challenging gender biases or training patterns, challenging cultural and familial patterns around the problem, and finding resources within those contexts to help change [are] important, too.

What role does a homework assignment have in this model?

I used to use homework all the time and now I don't. When I've found that clients didn't do their homework, we just discussed what wasn't working. I didn't assume resistance or anything, we just talked about it. Now, when I give homework, I spend a lot of time negotiating it in the session. For example, I saw this woman the other day and her job was to go home and think of three positive futures in a situation that she has been really worried about and to write those down and discuss them with her partner. She learned that when she starts to think of negative futures, she worries and gets anxious about how terrible life is going to be, and now instead of worrying, she just decides to remember these three positive or possible filled futures. This came right out of our conversation; she said, "When I focus on the worse stuff, I develop these anxiety attacks and I kept on thinking it's going to go badly this way. Then, I had this dream that everything was great and it worked out, and when I think of that dream, I calm right down and then I think, it's not going to be that bad—and even if it gets bad, I'll find a way to deal with it." So, I said, "Okay, I want you to think of three possibilities like your dream and that was the homework." It worked because it was client driven and she was highly motivated to do it.

What suggestions do you have for students learning this model?

New therapists are too positive. They don't acknowledge and validate, and don't listen and don't respond to where the client actually is in their overenthusiasm about discovering solutions. I think, sometimes, they grab on to a formula rather than have the relationship with people and the flexibility to respond to the moment.

Carl Jung said years ago, "To learn your methods, learn your theories—and then when you walk into the room, set them aside and marvel at the uniqueness of the human beings that are right in front of you." I would say, "Really do your homework, learn your stuff, practice it, and then go in the session and be yourself with this unique client or set of clients that is in front of you." That is the best training you can do, and to realize you are going to go through phases in your career, you're going to know, and then not know, and then know, and then relax a little about it. In summary, I would recommend you get your training and then bring your humanity into the conversation.

Is there anything that you would like to add?
When I was younger, I thought about what I was going to do with my life because I really didn't feel right about going to work for a corporation to make money or make products. And then I discovered this area of psychotherapy, and I thought, "Wow, what a privilege!" This is a sacred profession where we are doing something that contributes to people, that shows compassion. People will allow us into their lives and be vulnerable with us and ask us for help, and it's such an awesome responsibility. I think this profession is a sacred profession, and it's just an amazing privilege to get paid for doing this kind of work.

How do you see this model changing in the next 20 or so years?
I think we'll find out what this model or others do with the brain and we'll be able to integrate some of the new research from the brain sciences. I think we'll be able to incorporate more new methods. We'll find ways of making it more efficient and respectful. I think it will be somewhat like many other therapies and disappear as a separate approach. It will be somewhat like Carl Rogers, part of the mainstream. Everyone will learn to ask about strengths, and solutions, and competencies as part of whatever therapy they do, and it won't stand out so much as a separate approach or a separate school; and I think that would be one of the best outcomes that we could have.

Case Study

A mother calls and makes an appointment for her family to come to therapy. The family consists of the wife and her husband, both in their forties; their 15-year-old son; college aged daughter; and the woman's father, age 82. Three years after the woman's mother died, her father developed Alzheimer's. He moved in with the family six months ago. When his health began to deteriorate, the woman spent more time caring for him than for other members of the family. Three months ago, the 15-year-old, who has been treated for ADHD since age 7, began to refuse to take his medication, and is now being truant from school.

During the session, the wife cries and the husband reports that their relationship is strained, occasionally rolling his eyes as his wife becomes tearful. He reports that he has had to take on more work since his wife had to quit her job to attend to her father's needs. The daughter is away at college and the wife smiles as she describes her as a straight A student. The daughter was asked to attend the session but refused because she has a hard time with her grandfather's illness and dislikes the conflict that has developed at home.

Insoo Berg's Response to the Case Study

My first thought would be "What's missing here?" What might the clients consider as the most pressing issue for them? The mother called, so she must be the most concerned about things, so I would say she is sort of the instigator of this contact and could be the most invested in finding something that could work for them. I would most likely ask the mother, "What happened between the phone call and the first meeting?" I ask that because things might have caused the client's ideas to change about what might be the most pressing issue for them. In families with lots going on, I don't try to tackle it all at once. I am very mindful to consider what the most *pressing* issue is for the family.

Obviously, you would get some social talk started, small talk about the family, and then my first questions would be "What kind of work do you do for a living?" Then I would inquire who is doing what, and ask about the daughter away in school and how she was doing. I might ask, "Is she the first person going to college in the family? How about other children, how are they doing in school?" That is sort of the big picture of the family. Since mother quit her job to take care of the father, I would inquire about what kind of work did she do before, where was she working, what did she like about the job? Then I would ask what might be their best hope for the session. I focus on this meeting because it could be the last meeting—we don't know. So I want to know what they could get out of this meeting to make their effort worthwhile. What might be the outcome that they are looking for? What will be the pay off for their effort? Those are the kinds of things I would be most interested in, rather than all the problems, like the problem with the father and the 15-year-old boy.

Bill O'Hanlon's Response to the Case Study

It's interesting to read this case study because, generally, I don't have any interest in this information. In fact, if I'm asked to do a consultation, I say, "I don't want to know anything about this family, or this couple, before I see them." Years ago, I saw a cartoon in *The New Yorker* and it had a cab driver and a passenger. The cab driver said "Okay, you're going to 42nd St. and 7th Avenue," and the passenger looked a little startled. I think that's how therapy often starts. The therapist has a theory, an idea of where they are going, and the client comes in and the therapist begins to work their theory if you will. What I say is, "What is concerning you and what do you want?" Like a cab driver, "Where do you want to go, what's concerning you or anybody that's sitting in the room?" And then the second thing is, "What do you want that has to do with therapy? You know it's obviously not fun to have your relationship strained, it's not fun to have to take on more work, but what does that have to do with therapy?" That's this life so far, yep, your wife's taken in a parent and it's challenging, and your son is refusing to take his medication and he's being truant, but what do you want from therapy, what's the therapy part of this? Because if they say, "Well, we've got this difficult situation with Alzheimer's," I'll say "Yeah, that is really tough, that is a really tough situation, now what can I do as a therapist, what would you like from me?" So that is where I start every therapy case. I just keep searching for a motive or direction until they give me a direction, and the direction is set with two things: One is what they don't want, what they say they don't like, what they are concerned about and unhappy about, and the other is what they say they would like. I don't even move my cab until I get that stuff.

KEY TERMS

Client-defined goal   In solution-focused therapy (SFT), the goal is defined by the client, not the therapist. The therapist only aids the client in helping to visualize or describe the goal.

Compliments   Feedback given to clients designed to be supporting and normalizing.

Exception-finding questions   Questions that ask the client to think about a time when a problem did not occur or did not interfere with the client's life. The client's responses offer clues to help build more solutions.

First-session formula task   An assignment designed to help the client focus on the future and to create an expectation for change. It helps the client notice the positive aspects of his or her life. For example, "Between now and the next time we meet, I want you to observe, so that you can describe to me next time, something that happens in your family that you want to continue to have happen."

Future-oriented statements   Statements that help clients visualize a future in which they have achieved their solution.

Goal-oriented statements   Statements that help the client clarify or visualize a goal.

Miracle question   A question that explores what the solution might look like (not necessarily the elimination of the problem). For example, "Suppose that one night while you were sleeping, there was a miracle and this problem was solved. How would you know? What would be different when you woke up?"

Normalizing compliments   Comments by the therapist that help the client to realize that his or her reactions, feelings, or behaviors are normal and natural responses to certain life events.

Presuppositional questions   Types of questions designed to function as "interventions" by assuming that change will happen. For example, "Someday *when* you and your wife are communicating better, what *will* be different?"

Reframing   A technique that relabels a behavior by placing it in a new, more positive perspective; for example, labeling a client as "sad" rather than "depressed." This helps to change the perception of the behavior and invite new responses to the same behavior.

Resistance   Resistance refers to a client's inability or unwillingness to change. In SFT, resistance is attributed to the therapist not having found what works for the client, because, fundamentally, solution-focused therapists believe that clients want to change.

Scaling questions   Helpful questions where clients are asked to rate their progress on a scale of 1 to 10. The questions are used to see where the client is currently in regard to finding solutions. The questions also help to maintain and amplify change when the client sets goals to reach a certain point on the scale in a certain amount of time.

Solution-focused brief therapy (SFBT)   A strengths-based model of brief therapy that shifts the focus from problems to solutions, with little focus on why problems occurred and more focus on how the client has avoided similar problems in the past. Originally developed by Steve de Shazer and Insoo Kim Berg.

Solution-oriented therapy   A results-oriented therapy approach adapted from SFT and later developed by Bill O'Hanlon and Michelle Weiner-Davis. It is short term, meaning that goals are usually accomplished in a limited number of sessions, focus on times when the problem occurs less, and are task-oriented.

REFERENCES

Berg, I. K. (1994). Family based services: A solution-focused approach. New York, NY: Norton.

Berg, I. K., & De Jong, P. (1996). Solution-building conversations: Co-constructing a sense of competence with clients. *Families in Society: The Journal of Contemporary Human Services, 77,* 376–391.

Berg, I. K., & Dolan, Y. (2001). *Tales of solutions: A collection of hope-inspiring stories.* New York, NY: Norton.

Bozeman, B. N. (1999). *The efficacy of solution-focused therapy techniques on perceptions of hope in clients with depressive symptoms.* Unpublished doctoral dissertation, New Orleans Baptist Theological Seminary, New Orleans, LA.

Cade, B. (2005). Steve de Shazer obituary. *European Brief Therapy Association.* Retrieved from http://www.ebta.nu/page28/page32/page32.html

Cade, B. (2007). Springs, streams, and tributaries: A history of the brief, solution-focused approach. In T. S. Nelson & F. N. Thomas, (Eds.), *Handbook of solution-focused brief therapy: Clinical applications* (pp. 25–64). Binghamton, NY: The Haworth Press.

Campbell, J., Elder, J., Gallagher, D., Simon, J., & Taylor, A. (1999). Crafting the "tap on the shoulder": A compliment template for solution-focused therapy. *The American Journal of Family Therapy, 27*(1), 35–47.

Cockburn, J. T., Thomas, F. N., & Cockburn, O. J. (1997). Solution-focused therapy and psychosocial adjustment to orthopedic rehabilitation in a work hardening program. *Journal of Occupational Rehabilitation, 7*(2), 97–106.

de Shazer, S. (1982). *Patterns of brief family therapy: An ecosystemic approach.* New York, NY: The Guilford Press.

de Shazer, S. (1985). *Keys to solution in brief therapy.* New York, NY: Norton.

de Shazer, S. (1988). *Clues: Investigating solutions in brief therapy.* New York, NY: Norton.

de Shazer, S. (1991). *Putting difference to work.* New York, NY: Norton.

de Shazer, S. (1994). *Words were originally magic.* New York, NY: Norton.

Efran, J., & Schenler, M. (1993). A potpourri of solutions. How new and different is solution-focused therapy? *Family Therapy Networker,* 71–74.

Franklin, C., Moore, K., & Hopson, L. (2008). Effectiveness of solution-focused brief therapy in a school setting. *Children and Schools, 30*(1), 15–26.

Gingerich, W. J. (2005). *Strong studies of solution-focused brief therapy.* Retrieved from http://www.gingerich.net/SFBT/research/strong.htm

Gingerich, W. J., & Eisengart, S. (2000). Solution-focused brief therapy: A review of the outcome research. *Family Process, 39* (4), 477–498.

Greene, J., & Grant, A. M. (2003). *Solution-focused coaching: Managing people in a complex world.* Upper Saddle River, NJ: Prentice Hall.

Hoyt, M. F. (2000). *Some stories are better than others: Doing what works in brief therapy and managed care.* Philadelphia, PA: Brunner/Mazel.

Hoyt, M. F. (2002). Solution-focused couple therapy. In A. S. Gurman & N. S. Jacobson (Eds.), *Clinical handbook of couple therapy* (pp. 335–372). New York, NY: The Guilford Press.

Hoyt, M. F., & Berg, I. K. (1998). Solution-focused couple therapy: Helping clients construct self-fulfilling realities. In F. M. Dattilio (Ed.), *Case studies in couple and family therapy: Systemic and cognitive perspectives* (pp. 203–232). New York, NY; The Guilford Press.

Kim, J. S. (2006). *Examining the effectiveness of solution-focused brief therapy: A meta-analysis using random effects modeling.* Unpublished doctoral dissertation, University of Michigan–Ann Arbor.

Kingsbury, S. J. (1997). What is solution-focused therapy? *Harvard Mental Health Letter, 13*(10), 8.

LaFountain, R. M., & Garner, N. E. (1996). Solution-focused counseling groups: The results are in. *Journal for Specialists in Group Work, 21*(2), 128–143.

Lethem, J. (2002). Brief solution-focused therapy. *Child and Adolescent Mental Health, 7*(4), 189–192.

Lindforss, L., & Magnusson, D. (1997). Solution-focused therapy in prison. *Contemporary Family Therapy, 19*(1), 89–103.

Metcalf, L. (1995). *Counseling toward solutions: A practical solution-focused program for working with students, teachers, and parents.* West Nyack, NY: Center for Applied Research in Education.

Metcalf, L. (2008). *Counseling toward solutions: A practical solution-focused program for working with students, teachers, and parents* (2nd ed.). San Francisco, CA: Jossey-Bass.

Metcalf, L. (2010). *Solution-focused RTI: A positive and personalized approach to response-to-intervention.* San Francisco, CA: John Wiley & Sons.

Metcalf, L., Thomas, F. N., Duncan, B. L., Miller, S. D., & Hubble, M. A. (1996). What works in solution-focused brief therapy: A qualitative analysis of client and therapist perceptions. In S. D. Miller, M. A. Hubble, & B. L. Duncan (Eds.), *Handbook of solution-focused brief therapy* (pp. 335–349). San Francisco, CA: Jossey-Bass.

Miller, G. (1997). Systems and solutions: The discourses of brief therapy. *Contemporary Family Therapy, 19*(1), 5–22.

Miller, G., & de Shazer, S. (2000). Emotions in solution-focused therapy: A re-examination. *Family Process, 39*(1), 5–23.

Murphy, J. J. (1997). *Solution-focused counseling in middle and high schools.* Alexandria, VA: American Counseling Association.

O'Connell B., & Jones C. (1997). Solution-focused supervision. *Counselling, 8*(9), 289–292.

O'Hanlon, W. H. (1998). Even from a broken web: Brief and respectful, solution-oriented therapy for resolving sexual abuse. New York, NY: Wiley.

O'Hanlon, W. H. (2010). *FAQ about possibility therapy.* Retrieved from http://www.billohanlon.com/FAQS/questionsaboutpossibilitytherapy/billohanlon.html

O'Hanlon, W. H., & Weiner-Davis, M. (1989). *In search of solutions: A new direction in psychotherapy.* New York, NY: Norton.

Seagram, B. C. (1997). *The efficacy of solution-focused therapy with young offenders.* Unpublished doctoral dissertation, York University, Ontario, Canada.

Shilts, L., Rambo, A., & Huntley, E. (2003). The collaborative miracle: When to slow down the pace of brief therapy. *Journal of Systemic Therapies, 22*(2), 65–73.

Solution-Focused Brief Therapy Association 2007 Conference on Solution-Focused Practices.

Trepper, T. S., Dolan, Y., McCollum, E. E., & Nelson, T. (2006). Steve de Shazer and the future of solution-focused therapy. *Journal of Marital and Family Therapy, 32*(2), 133–139.

Visser, C. (2008). *A brief history of the solution-focused approach.* Retrieved from http://articlescoertvisser.blogspot.com/2008/02/brief-history-of-solution-focused.html

Walter, J. L., & Peller, J. E. (2000). *Recreating brief therapy: Preferences and possibilities.* New York, NY: Norton.

Yalom, V., & Rubin, B. (2003). Solution-focused therapy: An interview with Insoo Kim Berg. *Psychotherapy.net.* Retrieved from http://www.psychotherapy.net/interview/insoo-kim-berg

Zimmerman, T. S., Jacobsen, R. B., MacIntyre, M., & Watson, C. (1996). Solution-focused parenting groups: An empirical study. *Journal of Systemic Therapies, 15*(4), 12–25.

RECOMMENDED READING LIST

Books

Berg, I. K., & Steiner, T. (2003). *Children's solution work.* New York, NY: Norton.

Chevalier, A. J. (1995). *On the client's path: A manual for the practice of solution-focused therapy.* Oakland, CA: New Harbinger.

Connie, E., & Metcalf, L. (2009). *The art of solution focused therapy.* New York, NY: Springer.

De Jong, P., & Berg, I. K. (2002). *Interviewing for solutions* (2nd ed.). Pacific Grove, CA: Brooks/Cole.

de Shazer, S. (1986). An indirect approach to brief therapy. In S. de Shazer & R. Kral (Eds.), *Indirect approaches in therapy.* Rockville, MA: Aspen.

de Shazer, S., Dolan, Y., Korman, H., Trepper, T., McCollum, E., & Berg, I. K. (2007). *More than miracles: The state of the art of solution-focused brief therapy*. Binghamton, NY: The Haworth Press.

Insight Media. (Producer). (1998). *Family therapy with the experts—a video series: Solution oriented therapy with Bill O'Hanlon* [Motion picture]. (Available from Insight Media, 2162 Broadway, New York, NY 10024).

Macdonald, A. J. (2007). *Solution-focused therapy: Theory, research & practice*. Los Angeles, CA: Sage.

Miller, S. D., Hubble, M. A., & Duncan, B. L. (Eds.). (1996). *Handbook of solution-focused brief therapy*. San Francisco, CA: Jossey-Bass.

O'Hanlon, W. H. (1999). *Do one thing different: And other uncommonly sensible solutions to life's persistent problems*. New York, NY: Morrow.

O'Hanlon, W. H., & Weiner-Davis, M. (1989). *In search of solutions: A new direction in psychotherapy*. New York, NY: Norton.

Sharry, J., Madden, B., & Darmody, M. (2003). *Becoming a solution detective: Identifying your clients' strengths in practical brief therapy*. Binghamton, NY: The Haworth Clinical Practice Press.

Walter, J. L., & Peller, J. E. (1992). *Becoming solution-focused in brief therapy*. New York, NY: Brunner/Mazel.

Articles

Gingerich, W. J., & Eisengart, S. (2000). Solution-focused brief therapy: A review of the outcome research. *Family Process*, *39*(4), 477–498.

Murray, C. E., & Murray, T. L. (2004). Solution-focused premarital counseling: Helping couples build a vision for their marriage. *Journal of Marital & Family Therapy*, *30*(3), 349–358.

Newsome, W. S. (2005). The impact of solution-focused brief therapy with at-risk junior high school students. *Children & Schools*, *27*(2), 83–91.

Websites

European Brief Therapy Association
http://www.ebta.nu/

Solution-Focused Brief Therapy Association
http://www.sfbta.org

Narrative Therapy With Families

13

Carla Atkinson Leslie

In striving to make sense of life, persons face the task of arranging their experiences of events in sequences across time in such a way as to arrive at a coherent account of themselves and the world around them . . . The success of this storying of experience provides persons with a sense of continuity and meaning in their lives, and this is relied upon for the ordering of daily lives and for the interpretation of further experiences . . . the interpretation of current events is as much future-shaped as it is past-determined.

—Michael White and David Epston

INTRODUCTION

Narrative therapy is a postmodern approach that holds a deep respect for the client and acknowledges that the interactions and perceptions a person experiences throughout his or her life will result in certain actions and beliefs. Narrative therapy is based on the idea that a person's life and relationships are shaped by the "stories" that a person engages in with others. To assist the client in change, the therapist must help the client to alter or write new stories within new contexts of meaning.

The narrative therapist assists clients to resolve their problems by helping them to separate themselves from the problems that keep them from fulfilling lives, assisting them to challenge how they currently live, and negotiating a newer, more satisfying story. The narrative therapist empowers the client to "reauthor" his or her life with a new, preferred identity, thereby creating new beliefs, context, and promoting change.

Narrative therapy stands out among other family therapy models in that it promotes using the narrative metaphor as a guide to help family members understand the meanings they make about themselves and their relationships within their families. Through a process of learning from the family members how certain interactions have created the family's story and, thereby, dilemma, the narrative therapist invites family members to revisit their current roles and create together new ones that give new meaning to their individual and family lives.

HISTORY AND LEADING FIGURES

Michael White and David Epston were the cocreators and longtime collaborators in the continuing evolution of narrative therapy. Michael White was codirector with Cheryl White of Dulwich Centre, an independent center in Adelaide, Australia, which is involved in narrative therapy, community work, training, publishing, and supporting practitioners all over the world. David Epston and Michael White met in 1981 when White attended Epston's workshop at the Second Australian Family Therapy Conference in Adelaide. Epston had a reputation as a gifted storyteller, and his workshops were immensely popular. White reported being "immediately intrigued" by Epston's material and his style of delivery (White, 1995; White & Epston, 1990), and he recognized that their practices and ideas had much in common. Their meeting sparked the beginning of their professional collaboration and deep friendship. Before his death in 2008, White had provided workshops in narrative therapy to thousands of practitioners throughout the world. David Epston is codirector of The Family Therapy Centre in Auckland, New Zealand. He continues to work as a therapist, writer, trainer, and consultant.

David Epston was born in Canada in 1944, emigrated to Auckland, New Zealand, and trained as an anthropologist. Eventually, he gravitated to social work and obtained his first position as a family therapist at a child psychiatric outpatient unit in an Auckland hospital in 1977. He later moved to the Leslie Centre, run by Presbyterian Support Services in Auckland, where he worked as consultant family therapist from 1981 to 1987. From 1987 to the present, he has been a codirector of The Family Therapy Centre in Auckland. Epston is a colorful, energetic practitioner known for his storytelling. Along with White, he adds a creative flavor to narrative therapy with his letter writing to families and certificates of achievement to children and adolescents. He has authored, coauthored, and edited numerous books and articles on narrative therapy.

David Epston's early training in anthropology had a great influence on his practice as a therapist. Anthropologists are intrigued with curiosity about "what makes a human?" Narrative therapists are intrigued with how people define themselves as humans. Epston gravitated to the idea that how people define themselves directly affects how they live their lives. He established a practice of writing letters to his clients after seeing them and popularized some practices associated with rites of passage. For example, he might write a letter to parents, commending them for helping their children to grow up and escape from fears at night. He would enclose a list of solutions that the parents had developed and would compliment them on their efforts (Turner, 1969; van Gennep, 1960).

In the meantime, White was introduced to the interpretive method of social science by Gregory Bateson's *Steps to an Ecology of the Mind* (1972) and *Mind and Nature: A Necessary Unity* (1979; White, 1995; White & Epston, 1990). Both men became intrigued with the notion of using a text analogy to understand human lives rather than the systems metaphor, which was then widely in use by family therapists. The text analogy or narrative metaphor had become the guiding metaphor in the humanities and social sciences in the mid-70s, but it had not yet been critically examined in the field of family therapy (Bruner, 1986; Freedman & Combs, 1996). White's partner, Cheryl White, was also enthused with this approach, which was evident in her feminist reading and she encouraged them to pursue it. They read deeply in the areas of literary theory, anthropology, feminist theory, critical theory, and other areas. This included the works of Michel Foucault, a French philosopher whom White credits as being most influential in his thinking, as well as Gregory Bateson, psychologist Jerome Bruner, ethnographer/anthropologist Edward Bruner, anthropologist Clifford Geertz, psychologists Kenneth Gergen and Mary Gergen, and sociologist/anthropologist Erving Goffman (White, 1995).

After their initial meeting in 1981, Epston and White corresponded, meeting when they could to discuss their ideas as their unique approach to therapy began to take shape. In 1989, the two men published *Literate Means to Therapeutic Ends* (White & Epston, 1989) in Australia. The book underwent revision and was republished in the United States in 1990 as *Narrative Means to Therapeutic Ends* (White & Epston, 1990). Interest in their ideas and their approach grew rapidly, making inroads in Australia, New Zealand, the United States,

Canada, and Europe as early as 1989 (Tomm, 1989). In the ensuing years, White and Epston wrote extensively about their ideas, creating a cohesive theory and practice of narrative therapy.

Currently, narrative therapy flourishes in many parts of the world, helping clients with various issues that range from enuresis (bed-wetting), encopresis (passing stools), sexual abuse or assault, anorexia/bulimia, anger, depression, anxiety, and many more. Its application has been shown to be helpful with children, adolescents, families, and adults.

Other prominent narrative therapy centers include The Family Therapy Centre and the Family Centre in New Zealand; Yaletown Family Therapy in Vancouver, British Columbia; the Evanston Family Therapy Center in Evanston, Illinois; and Family Institute of Cambridge's Program in Narrative Therapies in Massachusetts.

INTRODUCTION TO NARRATIVE THERAPY

We live our lives through stories. These stories consist of events that are linked in sequence across time, according to a plot (Morgan, 2000, p. 5). Stories are the way that we map our experiences to create meaning over time. Following social constructionist thought, our stories are created within social contexts, in relationship with other people. Family members, friends, and others both inside and outside of our own culture, race, socioeconomic class, gender, sexual orientation, and religion influence our stories. "The interpretation of an event is determined by its receiving context, and events that can't be patterned are not selected for survival" (White & Epston, 1990). This concept is eloquently described by Edward Bruner (1986):

> . . . life experience is richer than discourse. Narrative structures organize and give meaning to experience, but there are always feelings and lived experience not fully encompassed by the dominant story. (p. 143)

Events that do not fit the existing plot tend to be omitted from the evolving story line. Over time, these stories become more constricting in our lives, seemingly narrowing the paths that we have available to us. For example, a young woman who has been sexually abused and labeled as a victim in therapy may see herself primarily as a victim, putting aside any other successful moments in her life. A narrative therapist would redescribe the word *victim* to *survivor* and assist the young woman in redefining who she is by seeking "unique outcomes" that show her strengths and abilities outside of the narrative of victim. Such change in thinking and believing about oneself leads to the construction of a new story. The phrase *unique outcomes* was borrowed from sociologist Erving Goffman (1961) to describe feelings and experiences that did not survive the dominant narrative, and which might provide the seeds for the generation of alternative stories (White & Epston, 1990). The process of locating unique outcomes and using them to plot alternative stories is called *reauthoring*, a term coined by Myerhoff (1986). Narrative therapy is sometimes called *reauthoring therapy*, or *restorying therapy*.

It may be hard to believe that mere conversations can be enough to begin working with families on various difficult issues such as violence, substance abuse, depression, anger, and others. However, narrative therapists believe that by altering language, meanings are also altered, and it is that process that catapults change within individuals and families. In the next section, the reader will gain more insight into how the narrative therapist working with families uses conversations to create a new context, which can lead to alternative stories.

THEORETICAL ASSUMPTIONS

The following list of assumptions serves to further explain the theory behind narrative therapy. Jill Freedman and Gene Combs have provided this list in workshops and detailed them on their website (Freedman & Combs, n.d.).

1. *Our lives are socially constructed.*
   - We become who we are through relationships—through the meaning we make of other's perceptions of us and interactions with us.

2. *We organize our lives through stories.*
   - We can make many different stories or meanings of any particular event.
   - There are many experiences in each of our lives that have not been "storied."
   - Each of those events could, if storied, lead to a different, often preferable, life narrative.

3. *The dominant discourses in our society powerfully influence what gets storied and how it gets storied.*
   - A *discourse* is a system of words, actions, rules, beliefs, and institutions that share common values. Particular discourses sustain particular worldviews. One might even think of a discourse as a worldview in action.
   - Discourses tend to be invisible and taken for granted as part of the fabric of reality.

4. *Locating problems in discourses helps us see people as separate from their problems.*
   - We seek to identify the discourses that support problematic stories. Once a problem is linked to a problematic discourse, we can more easily help people oppose the discourse or choose to construct their relationship in line with a different, preferred, discourse. (Freedman & Combs, n.d.)

View of the Family and Client

The narrative therapist views the family as possessing a rich history together that provides various unique outcomes due to family history, interactions, and cultural context. The narrative therapist does not label the family or the client; instead, he or she sees past meanings as the culprit in current problematic behaviors. For example, if a family labels a 17-year-old adolescent male as a "troublemaker," they will certainly see him as such and surround him with actions to curtail his behavior. However, if the family sees the adolescent as "merely stealing attention away from younger siblings as he searches for independence" with the help of the narrative therapist, the parents may begin noticing the younger siblings more, thereby giving less need to the 17 year old to act up (White & Epston, 1990).

View on How Change Occurs

Change occurs through the process of therapy, which promotes the clients storying their current situation, the interactions and actions around the situation, and then together, with the therapist restorying the situation. By doing so, clients leave sessions with new descriptions of themselves. The aforementioned example of the young woman who saw herself as a victim, leaves with a new story to consider that of a survivor. New meanings instigate new actions. The therapy, therefore, deconstructs unhelpful discourses that have taken over the person's life and suggests, during the session, new discourses that will direct the life more favorably. Narrative therapists use questions that assist clients in telling their story and generating alternative stories.

Another method used by narrative therapists is that of externalizing problems (White & Epston, 1990). Externalizing conversations separate the person from the problem and help the person to recognize how the problem has influenced his or her way of life. Then, the therapist uses deconstructive questioning to help persons question the values and beliefs that support the problem, thereby developing new ways to keep the problem from interfering in the future.

Therapist's Role

Narrative therapists typically take a not-knowing stance, like solution-focused therapists, making no assumptions about the client's current situation, values, or preferences. The therapist does not present himself or herself as an expert or authority, but as someone who is interested, curious, and intrigued by the successes in people's lives. The use of labels is avoided, and narrative therapists often avoid the word "client" in favor of "person" or "people." The therapist's role is to assist the client in discovering those events and meanings that contribute to his or her preferred story. The therapist collaborates with the client in rewriting his or her problematic stories or identities into preferred ones. The therapist is not neutral, but takes the side of the client and the client's preferred story. The therapist is decentered, with therapy focusing more on what the client is saying than what the therapist is saying. At the same time, the therapist must acknowledge that his or her work is influential, although most often, this acknowledgment is not made to the client.

Narrative Practices (Interventions)

Narrative therapists do not speak of their work with families as interventions, but instead as practices. The practices of narrative therapy are associated with hearing the person's story, helping to separate the person from the problem, coauthoring alternate preferred stories, and helping to propagate those stories within the person's family or community. The following are some commonly used narrative practices:

Problems and Externalizing Conversations

The person is not the problem. The problem is the problem.

Problems play a central role in narrative therapy. Problems are considered to be highly undesirable, in contrast to the ironic view in Milan systemic therapy that problems are useful (see Chapter 9; Epston & White, 1993; Tomm, 1989). The therapist's focus is not on solving problems in contrast with the solution-oriented approach (see Chapter 12). The narrative approach focuses on helping people deconstruct problems in a manner that robs those problems of their power and influence in their lives.

Instead of seeing problems as something that people *are*, problems are externalized, cast as villains that affect the person and the people around them. There are some distinct advantages to this approach. Externalizing conversations allow persons to see their own identity separate from problems or "problem-saturated or deficit-centered accounts of who they are" (White, 2000, p. 4). This alleviates the shame and guilt associated with *being* the problem, and instead allows individuals or families to consider themselves *in relationship* to the problem. Clients are asked to describe the problem, and together with the therapist and other significant persons, map the effects of the problem on everyone concerned. This approach is particularly useful in family therapy. Each family member can be asked to consider how they each keep the problem alive and how he or she can begin to lessen its impact on their lives. Conversations between family members sound much different when the problem no longer resides inside a person because they can unite together against the problem instead of blaming someone or each other.

Deconstruction

Michael White has described deconstruction as methods that "exoticize the domestic" (Bourdieu, 1988, pp. xi–xii; White, 1992, p. 121). Deconstruction is intended to put our commonplace assumptions and realities under scrutiny. "Deconstruction helps people unpack their stories or see them from different perspectives, so that how they have been constructed becomes apparent" (Freedman & Combs, 1996, p. 120).

"Disassembling and examining taken-for-granted assumptions" gives families a chance to change their perspective of each other and come together to redescribe themselves in a way that influences their future actions (Goldenberg & Goldenberg, p. 343). A common example, parents presenting to therapy with a 13-year-old adolescent with attention deficit hyperactive disorder (ADHD) and a list of school problems may encounter a narrative therapist who begins talking about other aspects of the adolescent's life when the "energy" is not in control of him. Such refreshing conversations lighten the mood of the session and begin to deconstruct the notion that the adolescent is doomed with an unmanageable diagnosis. The discovery of unique outcomes during the session helps the parents to see their adolescent differently and join in with the adolescent to help him gain control of the energy, and this collaboration results in better behavior.

Internalizing Other Questions

David Epston developed a practice that he originally called "cross-referential" questioning to help him in interviews with conflictual couples. Epston credits Karl Tomm with further refinements and renaming of the practice. Epston (1998) has each partner take turns in responding to questions that he poses to them while the other partner listens without responding. These questions can reduce hostile responses.

An example might be, "What would your husband say if I asked him about ___?" "What would your wife say about how you deal with_____?" And to an adolescent, "How would your teachers describe your reputation at school?"

Unique Outcomes

Unique outcomes are aspects of one's lived experiences that fall outside of the dominant story. "They include the whole gamut of events, feelings, intentions, thoughts, actions, etc., that have a historical, present, or future location and that cannot be accommodated by the dominant story" (White & Epston, 1990, p. 16). The identification of unique outcomes by the therapist and client creates an empowerment that catapults the client into believing in his or her own competencies and becomes strategies for stepping into an alternative story with new outcome. Talking about the unique outcome may take most of the time in the therapy session and is well worth the time because it helps the client to begin seeing his or her way out of the dominant story and realizing that alternative measures and steps are already available based on past experiences.

For example, an adolescent who has been diagnosed with ADHD may begin talking to the therapist about his "energy" and the times when he is in control of the energy instead of vice versa. He may describe classrooms where he pays attention better because he is seated near the front, or times at home when the noise level of the television is lower. Such important discoveries guide the session, providing material for strategies.

Reauthoring

When unique outcomes are identified, persons can be invited to ascribe meaning to them. Success in this ascription of meaning requires that the unique outcomes be plotted into an alternative story or narrative. Various questions can be introduced that assist in engaging persons in this ascription of new meaning, questions that actively involve them in, as Myerhoff (1982) would put it, the "reauthoring" of their lives and their relationships. (White & Epston, 1990, p. 16)

When persons have already ascribed a certain belief about their lives such as the sexual abuse victim that only sees herself as a "victim," there is a likelihood that she will take on that story and the story will lead her to isolate, not trust people similar to the perpetrator, and not take risks. If, however, she was given a chance to begin reauthoring her life and takes on a new label, such as sexual abuse survivor, there is a better chance that the mere label change could bring about personal change. Therefore, inviting clients to participate in the reauthoring of their lives means editing out those who caused them distress or harm and inviting new coauthors to participate in a more amenable story.

Extending the Conversation—Letter Writing

David Epston began the practice of letter writing after his very first therapy session with a client family. He said it seemed like the natural thing to do, "like an extension of the conversation we had been having." He put one copy in his or their file in lieu of case notes and he mailed the other copy to them. "The family was surprised and gratified to receive my letter, and we read it at the beginning of the next session to give us a jumping-off point. We were all so pleased with having a letter on hand to refer to, that I wrote to them again at the conclusion of the second session." (Epston, 1998, p. 96).

Letters and other documents were a prime force behind the first book on narrative therapy (White & Epston, 1990). Epston gradually expanded on his practice of mailing letters by creating other types of documents as well. He eventually composed certificates of merit to children and adolescents to commend them on new behaviors that then impacted their family and school interactions. The use of letters and documents serves to celebrate new stories that are created by clients and families and promote ongoing "performances" of the new stories.

Outsider Witness Groups or Reflecting Teams

Outsider witness groups are a form of reflecting team. The use of reflecting teams in narrative therapy originated in the work of Tom Andersen. (See Andersen, 1999, "The reversal of light and sound." In *Gecko* No. 2. Dulwich Centre Publications). The reflecting team often observes clients and families and then holds a conversation in front of the client and family in which they reflect on what they saw and heard. Together, they may arrive at new understandings of the family's experience and present it to the family for consideration. The family benefits from having an audience for their new preferred stories.

Definitional Ceremonies

Drawing on the work of Belgian anthropologist, Arnold van Gennep, White and Epston incorporated elements from traditional rites of passage to communicate, commemorate, and celebrate changes in a person's life. This could be as simple as a meal celebrating an accomplishment with a group of supporters, or a certificate commending a client or family on overcoming an issue. Epston and White's first use of this practice was with children. The children's responses were so encouraging that they continued to refine and develop additional written interventions for children, and eventually began using these with adolescents and adults (White, 2000). The letters that they wrote and the certificates that they presented to the children and adolescents served to solidify new meaning and descriptions that the children took on as their armor against the problem.

Silver, Williams, Worthington, and Phillips (1998) did a "retrospective audit of the therapy outcome of 108 children with soiling and their families. Fifty-four children were treated by externalizing and 54 comparison children and families were treated by the usual methods in the same clinic. The results from the externalizing group were better and compared favorably with standards derived from previous studies of soiling. Externalizing was rated as much more helpful by parents at follow-up."

Vromans (2008) did a study on the effectiveness of narrative therapy with depressed adults. "Therapy was effective in reducing depressive symptoms in clients with moderate and severe pre-therapy depressive symptom severity. Improvements in depressive symptoms, but not inter-personal relatedness, were maintained three months following therapy. The reduction in depressive symptoms and the proportion of clients who achieved clinically significant improvement (53%) in depressive symptoms at post-therapy were comparable to improvements from standard psychotherapies, reported in benchmark research."

Narrative therapy continues to be used with practically all concerns brought to therapy. It is particularly useful with grief, sexual abuse, anger, depression, and issues of childhood and adolescence.

NARRATIVE THERAPY WORKING TEMPLATE

The *narrative therapy template* is meant to be used as a guideline to learning the process of narrative therapy. The template provides the beginning therapist with steps to take and questions to ask that promote collaboration between the therapist and client. There are suggested questions under each heading to help start the process. After using the initial questions, guide the client through each process, asking questions that occur to you, as you stay within the family therapy theory. Although there is no one "script" for any therapy session, it is the hope of the author that the template serves as an impetus to learning this family therapy model.

Tools for Change

Tools for narrative therapy involve initially mapping the effects of the presenting problem on the person's life. The therapist may encourage the client to name the problem, externalize it, list the effects of the problem, evaluate the effects of the problem, and then strategize to minimize its effects on his or her life. The therapist may also focus on deconstructing the dominant story and creating an alternative story together with the client or family.

Here are some comments or questions that a therapist might use to evaluate the problem:

- *"What does the voice of (problem) tell you? How do these words influence your everyday life?"*
- *"How does (problem) affect your relationships?"*
- *"How does it affect your relationship with yourself?"*
- *"Who else is being affected by the problem?"*

Phase 1: Joining and Building Rapport

During this phase, the therapist should think of the encounter as an interview—be curious. Ask questions you do not know the answer to. Get to know the family in the context of their life, not just the problem. Listen for unique outcomes to the problem story. Establish a relationship where it is all right for the family to ask questions. Flatten the therapist–client hierarchy. One unique feature of narrative therapy is the use of letters or other documentations. After the first and subsequent sessions, the therapist may wish to summarize important elements of the conversation and ask therapeutic questions that occur after the session. Write a letter or leave a voice message for the family (if you get permission to do so). Letters may be mailed to the family (with their permission) or presented at the beginning of the next session.

Here are some comments or questions that a therapist might use during this phase:

- *"Would you mind telling me things about each of you besides the reason that you are here?"*
- *"What sort of things do you enjoy?"*
- *"You're deciding if you'd like to open up your life to me. Are there things about me that it's important for you to know?"*

Phase 2: Understanding the Presenting Issue

Although the narrative therapist is not concerned with understanding the presenting issue, he or she is interested in how the issue is maintained in such a dominant position. The therapist will ask each person individually about the problem because it may differ for each member of the family and how the problem interferes. The therapist will take notes using the exact words used by the clients and will use them throughout the session. (Let the family know that they can see your notes.) Begin talking about the problem as if it is external, and not the problem of any one person. When setting goals with the family, invite family members to name the problem that is affecting them. Listen for key words as the family describes the presenting issues.

Here are some comments or questions that a therapist might use during this phase:

- *"What brought you to see me?"*
- *"Tell me about the problem that has intruded in your lives."*
- *"What are your expectations for yourself when the (problem) intrudes?"*
- *"Would you like to continue talking about the problem or would you rather step out and talk about developing a new project where the problem is not allowed in?"*
- If the family members begin blaming each other or other individuals, ask, *"Is this more in the direction of the problem or the new project?"* to refocus on the preferred goal.

Phase 3: Assessment of Family Dynamics

In narrative therapy, the family members assess the problem and its effects on their lives, not the therapist. The therapist does not assume anything about the family or the problem; he or she believes that there is much more in the family waiting to be recognized, told, and circulated. The therapist may wonder whether invisible discourses are contributing to the problem. Deconstruction may be used to unpack the unspoken assumptions that contribute to the life of the problem. To do so, the therapist must ask questions that provide him or her with information on how the dominant discourse was created. The therapist also begins asking questions about unique outcomes.

Here are some comments or questions that a therapist might use during this phase:

- *"So, your view of yourself as a victim has harnessed you into isolating yourself from people and keeping you away from living life as you wish. Is that true?"*
- *"What is it that you think about that keeps this unfair view of yourself alive?"*
- *"What does your family do, if anything, that keeps this unfair view of yourself alive?"*
- *"How does this unfair view of yourself affect you and your family?"*
- *"Tell me about any times when the problem didn't have the upper hand?"*
- *"What is different about you during those times? How do you explain your ability to do that?"*
- *"What do other people in your life do at that time to avoid the problem's entrance?"*

Phase 4: Goals

Collaborate with the family in defining how life will be when the problem is no longer dominant. (Be sure to use externalizing language to separate the person from the problem.) Recognize that the problem's description may change over time, or that different family members may identify different problems. If so, come to an agreement with the family on which problem to focus on. Listen for what the family *does* want in their lives rather than what they do not want.

"How can I direct the conversation with the family so that they begin to formulate a new, alternative story where their interactions will be different?"

Here are some comments or questions that a therapist might use during this phase:

- *"What would you call this thing that you're struggling against?"*
- *"How will you know when you and/or your family members are in control and the problem has little chance of interfering?"*
- *"What will you each be doing on a small scale that would tell us all that the problem is no longer in control?"*

Phase 5: Amplifying Change

Lead the family to continue to focus on unique outcomes and experiences that some-how contradict the traditional family narrative. Stay curious and ask who does what to ensure that the unique experiences happen. As change occurs, stay "impressed" with their progress. Write notes to them, commending them on their journey out of the control of the problem. Stay curious with statements such as "I am unsure how you were able to maintain such a balance last week in spite of the chaos, but I look forward to your telling me about it." A unique feature of narrative therapy is the use of letters and other documentations. You may ask the family whether they wish to make a videotape or audiotape of their new story. Another technique is to ask them to write letters to others with the same problem. This is a way for the family to sustain their new story while also helping others.

Here are some comments or questions that a therapist might use during this phase:

- *"As we work together to change the course of the problem, who can help to sustain the preferred story or identity?"*

The therapist might also use a letter:

Dear Thomas family,

I am writing you this letter to express my deepest amazement at your ability to help your son control his energy. I learned from you today that Scott controlled his energy not only at home but also at school, under difficult circumstances. His obvious skill at knowing where to sit, when to ask for a pass to the library, or how to excuse himself from a chaotic situation in the cafeteria is by far the most impressive. Your ability as a family to see Scott for his creative self by encouraging his involvement in music after school has obviously shown him your support as a family. No wonder he is responding with such respect, I look forward to hearing more about how you have obviously given "energy" to the message that you are the ones who will direct it from now on.

Sincerely,

Narrative therapist

Phase 6: Termination

Do not assume that there will be a next meeting; let the family decide whether they think meeting again will be helpful and when they wish to return. It is common to meet less frequently over time. Finally, you may present them with a document of some kind, such as a certificates of achievement, diplomas, declaration of independence from (problem), or an honorary membership in the Society of (problem solvers—e.g., "Anger Busters"). This may be done together in a session, or prior to the last session, and presented as a way of solidifying their success.

Here are some comments or questions that a therapist might use during this phase:

- *"Has this time together been helpful today?"*
- *"What was most helpful?"*
- *"Would you like to meet again?"*
- *"When would you like to meet again?"*

JILL FREEDMAN

Jill Freedman, MSW, is a codirector of the Evanston Family Therapy Center and a faculty member of the Chicago Center for Family Health. She is an AAMFT-approved supervisor.

What attracted you to the theory behind narrative therapy?

I think what attracted me to narrative therapy had to do with the kinds of ways of relating. I saw Michael White in a small workshop before I had read anything about it. He did live interviews and I don't think I had any understanding of the ideas that were guiding him. But I was really attracted to the kind of relationships I saw him having with the people he was interviewing and the kind of feeling that went with those ways of relating. I was really excited and attracted by that. I remember thinking that it was playful and light on the one hand, and on the other hand, I thought I saw people thinking about things they hadn't before. I thought I saw it being very effective. I saw a lot happening, but in a way that felt very respectful and like a good experience. So I thought it would be a fun way to work and an interesting way to work, an energizing way to work. Really, I just liked the way it felt and looked. It had nothing to do with the ideas, although I think the ideas were reflected in that way of working. And I would contrast that to one of the things that I had seen a lot in therapy before, [and] that was confronting people. It was very different than that. Or instructing people. It was really different than that. Or challenging people in a way that it seemed like they didn't know what was going on, but the therapist knew what was going on. It was very different than that.

I think that narrative therapy is very relational. I think that a lot of the ideas that the family world thinks about are included, so if I had to put it into a category, that would be the category I would put it into, but I see it as somewhat different in that some of the assumptions are different than systems theory.

People story their lives and make stories, and stories involve a sequence of events over time[, which is] linked through plot. But that also involves meaning making. I think that we remember in terms of stories, what happened over time and what it meant. And that there are lots and lots and lots of events that happen every day, but most of them don't become stories. There are just certain events in our lives that are storied. Those mean a lot about our identity, and what our lives are like, and what is possible, and what our future is like. So that there are many, many, many other events that could be storied, could hold meaning, [and] that could add different strands to our lives. That's a really quick and dirty description of the narrative metaphor. Thinking about people's lives in terms of stories in that way helps me always be thinking that there are other events that could be storied. My job is to not let a problem story take on the meaning of reality, but to hold in mind that there are many other stories that would hold different implications. The second idea has to do with where the stories are located, in a sense, what it is that supports the stories, why certain things are storied and others aren't. And for me, one way that I would be thinking about it today has to do with normative judgments and the kinds of self-policing that we go through because of normative judgments.

How do you formulate your view of a family when they enter therapy?
When I first see people, I'm interested in finding out about them both individually and in terms of their relationship that has nothing to do with the problem. I'm interested in having an experience of them, a view of them that's bigger than what it is that brings them into therapy. So I might ask people what they're interested in, and what they like to do for fun. I might ask family members questions about each other, like to tell me about something that they really treasure about the other person. I'm interested in having a view that isn't colored by the problem that they've come for. Because if I start out directly finding out what the problem is, I think I miss a lot that could be very helpful in moving outside of the problem.

What kinds of families do you think benefit most from this model?
I would say that lots of times, people have this idea that narrative is a very intellectual kind of therapy, and I think they have that idea because of the writing, not because of the actual practice. My experience is that the more experience that people have had with other kinds of therapies, and expectations of what therapy will be like, the more likely it is that those people are the people I have the most difficult time with. So it's not about a kind of problem, it's not about whether people are verbal or not, it's not any of those kinds of things, it's that therapeutic expectations are very different. They think I'm going to be an expert, they think I'm going to give advice, they think I'm going to formulate things in terms of triangles. And, particularly, if people have had good and helpful experiences in other kinds of therapy and they're waiting to have that same kind of thing replicated, that's when I think it's less likely to go well. Now, sometimes, it goes great, because even though it's very different, they like it.

Different models of therapy require the therapist to be directive or nondirective. In your opinion, what are the necessary characteristics that a therapist should possess to be effective with this model?
One thing I would say is that the idea of identity, in terms of narrative ideas, is that people constitute themselves. So "characteristic" isn't a word that we would use, usually, and I actually don't use the words "directive" and "nondirective." I think of myself as being active in the process. I ask a lot of questions. I think curiosity is important to bring to this work. One of the things that I think is important is not being neutral. Being on the side of preferred stories and taking stands that have to do with that. I also think it's really important to be willing to critique your own work and to be involved in the critiquing of your work, and to be accountable in some way. Because I think it's a powerful position to be a therapist. I always hope that I'm letting people know that they can ask me questions about why I asked a particular question or where I'm coming from, and I think it's important to be willing to engage about that.

Michael White has talked about the position of the therapist being decentered but influential. And I really like that description. I'm very active as a therapist. I ask a lot of questions. I feel a lot of responsibility as a therapist, but I want to make sure that the people whose stories are honored and whose knowledge is honored are the people who come to consult, not me. So I see myself as asking questions to generate experience, and the people evaluating that experience are those people whose life we're talking about. I think transparency is really important.

How often does the client see you and for how long a period of time?

Because a lot of people want to use insurance, I do an hour. I don't think that's ideal. That's completely based on having it be reimbursable. I have had the experience with some people that it's not enough consistently, and so I might then say, "This is how it seems to me, does that fit with how it seems to you? Would you be interested in scheduling an hour and a half?" I also only make one appointment at a time, and at the end of the time, I say, "Was it useful? How was it useful? Would you like to meet again?" And "When would you like to meet again?" And then if they say, "Well, how often do you think I should come?" I say something like, "I think it's important that while we're working on this particular problem, that you come frequently enough, that you're thinking about some of the things that we talk about, that these are alive in the way that you're experiencing the world. I think it's important that you don't come so soon that you feel like we've just talked. That might be different at different times. So if you feel like we're right in the middle of something and you want to talk more about it, we might meet sooner. If you feel like something's changed in the way that you're thinking about that and you want to see what that's like in your life, maybe we won't meet again for much longer. So I'm interested in thinking about that with you at the end of each time."

What are you looking for when you are in the session?

When I start working with people, I'm interested in establishing a relationship that might be a bit different than a more traditional therapy relationship. I want it to be a collaborative relationship where—not that the hierarchy won't be there, but that perhaps it'll be somewhat minimalized, somewhat flattened, and also where we're talking as people, to some extent. I'll do a little small talk as we walk into the room, but one of the things that I want to do right at the beginning is get to know people outside of the problem. So I'm really aware of trying to create a context where we're going to talk about things that have to do with people and their lives, but they're not about the problem. Because I feel like problems really narrow people's sense of identity and possibilities. And I don't want to be taken in by that to begin with.

So I'll start a conversation by saying something like, "Is it okay if I get to know you outside of the problem, and we don't talk about it for a while?" And then I'll be interested in hearing what people are interested in and what they do for fun, things like that. It could be what they do for work, but I'm just more interested in getting a broader picture of what they're into. And usually people talk about some of those things and then begin to talk about the problem, and I'll say something like, "Before you tell me what brought you here, I just want to find out if there are any questions you want to ask me?" And they say "Well, what do you mean?" And I say something like, "Well you know, you're in this position of deciding whether you want to open your life to me, and there are probably some things [that] would be important for you to know in making that decision." You know, it's sort of an intake for them. Am I a person that they want to trust with their life in some way? And some people say, "Well, you know you got this really good referral, but other people ask me some interesting questions like, 'What do you like to read?'" I love having conversations about that. Or somebody said to me, "What do you love?" which I thought was interesting. Or, "Why do you do this kind of work?" I'm trying to signal right at the beginning that I'm going to ask questions, but they can ask questions, too. And I'm not the professional therapist. I'm not representing the whole world of professional therapy. I'm myself. And so they might want to know some things about me so they'll have some idea of how to take where I'm coming from. I'm thinking about all those kinds of things as a way of setting the scene for a different kind of relationship. I'm interested in that happening before we begin to have a conversation in which I'm hoping to understand and help name the problem. Then I'm thinking about hearing the problem in an externalized way, which might move into "statement of position" map. It might move to just talking about naming the problem.

What is the assessment process of this model?

The people who are coming for help are making the evaluation, both about what's problematic in their lives and about the therapy process itself. I'll make a point at the end of interviews, of saying, "How is this conversation going for you? Are we talking about what you want to be talking about?" At least at the end, and sometimes more than at the end, I'll say, "Has this been helpful? How has it been helpful? What has been most helpful?" I might also ask, "Are there things that haven't been helpful? Are there questions you want to ask me?" And that's all about signaling that I'm interested in the evaluation of the people who are coming for help. That has to do with the interpretive turn. I consider my job to be facilitating that. And if they say to me, "Well, what do you think?" I might say, "Well, the first time we met, you were saying that these kinds of things were problematic and you've talked about this, this, and this, which seems to me to really stand for something different." I might remind them of things like that, and I'd say, "So would you say then that you're more involved in this way of doing things instead of the problem's way of doing things?" Then I might ask questions to help that process. I'd say what I've noticed, but I'm still asking them to be making the evaluation.

Another really important thing that I haven't mentioned is thinking about the larger sociocultural context and locating problems, thinking about what it is that people might be trying to live up to, comparing themselves to what have they been recruited into believing, that's creating a groundwork for this problem to develop. So that people are not feeling good about themselves because they're comparing themselves to some sort of idealized notion about what they should be doing. So instead of calling that a problem—a self-esteem problem, for example—we can think about that as a problem having to do with modern power and the way people get recruited into thinking they have to live up to certain kinds of norms. So [it] would be part of something that I'd want to introduce into the evaluation of problems, questions asking people to think about experience-near ways that the larger sociocultural context is creating the ground for that particular problem.

Who sets the goals, the client or the therapist?

I came from an Ericksonian practice and Erickson was very focused on the future and he was interested in goals, and so I think that was one of the hardest things for me about switching to narrative—not starting out by asking people what they wanted and how they knew they'd get there. My understanding now has to do with the narrative metaphor and a number of things. One is the idea that if you set a goal, you're really sort of narrowing your conversation to get to it, and the narrative metaphor is more about unfolding, and it can go in different directions that you might not have predicted. So in terms of time, the future that we talk about is much more of a near future instead of a long future. In the narrative metaphor, we're finding moments that could be storied outside the problematic story, asking questions to develop those as stories. But we don't know where those stories are going to go. And so rather than trying to get to a particular goal, it's the telling and retelling of those stories and then the person's evaluation of whether those are helpful. So I'm thinking much more of adding more and more strands and thickening those strands of story rather than moving to a particular point I might think of as a goal.

However, one of the things that I've found extremely useful, one set of distinctions, is the distinction between problem and project, or plot and counterplot. After a problem is named, when we're talking about things outside of the problem, there might be a phrase that sticks out for me when they're talking about the meaning of something that we're storying that wouldn't have been predicted by the problem. And so, I might repeat back that phrase and say, "So, is this really the project that you're here to work on?" And they might say, "Yes." Now it's a counterpoint to the problem that's going in an opposite direction than the problem, but it's not a goal.

For example, somebody whose problem was named as the effects of abuse, and she named her project as "freeing her spirit." So that's not a goal exactly; that's not very specific, but it encapsulated, for her, the direction that this project that she was on had to do with. Naming the problem and the project was really helpful because as she would talk about something, one of the questions I could ask was, "Is that more on the side of the problem or the project? Is that more on the side of some of the effects of the abuse, or is that more on the side of freeing your spirit?" That was very helpful in clarifying preferred directions in life and how something that might not seem like it had to do with anything actually was contributing to a preferred direction in life.

What are some commonly used interventions with this model?
We don't talk about interventions. I think because it's something you do to people, and so that wouldn't be a word that we would use. We would talk about practices, so we have particular skills and practices that are involved in asking questions. One would be asking questions and that has to do with trying to have a collaborative relationship. I think it's very powerful to ask questions. You're creating the domain of possible response, but the person is still picking the response out of that domain. Another is outsider witness groups, if that's possible. Or other kinds of practices that have to do with other people being involved because there's this importance of community and other people's ideas about one. Another practice that I would use, when I'm working with a couple or family, is speaking with one person with the other person being in a witnessing position as a way of witnessing stories. If I'm thinking about couples, for example, I often think that if they're both going to be talking to each other, or talking to me, that when somebody says something, usually, or often, the other person feels like they either have to give their version or correct or respond. It's really hard to hear the other person's story, or witness the other person's story if you're thinking about how you need to respond. I think it puts people in a position where they're more likely to actually hear what the other person's experience is if they're not going to be directly responding. It's trying to create a format for listening in a particular way. And also, then I can ask questions that might help extend the preferred story. So I might say something like, "Were you surprised when your partner said that they were quite concerned about what this might mean to you? What do you think that might mean that you hadn't

recognized about the thinking that went on in this decision?" So I might ask things that could help thicken a particular part of the story rather than being just a rebuttal. Often when people come in conflict, they're thinking more about rebuttals, and so, it's often a chance to develop other parts of the story that might actually have more to do with what they want for their relationship.

I also ask permission to send a letter. Sometimes if I'm doing a document, I might save it until they come in, and then we read it together and then I can change it if they'd like it changed in some way. But often I send letters. They don't write back, but their response may take other forms. I've had people actually call and leave a message on my voice mail in response to a particular question. "I've been thinking about this for 3 days since I got this letter, and here's what I think." People really like getting letters, and that's the first thing they say when they come back. They comment on them, and if there were questions, they answer questions. Sometimes people give reports of keeping things with them and referring to them and reading them and rereading them.

What role does a homework assignment have in this model?
If you think about homework as being something assigned, then it implies a certain kind of relationship. Earlier in my work as a family therapist, I was more likely to give homework when I didn't think as much about the hierarchy. I do think there is a hierarchy in therapy. I'm not saying that there isn't. But I think in narrative work, one thing that's really privileged is the person's ideas, instead of expert ideas. And so, giving an assignment implies an expert idea of what should happen. So in that sense, I don't think the idea of homework fits. One of my practices is often asking people at the beginning of the time if they'd like to hear my notes from the time before. My notes are a document of how the stories are unfolding, so I would read those notes, and then I might ask a question at the end of the notes like, "I'm curious about where that's taking you." And so people relate that to experiences they have. It's not uncommon for people to say, "I thought you might ask this question."

How do you know when your client is ready to terminate?
I really think that they decide when to terminate. I know there are some models where there's a lead up and talking about and getting ready for termination. For me, it's more casual. People are only signing up for one time, each time, and I ask if it's useful, how is it useful, would they like to come back, when would they like to come back. And sometimes people say, "I don't know when I want to come back, can I call you?" and that's okay with me. Almost always, they do call. So usually, people tell me. However, one of the things that I think is really important for me in doing this work—I don't think I could do it in another way—is documenting our conversations and the stories as they're developing. And so at the beginning, I'm keeping a lot of notes that have to do with the problematic story, and as we go on, I'm also noting what the project is, the direction that people are developing, the alternative stories. Before each time I meet with people, I go back and read at least the notes from the time before. Sometimes I read all the notes, or sometimes I'll just go back and read the first note. If I have a sense that what was operating at the beginning, the problem that brought people in, is very different from where they are now, I might wonder with them about what we're still doing here, and if it's time for us to stop having these conversations. So I might bring up the possibility.

I often have people talk about how far they've come and what was it like when the problem was operating as opposed to now.

What have you found to be the limitations of this approach?

I guess maybe I would say the limitations that I've seen have to do with a conflict between the approach and the culture. For example, we get paid for, in terms of insurance, making diagnoses. That doesn't really fit with the approach. We get paid in blocks of an hour. Sometimes it would be much more useful to work for a longer period of time. We get paid by the hour, which makes it very difficult financially to assemble an outsider witness group, whereas if we got paid for the problem, we could do that. Or in other cultures, there's an expectation of working in teams.

What suggestions do you have for students?

David Epston said that he thought it took 3 years of practice and immersion to really learn how to do narrative therapy. Practice. Practice in teams. Find somebody else—at least one other person. I've repeated that a lot and people find it really helpful, the idea that it's going to take a lot of time. Some people talk about learning really well from watching. I think working in teams is really important. I think critiquing one's own work is really important, being willing to have people ask questions about where particular ideas come from that are informing your work, because I think that dominant discourses are invisible to us as therapists, so working with people who are willing to question those and are open to those questions, I think, is important. I think that narrative ideas are different than the usual ideas, so it's very, very helpful to be working with other people who are also immersing themselves in those ideas. It would be much easier to learn how to do narrative therapy as part of a group than it would be on one's own. I also think how much you've been immersed in traditional ideas of therapy makes it more difficult because you have things to fall back on instead of stretching yourself with new ways of doing things.

When I first started doing this work, Gene Combs and I were part of a group that met every other week, and somebody different each time brought in a person or a couple or a family that we saw using outsider witness groups. I think that was really important. We did that for maybe a year and a half. Reading and going to workshops, I think is important to do, to hear what people have to say who've organized it and been thinking about it, and to do the practice activities. I think it's also important to do the work as part of a community. And I think it's really helpful if it's possible at the end of the time to be able to ask each other questions like, "What were you thinking" or "I would have asked, at this point in the therapy, these kinds of questions, and I noticed you went in this other direction and I'm curious what led you to do that." Those sort of questions deconstruct the interview. I think that's very helpful. If there's nobody around to do that with, at least have somebody that you're corresponding with that you can send things back and forth and talk about it. I have the thought that if it was just me, I couldn't have learned how to do this work. I think it's also really helpful to tape your work—either videotape or audiotape it. And to be able to go back to points and think about what other questions I could have asked. Either what directions might it have gone in that would have been different, or how I could thicken this even more. So, not to look back to critique your work, but to think about ways in particular moments that you could have done some other things that can extend your possibilities. We've done that quite a lot, just sort of stopped the tape at certain points, and if you were going to ask six more questions, what six questions could you ask that would thicken things even more at this moment.

STEPHEN MADIGAN

Stephen Madigan, MSW, MSc, PhD, is the director of Yaletown Family Therapy, which provides therapy, consulting, and therapy training. He is an AAMFT-approved supervisor.

What attracted you to the theory behind narrative therapy?

What attracted me to it were the politics of it. I used to be very involved—and I still am—in grassroots political organizations. Its treatment of people and the philosophy and the working style of narrative were coherent with my political beliefs. I think without coherency in the politic[s] of narrative therapy, I think that it might be more of a challenge to do. I think that the construction of identity is a political act. I think therapy itself is a political act. I think that people come to know themselves as persons through the very structures that we live within. And these structures involve structures of power, and these structures of power help to organize how we come to think about ourselves as persons. So that the problems that people experience, or the overall experience that we have, are influenced through the language of a much larger discourse. And a short definition of discourse might be "what could be said, and who can say it, and with what authority." These are not the freethinking ideas of an individualized skin-bound person. We are in constant dialogue and interaction with the other in landscapes of power.

The majority of people that are coming to see me are having a crisis due to their position, location, and how they internally make sense of the culture that surrounds them. So where you are located within this cultural landscape and what ideas are privileged within this cultural landscape will in fact have an influence on how people come to see themselves as persons, be it mother, father, parent, teacher, employee. Bateson had this idea that we should stamp out nouns. And I think it was an idea we were all very enchanted with. However, family therapists name and categorize, so we moved from just naming individuals within certain categories—parent, teacher, student—to attaching other names: single-parent mother, Black urban youth, gay employee, a woman on social assistance. And so, these take on meanings, and it is those meanings that often dictate our treatment.

How do you formulate your view of a family when they enter therapy?

A woman came to see me recently. She is a woman who is on social assistance, living just at the poverty line, a sole parent, struggling with what her doctor says is depression. There would be many, many ways to look at this. But for me, not addressing the issue of the politics of poverty and the effect that has on how she sees herself as a parent, and the history of ideas that led up to her being located here, and the social pressures that keep sole-parent women there, then I think that would be unethical to not address those issues. So the issue—I don't really know what depression is—all I know is that there are certain apparatuses in place, structures if you will, in place, that are very much assisting in how this young woman has come to view herself and her situation. To say that it is depression means that, in some ways, it places the onus of responsibility on this person and treats her as an isolated strip, away from the culture within which she lives. So we're looking at a variety of the politics of poverty, of women or gender, of race—a variety that if we're looking at depression, we might miss.

It's like looking at a rainbow if you will. If I can look up at the sky and say to you, "Oh, look; isn't that a beautiful rainbow?" and "Look at that green in the rainbow" . . . And so we pretend for a moment that we can actually just see the green and we . . . as Erving Goffman says, we treat it as an isolated strip and take it away from its context. And so what we as family therapists often do is to forget to put the green back in its context in the rainbow, because there really isn't a green, it's a mixture of yellows and blues, and spectrums of light pollution, and water particles, and different issues that are making up this green. So to treat it as just a single solitary color, as green, is not an accurate description. I think that we are often led to believe that our descriptions of people in isolation are accurate, and I would say that they're not accurate.

Different models of therapy require the therapist to be directive or nondirective. In your opinion, what are the necessary characteristics that a therapist should possess to be effective with this model?
My sense is that I don't want to commit any therapeutic violence, like to help to perpetuate the problem, or to help the person feel less than they already feel; and to keep myself available to listening to the contradictions in the story being told. Persons often have a much lower opinion of themselves than the story suggests. People are actually far more interesting than they let on. I think that with these internal problem conversations that we all have, and we struggle with, that it closes off people from other experiences that they've had, that they're currently having, that they may wish to have. And those are the conversations that I wish to open up, a full rendering of the story being told, not just the problem story being told.

How often does the client see you and for how long a period of time?
I'll see couples for about two hours if it's the first session. Part of the reason is that it helps me, but also I find that [it helps] to get the fullness of the story with two people talking, and I find that it helps them as well. I would say the majority of the time people spend is between an hour and an hour and a half. I also work on teams, so that would be 2 hours, 2 hours and 15 minutes. That would be a reflecting team. That's how I train people as well. Actually, I'm participating in the session by offering their witnessing accounts or reflections back, and I really like working that way. If there's any luxury for therapists to work together, I think it's imperative because I think that the isolating effects of working one-to-one behind your therapy door for long periods of time can in some way lead you away from more refreshed looks at your work, and this provides an opportunity to have people comment on your work and be transparent about your work and [you] learn from their comments and your clients' comments. I often interview clients about how this is going and what they found valuable and what they didn't, whether courses or threads of conversation that we began to pursue but we

need to pursue further, so I suppose, it's getting supervision from the people that you're training and also from your colleagues and also from your clients. That really keeps me sharp, anyway, in what it is that I'm doing or hoping to do.

It's hard to give a specific number of sessions. When we did count the sessions, it was right around four sessions. People would come probably for—depends on the person and their time schedule—but in an idealized world, they might come once or twice that first week and then maybe a third time the following week or the week after, and then we'd really begin to look at where they're going. Oftentimes, people might come for three or four sessions and feel really good at where they are, continue down that track, come back 6 months later for a session just to catch up, to look at, to re-remember. That's why those letters are very important, because it's a text for them to remember. I often ask—I always ask people, and offer them the opportunity to tape our sessions as well. Audiotape it, so they can take it with them. Some people videotape to show their significant others, if they wish to show them. And I often have people who tape, bring other people in to listen to what's been said.

What are you looking for when you are in the session?
I'm very explicit in getting a full understanding of what the problem is and how it operates. And I'm very interested to know (a) what life has been like when they've lived outside of that problem, and (b) why is it that they would like to move away from this problem situation and what makes them think that they can? And who might be in their life that supports this idea of themselves as a person moving away from a problem? And my dedication to them is to live outside this idea that somehow the shame of diagnosis and the privatization of the problem is somehow inside of them, or the cause of the problem is inside of them. My work is to stay away from that dominant idea because I find, both from what my clients tell me and what I've experienced myself in therapy, but also in my own life, that that's not helpful. So I'm hoping to offer an alternative, because I think if we don't offer an alternative pathway with a person, then the results will be the same, which will further the strength of the problem in their life.

I don't work from a map of goals. It's more about looking at the struggles that they're having, the structures that support this, the histories of these struggles, and moving them to reremember aspects of themselves that were free of this and didn't think of themselves in these ways. And really looking at the internal conversations that they're having with themselves and the influence that the culture has had on how they've come to see themselves as people. So goals and that sort of thing [are] a bit of a foreign language.

What is the assessment process of this model?
There isn't one. In terms of how I understand the question and the use of the word assessment, what that means is that it's giving all power to the professional other—you and me. My sense is that that's an unequal distribution of power. To suggest that because we've been given this great privilege to name and assess, I think we really have to rethink that. So in terms of the way that you're using assessment and the way that I envision it, I don't use it. I ask people, and the people have come to look for changes, to see how things are different. To assess the effects of the problem—are they getting the upper hand on the problem, or is the problem getting the upper hand on them? This leads us into a whole other realm of questioning that has to do with appreciation of

the self. Given what is going on, and the problem's best attempt to kill your life, how do you explain your ability to survive, and not only to survive but to be free and to move toward a more preferred idea of who you are and managing your relationships in more preferred ways? To me, that might be more of an equal distribution of who gets to say what about how well this person's doing.

Who sets the goals, the client or the therapist?

To me, there's a goal in therapy and that is someone who comes to me, viewing me as having an ability to help. I take that position very seriously, and our contract is that I will do the very best I can to work alongside this person so that they can move towards a more preferred idea of themselves and their relationships. Period.

What are some commonly used interventions with this model?

Well, it's like a short form of a conversation that we've had between ourselves, the client and myself. Like it might sound like this dialogue, between a therapist, a client, and his wife, Mary:

Therapist: If you find Guilt really getting the better of you this week and you feel that it's pushing you towards actions that are detrimental to yourself, what kind of conversations do you think you might have with Guilt as a way of standing away from guilt and towards yourself? Would this be something to document and to remember as you try out having your relationship with Guilt in different ways?

Client: Well, what do you mean? Do you want me to write it down?

Therapist: I don't know, do you think that might be a good idea if you document, if you became an anthropologist in your own life and to survey the taken-for-granted place that guilt has in your life as it takes advantage of you?

Client: Yeah, I think that would be a good idea.

Therapist: Why do you think that would be a good idea?

Client: Well, maybe I have things that I'm doing already that I don't know that I'm doing.

Therapist: So why might that . . .

Client: Well, maybe I'm further ahead than I know.

Therapist: Why would this be a good knowing to know?

Client: Well, then I would be able to challenge this idea of myself as the problem having full control of my life.

Therapist: Well, that might be interesting. I'll be really interested to see what you come up with.

Therapist: And do you think, Mary, that this is a good idea?

Mary: Yep, yep, I think this is a good idea.

Therapist: And is there anything that you'd like to add if you notice guilt getting the better of Bob this week?

Mary: Well, I could point it out.

Therapist: Now, do you mean point it out to make Bob feel more guilty that he has guilt?

Mary: Oh right, that could happen.

Therapist: Right, do you think that there might be a way that you could be supporting of Bob, and not supporting of Guilt, when Guilt is getting the better of Bob?

Mary: Hmm, that's interesting. You know, I remember a time when I did that.

Therapist: Yeah, Mary, what was that like?

What role does a homework assignment have in this model?
Not homework. We have conversations about perhaps what they might want to pay attention to in terms of what it is that we've talked about, in terms of the problem getting the upper hand in their life, and asking them, "What would be a good way to document this?" Quite often people do it in written form. Either through writing about it, or writing point form, or diarying, or sometimes people come in with collages, sometimes people come in with artwork. Some people come in with articles from the newspaper that somehow they attach to their own experience.

What have you found to be the limitations of this approach?
I don't think there's any problem with where the approach can go. The limitation would be mine and not the client's or not the problem. I do think that we have to be fully accountable and responsible for the work that we're doing. Have there been tricky situations? Of course. That's when having a great collegial group around you can really help you sort through it. I always come back to there was a limitation in myself, that I didn't hear something, or I couldn't see something, or I couldn't figure out the pattern in a particular way, or that the problem had me thinking that perhaps this was unsolvable. And I think we all get to those places at certain times. But rather than blame the client as being untreatable or chronic, we need to look at what it is that we are implementing and how we are distributing this knowledge of therapy. It's not connecting with the person that we're working with, so we need to find a way to assist that.

What are your suggestions for students learning this model?
First of all, I think I would read the early work of Michael White and David Epston, the collected and the selected work, because at that moment, they were writing into history how they worked. And really, there's a lot of the work that is very familiar from back when they were creating this in the early and mid-80s, to the way in which they're working now. So if you read those stories, those letters, those questions, that structure of the interview, if you can get your hands on videotapes or transcripts, and you study them. I have a DVD out with an African American boy and his mother (*Narrative Therapy With Children [Child Therapy With the Experts Series]*, Stephen Madigan, PhD, psychotherapy.net) and you can study that. This is the way that I did it. You write down all the questions that people are asking and then as your great American anthropologist, Clifford Geertz, once said, eventually the copy originates. If you can get your hands on transcripts, videotapes, and just get the cadence and the structure of the questions that they're using and ask yourself why they're asking this question as opposed to all the other questions that other people might ask. Where is this going? And so eventually, it's like music. You begin to understand the structure a little bit more. David Epston says it takes a solid 3 to 4 years of intense study to learn it. Tape all the work that you do, if it's possible where you're working, and really, not from a critical point of view that is going to dampen your spirit and passion of therapy, but to really learn from yourself.

Case Study

A mother calls and makes an appointment for her family to come to therapy. The family consists of a husband and wife, both in their 40s; their 15-year-old son; a college-aged daughter; and the woman's father, age 82. Three years after the woman's mother died, her father developed Alzheimer's disease and moved in with the family 6 months ago. When his health began to deteriorate, the woman spent more time caring for him than for other members of the family. Three months ago, the 15-year-old son, who has been treated for ADHD since age 7, began to refuse to take his medication and is now being truant from school.

During the session, the wife cries and the husband reports their relationship is strained, while occasionally rolling his eyes as his wife becomes tearful. He reports that he has had to take on more work because his wife had to quit her job to attend to her father's needs. The daughter is away at college and the wife smiles as she describes her as a straight-A student. The daughter was asked to attend the session but refused because she has a hard time with her grandfather's illness and dislikes the conflict that has developed at home.

Jill Freedman's Response to the Case Study

I would begin the interview by saying, "I understand that you think there's a problem, and I'd be curious to know if other people in the family think that there's a problem." And if they do think there's a problem, I'd want to know what the problem is." I wouldn't make the assumption that there would be any agreement about what the problem was. I think the way this is written, there's an idea that there's a relationship between the 15-year-old son refusing to take medication and the father being with Alzheimer's. I wouldn't assume that there was a relationship between those things. At the beginning, I'm usually more open to how they would like to tell it. So if one person starts telling and then another person joins in, that's okay at the beginning unless I can't follow what's going on, and I feel like somebody is saying something and they don't get to finish what they're saying. In that case, I might say something like, "Would it be okay if I hear from so-and-so first, and I promise that I will be interested in what each of you has to say." And if they seem concerned, I might say, "I've been doing this for a while, and I've noticed that people have different versions, and I'd just like to hear from each of you whether you find something problematic, and if you do, what that is." So I'm creating a sense where people don't think that we're establishing what we're going to do with the first person and that I'll hear multiple stories. There can be multiple strands of the stories that we're telling. I don't have this idea that everybody's going to agree what the problem is.

Even if I had spoken with the woman on the phone for 20 minutes, I'm still assuming that there would be other stories that would be spoken by other people, and that she might be making different meaning at the time that they were all there together. So I don't have in my mind an idea of what a healthy family should be like, or a normal family. So I don't have something I'm trying to get to. So I'm really interested in hearing what each person might find problematic and listening to that in a way that's externalizing it and keeping in mind that there are many things that wouldn't be predicted by that. I'm hoping to create a context where we'll be able to hear some of those stories that couldn't be predicted. That's really what I'm bringing with me, but not an idea about what would be important to change, or what particular people, you know I'm not thinking about family configuration, or any of those kinds of things.

I might be curious about the son's decision to refuse to take medication. I wouldn't know whether that was a good thing or a bad thing. I would want to find out something about the effects that he's noticed, and that other people have noticed, and what they make of those effects. If they thought that was a bad thing, then I'd be interested in the timing of it, or if they thought it was a good thing, I'd also be interested in the timing of it. I would ask him if he thought there was a problem, and if he did, what he thought it was. And if that was something that concerned him, or if he thought it was more of concern to his parents. I would try to give the idea that I thought what he found problematic might be different, and that I would want him to be able to speak from his experience and evaluation . . . that it was okay. I wasn't taking sort of the "official version," I wanted everybody's version. I think that's particularly important. I can't tell what's of most importance to this family. I don't know. But if I'm working with children, I want to hear their evaluation, not just their parents or the school.

In general, what I'm interested in is getting to know people as people, trying to create a framework where they can ask me questions, so they can decide whether they'd like to open their life to me and invite them to create a relationship where questions can go both ways. And I'd be interested in what different people think of as a problem. I'd like to be creating a kind of a context or format where people can witness those stories that their family members or partners are telling. And what I'm *really* interested in is creating a context for this telling and retelling of preferred stories. I think lots of times it's important to understand what people find problematic and to deconstruct those a bit so that there's room to see beyond them to preferred stories.

I might ask about the man rolling his eyes. I'm interested in creating a context where people can hear and witness each other's stories, and I'm also interested, if something's problematic, not to repeat it. So if somebody's making faces at something somebody's saying because they've heard it a lot of times, I might ask a question because I don't have an understanding of what's going on, but I might also take it as an indication that I haven't created a context that's allowing for a different kind of hearing. So I might say something like, "Would it be okay, while Linda talks about this, for you, her partner, to listen to her the way you would listen to a friend." Because a friend is somebody who is on their side. I might ask them about their ideas about friendship, but my idea of friendship is that you care what they're saying, but what they're saying doesn't have a direct effect on you.

I might ask the father, "Would you say that the strain is what most concerns you, or is it the hardship of working the extra hours?" If it's the strain, I would have more ideas about what would be useful. Like if there's a strain, then I would be wondering what it means to her, that her partner is working these extra hours, and what difference that makes in her life, and if she's understood that it's a concern to him how they're not spending time together. So that might end up being something that would be a preferred story that they might treasure. If it's the actual working the extra hours, I'd be curious about some other kinds of things, like how the decision was made that that's the best way to make this possible, and who took the lead in that. Maybe they would want to rethink that. I don't know.

One of the things I might consider is whether it might be useful to write a letter to the daughter with some notes about what we talked about, and questions that we would have asked her if she had been here. I've found that to be useful sometimes.

> ## KEY TERMS
>
> **Deconstruction** "Discovering, acknowledging and 'taking apart' (deconstructing) the beliefs, ideas and practices of the broader culture in which a person lives that are serving to assist the problem and the problem story" (Morgan, 2000, p. 45).
>
> **Discourse** A system of statements, practices, and institutional structures that share common values.
>
> **Externalization** The process of developing a dialogue with a client about a problem as if the problem was external from the client. For example, "anger" could be externalized and the client could think about how to avoid its influence in his or her life.
>
> **Postmodernism** The view that there is no one objective "truth" and that there are many multiple possible interpretations of any event.
>
> **Reauthoring** The process in narrative therapy wherein the client and the therapist begin rewriting the client's story into an alternative story.
>
> **Social constructionism** A theoretical standpoint that takes the view that there is no objective reality. Our reality is constructed within social groups in the context of shared language, culture, history, and relationships.
>
> **Unique outcomes** Events that a person partakes in that shine or stand out in contrast to times when the person subjected himself or herself or others to the dominant, problem-focused story.

REFERENCES

Andersen, T. (1999). The reversal of light and sound. *Gecko: A Journal of Deconstruction and Narrative Ideas in Therapeutic Practice, 2,* 5–9.

Bourdieu, P. (1988). *Homo academicus.* Stanford, CA: Stanford University Press.

Bruner, E. M. (1986). Ethnography as narrative. In V. Turner & E. Bruner (Eds.), *The anthropology of experience.* Chicago, IL: University of Illinois Press.

Epston, D., & White, M. (1993). A proposal for a re-authoring therapy. In D. Epston, *Catching up with David Epston.* Adelaide, Australia: Dulwich Centre.

Freedman, J., & Combs, G. (1996). *Narrative therapy: The social construction of preferred realities.* New York, NY: Norton.

Freedman, J., & Combs, G. (n.d.). *Narrative worldview.* Retrieved from http://www.narrativetherapychicago .com/narrative_worldview/narrative_worldview.htm

Goffman, E. (1961). *Asylums: Essays on the social situation of mental patients and other inmates.* Garden City, NY: Doubleday Anchor.

Goldenberg, H., & Goldenberg, I. (2007). *Family therapy: An overview* (7th ed.). Pacific Grove, CA: Brooks Cole.

Morgan, A. (2000). *What is narrative therapy? An easy-to-read introduction.* Adelaide, Australia: Dulwich Centre.

Myerhoff, B. (1986). "Life not death in Venice": Its second life. In V. W. Turner & E. M. Bruner (Eds.), *The anthropology of experience* (pp. 261–286). Chicago, IL: University of Illinois Press.

Silver, Williams, Worthington, & Phillips (1998)

Silver, E., Williams, A., Worthington, F., & Phillips, N. (1998). Family therapy and soiling: An audit of externalizing and other approaches. *Journal of Family Therapy, 20*(4), 333–449.

Tomm, K. (1989). Externalizing the problem and internalizing personal agency. *Journal of Strategic and Systemic Therapies, 8*(1), 54–59.

Turner, V. (1969). *The ritual process.* Chicago, IL: Aldine.

Van Gennep, A. (1960). *The rites of passage* (M. B. Vizedom & G. Caffee, Trans.). Chicago, IL: University of Chicago Press.

Vromans, L. (2008). *Process and outcome of narrative therapy for major depressive disorder in adults: Narrative reflexivity, working alliance and improved symptom and inter-personal outcomes.* Unpublished doctoral dissertation, Queensland University of Technology.

White, M. (1992). Deconstruction and therapy. In D. Epston & M. White, *Experience, contradiction, narrative & imagination: Selected papers of David Epston and Michael White, 1989–1991.* Adelaide, Australia: Dulwich Centre.

White, M. (1995). *Re-authoring lives: Interviews and essays.* Adelaide, Australia: Dulwich Centre.

White, M. (2000). *Reflections on narrative practice.* Adelaide, Australia: Dulwich Centre.

White, M., & Epston, D. (1989). *Literate means to therapeutic ends.* Adelaide, Australia: Dulwich Centre.

White, M., & Epston, D. (1990). *Narrative means to therapeutic ends.* New York, NY: Norton.

RECOMMENDED READING LIST

Books

Bird, J. (2004). *Talk that sings: Therapy in a new linguistic key.* Auckland, New Zealand: Edge Press.

Brown, C., & Augusta-Scott, T. (2007). Narrative therapy: Making meaning, making lives. Thousand Oaks, CA: Sage.

Dulwich Centre. (n.d.) *Commonly asked questions about narrative therapy.* Retrieved from http://www.dulwichcentre.com.au/common-questions-narrative-therapy.html

Dulwich Centre. (n.d.). *Externalising: Commonly asked questions* (Ed. by Carey, M. & Russell, S.). Retrieved from http://www.dulwichcentre.com.au/externalising.html

Epston, D. (1993). Internalizing discourses versus externalizing discourses. In D. Epston, *Catching up with David Epston.* Adelaide, Australia: Dulwich Centre.

Epston, D. (1998). *"Catching up" with David Epston: A collection of narrative practice-based papers published between 1991 & 1996.* Adelaide, Australia: Dulwich Centre.

Epston, D., & White, M. (1992). *Experience, contradiction, narrative, and imagination.* Adelaide, Australia: Dulwich Centre.

Epston, D., & White, M. (1992). *Experience, contradiction, narrative, & imagination: Selected papers of David Epston and Michael White.* Adelaide, Australia: Dulwich Centre.

Freedman, J., & Combs, G. (1996). *Narrative therapy: The social construction of preferred realities.* New York, NY: Norton.

Freedman, J., & Combs, G. (2002). *Narrative therapy with couples . . . and a whole lot more!* Adelaide, Australia: Dulwich Centre.

Freeman, J., Epston, D., & Lobovits, D. (1997). *Playful approaches to serious problems: Narrative therapy with children and their families.* New York, NY: Norton.

Geertz, C. (1983). *Local knowledge: Further essays in interpretive anthropology.* New York, NY: Basic Books.

Maisel, R., Epston, D., & Borden, A. (2004). *Biting the hand that starves you: Inspiring resistance to anorexia/bulimia.* New York, NY: Norton.

Monk, G., Winslade, J., Crocket, K., & Epston, D. (Eds.). (1997). *Narrative therapy in practice: The archaeology of hope.* San Francisco, CA: Jossey-Bass.

Morgan, A. (2000). *What is narrative therapy? An easy-to-read introduction.* Adelaide, Australia: Dulwich Centre.

Parry, A., & Doan, R. (1994). *Story re-visions.* New York, NY: Guilford Press.

Ricoeur, P. (1983). *Time and narrative.* Chicago, IL: University of Illinois Press.

Smith, C., & Nylund, D. (1997). *Narrative therapies with children and adolescents.* New York, NY: Guilford Press.

White, M. (1995). *Re-authoring lives: Interviews and essays.* Adelaide, Australia: Dulwich Centre.

White, M. (1997). *Narratives of therapists' lives.* Adelaide, Australia: Dulwich Centre.

White, M. (2000). *Reflections on narrative practice.* Adelaide, Australia: Dulwich Centre.

White, M. (2005). *Workshop notes.* Retrieved from http://www.dulwichcentre.com.au/Michael%20White%20Workshop%20Notes.pdf

White, M. (2007). *Maps of narrative practice.* New York, NY: Norton.

White, M., & Epston, D. (1990). *Narrative means to therapeutic ends.* New York, NY: Norton.

Articles

Andersen, T. (1987). The reflecting team: Dialogue and meta-dialogue in clinical work. *Family Process, 26*(4), 415–428.

Anderson, H., & Goolishian, H. A. (1988). Human systems as linguistic systems: Preliminary and evolving ideas about the implications for clinical theory. *Family Process, 27*(4), 371–393.

Besley, A. C. (2002). Foucault and the turn to narrative therapy. *British Journal of Guidance & Counselling, 30*(2), 125–143.

Gremillion, H. (2004). Unpacking essentialisms in therapy: Lessons for feminist approaches from narrative work. *Journal of Constructivist Psychology, 17*(3), 173–200.

Hoffman, L. (1990). Constructing realities: An art of lenses. *Family Process, 29*(1), 1–12.

Markey, C. (2005). The goodbye feelings: Working with children living in two homes—one with mum and one with dad [Online]. *The International Journal of Narrative Therapy and Community Work, 2,* 62–71.

Monk, G., & Gehart, D. R. (2003). Sociopolitical activist or conversational partner? *Family Process, 42*(1), 19–30.

Tilsen, J., Russell, S., & Michael. (2005). Nimble and courageous acts: How Michael became the boss of himself. *Journal of Systemic Therapies, 24*(2), 29–42.

Journals

The International Journal of Narrative Therapy and Community Work, published by Dulwich Centre.

Videos/Media/Websites

http://www.baftta.com/

http://www.dulwichcentre.com

http://www.familyinstitutecamb.org/

http://www.kenwoodcenter.org

http://www.narrativeapproaches.com

http://www.narrativebooks.com/

http://www.narrativetherapycentre.com/index.htm

http://www.narrativetherapychicago.com

http://www.yaletownfamilytherapy.com/index.html

http://web.lemoyne.edu/~hevern/narpsych.html

Governors State University. (Producer). (1999). *Family Therapy with the experts—a video series: Narrative therapy with Stephen Madigan* [Motion picture]. (Available from Insight Media, 2162 Broadway, New York, NY 10024)

Master's Work Productions (Producer). (1996). *Partners in strength: A consultation with Jill Freedman & Gene Combs of the Evanston Family Therapy Center* [Motion picture]. (Available from Master'sWork Productions, Los Angeles, CA, *http://masterswork.com/shopsite_sc/store/html/index_1.html*).

Master's Work Productions (Producer). (1996). *The best of friends: A live interview with Michael White* [Motion picture]. (Available from Master'sWork Productions, Los Angeles, CA, *http://masterswork.com/shopsite_sc/store/html/index_1.html*).

Master's Work Productions (Producer). (1992). *Grandma's ghost spirits away family violence: A unique reauthoring with David Epston* [Motion picture]. (Available from Master'sWork Productions, Los Angeles, CA, *http://masterswork.com/shopsite_sc/store/html/index_1.html*).

Emotionally Focused Therapy

14

Edita Ruzgyte and Donald Spinks

We know too much and feel too little. At least, we feel too little of those
creative emotions from which a good life springs.

—Bertrand Russell

INTRODUCTION

Emotionally focused therapy (EFT) is an approach that entails influences from humanists' approaches, general systems theorists, and most importantly, attachment theory (Johnson & Greenman, 2006). Through the integration of the intrapsychic emotional responses and interpersonal interactional patterns, emotionally focused therapists work with couples, helping them to create a more secure bond between each other (Johnson, Hunsley, Greenberg, & Schindler, 1999). This approach allows clients to explore their feelings of hurt and longing, see how it plays out in close relationships, and then apply this new, discovered information to their relationship to build a stronger and emotionally secure bond with each other (Johnson, 2007).

The goals in EFT include dealing with projective identifications; providing attachment opportunities, constructing or rebuilding healthy couple relations, discovering and clarifying individual needs, encouraging autonomy as described by Bowen's theory of differentiation (see Chapter 3), and working in the developmental life task stages (Makinen & Johnson, 2006).

HISTORY AND LEADING FIGURES

From the 1930s to the 1950s, there was a change in American psychoanalysis that focused more on ego psychology. Led by such leaders as Erik Erikson who looked into the sociological arena, others like Eric Fromm talked about the individual struggle for individuality. Harry Stack Sullivan developed an interpersonal theory and emphasized the role of the mother (or caretakers) in developing anxiety in children. Just as Fromm led Bowen to his work on differentiation, Sullivan led the world toward family object relations and attachment theory, both of which have tremendously impacted family therapy (Scharf, 2000).

In the 1980s, before Susan Johnson introduced the idea of EFT, the field of family therapy focused on behavioral changes or training programs that were oriented toward learning how to solve marital problems (Johnson & Greenberg, 1987). To achieve empirically measurable results, therapists were focusing on specific behavior and clients' response to specific interventions. These approaches were effective in helping people change their behavior, but none of them addressed the issues of emotional connection, dramas, and pain that people experienced in close relationships (Palmer & Johnson, 2002).

To fill this gap, Johnson and Greenberg (1987) began to study different therapy sessions looking for patterns that created positive change for clients. During these observations,

Johnson and Greenberg noticed that in order for change to take place, clients had to work on their internal emotional processes as well as develop healthier interactional sequences (Greenberg, Ford, Alden, & Johnson, 1993). After observing a number of those patterns, Johnson and Greenberg identified the steps in the process of change and created specific therapeutic interventions that therapists could use to achieve those steps (Johnson & Greenberg, 1985). Once the process of change was mapped, therapists started to do empirical testing and create new ways to achieve change. These processes marked the beginning of a new therapeutic approach—emotionally focused therapy.

To fully understand the origin and history of EFT, it is important to present an overview of the theoretical approach that had the most influence in the origination of this model, attachment theory.

ATTACHMENT THEORY

In the early 1950s, John Bowlby began his work in Britain on attachment theory. Attachment theory has become one of the most prominent theories emanating from the history of psychodynamic thinking and in thinking about family systems. Bowlby's attachment theory is best represented in his trilogy, *Attachment* (1969), *Separation* (1973), and *Loss* (1980). Bowlby was trained in the object relations schools in Britain but did not receive the kind of recognition and following there compared to the United States. The difference is most notably recognized between the two countries because of the history of Bowlby's relationship with Melanie Klein. Klein was mostly interested in the internal world and fantasies of the child compared to Bowlby's interest in the environment in which the child developed (McDonald, 2001).

In 1950, Bowlby was invited by the World Health Organization to advise on the mental health of homeless children. This study supported the research and beliefs he had already formed from working with deprived children in London. It was in this study that Bowlby focused on the emotional issues of childhood more than the larger social or economic realities affecting them. It became a historically important piece of research (Bowlby, 1958) in which he surmised that the relationship of the "mother" (later interpreted by others as caregiver) to the child must be warm, nurturing, intimate, and continuous. This work ultimately led to attachment theory.

According to attachment theory, each individual develops consistent interrelational patterns to regulate his or her emotions in his or her relationships. These patterns are created based on the experiences the individual has in his or her present and past relationships (Rholes & Simpson, 2004). These strategic patterns are referred to as attachment orientations (Hazan & Shaver, 1987). Attachment orientations affect both the individual's internal processes as well external relational behavior. More secure individuals will have both more self-confidence in themselves and ability to connect to other people in a more open manner. Individuals who are insecure tend to lack self-confidence and their relationship patterns are usually driven by fear of abandonment or inability to get close to people in the relationships (Hazan & Shaver, 1987).

According to Johnson and Denton (2007), in recent years, the influence of attachment theory to EFT has become even more significant. The integration of these two theories proved to be particularly helpful in working with individuals who experienced depression or trauma (Whiffen & Johnson, 1998).

INTRODUCTION TO EMOTIONALLY FOCUSED THERAPY

EFT is aimed at reducing stress and anxiety in adult relationships and creating (or recreating) more secure attachment bonds (Makinen & Johnson, 2006). Emotionally focused family therapy is a variant of EFT that can be used with families. Focusing on emotion is the key and essential transforming element in EFT. By focusing on emotion in an egalitarian fashion, the therapist creates a "safe environment" for all participants (Greenberg et al., 1993).

As mentioned earlier, EFT is based in attachment theory. However, EFT also uses elements of Gestalt therapy and systems theory. As noted by Greenberg and Johnson (1988), both theories see the human as "becoming" and not "being," capable of living in a flux between what is and what can be. Both Gestalt and systems theory also focus on the "here and now" more than on the historical constructs often found in more traditional psychodynamic approaches to therapy.

EFT presents, as a theoretical basis, that therapy needs to engage the "real relationship of the inner psychological world of both partners to their interaction" (Greenberg & Johnson, 1988, p.36) and the contextual relationship as also a basis of each person's behavior in relationship to his or her intrapsychic experience. The following is the summary of the principles that determine and guide the therapeutic process:

1. The therapist acts as a process consultant and helps couples to create collaborative alliances that will allow them to create a secure bond and explore their emotions.

2. Emotions are the key element in relationships. It governs attachment behavior and influences how people feel about themselves and how they experience intimate relationships.

3. Most of the time, attachment needs and desires are healthy and adaptive. Problems occur when people are not able to enact those needs or perceive their partner's needs in a secure way. For example, a daughter wants to get closer to her mother (which is a very appropriate desire), but she does it by acting out (insecure behavior pattern).

4. Problems occur when people develop their interaction patterns based on negative emotions and experiences that each of them have in the relationship. According to Johnson (1996), emotions and interactional patterns develop a self-reinforcing feedback loop.

5. Change occurs by creating new emotional experiences in the present relationships that are based on secure attachment-driven interactions. This theory does not focus on the insight to the past, catharsis, or negotiation.

6. The therapist views the relationship between the partners as a "client" in the session. The goal of therapy is to create a relationship that is based on secure bonding (Johnson, 1996).

Emotionally focused therapists believe that a "bond" exists between persons, and if a couple or family comes in for therapy, this bond has been compromised in some form (Johnson & Talitman, 1997). Trust may be broken, people may feel insecure in the relationship, and family members may not believe that others are trustworthy or even safe. ("Safe" in this context means that the other can be counted on regardless of difficulty and that the relationship is a safe and secure place in which one feels cared for and about.) Based on this belief, the treatment strategy in EFT is to heal the broken bond, to repair the trust, and help recreate a safe environment for its members, and not to resolve childhood introjects and projections (Johnson & Talitman, 1997).

The therapist using EFT has three main tasks: first, to create and maintain a therapeutic alliance: a "safe base" in the therapeutic environment for each member of the family to explore his or her self and others. The second task is to access client emotions and then to reformulate those emotions into a new and more positive basis between the family members. The third task is the restructuring of the interactions between family members, in essence, changing problematic patterns of behavior into more positive patterns (Johnson et al., 2005). This, in turn, addresses the positive and negative feedback loops within the system and the contextual environment.

To accomplish these tasks, the EFT therapist takes a three-stage and nine-step process (Johnson et al., 2005). The three stages of EFT are as follows:

Stage 1: Cycle de-escalation
  Step 1: Identify the relational conflict issues between partners.
  Step 2: Identify the negative interaction cycle where these issues are expressed.
  Step 3: Access the unacknowledged emotions underlying the interactional position each partner takes in this cycle.
  Step 4: Reframe the problem in terms of the cycle, accompanying underlying emotions, and attachment needs.

Stage 2: Changing interactional positions
  Step 5: Promote each partner's identification with disowned attachment needs and aspects of self (. . .).
  Step 6: Promote acceptance by each partner of the other partner's experience (. . .).
  Step 7: Facilitate the expression of needs and wants to restructure the interaction based on new understanding and create bonding events.

Stage 3: Facilitate consolidation and integration
  Step 8: Facilitate the emergence of new solutions to old problems.
  Step 9: Consolidate new positions and cycles of attachment theory (Johnson & Denton, 2008, p. 230).

Each of the stages has goals that the therapist helps clients achieve. The first step involves assessment and de-escalation of problematic encounters. During this stage, clients gain broader understanding of their relationship patterns. Each person in the couple starts viewing the cycle of interactions as a problem, and stop putting blame on each other. The therapist and clients shape a new version of their problem. This version validates each person's reality and encourages them to cooperate in overcoming this negative cycle (Johnson et al., 2005).

At the end of stage 2, partners who are withdrawn from the relationship are encouraged to reconnect, and partners who maintained a blaming response cycle learn to "soften" and have their attachment needs met from more positive interactions. When both partners complete all steps in stage 2, bonding events start to occur and clients are ready to create different forms of emotional engagement (Johnson et al., 2005).

In the final two steps that take place in stage 3, the therapist reviews the couple's achievements in the session and promotes consolidation of new relationship responses and cycles of interactions. At this stage, the therapist consults clients while they review the specific problems that created hurts in their relationship and helps them to apply new interactional cycles to different situations (Johnson et al., 2005).

THEORETICAL ASSUMPTIONS

View of the Family and Client

EFT's view of psychopathology and health influences its view of the family or the client(s) (Johnson, 2004). EFT defines "health" as flexibility, instead of being caught into tight patterns of emotional and behavioral responses. When an individual is healthy, there is fluidity to his or her responses and repertoire of behavioral choices. The healthy individual also has an ability to regulate emotional responses and connect with other people, which create a sense of safety within the person and within his or her relationships (Johnson, 2002). This includes the ability to access, accept, and understand one's own emotions. Pathology, in EFT terms, refers to repetitive emotional, behavioral, cognitive, and perceptual responses that do not account for the reality of the current context (Johnson, 2002).

When a family or couple enters into therapy, EFT views the family as healthy but with currently stuck patterns of repetitive behaviors that are based in an attachment injury, or some other loss of a sense of safety and security. The therapist focuses on looking at the cycles of behavior and interaction between members that create the ongoing system (Greenberg & Johnson, 1988; Johnson, 1996). By examining the communication behaviors through the frames of attachment theory, the EFT therapist experiences the family in their assumed roles and patterns of behavior that create the sense of being "stuck" in repetitive cycles of interaction. This view of the family is not pathologically based, but instead is a view of the family/couple that has a habitual negative interactional cycle that typifies the client's complaint (Johnson & Denton, 2007). The system is healthy and whole, only caught currently in unproductive and repetitive cycles of behavior that can be interrupted with new patterns of emotional, cognitive, and perceptual experiences—experiences that will create a new homeostasis within the relationship (Johnson et al., 2005).

View on How Change Occurs

According to EFT, change happens when the family is able to restructure their interactions so that affiliation and autonomy are both accepted and nurtured in the relationship (Moser & Johnson, 2008). Change occurs in the therapy relationship when the therapist is first able to create a safe environment for each member to acknowledge and explore his or her own primary emotions and find acceptance and understanding (Johnson et al., 2005). Then the therapist consults the couple through the process of nine stages that are described earlier. The change process is illustrated in the following case study:

> Susan and Tom have been married for 5 years. They had a close and safe bond at the beginning of their marriage, but it all changed when Tom lost his job and Susan got pregnant with their first child. Susan and Tom made a conjoint decision that, after the birth of the child, Tom will stay home and Susan will pick up a few more shifts in the hospital. This arrangement turned out to be very stressful for both partners, but in the decreasing economy, Tom's attempts to find a job were unsuccessful and Susan had to continue picking up more shifts and spending less time with her family. After 2 years of this arrangement, the couple sought therapy.
>
> During the first session, Tom shared that he continuously experienced Susan as angry and not available emotionally, and he was concerned that she was going to leave him. Every time he would bring up his concerns, Susan would get upset, complain that she was not able to spend more time with the child (according to Tom, she never talked about her desire to spend more time with him), and then distanced herself from Tom. In the same session, Susan shared her doubts about not being an adequate mother and said that her feelings of unworthiness led her to react in an angry and withdrawn manner toward her husband.

To serve as a consultant in this session and lead the couple through the process of change, the therapist spent the first two sessions building a therapeutic alliance, closely observing the couple's interactions and identifying their problematic cycles. Tom complained about Susan's unavailability, and she would translate his complaint as a criticism of her as a mother and become angry. She would then withdraw, which would increase Tom's feelings of insecurity in the relationship. Before change could occur, both partners had to realize each other's emotional experiences in the relationship, learn that they were not enemies, and that the negative cycle of their interactions was causing them to feel pain and insecurity. These conceptualizations and preparation for change take place in the first stage of EFT therapy.

During the second stage of therapy, Tom and Susan were encouraged to reunite against their negative cycle of interactions and conceptualize that this cycle is maintained by their unmet attachment needs. (Tom would criticize and then be afraid, and Susan would get angry and then withdraw.) Once the couple understands the cycle and are ready to reunite against it, the therapist starts to restructure the couple's interactions, where they become more open and responsive to each other. These new interactions will lead Tom and Susan to form a more secure emotional bond.

In stage 3, the process of change continues and the couple is able to apply new learned cycles to specific situations. Tom and Susan were able to recognize and identify their response patterns that trigger negative cycles and feel secure with each other to openly discuss it and ask for specific reassurance from each other.

This example illustrates using EFT in the process of change in therapy. During these sessions, the couple learned that by expressing fear, vulnerability, and the need for each other's contact and support, they were able to create a real language of relationships that promoted acceptance, understanding, and change in responsiveness (Johnson & Greenman, 2006). By focusing on the interaction processes instead of the content of the discussion, the therapist can work on the patterns that support the problems and change them into patterns that support the solutions (Johnson et al., 2005). By viewing each partner's behavior in response to the other partner, the therapist is promoting change by altering the awareness of what is being communicated and what is needed by each person. This example also illustrates that the therapist does not need to be caught in the problem content but can effectively address the problem process to effect change (Johnson et al., 2005).

All this is directed at bringing about a restructuring of the interactions by using newly discovered or at least newly accessed and discussed emotions to motivate new behavior responses (Johnson & Greenman, 2006). When one member is really aware of the other member's needs and can understand those needs within themselves and the relationship, they are motivated to provide new behaviors found in new emotional responses. As this restructuring of cycle of behavior begins to take hold, emotional experience gives way to discussions and behaviors that promote connectedness and separateness. Change occurs through the focus on and restructuring of emotional experience (Johnson & Greenman, 2006).

Therapist's Role

Susan Johnson describes the EFT therapist as a "process consultant" (Johnson, 2004). The therapist takes a collaborative role, not one of authority or expertise. The therapist is to be egalitarian, to have respect for the client's experience and need, and to work with the client in forming an understanding of and about his or her setting and situation (Johnson et al., 2005).

As a process consultant, the therapist is to reflect back to the couple, the processes, and the emotions they are enacting in the therapy environment. The therapist is not an advice giver nor is he or she the final authority on a couple's relationship or a family's relationship (Johnson & Denton, 2007). Pronouncing any judgment on the relationships is outside the purview of the therapist's role. On the contrary, the therapist's role is that of providing a safe place for the clients to express their most inner emotional realities and find support and care (Johnson, 2004). As a process consultant, the therapist is reflecting back to the client the dance he or she is engaged in with his or her significant other, the potential outcome of that dance, and the possibilities of expression of emotion that create a new step in time (Johnson, 2006). The therapist shows the clients choices, makes the choices explicit, helps them process the choices available to them, and then enables the client to make choices that are best for him or her and others.

Interventions

In creating and maintaining a therapeutic relationship with the client, the emotionally focused therapist must include an emphasis on empathy, genuineness, and respect and have the ability to focus on and join in the systems' interactional nature (Johnson et al., 2005). Beyond creating the therapeutic alliance, EFT focuses on expression and restructuring of emotions. This requires skills in emotional accessing and reformulation. Greenberg and Johnson (1988) summarized these skills as attending, refocusing, immediacy, expression analysis, intensification, symbolization, and establishing intents.

- Attending involves helping the client to pay attention to new experiences with the therapist.
- Refocusing is a technique in which the therapist asks the client to stay with an inner experience and intensify it.
- Immediacy means that the focus is in the here and now of experience.
- Expression analysis teaches the client to pay attention to nonverbal communications.
- Intensification is the experience of heightened awareness through repetition or metaphor.
- Symbolization is helping the client to grasp the essence of what has happened in the therapeutic environment.
- Establishing intents means the client is able to formulate new behaviors based on new experiences found in the therapeutic environment.

EFT is one of the best empirically validated models in the field of couples therapy (Baucom, Shoham, Mueser, Daiuto, & Stickle, 1998). The originators of the EFT consistently supported their progress through empirical research. Their first studies tested and supported the overall efficacy of EFT (Greenberg & Johnson, 1985). Later studies (Greenberg & Johnson, 1988) addressed the process of change in the therapy sessions and analyzed successful and unsuccessful EFT treatment factors. Later studies (Johnson & Talitman, 1997) continued to support efficacy of EFT. Meta-analysis conducted by Johnson et al. (1999) demonstrated that EFT is effective in treating couples who experience marital distress.

EFT studies, which were discussed earlier, as well as broad range of other studies conducted for this treatment modality, indicate that, on average, 90% of couples who were treated using this model reported significant improvements in their relationships in comparison to couples who did not receive any treatment. Similar research provides evidence that 70% to 73% of couples recover from emotional distress after EFT treatment (Johnson et al., 1999).

EFT research and practice suggest that this model can be used with various different populations and issues that clients bring to therapy. There is evidence that EFT is effective while working with couples who struggle with hypersexual behavior (Reid & Woolley, 2006), depressed partners (Dessaulles, Johnson, & Denton, 2003), families who have chronically ill children (Kowal, Johnson, & Lee, 2003; Walker, Johnson, Manion, & Cloutier, 1996), and families who have a member suffering from bulimia (Johnson, Maddeaux, & Blouin, 1998). Research also suggests that EFT effectiveness is not affected by client's age, education, income, or cognitive complexity (Denton, Burleson, Clark, Rodriguez, & Hobbs, 2000).

EMOTIONALLY FOCUSED THERAPY WORKING TEMPLATE

The *EFT template* is meant to be used as a guideline to learning the process of emotionally focused family therapy. The template provides the beginning therapist with steps to take and questions to ask that promote collaboration between the therapist and client. There are suggested questions under each heading to help start the process. After using the initial questions, guide the client through each process, asking questions that occur to you, as you stay within the family therapy theory. Although there is no one "script" for any therapy session, it is the hope of the author that the template serves as an impetus to learning this family therapy model.

Tools for Change

The emotionally focused therapist encourages engagement with disowned or unrecognized attachment emotions throughout the session. The therapist creates a warm and inviting space where the couple can express their emotions to each other, intensifying their emotions when necessary so that each person is heard. The therapist helps each partner to accept and understand the other's emotional experience as the therapy process continues and enables each partner to respond to the other's experience with authenticity. The therapist uses the new emotional experiences and the client's ability to express them to change interactional positions.

Phase 1: Joining and Building Rapport

During this phase, the therapist's objective is to connect with the family and to build an alliance where they feel safe, accepted, and understood. This is done by the therapist listening to each family member's story to understand how the relationship evolved and why they are seeking therapy. The therapist assesses attachment history and looks for blocks to attachment between partners. The therapist joins with each person to discover how he or she is constructing his or her own experience in the relationship.

The following is a question that a therapist might ask during this phase:

- *"What has brought you in to talk with me? I would like for each one of you to tell me what you came to talk to me about."*

Phase 2: Understanding the Presenting Issue

The therapist assesses the nature of the presenting problem and how it is maintained by the emotional roadblocks that the family members have constructed. To understand and assess, the therapist must push the family emotionally. The therapist tracks the typical and recurring systemic sequences of interactions that continue the distress and constitute the negative interaction cycle. The cycle may be discussed or may be actually demonstrated in the session. The therapist accesses and acknowledges the underlying emotions and experience of each partner in the negative interaction cycle, relates these underlying emotions to the interactional patterns being enacted, reframes the "problem" in terms of underlying emotions for each person, and relates the underlying emotions to actual attachment needs of each person.

Here are some comments or questions that a therapist might use during this phase:

- *"Susan, when you try to engage Dave in an intimate way, what happens, and then what happens after that?"*
- *"Pretend that I am a fly on the wall. Describe to me what I would see when the two of you argue?"*
- *"You become aware of a problem and when you bring it up, somehow (to the other partner) you feel criticized, and you were telling me that you have found that the best thing to do is just say nothing and (to the first partner) you told me this drives you crazy and try harder to get a response until (to second partner) you end up leaving."*

Phase 3: Assessment of Family Dynamics

The presenting issue or problem is reframed in terms of the negative interaction cycle, underlying emotions, and attachment issues. During this phase, the therapist notices how such interactions affect the other person and encourages the person to explain the effects to his or her partner.

Here are some comments or questions that a therapist might use during this phase:

- *"What happens to you when your partner clams up? What are you experiencing right now as your partner is saying these things?"*
- *"Susan, when you see Dave withdraw and become quiet, what happens to you?"*
- *"Can you tell Carl about the fear you have that is upsetting you?"*
- *"Can you tell him that you are afraid you might lose the closeness, the connection you have together now?"*

Phase 4: Goals

The goal of EFT is directed at bringing about a restructuring of the interactions of family members by using newly discovered emotions that the family discovers during the process. As the therapist begins to see that the negative interaction cycle has begun to change to a new, more satisfying cycle where both partners are having their attachment needs met, the couple is ready to discuss solutions to the presenting problems, which, by this point, are obvious.

Here are some comments or questions that a therapist might use during this phase:

- *"Now that you have shared with Susan that it is hard for you to think of taking the new job when you are not sure you can depend on her, what can she do to show you she is there for you?"*
- *"Susan, now that you know how important it is to your husband to have your support, what do you need your husband to do so that you can be there for him?"*
- *"Don, now that you know why it is hard for your wife to forgive you (she could never forgive her father for leaving her as a child), what do you think she needs from you to show her that forgiveness is something she should invest in?"*

Phase 5: Amplifying Change

In this phase, the therapist summarizes the discoveries that the family makes in the process of therapy and helps the family to choose new interactional methods of relating to each other. The therapist reminds the family members of the discoveries about each other that each person has made and encourages each person to consider such discoveries as he or she formulates new ways of relating. This amplification of the process continues as the therapist again facilitates new strategies with the family so that they feel supported and encouraged emotionally.

Here are some comments or questions that a therapist might use during this phase:

- *"Tom and Susan, now that you are able to recognize and identify emotions, words, or actions that trigger negative responses to each other, what do you suggest doing together when you make decisions together?"*

- *"Julie, now that you recognize how your words have impacted your daughter, what do you think would be some new strategies to use when she comes to you to discuss her future plans?"*

Phase 6: Termination

In this phase, the therapist helps the family to consolidate the gains that have been made in therapy. The therapist does this by identifying and giving support to new patterns of interaction and helps the family to create a shared narrative that identifies the progress that has been made in creating a secure relationship. The therapist also addresses any fears of termination and its effect on the couple's relationship, and guides the couple in discussion of how they will exit the previous negative cycle when it reoccurs to head off a reescalation of the old cycle.

- *"Tom and Susan, now that you have discovered how you both feel emotionally and have discussed what you need from each other, how will you use these discoveries after we complete our sessions and you feel stuck?"*

- *"How will you keep a lookout for the negative cycles that trapped you into feeling separate and alone, and how will you keep the cycles away when they threaten to interfere?"*

- *"I have learned that both of you desire the warm relationship you once had and am impressed that you have found a way back to each other. You have done this through identifying negative behaviors that kept you apart and discovered better ways of keeping in touch with each other."*

board of the Journal of Marital and Family Therapy, the Journal of Couple and Relationship Therapy, and the Journal of Family Psychology. She is a research professor in the Marital and Family Therapy Program at Alliant University in San Diego.

Her 2004 book (2nd ed.), The Practice of Emotionally Focused Couples Therapy: Creating Connection, *is the basic text on EFT for couples. She is the senior editor of the 2003 book* Attachment Processes in Couples Therapy *and the 1994 book* The Heart of the Matter. *Her 2002 book on couples therapy with trauma survivors applies EFT to different kinds of trauma. Her most recent edited book (2005) is the* EFT Workbook, Becoming an EFT Couples Therapist.

Dr. Johnson is an approved supervisor for the American Association of Marriage and Family Therapy and is internationally known for her workshops and presentations on practice, theory, and research in couples therapy, adult attachment, and emotion in psychotherapy. She maintains a private practice and lives in Ottawa, Canada.

What attracted you to the theory behind emotionally focused therapy?

I was attracted to a more experiential approach to creating change, but somehow the behavioral approaches didn't seem to have the vibrancy. They didn't seem to really address people's emotional realities. Sometimes they seemed to be very mechanical, and they didn't seem to go to the heart of the matter. Whereas the experiential techniques, when you really try to empathize with somebody's emotional experience, and you really try to help them touch that experience and taste it, and synthesize it so that they could grasp it as a whole—then my experience of that, it was very dramatic. It was very compelling. Emotion comes from the Latin word [*emovere*, which means] "to move." And people were moved by it, literally. It changed the meaning they made of things, it changed what they were motivated to do. It was much more alive for me. So I was much more interested in the experiential techniques.

In Vancouver in the '70s, Fritz Pearls had been there a lot just before he died, and so there was a huge movement of experiential therapists. But I think it then got sort of stuck. It got stuck because the emotion got all caught up in the idea of catharsis, which was, you just let it all out and then everything's fine. At that time, I went to the University of British Columbia. I worked with Les Greenburg, who was trying to look at Rogers and look at Gestalt. I first trained working with emotionally disturbed adolescents. Trying to get them on behavioral programs was one thing. But sometimes if you just sat down and talked to them about their realities and connected with their emotions, I found that you could get further with them. So it was that, it was the aliveness, the relevance of working with emotion. And helping people have a corrected emotional experience. It still fascinates me. It connects me with my deepest parts of being human. I still have that bias towards that. So that part, the experiential part of EFT was an easy choice for me.

The attachment piece, which is how we understand relationships, I had read John Bowlby. I had thought he was fascinating. But I'd read him and sort of thought about parent, mother, child, you know. I hadn't really connected it with that out loud. And I didn't until I finished my thesis, about the beginning of the '80s. When suddenly it became really obvious to me that the reality that we were dealing with in couples therapy was all about attachment. And that's what adult love is all about. And for me, that theory just made so much sense. I was looking at this drama unfolding in front of me with these couples. And it was like attachment theory was the only theory that really told me what that drama was all about. That really helped me make sense of that drama. It gave me the plot, the main story line, the scenes. It helped me understand why people felt so fearful and threatened by their partner's criticism. [I] Understand how people reacted like they were dying when their partner closed them out, shut them out, and would not respond to them. It helped me understand people's rage.

At that time that theory wasn't anywhere near[ly] as developed as it is now because it's been researched for the last 15 years by folks like Phil Shafer, who is a social psychologist. And I've come to understand it on a much deeper level. We've sort of developed Bowlby's original ideas. So when you put both of those things together, when you work with the patho-emotional and experiential level, and when you put those patho-emotions and that experience into the frame of an attachment view of adult love, it seems to me that you have a map for what close relationships are all about and why they matter so much to us, and why they're such a source of our meaning in life, our happiness, our sorrow. And also you have a map for how to change them. So, those two things meshed for me beautifully. And they just fit for the reality I saw.

They also fit for me as a person. I think no matter how much we argue about what's the best approach, there'll always be a number of approaches because clients are different and therapists are different. I'm a relatively intense, rather passionate person. So, I get bored easily. So for me to go to the heart of the matter of something, to go to the emotional meat of the matter, is what enthralls me.

How do you formulate your view of a family when they enter therapy?

I look at the family and I look at the cycles between them. The way they communicate—not what they're communicating about. I don't get stuck in problem-solving content, I look at the patterns of their communication and I use an attachment frame for that. I ask, if [a] family can respond to each other, is there someone who's always the critic, judging in this family? Is there someone who's always shutting down and withdrawing in this family? Is there a safe, loving attachment relationship in this family? Between who? Where are the negative patterns in this family where they get stuck? I might look at a family and see that the father is very distant, from both mother and daughter. And the daughter is caught in an incredible negative pattern with the mother, where the mother constantly tells the daughter she's a disappointment, that it's a shame to the family that she has this eating disorder, and the mother constantly criticizes the daughter and tells the daughter to shape up. The daughter sometimes rebels by doing things that will really offend the mother, like going out and getting a nose ring. It's all about telling the mother that she can't control her. So you've got an incredibly negative cycle between the mother and the daughter, but it's also a very, very negative attachment where the daughter cannot get any approval from the mother. You can see that she wants some emotional connection with the mother, but she can't get it. And she has nothing with the father.

What we would do in that situation is we look at the whole family, we look at the patterns, try to de-escalate the negative patterns, try to bring the father in more and have him connect with his daughter. Instead of not talking at all, have him be able to tell her, for example, "I'm silent because I don't know what to do. I don't know how to be a good father to you, so I stay quiet." And you know, and it's for the daughter to say, "But you've let me down. I needed you to be with me. Don't you understand?" The father weeps, and the daughter and him create a new space in their bond that they can come close together to talk about the mother and father, so father can come into the family and start helping the mother so she's not so overburdened by the daughter's problems. And she doesn't feel so much like a bad mom.

The goal is to diffuse the negative patterns between the mother and daughter, and then build more connection where the daughter says to the mother instead of refusing to speak, the daughter says, "I can never please you. It doesn't matter what I do. I can never please you." And weeps. At that time, the mother goes into total confusion. If the therapist isn't there, the mother will probably just wipe that out because she doesn't know what to do with it, but the therapist is there, so the therapist helps the mother stay focused on the daughter, listen, and process the information, [and] connect with her daughter. The fact that her daughter is actually wanting her approval and vulnerable, and then help the mother respond to the daughter by talking about that, the mother feels overwhelmed, she feels like a bad mother. This will start to connect that bond. So you go around and you look at the resources in the family to stop cycles, and then you look at the whole thing from the attachment frame, and you start de-escalating those stuck cycles and building moments of attachment, change events that create different kinds of attachments. So at the end of therapy, what you have is a mother and a father who are more of a team, and you understand that they probably need to go for couples therapy because they're so distant from each other, but they can support each other. You also have a daughter who can go to her father for support, and the father will support her.

What kind of families do you think benefit most from the model?
Well, that's a tricky one. The belief is that if you're going to use an emotionally focused approach, you have to have people who can talk about emotion. This isn't our experience at all. In fact, the research on couples therapy says that EFT works very well with men who are described as "inexpressive" by their partner. EFT is now being used in Eastern cultures like Japan and China. They have different ways of expressing emotion, but the bottom line is emotion is universal, and so is attachment. So, culturally, I think EFT can be adapted and used pretty universally. I think the kinds of couples and families who might have a hard time in EFT are the same couples and families that might have a hard time in any marital and family therapy approach. If we're working with a trauma couple or family, I go much slower. We pace it to peoples' needs, you have to slice it thinner, you have to contain emotion and help people work at a level that they can tolerate.

I think it's how it's done, not just the approach. As long as you have a therapist who knows how to stay close to peoples' experience, which we teach people to do in EFT, knows how to connect impassively with the client, and tailors the interventions to the client, and works very collaboratively with people. We don't have any issues around men having trouble in EFT, or women, being more responsive to EFT. We don't really have any of that. But it's about tailoring your interventions to the specific needs of the couple. If you have a skilled therapist, I think that EFT can be used very extensively.

Different models of therapy require the therapist to be directive or nondirective. In your opinion, what are the necessary characteristics that a therapist should possess to be effective with this model?
Well, the EFT therapist is a process consultant. The EFT therapist has a collaborative alliance with the couple and family. For example, I never allow clients to call me

Dr. Johnson. That's not just a personal preference. It's about an egalitarian, respectful, collaborative relationship. If you go to any basic EFT training that's done across the U.S., usually, the person that's training you will come across as very open, collaborative, and nonhierarchical. And I don't think that's an accident—the model promotes that. So, the EFT therapist is a process consultant.

So, for example, I reflect back peoples' process. I say . . . they're having a fight . . . I'll say, "Can we stop for a second? What's happening here? Let's look at what's happening here." And I'll reflect that, the way that they move in the dance, their steps in the dance, the emotions in the dance, how the emotions are, how they're getting stuck, [and] the consequences of the steps. Then, I might turn to one person and ask a question. A good EFT therapist leads sometimes, and follows sometimes, but basically you always have that collaborative alliance with people. When we lead the most, when we're the most directive, is when we're trying to create key change events in the second stage of EFT. When we're actually trying to create these bonding events [is] when people become more vulnerable to each other, more open, and they reach for each other and create this emotional responsiveness that is the essence of a good attachment bond. And which the research says is the essence of a good marriage. Houston (2001) looked at what predicted whether newlyweds were together and happy 4 years later. And what he found was that the main thing that predicted it was the emotional responsiveness.

So, the most directive the EFT therapist will be is when you've got this drama unfolding in front of you, and you've got this possibility for creating this emotional responsiveness. But generally, you're a collaborator. I absolutely wince when I hear things like people tell people that they should get a divorce, or they shouldn't be in the marriage. For me, that is an absolute unprofessional thing to do. You don't make peoples' choices for them. That's none of your business. You are there [to] help people see the choices they are making, ipso facto making, by the way they live their lives. And you are there to show people those choices, to make those choices explicit, to help them process those choices, to help them look at the implications of their actions, and then to crystallize those choices in a way that is good for them and for the people around them. You're not making those kinds of choices for people. I never, in all my years of working with families and couples, I have never told anyone that they should separate. That's not my decision to make.

I think it helps if you have a natural empathy. However, I want to say that you can train that. I think, when I first went to graduate school, doctoral school, I thought that I had quite a lot of empathy. I actually resented having to go and do a basic training on empathy. I had to do it I think because they weren't quite sure about me, and they wanted to make me go through this hoop. But I did it, and it taught me a lot. I think you learn how to be empathic. Especially if you've got a map. See, an attachment theory gives you a map to peoples' emotions. It helps if you are comfortable with emotions. Although I must say that one of the best therapists I ever trained was highly intellectual. When I first met her, I didn't think that she'd make a good EFT therapist, but she did. When she was with clients, she just used her intellect to really understand where they were at, and then she came down and stayed with them in their emotion brilliantly.

So it's hard to tell. I think you have to like to have that emotional connection with people. It's what you're promoting. If you're much more comfortable with the distant expert role, I don't think that you're going to like EFT. After all these years, I basically am a researcher, a writer. And basically a clinician. I can't do any of those things without being a clinician because I love doing the therapy. You have to have somebody who kind of likes that kind of emotional connection with people. If you get somebody who really finds that distasteful and wants to stay in a more distant, cognitive role, then I think they might not take to EFT.

How often does the client see you and for how long a period of time?
Most people take an hour. Personally, I like a little longer, I like an hour and 10 minutes.

We try to see people once a week, if we can. In research studies, we've seen them 10 to 12 times and we're very focused. And we try to make every session count, because we have to. In clinical practice, people are seen anything from 10 to 15 to 20 times. It is very important to make a distinction between research and practice because people mustn't feel that they've got to have it done in the same number of sessions that they see in the research studies. Like that's not feasible for most folks.

What are you looking for when you are in the session?
You'll ask people what the fight between them looks like, or what the distance between them looks like. You want people to describe the steps and their negative interaction so that you can really understand it in detail. You ask people if there are ever times they feel safe together. Do they have any positive cycles? Do they ever feel safe and connected? What are those times? You really want to know if people even know what you're talking about when you talk about safe connections. Sometimes, they don't. So you might ask people, do they know what it feels like to turn to someone else in times of uncertainty? John Bowlby talks about the times of uncertainty, or doubt, or vulnerability, change, painful events . . . that are when attachment needs really, really become front and center. So, you might say to somebody, "Who would you turn to in your family?" You want to know [if] are they used to the idea that they could turn to somebody and hold them close. Do they even know what that looks like? And sometimes people will tell you in no uncertain terms, they don't know what that looks like. That in fact, to do that would be weak and pathetic.

Then I understand then what I'm going to have to accommodate because they don't even know what I'm talking about when I talk about a safe emotional connection. They don't have any picture of it. So I'm going to have to help them, more than somebody who says, "Sure, I used to have that with her. I used to be able to come home and tell her about how overwhelmed I was at work, and she'd hold me, and now, we can't do that anymore." Well, that couple's probably going to be a lot easier, because they know what safe attachment looks like. You're going to get them back there faster. There are specific questions that you look [to answer] and those things are all laid in *Becoming an Emotionally Focused Couple Therapist: Workbook* (Johnson et al., 2005).

What is the assessment process of this model?
Once the therapist has looked at the couple, we usually see the couple together twice, look at the negative cycles, and then we see each person together once. And we try to use that session to create a real bond between each person and the therapist. After those, which will be session five, we really collaboratively set goals for the couple. We talk about what this process is all about, how they understand their image of their problems, which might be different than when they came in.

Who sets the goals, the client or the therapist?

A couple I just saw came in and said, "The problem is that he wants to visit his mother all the time, and I've told him if he visits his mother, I'll divorce him. The problem is his relationship with his mother. And I want you to problem solve that." Well, that's her view of the problem. Well, by the end of the second session, we've already moved that goal to talking about the fact that, actually, it's not his mother that's the problem, it's the fact that when they become vulnerable on any level, they can't communicate, and they get stuck in very rigid positions. When she addresses that he feels attacked, and he withdraws, and then he turns and becomes enraged and goes for her. And she becomes what she calls "biker lady." She becomes impermeable, cold, and sarcastic. And this is the problem, and it happens all the time—not just with the mother.

So by the fifth session, we're talking about that the goal is for them not to get stuck in this pattern. And they start to understand how much it's costing them. And she starts to hear for the first time what happens to him in the few minutes before his rage. Which is that he's devastated. She starts to understand for the first time that he sees her as this biker lady. And she starts to be able to talk about what that biker lady image is all about for her. And how terrified she is of what she calls the big D—the specter of divorce.

In other words, you make the basic goals of EFT, which in a sense are always the same, specific to the couple. But we're going to help them get out of this negative cycle, and then what we're going to do is promote those times that they've had a few of, but not many, where they can actually turn to each other for support and comfort, and they can hold each other and connect and share vulnerabilities. And we're going to help them create that deeper intimacy and closeness.

What are some commonly used interventions with this model?

Basically, we use a set of interventions to help people process their emotion further. A lot of empathic reflection where we reflect the emotional processing that they're going through. We use evocative questions like, "What's happening for you as he talks about this? What's it like for you to hear this?" We use what we call interpretation, but it's very close to the client's experience. Interpretation is [when] somebody says, "I'm upset," and the therapist says, "Could you help me? I don't quite understand. Is that sort of upset . . . what is that like? Would you help me with that? Is that almost like perhaps it's a little scary?" And if the person says, "No, it's not scary," we listen. But that's an interpretation. In other words, you just go one step further than the client, okay? We use lots of validation.

What you'd see in the EFT therapist is you'd see them reflecting a cycle, going in at some point and working with somebody on their emotions, and leading to the positions that they take in that cycle. So I understand when you're scared, then I guess it's a natural thing for you to kind of close the door between you and him. And you sort of shut down. But unfortunately he experiences that as being shut out, if I've got that right. We use very simple language. We evoke their emotion. That's one set of interventions.

The second set of interventions is more specifically focused on interactional shifts. Changing interactions. Then we'll track a process of interactions. We'll say, "Look at what just happened here right there. What happened right there in [those] 3 seconds between the two of you. You know, he turned to you. You asked him a question. He turned away. You upped the ante, and when he turned further away from you, you came out with this very powerful remark. It was almost like you smacked him to get his attention." And the woman says, "Yes." And that's what happens all the time. So you track the process. Then you might refrain some of that. You use reframes where we say, "He's shutting you out right now, not because you don't matter, but because you matter so much to him. He can't bear to look and see the disappointment in your eyes." That's a very usual reframe.

And we use enactments. They're very attachment oriented. They're not just any enactment where you're trying to change the interaction in any direction. You're trying to change it in a very specific direction, where people can express their vulnerability in a way that pulls the other person towards them. So somebody will say, "If I'm hearing you right, you're feeling very overwhelmed right now. This is one of these times when you just feel hopeless and helpless and you want to give up." And the person says, "Yes." And you say, . . . this is a withdrawn person who is described as just indifferent by their partner, you do an enactment, you crystallize the person's experience, and then you say, "Could you turn and tell her? Could you turn and tell her, 'I do shut down because I just feel so helpless and hopeless'?" And he does. And then you help him process what that felt like. You help her process what happens to her when he says that. So you're creating enactments, and those enactments start to become the basis of a new drama between the couple.

How do you know when your client is ready to terminate?
You can see it. If you have a very clear model and you have a map, you can see that they've gone through change events. You can see that they interact with each other differently. They'll tell you that they can step out of the negative models, and you can see them do it in front of you. They start to get stuck and you watch and see if they can step out. You see if they can take risks with each other and pull each other close. If you're a good EFT therapist and you're in the final stage of therapy, you don't say, "Show me," but you set it up. You say, "So, right now you're telling me that you're very threatened by this particular thing that's happening to you. Have you talked to Harry about it? Could you talk right now to him?" And you watch and you see how they do it.

You see that they are able to do what research says that people with a safe, strong bond can do (i.e., be open with the other person, be clear about their emotional needs and longings, ask the other person very clearly for what they want, stay emotionally connected and engaged, and ask the other person in a way that pulls the other person towards them, and that they can also respond to the other person).

The research tells us that this is what secure attachment is about. What we know is that securely attached people communicate better. They can be more assertive. They can be more expressive. They can confide more. They're much better at seeing patterns, meta-communicating about patterns. And this is not therapy research. This is the research on adult attachment. That securely attached people can do all these things. And that's what you see people do in the final stages of EFT. You watch them, you can see that they're very different than when they came in. You know when they're ready. And also, it's collaborative. If you're tuned in to the couple, you turn and say, "Well, I'm not sure you guys really need me anymore." They'll say, "Well, we were talking about that here in the car." Because they know that they're able to create that connection for themselves.

By the way, that connection, that need for a strong attachment bond, is wired in by millions of years of evolution. One of the reasons why we don't seem to have a problem with relapse in EFT, which is a big issue in couples and family therapy, is perhaps that once the couple are able to create these powerful moments of bonding, they are intoxicating. That's what gets people to risk and fall in love in the first place. Those moments of bonding are intoxicating. They are thrilling. People will keep doing them, just because they feel so good. They're wired in by millions of years of evolution.

What have you found to be the limitations of EFT?
I don't think that we know yet. We're still finding them out. There might be cultures where marriages are not seen as attachment bonds. I think arranged marriages, where people don't even know each other before they marry, might be different.

What suggestions do you have for students?
You need to have some sort of intense exposure to EFT. Not just one class in a graduate program. We do 5-day externships where you are given the theory, you see live sessions. In other words, you see the model used as well as read the theory. We have a workbook so that you could experience some of doing EFT (Johnson et al., 2005). There are tapes of EFT. You have to watch any therapy to see how it's done. You can't learn ballet from a book, and you can't learn therapy from a book. So, you have to have some intense exposure. You also need some formal supervision in EFT. That's getting not difficult to find these days because there are more and more people doing it. In most areas of the states, there are people who can do it, and also there are people on our website (www.iceeft.com).

Is there anything that you would like to add?
I really believe that couples therapy has a very important role to play in the treatment of depression, and the treatment of anxiety, and PTSD. Because I believe that the quality of your intimate relationship has very clear links to how you deal with depression and anxiety. And perhaps, sometimes, the best thing we can do for people is, rather than putting them on long-term antidepressants, is to look at the quality of their most intimate relationships. If you can create a safe haven, a secure base for people, that is a healing environment. And what we know is that secure bonds with the people we love are the natural antidote, for example, to trauma. Men don't fight wars alone. They fight wars with their battle buddies. So, that's what allows men to face death, that somebody faces it with them. So, couples therapy has a big role to play in addressing those two things, which we tend to think of as interpsychic issues.

Case Study

A mother calls and makes an appointment for her family to come to therapy. The family consists of a husband and wife, both in their 40s; their 15-year-old son; college-aged daughter; and the woman's father, age 82. Three years after the woman's mother died, her father developed Alzheimer's disease and moved in with the family 6 months ago. When his health began to deteriorate, the woman spent more time caring for him than for other members of the family. Three months ago, the 15-year-old son, who has been treated for attention deficit hyperactivity disorder since age 7, began to refuse to take his medication. The school is now calling home to report truancy by the 15-year-old boy.

During the session, the wife cries and the husband reports their relationship is strained, while occasionally rolling his eyes as his wife becomes tearful. He reports that he has had to take on more work because his wife had to quit her job to attend to her father's needs. The daughter is away at college and the wife smiles as she describes her as a straight-A student. The daughter was asked to attend the session but refused because she has a hard time with her grandfather's illness and dislikes the conflict that has developed at home.

Dr. Susan Johnson's Response to the Case Study

An emotionally focused couple and family therapist would view this case through the lens of attachment and bonding theory (Johnson, 2004, 2008). The therapist would take an integrated experiential and systemic approach to changing negative patterns of interaction and affect regulation strategies and creating more secure positive connections between the son and his parents and within the couple['s] relationship.

In systemic terms, emotion as experienced and expressed is seen as the organizing element in the dance—the patterned interactions between family members, and so is a key target and agent of change. The grandfather moving into the family would be seen as likely to impact the relationships in the family in the following ways:

- The son would experience a less secure connection with his mother as a result of her stress and preoccupation with her sick father. His acting out would be seen in terms of protesting this threat to his connection with his mother.

- The wife and mother would be overwhelmed and so in much greater need of a safe haven with her husband and his emotional responsiveness. If this is not forthcoming, conflict in this relationship is inevitable and will then exacerbate the wife's stress.

- The husband and father probably resents the extra load on the family and appears to dismiss his wife's distress, setting up a pattern of "wife demand and husband withdraw" that will erode any safe connection this couple has.

A spiral of negative interactions and emotional injury and isolation is then in place that can only exacerbate stress, reactivity, and loss of connection. The wife and mother seem especially isolated in this scenario. She might be at risk for depression or anxiety problems since she is unable to count on her husband or her daughter for emotional support. The EFT therapist's goal is to reprocess the key emotional responses and signals that cue and maintain negative interactions and to shape positive patterns of responsive bonding interactions.

The family would be seen as a whole, a collaborative alliance created with each person, a history taken and the moment-to-moment process of interaction noted. Sessions might then proceed as follows: Mother and son would be encouraged to explore attachment issues such as the son's sense of abandonment, his reactive anger at his mother, and how this fits with his truancy. Emotions and emotional signals would be clarified and enactments shaped where the mother can reassure her son of her caring, and he can talk about his attachment fears and needs.

A session with son and father might explore their relationship and how the father might offer safe emotional connection to his son. The couple would then be offered a number of sessions and encouraged to reframe their problems in terms of the cycle of distance and conflict that victimizes them both. The emotional music that directs their dance would be clarified and new response patterns created. For example, the therapist might unfold the moment where the wife (Sarah) weeps and the husband (Jeff) rolls his eyes by slowing down this process, reflecting, validating, and evoking deeper levels of emotion that are then shaped into clear signals about attachment distress and attachment needs. This may unfold as follows:

Therapist: So Jeff, when your wife weeps and says that she is overwhelmed, what happens for you? I notice that you sighed and kind of raised your eyes. Somehow, it is hard for you to tune into Sarah's distress, her sense of burden, her sadness?

Jeff: There is no point. The only way to deal with all this is to just suck it up. I have had to take on more projects. It's hard on everybody. I just try to roll with it.

Therapist: This is the only way that seems clear to you, to put your head down and keep cool, and when Sarah weeps and isn't "cool," then that seems pointless to you. You are too busy coping yourself to let yourself tune into her feelings and offer her comfort? (He nods in agreement and puts his hand on her knee. She moves away.)

Sarah: He isn't there for me. (She weeps more.)

Therapist: And that means that you are dealing with this—your father and your son's behavior and your own stress and grief all alone? (She nods.) And that adds 10 tons to the burden, doesn't it? (She nods empathically.) This is a time when the best or only "solution" is for you to feel close to Jeff and for you both to comfort each other. (She nods again.) When he says expressions of upset are pointless, how do you feel?

Sarah: I feel just left. It's like he walks away when I need him the most. Abandoned. Then I get mad at him and yell—and that pushes us even deeper into this dark hole.

Therapist: (First recaps the negative cycle where she yells and demands and he withdraws)— And underneath all this yelling, you feel alone and "left"? That is scary? (She agrees.) After a while, even if he does reach out—he just put his hand on yours—it's hard to take in. Yes? Can you tell him, "I am so alone here. And that is so scary. This is when I need you the most. But it is hard to let you in right now."

Sarah tells him this and goes on to elaborate on her need for connection with Jeff. With the therapist's help, Jeff is able to stay accessible and responsive and talk of his own desire to numb out so as to not be "a wimp" and avoid his sense of failure that he cannot "fix" this situation and make his family "all better." Jeff and Sarah begin a positive bonding cycle of sharing and connection that offers an antidote to the stress and distress they both feel. They see the stress and their negative cycle as the enemy, not each other. They can then collaborate more effectively as parents and caregivers.

Therapy continues with a session with both parents and their son to help the parents come together to create a safe haven attachment bond with their son where he can reach for them and they can respond empathically to his needs. A final session would bring all the family together, including the daughter if she would come, to consolidate gains and to help everyone create a positive frame on caring for the grandfather and each other.

KEY TERMS

Attachment   The theoretical concept proposed by John Bowlby that emphasizes the human tendency to reach out for closeness to other people, especially caregivers. Attachment theory is used heavily in emotionally focused therapy as a means to understand close relationships.

Attachment orientations   The habitual response strategies that a person creates to regulate his or her emotions in a close relationship. These response patterns are influences by past and present relationships.

Introjects   An individual's internal image that has a direct influence on his or her behavior in relationships but is outside of his or her awareness.

Introjective identification   A phenomenon where an individual will take a part of another person's identity that he or she finds attractive and adopt as part of his or her own ego. This allows an individual to feel more like a person that he or she admires or likes.

Mutual attribution   A situation where an individual who is in negative or destructive relationships tends to perceive the person in the current relationship as a hurtful person from his or her past.

Mutual projection   A process in which one individual unconsciously projects "bad" objects within himself or herself onto another person.

Parental projections   These are the projections of traits, talents, wishes, failures, and negative aspects from the parent onto his or her child. The children often confirm these projections by acting out behaviorally to the expectations.

Projective identification   A process during which an individual projects bad thoughts and beliefs onto another person and relates to that person as if such projections were truly a part of that person.

Unconscious contracts   Marital bargains where each person in the relationship behaves in accord with the other's perceptions and manipulative demands for the purposes of getting the other partner to behave as he or she wants.

REFERENCES

Baucom, D. H., Shoham, V., Mueser, K. T., Daiuto, A. D., & Stickle, T. R. (1998). Empirically supported couple and family interventions for marital distress and adult mental health problems. *Journal of Consulting and Clinical Psychology*, *66*(1), 53–88.

Bowlby, J. (1958). The nature of the child's tie to his mother. *International Journal of Psychoanalysis*, *39*(5), 350–373.

Bowlby, J. (1969). *Attachment and loss: Vol. 1. Attachment.* London, United Kingdom: Hogarth Press.

Bowlby, J. (1973). *Attachment and loss: Vol. 2. Separation: Anxiety and anger.* London, United Kingdom: Hogarth Press.

Bowlby, J. (1980). *Attachment and loss: Vol. 3. Loss: Sadness and depression.* London, United Kingdom: Hogarth Press.

Denton, W. H., Burleson, B. R., Clark, T. E., Rodriguez, C. P., & Hobbs, B. V. (2000). A randomized trial of emotion-focused therapy for couples in training clinic. *Journal of Marital and Family Therapy*, *26*(1), 65–78.

Dessaulles, A., Johnson, S. M., & Denton, W. H. (2003). Emotion-focused therapy for couples in the treatment of depression: A pilot study. *American Journal of Family Therapy*, *31*, 345–353.

Greenberg, L. S., Ford, C. L., Alden, L. S., & Johnson, S. M. (1993). In-session change in emotionally focused therapy for couples. *Journal of Consulting and Clinical Psychology, 61*(1), 78–84.

Greenberg, L. S., & Johnson, S. M. (1985). Different effects of experiential and problem-solving interventions in resolving marital conflict. *Journal of Clinical and Consulting Psychology, 53*(2), 175–184.

Greenberg, L. S., & Johnson, S. M. (1988). *Emotionally focused therapy for couples.* New York, NY: The Guilford Press.

Hazan, C., & Shaver, P. R. (1987). Romantic love conceptualized as an attachment process. *Journal of Personality and Social Psychology, 52*(3), 511–524.

Johnson, S. M. (1996). *The practice of emotionally focused marital therapy: Creating connection.* Florence, KY: Brunner-Mazel.

Johnson, S. M. (2002). Emotionally focused couple therapy with trauma survivors. New York, NY: The Guilford Press.

Johnson, S. M. (2004). *The practice of emotionally focused couple therapy: Creating connection.* New York, NY: Brunner-Routledge.

Johnson, S. M. (2006). Integration in emotionally focused therapy: A reply to Simon. *The Family Journal: Counseling and Therapy for Couples and Families, 14*, 1–4.

Johnson, S. M. (2007). The contribution of emotionally focused couples therapy [Special edition]. *Journal of Contemporary Psychology: Humanistic Psychology.*

Johnson, S. M., Bradley, B., Furrow, J., Lee, A., Palmer, G., Tilley, D., & Woolley, S. (2005). *Becoming an emotionally focused couple therapist: The workbook.* New York, NY: Brunner-Routledge.

Johnson, S. M., & Denton, W. H. (2007). Emotionally focused couple therapy: Creating secure connections. In A. S. Gurman & N. S. Jacobson (Eds.), *Clinical handbook of couple therapy.* New York, NY: The Guilford Press.

Johnson, S. M., & Greenberg, L. S. (1985). Differential effects of experiential and problem-solving interventions in resolving marital conflict. *Journal of Consulting and Clinical Psychology, 53*(2), 175–184.

Johnson, S. M., & Greenberg, L. S. (1987). Emotionally focused marital therapy: An overview. *Psychotherapy: Theory, Research & Practice, 24*, 552–560.

Johnson, S. M., & Greenman, P. (2006). The path to a secure bond: Emotionally focused couple therapy. *Journal of Clinical Psychology: In Session, 62*(5), 597–609.

Johnson, S. M., Hunsley, J., Greenberg, L. S., & Schindler, D. (1999). Emotionally focused couples therapy: Status and challenges. *Journal of Clinical Psychology: Science and Practice, 6*, 67–79.

Johnson, S. M., Maddeaux, C., & Blouin, J. (1998). Emotionally focused family therapy for bulimia: Changing attachment patterns. *Psychology: Theory, Research and Practice, 35*, 238–247.

Johnson, S. M., & Talitman, E. (1997). Predictors of success in emotionally focused marital therapy. *Journal of Marital and Family Therapy, 23*(2), 135–152.

Kowal, J., Johnson, S. M., & Lee, A. (2003) Chronic illness in couples: A case for emotionally focused therapy. *Journal of Marital and Family Therapy, 29*(3), 299–310.

Makinen, J. A., & Johnson, S. M. (2006). Resolving attachment injuries in couples using EFT: Steps towards forgiveness and reconciliation. *Journal of Consulting and Clinical Psychology, 74*(6), 1055–1064.

McDonald, S. G. (2001). The real and the researchable: A brief review of the contributions of John Bowlby (1907–1990). *Perspectives on Psychiatric Care, 37*(2), 60–64.

Moser, M. B., & Johnson, S. M. (2008). The integration of systems and humanistic approaches in emotionally focused therapy for couples. *Person-Centered and Experiential Psychotherapies, 7*(4), 262–278.

Palmer, G., & Johnson, S. M. (2002). Becoming an emotionally focused therapist. *Journal of Couple and Relationship Therapy, 1*(3), 1–20.

Reid, R., & Woolley, S. R. (2006). Using emotionally focused therapy for couples to resolve attachment raptures created by hypersexual behavior. *Sexual Addiction & Compulsivity, 13*, 219–239.

Rholes, S. W., & Simpson, J. A. (2004). Adult attachment: Theory, research, and clinical implications. New York, NY: The Guilford Press.

Scharf, R. S. (2000). *Theories of psychotherapy & counseling: Concepts and cases.* Belmont, CA: Brooks/Cole.

Walker, J. G., Johnson, S. M., Manion, I., & Cloutier, P. (1996). Emotionally focused marital intervention for couples with chronically ill children. *Journal of Consulting and Clinical Psychology, 64*(5), 1029–1036.

Whiffen, V., & Johnson, S. M. (1998). An attachment theory framework for the treatment of child bearing depression. *Clinical Psychology: Science and Practice, 5,* 478–493.

RECOMMENDED READING LIST

Books

Greenberg, L. S., & Johnson, S. M. (1988). *Emotionally focused therapy for couples.* New York, NY: The Guilford Press.

Hertlein, K. M., & Viers, D. (2005). *The couple and family therapist's notebook: Homework, handouts, and activities for use in marital and family therapy.* Binghamton, NY: Haworth Clinical Practice Press.

Johnson, S. M. (1996). *Creating connection: The practice of emotionally focused marital therapy.* Florence, KY: Brunner-Mazel.

Johnson, S. M. (2002). *Emotionally focused couple therapy with trauma survivors: Strengthening attachment bonds.* New York, NY: The Guilford Press.

Johnson, S. M. (2004). *The practice of emotionally focused couple therapy: Creating connection* (2nd ed.). New York, NY: Brunner-Routledge.

Sandler, J. (1995, July). *On attachment to internal objects.* Paper presented at the conference: Clinical Implications of Attachment: The Work of Mary Main, University College, London, United Kingdom.

Wexler, D. (1991). *The adolescent self: Strategies for self-management, self-soothing, and self-esteem in adolescents.* New York, NY: Norton.

Wolf, E. (1988). *Treating the self: Elements of clinical self psychology.* New York, NY: The Guilford Press.

Articles

Bartholomew, K., & Horowitz, L. M. (1991). Attachment styles among young adults: A test of a four-category model. *Journal of Personality and Social Psychology, 61*(2), 226–244.

Dankoski, M. E. (2001). Pulling on the heart string: An emotionally focused approach to family life cycle transitions. *Journal of Marital and Family Therapy, 27*(2), 177–187.

Denton, W. H. (2008). Conducting an initial session in emotion focused therapy for couples. Suggestions for beginning EFT therapists. *Journal of Couple and Relationship Therapy, 7*(2), 113–135.

Diamond, G. S., Siqueland, L., & Diamond, G. M. (2003). Attachment-based family therapy for depressed adolescents: Programmatic treatment development. *Clinical Child and Family Psychology Review, 6*(2), 107–127.

Doherty, N. A., & Feeney, J. A. (2004). The composition of attachment networks throughout the adult years. *Personal Relationships, 11,* 469–488.

Harvey, A. M. (2003). Interview with Dr. Sue Johnson: Emotion in family therapy. *Journal of Feminist Family Therapy, 15*(1), 53–63.

Henderson, A. J. Z., Bartholomew, K., & Dutton, D. G. (1997). He loves me; He loves me not: Attachment and separation resolution of abused women. *Journal of Family Violence, 12*(2), 169–191.

Jencius, M. (2003). This thing called love: An interview with Susan Johnson. *Family Journal, 11*(4), 427–434.

Johnson, S. M. (1998). Listening to the music: Emotion as a natural part of the systems theory. *Journal of Systemic Therapies, 17*(2), 1–17.

Johnson, S. M., & Greenman, P. (2006). The path to a secure bond: Emotionally focused couple therapy. *Journal of Clinical Psychology, 62*(5), 597–609.

Johnson, S. M., & Talitman, E. (1997). Predictors of success in emotionally focused marital therapy. *Journal of Marital and Family Therapy, 23*(2), 135–152.

Luke, M. A., Maio, G. R., & Carnelley, K. B. (2004). Attachment models of the self and others: Relations with self-esteem, humanity-esteem, and parental treatment. *Personal Relationships, 11*(3), 281–303.

Middelberg, C. V. (2001). Projective identification in common couple dances. *Journal of Marital and Family Therapy, 27*(3), 341–352.

Morgan, B., & Mac Millan, P. (1999). Helping clients move toward constructive change: A three-phased integrated counseling model. *Journal of Counseling & Development, 77*(2), 153–159.

Peluso, P. R., & Macintosh, H. (2007). Emotion-focused couples therapy and individual psychology: A dialogue across theories. *The Journal of Individual Psychology, 63*(3), 247–269.

Pickover, S. (2002). Breaking the cycle: A clinical example of disrupting an insecure attachment system. *Journal of Mental Health Counseling, 24*(4), 358–366.

Thweatt, R. W. (1980). Divorce: Crisis intervention guided by attachment theory. *American Journal of Psychotherapy, 34*(2), 240–245.

Medical Family Therapy

15

Teresa Masdon

There are no psychological problems without biological features and there are no biomedical problems without psychological features.

—George Engel, MD

INTRODUCTION

Coined in 1992, the term *medical family therapy* refers to the "biopsychosocial treatment of individuals and families who are dealing with medical problems" (McDaniel, Hepworth, & Doherty, 1992, p. 2; emphasis added). Illness makes unpredictable visits, which can disrupt family relationships in significant ways (Watson & McDaniel, 2005). Because sickness contains biological components as well as psychosocial dimensions, any illness may have a systemic impact on a family's life (Wright, Watson, & Bell, 1996).

For example, the father who defines himself by his hard work and ability to provide for his family may find his self-value shattered with a diagnosis of Lou Gehrig's disease (muscular degeneration). This father not only fights the physical changes overtaking his body, but he also fights the depression that can occur due to the loss of his identity as a "provider." His faith may be shaken and the roles among his family members may be forced to change as he becomes more dependent on his wife and children for support. In this way, illness not only affects every aspect of who people are as individuals, but it also creates relational issues (McDaniel, Hepworth, & Doherty, 1999).

It is important to understand that illness means different things to different people. For most of the modern developed world, illness can include acute sickness, disabilities, terminal diagnosis, and chronic disease (McDaniel et al., 1999). Medical science has made such advanced strides in the successful treatment of many diseases that families now face new challenges; for example, illnesses such as AIDS or certain cancers, which were at one point fatal, can now be managed as chronic diseases. Living with these diseases presents its own challenges for both the patient and his or her family.

Statistics show that nearly 50% of Americans suffer from a chronic condition, and they represent more than 80% of health care spending. People with functional limitations and chronic conditions need more assistance and help with daily living, placing heavy demand on services (The Lewin Group, 2010).

Although still below 2 percent, the proportion of people ages 50–64 who reported needing help with personal care activities increased significantly from 1997 to 2007. The proportions needing help with routine household chores and indicating difficulty with physical functions were stable. These patterns contrast with reported declines in disability among the population age sixty-five and older. Particularly concerning among those aged 50–64 are significant increases in limitations in specific mobility-related activities, such as getting into and out of bed. Musculoskeletal conditions remained the most commonly cited causes of disability at these ages. There were also substantial increases in the attribution of disability to depression, diabetes, and nervous system conditions for this age group. (Martin, Freedman, Schoeni, & Andreski, 2010)

According to the American Society of Consultant Pharmacists, the most common chronic diseases afflicting older people are as follows:

- Adult-onset diabetes
- Arthritis
- Kidney and bladder problems
- Dementia
- Parkinson's disease
- Glaucoma
- Lung disease
- Cataracts
- Osteoporosis
- Enlarged prostate
- Alzheimer's disease
- Macular degeneration
- Depression
- Cardiovascular disease (ParentGiving, 2010)

Older people often become disenchanted when diagnosed, as if the doctor attempts to take away their freedom when he or she gives them the diagnosis. While health care costs rise, so do caregivers' fees, and family members are often called on to take charge of care.

Between 2000 and 2020, the number of Americans with chronic conditions is projected to increase from 125 million to 157 million, and the number of Americans with two or more chronic diseases is projected to increase from 57 million to 81 million. People with chronic conditions accounted for more than 78% of health care expenditures in 2000, and this percentage is expected to increase in the coming decades (Anderson, 2003).

A need has surfaced today for a family therapist who can address families affected by medical problems using a biopsychosocial perspective (Blount & Bayona, 1994; Campbell, McDaniel, & Seaburn, 1992). The next section will briefly discuss the historical developments in both medicine and psychology that led to this development.

HISTORY AND LEADING FIGURES

The medical model is the traditional approach to the diagnosis and treatment of illness as practiced by physicians in the Western world since the time of Koch and Pasteur. The physician focuses on the defect, or dysfunction, within the patient, using a problem-solving approach. The medical history, physical examination, and diagnostic tests provide the basis for the identification and treatment of a specific illness. The medical model is thus focused on the physical and biologic aspects of specific diseases and conditions. (Mosby's Medical Dictionary, 2009)

When viewed through a mental health lens, the "medical model" represents an approach to issues of mental health that incorporates aspects of both science and biology without being synonymous with either (Grobstein & Cyckowski, 2006).

One critic of the medical model was a biologist named von Bertalanffy who developed general systems theory. He stipulated that science had become too reductionistic by breaking phenomena into such small units, and that the analyses were no longer meaningful (von Bertalanffy, 1960). The disease model of medical science was too simplistic and inadequate to explain the complexities of human relationships. Instead of reducing an organism into the properties of its parts, systems theory concentrates on the interaction between the parts that connect them to a whole.

Interestingly, family therapy was heavily influenced by two former biologists, Gregory Bateson and Murray Bowen (Doherty, McDaniel, & Hepworth, 1994). Considered the founders of family therapy, Bateson and Bowen joined psychotherapy's "flight from biology." Symptoms in an individual began to be viewed as part of the interactions within an entire system, such as a family. Family system scientists began to explore the correlation of the disease process and family interactions. In the 1970s, family therapists Salvador Minuchin and Bernice Rosman, together with pediatrician Lester Baker (1978), studied the interconnection between family systems and the psychosomatic childhood diseases of diabetes, asthma, and anorexia nervosa (Minuchin et al., 1975).

In 1977, George Engel, an internist, published a theory—the biopsychosocial model—that was a foundational step toward a shift in perspective on medical illness. Engel proposed that a fully comprehensive and scientific model of medicine involves the simultaneous consideration of biological, psychological, and social issues (Engel, 1977, 1980). Dr. Engel insisted that all medical issues have psychological components and all psychosocial issues have biological features.

In the 1980s and early 1990s, a substantial amount of research explored the relationships between family factors and health. These endeavors resulted in a greater recognition of the importance of the family's dynamics in all aspects of health care (see, for example, Aronson, 1996; Campbell, 1986; Fisher, Ransom, Terry, Lipkin, & Weiss, 1992; Turk & Kerns, 1985). It became evident that the exclusively biological focus of medical science was too limited to help families dealing with chronic illnesses, which are rising in incidence (Doherty & Campbell, 1988). Nor has the biomedical model been successful in assisting individuals in making healthy lifestyle modifications. Indeed, as presented by the Centers for Disease Control (2010), 7 of the 10 leading causes of death in the United States could be substantially reduced by improving just five habits: diet, smoking cessation, exercise, moderate alcohol intake, and correct use of antihypertensive medications (Doherty & Campbell, 1988). Nearly half of all causes of morbidity and mortality in the United States are linked to behavioral and social factors.

Unfortunately, although the importance of psychological and social factors in health has become more obvious, doctors have become more limited in their abilities to effectively address such concerns. To effectively run a business, family practitioners have had to increase the number of patients who come to their offices, which has reduced their available time with each patient (Aronson, 1996). Virtually all areas of health care have been widely altered with the rapid expansion in health maintenance organizations (HMOs), preferred provider organizations (PPOs), and other health care organizations. Given financial and time constraints, many physicians may overlook the influence of family as well as the patient's emotional needs.

Based on the biopsychosocial systems theory developed from Engel's model, medical family therapy has emerged to address the behavioral and social factors affecting health

(McDaniel et al., 1992; Watson & McDaniel, 2005). Many players have had a part in promoting medical family therapy, which are too numerous to list. Among the key leading figures that helped define this perspective were Susan McDaniel, William Doherty, Thomas Campbell, Jerri Hepworth, Dennis Turk, Robert Kerns, and John Rolland. Over the past two decades, a growing body of literature confirms the need for collaboration between mental health care professionals and medical health care professionals to provide optimal patient care (Blount & Bayona, 1994; McDaniel et al., 1992; Rolland, 1994; Seaburn, Lorenz, Gunn, Gawinski, & Mauksch, 2003; Turk & Kerns, 1985).

Leading Figures

Susan McDaniel, PhD, is the director of the Institute for the Family in Psychiatry at the University of Rochester. She enjoys the many philosophical, theoretical, and clinical commonalities between family therapy and family medicine and their integration into the practice of biopsychosocial medicine. Her special interests are in family medicine and collaboration between mental health specialists and primary care practitioners. Her publications include books entitled *Integrating Family Therapy: Handbook of Family Psychology and Systems Theory* (1995) with Richard Mikesell and Don-David Lusterman, *The Shared Experience of Illness* (1997) with Jeri Hepworth and Bill Doherty, *A Casebook for Integrating Family Therapy* (2002) with Don-David Lusterman and Carol Philpot, *Primary Care Psychology* (2004), and *Family Therapy* (2009).

William J. Doherty, PhD, is a professor of family social science and the director of the Marriage and Family Therapy Program at the University of Minnesota. He is the past president of the National Council on Family Relations and a pioneer in the field of family therapy, particularly as it pertains to illness. Along with Mendenhall, he is the coauthor of *Partners in Diabetes: A New Initiative in Diabetes Care* (2005) and *Citizen Care: A Model for Engaging Patients, Families and Communities as Coproducers of Health Care* (2006; Doherty & Mendenhall, 2006).

INTRODUCTION TO MEDICAL FAMILY THERAPY

What is meant by the term *family*? One broad definition given by Turk and Kerns (1985) states that "families are groups composed of members who have mutual obligations to provide a broad range of emotional and material support" (p. 2). In today's society, families are not limited to blood relatives or members who live together; thus, the operative phrase is "mutual obligations." Families behave with a set of fairly well-defined beliefs, which are the lenses to view the world and thereby attach meanings (Wright et al., 1996). To facilitate change requires the consideration and understanding of the individual and family's beliefs. The focus of medical family therapy is to magnify the families' beliefs that sustain hope and aid in their empowerment while minimizing the ideas that foster blame, shame, or guilt.

Medical family therapy actually represents a metaframework that encompasses overarching principles within which any model of psychotherapy can be practiced (McDaniel et al., 1992, 1997; Ruddy & McDaniel, 2003). What sets medical family therapy apart from all other family therapy theories is the routine collaboration with medical professionals as well as seeing illness as part of the system (McDaniel et al., 1992). Collaboration is a primary aspect; medical family therapists need to have an understanding of the medical system to embrace a multidisciplinary team approach with physicians and other health care providers (Ruddy & McDaniel, 2003). Sometimes, these collaborations take place across settings, such as in private practice, a medical clinic, or perhaps within the same institutional setting. To successfully integrate illness into the therapy, the family therapist needs to have a working knowledge of diseases and their influence on individuals and families (Doherty et al., 1994).

McDaniel et al. (1992) identify the two major goals of medical family therapy as promoting agency and communion. Agency is the active participation of the patient and family, as well as self-determination for the patient's own care. There are times when a family therapist will promote agency by helping "the patient and family set limits on the amount of control the illness or disability has over their lives" (Doherty et al., 1994, p. 39). Within the family itself, the therapist can encourage the agency of the patient in relation to other family members by assisting them to set boundaries on a family member's helpfulness or in supporting the patient's efforts to assertively ask for help.

Communion refers to the emotional interconnections that are often torn by illness, disability, and interaction with the health care system. For patients, communion represents the sense of loving care and support by family members, friends, and professionals. In helping patients and families obtain communion, the medical family therapist guides families to band together to cope with an illness while securing maximum autonomy.

The psychosocial model of illness designed by John Rolland facilitates the examination of individual and family dynamics surrounding the disease (Rolland, 1994). His conceptual model identifies the components of different illnesses that stress families in various ways. Rolland divided these dimensions into four categories: onset, course, outcome, and degree of incapacitation. In this integrative model, Rolland emphasizes the powerful influence of a family's belief systems, especially those associated with ethnicity, gender, and culture.

When a family's belief system conflicts with the belief system of the health care provider's, then noncompliance with medical recommendations can be expected. This may present as rejection of the treatment plan by the patient or family members.

To affect change in a family system, the skills of a medical family therapist need to include the ability to solicit the illness history, listen empathetically, respect the patient's defenses, and normalize negative feelings (Doherty & Campbell, 1988). Family therapists can also help families embrace a broader perspective and reduce the tendency to become entirely focused on the illness (Sholevar & Sahar, 2003). Frequently, an illness can overcome a family and disturb prior roles among the members. The role that gender plays in a particular family can present just one difficulty in a family's ability to adjust to the demands of illness (Watson & McDaniel, 2005):

> For example, unacceptable feelings may arise related to ways in which men or women respond to illness that run counter to their gender script. A man who is weepy or a woman who is angry in response to a new diagnosis may feel the additional burden of criticism from others. Medical family therapy works to counteract the dehumanizing experience of these gender scripts. (p. 258)

Even with the increased focus on psychosocial issues in the training programs of physicians, doctors may not be able to equally attend to psychosocial and medical issues. Medical family therapy offers a possible middle ground (McDaniel et al., 1992). Family therapists can possibly increase a family's awareness of these issues, thus enlarging the beliefs influencing role options (Lyness, 2003). Collaboration with medical providers is an essential element of medical family therapy; yet, most family therapists may still be uncomfortable with this approach. However, exclusive focus on psychosocial issues minimizes the important role that illness can play on the family system. Omitting consideration of biological issues prevents the therapist from adhering to a true "systems" approach.

Training

Training plays a major role in developing this systemic perspective. In some states, for example, marriage and family therapists are required to learn about disease processes. However, most are not required to study the interconnection of health issues and families. Therefore, family therapists may feel uncomfortable in addressing illness with families. What is helpful for the family therapists to recognize is that they do not need medical expertise to be helpful to a family dealing with a disease or chronic condition. Family therapists have skills that physicians do not have, and thinking about one's expertise in that way often provides reassurance.

Medical family therapy is distinguished from other therapies in that family therapists pay "mindful attention to the systemic and reciprocal influences among the illness, the individual, the family, and the medical system (including insurance providers) to help clients achieve their particular goals for therapy" (Brucker et al., 2005, p. 132). These goals might include help with lifestyle changes, better coping with a chronic illness or disability, greater ability to handle a medical regimen, more effective communication with physicians, and increased flexibility in facing a terminal medical diagnosis (Campbell et al., 1992). For the medical family therapist, the systemic impact of illness is thoroughly explored. Doherty et al. (1994) assert that "the fundamental tenet of medical family therapy is that _all human problems are biopsychosocial systems problems_" (p. 34; emphasis added). More than ever, families are becoming aware that problems on the physical level are connected to every other aspect of the individual and the family. Working alongside the health care team, medical family therapy has emerged to assist families to obtain optimal health in the complex systems of life.

Historically, medical preparation has emphasized the hard sciences, including anatomy, physiology, biochemistry, pathology, microbiology, and pharmacology (Doherty & Campbell, 1988). According to Campbell (1986), "most physicians are not trained in dealing with the psychosocial aspects of health care and are more comfortable ignoring it" (p. 137). However, currently, family practice residency programs across the United States strive to broaden the physician's awareness of the family system. These programs include consideration of the patient's life outside the hospital and what sickness means as a life experience for the patient and family (Moore, Block, Style, & Mitchell, 1994). In the case of families with ill children or children whose parents are ill, the medical family therapist can be of enormous help. For example, the American Cancer Society states:

> _Children take cues about cancer from parents and other adults. How a child reacts to a cancer diagnosis often depends on how their parents or other close adults handle the crisis. Kids learn through their parents' behavior. Although parents know this, they still are under a great deal of stress and have their own intense feelings of fear and uncertainty. Sometimes, with the right kind of help, parents and their children_ can _and_ do _learn to cope well with cancer and its treatments. (Christ & Christ, 2006; emphasis added)_

The impending death of a child affects every member of the family. Parents may be overwhelmed by the decisions they must make about the child's terminal care. Parents, siblings, and the dying child may experience an array of emotions, including sadness, anger, and guilt. Dying children, especially, may have difficulty expressing their feelings and become upset with parents, or siblings are upset. By giving family members the information they need, family therapists provide an opportunity for the family to talk about their feelings and suggestions for making the last days count (Lewis, Brecher, Reaman, & Sahler, 2010).

THEORETICAL ASSUMPTIONS

Most patients and families who present to medical family therapy have become stuck in or around an illness or health condition. As mentioned earlier in the chapter, medical family therapy is a metaframework that encompasses overarching principles within which any model of psychotherapy can be practiced. For example, there are medical family therapists who take a narrative approach (see Chapter 13 for more on narrative therapy) in assisting families facing complicated illness issues. The therapist may help that family re-story their lives in such a way that the illness is no longer in charge. Alternatively, perhaps a therapist may prefer to use a Bowenian approach (see Chapter 3) and examine how anxiety perpetuates the interactions of families faced with disease. There are truly no limits to this perspective.

There are two aspects that set medical family therapy apart from the other models of family therapy. The primary distinguishing feature of medical family therapy is that therapists comfortably address the influential role that illness has on the family system.

Therapists can do this in several ways, as in exploring a medical genogram or simply discovering the meanings that each family member has attached to the intruding disease process.

The medical genogram provides a quick and useful context in which to evaluate an individual's <u>health risks</u>. (Genograms were introduced in Chapter 1.) Knowledge of diseases and conditions that occur within a family can give a health care team invaluable information that may aid in a swift, accurate diagnosis and treatment of health problems. In addition, knowledge of diseases and illnesses that "run" in families can give individuals an important head start in pursuing effective preventive measures. A medical genogram is helpful in determining patterns of disease or illness within a family. Medical genograms can include many generations; however, four generations may prove to be enough detail. See Figure 15.1 for some common symbols used in medical genograms.

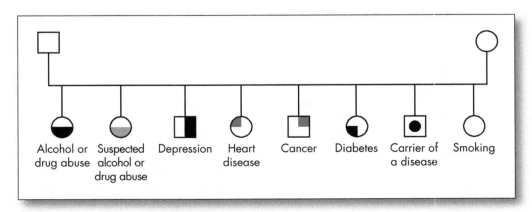

FIGURE 15.1 ■ Medical genogram legend.
Source: GenoPro®. http://www.genopro.com/Newsletters/2007/02/MedicalGenogramLegend.gif

The other key component of medical family therapy is collaboration, which has been discussed earlier. The medical family therapist must be comfortable in a multidisciplinary team approach with physicians and other health care professionals. Typically, collaboration means being available or "on call" when physicians in an acute care setting need the family therapist to talk to a patient. On one occasion, for example, a young woman who was engaged to be married was told she had terminal cancer and only 6 months to live. After the doctor told her the prognosis, he asked the family therapist, Michelle, to talk with the patient and her fiancée. After an hour of conversation, the young woman and her fiancée left the hospital to get married. Thereafter, Michelle was there while she entered care and when she passed away as a support.

Collaboration between the family therapist and medical staff often means attending staff meetings where the family therapist provides input into the social and psychosocial states of the patients. On some occasions, the family therapist is educated by the physician to better understand the treatments. In general, the family therapist is the support that the system needs when a problem enters a family and can help the family find ways to deal with and support the patient.

View of the Family and Client

The medical family therapist views the client and family as interconnected to each other as well as to the presenting physical illness. With this perspective, it is left to the client and family to define who makes up the family. Many times, illness can disrupt a system and change previous roles. For example, a man who becomes paralyzed after a stroke may have a wife who is uncomfortable assisting with his personal care needs. A distant relative or even a close friend who steps in to provide this care then is considered an important member of this redefined family. The family therapist will offer support and acknowledgment to the primary caregiver who often feels very stressed and alone in care. By providing the caregiver with information on resources and encouraging the caregiver to take time for himself or herself, the caregiver gets a welcome relief with less guilt. As with any family dynamic where one person carries the most burden, the helpful family therapist will encourage the primary caregiver to delegate and discuss with other family members what his or her needs are so that he or she has family support, too.

View on How Change Occurs

The medical family therapist views change as occurring throughout multiple systems. For example, change on the physical level would be expected to precipitate change on the emotional, mental, and relational levels in an individual and the family. In this respect, a medical family therapist may address a specific issue relating to one system with the intent of fostering change throughout every dimension.

For example, the medical family therapist might address the mental anguish of a wife whose husband suddenly has to deal with a chronic illness. The wife takes on all of the responsibility for the husband's medication and doctor's appointments, putting aside her personal activities and jeopardizes her job. She becomes irritable with her husband who then feels worse. The family therapist could intervene and speak with the husband about how he could begin taking care of himself more so that the wife could live her life slightly as she had before. This eases the relationship between the spouses; the husband feels less helpless and more independent, which pleases the wife, who then feels relaxed enough to pursue an occasional outing.

Therapist's Role

The role of the medical family therapist is one of collaboration with other health care providers and to be a curious, unbiased observer of the biopsychosocial systems of the client and the family. Included in this role, the family therapist must be able to obtain a thorough illness history for the medical genogram and be comfortable in discussing disease process and treatment, even though the family therapist has little to do with the actual medical treatment. He or she is there to provide a layman's explanation or psychoeducation (see Chapter 16) to the family of what is occurring with the patient, as explained to him or her by the physician. Then, using the specific interventions of any family therapy model, the medical family therapist works to magnify the families' beliefs that sustain hope and aid in their empowerment while minimizing the ideas that foster blame, shame, or guilt. The work of the medical family therapist is to help the family expand their understanding of the "problem" and help them explore possible solutions that best fit their family where they are right now.

Interventions

Flexibility is needed for the medical family therapist to not only maneuver across various systems in an individual and family—the biological, psychological, emotional, and relational—but the therapist must also be flexible to the setting where therapy takes place. A medical family therapist may find intakes requested while the patient is still in the acute care facility, for example. There are other times that it may benefit a medical family therapist to visit the family at their residence because the ill family member has terminal or incapacitating illness that prevents him or her from leaving their home. Being able to adapt to many different scenarios, as well as working with many different players, helps to ensure successful outcomes for the medical family therapist.

The specific interventions of a medical family therapist will reflect on the particular model of family therapy that is used. For example, if a medical family therapist prefers a narrative approach (see Chapter 13), then the therapist will assist the client and family to re-story their lives around the illness. The interview process will include a detailed illness history, which may be represented in a medical genogram. The medical family therapist will also interview and gather information from other health care practitioners working in collaboration.

MEDICAL FAMILY THERAPY WORKING TEMPLATE

The *medical family therapy working template* is meant to be used as a guideline to learning the process of medical family therapy. The template provides the beginning therapist with steps to take and questions to ask that promote collaboration between the therapist and client. There are suggested questions under each heading to help start the process. After using the initial questions, guide the client through each process, asking questions that occur to you as you stay within the family therapy theory. Although there is no one "script" for any therapy session, it is the hope of the author that the template serves as an impetus to learning this family therapy model.

Tools for Change

Because medical family therapists may use various family therapy models, there is no one-size-fits-all set of interventions. Using any model of choice, the medical family therapist will assist the patient/family in gaining a direction by finding new ways to approach their difficulties. Limit interventions to the current stated goal/problem/need and remember that the illness is now part of the family.

Phase 1: Joining and Building Rapport

The initial setting may occur in various settings: a clinic, emergency room, acute care facility, or patient's home, for example. The therapist should determine how the illness affects relationships and the family system. Since all systems are comfortably addressed (biological, psychological, and social), let families know that any topic of concern can be freely discussed. Explore the family's understanding of the illness and its effects on the patient and the family, and begin drawing a medical genogram to capture these issues. Interview the patient, family, and/or the medical team to become aware of how to help the family gain relief from the problem.

Here are some comments or questions that a therapist might use during this phase:

- *"What are some of your concerns today?"*
- *"Who lives in the household? Is there extended family support? Who will be the caregiver?"*
- *"Tell me the story of how this _____ (illness/condition) has affected your life/lives?"*
- *"Have there been times when you have experienced illnesses like this in the past? When and with whom?"*
- *"Has there been prior treatment? And if so, was this helpful?"*
- *"Are you and your family getting all the support that you need?"*
- *"Are resources/funding available for adequate treatment?"*

Phase 2: Understanding the Presenting Issue

Assess family understanding of illness and the reaction of family members; process the family's feelings (angry, sad, denial, depressed, hopeless, helpless, warm, affectionate, playful, optimistic, etc.)

Here are some comments or questions that a therapist might use during this phase:

- *"How has your family changed as a result of _____ (illness/condition)? How have roles in the family been affected? How have roles shifted?"*
- *"Has the family begun to grieve the loss of functioning/changes in physical condition and the medical routine needed to treat the illness?"*
- *"How do family members feel that the illness/condition has affected the inflicted family member? What do you believe is the cause of this illness?* (To each person) *Does everyone think the same or differently about this?"*
- *"Who would you say is having the easiest time adjusting to this recent diagnosis? Who is having the hardest time?"*

- *"How do the patient's expectations of the illness compare with the health professional's? How do each family member's expectations of the illness compare with the health professional's?"*
- *"Who is the person most responsible for caregiving? How was this decided? Is there equal sharing?"* Educate family members regarding the increased stress for those in caregiving roles and the importance of their own self-care.

Phase 3: Assessment of Family Dynamics

Assess whether the family members talk directly and/or openly with each other. Examine how the family defines the illness in their system and how they make sense of it all. Learn to read body language, eye contact, and tone of voice to determine the true feelings of family members regarding the illness and its impact. Pay attention to how the illness is discussed among the family. Who speaks and to whom, and who seems more comfortable discussing the surrounding issues? Who is least comfortable discussing any related issues? Are the family members educated about the course of the illness and what to expect? Have they connected with their treatment team? Do they have the information needed to make decisions regarding the illness?

Here are some comments or questions that a therapist might use during this phase:

- *"When someone in your family is sick, what is the expected role of each family member?"*
- *"Which relationships have become closer? How? Which relationships have become more distant? In what way?"*
- *"How can the family work together to support the changes needed?"*
- *"What feelings seem the easiest or the most difficult for the family to express?"*
- *"What are some of your concerns related to the illness that you have? Have you shared these with anyone else?"*
- *"Is there any family member protected or excluded from these discussions?"*
- *"With whom in the family does each member feel most and least comfortable in sharing feelings about the ill member's condition? To whom are the frustrating feelings about the illness expressed?"*
- *"Do these feelings get expressed to the affected member? If not, how does the patient feel about being protected in this way?"*

Phase 4: Goals

Generally, goals in medical family therapy are short term, measurable, and linear in nature. Goals can be long term if the patient returns regularly to the clinic for follow-up care. Typical goals may be voiced by both the medical staff (such as "this diabetic will not take his insulin and needs to start doing this") or by the family (such as "Mom wants to die at home, but none of us are ready").

Here are some comments or questions that a therapist might use during this phase:

- *"Do the family and medical team agree on the goals of treatment? If not, how can the issues be resolved?"*
- *"Do family members agree on goals of treatment?"*

Phase 5: Amplifying Change

The work of the medical family therapist is to help the family expand their understanding of the "problem," weigh pros and cons, facilitate problem solving, and increase communication among family members. As the family begins to adapt or conform to their new roles, compliment them on their abilities to adapt and encourage them to talk about how they managed to step up when needed by the patient. Be there as a support to each member who feels things are stabilized when that happens so stability is maintained. Refer back to the original interview with the patient, family, and/or the medical team to determine how progress is being made. Since this therapy is normally very brief, change resulting in such relief may be sooner than what would be expected in another type of therapy. Progress is defined by those who presented with the initial concern; the therapist refrains from imposing his or her idea of progress.

- *"It seems as if you are more relaxed this week as you talk about your role as a caregiver. Talk to me about how you have helped that happen."*
- *"It seems like _____is complying better with the doctor's treatment plan. Tell me who is helping him to do this."*
- To patient: *"How is it that you are able to remember your medication and doctor's appointments so that Sherry could take you there last week?"*

Phase 6: Termination

In an acute care setting, termination may not be a formal process. Clients come and go, and may be discharged before you have completed your goals. Prior to the patient's discharge, a medical family therapist may want to arrange follow-up care with the patient and/or family after going home.

Calling the patient and/or family is a respectful way to check on their continued relief and, if needed, set up ongoing therapy sessions. Many times, family members get the closure they need from having follow-up contact.

The therapist will also need to follow up with the health professionals involved with the patient's case. Make sure that the patient has obtained needed medications, equipment, and all the tools required for a positive recovery. Make sure the treatment team has all the important information.

MASTER THERAPIST INTERVIEW

SUSAN MCDANIEL

Dr. Susan McDaniel is a clinical psychologist who has been trained in family therapy and currently works on faculty at the family residence program at the University of Rochester in New York. She is a professor of psychiatry (psychology) and family medicine at the University of Rochester School of Medicine and Dentistry in Rochester, New York, where she is the director of the Division of Family Programs in Psychiatry and codirector of Psychosocial Programs in Family Medicine. Dr. McDaniel received her doctorate in clinical psychology from the University of North Carolina at Chapel Hill, and completed an internship at the University of Texas Medical Branch in

Galveston, Texas, and a postdoctoral fellowship in family therapy at the Texas Research Institute for Mental Sciences in Houston, Texas. Dr. McDaniel's career has focused on teaching, research, and developing clinical approaches for psychologists, family therapists, and physicians in the area of families and health. She is the author of six books, including Medical Family Therapy: A Biopsychosocial Approach for Families With Health Problems *(with Jeri Hepworth and William Doherty, 1992),* Integrating Family Therapy: Handbook of Family Psychology and Systems Theory *(with Richard Mikesell and Don-David Lusterman, 1995), and* The Shared Experience of Illness: Stories of Patients, Families, and Their Therapists *(with Jeri Hepworth and William Doherty, 1997). Dr. McDaniel is also coeditor of the journal,* Families, Systems & Health. *Since 1986, she has been an active member of the Board of the Division of Family Psychology (Division 43) of the American Psychological Association. In 1995, she was named Family Psychologist of the Year by Division 43.*

Can you tell me about your professional background and what has connected you to medical family therapy?

I grew up in a home where my father was an OB/GYN physician and some of my great aunts and great uncles were also physicians. I married a physician so I am used to issues about health and illness and also in dealing with physicians as well. I started working in family medicine in 1982 teaching residents. I spent probably the first 5 or 6 years trying to articulate and operationalize family systems concepts, and what primary care physicians needed to know about families and family systems to be good doctors, and how practically that could be implemented, which is obviously very different from doing family therapy. From 1988, I was working fairly hard to figure out how to help physicians notice the emotional and interpersonal problems of their patients and what to do about it and how to use the family as a resource in health care. I began realizing that the biopsychosocial model that I think health care should be based on was equally applicable to psychotherapy. Rarely was the biological or physical illness taken into account in the typical mental health visit, although psychiatrists probably did a better job of taking a physical history than most therapists.

Around this time, I was at a meeting in Costa Rica along with Bill Doherty and Jeri Hepworth. The three of us were outside at a pool talking about our work in family medicine because they also worked in family medicine at that time. We all thought we were getting pretty good at teaching the physicians what they needed to know, but we were having a horrible time getting our mental health colleagues to collaborate appropriately. Furthermore, we were beginning to realize that the biopsychosocial model integrated well with the family systems theory and should be a kind of metaframework for any kind of psychotherapy. As it turned out, we were actually flying to another meeting together—so by the time we touched down in Jacksonville, Florida, we had an outline for medical family therapy. We did not have a name for it yet, but we knew that we wanted to try to influence the mental health field to take a biopsychosocial systems approach.

How did you coin the term, medical family therapy?

Bill, Jeri, and I debated what we should call it, but I can't remember which of the three of us originally thought of it. We actually didn't think "medical family therapy" was the best name because some nurses reacted strongly against using the term "medical" because they thought it meant physicians instead of health. It turned out that Bill was doing a plenary in the next few months, so we decided he would try it out and test it, and it immediately took off with the participants and has stayed.

What is the theory that defines how the model works?

One element of the theory is based on the biopsychosocial model that George Engel published in 1977. He tried to point out to physicians that illness and disease happens in a person who lives in an even larger context. He was really interested in the person of the physician and the person of the patient, but his theory really is larger than that. It goes from the molecular level all the way up to the biosphere, which I believe is the last level of his model.

The other element came from my interactions with Lyman Wynne, who was a pioneering family therapist deeply rooted in family systems. He and George Engel both worked in our psychiatry department from 1973. It is interesting that both the biopsychosocial model and family systems have common intellectual roots in general systems theory, and yet these theories worked in parallel worlds not really influencing each other much. In other words, it is systemic in terms of family therapy orientation, and it is systemic in terms of bringing the organic or physical or biological part of problems into focus. What seemed to be amiss was the idea that if you deal with a person's emotions, then you are being fully systemic, and that is not really true. A whole other level is left out unless the medical component is dealt with as well.

What are the necessary agents of change in this model?

One of the important features is collaboration with other health professionals. It's hard to implement a comprehensive biopsychosocial approach to psychotherapy if you don't include other health providers, and in return, it is often hard for them to implement a comprehensive biopsychosocial approach without the mental health provider. One of the agents of change is in having the ability and the understanding to collaborate, whether it's just by phone or seeing the patient together but conceptualizing the health professionals as part of the treatment system.

Another important feature is the interaction with the patient by asking about both emotional and biological problems, which gives the patient the idea that both are important and can be related. This is quite different [from] interviewing somebody by asking psychosocial questions and then asking them the biological questions, which communicate that they are separate entities. In the initial interview with the patient, it is important to include the illness history and the experience of it. It is also important to learn how the family is responding to it as well.

What kinds of families do you think benefit most from this model?

All kinds of families and all kinds of issues. Some issues may not have direct relevance to the health problem or a child behavior problem or a marital problem, but it is really important to make sure that is the case. I can remember a case where I saw parents bringing in their 16-year-old daughter who had a 2-year-old daughter, and they were frustrated that she wasn't taking care of the baby. It looked like a pretty obvious case of a kid having a kid and trying to deal with leaving-home issues and not being responsible with the child. But it turned out when I took the genogram that the mother had gotten pregnant with this girl and while the mother was pregnant, the father had left her so her daughter didn't know the father's name. She thought her father's name was Bob, and while I'm drawing the genogram, the mother says the father's name [is] Fred. The stepfather had really raised her, and was the partner of the mother while she was pregnant. The stepfather had a myocardial infarction (MI) almost 3 years before. It turned out that the girl had gotten pregnant a few months after the stepfather had the MI. So the stepfather actually recovered, but the issue of men leaving her and then a pregnancy and having a baby was in some way a response to the threatened loss of a father. I think I would have missed that dynamic if I hadn't taken the physical history as well as the girl's family history.

Different models of therapy require the therapist to be directive or nondirective. In your opinion, what are the necessary characteristics that a therapist should possess to be effective as a medical FT?
The family therapist definitely has to be directive, otherwise, the family will just dominate the family therapist. I think people need very good, solid family therapy training and to be able to understand individual dynamics and know a fair amount about health and illness. They need to be able to deal with other kinds of professionals, especially health professionals. They also need to understand the cultures of nursing and medicine and know to be respectful but not intimidated when they need to know something about the health care system.

How often does the client see you and for how long a period of time?
Probably about 50 minutes. The kinds of patients I see at this point are usually either really complicated or those that I've known for a long time. Some of them I see for 2 hours because they come from farther away. I think a typical length of time in the average clinic is about seven to eight sessions.

Who sets the goal in this model, the client or the therapist?
I work with the client and ask her for goals, but I often shape what she may say because, usually, the way a person puts it, it's impossible to achieve. I can remember a patient with psychogenic seizures, and her goal was to get her family to stop blaming her for things. So I suggested that the goal was to get her family to stop blaming her for things and to get her to stop accepting the blame. That's an example of making the goal into something that is actually achievable.

What role does a homework assignment have in this model?
I do set goals and I do give homework assignments. I might do the homework in the session if I think it's important because maybe they need my support in order to do it.

What have you found to be the limitations of this approach?
If the other health professional(s) won't collaborate with the family therapist, that can make things difficult, although I rarely see that happen. Perhaps working on the collaborative relationship between health professional and family therapist is of paramount importance.

Can you tell me some suggestions for students learning this model?
The most common mistake is being intimidated by physicians and not developing relationships with them and feeling insecure about their own skills. They need to recognize that, in a training environment, the residents are insecure about their skills, too, and they just may cope with it differently. It is helpful to do some role playing with family therapists so that they learn to pretend that they are confident. Physicians definitely know how to pretend that they are confident. I try to train therapists that they should not enter the collaborative relationship from a one-down position.

Wayne Denton

*Dr. Wayne Denton is a medical doctor (MD) who completed his residency in psychia-
try and then obtained a PhD in family therapy. He is now the director of the Family
Studies Center at the University of Texas Southwestern Medical Center at Dallas.
Dr. Denton has a dual background in psychiatry and marriage and family therapy,
and his interest is in the interface of couple/family relationships with health and illness. Dr. Denton provides clinical training to trainees from various professional backgrounds. Trainees from the Family Studies Center work with patients and families at
the center's clinic as well as in various clinical locations across the medical center. He is
the past president of the North Carolina Association for Marriage and Family Therapy,
which awarded him the David and Vera Mace award in 2002 for his outstanding contributions to the profession of marriage and family therapy. He has also served as chair
of the North Carolina Marriage and Family Therapy Licensure Board.*

**Can you tell me about your professional background and what has connected you to
medical family therapy?**

I grew up with the profession of marriage and family therapy. My father was a marriage
and family therapist, and he would talk at the dinner table and tell us what was going
on in the professional associations. I was interested in the mental health field in general,
and psychology held a greater appeal for me. So I ended up in medical school and I did
medical training as well as psychiatric training. I wanted to pursue an academic career
and needed an area to specialize in, and family therapy felt right. Also, when I was in my
general psychiatric residency, I knew I needed some more clinical training to work with
families. I went back to graduate school and got a PhD in marriage and family therapy.
Medical family therapy just seems to be a natural blending of those two backgrounds.

What are the necessary agents of change in this model?

It is going to depend largely on what type of therapy you choose to work within.

What kinds of families do you think benefit most from this model?

I think there are two groups that would greatly benefit because both groups would have an
issue of illness. The first group would be those who have preexisting family systems dysfunction before the illness arose. The second group would include those who were functioning well until the illness came along but then they begin to have coping problems.

**Different models of therapy require the therapist to be directive or nondirective. In
your opinion, what are the necessary characteristics that a therapist should possess to
be effective as a medical FT?**

I think therapists need to be more on the directive end with short-term treatment.

How long is your typical session?

It's hard to say that there is a typical amount of time. We have some work going on at
medical clinics that's going to be very brief because it may just be one time that you see
that family, yet if I see them a handful of times, that would probably amount to a lot. In
those cases, it's not going to be 50 minutes because you may have just 15 minutes, so you
have to work more quickly and with limited goals. Yet, at other times, the family might
transition to the outpatient psychotherapy clinic. Then it would be open-ended.

Who sets the goal in this model, the client or the therapist?

It's a collaborative process to find out what the family's goals are and to decide if that is something I feel comfortable helping them work towards. It's always going to be something which the client wants to work on. At other times, if [a] man wants to work on saving his relationship and being together when his wife says she has already decided to leave him, I'm here to make that process as smooth as possible. Both of these goals can't happen. So I ask them, what else can we do here?

What are some commonly used interventions in this model?

In medical clinics, the family therapist meets with the patient and family who may all be waiting for the physician, which is the case in clinics many times. The family therapist may have only 15 or 20 minutes, since it was a quick referral and there might not be enough chairs so some people have to stand. It can be awkward, but it is a beginning for the family to deal with medical issues as a system. In this kind of clinic work, you may not really ever know if it's a first or last session. Most people have chronic illnesses that they live with or that they may die from, so you may not know, particularly with some of the clinics we have, which is which. Each session should be treated like it might be the last one. That's true of all therapy, but more so in medical family therapy than the traditional outpatient psychotherapy setting.

What role does a homework assignment have in this model?

I don't really see it as a role per se. None of the models I generally use utilize homework, but probably in the clinic setting, it's a little more focused. Someone might be struggling with a diagnosis and there is some practical problem that the family system interaction is interfering with. In that case, it is important to work so that the problem gets resolved. And you try to do that in one session because it is a pressing problem with their health care and it may be the last time you see them. In other words, a family therapist can't just do an assessment today and then schedule 12 sessions. He would want to pick one specific aspect. For example, maybe the father is the patriarch of the family and he is dying of cancer, and the medical team has recommended that he go on to hospice but the family wants him cared for at home. Yet they don't have the resources to do that because the mother is elderly and frail. There, the family system is blocking what really needs to happen for his care, so the therapist might help them to process the change that's happened in the family system, that this strong powerful father is not like that anymore and the system is going to have to change, and other people are going to have to step up and take some of the authority, etcetera.

What have you found to be the limitations of this approach?

Most medical professionals don't think of family therapy as having something important to offer in the medical setting, so you have to sell the idea. Whereas with traditional social work, the need is obvious because you have patients and they need placement or they need services. Professionals don't know what family therapists are or what family therapy is and how can they help, so you have to explain yourself before you ever get to see a patient. The other limitation would be reimbursement and how a family therapist is going to make a living because so much of our health care is fee-for-service. What's most ideal is that you can drop in and out and see this person for half an hour and this one for 15 minutes and if you are on salary, then you don't have to worry about billable service.

Can you tell me some suggestions to offer students learning the model?
Family therapists need to have training done in a medical context. Some family therapists have this mind-set that their way is the best way or the only way to help people, and that doesn't really work in a medical setting because there are too many different kinds of professionals. That type of attitude simply would not make it in the medical setting. Be collaborative and work as a team member. Then they need to be able to get clinical experience working with patients and families who are dealing with medical or psychiatric problems. The medical world is a different culture than the family therapy world. The medical culture tends to be more hierarchal than what family therapists are used to. Primary care practitioners are extremely busy and they have many patients to see every day and a lot of pressure. If a family therapist is going to give them feedback, they need to be succinct and not too theoretical. The information needs to be practical in everyday language. Another aspect is that primary care providers are used to referring their patients to experts all the time, such as cardiologists, surgeons, endocrinologists, and they expect feedback. Some family therapists feel like that information is confidential. This can make the physician unhappy. They want and need feedback that is brief, succinct, and practical.

Case Study

A mother calls and makes an appointment for her family to come to therapy. The family consists of a husband and wife, both in their 40s; their 15-year-old son; a college-aged daughter; and the woman's father, age 82. Three years after the woman's mother died; her father developed Alzheimer's disease and moved in with the family 6 months ago. When his health began to deteriorate, the woman spent more time caring for him than for the other members of the family. Three months ago, the 15-year-old son, who has been treated for attention deficit hyperactivity disorder since age 7, began refusing to take his medication. The school is now calling home to report truancy by the 15-year-old son.

During the session, the wife cries and the husband reports that their relationship is strained, occasionally rolling his eyes as his wife becomes tearful. He reports that he has had to take on more work because his wife had to quit her job to attend to her father's needs. The daughter is away at college and the wife smiles as she describes her as a straight-A student. The daughter was asked to attend the session but refused because she has a hard time with her grandfather's illness and dislikes the conflict that has developed at home.

Dr. Susan McDaniel's Response to the Case Study

I would certainly have all of the family members in the room. I would compose a genogram. I would ask about who lives in the house, and when the grandfather came up in the conversation, I would then spend a fair amount of time on that. I would ask the 15-year-old son what he thought about the grandfather and get him to comment on the grandfather and the parents' dynamics. This way, once I've gotten to the presenting complaint, which is the son, I would have a fairly good idea about the Alzheimer's situation and what sounds like a bid for attention and a concern about how his parents are doing in the fate of this grandfather. I would then start trying to build the connections and find out if the family needs some relief for the grandfather and whether they have enough help. I would inquire about their support system around the grandfather's chronic illness. I would want to know who's prescribing the medication for the ADHD, and I would probably want to get in touch with that person. I would want to know what the 15 year old thought about his medication. How able is he to have some internal structure now that he is 15 if he started the medication when he was 12? Can the parents provide more structure? Can the school provide more structure? I would watch for reactions as I am hearing about the truancy, where he was going, and ask if there were other drugs involved. Are any substances being used by the parents? What's the family's response to his truancy? Is there appropriate limit setting, etcetera? I think it's important to try to understand all the different stresses and strains by doing a time line to see when things started to fall apart, and that might be a way also to connect the grandfather's deterioration with some of the other stresses in the family. I would try to find out if the wife has siblings who might be able to pitch in and help. I may suggest that the husband take the wife out for a date to get some relief from her caregiving. Perhaps there are caregivers' support groups that the mother might be involved in. Those are just some initial thoughts. I think the main focus would need to be getting the 15-year-old back into school on a regular basis and try to assess whether he does need to be on the medication and, if so, trying to influence him about that. I suppose I would look for the next possible vacation so that the college daughter could be involved in the treatment.

Dr. Wayne Denton's Response to the Case Study

It seems the truancy might be what brought the family in, but it is not clear. The daughter won't come to the session. There is a medical aspect in that the wife's father has Alzheimer's and he lives with them, but I don't know if he came to the session. It looks like the parents and the boy came, so there's a medical aspect to the Alzheimer's as well as the ADHD. It says that the boy has been more of a problem since the mom has not spent time with him. The boy has not been taking his meds and that appears to be just one piece of the problems, so I wouldn't start with that because that is a losing battle. The mother is stressed because she has had to care for her father, and the father is stressed because he has had to work more because mom quit her job. They are both under increased stress, and they're giving less attention to the boy who is now creating trouble, and the trouble is serving a function of getting more attention from his parents, and now, they are all coming together for these sessions. Generally, I would be cautious about focusing on the couple when they have presented that the problem is their son because families can be run off that way. My belief is that there is a reason that they are holding this son out as an identified patient. I'm more respectful of that than I used to be. I'm seeing this from a structural standpoint; this strain that this father brought in to the family has disturbed the family's homeostasis, and the parents are under increased stress from real-life burdens, and now it's hurting their relationship. The son is not getting the attention he needs and he is starting to act up, and the family is faltering under the pressure, so I might start by pointing this out. As far as goals, as in any structural therapy, I would attempt to change the structure because the boy needs more attention and more involvement from the parents. The parents need some relief, so that would be a goal that I would be looking at. There are many services for folks with Alzheimer's, and I would wonder if the parents knew about these. Partly I would want to know how things were before the grandfather moved in because it sounds like things were going better. That would make me feel more optimistic that only a few changes are needed for the family to be able to function again. Maybe mom could start working again, which would take some of the burden off of the father, and they would have more time and devote more time to the son, and hopefully, he would do better at school. So it seems to be more of a medical family therapy case since it's the introduction of the Alzheimer's that has disrupted the family.

KEY TERMS

Agency   In medical family therapy, agency refers to the family's power to set limits on the amount of control an illness or disability has over their lives.

Biopsychosocial   A systemic perspective that considers an interlinking of the biological, psychological, and social processes in an individual or family system.

Collaboration   A process of recursive interaction of knowledge between two or more people who are working together toward a mutual goal. In medical family therapy, this may include collaboration with the health care practitioners involved in a client's case.

Communion   In medical family therapy, communion refers to the support and connection experienced by patients and family members along with a balance of autonomy.

Diagnosis related groups (DRGs)   This is a reduced classification system of all the diseases identified in the *ICD-9 International Classification of Disease*: The *ICD-9* lists around 18,000 medical and 5,000 surgical codes, and these were simplified to about 700 DRGs.

Family medicine   The area of study that prepares a physician for family practice (see family practice).

Family practice (FP)   The field of specialized medicine where a physician provides primary care for essentially all members of a family, which includes all ages and both sexes. Some FPs also provide care for their hospitalized patients and do minor surgery and/or obstetrics.

Family therapy   A branch of psychotherapy that takes the broader view that individual behavior is better understood as occurring within a family social system.

General systems theory   A theory that concentrates on the interaction between parts that connect them to a whole as opposed to examining each part individually.

Genogram   A pictorial display of the members and relationships of a family system. In medical family therapy, the genogram will also diagram the patient and family's medical history.

Health maintenance organization (HMO)   This is a type of managed care organization that provides a form of health insurance coverage in the United States.

Medical   refers to the field of medicine, which is the science of maintaining and/or restoring human health through the process of observation, diagnosis, and treatment.

Medical family therapy   A family therapy approach that addresses the biomedical along with the emotional, psychological, and relational processes affecting a client and the family, which includes the collaboration with other health care practitioners.

Medical model   The term cited by psychiatrist Ronald D. Laing in his book, *The Politics of the Family and Other Essays* (1971), for the "set of procedures in which all doctors are trained." This set includes complaint, history, physical examination, ancillary tests if needed, diagnosis, treatment, and prognosis with and without treatment.

Metaframework   An overarching set of assumptions, concepts, values, and practices that constitute a way of viewing reality. Medical family therapy provides these overarching principles where any model of therapy may be practiced.

Preferred provider organization (PPO)   A type of managed care organization similar to HMOs. PPO members are reimbursed for utilization of nonpreferred providers, usually at a reduced rate, which may also be accompanied by higher deductibles, co-payments, lower reimbursement percentages, or a combination of all of these.

Psychoeducational   An intervention evident in a therapeutic setting where educational programs and information are provided to assist clients and families to better understand and learn skills for coping with specific problems.

REFERENCES

Anderson, G. F. (2003). Physician, public, and policymaker perspectives on chronic conditions. *Archives of Internal Medicine, 163*(4), 437–442.

Archives of Internal Medicine. (2003, February).

Aronson, J. (1996). *Inside managed care: Family therapy in a changing environment.* New York, NY: Brunner/Mazel.

Blount, A., & Bayona, J. (1994). Toward a system of integrated primary care. *Family Systems Medicine, 12,* 171–182.

Brucker, P. S., Faulkner, R. A., Baptist, J., Grames, H., Beckham, L. G., Walsh, S., & Willert, A. (2005). The internship training experience in medical family therapy of doctoral-level marriage and family therapy students. *American Journal of Family Therapy, 33*(2), 131–147.

Campbell, T. L. (1986). Family's impact on health: A critical review and annotated bibliography. *Family Systems Medicine, 4*(2/3), 135–328.

Campbell, T. L., McDaniel, S. H., & Seaburn, D. B. (1992). Family systems medicine: New opportunities for psychologists. In T. J. Akamatsu & M. A. Stephens (Eds.), *Family health psychology* (pp. 193–215). Washington, DC: Hemisphere Publishing Corp.

Centers for Disease Control. (2010). Ten leading causes of death and injury. Retrieved from http://www.cdc.gov/injury/wisqars/LeadingCauses.html

Christ, G. H., & Christ, A. E. (2006). Current approaches to helping children cope with a parent's terminal illness. *CA Cancer Journal for Clinicians, 56*(4),197–212. Retrieved from http://caonline.amcancersoc.org/cgi/content/full/56/4/197

Doherty, W. J., & Campbell, T. L. (1988). *Families and health.* Beverly Hills, CA: Sage.

Doherty, W. J., McDaniel, S. H., & Hepworth, J. (1994). Medical family therapy: An emerging arena for family therapy. *Journal of Family Therapy, 16,* 31–46.

Doherty, W., & Mendenhall, T. (2005). *Partners in diabetes: A new initiative in diabetes care.* Baltimore, MD: Johns Hopkins University Press.

Doherty, W., & Mendenhall, T. (2006). Citizen care: A model for engaging patients, families and communities as coproducers of health care. *Families, Systems and Health, 24,* 251–263.

Engel, G. L. (1977). The need for a new medical model: A challenge for biomedicine. *Science, 196,* 129–136.

Engel, G. E. (1980). The clinical application of the biopsychosocial model. *American Journal of Psychiatry, 137,* 535–544.

Fisher, L., Ransom, D. C., Terry, H. E., Lipkin, M., & Weiss, R. (1992). The California family health project: 1. Introduction and a description of adult health. *Family Process, 31,* 231–250.

Fried, L. P., & Guralnik, J. M. (1997). Disability in older adults: evidence regarding significance, etiology, and risk. *Journal of the American Geriatrics Society, 45*(1), 92–100.

Grobstein, P., & Cyckowski, L. (2006). Common chronic conditions and aging at home: Chronic illness impacts some seniors' ability to live at home. *Serendip/SciSoc Group Summer 2006.*

Laing, R. D. (1971). *The politics of the family and other essays.* London, United Kingdom: Tavistock Publications.

Lewin Group. (2010, January). Individuals living in the community with chronic conditions and functional limitations: A closer look. *U.S. Dept of Health and Human Services.* Retrieved from http://aspe.hhs.gov/daltcp/reports/2010/closerlook.pdf

Lewis, L., Brecher, M., Reaman, G., & Sahler, O. (2010). *When children are dying.* Retrieved from http://www.beachpsych.com/pages/cc87.html

Lyness, A. M. (2003). *Feminist perspectives in medical family therapy.* New York, NY: Haworth Press.

Martin, L. G., Freedman, V. A., Schoeni, R. F., & Andreski, P. M. (2010). Trends in disability and related chronic conditions among people ages fifty to sixty-four *Health Affairs, 29*(4), 725–731. doi:10.1377/hlthaff.2008.0746

McDaniel, S. H., Harkness, J. L., & Epstein, R. M. (2001). Differentiation before death: Medical family therapy for a woman with end-stage Crohn's disease and her son. In S. H. McDaniel & D. Lusterman (Eds.), *Casebook for integrating family therapy: An ecosystemic approach* (pp. 323–336). Washington, DC: American Psychological Association.

McDaniel, S. H., Hepworth, J., & Doherty, W. J. (1992). *Medical family therapy: A biopsychosocial approach to families with health problems.* New York, NY: Basic Books.

McDaniel, S. H., Hepworth, J., & Doherty, W. J. (1997). *The shared experience of illness: Stories of patients, families, and their therapists.* New York, NY: Basic Books.

McDaniel, S. H., Hepworth, J., & Doherty, W. J. (1999). The shared emotional themes of illness. *Journal of Family Psychotherapy, 10*(4), 1–8.

Minuchin, S., Baker, L., Rosman, B. L., Liebman, R., Milman, L., & Todd, T. C. (1975). A conceptual model of psychosomatic illness in children. Family organization and family therapy. *Archives of General Psychiatry, 32,* 1031–1038.

Minuchin, S., Rosman, B. L., & Baker, L. (1978). *Psychosomatic families: Anorexia nervosa in context.* Cambridge, MA: Harvard University Press.

Moore, G. T., Block, S. D., Style, C. B., & Mitchell, R. (1994). The influence of the new pathway curriculum on Harvard medical students. *Academic Medicine, 69*(12), 983–989.

Mosby's medical dictionary (8th ed.). (2009). Philadelphia, PA: Elsevier.

ParentGiving. (2010). *Common chronic conditions and aging at home: Chronic illness impacts some seniors' ability to live at home.* Retrieved from http://www.parentgiving.com/elder-care/common-chronic-conditions-and-aging-at-home

Rolland, J. S. (1994). *Families, illness, & disability: An integrative treatment model.* New York, NY: Basic Books.

Ruddy, N. B., & McDaniel, S. H. (2003). Medical family therapy. In T. L. Sexton & G. R. Weeks (Eds.), *Handbook of family therapy: The science and practice of working with families and couples* (pp. 365–379). New York, NY: Brunner-Routledge.

Seaburn, D. B., Lorenz, A. D., Gunn, W. B., Gawinski, B. A., & Mauksch, L. B. (2003). *Models of collaboration: A guide for mental health professionals working with health care practitioners* (2nd ed.). New York, NY: Basic Books.

Sholevar, G. P., & Sahar, C. (2003). Medical family therapy. In G. P. Sholevar (Ed.), *Textbook of family and couples therapy* (pp. 747–767). Washington, DC: American Psychiatric Publishing.

Shute, N. (2002). That old-time, medicine. Innovative doctors are rethinking the office visit to put the care back in healthcare. *U.S. News & World Report, 132*(13), 54–58; 60–61.

Smolan, R., & Moffitt, P. (1992). *Medicine's great journey: One hundred years of healing.* New York, NY: Callaway Editions.

Turk, D. C., & Kerns, R. D. (Eds.). (1985). *Health, illness, and families: A life-span perspective.* New York, NY: John Wiley & Sons.

von Bertalanffy, L. (1960). *Problems of life: An evaluation of modern biological and scientific thought.* New York, NY: Harper.

Watson, W. H., & McDaniel, S. H. (2005). Managing emotional reactivity in couples facing illness: Smoothing out the emotional roller coaster. In M. Harway (Ed.), *Handbook of couples therapy* (pp. 253–271). New York, NY: John Wiley & Sons.

Wright, L. M., Watson, W. L., & Bell, J. M. (1996). *Beliefs: The heart of healing in families and illness.* New York, NY: Basic Books.

RECOMMENDED READING LIST

Books

Atkinson, B. J. (2005). *Emotional intelligence in couple therapy: Advances from neurobiology and the science of intimate relationships.* New York, NY: Norton.

Broyard, A. (1992). *Intoxicated by my illness and other writings on life and death.* New York, NY: Clarkson Potter.

Cousins, N. (1979). *Anatomy of an illness as perceived by the patient.* New York, NY: Norton.

Cozolino, L. (2006). *The neuroscience of human relationships: Attachment and the developing social brain.* New York, NY: Norton.

Crane, D. R., & Marshall, E. S. (2005). *Handbook of families and health: Interdisciplinary perspectives.* Thousand Oaks, CA: Sage.

Damasio, A. (1999). *The feeling of what happens: Body and emotion in the making of consciousness.* San Diego, CA: Harvest Book.

Dement, W. C. (1999). *The promise of sleep.* New York, NY: Delacorte Press.

Gitlin, M. J. (1996). *The psychotherapist's guide to psychopharmacology.* New York, NY: Free Press.

London, O. (1987). *Kill as few patients as possible.* Berkeley, CA: Ten Speed Press.

Morrison, J. (1997). *When psychological problems mask medical disorders: A guide for psychotherapists.* New York, NY: Guilford Press.

Patterson, J., Peek, C. J., Heinrich, R., Bishoff, R., & Scherger, J. (2002). *Mental health professional in medical settings: A primer.* New York, NY: Norton.

Smith, E. O. (2002). *When culture and biology collide: Why we are stressed, depressed, and self-obsessed.* New Brunswick, NJ: Rutgers University Press.

Sarno, J. E. (1991). *Healing back pain: The mind-body connection.* New York, NY: Warner Books.

Articles

Black, P. H. (2006). The inflammatory consequences of psychological stress: Relationship to insulin resistance, obesity, atherosclerosis and diabetes mellitus, type II. *Medical Hypotheses, 67*(4), 879–891.

Kemeny, M. E. (2003). The psychobiology of stress. *Current Directions in Psychological Science, 12*(4), 124–130.

Lundberg, U. (2005). Stress hormones in health and illness: The roles of work and gender. *Psychoneuroendocrinology, 30*(10), 1017–1021.

Mendenhall, T. J. (2006). Trauma-response teams: Inherent challenges and practical strategies in interdisciplinary fieldwork. *Families, Systems, and Health, 24*(3), 357–362.

Padgett, D. A., & Glaser, R. (2003). How stress influences the immune response. *Trends in Immunology, 24*(8), 444–448.

Robinson, W. D., Barnacle, R. E., Pretorius, R., & Paulman, A. (2004). An interdisciplinary student-run diabetes clinic: Reflections on the collaborative training process. *Family Systems & Health*, *22*(4), 490–496.

Scollan-Koliopoulos, M. (2005). Managing stress response to control hypertension in type 2 diabetes. *Nurse Practitioner*, *30*(2), 46–49.

Sternberg, E. M., & Gold, P. W. (2002). The mind-body interaction in disease. *Scientific American Special Edition*, *12*(1), 82–89.

Taylor, A. N., Chiappelli, F., Tritt, S. H., Yirmiya, R., & Romeo, H. E. (2006). Fetal alcohol syndrome, fetal alcohol exposure and neuro–endocrine–immune interactions. *Clinical Neuroscience Research*, *6*(1/2), 42–51.

Werner, R. (2006). Touch and the stress response system. *Massage & Bodywork*, *21*(1), 122–126.

Websites

Larkin, C. (2001). All in the family. *WGBH Educational Foundation and Clear Blue Sky Production.* *http://www.pbs.org/wgbh/evolution*

The Lewin Group for the Department of Health and Human Services *http://aspe.hhs.gov/daltcp/reports/2010/closerlook.pdf*

Family Psychoeducation

16

Fallon Cluxton-Keller

When you blame others, you give up your power to change.

—Dr. Robert Anthony

INTRODUCTION

Family psychoeducation is an eclectic approach that is primarily based on family systems theory, behavior therapy, structural family therapy, and educational psychology. Family psychoeducation was first developed to be used for families with mentally retarded members. Since that time, it has proven to be an effective treatment for people diagnosed with severe mental illnesses and their families. Proponents of the family psychoeducation model believe that for the treatment of such illnesses, medication alone is not effective, and family psychoeducation is also required. Although there are many different types of family psychoeducational programs, this chapter only addresses two evidence-based practice family psychoeducational approaches. Therefore, this chapter only addresses the family psychoeducational approaches used as treatments for families with members who are diagnosed with schizophrenia and bipolar disorders.

Family psychoeducation is an evidence-based practice for people diagnosed with severe mental illnesses and their families. Evidence-based practices are those types of treatments that have been documented numerous times in many different research studies and have been clinically proven to be effective treatments for specific clinical problems. You will learn more about evidence-based practices in the research chapter. Some researchers state that "evidence-based practices offer great promise for helping individuals who have severe mental illnesses accomplish their life goals" (Corrigan, Steiner, McCracken, Blaser, & Barr, 2001, para. 56).

The two family psychoeducational models that receive the most attention included multifamily psychoeducation (involving groups of five to six families) and family-focused therapy (FFT). Multifamily psychoeducation is an evidence-based practice for treatment of people diagnosed with schizophrenia and their families. FFT is an evidence-based practice for treatment of people diagnosed with bipolar disorder and their families. Research for multifamily psychoeducation groups (i.e., Dixon, McFarlane, et al., 2001; Dyck, Hendryx, Short, Voss, & McFarlane, 2002; McFarlane, Dixon, Lukens, & Lucksted, 2003; McFarlane, Link, Dushay, Marchal, & Crilly, 1995; McFarlane Lukens, et al., 1995) and research for FFT (i.e., Miklowitz et al., 2007; Miklowitz, Rea, et al., 2003; Miklowitz, Richards et al., 2003; Miklowitz et al., 2000) indicate that both of these models are evidence-based practices.

HISTORY AND LEADING FIGURES

Research studies have confirmed that the levels of conflict within the family environment of people with schizophrenia play a central role in the relapse rates of people diagnosed with schizophrenia (e.g., Dixon et al., 1999; Dixon, Lyles, et al., 2001; Miklowitz, Goldstein, & Nuechterlein, 1995). The EE studies (Leff & Vaughn, 1985) provided clinicians with the necessary evidence that laid the foundation for practicing family psychoeducation.

> *Critical, hostile, or emotionally overinvolved attitudes held by key relatives about a hospitalized patient, termed high expressed emotion (EE), are associated with high rates of patient relapse over 9-month to 1-year periods in schizophrenia . . . negative parent-to-patient verbal interactional behaviors (i.e., criticism, intrusiveness) during the post discharge period, termed negative affective style (AS), prospectively predict relapses of schizophrenia. (Miklowitz et al., 1995, para. 2)*

Family psychoeducation programs advocate the importance of eliminating high expressed emotion (EE) in these families to decrease relapse rates.

William R. McFarlane, a psychiatrist, is known as one of the main proponents of the multifamily psychoeducation model. His approach is based on the work of Carol Anderson and Peter Laqueur. Peter Laqueur is a pioneer of multifamily groups (McFarlane, 2002, p. xv), an approach, which suggested that families, in addition to the patients, need treatment (McFarlane, 2002, p. xv). Multifamily groups provided families with much-needed information, guidance, respect, and empathy (McFarlane, 2002, p. xv). The first ongoing multifamily psychoeducational group for treatment of schizophrenia began in 1979 (McFarlane, 2002, p. xvi).

In 1978, Michael J. Goldstein, a licensed psychologist at the University of California at Los Angeles, introduced a program to help families with members diagnosed with schizophrenia to understand the illness and to plan how future crises could be managed within the framework of available community services (Goldstein, Rodnick, Evans, May, & Steinberg, 1978). Goldstein had been the first to demonstrate the effectiveness of a short-term psychoeducational, crisis-oriented intervention for patients with schizophrenia (Goldstein et al., 1978).

Shortly after Goldstein's research laid the foundation for family psychoeducational approaches for people with schizophrenia, Carol Anderson and her colleagues developed a similar program in 1986. Anderson et al., (1986) developed the single-family psychoeducation programs called Survival Skills Workshops. This approach assumes that families and patients are all struggling with schizophrenia because the illness affects the family system, not just the patient. The approach developed by Anderson et al. (1986) is further explained later in this chapter.

Miklowitz, Goldstein, Neuchterlein, Snyder, and Mintz (1988) conducted research on the effects of the family environment on bipolar disorder through examining a cohort of hospitalized patients with bipolar disorder and mania whom they followed for more than a 9-month outpatient period. Miklowitz et al. found that when recently manic patients returned from the hospital to high EE homes, their chances of relapse were much higher than patients who returned to low conflict, relatively benign homes (Miklowitz & Goldstein, 1997, p. 5). Miklowitz and Goldstein (1997) developed a psychoeducational family-focused treatment in the early 1980s. This treatment is described in further detail in the next section of this chapter.

McFarlane started the Early Detection and Intervention for the Prevention of Psychosis Program (EDIPPP), which is a multifamily group prevention program for kids who exhibit prodromal symptoms of psychosis. McFarlane was featured in the June 2009 issue of

Time Magazine for receiving a $15 million grant from the Robert Wood Johnson Foundation for the national expansion of the EDIPPP. According to McFarlane (2002), researchers are conducting studies for the use of multifamily groups with people diagnosed with bipolar disorder, major depressive disorder, borderline personality disorder, obsessive–compulsive disorder, and chronic medical disorders. However, this treatment is only an evidence-based practice for treatment of schizophrenia.

INTRODUCTION TO FAMILY PSYCHOEDUCATION

Family psychoeducation is not based on one particular theory; it is an eclectic approach primarily based on family systems theory (see Chapter 3), behavior therapy (see Chapter 5), structural family therapy (see Chapter 10), and educational psychology.

As discussed in Chapter 3, family systems theory is a " . . . theory advanced by Bowen that emphasizes the family as an emotional unit or network of interlocking relationships best understood from a historical or transgenerational perspective" (Goldenberg & Goldenberg, 2000, p. 439). In behavior therapy, the goal is to change a patient's problematic behaviors. Structural family therapy focuses on a primary therapeutic goal, which is " . . . to challenge the family's patterns of interaction, forcing the members to look beyond the symptoms of the identified patient in order to view all of their behavior within the context of family structures" (Goldenberg & Goldenberg, 2000, p. 205). Educational psychology entails an "evaluation of cognitive processes . . . teaching methods . . . curriculum development and special education" (Barker, 2002, p. 28). In addition to these elements, family psychoeducation is also based in learning theory.

Family psychoeducation is also based on a medical model called the diathesis-stress model. The diathesis-stress model is "the theory that genetic predispositions and/or biochemical imbalances make stressed individuals vulnerable to specific illnesses" (Barker, 2002, p. 647). Severe mental illnesses may require pharmacological treatment education and medical management. Medication compliance is strongly encouraged in the family psychoeducation model.

Family psychoeducation is an evidence-based practice for schizophrenia, which makes it attractive to insurance companies and others, who will often only fund treatments that are effective. "Family psychoeducation is an evidence-based practice that has been shown to reduce relapse rates and facilitate recovery of persons who have mental illnesses" (Dixon, McFarlane, et al., 2001, para. 1). According to Dixon, McFarlane, et al. (2001), family psychoeducation has been proven to reduce relapse by 50% in patients with schizophrenia.

THEORETICAL ASSUMPTIONS

In the family psychoeducational model, every family is assumed to be functional, until proven otherwise. The focus of this model is on family strengths and resiliency. Family psychoeducation helps families to connect with larger community support systems through recognizing that patients and their families need assistance in the patient's transition back into the community.

There are two main types of family psychoeducation: single-family and multifamily. According to McFarlane (2002), multifamily groups have consistently yielded lower morbidity and better vocational outcomes than single-family psychoeducation when the comparison is only the format of the treatment. McFarlane also reported that multifamily group approaches are more effective than single-family approaches for first-episode and high-risk patients, poor responders to medication, or patients with highly stressed families. Typically, five to six families participate in a multifamily group session.

Regardless of the format, the goals remain the same, which are to achieve the best possible outcome for the patient through treatment management that involves a collaborative and supportive relationship, in addition to alleviate suffering among family members by supporting them in their efforts to foster their loved one's recovery. It is important to note that the goal of family psychoeducation is not to cure the mental disorder, but rather to help the patient and family live with it.

View of the Family and Client

Most of the research and books written about family psychoeducation have focused on this model in the treatment of schizophrenia. Therefore, this chapter will explain how the "problem" is conceptualized in family psychoeducation as a treatment for schizophrenia. The problem is usually viewed as a particular mental disorder (e.g., schizophrenia) and not the identified patient or any of his or her family members. The family psychoeducation model takes a blame-free view that family functioning is not the cause of the severe mental illness. Mental illnesses are viewed as biological diseases; however, it is understood that certain environmental factors can trigger symptom relapse.

Therapists need to take a "blame-free" stance throughout therapy. It is important to be aware of the resentment, anger, and general distress that families may be experiencing and to make each family feel validated and accepted. During family psychoeducation, therapists should normalize the functioning of families, since the family may ordinarily function well, but the illness may cause temporary disruptions to the system (D. Miklowitz, personal communication, April 28, 2007).

Miklowitz and Goldstein (1997) developed a psychoeducational family-focused treatment for people diagnosed with bipolar disorder in which they outlined three assumptions of their approach. First, each episode of bipolar disorder represents a disaster for the whole family. Second, each episode of the disorder produces a state of disorganization in the family. Third, the overall goal of the family-focused program is to assist the family to achieve a new state of equilibrium.

View on How Change Occurs

Family psychoeducation does not follow a typical family therapy format; therapists may utilize different interventions, such as cognitive behavioral therapeutic interventions. Instead, this model utilizes education, stress management, and coping skills for patients and their family members. Dixon, McFarlane, et al. (2001) found that the central components in family psychoeducation include emotional support, education, crises intervention, and problem-solving skills. Also, many of the interventions in family psychoeducation are manualized, which allows practitioners to follow a consistent step-by-step format.

These programs last longer than other therapeutic treatments because the change process tends to take longer (Dixon, McFarlane, et al., 2001). Many times, the families are resistant to change, and part of the therapeutic process must address reducing that resistance (Dixon, McFarlane, et al., 2001). Secondly, much time may be spent on educating families about the course and prognosis of the illness, particularly if the illness is severe and involves extreme behaviors and disruptions. There is also a considerable amount of time spent on teaching families coping skills so that they can handle symptomatic stressors when they arise. Finally, these programs spend a lot of time educating families and patients about the benefits of medication compliance. For all these reasons, family psychoeducation programs may last anywhere from 9 months to 5 years (Dixon, McFarlane, et al, 2001). However, some of the multifamily psychoeducation groups are ongoing, and families can choose when they want to terminate.

Change is typically measured through increases and decreases in relapse rates (Dixon, McFarlane, et al., 2001). Change is also measured through improvements in patients' social functioning and whether or not family stress has decreased over a period (Dixon, McFarlane, et al., 2001).

Therapist's Role

Family psychoeducation helps families to connect with larger systems through recognizing that patients and their families need assistance in the patient's transition back into the community. Family psychoeducational therapists help families to acquire various services, such as medical services and welfare services, in an effort to reduce stress for families and to help family members to be proactive. Dixon, McFarlane, et al. (2001) suggest that family psychoeducation programs last 9 months to 5 years. However, some of the multifamily psychoeducation groups are ongoing, and families can choose when they want to terminate. Family psychoeducation programs for people with severe mental illnesses and their family members can last 6 months to 5 years. It usually takes about 1 year for a person to recover from an acute psychotic episode because the brain has been traumatized. Therefore, some patients may not participate with their families in the initial stages of family psychoeducation.

Family therapists with the psychoeducational orientation build a supportive and non-judgmental therapeutic environment. In this model, family therapists collaborate with the patient and his or her family to provide the maximum therapeutic help. In family psychoeducation, the family therapist joins with the family to establish alliances with family members. Family therapists who adopt this model tend to be directive and use a "matter-of-fact approach" in educating family members, and they maintain neutrality.

Interventions

Family psychoeducation is primarily used in conjunction with medication as a treatment for people with severe mental illnesses and their family members.

As mentioned earlier in the chapter, family psychoeducation can be done with a single family or with multiple families. Single-family psychoeducation was developed by Carol Anderson and her colleagues. Anderson's version typically entails "a day-long Survival Skills Workshop," which consists of a therapeutic team providing education about the illness, treatments, prognosis, discussion of patient and family needs, and coping skills (Anderson et al., 1986; see Table 16.1 for further detail of the stages in this family psychoeducation program).

Multifamily psychoeducation was developed by William R. McFarlane, MD. Typically, it consists of five to six different families. In some sessions, the entire families, including patients, will attend; in others, the families will attend without the patients. McFarlane believes that multifamily psychoeducation increases social support for participating families. After 2 to 3 years, the group shifts from being leader centered to group centered to empower the group members. McFarlane's (2002) multifamily psychoeducation program is outlined in Table 16.2.

TABLE 16.1 ▨ Stages of Family Psychoeducation

1. Engagement	2. Education	3. Community Reentry	4. Social and Vocational Rehabilitation
• The family therapist meets with the family members within 48 hours after the patient has been admitted to the hospital.	• The family members attend an 8-hour workshop conducted by a family therapist and other staff.	• The patient enters family psychoeducation in this stage.	• This stage occurs 1 year after the acute psychotic episode. Sessions are usually once a month (except in emergencies).
• The family therapist asks the family to join with him or her in a partnership.	• Information about schizophrenia is taught, and families are given guidelines to manage the illness.	• The family therapist meets with the family and the patient twice a month.	• Patients are taught social skills.
• Family members are invited to several meetings in which they are helped to work out a strategy that suits their needs and desires.	• Families are also encouraged to exchange thoughts and feelings with other families going through similar situations because this enhances the group's effectiveness.	• The family therapist helps the family and the patient to develop effective coping skills.	• Employment issues are addressed.
• Family therapist provides advice and information in this stage.		• Medication compliance is emphasized in this stage.	• Situations that are likely to cause the patient stress are rehearsed.
		• Family members are told to lower their expectations of the patient and they are told to be tolerant of the negative symptoms of schizophrenia (such as avolition—inability to initiate and persist in goal-directed activities; affective flattening—diminished range of emotional expressiveness).	• The family therapist helps the family to rebuild social networks.
		• Problem-solving and communication skills training are provided.	• Family members are taught how to assist the patient in rehabilitation at home.

Source: Anderson, Reiss, and Hogarty (1986).

TABLE 16.2 ■ Multifamily Psychoeducation Program

1. Joining with Individual Patients and Families	2. Conducting an Educational Workshop for Families	3. Preventing Relapse Through Problem-Solving Groups Attended by Patients and Families	4. Pursuing Vocational and Social Rehabilitation
• Build an alliance with the patient and his or her significant other(s). • Create a collaborative treatment system in which the family members become engaged and experts on the daily life of their ill family member.	• Lasts approximately 1 day and patients do not usually participate in the workshop. • Workshop topics include brain function, medication effects, symptoms, and signs of schizophrenia.	• Families and patients meet on a biweekly basis, and problem-solving methods are taught to them. • Stages of problem solving include the following: 1. Define the problem; 2. List all possible solutions; 3. Discuss advantages and disadvantages; 4. Choose the solution that best fits the situation; 5. Plan and carry out this solution in detail; and 6. Review implementation.	• This stage begins about 6–8 months to 1 year after the educational workshop stage. • Continue doing problem-solving exercises. • Groups members collaborate to enhance each patient's psychosocial functioning. • Goal is for the group to be supportive and offer encouragement as each patient emerges from the family environment to the work and social domains.

Miklowitz's and Goldstein's multifamily model is similar to McFarlane's model. It consists of three phases and the duration of treatment is usually 9 months. There are six biweekly sessions and three monthly sessions spread through the 9-month period (Miklowitz & Goldstein, 1997, p. 12). Miklowitz and Goldstein (1997) identified six objectives for their model:

1. Assist the patient and relatives in integrating the experiences associated with bipolar episodes.
2. Assist the patient and relatives in accepting the notion of vulnerability to future episodes.
3. Assist the patient and relatives in accepting a dependency on psychotropic medication for symptom control.
4. Assist the patient and close relatives in distinguishing between the patient's personality and the bipolar disorder.
5. Assist patients and families in recognizing and learning to cope with stressful life events that trigger recurrences of bipolar disorder.
6. Assist family in reestablishing functional relationships after the episode.

Two interventions commonly used in family psychoeducation include validation and problem solving. According to Linehan (1993), a therapist communicates validation to the client that his or her responses make sense and are understandable within his or her current life context or situation; the therapist actively accepts the client and communicates this acceptance to him or her. In general, specific skills that a therapist teaches clients will help them to resolve their problems on their own. According to McFarlane (2002), problem solving in multifamily groups organizes experiences, values each person's possible contributions, and prevents premature closure before family members carefully plan a new approach.

FAMILY PSYCHOEDUCATION WORKING TEMPLATE

The family psychoeducation working template is meant to be used as a guideline to learning the process of family psychoeducation. The template provides the beginning therapist with steps to take and questions to ask that promote collaboration between the therapist and client. There are suggested questions following each heading to help start the process. After using the initial questions, guide the client through each process, asking questions that occur to you, as you stay within the family therapy theory. Because there is no one "script" for any therapy session, it is the hope of the author that the template serves as an impetus to learning this family therapy model.

Tools for Change

The primary intervention is to provide families and patients with education about the disorder. Therapists utilize a variety of other interventions in family psychoeducation, which include validation, reframing, problem solving, role-plays, and empathy in addition to positively reinforcing healthy changes.

The therapist may provide families and patients with handouts that include information about what they can expect from the treatment, education, definitions of communication and problem solving, and homework assignments.

Phase 1: Joining and Building Rapport

Therapists operate in multiple roles during this phase (D. Miklowitz, personal communication, April 28, 2007):

- *Builder of a supportive alliance*—The therapist must build a supportive alliance with the families and patients.
- *Engager*—The therapist actively listens and validates clients' experiences. The therapist is nonjudgmental, sympathetic, and empathetic.
- *Educator*—The therapist educates the family about the illness and ways to cope with emerging symptoms (e.g., how to arrange emergency help from the physician or hospital if symptoms worsen).
- *Consultant or coach*—The therapist acts as a consultant or coach for families and patients.

Here are some comments or questions that a therapist might use during this phase:

- *"How does this disorder affect the family members?"*
- *"What has it been like to live with this?"*
- *"What was the person like before the illness?"*
- *"How does the family relate to the fact that their family member has been diagnosed?"*
- *"How hopeful is the family that some peace will come back?"*
- *"Who has stood by you through all of this?"*

Phase 2: Understanding the Presenting Issue

Families present to treatment wanting to learn about the illness, as well as how to cope with it. The therapist should provide family members and patients with education about the illness in addition to teaching them effective ways to cope with it (D. Miklowitz, personal communication, April 28, 2007).

Phase 3: Assessment of Family Dynamics

Think about the ways in which the onset of the disorder has affected the family's structure, interaction patterns, and problem-solving styles. Early on, assess what the family wants out of treatment. It is important for therapists to recognize any risk factors (i.e., high EE) in the family environment that may contribute to the patient relapsing and how these risk factors can be addressed in treatment (D. Miklowitz, personal communication, April 28, 2007).

The assessment process is ongoing and it includes the following elements:

1. Understand the precipitants for the episodes.
2. Understand the early warning signs of onset.
3. Assess high EE. In addition, pay attention to the way family members understand the disorder and its associated impaired behaviors—do they think the patient is doing this on purpose?

4. Identify families that are isolated. The families that are the most isolated are the most vulnerable to becoming very angry and resentful, and this can lead to family fragmentation. Encourage patients and relatives to build support systems—sometimes through participation in illness support organizations—to decrease their isolation.

5. Look for opportunities to help families develop effective communication and problem solving in the family as related to the disorder.

Here are some comments or questions that a therapist might use during this phase:

- *"Are symptoms diminishing?"*
- *"Are patients keeping their follow-up appointments with psychiatrists and other practitioners involved in treatment?"*
- *"How are patients functioning socially and occupationally?"*

Phase 4: Goals

Goal setting is a dialogue between the therapist, the patient, and family. The overall goal is that the patient does not relapse, has fewer symptoms, and maintains healthy community functioning (as measured by relationships, employment, and quality of social and family life). Therapists usually ask the patient and the family what they want to get out of the treatment. The goals must be realistic.

Here are some questions that a therapist might use during this phase:

- *"If your life were better in the next 3 to 6 months, what would it look like?"*
- *"What would you like to see happen in the next 3 to 6 months?"*
- *"How about during the time we are working?"*
- *"What would you consider a good outcome?"*

Phase 5: Amplifying Change

As families gain more knowledge about the illness, their attitudes and behaviors may change. Behavioral changes may include enhanced communication, improved emotional behavior, and effective coping skills (such as the ability to recognize and intervene early with warning signs of recurrence).

The therapist should continue to encourage families to practice communication and problem-solving skills with each other outside of sessions to increase familial cohesion and decrease conflict (D. Miklowitz, personal communication, April 28, 2007).

Phase 6: Termination

Dr. Miklowitz's treatment has 21 sessions.

WILLIAM MCFARLANE

William McFarlane, MD, is a psychiatrist and the director of the Center for Psychiatric Research, Maine Medical Center and Spring Harbor Hospital; the principal investigator of the Portland Identification and Early Referral Program (PIER), and professor of psychiatry at the University of Vermont, Department of Psychiatry. Dr. McFarlane has published more than 40 articles and book chapters (McFarlane, 2002).

What attracted you to the theory behind the psychoeducation model?
Fundamentally, it was that family therapy didn't work. It really was not at all helpful to families or patients who had severe mental illness, in particular, schizophrenia. I'd been doing a lot of work with families using (at the time) conventional models and approaches, which, of course at that time, were also fairly new, but they really didn't work. In fact, some of us began to get worried that in spite of all the wonderful theories that we heard about, schizophrenogenic mothers and double binds and all that, that we might even actually be doing some damage to these families.

It was about that time that a couple of things happened. One is that Michael Goldstein published a study showing that some difficulties in families, but not the ones that were targeted in family therapy, predicted the onset of schizophrenia. Also, Carol Anderson was beginning to publish some of her views and approaches going at it almost diametrically the opposite direction; that is, assuming that the families were essentially beleaguered and victims of the disease as much as anybody else, including the patients, if not maybe more so. I was also heavily influenced by the British research on expressed emotion. So, those were the main theoretical foundations.

The other influence was somewhat accidental, and that is that I had spent 2 years working as a fellow under Peter Laqueur in Vermont, who was one of the developers of multiple family group therapy. So, I suppose the strongest influences were the fact that family therapy didn't work and multifamily group therapy did, and then the influence of expressed emotion research all me got started. We started running these groups and experimenting, aiding and supporting, and guiding families rather than trying to fix them. Within months, we knew this was going to be dramatically more successful than anything we tried before. That's always the test of a theory, at least in clinical sciences: Do the people get better?

How do you formulate your view of a family when they enter therapy?
I think one of the characteristics of family psychoeducation is that we don't assume that the family is of any particular type because the disease seems to happen to all kinds of different people, the same way pneumonia does. So to have a formulation of family, in general, is almost contrary to the model. However, we're always looking for resentment, anger, and general distress. In other words, our present perception is that the disorder, the early symptoms of the disorder, actually elicit[s] from the family the very responses that make the disorder worse. So it's a double feedback loop, if you will.

What kinds of families do you think benefit most from this model?
The families that benefit the most are the most confused and, therefore, out of that confusion, are the most critical of the person with the disorder. That's expressed emotion,

and if it changes, and it almost always does, that's going to lead to very rapid improvement of the patient and also very much longer term outcome. Probably, the second most likely candidate would be families that are confused and distressed, and that's almost everybody. So it's pretty much every family of somebody with a severe mental illness.

Different models of therapy require the therapist to be directive or nondirective. In your opinion, what are the necessary characteristics that a therapist should possess to be effective with this model?
There's very little room for just sort of letting people talk, given the process. There is a tendency for families to criticize each other, or criticize other family members in the group, and we don't allow that to happen anymore; it's kind of off-limits, just bad behavior. So most of what one does in a group is directive. There's even a program for each group session and it's even timed, so it's fairly highly structured. It is complex because the first responsibility is to establish a therapeutic process; it's not always going to happen automatically. So the first role is to convene effort on the part of the patient and the family, and that often requires a lot of explanation. The second role is then the engager in the usual sense as in almost any therapy, being nonjudgmental, sympathetic, empathetic, and listening to people. The next role is being an educator. You have to stand up and give a talk to a group of families about these disorders and what to do about them; what skills the family members can develop to make a difference. Then you have to learn to run a multifamily group, which is different than doing family therapy. You turn a lot of therapeutic effort over to the families. What's odd about these groups in the end is that you become almost symmetrical with the families and the patients, and it feels a little bit like just a meeting of good old friends, except you still have clinical responsibilities for the patients. One of the things we try and teach is that in order to do family psychoeducation groups, you've got to learn several roles and be comfortable evolving from one to the other.

How often does the client see you and for how long a period of time?
The sessions are pretty much an hour and a half. In some settings, because people have transportation difficulties, the therapists might do the equivalent of two sessions at once, and that will run almost 2 hours.

What are you looking for when you are in the session?
We're very concerned about family members who, out of misunderstanding about the disorder, are very angry at the person with the disorder. That's a target, and that's highly amenable to support and education and guidance.

I think in the larger sense, we're looking for opportunities to help families develop special approaches to the patient and the disorder that are going to be effective. The other thing we're looking for is evidence that the family is really isolated, because our experience is that the families that are the most isolated are the ones who are the most vulnerable to becoming angry, resentful, having things melt down and often leading them to family fragmentation. Our view is that, that's a catastrophe. Losing family contact is often the final step to homelessness for a lot of people, and I don't need to tell you what the effects of homelessness are. I'm always thinking in the back of my mind, how can I keep this family together? How can we make this thing manageable and tolerable for everybody so that the fundamental integrity of the family is maintained?

The patient wants help from their family. They're always returning to them and the family is always looking for help, usually from the professional community, usually to ask what can we do to help their ill relative.

What is the assessment process of the model?
It's important to remember that the family assessment is part of an ongoing psychiatric treatment program. The same kind of assessments that any clinician, particularly psychiatrists, would apply are relevant to this approach. Obviously, we're interested in the families getting less angry and less preoccupied with the illness and starting to pay attention to their lives and even in some cases, the marriage of the patient's parents. If you look at a whole group or a whole group of groups, you're looking at rehospitalization rates, symptom ratings and usually employment, and social functioning in a group. One other measure is actually the physical and mental well-being of the family members, which seems to be dramatically improved by this experience.

Who sets the goals, the client or the therapist?
It's a dialogue. Our goal is that the patient[s] not have relapses, have fewer symptoms, and get a diploma or a job. But, we also start with a question to the patient and the family: What do you want to get out of this? There's a contracting process, the melding of those approaches, of those goals.

What are some commonly used interventions with this model?
Well, the most commonly applied intervention is problem solving, and that's derived from behavioral family therapy and organizational dynamics. The others are all described in my book, *Multifamily Groups in the Treatment of Severe Psychiatric Disorders* (Guilford Press, 2002).

What role does a homework assignment have in this model?
At the end of problem solving, there is a homework assignment, and it's really expected that the family go and try it out. We don't expect that necessarily it's going to work, but the whole group has participated in helping the family develop some strategies, and there's kind of an obligation to at least try it and report back. So that's a key piece in each session. The next session you turn to the family and ask, "How did it go? Did it work?"

How do you know when your client is ready to terminate?
I think they just decide on their own. Most people don't terminate, they keep coming for years; it's quite remarkable. That's one of the reasons we know its effective.

What have you found to be the limitations of this approach?
Probably, the biggest limitation so far has been the clinicians' reluctance to use it. A couple of surveys have been done nationally, and they keep coming up with a 5% to 15% application rate across the United States. So there's something really wrong somewhere about the mental health field's application of evidence-based psychosocial treatments and especially the family-based versions. We're struggling to figure out what to do about it. It's a field biased against evidence or effectiveness. The relevance of the evidence is to everyone's individual practice.

There may be a limitation of the group being difficult for some families and some patients, but they tend to get over that. I think there may be some limitations of the model in certain cultures. The evidence for that is nonexistent, because it's actually much more widely applied in Japan, Europe, Australia, and now, in China. Thousands of people are receiving family psychoeducation in China and Japan. So maybe the culture that family approaches don't fit well is ours, and that's a little disturbing.

What suggestions do you have for students learning this model?

I'm kind of old-fashioned; I say first reading about it, and look at some of the research outcome studies so that you're convinced that it is worth doing. Second, just read the book. Read my book (McFarlane, W. R. [2002]. *Multifamily Groups in the Treatment of Severe Psychiatric Disorders.* New York, NY: The Guildford Press), Carol Anderson's book (Anderson, C. A., Reiss, D. J., & Hogarty, G. E. [1986]. *Schizophrenia and the Family: A Practitioner's Guide to Psychoeducation and Management.* New York, NY: The Guilford Press), Ian Falloon's book (Falloon, I. R. G., Boyd, J. L., & McGill, C. W. [1984]. *Family Care of Schizophrenia: A Problem-Solving Approach to the Treatment of Mental Illness.* New York: Guilford), David Miklowitz's book (Miklowitz, D. J. [2002]. *The Bipolar Disorder Survival Guide: What You and Your Family Need to Know.* New York, NY: The Guilford Press).

There are slight differences between Anderson and Falloon that I think are worth students knowing about. We've integrated those two approaches in our multifamily group. So, to some degree, you might want to start with my book (*Multifamily Groups in the Treatment of Severe Psychiatric Disorders*) if you think you might want to do groups. Then get trained. It's a 2- or 3-day exercise with extensive role-playing. We found that most people won't be that effective unless they have had a year of at least monthly supervision. We found that people have fairly good results if they have an opportunity to have a 2- or 3-day training experience. That's usually pretty intensive, mostly skill-oriented training, and followed about a year of supervision. This is all still in process. We still don't know exactly what's ideal. It's really designed to be used in ordinary mental health center settings where the patient is treated.

MASTER THERAPIST INTERVIEW

DAVID J. MIKLOWITZ

David Miklowitz, PhD, is a psychologist and a psychology professor at the University of California at Los Angeles. Dr. Miklowitz's research has been funded by the National Institute of Mental Health in addition to the MacArthur Foundation, and he has published more than 90 journal articles and book chapters (Miklowitz & Goldstein, 1997).

What attracted you to the theory behind the family-focused therapy model?

I was working with Michael Goldstein, a mentor who was interested in schizophrenia and the family. He did much of his seminal work in the late 70s and I started graduate school in '79. The prevailing model at the time was a combination of family systems and a kind of crisis-oriented psychoeducational model, which was starting to crop up. The idea was that you didn't think about families as causative agents in the illness as much as allies in the treatment process. The idea was these were families, basically, that were going through a rough time, and if they understood more about the disorder, how to cope with it, then there wouldn't be so much high expressed emotion and negativity in the family environment. So I think what really attracted me was this idea that families weren't pathological as much as just going through a rough time and needing to learn coping skills.

How do you formulate your view of a family when they enter therapy?

I usually start with the assumption that, unless I am proven wrong, the family is not pathological. I think that is a very important difference from traditional forms of family therapy. I view them very much the way I would view a family dealing with diabetes, Alzheimer's, multiple sclerosis, or cancer, or any kind of biological disorder that is going to disrupt the family's functioning. That having an illness in one member is going to cause a disruption in the family's functioning, and they're going to try to normalize their functioning as best as they can. And this is where treatment comes in and how are they going to cope with this new source of information, which is that one member has a psychiatric disorder. So what I am going to do is access what their strengths and weaknesses are, how they understand the disorder already, and what can I do to improve upon the situation. What I don't do is assume that the family is in any way causal of the onset of the disorder. I don't believe that family environment causes people to become bipolar or schizophrenic. However, I do believe they are important whether people have recurrences once they're already diagnosed.

What kinds of families do you think benefit most from this model?

I think the ones that are highest in conflict. That, if there is a high degree of expressed emotion, and a lot of negative interchanges swinging back and forth, then that's where communication training and problem solving and education can have its strongest impact. In fact, we have some data on that. That patients who improve the most are often the ones from high expressed emotion families.

Different models of therapy require the therapist to be directive or nondirective. In your opinion, what are the necessary characteristics that a therapist should possess to be effective with this model?

First, you need to be warm and genuine. You have to be sympathetic and validating of the family's plight, both the patient and the relatives. You do have to be directive and have an agenda, and generally, I think the treatment works better when you stick to your agenda. But you also have to be flexible. You have to be ready to depart from your agenda as situation calls for it.

I see myself more of a consultant; like a coach. I don't see myself becoming part of the family system. It's more coping oriented. The reality is that, I am seeing them once a week for an hour. And I'm a consultant in the same way that other people they consult in their life are influential. That doesn't mean that they aren't going to try to incorporate me into their system, but I don't see that as part of the process of therapy. It is a good idea to self-disclose once in awhile, not on a very personal level but to admit one's own vulnerabilities.

You have to be willing to deal with affective reactions including to the therapeutic interventions. To be understanding, a good listener, to stay away from deep interpretations, even though you may see opportunity to do so in general, that is not what this model is about. You should use reframing interventions as often as possible. There's very little trickery. I think that traditional family therapy sometimes relied upon tricky interventions to bring about change, and that is not what this model is about.

How often does the client see you and for how long a period of time?
Our treatment is 21 sessions long. Weekly for 12 weeks, then it goes biweekly for 12 weeks, and then it goes monthly for 12 weeks. So it is titrated over time and the sessions are usually an hour long.

What are you looking for when you are in the session?
First, I am looking for evidence of high expressed emotion. Lots of criticism, hostility, overprotectiveness. I'm interested in problem solving and how they solve problems as a family. I'm interested in whether the communication is healthy and bidirectional. And whether there is any active listening going on, or clear communication, or whether it is kind communication is vague and frustrated. Whether they seem to be maintaining a focus of attention when they talking about a topic, or are they going off in different directions. How well do they understand the disorder? Is their understanding accurate? To what extent has the patient accepted that he or she has a disorder? And to what degree is the family brought into that? Or, are there implications that somehow the person is faking it or not trying hard enough?

What is the assessment process of this model?
Well, in our research, we have an independent evaluator who assesses the family and the patient for both independent and systematic progress and also family functioning. That's done every 3 months during treatment, and then during the second year, they go to every 6 months . . . That's different from the informal assessments I'm making along the way. Do I think the patient's improving? Do I feel I'm stuck? Does it feel like the family is improving? Keeping in mind that sometimes you don't see any change in the first 3 to 6 months and then sometimes it comes later.

Who sets the goals, the client or the therapist?
We have six goals in FFT: to assist the patient and family members in understanding the current mood disorder episode, understanding his or her vulnerability to future episodes, accept the role of mood medications in maintaining stability, distinguish the patient's personality from the disorder, identify and cope more effectively with stressors that provoke episodes, and enhance the functioning of the family. I try to make it clear that the goals are not just for the patient but also for the relatives. A good outcome for me would be them having a more satisfying [and] less stressful life, not just that the patient gets better.

What are some commonly used interventions with this model?
Psychoeducation is the first module. Relapse prevention drills where you get family to identify the early warning signs of the disorder and how do you intervene when you see those start to occur. What are the early interventions you can do to keep it from spiraling out of control? Reframing, I think is very important. For example, if there are fights about the disorder, you frame it as part of the natural process that the family

goes through developmentally in trying to come to terms with the illness. Not that they are pathological, but this is just part of the developmental transition of adapting to this disorder. So reframing [and] relabeling, I think are very important. Communicating hopefulness.

Once in a while, we will bring in ancillary interventions like working with the school systems. So we might, for example, attend an IEP (Individual Education Plan) meeting. We might have a conversation with the schoolteacher or counselor. We might, if the person is in legal trouble, with their permission, talk to their attorney. We would work with their psychiatrist, of course, in terms of sharing information about side effects or clinical progress. The psychiatrist may not be seeing them as often as we do. So being an ally, really, to the family in advocating for other services.

What role does a homework assignment have in this model?
It's very important. We try to assign homework every week. Homework can be any number of things, such as the family sitting down and watching the [movie] about bipolar disorder. It might be keeping a mood chart. It might be keeping a sleep/weight chart. It might mean practicing a communication skill or going to a problem solving exercise. But in general, we think that the people who do stuff between sessions, work between sessions, and practice the skills are going to do better.

How do you know when your client is ready to terminate?
We have a preset protocol, so it is 21 sessions long, followed by trimonthly booster sessions. When I do this in private practice, I may not carry it out 21 sessions. It depends upon whether they need that much; sometimes they need more, sometimes they need less. I think when I feel like they are coping fine without me and they're using the skills spontaneously, and the bipolar disorder is under control and it is not really an issue for them right now other than just day-to-day living. If I feel [that] sessions are starting to feel flat, there is not as much to talk about, and we're sort of going over the same ground, I might suggest that they either take a break or terminate. These are multiproblem families and their functioning varies considerably over time. It's rare that people are done after a short period of time.

What have you found to be the limitations of this approach?
First, not everybody has a family. Although that may seem obvious, I think it is often underplayed by family therapists. That there are a lot of psychiatric patients that are disconnected from the family. Their families don't want anything to do with their therapy or their families are burnt out. They live far away or their families wrote them off a long time ago, so that is one limitation. Obviously, to do family therapy, you have to have a family.

I think there are some people who really have long-standing personality issues that are not particularly amendable to skill training. They have personality disorders, for example, and have gotten into trouble with one person after another. And their spouses are just sort of the most recent victim, and sometimes, I think that they need a different approach, maybe something like individual DBT would be helpful (see Chapter 5), or group skills training. People have had severe traumas, where the issue isn't really bipolar disorder as much as their early childhood. They might need some treatment for PTSD. Another thing is severe substance abuse. Our model is not for people who are concurrently abusing drugs. And if we can't get the substance abuse under control, somehow, either through an ancillary rehabilitation treatment, or AA or Antabuse, or whatever it is they need if they are actively using, our approach by itself will be pretty limited.

What suggestions do you have for students learning this model?

First, I think you have to be used to working with families. The toughest part, really, is getting used to think about psychological problem and transactional models. To think not so much about intrapsychic forces but how does one person's behavior, thinking, and feeling have upon another person. Not to think about one person causing another person's behavior, but there's a mutual influential causal process that involves them and other people who may not even be there. So partly, I think it's learning to be with a family, learning to target your interventions at the family rather than at individuals. Once you get used to working with families, then learning psychoeducation is actually fairly easy because of a prescribed set of steps, session by session that you want to accomplish. The hardest part is learning to work with families, some of whom are really disturbed. Read the research literature on family therapy. Students have to get to the point where they believe in what they're doing, not just following the manual, but that they actually believe that it will genuinely help the family and knowing the reasons for what they are doing. Maybe that's another way that therapists get into trouble is that they say, "You're supposed to do that just because that is what the manual says I have to do. But what I really want to be doing is this other thing but the manual says I have to do that." You really have to believe that you're doing the right thing. I think that involves reading the research literature and knowing that this is likely going to help a person.

Case Study

A mother calls and makes an appointment for her family to come to therapy. The family consists of the wife and her husband, both in their 40s; their 15-year-old son; a college-aged daughter; and the woman's father, age 82. Three years after the woman's mother died, her father was diagnosed with Alzheimer's disease and moved in with the family 6 months ago. When his symptoms got worse, the woman spent more time caring for him than for other members of the family. Three months ago, the 15-year-old son, who has been treated for bipolar I disorder since age 7, began to refuse to take his medication. The school is now calling home to report truancy by the 15 year old.

During the session, the wife cries and the husband reports that their relationship is strained, occasionally rolling his eyes as his wife becomes tearful. He reports that he has had to take on more work because his wife had to quit her job to attend to her father's needs. The daughter is away at college and the wife smiles as she describes her as a straight-A student. The daughter was asked to attend the session but refused because she has a hard time with her grandfather's mental illness and dislikes the conflict that has developed at home.

Dr. David Miklowitz's Response to the Case Study

The first step in this case is to make a careful diagnostic assessment of the 15 year old. He has been diagnosed with bipolar disorder at age 7, but what do we know about the validity of this diagnosis? Is his recent bout of truancy a manic or mixed episode, or is it a way of forcing his parents to join together around his care and redirect some of their emotional energy (especially his mother's) back onto himself? What is the history of the parent's marriage, and is the strain they are now experiencing the direct result of the father's Alzheimer's, or was it present before he got ill? An assessment of their communication and problem-solving styles would be helpful.

The mother must be enduring considerable grief, given the loss of her mother, the impending loss of her father, and the potential loss of her husband and family. She will need considerable emotional support and validation from the family therapist. Perhaps family treatment sessions could be supplemented by individual support sessions for the mother. Are the parents conjointly raising the boy, or is this primarily the mother's job? What is the father's role in his day-to-day life? How do the parents resolve disagreements about limit setting, disciplining, [and] school truancy? A useful experiment might be to put the father in charge of managing the boy's activities for the next week, making sure he gets to school, making sure he takes his medications and does his homework, to assess the how malleability of the preexisting alliances in this family (possibly, an enmeshed relationship between mother and son and disengagement between father and son).

How much do the parents understand about the two disorders they are dealing with—Alzheimer's and bipolar disorder? What medication does the child take, and is it appropriate? Can he clarify his reasons for discontinuing it—perhaps he is noncompliant because he misunderstands why he is taking it (as well as acting out against his parents).

In family therapy sessions, I would reframe and normalize what is going on in this family. I would underline how difficult it is for parents to cope with the aging and illness of their own parents, how this transition strains marriages, and how children often act out when their parents' emotional attention is drawn elsewhere. I would educate them about how bipolar disorder episodes can be provoked by stress in the family, and how symptoms can be the by-product of genetics, neurotransmitter imbalances, and psychosocial stress, for example, the stress of the grandfather's move into their home. I would encourage the parents to problem solve about rules for the child's behavior that they both agree on and are willing to enforce: How is he to be rewarded if he consistently attends school? How is he to be disciplined if he doesn't? I would also encourage them to problem solve about how the mother and son can spend more "quality time" away from the rest of the family; perhaps they could have a certain weekend afternoon that is just theirs, in which the father agrees to take care of the grandfather. The young son may also benefit from psychoeducation about the grandfather's illness, what to expect, and how the stress of an illness can affect his parents. Finally, the mother and father could probably benefit from a support group for caregivers of Alzheimer's patients. They, too, need uninterrupted time together, without the child or grandfather present. Is the daughter living close enough that she could stay with the teenage son once a week to allow them some time to escape the stress and eventually rediscover their relationship?

KEY TERMS

Behavior therapy   See Chapter 5.

DBT   Dialectical behavior therapy.

Diathesis-stress model   The diathesis-stress model is defined as "the theory that genetic predispositions and/or biochemical imbalances make stressed individuals vulnerable to specific illnesses" (Barker, 2002, p. 647).

Expressed emotion (EE)   Family members' emotional responses to the patient's symptoms. EE has been linked to relapse rates for people diagnosed with schizophrenia. According to Leff and Vaughn (1985), families that exhibit high EE tend to be critical, hostile, and emotionally overinvolved with the schizophrenic patient.

Family-focused therapy (FFT)   Miklowitz and Goldstein (1997) developed psychoeducational family-focused treatment in the early 1980s.

Family psychoeducation   Family psychoeducation is an eclectic approach that is primarily based on family systems theory, behavior therapy, structural family therapy, and educational psychology.

Family systems theory   See Chapter 3.

Multifamily psychoeducation groups   According to McFarlane (2002), five to six families participate in the groups, and the treatment includes the following stages: joining, education about the illness, problem solving, and vocational as well as social rehabilitation. These groups are designed to increase social support and reduce isolation.

Single-family psychoeducation   Single-family psychoeducation was developed by Carol Anderson and her colleagues. According to Anderson, Reiss, and Hogarty (1986), this approach includes a day-long Survival Skills Workshop that consists of education about the mental illness, current psychopharmacological and psychosocial treatments, prognosis, discussion of patient and family needs, and family coping skills.

REFERENCES

Anderson, C. M., Reiss, D. J., & Hogarty, G. E. (1986). *Schizophrenia and the family: A practitioner's guide to psychoeducation and management.* New York, NY: The Guilford Press.

Barker, L. (2002). *Psychology.* Upper Saddle River, NJ: Prentice Hall.

Corrigan, P. W., Steiner, L., McCracken, S. G., Blaser, B., & Barr, M. (2001). Strategies for disseminating evidence-based practices to staff who treat people with serious mental illness. *Psychiatric Services.* Retrieved from http://psychservices.psychiatryonline.org/cgi/content/full/52/12/1598

Dixon, L., Lyles, A., Scott, J., Lehman, A., Postrado, L., Goldman, H., & McGlynn E. (1999). Services to families of adults with schizophrenia: From treatment recommendations to dissemination. *Psychiatric Services.* Retrieved from http://ps.psychiatryonline.org/cgi/content/full/50/2/233

Dixon, L., Lyles, A., Smith, C., Hoch, J. S., Fahey, M., Postrado, L., . . . Lehman, A. (2001). Use and costs of ambulatory care services among Medicare enrollees with schizophrenia. *Psychiatric Services.* Retrieved from http://ps.psychiatryonline.org/cgi/content/full/52/6/786

Dixon, L., McFarlane, W. R., Lefley, H., Lucksted, A., Cohen, M., Falloon, I., . . . Sondheimer, D. (2001). Evidence-based practices for services to families of people with psychiatric disabilities. *Psychiatric Services.* Retrieved from http://psychservices.psychiatryonline.org/cgi/content/full52/7/903

Dyck, D. G., Hendryx, M. S., Short, R. A., Voss, W. D., & McFarlene, W. R. (2002). Service use among patients with schizophrenia in psychoeducational multiple-family group treatment. *Psychiatric Services*. Retrieved from http://ps.psychiatryonline.org/cgi/content/full/53/6/749

Falloon, I. R. G., Boyd, J. L., & McGill, C. W. (1984). *Family care of schizophrenia: A problem-solving approach to the treatment of mental illness*. New York, NY: Guilford.

Goldenberg, H., & Goldenberg, I. (2000). *Family therapy an overview* (5th ed.). Belmont, CA: Wadsworth/Thomson Learning.

Goldstein, M. J., Rodnick, E. H., Evans, J. R., May, P. R., & Steinberg, M. R. (1978). Drug and family therapy in the aftercare of acute schizophrenics. *Archives of General Psychiatry, 35*, 1169–1177.

Leff, J., & Vaughn, C. (1985). *Expressed emotion in families: Its significance for mental illness*. New York, NY: The Guilford Press.

Linehan, M. (1993). *Cognitive behavioral treatment of borderline personality disorder*. New York, NY: The Guilford Press.

McFarlane, W. R. (2002). *Multifamily groups in the treatment of severe psychiatric disorders*. New York, NY: The Guildford Press.

McFarlane, W. R., Dixon, L., Lukens, E., & Lucksted, A. (2003). Family psychoeducation and schizophrenia: A review of the literature. *Journal of Marital Family Therapy, 29*, 223–245.

McFarlane, W. R., Link, B., Dushay, R., Marchal, J., & Crilly, J. (1995). Psychoeducational multiple family groups: Four-year relapse outcome in schizophrenia. *Family Process, 34*(2), 127–144.

McFarlane, W. R., Lukens, E., Link, B., Dushay, R., Deakins, S. A., Newmark, M., . . . Toran, J. (1995). Multiple-family groups and psychoeducation in the treatment of schizophrenia. *Archives of General Psychiatry, 52*, 679–687.

Miklowitz, D. J., & Goldstein, M. J. (1997). *Bipolar disorder: A family focused treatment approach*. New York, NY: The Guilford Press.

Miklowitz, D. J., Goldstein, M. J., & Nuechterlein, N. H. (1995). Verbal interactions in the families of schizophrenic and bipolar affective patients. *Journal of Abnormal Psychology*. Retrieved from http://spider.apa.org/ftdocs/abn/1995/may/abn10422628.html

Miklowitz, D. J., Goldstein, M. J., Neuchterlein, K. H., Snyder, K. S., & Mintz, J. (1988). Family factors and the course of bipolar affective disorder. *Archives of General Psychiatry, 45*, 225–231.

Miklowitz, D. J., Otto, M. W., Frank, E., Reilly-Harrington, N. A., Wisniewski, S. R., Kogan, J. N., . . . Sach, G.S. (2007, April). Psychosocial treatments for bipolar depression: A 1-year randomized trial from the Systematic Treatment Enhancement Program. *Archives of General Psychiatry, 64*(4), 419–426.

Miklowitz, D. J., Rea, M. M., Tompson, M. C., Goldstein, M. J., Hwang, S., & Mintz, J. (2003, June). Family-focused treatment versus individual treatment for bipolar disorder: Results of a randomized clinical trial. *Journal of Consulting and Clinical Psychology, 71*(3), 482–492.

Miklowitz, D. J., Richards, J. A., George, E. L., Frank, E., Suddath, R. L., Powell, K. B., & Sacher, J. A. (2003, February). Integrated family and individual therapy for bipolar disorder: Results of a treatment development study. *Journal of Clinical Psychiatry, 64*(2), 182–191.

Miklowitz, D. J., Simoneau, T. L., George, E. L., Richards, J. A., Kalbag, A., Sachs-Ericsson, N., & Suddath, R. (2000). Family-focused treatment of bipolar disorder: 1-year effects of a psychoeducational program in conjunction with pharmacotherapy. *Biological Psychiatry, 48*, 582–592.

RECOMMENDED READING LIST

Books

American Psychiatric Association. (2000). *Diagnostic and statistical manual of mental disorders* (4th ed., text rev.). Washington, DC: Author.

American Psychological Association. (2001). *Publication manual of the American Psychological Association* (5th ed.). Washington, DC: Author.

Miklowitz, D. J. (2002). *The bipolar disorder survival guide: What you and your family need to know.* New York, NY: The Guilford Press.

Nichols, M. P., & Schwartz, R. C. (2004). *Family therapy concepts and methods* (6th ed).Boston, MA: Pearson Education.

Articles

Bateson, G., Jackson, D., Haley, J., & Weakland, J. H. (1956). Toward a theory of schizophrenia. *Behavioral Science, 1*(4), 251–264.

Falloon, I. R. (1999). Rehab rounds: Optimal treatment for psychosis in an international multisite demonstration project. *Psychiatric Services.* Retrieved from http://ps.psychiatryonline.org/cgi/content/full/50/5/615

Fromm-Reichmann, F. (1948). Notes on the development of treatment of schizophrenics by psychoanalytic psychotherapy. *Psychiatry, 11*(3), 263–273.

Lidz, R. W., & Lidz, T. (1949). The family environment of schizophrenic patients. *American Journal of Psychiatry, 106,* 332–345.

Lidz, T., Cornelison, A. R., Fleck, S., & Terry, D. (1957). The intrafamilial environment of the schizophrenic patient. II. Marital schism and marital skew. *American Journal of Psychiatry, 114*(3), 241–248.

Miklowitz, D. J. (2007, August). The role of the family in the course and treatment of bipolar disorder. *Current Directions in Psychological Sciences, 16*(4), 192–196.

Miklowitz, D. J, George, E. L., Axelson, D. A., Kim, E. Y., Birmaher, B., Schneck, C., . . . Brent, D. A. (2004, October). Family-focused treatment for adolescents with bipolar disorder. *Journal of Affective Disorders, 82*(Suppl. 1), S113–S128.

Miklowitz, D. J., George, E. L., Richards, J. A., Simoneau, T. L., & Suddath, R. L. (2003). A randomized study of family-focused psychoeducation and pharmacotherapy in the outpatient management of bipolar disorder. *Archives of General Psychiatry, 60*(9), 904–912.

Simoneau, T. L., Miklowitz, D. J., Richards, J. A., Saleem, R., & George, E. L. (1999). Bipolar disorder and family communication: Effects of a psychoeducational treatment program. *Journal of Abnormal Psychology, 108,* 588–597.

Websites

CMHS Programs: Toolkit—Family Psychoeducation
http://mentalhealth.samhsa.gov/cmhs/communitysupport/toolkits/family/

The Early Detection and Intervention for the Prevention of Psychosis Program (EDIPPP) has launched *ChangeMyMind.org,* an information and resource hub for professionals working with adolescents and young adults.

Website for McFarlane's Portland Identification and Early Referral Program (PIER), which includes research and information for professionals
http://www.mmc.org/pier_body.cfm?id=2102

Supervision in Marriage and Family Therapy

17

Sean B. Stokes and Billee K. C. Molarte

The power of accurate observation is frequently called cynicism by those who don't have it.

—George Bernard Shaw (1856–1950)

HISTORY OF SUPERVISION IN FAMILY THERAPY

In 1961, David Mace, then the executive director of the American Association for Marriage Counseling (AAMC) created the concept of forming a group of supervisors to oversee the clinical training of interns in marital counseling. His aim was to raise the standard of marriage counseling and to promote membership into the AAMC, which later became known as the American Association for Marriage and Family Therapy (AAMFT). Although most of his colleagues agreed that there was a great need for supervision in the training of marital counselors, they did not want supervision to replace formal training and education (Todd & Storm, 2003).

The first supervisors were originally

designated by the membership committee or the executive director to provide supervision for individuals seeking membership in the organization. The process was formalized in 1971, when a list of Approved Supervisors was compiled by the committee on training and standards and approved by the organization's Board of Directors. The list consisted almost entirely of individuals who were working in educational and training programs approved by the association. (Nichols, Nichols, & Hardy, 1990, pp. 275–276)

In the 1970s, therapists agreed on three family therapy skills that were considered crucial:

(a) *perceptual skills, the ability to see and describe accurately the behavioral data of the therapy session*

(b) *conceptual skills, the ability to translate clinical observations into meaningful language*

(c) *intervention skills, in-session behaviors that allow trainees to modify family interactional patterns. (Cleghorn & Levin, 1973)*

Also, during this period, training models became more specific to schools of family therapy. Finally, various teaching modalities such as viewing live sessions, videotaping, and group sessions became more popular. These modalities have become a trademark for marriage and family therapy training. They offer direct observation and the means for instant interaction between supervisor, therapist, trainee, and client (Beavers, 1985).

In the 1980s, evaluation and critical appraisal of supervision were emphasized, and the number of published articles about training and supervision models increased as well as reviews, critical analyses, and recommendations for future guidelines (Anderson, Rigazio-DiGilio, & Kunkler, 1995). In "Training With O (Observing) and T (Treatment) Teams in Live Supervision: Reflections in the Looking Glass," the importance of working with a treatment team behind the one-way mirror was touted as an excellent way of combining two family therapy models simultaneously, providing feedback to the therapist and the group behind the mirror who were processing the session (Roberts et al., 1989).

Many experts called for the examination of the effectiveness of the existing training procedures. Liddle, Breunlin, Schwartz, and Constantine (1984) stated:

> Considerable clinical experience does not automatically qualify one to be a supervisor, but rather, just as the skills of family therapy can be taught, so also a separate and definable set of supervisory skills can and should be taught systematically to therapists who wish to be competent supervisors. For our field to advance, supervision, like therapy, must be conceived as a teachable enterprise, and more basically, it must be deemed necessary to teach. (p. 140)

Issues of ethnic and cultural diversity were interjected into training, as well as individual learning styles (Anderson et al., 1995). Nichols and Schwartz (1998) have stated that ethnicity is one factor that therapists may overestimate. However, Hardy and Laszloffy (1992)

> maintain that unaware therapists may seriously underestimate the impact of race on clients and actually impede or damage the therapeutic process by not discussing issues of race with black clients. They clearly advocate addressing race and maintain that it may be crucial in establishing a therapeutic relationship. (Nelson et al., 2001)

Conversely, Nichols and Schwartz (1998) stated that it is difficult to learn about all ethnic groups, and client families are usually cooperative about providing needed information when asked.

Supervisor Standards

It took an entire decade for leaders in marital therapy to create the qualifications for supervisors, who were originally instructors in the field of family therapy, nominated by their peers.

The following are the current Standards for Supervisors for the AAMFT approved supervisor designation:

Approved supervisors must:

1. *Be familiar with the major models of marriage and family therapist (MFT) and supervision, in terms of their philosophical assumptions and pragmatic implications.*

2. *Articulate a personal model of supervision, drawn from existing models of supervision and from preferred styles of therapy.*

3. *Facilitate the coevolving therapist-client and supervisor-therapist-client relationships.*

4. *Evaluate and identify problems in therapist-client and supervisor-therapist-client relationships.*

5. *Structure supervision, solve problems, and implement supervisory interventions within a range of supervisory modalities (for example, live and videotaped supervision).*

6. *Address distinctive issues that arise in supervision mentoring.*

7. *Be sensitive to contextual variables such as culture, gender, ethnicity, and economics.*

8. *Be knowledgeable of ethical and legal issues of supervision.*

9. *Be aware of the requirements and procedures for supervising trainees for AAMFT Clinical Membership. (AAMFT, 2007, pp. 5–6)*

Description of Supervision

For this chapter, supervision is defined as a face-to-face method by which a supervisor evaluates the skills, knowledge, and abilities of a therapist in training. This definition is applicable to both practicum students and postgraduate, prelicensure interns.

Roughly 70 articles have been published over a 12-year period in three family therapy journals on the topic of supervision (Feinauer, Pistorius, Erwin, & Alonzo, 2006). This is not counting the number of books or other professional counseling journals that address the topic of supervision. Because of this, one of the difficulties becomes describing what is involved in supervision. There are multiple perspectives of supervision, which, in turn, creates many variations in both definitions and descriptions of what exactly "is" supervision (Morgan & Sprenkle, 2007; Powell & Brodsky, 2004; Storm, Todd, Sprenkle, & Morgan, 2001; White & Russell, 1995). Descriptions range from the general—to simply "oversee" the work of a student or intern to the specific—"live observation and/or face-to-face contact with the MFT trainee . . ." (AAMFT, 2007, p. 17) that provides direct feedback to the trainee and increases his or her ability to help a client (Ratanasiripong & Ghafoori, 2009; Watkins, 1997). Supervision arrangements can occur in either one-on-one or group settings (Campbell, 2000). Although most training programs use both approaches, they are especially used in those accredited by the Commission on Accreditation for Marriage and Family Therapy Education (COAMFTE; Anderson, Schlossberg, & Rigazio-DiGilio, 2000).

According to the AAMFT, supervision of marital and family therapy is expected to have the following characteristics:

- *Face-to-face conversation between the MFT/MFT trainee and the supervisor, usually in periods of approximately one hour each.*

- *The learning process should be sustained and intense.*

- *Appointments are customarily scheduled once a week; three times weekly is ordinarily the maximum and once every other week the minimum.*

- *Supervision focuses on raw data from a MFT's/trainee's continuing clinical practice, which is available to the supervisor through a combination of direct live observation, cotherapy, written clinical notes, audio and video recordings, and live supervision.*

- *It is a process clearly distinguishable from personal psychotherapy and is contracted in order to serve professional goals.*

- *It is normally completed over a period of one to three years. (AAMFT, 2007, p. 11)*

Additional Types of Supervision

During the 1980s, live supervision was a popular way to supervise (Roberts, 1983; Schwartz, Liddle, & Breunlin, 1988), because it allowed the supervisor to directly affect the therapy session through his or her supervisee, who was often on the other side of a one-way mirror. This method gave the new therapist in training support and a way of better understanding the family therapy model of their choice, as he or she literally learned how to work the model with direct instructions from the supervisor who might use a telephone to converse with the therapist in the room. Live supervision also provides the supervisor or instructor with a view of how the student or supervisee is conducting therapy and gives the therapist the support needed to do an efficient job.

Other methods of supervision for MFTs include group supervision, where a group of supervisees gather on a consistent basis, as stated by the state licensing board, with a designated supervisor to discuss cases and get support for practice in the field. Other supervision arrangements include individual supervision, where a supervisee meets one-on-one with a designated supervisor on a consistent basis, according to state regulations. Additionally, since the 1980s, supervision and training has become more specific to the individual models (such as structural, strategic, functional, and behavioral) that are discussed in this volume. Supervisors are encouraged to do supervision within family therapy models of their expertise.

Today, with technology expanding the resources to MFTs and other mental health practitioners, e-supervision has an obvious advantage for supervisees and supervisors to work together, even if located in different geographical locations.

> There are areas in the United States where finding a family therapist supervisor is prohibitive or not accessible. A bright intern on a tight budget ready to start her internship and doing family therapy outreach in Williamsport, PA, would need to drive 100 miles every week if she were to obtain all her supervision hours in the traditional format. E-supervision fits perfectly well in making the seemingly impossible possible and expanding our services into areas that really need them. Another example of e-supervision's possibilities is a supervisee, able to obtain supervision or consultation from an expert in an area of expertise not available in her state or locality. (Bacigalupe, 2010, p. 37)

Practicum Setting Versus Intern Setting

In an academic setting, a practicum student (trainee) is often afforded the opportunity to experience multiple types of supervision: (a) live observation occurring with the practicum instructor being behind a one-way mirror; (b) audio or video supervision, whereby the practicum student presents a recorded case to the supervisor and his or her assigned practicum group; (c) case-note only; and (d) co-therapy with the student's practicum supervisor being "in the session" with the client and the student therapist. The co-therapy opportunity appears to be growing in popularity with many practicum students, because it not only provides immediate feedback but also provides the student trainee a chance to work side-by-side with his or her supervising faculty member (Bernard, Babineau, & Schwartz, 1980; McGee & Burton, 1998; Powell & Brodsky, 2004).

Most, if not all, university training programs require a student trainee to have amassed a certain number of hours of classroom experience and course work before entering into the clinical training portion of the program. Once the clinical training portion has begun, the student trainee is assigned to a practicum group and a supervisor. It is with this group that the student trainee will spend the next 3 to 4 months (usually one semester) before being assigned to a new practicum group at the beginning of the next semester. However, for some training programs, the students are considered a "cohort," meaning the group of students will start and finish the graduate program together and not be reassigned to new practicum groups each semester.

Regardless of how a student trainee enters practicum, the student trainee is often required to complete a certain number of clock hours, usually ranging between 100 and 150 per semester with between 40 and 50 of those hours being direct client contact hours (COAMFTE, 2002; Council for Accreditation of Counseling and Related Educational Programs [CACREP], 2009). Northey (2005) describes a paradigm shift occurring in MFT training programs that is moving toward "documenting what students are able to do, rather than what they have done (e.g., go to class, spend 500 hours with clients)" (p. 11) as part of the new core competencies that are being instituted in MFT training programs. At present, however, all practicum students are to have weekly supervision during the accumulation of the necessary practicum hours. On average, the supervision is with the other members of the practicum group, not primarily one-on-one with the practicum instructor or supervisor. In most training programs, there is a set day and time of the week when the practicum group meets. Topics of supervision usually involve current client issues where the trainee might be struggling or have questions as to a proper course of action. Examples of topics can include parent–child relationship issues, couple relationship issues, ethical concerns, and self-of-therapist issues. Additionally, any audio or video presentation of cases can also occur.

As a way for supervisors to track the growth of a student trainee, Briggs, Fournier, and Hendrix (1999) developed the "Family Therapy Skills Checklist" that tracks progress on three major domains: conceptual skills, behavioral skills, and the use of supervision (see Figure 17.1). By using it at the beginning of a practicum term, midpoint, and finally at the conclusion of the practicum term, a student trainee and his or her supervisor are able to gain an accurate picture of the student trainee's professional development over time.

The requirements of supervision for those who have graduated from a training program and are now seeking licensure as a licensed marriage and family therapist (LMFT), or a licensed professional counselor (LPC) vary by practice setting as well as by state (Campbell, 2000). As with the student trainee, an intern is usually required to meet with his or her supervisor on a weekly basis. Each state has a regulatory board that will dictate what is required to obtain licensure. For example, for those interns seeking to be licensed in Texas as an LMFT, the supervisee must:

Be licensed as a Licensed Marriage and Family Therapist Associate; be working under an approved supervision contract [that is] is provided by the board; the supervision must occur over a minimum of 24 months; Over the minimum of 24 months, the supervisee must have provided a minimum of 3,000 hours of marriage and family therapy services; of the 3,000 hours of service, at least 1,500 hours must be direct clinical services; of the 1,500 hours of direct clinical services, 750 hours must be direct clinical services to couples or families; of the 3,000 hours, up to 500 hours may be transferred from a COAMFTE accredited doctoral program; the supervisee must accrue at least 200 hours of direct supervision; of the total 200 hours of direct supervision, at least 100 hours must be individual supervision. (Texas Department of State Health Services, 2008)

Oftentimes, the supervision setting for postgraduate interns is limited to case-note review in a one-on-one setting or, should the supervisor have more than one intern,

Name:					Semester:
					Year:

Work Area	Acceptable		Strength
1	2	3	4	5

Conceptual Skills

The therapist is able to

Recognize family strengths.

Therapist: ＿＿   Supervisor: ＿＿

Recognize hierarchy problems.

Therapist: ＿＿   Supervisor: ＿＿

Define family problems in systematic terms.

Therapist: ＿＿   Supervisor: ＿＿

Formulate systemic hypotheses.

Therapist: ＿＿   Supervisor: ＿＿

Distinguish between content and process.

Therapist: ＿＿   Supervisor: ＿＿

Use systemic understanding of family interactions to design interventions.

Therapist: ＿＿   Supervisor: ＿＿

Behavioral Skills

The therapist is able to

Focus interview.

Therapist: ＿＿   Supervisor: ＿＿

Control/structure interactions during session.

Therapist: ＿＿   Supervisor: ＿＿

Establish the therapeutic contract with family.

Therapist: ＿＿   Supervisor: ＿＿

Keep the family connected with the therapy process.

Therapist: ＿＿   Supervisor: ＿＿

Handle toxic causes sensitively.

Therapist: ＿＿   Supervisor: ＿＿

Use genograms.

Therapist: ＿＿   Supervisor: ＿＿

Design and carry out appropriate interventions.

Therapist: ＿＿   Supervisor: ＿＿

Use of Supervision

The therapist is able to

Appropriately use AAMFT ethical guidelines.

Therapist: ＿＿   Supervisor: ＿＿

Come prepared for individual and group supervision.

Therapist: ＿＿   Supervisor: ＿＿

Set appropriate supervision goals.

Therapist: ＿＿   Supervisor: ＿＿

Accurately assess his or her part in the therapeutic system.

Therapist: ＿＿   Supervisor: ＿＿

Incorporate input from supervision during session.

Therapist: ＿＿   Supervisor: ＿＿

Make use of phone-ins during therapy sessions.

Therapist: ＿＿   Supervisor: ＿＿

Make use of midsession breaks.

Therapist: ＿＿   Supervisor: ＿＿

The above rating scale was shared with the therapist on the date below. Therapist's and supervisor's signature are not meant to imply agreement, only that the information was discussed during a supervision session.

Therapist's Signature/Date ＿＿＿＿＿＿ /＿＿＿＿   **Supervisor's** Signature/Date ＿＿＿＿＿ /＿＿＿＿

FIGURE 17.1 ■ Family therapy skills checklist.
Source: With kind permission from Springer Science+Business Media: *Contemporary Family Therapy*. Evaluating Trainees' Skill Development: The Family Therapy Skills Checklist, 21, 3, 1999, Kathleen Briggs.

case-note review in a group setting. It is the rare agency setting that has the ability to videotape sessions and incorporate video supervision with the intern. Further, although co-therapy with the supervisor is always a possibility for interns in either an agency setting or private practice setting, the exact number of occurrences in these settings is not known.

One major difference between practicum status and intern status is that the LMFT or LPC intern has the ability to choose his or her supervisor whereas, stated previously, the practicum student is usually assigned to a supervisor and practicum group. This requires the use of a formal contract establishing the supervision relationship. Each state licensing board will often have a form that is required to be completed prior to the "temporary" license being issued. Using Texas as the example again, there is a two-page contract that must be notarized and submitted with the other documents necessary for applying for a license (see Figure 17.2).

Additionally, many supervisors will require a written contract be established between the LMFT or LPC intern and the supervisor. Oftentimes, this contract will supplement the state contract in that it will provide more details as to exactly when and where supervision will occur, how much the supervision will cost (if anything), the responsibilities of the intern and the supervisor, and how the intern will be evaluated. Sutter, McPherson, and Geeseman (2002) developed a formalized contract designed to aid both the supervisor and intern with developing the supervisory relationship (see Figure 17.3).

Benefits

Supervision carries with it certain benefits for the trainee or intern. It is a way in which to provide not only desired feedback (Briggs et al., 1999) but also support and encouragement to the therapist in training (Bernard & Goodyear, 2009). As mentioned previously, many students have expressed their support for co-therapy with their supervisor (Powell & Brodsky, 2004) because this affords them a way to observe and learn in a collaborative environment (Goolishian & Anderson, 1991 as cited in Ratliff, Wampler, & Morris, 2000). When the question of "What have been the benefits of supervision for you during your practicum training?" was posed to practicum students, the following answers were found:

> I found [out that] one of the benefits of supervision was having an experienced person, who had the ability to help me see things and life through the lenses of a different set of eyes and not just through my own. Supervision has helped me grow not only professionally, but personally as well. (D. Eunice, personal communication, August 24, 2010)

> Helps protect my clients from any oversight of my behaviors, thoughts, and feelings that may become an issue in the session. This has been ongoing for me. [It] has also helped me to manage my frustrations and tensions associated with my clients. (B. Danz, personal communication, August 23, 2010)

> Supervision helps therapists see different perspectives, broaden their realm of knowledge and level of comfort, as well as challenges therapists to look deep within themselves to face the individual biases which can affect productive counseling. (S. Keck, personal communication, August 23, 2010)

Other benefits include encouragement of new therapeutic techniques, a chance to observe the work of fellow practicum students (i.e., learning from peer supervision), and an opportunity to socialize with the practicum instructor (Anderson et al., 2000).

CULTURAL DIFFERENCES IN SUPERVISION

MFTs will increasingly be called on to assist individuals, couples, and families who possess markedly different cultural backgrounds than the therapists and also different worldviews. The worldviews of the clients directly affect their understanding and processing of

FORM III
Required for issuance of
Associate license.

TEXAS STATE BOARD OF EXAMINERS
OF MARRIAGE AND FAMILY THERAPISTS

SUPERVISORY AGREEMENT FORM
Complete Both Pages
THIS IS NOT A CONTRACT BETWEEN SUPERVISEE AND SUPERVISOR

Mail this correspondence (no fees enclosed) to:
Texas State Board of Examiners of Marriage and Family Therapists
Mail Code 1982
P.O. Box 149347
Austin, Texas 78714-9347
Phone: 1-512-834-6677   FAX NO. 1-512-834-6677

I. Supervisee Information

Name: _____ Associate License Number: _____
   Where will the marriage and family therapy services be provided?
      Name/address/phone number of agency: _____
      _____
   Type of setting: ___ Private practice; ___ Hospital; ___ School; ___ Governmental agency;
      ___ Nonprofit; or ___ other: _____

Work schedule: ☐ Full time (30hrs/week) or more ☐ Part time (Hours per week _____)

II. Supervisor Information (supervisor must meet the board's criteria)

Name: _____ License Number: _____
Business Name: _____
Business Address: _____
Business Phone: _____
Are you a board-approved supervisor?   Are you an AAMFT-approved supervisor?
☐ Yes ☐ No   ☐ Yes ☐ No

III. Clinical Supervision Schedule
Beginning Date of Supervision: _____
Supervision Format: ☐ Individual ☐ Group ☐ Combination
Supervision Sessions per Month: ___ Hours Individual + ___ Hours Group = ___ Total Hours/Month

IV. Affidavit of Understanding and Signatures

   I, as applicant, affirm that all information provided by me on this form is true and accurate,
   and I affirm the following:
   • That I have read the board rules relating to supervised experience and that all supervised
     experience will be completed in accordance with the section of the board rules relating to
     supervised experience.

FIGURE 17.2 ■ Texas supervisory agreement form.
Source: Texas State Board of Licensed Marriage and Family Therapists.

- That I will meet with my supervisor for a minimum of one hour of supervision every two weeks.
- That I will abide by all rules of the board including ethics requirements.
- That I understand the associate license does give me the authority to engage in the independent practice of marriage and family therapy under supervision.
- That I understand the professional responsibility for the service of the supervisee shall be a joint responsibility of the supervisor and supervisee.
- That I will notify the board if the supervisory arrangement is terminated.

_____   _____
Printed Name of Notary   Signature of Applicant

_____   _____
Signature of Notary   Date

(SEAL)

I, as supervisor of the above named applicant's experience, affirm that all information provided by me on this form is true and accurate, and I affirm the following:
- That all supervised experience will be completed in accordance with the section of the board rules relating to supervised experience and all subsequent board rules.
- That I will meet with the supervisee for a minimum of one hour of supervision every two weeks.
- That I understand the professional responsibility for the services of the supervisee shall be a joint responsibility of the supervisor and the supervisee.
- That I understand the supervisee can engage in the independent practice of marriage and family therapy under supervision until he or she obtains a regular license as a licensed marriage and family therapist.
- That I understand the supervisory arrangement <u>must</u> be reflected on <u>all</u> billing documents.
- That I will notify the board if the supervisory arrangement is terminated.

_____   _____
Printed Name of Notary   Signature of Applicant

_____   _____
Signature of Notary   Date

(SEAL)

TEXAS Department of State Health Services

PRIVACY NOTIFICATION: With few exceptions, you have the right to request and be informed about information that the State of Texas collects about you. You are entitled to receive and review the information on request. You also have the right to ask the state agency to correct any information that is determined to be incorrect. See http://www.dshs.state.tx.us/ for more information on Privacy Notification. (Reference: Government Code, Section 552.021, 552.023, 559.003 and 559.004).
Paper Publication #:F 73-10753   **Rev. 6/09**

FIGURE 17.2 ■ Texas supervisory agreement form. *(Continued)*

Supervision Agreement: MFT Intern/Associate

APPLICANT INFORMATION

Name: _____

Preferred Mailing Address: _____

City: _____ ST: _____ Zip Code: _____

Telephone Number: (_____)_____

SUPERVISOR INFORMATION

Name: _____

Type & Title of License Held: _____ Lic. #: _____ Exp. Date: _____

Date Original License was Issued: _____ State in which Lic. was Issued: _____

Preferred Mailing Address: _____

City: _____ ST: _____ Zip Code: _____

Telephone Number: (_____)_____

Are you an AAMFT Approved Supervisor? Yes _____ No _____

State Approved? Yes _____ No _____

INFORMATION RELATING TO SUPERVISED EXPERIENCE

Name and address of organization or agency where experience will be gained:

_____

_____

Average number of client contact hours expected to be gained per week:

I, as applicant, affirm that all information provided by me on this form is true and

accurate and I affirm the following: (initial)

_____ That I have read the AAMFT Code of Ethics.

_____ That I have read the Board Rules relating to supervised experience in my State and

that all supervised experience will be completed in accordance with the section of the Board Rules

relating to supervised experience.

_____ That I will typically meet with my supervisor for at least one hour during each week

of documented experience.

_____ That I understand the MFT Associate or MFT Intern Certification does not give me

the authority to engage in the independent practice of marriage and family therapy.

_____ That I will notify the Board if the supervisory arrangement is terminated.

_____   _____

Signature of Applicant   Date

FIGURE 17.3 ■ Supervision agreement.

Sworn to and Subscribed before me this the _____ day of _____, 20_____

Signature of Notary My Commission Expires

I, as the supervisor of the above named applicant's experience, affirm that all information provided by me on this form is true and accurate and I affirm the following: (initial)

_____ That all supervised experiences will be completed in accordance with the section of the Board Rules relating to supervised experience and all subsequent Board Rules.

_____ That I will typically meet with the supervisee for at least one hour during each week of documented experience.

_____ That I understand the full professional responsibility for the services of the supervisee shall rest with the supervisor, except that the supervisee shall pay their premium for any malpractice insurance covering the services.

_____ That I understand the supervisee cannot engage in the independent practice of marriage and family therapy until he or she obtains a regular license as a licensed marriage and family therapist.

_____ That I will notify the Board if the supervisor arrangement is terminated.

_____   _____

Signature of Supervisor   Date

Sworn to and Subscribed before me this the _____ day of _____, 20_____

Signature of Notary My Commission Expires

FIGURE 17.3 ▦ Supervision agreement. *(Continued)*

mental health services. The comfort level of the process must be designed with care through sensitivity, which will impact how a client self-discloses to the therapist. It is the effective, efficient MFT who recognizes the need to understand different worldviews.

Marriage and family therapy is successful with multicultural clients and families when the therapist spends time at the beginning of therapy assessing the client's concerns and inquiring about how the client feels to be working with a therapist of a different culture. Will the therapist understand the client's concern? Does the therapist know enough about the client's culture so as not to suggest strategies that would be offensive? Additionally, there might be uneasiness about the therapist's ability to view them as unique individuals, as a social unit within a family, and as a member of a cultural group (Ponterotto & Casas, 1991).

Additionally, it is important for supervisors to pay attention to cultural differences between them and their supervisees and between supervisees and clients. If not, both the supervisees and clients are left extremely susceptible to emotional harm. Therefore, as scholarly students, we must set three standards for ourselves:

- We must learn what our cultural lens is.
- We need to understand our blind spots with certain cultures.
- We need to know our own prejudices and should expect and request that our supervisors aid us in that process of self-assessment. (Banks, 2001)

Therefore, to summarize, supervisors should inquire about their marriage and family supervisees' knowledge about working with multicultural families. The supervisor should encourage supervisees working with diverse families to ask the family to teach the supervisee about their culture, ethnicities, orientations, and beliefs. Not only does the supervisee learn from this experience, but also the relationship between supervisee and client grows in the process, creating an atmosphere of sincerity and respect. It is the competent therapist that allows clients to grow and change and reach their full potential in a culturally sensitive therapy environment (Jordan, 2001).

ETHICAL ISSUES IN SUPERVISION

Storm and Todd (2003) raise penetrating questions about our standards, such as, "While none of us would like to believe that we overreact or underreact to unethical behavior, to which extreme are you more likely to gravitate?" and, "Are there 'hot button' issues where your ethical judgment would be less objective?" and finally, "Do you have a clear and systematic plan of action when you hear of possible unethical behavior on the part of another helping professional?" (p. 1). These are questions that a beginning MFT should evaluate and take to heart as he or she enters the field.

In 2001, when the AAMFT revised its ethics code, Hovestadt (2001) stated that supervisors should discuss ethical principles with their supervisees but go beyond just reciting them. In addition, supervisors should discuss how understanding the ethics code can guide their practice as a family therapist. Hovestadt suggests that supervisees review the following revisions of the code. Code number is in parentheses:

Dual relationships: Supervisees do not engage in outside activities or business transactions with clients at anytime. "The concern is not the mere existence of a dual relationship, but the risk of the therapist's judgment being impaired or of the client being exploited. The prohibition against sexual intimacy with clients is emphasized (1.4), and there is still an absolute prohibition for 2 years following therapy."

Length of therapy: Therapists will continue seeing a client only so long as the client will benefit (1.7) and will appropriately refer any client the therapist cannot help (1.8). Not every therapist is good for every client, a notion that is often overlooked as trainees strive to demonstrate their competence.

Confidentiality: This issue can be complex in real practice and during training. Areas to emphasize in a supervisory discussion include ensuring that clients understand possible limits to confidentiality (2.1), maintaining confidentiality when transferring records (2.5), and managing confidentiality when consulting with colleagues or referral sources (2.6).

Practicing therapy models: Therapists should not practice new techniques or specialties without the proper education and supervision (3.6) and reminds therapists that there is an ethical obligation to stay abreast of developments in the field (3.5).

Intimate/dual relationships: The code prohibits the supervisor from providing therapy to students and supervisees (4.2) and against sexual intimacy with students and supervisees (4.3). Additionally, the code prohibits the acceptance of students and supervisees with whom the supervisor has a prior or existing relationship, which could compromise the supervisor's objectivity (4.5).

Employment conflict of code: On occasion, a supervisee may encounter a conflict where their employing agency's policy conflicts with the code (6.1). Specifically, the therapist is obliged to notify the employer of the conflict and his or her desire to abide by the code, and to make every effort to resolve the conflict in a way that adheres to the code.

Financial cost of therapy: Supervisees should inform their clients about what therapy will cost through their agency and what will happen if the client becomes unable or unwilling to pay for services (7.2). For example, therapists generally cannot withhold records solely because payment has not been received (7.6).

It is advisable that all supervisees in training review the AAMFT Ethics Code, located at AAMFT.org.

Supervision Suggestions for Students and Supervisors

Instead of the template in this chapter, checklists are provided for both the supervision relationship and the supervisee.

Prior to the first session of supervision, meet with your perspective supervisor to determine if the supervisor has the capacity to suit your needs as a supervisor. Ask the supervisor about his or her expertise with the family therapy model you have chosen to practice. Ask about his or her availability for supervision on a consistent basis. Ask about the cost of supervision per hour. Find out about his or her practice and beliefs of supervision. If the supervisor has group supervision, ask if you can sit in on a group and observe. It is also important that your supervisor is available for consultation on an as-needed basis by phone or e-mail.

Some supervisors prefer live supervision whereas others are fine with viewing the supervisee on a videotape or simply listening to audiotapes of their sessions. Sometimes, therapists will have a choice of which way they prefer to be supervised, and sometimes, clinics or institutions have set rules about how supervision will be conducted. However, deciding what modality a supervisor uses ought to be based on the needs of the supervisee and their clients (Prest & Schindler-Zimmerman, 1997, p. 210).

During supervision, therapists seek to develop more skills and a knowledge base. When limitations of a supervisee arise during a supervisory session, it is the responsibility of the supervisor to provide the supervisee with an atmosphere where he or she feels comfortable investigating and discussing skills. Rather than focusing on deficiencies, therapists and supervisors should be encouraged to recognize and develop them (Prest & Schindler-Zimmerman, 1997, p. 198).

It is probable that the supervisee will become more skillful in facilitating change in their client families throughout the supervision process. The supervisor should identify goals that are not being met during supervision, as well as allow the supervisees to self-evaluate and notice their own need for personal development. It is very important to remain positive and recognize even small steps in the right direction (Prest & Schindler-Zimmerman, 1997, p. 117–118).

The supervisor and supervisee need to decide if they want their contract completed prior to the first session or if they want it to evolve as needs arise during the normal processes of supervision. This is a matter of preference. The "Supervision Checklist" (Figure 17.4) is

Supervision Checklist

Examine the Supervisee's Educational History

_____ Discuss the supervisee's educational background and degrees

_____ Discuss the supervisee's training experience

_____ Inquire about the supervisee's years or service and setting

_____ Discuss the supervisee's theoretical orientation

_____ Discuss the supervisee's experience with certain issues in therapy and theoretical competencies with certain techniques

_____ Inquire about the supervisee's sense of mission and purpose in the field of marriage and family therapy

_____ Inquire about the supervisee's academic and professional goals

_____ Examine the supervisee's training and awareness of cultural and contextual issues in therapy

Explore the Philosophy of Supervision

_____ Discuss the philosophy of therapy and change

_____ Discuss the supervisor's and supervisee's role and purpose of supervision

_____ Inquire about the supervisee's expectations of supervision

Review Previous Supervision Experiences

_____ Inquire about prior supervision experiences in regard to format, setting, and what was helpful/not helpful

_____ Identify the strengths and weaknesses as a therapist of the supervisee and of the supervisor

_____ Talk about the supervisee's competence with stages of therapy

_____ Discuss the supervisee's understanding of case planning, keeping notes, gathering resources, and networking

_____ Discuss supervisory competence with various issues, models, techniques, populations, therapy groups, and modalities to see if they match the supervisee's needs

_____ Discuss strategies for managing any supervisor–supervisee differences

Supervision Goals

_____ Identify the supervisee's goals (personal and professional)

_____ Determine the process of goal evaluation

_____ Discuss the reasons for which supervisee is seeking supervision (e.g., licensure, professional certification) and the help that the supervisee needs from the supervisor

_____ Discuss the requirements to be met by supervisor in regard to total hours, and whether individual or group supervision applies

Supervision Style and Techniques

_____ Discuss together the kind of supervision that would facilitate clinical growth of the supervisee

_____ Discuss the supervision style of the supervisor

FIGURE 17.4 ■ Supervision checklist.

_____ Discuss the similarities between therapy and supervision models and how the supervisor may use the similarities

_____ Discuss how cases will be reviewed for crisis management or ongoing cases

_____ Discuss methods of case presentation such as videotapes

Theoretical Orientation

_____ Discuss and explore the models and specific theories in which supervisee and supervisor have been trained, practiced, and/or conducted supervision to see if there is a good fit

_____ Discuss with the supervisee which populations, presenting problems, and/or family situations that he or she sees the model of choice working best or if the model is applicable to all cases

_____ Inquire whether the supervisee is interested in learning new approaches

Legal and Ethical Considerations

_____ Describe, in detail, the supervisor and supervisee's responsibility for clients discussed in supervision in different contexts such as private practice, school setting, and agencies

_____ Discuss the number of cases for which the supervisee will see

_____ Provide emergency and backup procedures

_____ Inquire of the supervisee's awareness of professional ethical codes

_____ Discuss confidentiality regarding the information discussed in supervision

_____ Check out specific issues in situations where dual relationships may exist

_____ Discuss self-care and a process for addressing supervisee issues

FIGURE 17.4 ■ Supervision checklist. *(Continued)*

provided here as a tool for both supervisor and supervisee to examine and ensure that the supervisee's needs are addressed by the supervisor.

Using the checklist to get to know one another is ideal. It will lead both the supervisor and the supervisee into discussions about education, training levels, clinical experiences, as well as competence with various issues such as models, abortion, gender, and ethnicity.

Contracts

Contracts can be helpful for both the supervisor and the supervisee (Prest & Schindler-Zimmerman, 1997, p. 118). Figure 17.3 displays a contract that can be helpful for supervisors to use with their supervisees. Note that some states have their own supervisory agreement for supervision for MFT.

Typically, supervision ends when a supervisee has completed the hours required for his or her licensure in his or her state. The supervisor then signs the papers documenting that the supervisee has indeed conducted the hours required and may request a spreadsheet of the hours for her files. Sometimes, supervision continues as the supervisee may desire to continue to grow and develop her MFT skills. It is advised that all MFTs who complete their licensure requirements continue to seek either peer supervision on an occasional basis or occasional supervision with the past-designated supervisor to keep abreast of new developments in the field and to ensure that she maintains a high degree of integrity in the field.

INTERVIEW WITH AN APPROVED SUPERVISOR

CHERYL STORM

Cheryl Storm, PhD, is a professor of family therapy at Pacific Lutheran University. She is well known for two excellent books on supervision that she coauthored with Thomas C. Todd: The Complete Systemic Supervisor: Context, Philosophy, and Pragmatics *(January 2003) and* The Reasonably Complete Systemic Supervisor Resource Guide *(January 2003).*

What attracted you to the field of supervision?

Like many new supervisors, I wanted to pass on what I had learned about therapy and my excitement about the field of couple and family. At the time, I felt I was a part of a group of therapists who were going to revolutionize mental health and who had the "answers." Although I am still passionate about relational therapy, I am less arrogant and [I] believe [that] there are no answers to pass down. Today, I enjoy supervision as a process whereby each supervisee is finding the best answer for him or herself about what ways of practicing therapy he or she prefers and how to do so ethically within a professional culture where there are many competing claims for what is best.

What is your personal theory about how supervision works best?

One of my first publications in 1985 with Tony Heath, "Models of Supervision: Using Therapy Theory as a Guide," discussed the isomorphic relationship between therapy and supervision and how beginning supervisors could use their preferred ideas of therapy to guide the development of a supervision philosophy (Heath & Storm, 1985). For example, I believe supervision "works best" when it is based on a trusting, mutually respectful relationship similar to the central role of the therapeutic relationship in therapy. However, as I engaged in this process, I began to distinguish ways in which the supervision context was different from the therapy context. There is a significant difference between therapy and supervision. As a supervisor, I am assisting supervisees in learning what they will need to pass through the gate into the profession to become a competent colleague of mine, or, if necessary, close the gate for whatever reason to those not yet able to provide adequate services. This role does not exist for me as a therapist.

Thus, my supervision philosophy evolved and moved beyond my ideas of therapy into the new territory of paying attention to how people learn. I became interested in creating a learning context that encourages the development of life-long self-learners, discovering my supervisees' preferred ways of learning and drawing on various educational ideas and pedagogue (e.g., active learning, adult learning, competency-based education) in my work as a supervisor. In my experience, supervisees appreciate having a supervisor who is willing to discuss with them their process of learning and whether being a therapist as a career fits for them. My current philosophy of supervision is relationally focused, based on a mix of systems and postmodern ideas; integrates some ideas from solution-focused and collaborative language ideas about therapy; focuses on power, privilege, and multiculturalism; and incorporates ideas about learning cited above [previously].

What are the necessary attributes of a supervisor?
In my opinion, supervisors must be able to establish supervisory alliances, be open to and excited about many ways that therapy can be practiced, interested in the overall professional development of their supervisees, be able to handle their ascribed power benevolently, be respectful, and be focused on the supervisory relationship.

How do you see your involvement in the therapeutic process?
Although I am legally accountable for the supervision I provide, I am not expected nor would I want to walk in the shoes of my supervisees. My role is to provide the best supervision I can using my experience and knowledge to look down the road for problems or areas that should be attended to, and facilitate a supervisory context where supervisees build on their strengths, challenge their growth, and develop their preferred ideas, methods, and styles of being therapists.

How would you define the effective supervisor?
In my view, an effective supervisor is someone who helps their supervisees become better therapists than their supervisees believed possible. I feel I am effective when my supervisees leave supervision confident and having an ability to articulate their preferred ideas and methods along with their clients expressing satisfaction with therapy they are receiving and reaching their goals. It can also include helping a supervisee come to the conclusion that therapy is not the best career choice for him or her, or taking the difficult stance of sharing serious concerns about someone's ability to be a therapist but doing so kindly, respectfully, and carefully.

How do you determine your own sense of effectiveness with supervisees?
In addition to asking for feedback along the way and the formal evaluations of my supervision required by my educational context, I ask my supervisees to evaluate my supervision in our evaluation session together. I believe this decreases somewhat the power inherent in the evaluation process and sets a slightly more mutual tone to it. I come prepared with my evaluation of my work; things I thought went well and things I think I could have done differently to share with my supervisees. I listen extra carefully to what my supervisees say because I believe it is difficult for some, if not all, supervisees to tell me when I have not met their learning needs due to the power differential that exists in supervision.

What training and experience do you feel is necessary to become an effective supervisor?
In terms of supervisory training, I support the overall training program that was developed in 1971 by the AAMFT for approved supervisors. The training components include a course on supervision, experience in doing supervision for an extended period of time, and an experienced supervisor who is serving as a mentor and providing supervision of the individual wishing to become a supervisor. Regardless of whether a person interested in becoming a supervisor decides to be designated as an approved supervisor of AAMFT or not, I believe these three components, in some form, comprise quality supervision training.

In my opinion, being a supervisor is about facilitating the professional development of a therapist in some way; however, the supervision context can be very seductive. Supervisors can easily find themselves either telling supervisees how to practice therapy as if it is their own case or creating clones of themselves. The various training components assist supervisors in dealing with this seduction and in identifying and developing their preferred ideas, methods, beliefs, and styles of supervision. The course provides theoretical and informational background and broadens one's view of supervision beyond local experience. The doing of supervision in a mentoring relationship provides opportunities to process the experience with someone who is able to move to the supervision context rather than the therapy context. During the training process, supervisors take on the new role of supervisor and receive support and guidance as they develop themselves as supervisors.

How long is your typical session with a supervisee? How often does the supervisee see you and for how long a period of time? Can you describe your thoughts and approach to communicating with supervisees between sessions?
All of these questions are determined mostly by the context in which supervision occurs and [by] the experience levels of the supervisees. Most of the supervision I do is in a couple and family therapy masters' program, where the program parameters set the length and frequency of supervision, and I supervise brand new therapists. Between supervision sessions, I try to find a balance between being available to respond to my supervisees' needs without being so available that they do not have a sense of practicing as a professional. In addition, supervision is only a small part of my overall responsibilities that I must attend to in my position.

When I have supervised in private contracts, the frequency and length of supervision is based more on the amount of therapy the therapist is doing, in what context (i.e., agency or private practice), and for what reason (i.e., for professional development, for licensure, for an educational requirement, or some combination of these). An ethical responsibility of supervisors is to provide timely and ethical supervision while ensuring that clients are receiving adequate care and supervisees' appropriate guidance. Regulatory bodies and educational programs also set these parameters. Thus, each situation is unique and a supervision structure [is] set accordingly.

What are you looking for with individual supervisees when you are supervising them?
What I look for is evidence that a supervisee is showing the competencies as defined by the educational program where I teach. We developed an evaluation tool that defines competencies, [which] we feel are important based on supervisory and training experience of our supervisors, the literature on training and supervision, and generally accepted standards in the field. Personally, the areas that I highlight because they are especially important to me are that supervisees show a relational perspective to therapy, are using a multicultural lens throughout their work, are grounded in some organizing theoretical framework, can develop solid, respectful therapeutic relationships, and have a sense of their emerging professional development as therapists.

Who sets the goals for supervision?
Supervisors vary regarding whether goals are more supervisor-directed, supervisee-directed, or mutually set depending on their supervision philosophy. For example, supervisors who lean more towards skill building will work with supervisees to develop goals that are more defined by the supervisor, while postmodern supervisors will work at setting goals that are supervisee centered. However, experienced supervisors seem to believe supervisees always participate in the goal-setting process regardless of the supervisor's philosophy, and that goals are more supervisee-directed as supervisees' experience level increases.

In my situation with new supervisees in my educational context, we develop goals along the way together, but I often am leading the way. Many have never seen a client, so they do not know what they do not know! I begin by asking my supervisees about ways they learn best, what they need from me, and goals they have for supervision. For example, with a recent supervisee, the supervisee requested that we focus on diagnosis and doing intake paperwork expressing that she was feeling anxious about these responsibilities. Although we spent a fair amount of time on these areas, I also targeted helping her feel more comfortable conversing with clients around their relationships so she could adopt a more relational viewpoint than the individually oriented one I saw when I viewed her therapy tapes. At this point in her training, if I had suggested [that] we focus on her developing a relational perspective (something she felt very confident about), I believe I would have added to her anxiety. As my questions focused on the relationships in her cases, she began to experience the difference in an individually oriented and a relational view leading, to a mutually defined stated goal of developing her ability to conceptualize relationally. As we developed a more process-oriented goal around her competency as a therapist, her confidence increased, anxiety decreased, and her written intakes improved. But, clearly, I led us in this direction.

When you have a concern about a supervisee, how do you approach the issue?
At the first sign of a concern, I try to bring it up in a direct, firm, respectful way with specific examples supporting my concern in an empathetic atmosphere of searching for understanding and solutions. My goal is to create a context where my supervisee and I can begin to understand each other's perspective on the issue, so we can be on the same page, and hopefully find a way to address it in a mutually satisfactory manner. I have learned the hard way that sometimes, concerns do disappear over time, but that if they do not, supervisees feel understandably betrayed if a supervisor has not shared a concern until it has become a problem.

What role does a homework assignment have in supervision with supervisees? What happens if the supervisee does not do the homework and ignores your suggestion?
Some supervisors use homework assignments as their method of choice while others, rarely, if ever, do. I occasionally use homework assignments in my supervision, but typically only when supervisees have indicated they learn best by specific directions from me and they want guidance on what they could do between sessions to develop their abilities. This stems from my personal philosophy of supervision. If a supervisee does not do a homework assignment, I have learned not to continue to "do more of the same," but to view it as an indication that I have not matched my supervisee well or that our supervision relationship needs attention.

How do you know when your supervisee is ready to terminate the supervision relationship?
Again, the context in which the supervision occurs, as well as the reasons for supervision, seems to shape this a great deal. My educational context sets the ending of my supervision relationships; every 15 weeks, I end with my current supervisees and am assigned two new supervisees. For supervisees and supervisors entering into private contracts with one another, many report that having a specified ending date discussed in their initial supervision agreement can be helpful. This allows a way for supervisees to leave a supervision process that is not meeting their needs gracefully.

Why do family counselors need supervision?

This question goes to the heart of the matter by essentially asking about the value of supervision. One important reason is that the couple and family therapy field, like the other mental health fields, have sold (and I use the term sold intentionally) the idea of supervision to the public as a way for partially qualified clinicians to provide therapy to those in need because there is a fully trained therapist involved. Thus, supervision is a way to help new therapists gain the trust of the public.

A second reason is the belief in the field that supervision is a valuable process that facilitates the development of effective clinicians. Interestingly, there is little research that actually indicates supervision is effective. Surveys of supervisees find that supervisees report supervision as helpful particularly in gaining confidence (Bischoff, Barton, Thober, & Hawley, 2002), and most clinicians identify a supervisor as important in helping them grow as a clinician. As I listen to couple and family therapists' stories about their supervision experiences, it is clear to me that "helpful" supervision is inspiring, confidence generating, and leads to creative, grounded clinicians. In contrast, "unhelpful" supervision can lead to self-doubt and sometimes painful, even traumatic, experiences that can affect clinicians for years. Some authors, such as White (1997), have hypothesized that the dominant professional discourse itself can separate therapists from their initial vision of helping people that invited them to become a therapist. Hopefully, supervision for most therapists is of the first rather than the second variety.

Supervisors believe [that] by focusing on the therapy process in a few cases, supervisees are learning things that can be generalized to other cases. Supervisees sometimes believe that supervisors have more answers and a clearer vision for the best way to do therapy that can be easily transferred to them than they do. Clients often believe [that] supervisors are much more involved in monitoring their therapy than supervisors actually are. Most supervisors only have intricate knowledge about a few of their supervisees' cases, especially during postgraduate supervision. As a result, my colleagues and I recommend (Storm et al., 2001) that supervisors (and supervisees) be more modest about the value of supervision and the benefits of it to both supervisees and clients.

How could or should therapists inform their clients that they are being supervised?

I believe, if you understand the reasons why the field believes [that] supervision is needed, then telling clients that you are being supervised becomes easier. The trick is to present it in a balanced way that highlights the benefits of supervision to the clients without detracting from the competence of the supervisee. For example, you can explain that someone with more experience is working alongside you and them to ensure they are receiving the best possible services, and that supervision is an integral part of the training process that helps therapists develop and expand their abilities. You may want to note that you and your supervisor may spend significant time talking about their situation or maybe not much at all depending on how well therapy is going.

How long must a trainee therapist be supervised?

The answer to this question depends on how you define supervision and the reason for the supervision. If you are seeking supervision for professional growth and development, you may be supervised (I tend to define this more as consultation once a therapist has become "fully qualified") on and off your entire career. If you are being supervised to fulfill educational requirements, the amount is dependent on the educational setting and the accrediting bodies involved. The Commission on Accreditation for Marriage and Family Therapy Education typically requires a minimum of a year of supervision. During this time, supervisees are to receive 100 hours of supervision on 500 hours of clinical contact. If you are seeking licensure, then the state or provincial laws and regulations specify the requirements. Many of these laws have used the requirements of AAMFT's clinical membership as their guide, which are 1,000 hours of therapy and 200 hours of supervision. I recommend strongly that my supervisees are proactive and research the requirements for becoming "fully qualified" regarding where they ultimately wish to practice. Each local context is unique. In my opinion, it is a mistake to assume that your supervisor is "all-knowing." The saddest cases are supervisees who believe they are receiving appropriate supervision only to find out it will not satisfy the requirements. For example, I know of several local therapists who thought they had all the supervision hours they needed to become licensed and then found out their supervisor did not have the "right" credentials for the supervision to count.

How should a trainee choose a supervisor?

When you are in a position of selecting a supervisor, I encourage you to define the learning experience you are looking for and be proactive about finding it. Ask questions regarding potential supervisors' philosophy of supervision, availability to you, knowledge of any regulatory requirements or issues, and supervisory training. Someone who is well-known as a therapist in a community is not necessarily an excellent supervisor.

What if the supervisor does not understand the trainee's therapy model?

As a supervisor, one of my most difficult experiences was with a postgraduate supervisee whose preferred therapy ideas were very different from mine. At first, I thought my respect for her work and my philosophy of supervision could easily address this difference. In the end, supervision was a mutually frustrating experience, and we agreed another supervisor would be better for her. This experience led me to think carefully about the fit between the supervisees' and supervisors' preferred models. Some supervisors take a stance that supervisees are coming to learn from them so should work from their models, while others feel that supervisors should adapt to supervisees' models. I have decided for me that I can work with supervisees in a fairly wide range of models as long as they are relationally based, but that there are some models that are outside of this range. When someone requests supervision from me that is not within my comfort zone, we talk honestly about our differences and to what degree either of us wants to stretch ourselves.

If your supervisor does not understand your model, I encourage you to bring up your concerns in a professional manner. Your supervisor is probably already aware that you are not always seeing things similarly. In addition, I encourage you to look at what you can learn from a particular supervisor that can advance your development as a therapist. In my opinion, the specific model of therapy is not as important as many other abilities that cut across models that you may be able to learn from your particular supervisor.

What if a trainee disagrees with the supervisor?

Disagreeing with your supervisor is inevitable. I tell my supervisees that I am providing them with only one perspective that reflects a particular historical point in time and that not everyone agrees with it. At the same time, I hope they will consider my point of view seriously because it reflects a point of view that they chose to receive, and it reflects my experience in the field. I invite them to express their point of view and to challenge me. When my supervisory alliance is strong, supervisees feel free to challenge me, have forgiven me for many blunders, and we have been able to work out any number of differences of opinion. The harder times have been when I have not had such a positive supervisory relationship.

Although it is best if a supervision relationship exists where supervisees feel comfortable expressing their concerns, supervisors are in a powerful and privileged position that create a context where it can be difficult for supervisees to fully discuss their concerns or "fire" their supervisors! As a result, I listen very carefully to what my supervisees are saying about their experience along the way. I ask them if something I am doing is useful or suggest things I could do in order to obtain specific feedback from them, and request a formal evaluation from them at the end of supervision. Frequently, supervisees will say, "I wish we could have . . .," "It might be better if . . .," "Maybe this would have . . .," or "Nothing really other than maybe . . ." I crank up the volume and hear these statements as, "Supervision would have met my needs better if you had . . ."

Can I change supervisors?
Changing supervisors is a big step. I believe it is almost always better to work through disagreements if possible than to switch supervisors. I encourage supervisees who consult with me about problems in their supervision experiences to (a) focus on describing the issue to their supervisor in a professional, nonblaming way; (b) note their part in the disagreement and ways they can change to resolve the issue; and (c) use the situation as a learning experience for conflict resolution in a professional context. In my experience, most supervisors respond quite positively to this approach, and they will go beyond the call of duty to work the situation out. On rare occasions, a third party can be helpful to facilitate the discussion. If this occurs, you may want to invite a supportive colleague to the discussion.

What are the requirements in becoming a supervisor?
The best way to answer this question is for you to determine what context you wish to supervisee in and then to check out the various requirements. State or provincial regulation, professional organizations, such as AAMFT, and institutional settings (e.g., educational programs, agencies) will answer these questions very differently. In general, in the field of couple and family therapy, the standard appears to be that someone is ready to be a supervisor after having practiced as a therapist for a few years. I encourage couple and family therapists to consider becoming designated as an approved supervisor of the AAMFT because the training program is excellent in my opinion.

What do you think about electronic supervision?
I have not done electronic supervision. Janie Long and I have spent some time thinking about the issues related to online supervision. Supervisors are beginning to experiment with using e-mail as an adjunct to supervision and to delivering supervision online (Ambrose, 2004). There [are] a number of compelling reasons to consider doing so. Online supervision can provide more timely supervisory guidance in the moment where the most learning can take place and when the guidance is most needed. Supervision can accommodate each participant's work schedules, be provided to clinicians in rural or isolated settings, and is cost effective after the initial outlay of funds. It creates the opportunity for supervisees to work with supervisors whom they really want to work with on cases. A supervisee may select a supervisor because of an expertise in a

certain arena. Some supervisees learn best by writing their thoughts rather than talking about them, and writing for some supervisees promotes more openness contributing to a deeper engagement in supervision. E-mail exchanges automatically build in self-reflection by supervisees as they wait for replies or consider supervisors' questions and comments. Certain therapy models, such as the narrative approach, emphasize written language and may be most consistent with the use of online technology in supervision. Supervision documentation is easily done because there is an ongoing written record.

However, there are several obstacles to conducting supervision online. First, supervision is currently defined as a personal encounter between supervisor/supervisee (cf., definitions of supervision in regulatory laws, in AAMFT standards, and the literature). Although the "face-to-face" part of the common definition of supervision may be between a supervisor and a supervisee in his or her own offices, using technology challenges us to redefine the supervisory relationship.

Second, client and supervision communication is deemed confidential. Although some steps can be taken to change the specifics of cases to make them anonymous, this process raises serious questions about whether the supervision that is needed is actually occurring. Do the real supervisory issues emerge when cases are disguised? Do supervisees receive the assistance they need? And, do consumers receive the protection they deserve? Informed consent by clients seems imperative.

Third, supervisors are faced with figuring out a new pricing strategy as they determine the amount of supervision that has occurred. This is especially critical when supervision is occurring as part of an educational, credentialing, or regulatory requirement and when supervisees contact supervisors outside of the already paid for supervision period. Answering frequent and lengthy e-mails can be time consuming. Also, having such a complete written record may increase liability risks for the supervisor. Finally, determining professional accountability for supervisors and clinicians is challenging. Supervisors working with supervisees in other locales may be accountable to laws of both places. Supervisors may face new expectations for responsiveness and supervisees for keeping their supervisors informed.

How do you handle spiritual issues in supervision?
I consider spiritual issues to be one of many aspects of multiculturalism that must be considered with every supervisee and with every case. The challenge for supervisors will be to help supervisees navigate when their values based on their faith, whatever it may be, are in some way contradictory of that of their clients. Simultaneously, supervisors will need to navigate when their own values are contradictory to those of their supervisees.

What about dealing with different races and cultures?
This is one of the most important areas facing supervisors today. I believe that supervisors, like therapists, need to have a multicultural lens to their work that considers at all times the shifting intersecting social identities of the clients, their supervisees, and themselves, and the effects of them on the therapy and supervision process. Being a supervisor means facilitating the development of this multicultural perspective in their supervisees also.

In addition, the field of couple and family therapy continues to reflect the dominant culture (i.e., predominantly European centric, Caucasian, heterosexual, and middle class) both in membership and in the ideas prevalent in the field. My colleagues and I challenged supervisors to consider these questions: Who is creating and benefiting from the knowledge upon which we base our work? In what ways do we, as supervisors, maintain the status quo of the field as reflecting majority culture in the way we pass on our ideas and therapy practices?

As supervisors, I also believe we have responsibility to address power and privilege that exists in the larger culture, the professional culture, and that which comes with being a supervisor. This includes (a) promoting inclusivity and supporting marginalized voices (anyone whose voice is silenced within the larger global and local community, such as supervisees of color); (b) acknowledging the Euro-centricity of the field's ideas and practices; (c) confronting racism, heterosexism, classism, and so on when it occurs in supervision and assisting supervisees to do so in their therapy sessions; and (d) preparing supervisees from marginalized groups, especially those of color, for a mental health system dominated by the dominant culture. And finally, supervisors must figure out for themselves and also help their supervisees figure out where they stand on the role of social justice in their respective practices.

How do you feel about group supervision?

Group supervision, as all structures of supervision, has its benefits, constraints, and challenges for supervisors and supervisees. In general, I believe group supervision can be a wonderful way to develop participants' ideas, expand participants' repertoires, and create new of possibilities in their clinical work. A group can often find creative ways to work with a specific case that are less likely to occur if supervision is in an individual format. A trusting, respectful atmosphere is needed where confidentiality is honored in group supervision, and group dynamics must be addressed by all. It can be difficult for supervisees to receive individual attention they may need in group supervision, and there are some areas that are best brought up and dealt with in a more private setting.

INTERVIEW WITH AN APPROVED SUPERVISOR

Thomas C. Todd

Thomas C. Todd, PhD, is the director of the Marriage and Family Therapy Program at the Adler School of Professional Psychology and the coauthor, with Cheryl Storm, of The Complete Systemic Supervisor: Context, Philosophy, and Pragmatics *(January 2003) and* The Reasonably Complete Systemic Supervisor Resource Guide *(January 2003).*

What attracted you to the field of supervision?

Supervision was enormously helpful to me starting out as a young therapist. After grad school, I went to a major MFT training center, the Philadelphia Child Guidance Clinic, where there was a lot of interest in training and supervision, particularly live supervision and videotape. It was a very exciting time, particularly with all the innovations in live supervision, and I definitely wanted to be part of it. It has continued to be an exciting and stimulating part of my professional life ever since.

What is your personal theory about how supervision works best?

I think it helps a lot if the supervisee and I have similar goals, achieved collaboratively, that excite and intrigue both of us. I like for supervisees to begin each meeting with a question for supervision, which get more focused and useful as our work together progresses.

The supervisory relationship is very important, which includes support and encouragement, a constructive focus on the clinical work to be done, and a sense that we are in this together. For me, a sense of humor is a huge help, starting with my being able to laugh at myself and not take myself too seriously. While supervisees usually start out quite anxious, especially beginners, I hope to help them lighten up as supervision progresses.

What are the necessary attributes of a supervisor?

Supervisors should take supervision seriously, but not take themselves too seriously. They should share their knowledge and approaches, but be aware that one person's way of doing something can never work the same for anyone else, and that we often don't know all the critical variables that make something work. It is important to be encouraging toward supervisees and help them be easier on themselves and less anxious, while expecting their best. Supervisors should be genuinely collaborative, which means that both parties will learn from the process.

How do you see your involvement in the therapeutic process?

I definitely want to help supervisees solve problems they experience in being more effective with a case, but even then, I see my involvement as mostly indirect. I resist being heavily directive, and I often present my ideas as analogies by telling stories about other cases. That doesn't work with everyone, especially anxious beginners, but I am impressed by how often supervisees will take from the story what they need, which would be lost if I were too directive. I will intervene to break up what I consider destructive patterns or stuck points, but even there, I would like to think that I am respectful and indirect.

How would you define the effective supervisor?

Someone who helps supervisees to grow and become more autonomous while protecting the welfare of their clients.

What training and experience do you feel is necessary to become an effective supervisor?

I believe that grounding in clinical experience is important, followed by formal theoretical training in supervision, and finally, performing supervision with feedback from an experienced supervisor. I recognize that there may be compromises, such as having the supervision course occur before the potential supervisor has an opportunity to do actual supervision, or having doctoral marriage and family therapists need to be credentialed as supervisors in order to be employable within COAMFTE programs. Eventually, all three components are critical.

How long is your typical session with a supervisee?

Individual sessions are the same as a "therapeutic hour." For group supervision, I prefer an hour and a half.

How often does the supervisee see you and for how long a period of time?

The most common pattern is weekly for an academic year.

What are you looking for with individual supervisees when you are supervising them?

I want to know what they are capable of doing, both in terms of intervention and assessment. Most crucial, I need to know to what extent I can trust their reports of dangerous issues such as suicidal potential or risks of family violence. More generally, I want to trust that we can move beyond hour-for-hour live supervision to a looser structure in which supervisees can report accurately and prioritize what they need from supervision.

In terms of interventions, can they contract for safety with a potential suicide? Can they de-escalate a potentially violent situation? How explicitly do I need to instruct a supervisee about necessary interventions? Can the supervisee follow a more general plan for a session or for several sessions?

What are your suggestions for students seeking supervision?

Consider yourself a full partner in the supervision process. That includes asking any questions you have, even if they seem elementary. If you have any question about how to handle a dangerous situation, or if you have any impressions of dangerousness, no matter how vague, you should let your supervisor know, so the supervisor can sort this out.

Who sets the goals for supervision?

It is a mutual process with involvement of both parties. For any supervisee, no matter how inexperienced, I want the supervisee to come to supervision with a question or goal for the session. I will help the supervisee to refine these questions, but I believe that such questions give important information about what the supervisee is ready to learn.

When you have a concern about a supervisee, how do you approach the issue?

I am very careful not to jump the gun, and initially, I do not approach the situation as if my perspective were completely objective. We will discuss my concerns and what would be necessary to reduce my concerns. If there continue to be issues, I want to get the perspectives of other supervisees, whether at the training site or within the academic program. At every level, my ideal outcome is a specific remediation plan that we can all agree upon.

What role does a homework assignment have in supervision with supervisees?

Most of my homework assignments are not mandatory, such as reading about a particular population or therapeutic approach. Even interventions are not usually mandates unless they are directives about a particular case.

How do you know when your supervisee is ready to terminate your supervisory relationship?

"Termination" is not usually the issue. The more typical (and more difficult) issue is whether the supervisee is ready to move to the next level of independence— getting a terminal degree or being ready for licensure. It is very difficult to quantify, but basically, the issue is what degree of supervision the supervisee still requires. I prefer to have this spelled out as much as possible with clearly defined levels of competence, but even so, it takes a lot to decide to delay graduation or readiness for licensure.

Case Study

You are a therapist under supervision and you take on the following case: A mother calls and makes an appointment for her family to come to therapy. The family consists of a husband and wife, both in their 40s; their 15-year-old son; a college-aged daughter; and the woman's father, age 82. Three years after the woman's mother died, her father developed Alzheimer's disease and moved in with the family 6 months ago. When his health began to deteriorate, the woman spent more time caring for him than for the other members of the family. Three months ago, the 15-year-old son, who has been treated for attention deficit hyperactivity disorder since age 7, began refusing his medication. The school is now calling home to report truancy by the 15-year-old son.

During the session, the wife cries, and the husband reports that their relationship is strained, occasionally rolling his eyes as his wife becomes tearful. He reports that he has had to take on more work because his wife had to quit her job to attend to her father's needs. The daughter is away at college and the wife smiles as she describes her as a straight-A student. The daughter was asked to attend the session but refused because she has a hard time with her grandfather's illness and dislikes the conflict that has developed at home.

Dr. Thomas C. Todd's Response to the Case Study as a Supervisor

As a supervisee in this situation, here is what I would suggest thinking about: How was this case assigned to you? Would you have any other information before the session? Are you expected to obtain more information? As far as supervision, would you be expected to discuss the case before the first sessions? How do you imagine approaching the case? What are your supervisor's ideas? What expectations does the supervisor have about how you will conduct the first session? In your setting, would you be likely to tape the session? Would the supervisor watch behind the one-way mirror?

If the supervisor were watching this session live, what input would be likely? How would suggestions be negotiated with you [as] the treating therapist? After the session was over, what would you be expected to do in order to prepare for supervision? What are your questions and goals for supervision? What theories inform your approach and/or your supervisor's approach? What is likely to be the focus of the supervision session?

KEY TERMS

AAMC   The American Association for Marriage Counseling; now known as the American Association for Marriage and Family Therapy (AAMFT).

AAMFT   The American Association for Marriage and Family Therapy, Inc.; the primary national professional association of marriage and family counselors.

Approved supervisor   Professionals who have obtained the educational, experiential, and supervisory training required for the competent supervision of marriage and family therapists (MFTs) and trainees.

CACREP   Counsel for the Accreditation of Counseling and Related Programs; an independent agency that accredits master's degree programs in career counseling; college counseling; community counseling; gerontological counseling; marital, couple, and family counseling/therapy; and many others.

Clinical training   Clinical training is designed to give the therapist an opportunity to obtain valuable clinical skills, to meet professional development goals, to learn from, and to network with other experienced therapists. Clinical training may occur at practicum sites, in practicum classes, as well as through workshops, conferences, and training programs.

COAMFTE   The Commission on Accreditation for Marriage and Family Therapy Education; an organization that accredits master's, doctoral, and postgraduate degree clinical training programs in marriage and family therapy throughout the United States and Canada.

COS   The Committee on Supervision, which was formed by the AAMFT board in 1974, to designate those people who received the title of approved supervisor. The COS helped classify the philosophies and establish the customs of MFT.

Contract   Supervision contracts are used to detail how, and under what conditions, clinical supervision will be provided.

Licensure   Licensure or certification laws for MFTs provide a mechanism for the public and third-party payers to identify qualified practitioners of marriage and family therapy as well as their supervisors.

Live supervision   Supervision that occurs when the supervisor observes a live therapy session from behind a one-way mirror or through live video feed.

Modalities   The methods used to supervise the supervisee and his or her client(s). Those modes include (but are not limited to) live supervision behind a mirror or through live video feed, videotaped session, and audiotaped sessions.

Supervise   The act of direct supervision provided to an MFT or MFT trainee through live observation of the MFT or MFT trainee and/or face-to-face contact between the supervisor and the MFT or MFT trainee about cases of a marriage and family therapy nature.

Supervisee   An MFT intern or trainee with whom a supervisor has agreed to conduct supervision of therapy sessions and progress toward licensure.

Supervisor   A professional who has met the AAMFT requirements or individual state requirements to provide MFT supervision. It is a designation to identify qualified supervisors, and it is not an advanced clinical credential.

Systemic supervision   A supervisory process that takes into account the role ethnicity, culture, gender, and power play in the supervisory relationship, as well as the relationship between a therapist and a client.

REFERENCES

Ambrose, H., & Hicks, R. D. (2004). Clinical supervision of counselors in Appalachia: A culturally appropriate model. Unpublished manuscript

American Association of Marriage and Family Therapy. (2007). *Approved supervisor designation standards and responsibilities handbook.* Alexandria, VA: Author.

Anderson, S. A., Rigazio-DiGilio, S. A., & Kunkler, K. P. (1995). Training and supervision in family therapy: Current issues and future directions. *Family Relations, 44,* 489–500.

Anderson, S. A., Schlossberg, M., & Rigazio-DiGilio, S. A. (2000). Family therapy trainees' evaluations of their best and worst supervision experiences. *Journal of Marital and Family Therapy, 26*(1), 79–91.

Bacigalupe, G. (2010, January/February). Supervision 2.0: E-supervision a decade later. *Family Therapy Magazine, 9*(1), 38–41.

Banks, A. (2001). Tweaking the Euro-American perspective: Infusing cultural awareness and sensitivity into the supervision of family therapy. *The Family Journal: Counseling and Therapy for Couples and Families, 9*, 420–423.

Beavers, W. R. (1985). Family therapy supervision: An introduction and consumer's guide. *Journal of Psychotherapy and the Family, 1*(4), 15–24.

Bernard, H. S., Babineau, R., & Schwartz, A. J. (1980). Supervisor-trainee cotherapy as a method for individual psychotherapy training. *Psychiatry, 43*(2), 138–145.

Bernard, J. M., & Goodyear, R. K. (2009). *Fundamentals of clinical supervision*. Upper Saddle River, NJ: Pearson/Merrill.

Bischoff, R. J., Barton, M., Thober, J., & Hawley, R. (2002). Events and experiences impacting the development of clinical self-confidence: A study of the first year of client contact. *Journal of Marital and Family Therapy, 28*(3), 371–382.

Briggs, K., Fournier, D. G., & Hendrix, C. C. (1999). Evaluating trainees' skill development: The family therapy skills checklist. *Contemporary Family Therapy, 21*(3), 353–371.

Campbell, J. M. (2000). *Becoming an effective supervisor: A workbook for counselors and psychotherapists*. New York, NY: Routledge/Taylor & Francis Group.

Cleghorn, J. M., & Levin, S. (1973). Training family therapists by setting learning objectives. *American Journal of Orthopsychiatry, 43*(3), 439–446.

Commission on Accreditation for Marriage and Family Therapy Education. (2002). Standards of Accreditation Version 10.3. Retrieved from http://www.aamft.org/about/coamfte/standards_of_accreditation.asp

Council for Accreditation of Counseling and Related Educational Programs. (2009). 2009 Standards. Retrieved from http://www.cacrep.org/doc/2009%20Standards%20with%20cover.pdf

Feinauer, L. L., Pistorius, K. D., Erwin, B. R., & Alonzo, A. T. (2006). Twelve-year review of major family therapy journals: Topic areas, authors' characteristics and publishing institutions. *The American Journal of Family Therapy, 34*, 105–118.

Heath, A. W., & Storm, C. L. (1985). Models of supervision: Using therapy theory as a guide. *The Clinical Supervisor, 3*(1), 87–96.

Hovestadt, A. (2001, Winter/Spring). New ethics code provides opportunities. *AAMFT Supervision Bulletin*, 1–3.

Jordan, K. (2001, Summer). Promoting multicultural competence in marriage and family therapy supervisees. *AAMFT Supervision Bulletin*, 9–10.

Liddle, H., Breunlin, D., Schwartz, R., & Constantine, J. (1984). Training family therapy supervisors: Issues of content, form and context. *Journal of Marital and Family Therapy, 10*(2), 139–150.

McGee, M., & Burton, R. (1998). The use of co-therapy with a reflecting mirror as a supervisory tool. *Journal of Family Psychotherapy, 9*(4), 45–60.

Morgan, M. M., & Sprenkle, D. H. (2007). Toward a common-factors approach to supervision. *Journal of Marital and Family Therapy, 33*(1), 1–17.

Nelson, K. W, Brendel, J. M., Mize, L. K., Lad, K., Hancock, C. C., & Pinjala, A. (2001). Therapist perceptions of ethnicity issues in family therapy: A qualitative inquiry. *Journal of Marital and Family Therapy, 27*(3), 363–374.

Nichols, M. P., & Schwartz, R. C. (1998). *Family Therapy: Concepts and Methods* (4th ed.). Boston, MA: Allyn & Bacon.

Nichols, W., Nichols, D., & Hardy, K. (1990). Supervision in family therapy: A decade restudy. *Journal of Marital and Family Therapy, 16*(3), 275–285.

Northey, W. F. (2005, July/August). Are you competent to practice marriage and family therapy? *Family Therapy Magazine, 4*(4), 10–13.

Ponterotto, J. G., & Casas, J. M. (1991). *Handbook of racial/ethnic minority counseling research*. Springfield, IL: Charles C Thomas.

Powell, D. J., & Brodsky, A. (2004). *Clinical supervision in alcohol and drug abuse counseling* (Rev. ed.). San Francisco, CA: Jossey-Bass.

Prest & Schindler-Zimmerman. (1997). A guide: The initial supervision session checklist. In C. L. Storm & T. C. Todd (Eds.), *The reasonably complete systemic supervisor resource guide* (pp. 158–160). Boston, MA: Allyn & Bacon.

Ratanasiripong, P., & Ghafoori, B. (2009). Setting up the on-site marriage and family therapy clinical training course. *Journal of Instructional Psychology, 36*(4), 347–351.

Ratliff, D. A., Wampler, K. S., & Morris, G. H. (2000). Lack of consensus in supervision. *Journal of Marital and Family Therapy, 26*(3), 373–384.

Roberts, J. (1983). Two models of live supervision: Collaboration team and supervisor guided. *The Journal of Strategic and Systemic Therapies, 2*(2), 68–83.

Roberts, J., Matthews, W. J., Bodin, N. A., Cohen, D., Lewandowski, L., Novo, J., . . . Willis, C. (1989). Training with o (observing) and t (treatment) teams in live supervision: Reflections in the looking glass. *Journal of Marital and Family Therapy, 15*(4), 397–410. doi: 10.1111/j.1752-0606.1989.tb00825.x

Schwartz, R. C., Liddle, H. A., & Breunlin, D. C. (1988). Muddles in live supervision. In H. A. Liddle, D. C. Breunlin, & R. C. Schwartz (Eds.), *Handbook of family therapy training & supervision* (pp. 183–193). New York, NY: Guilford Press.

Storm, C. L., & Todd, T. C. (2003). Supervisory ethics and standards of practice. In C. L. Storm & T. C. Todd (Eds.), *The reasonably complete systemic supervisor resource guide* (pp. 1–10). New York, NY: Authors Choice Press. (Original work published 1997)

Storm, C. L., Todd, T. C., Sprenkle, D. H., & Morgan, M. M. (2001). Gaps between MFT supervision assumptions and common practice: Suggested best practices. *Journal of Marital and Family Therapy, 27*(2), 227–239.

Sutter, McPherson, & Geeseman (2002). Contracting for supervision. *Psychology: Research and Practice, 33*, 495–498.

Texas Department of State Health Services. (2008). *Requirements for Licensure as a Licensed Marriage and Family Therapist/Associate in Texas.* Retrieved from http://www.dshs.state.tx.us/mft/mft_require.pdf

Todd, T. C., & Storm, C. L. (2003). Thoughts on the evolution of MFT supervision. In T. C. Todd & C. L. Storm (Eds.), *The complete systemic supervisor: Context, philosophy, and pragmatics* (pp. 1–16). New York, NY: Authors Choice Press. (Original work published 1997).

Watkins, C. E., Jr. (1997). Defining psychotherapy supervision and understanding supervisor functioning. In C. E. Watkins, Jr. (Ed.), *Handbook of psychotherapy supervision* (pp. 3–10). Hoboken, NJ: John Wiley & Sons.

White, M. (1997). *Narratives of therapists' lives.* Adelaide, South Australia: Dulwich Centre.

White, M. B., & Russell, C. S. (1995). The essential elements of supervisory systems: A modified Delphi study. *Journal of Marital and Family Therapy, 21*(1), 33–53.

RECOMMENDED READING LIST

Books

Long, J., & Storm, C. (in press). Historical, present, and future influences on training and supervision: The journey from one way mirrors to cyberspace. In C. Cole, A. Cole, & V. Frusha (Eds.), *Marriage and family therapy in the new millennium.* Galena, IL: Geist & Russell.

McGoldrick, M., Giordano, J., & Pearce, J. K. (1996). *Ethnicity and family therapy* (2nd ed.). New York, NY: Guilford Press.

Articles

Anderson, H., & Swim, S. (1995). Supervision as collaborative conversation: Connecting the voices of supervisor and supervisee. *Journal of Systemic Therapies, 14*(2), 1–13.

Barton, C., & Alexander, J. (1977). Therapist's skills as determinants of effective systems-behavioral family therapy. *International Journal of Family Counseling, 5*, 11–20.

Beal, E. W. (1976). Current trends in the training of family therapists. *American Journal of Psychiatry, 133*, 137–141.

Bernard, J. M. (1994). Multicultural supervision: A reaction to Leong and Wagner, Cook, Priest, and Fukuyama. *Counselor Education and Supervision, 34*(2), 159–171.

Biever, J. L., & Gardner, G. T. (1995). The use of reflecting teams in social constructionist training. *Journal of Systemic Therapies, 14*(3), 47–56.

Bobele, M., Gardner, G., & Biever, J. (1995). Supervision as social construction. *Journal of Systemic Therapies, 14*(2), 14–25.

Cantwell, P., & Holmes, S. (1995). Cumulative process: A collaborative approach to systemic supervision. *Journal of Systemic Therapies, 14*(2), 35–46.

Cook, D. A. (1994). Racial identity in supervision. *Counselor Education and Supervision, 34*, 132–141.

Daniels, J., D'Andrea, M., & Kim, B. S. K. (1999). Assessing the barriers and changes of cross-cultural supervision: A case study. *Counselor Education and Supervision, 38*, 191–204.

Edwards, J. K., & Chen, M. (1999). Strength-based supervision: Frameworks, current practice, and future directions. *The Family Journal: Counseling and Therapy for Couples and Families, 7*, 349–357.

Ellis, M. V., & Douce, L. A. (1994). Group supervision of novice clinical supervisors: Eight recurring issues. *Journal of Counseling and Development, 72*, 520–525.

Falicov, C. J. (1995). Training to think culturally: A multidimensional comparative framework. *Family Process, 34*(4), 373–388.

Goodyear, R. K., & Bernard, J. M. (1998). Clinical supervision: Lessons from the literature. *Counselor Education and Supervision, 38*, 6–22.

Goodyear, R. K., & Bradley, F. O. (1983). Theories of counselor supervision: Points of convergence and divergence. *Counseling Psychologist, 11*, 59–67.

Granello, D. H., Beamish, P. M., & Davis, T. E. (1997). Supervisee empowerment: Does gender make a difference? *Counselor Education and Supervision, 36*(4), 305–317.

Greenwald, B. C. (2001, Summer). Cybersupervision: Some ethical issues. *Supervision Bulletin*, 1–3.

Hoffman, L. (1998). Setting aside the model in family therapy. *Journal of Marital and Family Therapy, 24*, 145–156.

Holloway, E., & Johnston, R. (1985). Group supervision: Widely practiced but poorly understood. *Counselor Education and Supervision, 24*, 332–340.

Juhnke, G. A. (1996). Solution-focused supervision: Promoting supervisee skills and confidence through successful solutions. *Counselor Education and Supervision, 36*, 48–57.

Kurpius, D., Gibson, G., Lewis, J., & Corbet, M. (1991). Ethical issues in supervising counseling practitioners. *Counselor Education and Supervision, 31*, 48–57.

Lee, R. E., Nichols, D. P., Nichols, W. C., & Odom, T. (2004). Trends in family therapy supervision: The past 25 years and into the future. *Journal of Marital and Family Therapy, 30*(1), 61–69.

Leong, F. T. L., & Wagner, N. S. (1994). Cross-cultural counseling supervision: What do we know? What do we need to know? *Counselor Education and Supervision, 34*, 117–131.

Marek, L. I., Sandifer, D. M., Beach, A., Coward, R. L., & Protinsky, H. O. (1994). Supervision without the problem: A model of solution-focused supervision. *Journal of Family Psychotherapy, 5*, 57–64.

Merl, H. (1995). Reflecting supervision. *Journal of Systemic Therapies, 14*(2), 47–56.

Montalvo, B. (1973). Aspects of live supervision. *Family Process, 12*, 343–359.

Nelson, M. L. (1997). An interactional model for empowering women in supervision. *Counselor Education and Supervision, 37*, 125–139.

Presbury, J., Eechterling, L. G., & McKee, J. E. (1999). Supervision for inner vision: Solution-focused strategies. *Counselor Education and Supervision, 39*, 146–155.

Prest, L., Schindler-Zimmerman, T., & Sporakowski, M. (1993). The initial supervision checklist (ISSC): A guide for the MFT supervision process. *The Clinical Supervisor, 10*, 117–133.

Priest, R. (1994). Minority supervisor and majority supervisee: Another perspective of clinical reality. *Counselor Education and Supervision, 34*, 152–158.

Prieto, L. R. (1996). Group supervision: Still widely practiced but poorly understood. *Counselor Education and Supervision, 35,* 295–305.

Ronnestad, M. H., & Skovholt, T. M. (1993). Supervision of beginning and advanced graduate students of counseling and psychotherapy. *Journal of Counseling and Development, 71,* 396–405.

Selekman, M. D., & Todd, T. C. (1995). Co-creating a context for change in the supervisory system: The solution-focused supervision model. *Journal of Systemic Therapies, 14*(3), 21–33.

Stewart, K., & Amundson, J. (1995). The ethical postmodernist: Or not everything is relative all at once. *Journal of Systemic Therapies, 14*(2), 70–78.

Thomas, F. N. (1994). Solution-oriented supervision: The coaxing of expertise. *The Family Journal: Counseling and Therapy for Couples and Families, 2,* 11–18.

Wetchler, J. L. (1988). Primary and secondary influential theories of family therapy supervisors: A research note. *Family Therapy, 15,* 69–74.

Wetchler, J. L. (1990). Solution-focused supervision. *Family Therapy, 17,* 129–138.

Wilbur, M. P., Roberts-Wilbur, J., Morris J. R., Betz, R. L., & Hart, G. M. (1991). Structured group supervision: Theory into practice. *The Journal for Specialists in Group Work, 16,* 91–100.

Worthington, E. L., Jr. (1987). Changes in supervision as counselors and supervisors gain experience: A review. *Professional Psychology: Research and Practice, 18,* 189–208.

Websites

American Association for Marriage and Family Therapy Ethics Code
AAMFT.org

Approved Supervisors Evaluation
http://www.aamft.org/membership/approved%20supervisor/approved%20supervisor%20evaluation.pdf

Approved Supervisor Overview
http://www.aamft.org/membership/approved%20supervisor/as_becoming_as.asp

Directory of State Marriage and Family Therapy Licensing/Certification Boards
http://www.aamft.org/resources/Online_Directories/boardcontacts.asp

How to File an Ethical Complaint Against a Marriage or Family Therapist
http://www.aamft.org/resources/LRMPlan/Ethics/eth_Complaint.asp

Information About Training for Candidates for the Approved Supervisor Designation
http://www.aamft.org/membership/approved%20supervisor/sample%20training%20plan.pdf

Professional Development Resources for Supervisors
http://www.aamft.org/membership/approved%20supervisor/as_resources.asp

Responsibilities and Guidelines for AAMFT Approved Supervisors and Supervisor Candidates
http://www.aamft.org/membership/approved%20supervisor/as_responsibilities.asp

Supervision Contract Tips
http://www.aamft.org/membership/approved%20supervisor/as_contract_tips.asp

Supervision Mentoring Report
http://www.aamft.org/membership/approved%20supervisor/supervision%20mentoring%20report.pdf

The Essentials of Marriage and Family Therapy Supervision
http://www.aamft.org/institutes/2006%20wi/supervision.asp

Research in Marriage and Family Therapy

18

Elizabeth M. Goodson Beasley

*Researchers who are very successful are mostly successful because
they are able to manage their time well.*

—Ron Chenail

INTRODUCTION

William E. Powell, editor of *Families in Society: The Journal of Contemporary
Human Services*, once wrote, "Training earthworms to tap-dance seems a less
onerous task than getting people in the helping professions to read professional literature and then apply what they have learned in their practices" (Powell, 2001, p. 437). It
is easy for those outside the academic world and in the field to become disconnected
from current research in marriage and family therapy (MFT). Perhaps academic journals are not readily available to clinicians, or perhaps, and more likely, our curiosity
has fallen victim to daily routine and the never-ending entourage of deadlines and time
restraints.

Even so, research is important. As marriage and family therapists, research is
crucial to our field. Not only does research provide us with the know-how to bestow
the best possible care for our clients, but it also validates the effectiveness of our
chosen field.

This chapter aims to explain this importance, provide a history of research in MFT
and explore the future of such research, present philosophical frameworks for research
methodology, explain methodologies as well as research techniques, provide practical
knowledge for those interested in doing research, and discuss current research that is
impacting our field.

HISTORY OF RESEARCH IN MARRIAGE AND FAMILY THERAPY

Research in MFT can be broken into three distinct phases (Gurman & Fraenkel, 2002):
Phase I—an approach in search of some data (1930–1974), Phase II—groundless enthusiasm (1975–1992), and Phase III—prudence and expansion (1993–present).

Phase I: An Approach in Search of Some Data (1930–1974)

Marital and family therapy research during this time was scarce at best. Not only was there
little data, but also there was little theory involved in practice. In 1957, Mudd published an

article entitled, "Knowns and Unknowns in Marriage Counseling Research." In the article, Mudd stated the following:

> For reasons of poor design, difficulty in data collection, insufficient funds, lack of communication with other research, abortive endings due to mobility of personnel or rigid time limits, some research projects have been disappointing in their conclusiveness for theoretical concepts or their guidance potential in the practice fields. (p. 75)

Furthermore, the research that was conducted during this time was overwhelmingly descriptive in nature (Olson, 1970). After examining existing research in marital therapy from 1931 to 1968, Goodman (1973) concluded that the "usual standards for evaluation research could not be applied to the marriage counseling papers" (p. 113). Though at this time, separate fields, marital therapy research, and family therapy research were running into the same problem. The limited research being done in both fields was both methodologically and conceptually weak and relied too heavily on self-report measures as opposed to outcome studies (Gurman & Fraenkel, 2002; Olson, 1970). Essentially, the first 40 years of research in marital and family therapy had little to no empirical research to validate the two fields.

Phase II: Groundless Enthusiasm (1975–1992)

The mid-1970s marked a turning in MFT research. During this time, MFT was largely cited together as a united field and numerous comprehensive reviews were published describing important research (Gurman & Kniskern, 1981; Gurman, Kniskern, & Pinsof, 1986). The extensive research during this period succeeded in putting MFT on the map as effective therapy. After an extensive review, Piercy and Sprenkle (1990) described four conclusions that can be drawn about MFT in accordance to the research of this period:

1. With the exception of behavioral approaches, marital and family therapies produce favorable outcomes in about two thirds of cases.
2. Conjoined therapy for marital problems is more beneficial than individual therapy for marital problems.
3. Favorable outcomes typically occur in a short period (within 1–20 sessions) for both marital and family therapy.
4. For problems related to family conflict, family therapy is as effective, if not more effective, than individual treatment models.

Clearly, research during this period demonstrated the helpfulness of MFT in dealing with marital and family problems. Although these findings put MFT on the mental health map, MFT still has a way to go before it can be fully accepted as a scientifically valid discipline in the mental health field (Gurman & Fraenkel, 2002).

Phase III: Prudence and Expansion (1993–present)

Although past research has demonstrated the helpfulness of MFT, the field has several challenges. First and foremost, there has been a limited amount of MFT research that can be considered empirically based according to American Psychological Association's (APA) standards for empirical research that was set in the 1990s, and, with this new standard, there has been a recent push in MFT research to become more empirically based. The empirically supported treatment criteria as outlined by APA are as follows (Sprenkle, 2003):

1. Empirically supported treatment requires that clinical subjects be randomly assigned to treatment, no treatment control, and an alternative treatment or placebo control group.

2. The therapy must exhibit a statistically significant improvement above the no treatment group or placebo and must be at least equally as effective as the previously determined alternative treatment.

3. The research should exhibit treatment manuals, specific research criteria in dealing with subjects, outcome measures for reliability and validity, and appropriate statistical analysis.

4. For a study to meet the criteria of "efficacious," it must have at least two independent investigations finding that the criteria stated previously have been met.

5. For a study to meet the criteria of "possibly efficacious," only one independent study is required.

6. For a study to meet the criteria of "efficacious and specific," the study must demonstrate that it is superior to the specified alternative treatments in at least two independent investigations while meeting the standards described earlier.

The movement toward empirically based investigations has improved the research standards in the field. Treatment research has benefited from uniform standards, as well as new methodological developments are being designed to meet these standards (Liddle, Bray, Levant, & Santisteban, 2002).

> The past decade has demonstrated that family-based treatment and family prevention studies can be done, and they can be done in a way that conforms to the rigorous standards of contemporary intervention science. The challenges to conducting these studies can be surmounted, and advances in family psychology intervention science are numerous. (p. 5)

Current MFT research has made great strides particularly in improving assessment tools. Historically, MFT has had difficulty producing empirically based research as a result of its systemic approach to therapy. Unlike linear measurement, systemic measurement requires highly sophisticated statistical methods that can measure multiperson, multilevel, and multicontext over multiple time points with an extended follow-up assessment. Many gains have been made to develop such assessment tools (Liddle et al., 2002).

Future Research

The current trend toward more empirically based research is expected to continue for years to come, and with this endeavor comes new challenges for MFT researchers. Sprenkle (2003) identified four challenges for future MFT researchers:

The ability to transfer MFT models into specialized clinical settings. Although systemic therapy has been found to be effective in several areas in mental health, MFT has had difficulty infiltrating many clinical settings. More efforts need to be made in training for specific clinical settings and increasing research with specific focus on external validity in specialized clinical settings.

Cultural acclimation and individual/family differences. Future MFT researchers must address our ever-changing cultural adaptation and relational differences. More research needs to be done to address cultural and ethnic differences as well as cohabitation, stepfamilies, and gay and lesbian couples.

The Common Factors Movement. Past research has demonstrated the effectiveness of different marriage and family models, and although it is clear that it works, it is unclear why it works (Sprenkle, 2003). "The same comparative efficacy research has yielded another clear conclusion—when therapy works, the vast majority of the outcome is not due to the unique contributions on any one model" (Davis & Piercy, 2007b, p. 344).

Although this movement is somewhat controversial, many scholars in the MFT field believe that future research must explore the commonalities among different models so that we better know what lead to change. The goal of such research would be to create an empirically derived metatheory on how change occurs that encompasses common factors of effective therapies. Sexton, Ridley, and Kleiner (2004) discussed the implications for such a find as follows:

> Some scholars have proposed that common factors should define the future direction of MFT. Without question, finding a common core of factors to explain successful therapy would be a major breakthrough. This finding would simplify practice, training, and research. It would unify the theoretical schools of MFT, which often compete against one another and find themselves in contentious struggles. In essence it would serve as a shorthand explanation for the complexity of practice and the diversity of clients' settings, and the sometimes disparate research findings. (p. 131)

Funding for MFT research. The fourth challenge of future MFT research is the everlasting quest for research grants. Because MFT researchers compete with many other social science disciplines for research funds, the MFT piece of the funding pie is often less than appetizing. Researchers can increase their chances of funding by researching topics that are typically well funded. Otherwise, researchers can look to their colleagues who demonstrated successful research on limited funds. Unfortunately, there is not an easy fix for this ongoing problem (Sprenkle, 2003).

THE PURPOSE OF RESEARCH

Research allows family scientists to explore topics of interest or, at the very least, it allows a family scientist to become more familiar with a topic that affects his or her professional life. Exploration is often where research begins. For instance, suppose as a family and marriage therapist, you have seen an influx of clients who cohabitate but are not married. As a clinician, you want to provide the best possible care for your new clients. So, in an effort to do this, you might want to conduct research to further understand this phenomenon, or at the very least, it might be helpful to explore research done by others on this topic. Those who become familiar and explore current research in their field continuously build on their knowledge to become better and more knowledgeable in their own practice.

Another purpose of social research is to describe phenomenon. In descriptive studies, the researcher serves as the observer and then describes these observations. Using the example of unmarried cohabitation, you might be interested to know whether or not the current influx of cohabitating clients in your geographic area is consistent with national trends. If so, you could look to current U.S. Census data to provide you with demographics for unmarried cohabitation. This type of research would be considered descriptive research.

Although descriptive research answers questions like "who," "what," "where," "when," and "how," explanatory research asks the question "why." This would be a linear approach to research where the researcher's aim is to find the cause and effect of certain phenomenon. For instance, as a clinician, you might be interested to know if alcohol consumption is a causal factor for family violence. Explanation research generally provides statistical data about a phenomenon that can be helpful to clinicians working with a population that is statistically connected to a specific phenomenon. Using the earlier example, if you worked extensively with alcoholics, it would be an important safety precaution to know if there was a link between alcohol and family violence. This type of research provides the marriage and family therapist with important factors to investigate.

THE PHILOSOPHY BEHIND RESEARCH

It is easy for students to be bogged down by philosophical terms like *positivism*, *postpositivism*, and *postmodernism*. Why are they important anyway? As a marital and family therapist, you would never tell a client that you believe in the "postpositivism approach to knowledge." Most of us go through our daily lives without giving philosophy much thought. Philosophers would term the way we think on a daily basis as *naïve realism*, meaning most of us do not really question reality. For instance, when we drink our coffee in the morning, we do not think about the fact that the cup that we use to protect us from this hot beverage is made up of atoms, which is in itself mainly empty space (Babbie, 2004). However, as family scientists, whether you plan to conduct research or not, philosophical knowledge is important. Philosophy provides us with a way of questioning that produces bewilderment and uncertainty about our previous assumptions about the world. In essence, philosophy allows us to grow intellectually (Smith, 1998).

Reevaluating assumptions about certain phenomenon is also essential when planning a research study. According to Easterby-Smith, Thorpe, & Lowe (1997), exploring philosophy while doing research may be important for three reasons:

1. It helps the researcher to narrow his or her choices of research methodologies to find the most useful approach and strategy to investigate the phenomenon under investigation.

2. If a researcher is knowledgeable about the philosophies behind research, then he or she will be more familiar with the strengths and weakness of the different methodologies. This knowledge will assist the researcher in choosing the most appropriate methodology.

3. Philosophical knowledge provides the researcher with the ability to be more creative and/or innovative, leading him or her to use methodologies that he or she may not have considered in the past.

Research methods can be classified on a number of different levels; however, the most basic distinction is the philosophical level. The most common philosophical distinctions focus on the differences between quantitative research, most commonly allied with positivism, and qualitative research, most commonly associated with postpositivism and postmodernism philosophical approaches. Later in this chapter, we will provide more detail about quantitative and qualitative research methodologies and definitions. However, for our purposes here, we will define quantitative research as research that makes use of numbers and statistical methods, whereas qualitative research makes use of words or pictures when analyzing data.

Positivism

Positivism laid down the groundwork for what we think of as the traditional scientific approach to research. In social science, a positive researcher "strives to know reality as it really is, rather than the way human beings make it to be" (Gale, 1993, p. 77). This research philosophy works under the assumption that phenomenon can be broken up and studied as hard facts and the relationship among these facts can lead to the establishment of scientific laws. According to the positivist view, scientific laws are considered truths (Smith, 1998).

Positivist researchers aim to rid science of speculation and bias using mathematics and formal logic. When making observations about a phenomenon, a positivist researcher will use either *inductive* or *deductive* reasoning. Inductive reasoning is the process of moving from the specific to the more general. For example, if a hypothetical survey found that among those who attend regular church service, 75% were in a marital relationship, then inductive reasoning would lead the researcher to believe that marriage and church attendance are linked in the general population. Deductive reasoning moves from the general to the more specific. An example of deductive reasoning would be if researchers decided to test the generally accepted idea that high sugar intake results in hyperactivity in children.

The elements of the positivist philosophy have the following suggestions for social research (Easterby-Smith et al., 1997; Hughes, Sharrock, & Hughes, 1994):

1. According to the positivist approach, all research should be done quantitatively with the goal of establishing or validating scientific laws and generalizations.
2. The choice about what is studied and the methodologies used should be determined by objective criteria as opposed to human interests.
3. The goal of positivist research should be to pinpoint causal factors that explain human behavior.
4. Analysis must be organized in a manner that allows the data to be measured quantitatively.
5. Researchers must remain independent from the subject under investigation.
6. Phenomenon is better understood if reduced to the simplest possible components.

Postpositivism

The postpositivist approach to research presents an alternative to the more traditional positivist research philosophy. Postpositivists "modify the positivist stance by maintaining that a real world exists, but they add that we must carefully account for human bias and sensory limitations when attempting to understand it" (Gehart, Ratliff, & Lyle, 2001, p. 263). Postpositivism does not believe that, as humans, we have the capacity to set aside bias and contextual issues to find one single reality. According to this philosophy, reality is shaped by an individual's frame of reference. This allows for different interpretations of reality. Postpositivists view the objective reality proposed by the positivist approach as only one dimension of reality (Hughes et al., 1994). Postpositivism is concerned not with an absolute linear truth, but with evidence that a phenomenon exists. This approach is in direct contrast to the positivist goal of establishing scientific law and creating generalizations (Smith, 1998).

In postpositivist research, the researcher interacts with participants in the study. It is these interactions that assist the researcher in interpreting the meaning of certain phenomenon. This meaning is not intended to go beyond the scope of what is under investigation. For instance, if a researcher were conducting a study of one family qualitatively, then he or she would not attempt to replicate the same research technique on another family to get the same result.

The postpositivist approach to research includes two theories of assessment: *phenomenology* and *ethnoscience*. Phenomenology attempts to identify the lived experience around a given phenomenon. The goal of phenomenology research is to gather a detailed description of phenomena but not an explanation of the phenomena (Moustakas, 1994). Ethnoscience focuses on the study of culture. It scrutinizes the use of language to determine patterns in social thought (Sells, Smith, Coe, Yoshioka, & Robbins, 1994).

Postmodernism

Postmodernism considers knowledge construction about the real world at the individual and interpersonal levels. It can be divided more specifically into social constructionism, constructivism, and hermeneutics (Gehart et al., 2001). Social constructionalists believe that reality is constructed through human activity; and thus social constructive research analyzes human interaction and how meanings are created and interpreted on the interpersonal level. Constructivism research also aims to interpret meaning; however, it focuses on individual cognitions. It is believed by constructivists that individuals gain meaning through individual life experiences. Hermeneutics, like both social constructionism and constructivism, focuses on interpretive meaning, but what distinguishes it from the other postmodern theories is that it emphasizes interpretation as a basic and fundamental part of the human existence (Gehart et al., 2001).

RESEARCH METHODS

Quantitative Research Methods

As mentioned earlier, quantitative research makes use of numbers and statistics when conducting research. "It tends to be based on numerical measurements of specific aspects of phenomena; it abstracts from particular instances to seek general description or to test causal hypothesis; it seeks measurement and analysis that are easily replicable by other researchers" (King, Keohane, & Verba, 1994, pp. 3–4).

Surveys

Surveys involve the collection of data pertaining to the current status of a *targeted variable* within a specific *collectivity* (Thomas, 2003). The *targeted variable* refers to the specific attribute or attributes that are being analyzed by the researcher. For example, a researcher might conduct a survey to determine the average number of children per household among a specific population. The term *collectivity* refers to the group or combination of groups, including people, objects, places, institutions, events, or periods that are under investigation in the survey. Using the previous example, the researcher might be conducting this survey to determine the average number of children (people) living in a household where at least one child has sought medical attention at a governmentally funded pediatric clinic (institution) located in Houston (place) during the last 12 months.

Strengths

- Surveys reveal up-to-date information about the specific group being studied.
- Surveys provide very specific data in numeric form.

Weakness

- Surveys provide averages and percentages that lead to generalizations of groups and neglect individual uniqueness among the group.

Correlation Analysis

Correlation studies attempt to answer questions like, To what extent can variable A be explained by variable B? (Bold, 2005). For example, a correlation analysis might try to answer the question: Does childbearing increase the chances for parental divorce? If a correlation does exist, it will be either positive or negative. In a positive correlation, an increase in variable B would lead to an increase in variable A. An example would be if a study found that as the number of children in a family increases, so does the likelihood for parental divorce. In a negative correlation, an increase in variable B would lead to a decrease in variable A. If our previous example had shown a negative correlation, an increase in the number of children within a family would lead to a decrease in the likelihood of parental divorce.

In correlation studies, the data is analyzed statistically using the Pearson's correlation coefficient. If a correlation does exist, statistical analysis determines whether a positive or negative correlation is statistically significant. If the correlation is found to be statistically significant, it is determined what percentage of variable A can be determined by variable B (Bold, 2005). This analysis would answer the question: What percentage of families with five or more children get divorced?

Strengths

- Using statistical analysis to determine relational percentages provides specific data about variables that can be more helpful than simple correlation statements such as this: Families with more than three children are usually intact.
- Technology makes correlation analysis relatively easy to do.

Weaknesses

- The trustworthiness of the correlation coefficient is completely dependent on the trustworthiness of the data. If the data is not reliable and valid, the correlation coefficient will be worthless.
- Many phenomena investigated by researchers cannot be accurately measured. Using our previous example, many more variables can lead to divorce than the number of children in a family. It would be impossible for a researcher to investigate all the variables that can correlate with divorce.

Experiments

An experiment is the process of applying some type of *treatment* to *objects* in a specific manner and then evaluating the treatment outcome. The goal of the experimental research is to determine whether or not the treatment had an effect on the object under study, and if so, why did it have this effect? In an experimental research, the term *objects* refers to what is under investigation. Objects can be almost anything from people, wildlife, physical structures, chemicals, and so forth. Experiments consist of five major components: the object or objects under study, preobservation of the object, a treatment of the object, a postobservation of the object, and the use of a control group (Babbie, 2004).

Experimental Versus Quasi-Experimental Research. The distinguishing factor that differentiates experimental research from quasi-experimental research is *randomization*. Experimental research requires randomization, a treatment (experimental) group, and a control group, whereas quasi-experimental research provides both a treatment and control group but lacks randomization. Randomization is the technique of assigning the objects under investigation indiscriminately. Randomization can be achieved by assigning numbers to subjects serially and then selecting numbers at random to determine experimental and control groups.

Experimental Research Design

R = represents Randomization

X = represents Treatment

O = represents Observation

Example 1:

| Experimental group | → R O X O |
| Control group | → R O   O |

In this example, there are two groups—the experimental group and the control group. The "R" tells us that both groups were randomly selected. The initial "O" lets us know that both groups received some kind of preobservation or pretest initially. The first group (experimental group) was given the treatment as represented by the "X," whereas the second group (control group) was not. This design represented experimental research because it possessed a treatment group, a control group, and randomization.

Example 2:

| Experimental group | → O X O |
| Control group | → O   O |

This example is similar to the first example; however, this research will be termed quasi-experimental because it has a treatment and a control group but lacks randomization.

The classic research design is termed *The Solomon*:

Experimental group (1)	→ R O X O
Control group (1)	→ R O O
Experimental group (2)	→ R X O
Control group (2)	→ R O

The Solomon design includes two experimental groups and two control groups. The first experimental group includes a pretest or preobservation, whereas the second does not.

The same is true for the control groups (1) and (2). The design allows the researcher to determine whether or not the pretest or preobservation influences the outcome of the experiment. All groups receive the posttest or postobservation (Bold, 2005).

Strength

- Experimental research is a useful way to gather information about targeted characteristics of a group as well as the apparent causes for changes among these characteristics.

Weaknesses

- Experimental research does not depict patterns or unique qualities among participants or groups.
- Conducting experimental research requires a large number of participants and researchers and can be quite expensive.

Qualitative Research Methods

Unlike quantitative research, qualitative research seeks to discover in-depth information about individuals or groups. For our purposes as family scientists, Jane F. Gilgun (1992) defined qualitative family research as "research with a focus on experiences within families as well as between families and outside systems; data and words or pictures and not numbers" (p. 24).

Ethnography

Ethnographic research is associated with *naturalistic inquiry,* defined as an approach to research that is based on the assumption that a concrete social reality exists and can be observed and recorded accurately. Ethnography focuses on detailed and accurate description of social phenomena as opposed to finding a causal explanation of the phenomena (Thomas, 2003). An ethnographer is often referred to as a "fieldworker," and he or she often lives among the population that he or she is studying. Ethnography relies heavily on interviews and observation to understand a culture or phenomenon within a certain context.

Strengths

- Ethnographic research provides valuable information about how a group defines itself and differs from other groups.
- It gives insight to the internal structure and hierarchy of a group.

Weaknesses

- It is impossible for a researcher to interpret the event outside his or her own worldview. There could be more than one interpretation of the same event.
- Generalizations cannot be carried from one group to another without considerable margin of error.
- The researcher must be able to immerse in the group while not losing the ability to be objective about his or her perceptions. This can be enormously difficult to achieve.

Narrative Inquiry

Narrative inquiry is both a phenomenon and a research methodology. "Narratives are stories about influential incidents in a person's own life" (Thomas, 2003, p. 38). Its aim is to understand how individuals think and act as they tell their stories. The biggest challenge to the researcher is to determine the degree to which the participant alters his or her story because of the researcher's presence.

Strengths

- Narratives convey both the uniqueness and similarities among situations.
- They enable researchers to participate vicariously in the lives of those who are a part of the research study.
- Narrative inquiry indicates similar emotions and responses during different life course events.

Weaknesses

- Narratives are so individualized that they cannot be generalized to fit other situations. Things learned from narratives cannot be used, in most cases, as tools to help others with their own unique problems.
- Narratives cannot effectively demonstrate characteristics of a group or population.

Case Studies

There are three types of case studies: intrinsic, instrumental, and collective. The purpose of intrinsic case studies is not to build theory. Rather, the case itself is the interest. For instance, if someone were to do a case study about President Clinton and his wife Senator Clinton, the case study would most likely be intrinsic because the interest would be about their specific relationship. Instrumental case studies examine a particular case to provide insight into an issue or to refine a theory. If someone wanted to investigate what life was like for a family living through a devastating hurricane, he or she might do an instrumental case study on a family that survived Hurricane Katrina. A collective case study investigates several case studies to better theorize about a phenomenon. This would be the case if someone decided to conduct 100 case studies on families that survived Hurricane Katrina with the goal of establishing a theoretical basis on how families cope with severe devastation caused by Hurricane Katrina.

Strengths

- Case studies emphasize the uniqueness of each phenomenon under study. They highlight the multiple factors that contribute to the event or events.
- Case studies are effective as teaching tools for students and experts alike. They give insight as to how a theory or technique can be applied.

Weakness

- When conclusions from one case study are generalized and applied to another circumstance, the margin for error is high. It is an error to assume that what works in one circumstance will automatically have the same result in another similar circumstance.

Grounded Theory

Researchers using grounded theory use an inductive approach to research because they study a phenomenon first and later determine a theoretical framework. This occurs after the researcher continuously compares repeated observations. The theory is determined solely from the examination of gathered data (Babbie, 2004; Woolley, Butler, & Wampler, 2000). Although this chapter categorizes grounded theory within the qualitative research section, the grounded theory can also be analyzed quantitatively.

Strengths

- Grounded theory is very useful when little is known about the phenomenon under investigation. It allows researchers to provide and interpret information about a phenomenon before looking at it through theoretical lenses.
- Before imposing a theoretical framework, the interpretation of the phenomenon can be evaluated by both the researchers and those participating in the research study.
- Grounded theory, when it is done quantitatively, allows for broader interpretation of the event, and that interpretation can often be applied to other similar events.

Weaknesses

- It can be difficult for researchers to disregard their own biases when interpreting the information.
- The researcher must be able to separate himself or herself from the study to analyze it critically.
- While maintaining a distance, the researcher must rely on experience and theoretical knowledge when interpreting the data.
- The researcher must possess shrewd observation skills while interacting well with those being studied.

Participant Action Research

Participant action research is an approach to social research where the people under study are given control over the purpose and procedures of the study. This method of research is intended to counter the idea that researchers are superior to those being studied (Rodgers-Farmer & Potocky-Tripodi, 2001).

Strengths

- Participant action research works well with populations that have historically been "exploited." The reason it works well with these populations is that it allows those who are being studied to act as the expert of their own culture or community. They are the ones who decide and identify what needs to be studied and provide the goal for the study. This helps in achieving a positive outcome.
- When people are given certain amounts of control in the research, they are more likely to participate.
- Participant action research allows participants to use their special skills and provides an arena where they can learn from one another.

Weaknesses

- Researchers must have the ability to remain distant when observing, while at the same time, they must have the ability to meticulously scrutinize and correctly interpret events.
- This type of research depends heavily on the insights of those being studied. Without active and insightful participation of the participants, this approach is pointless.

Data Collection Procedures

Questionnaires

Questionnaires consist of printed questions regarding a certain topic that are to be answered by a targeted population. Questionnaires are typically interested in finding either facts or opinions. Facts, in this context, refer to the information for which the targeted population has knowledge, and opinions refer the respondent's viewpoints and preferences. Questionnaires can be divided into subcategories: factual questionnaires and inventories. As you can imagine, factual questionnaires aim to find facts about respondents, whereas inventories ask for opinions (Babbie, 2004; Thomas, 2003).

Strengths

- Questionnaires provide large quantities of information in short periods.
- Researchers are not required to be present when a participant completes a questionnaire.
- Questionnaires can be easily dispersed to target populations locally or even globally.
- Responses can be categorized easily. This is especially true when the questions are formatted as multiple choice.

Weaknesses

- Without supervision, respondents can easily avoid certain questions and not fully answer other questions.
- To be useful, a large quantity of questionnaires must be returned to the researcher. Oftentimes, this can be quite difficult to achieve.
- Respondents are not able to ask questions about confusing questions or words.

Interviews

The process of interviewing usually involves the researcher asking questions and the interviewee answers. Interviews are usually done orally either in person or by phone; however, they can be done via e-mail as well. Before conducting an interview, the researcher must decide what kind of questions he or she will ask. They can use the *loose-question approach*, the *tight-question approach*, the *converging-question approach*, or the *response-guided approach*. When deciding what type of questions to ask, the researcher can use a combination of question types (Thomas, 2003).

Loose-question approach. The loose-question approach is used to gather the participant's interpretation of a broad inquiry. For instance, a researcher using the loose-question approach might ask: What does the word *love* mean to you? This gives the participant complete control over the way he or she answers the question.

Tight-question approach. The tight-question approach requires the interviewee to choose a response from a given number of options. Tight questions often require a yes/ no or like/ dislike response. Examples would be questions like: Are you a smoker? Are you married? Tight questions can also be used to pigeon-hole respondents by asking questions like the following: Are you for or against gay marriage? Will you vote for Candidate A or Candidate B in the upcoming mayor's election?

Converging-question approach. The converging-question approach combines loose questions with more specific questions. The researcher usually starts with a loose question to determine the respondent's utmost beliefs about a subject, and then follows with a more specific question or series of questions. For example, a clinician might first ask clients what they think about therapy, and then ask their opinion of their particular therapist. Converging questions allow researchers to learn about the participant's broad and specific opinion about a topic.

Response-guided approach. Using the response-guided approach, the researcher begins by asking a preprepared question and then follows with a spontaneous question or series of questions that are in line with the participant's response. This type of question allows the researcher to gather detailed information. For instance, if someone were conducting an interview to learn about coping skills of mothers who have children with severe autism, he or she may conduct an interview as follows:

Interviewer: *Suppose Sally is having a really rough day and you are at your wits end, what kind of things do you do to calm yourself down?*

Sally's Mother: *I first try to find a way to distance myself from the situation and then ask God for the strength to make it through this day.*

Interviewer: *Does this technique usually provide you with the strength that you are asking for?*

Sally's Mother: *I'm always hesitant as to whether it will work or not because at that moment, I really think that I might go crazy; but somehow, I always pull through. So, to answer your question, I guess it does work.*

Interviewer: *You mentioned asking God for assistance. Do you consider yourself to be a very religious person?*

Sally's Mother: *Yes, I attend church regularly and [I] am very involved in Sunday school. In fact, my church also helps me out with Sally 2 nights a month. They provide us with respite care. Donald and I can actually go out for a "night on the town" without worrying about whether Sally is in good hands.*

This example illustrates how the response-guided approach can provide the interviewer with an extended amount of information.

Strengths

- Interviews give the researcher elasticity when gathering information.
- Interviewees can provide extensive information regarding the topic.

Weaknesses

- Because interviewers normally meet participants individually, interviews can be very time consuming.
- Interviews might be less accurate when asking about topics that may be uncomfortable to the interviewee.

Tests

The term *test*, as related here, is the organization of printed questions that aim to measure a person's specific realm of knowledge about a subject. They can be administered traditionally with pen and paper or on computers. Tests can also be used to gather either quantitative or qualitative data (Thomas, 2003).

Strengths

- Test results can be used in a number of different contexts and for many different purposes.
- Depending on the form used, test results can be easily analyzed.

Weaknesses

- Many people are prone to test anxiety. Such anxiety can skew test results.
- Some test forms, like true/false and multiple choice provide the participant with the option to guess if the answer is not known. This also can result in a skewed score.

Observations

Observation is the process of collecting data by way of viewing and/or listening to and then documenting a phenomenon. Observation is important to any research, but it is especially important when doing qualitative research. In quantitative research, the researcher must remain objective so as not to influence the research outcome, whereas in qualitative research, the observer's analysis determines the outcome of the study. In qualitative research, the observer is termed the *participant observer*. This is because, as the name suggests, the observer joins the phenomenon in some fashion.

The Role of the Observer. Participant observation is broken into four categories: *complete observer*, *observer as participant*, *participant as observer*, and *complete participant* (Gold, 1958).

Complete observer: The complete observer purposely acts passively. The participants may or may not know about their presence. If the participants are made aware of the researcher's presence, it is understood that they will not play any part in what is under investigation. Complete observers often use audio and/or video equipment to record a phenomenon.

Observer as participant: An observer as participant might have limited contact with participants in a study. Relationships, however, are not established between the observer and the participants. This type of observation is often used when conducting in-depth interviews.

Participant as observer: A participant as observer engages with the participants while observing them. The participant as observer is often assigned a role in the phenomenon being examined. Usually, participants are made aware that the observer is indeed a researcher.

Complete participant: In studies that use a complete participant, the true identity of the observer is hidden. In essence, the complete participant acts as research "spy." This type of observer is often used when researching topics that are controversial or involve some form of deviance.

Strengths

- Observation can provide information about an unprompted or unexpected event.
- Observation does not require any special or highly technical equipment.
- Observations can occur in otherwise difficult areas to study, such as areas where audio recording devices would not work well because of noise or crowds.

Weaknesses

- Because of human error, the observer cannot provide flawless documentation of the phenomenon.
- The presence of the observer might have some impact on the phenomenon itself.

ETHICS IN RESEARCH

More and more, it has become important in the field of MFT to provide outcome-based research. MFT continuously strives to find its place among other mental health fields. However, regardless of the importance of validation research in our field, MFT researchers must adhere to ethical codes when conducting research. The AAMFT Code of Ethics (found at the organization's website, AAMFT.org) outlines certain guidelines taken from *The Belmont Report* (Cain, Harkness, Smith, & Markowski, 2003; National Commission for the Protection of Human Subjects of Biomedical and Behavioral Research, 1979) about how to ensure that research is done ethically.

Respect for Persons

Respect for persons acknowledges the independence and self-respect of an individual. This principle allows participants the freedom to volunteer to be a research participant without duress or pressure from others. Special protections must be provided for individuals who are not mentally capable of understanding what is being asked of them.

Beneficence

Beneficence means that the researcher must do whatever is necessary to prevent or minimize harm to individuals in the study. The goal should be to maximize benefits.

Justice

In this context, justice refers to the requirement that researchers represent social and ethnic groups impartially and equally regarding benefits in the study. This requirement applies to members of a social, racial, sexual, or ethnic group.

THE GAP BETWEEN CLINICAL PRACTICE AND RESEARCH

In the beginning of this chapter, the gap between researchers and practicing therapists was briefly discussed. In an effort to understand this gap, Sandberg, Johnson, Robila, and Miller (2002) surveyed 326 clinical members of American Association for Marriage and Family Therapy (AAMFT) to discuss common barriers between research and clinical practice. Of the 326 surveys sent, 128 were completed and returned. The following is a list of recommendations for both clinicians and those doing research:

1. Clinicians need to have a set amount of time dedicated to reading current research.
2. Researchers need to provide more research that is relevant to clinicians. Clinicians discussed the need for more problem-centered research. Specific topic areas mentioned included depression, violence, divorce adjustments, gender issues, religion, race, and cultural issues.
3. Clinicians consistently felt that it would be more helpful if they were doing more research themselves. This is opposed to the current status of dividing the field into clinicians and researchers. Some thought that this should be required by managed care.
4. Clinicians complained that there needs to be improvements in research design and methods and that research should be grounded by theory.
5. Clinicians asked that researchers write shorter articles that are easier to "digest." They asked for less statistical information and more narrative form.

TIPS FOR GETTING PUBLISHED IN AN ACADEMIC JOURNAL

In 1997, the then editor, Douglas Sprenkle, and the assistant editor, C. Everett Bailey, of the *Journal of Marital and Family Therapy (JMFT)* coauthored an article providing publishing tips for MFT researchers. They have been outlined as follows:

1. *Be aware of the journal's editorial purpose.* Before submitting a manuscript, carefully read the "Instructions for Authors" section of the journal where you are submitting. According to Bailey and Sprenkle (1997), 20% of articles submitted to the *JMFT* are rejected immediately because they do not match the journal's editorial purpose.
2. *Include significant MFT sources in the literature review.* For a manuscript to be published, it is important that the research cited in the literature review be both current and well known in the area of interest.
3. *The manuscript must be an original contribution to the field.* Although the article must demonstrate knowledge of prior contributions in the particular area of interest, in order to get published, it must extend beyond research done previously.
4. *The research must be done well.* For research to be publishable, it must demonstrate solid design, methodology, and data collection. It also must sufficiently describe the sample and discuss clinical applicability as well as weaknesses of the study.
5. *Manuscripts must be well written and grammatically correct.* If a document is not well written, editors will question the credibility of the research being done. To avoid immediate document rejection, proofread articles before submitting them.

6. *Authors should resubmit manuscripts given "revise and resubmit" status.* According to Bailey and Sprenkle (1997), articles given this status are already 60% ahead of other articles being submitted. If the author follows the reviewers' instructions and resubmits the manuscript, the article has a good chance of being published.

7. *The blind process is beneficial.* Because the authors' names are not shown during the review process, there is no bias toward certain researchers for articles that get published.

How to Submit an Article

The guidelines in this section are set by the *JMFT*. *JMFT*, the flagship journal of the AAMFT, is published four times a year by Wiley Blackwell. It is the most widely read and influential family therapy journal with more than 20,000 subscribers. The purpose of *JMFT* is to advance "the professional understanding of marital and family functioning and the most effective psychotherapeutic treatment of couple and family distress" (AAMFT, n.d.). *JMFT* publishes articles dealing with "research, theory, clinical practice, and training in marital and family therapy." Writers considering submission should check often on the AAMFT website, AAMFT.org, for any changes to manuscript submission standards.

Evaluation of Manuscripts

In order to submit a manuscript to *JMFT* for publication, it must not have been published previously, and it must not be currently submitted for publication elsewhere. *JMFT* reserves the right to reject any manuscript as well as to return manuscripts for further editing. The author's name as well as other identifying characteristics should appear only on the title page and not in the manuscript itself. Manuscripts are accepted online at http://mc.manuscriptcentral.com/jmft.

JMFT will then acknowledge receiving the manuscript, and in the shortest possible time, will inform the sender whether the manuscript has been accepted or rejected. If accepted, proofs will be sent to authors and must be returned within 48 hours. No changes can be made beyond typographical errors.

Manuscript Format

Manuscripts must be formatted to standard paper size (8.5″ × 11″) with 1-inch margins. The manuscript must use a 12-pt. font, and its entirety must be double spaced. Manuscript should not, under normal circumstances, be more than 30 pages in length.

Organization of Manuscript

1. *Title page.* The title page should include the title of the article, each author's name, and current professional affiliation. The following should be included below a small division line at the bottom of the page.
   - A sentence including each author's name, highest earned degree, current professional or department affiliation, and location.
   - Any changes in affiliation following the time of the study.

- Previous presentations of the manuscript, grants, and/or thanks and acknowledgments.
- Author contact information including mailing address and e-mail, if preferred.

2. *Abstracts.* The abstract should be written on a separate sheet of paper and not exceed 120 words. The abstract should include a description of the paper's topic, method, findings, and implications. All words in the abstract should be italicized.

3. *Text.* The text should be organized into logical sections with headings. The "first-order" headings must be centered on one line in all caps and bolded. "Second-order" headings should also be placed on a separate line. They should begin at the left margin and be italicized. "Third-order" headings should be on the same line as the first sentence of the section. They should be indented five spaces, have the first word capitalized only, end with a period, and be italicized.

4. *References.* The citations in the text must follow most current *Publication Manual of the American Psychological Association* (APA Style Manual; APA, 2001).

5. *Figures* (charts, tables, graphs). Figures should be minimal and kept on a separate sheet. The desired location of the figure should be explained. The figure should be labeled and numbered appropriately.

6. *Style.* For style issues, please refer to the current APA Style Manual.

For additional information and tips for authors, visit the following AAMFT website link: http://www.blackwellpublishing.com/journal.asp?ref=0194-472X&site=1

MASTER RESEARCHER INTERVIEW

RON CHENAIL

Ron Chenail, PhD, is the vice president for Institutional Effectiveness and a professor of family therapy at Nova Southeastern University. He is also the editor of Journal of Marital and Family Therapy, *the flagship journal of the American Association of Marriage and Family Therapy, and coeditor of* The Qualitative Report, *a peer-reviewed, online journal devoted to writing and discussion of and about qualitative, critical, action, and collaborative inquiry and research.*

What attracted you to research in family sciences?

I first became interested in research as a focus in my master's program at the University of Houston. That was in counseling. I was more interested in studying processes and the outcomes instead of opening up a private practice or doing counseling or therapy, per se. And then when I went to Texas Tech University for my doctorate in family therapy, they were really starting to do qualitative research, and so I gravitated towards that because that seemed to fit with a lot of the systemic ideas that we were learning at that time. And I was interested in the discovery-oriented aspects of it, too. That and I'm interested in family communication. So specifically in therapy that was an interest also. That always seemed to be of more interest to me and more fun, too, rather than doing therapy.

What is your personal theory about how research should be done in family sciences?
I encourage people to think of the big picture in terms of the individual research projects and thinking more about their research program. And even maybe beyond thinking about your research program is to think about how your particular focus, say for example, in the clinical area or [in] an applied area, is based upon more basic research. And then also, what you can be doing in your clinical research to see if that can be translatable into your clinical practice. And so, the fancy word for that is just "translational research" that is very popular in medicine right now. Their expression is "research that can go from the bench to the bed or to the bedside." And so, if you extend that into the area of technology transfer, and even economic development, so in medical research you see that they take the basic research, they go to the clinical trial, they develop new protocols, new materials, new inventions, and then they look to patent those and to license them. So, I'm interested in those kinds of things in family sciences, too. The kinds of technology that we develop are very, very useful in a variety of areas.

Secondly, is that I think that research should address the important questions. For example, in marriage and family therapy, there is just an awful lot of interest in studying themselves in terms of their academic programs, what's happening in the curriculum. Those are great things, but I think they are really limited and they are not answering the big questions in terms of how do families interact, how do they function, what does it take to help them improve their health and so forth. It seems that those are bigger questions and they can't be answered in a single project. So, I would like people to think more about that, and that is what I try to aim for with my students and work. I guess the other thing is that I don't think you can do it all and as I talk later about teaching and so forth, I think we have taught our students too much in using the lone ranger approach . . . that you're going to be just the principle investigator and you're going to be doing all your work. Anybody that I know that has had an extended career in research has always been in teams. They may be the leaders of the team, but they are working with teams. And I think that in terms of how research should be done, we should be looking to be more collaborative; we should be looking to work more in teams and so encouraging people to be both a generalist and a specialist understanding in general what the research endeavor is about, how it can be applied to policy or to practice but then also have very specific skills that you bring to the overall enterprise so that you can be a value member, but knowing that you can't do everything well.

What are the necessary attributes of a researcher?
Well, one is to be curious. And I guess it combines with the second one, [that] is, to be courageous. I had a chance to meet Jack Horner. He is a paleontologist that advises Steven Spielberg when he does a Jurassic Park movie. Actually, he gave a talk at the Family Counseling Program up in Montana State. And part of the thing is I got to meet him there. And so, he took us down into the labs and he was showing us all of his good stuff. And we were talking about his theories because he has some very interesting and very often, very controversial theories. And he said, "If anyone is going to disprove my theory, I hope it's me." And I thought, "Wow, that's really what science is about." It's not establishing yourself as the expert, it's really always being humble enough to let the data take its course and your findings and not be so wedded to your theory or so defensive of your theory, that as a matter of fact, you should be the one who is attacking it the most. And I think that takes a lot of courage and a lot of integrity. And last, I think there is a

lot of ethical concerns going on now in terms of treatment of participants in a study and how well you maintain confidentiality and with all the pressures of specialist funding and promotion and so forth, that you make sure you are doing the best science that you can and not sort of fudging with your results and the results of others.

How would you define the effective researcher?

Well, I guess it is to stay focused on the big picture while attending to the local details. Here at the university, I also, besides doing the family therapy, I also am vice president for research and planning governmental affairs. So the office of grants and contracts reports to me. And the institution of the review board reports to me. And so you find all the time that researchers can be wonderful scientists, but they are a terrible manager of people. They are terrible managers of budgets. And sometimes, they are terrible managers of the hierarchy aspects of things. And so you really have to understand the big picture of things, not just that you're this wonderful scientist who is working on results, but that you are also an effective manager, and that you attend to the details of your projects. So I think that in defining an effective researcher, we have to look at the big picture and all the different skills that you have to be a good manager not only in your methodology in the science but also the people and the budget. It's just basically the responsibilities that you have. Also, to be an effective researcher, you have [to] keep [yourself] up to date with the latest findings. To be up to date with the latest finding in your area and sometimes outside your area, where [we're] going back to some of our earlier questions of "what does the basic science say in this area?" And then "what are the methodological improvements?" I see this all the time, especially in qualitative research where I think there's some great strides being made in terms of improving the quality of qualitative research. And people are still going back to books written in the 60s and 70s or earlier stuff. And you know they are not really going to be transparent in terms of what the methodological choices they are making were. They say they are using one method; a classic example is people say, "I'm doing grounded theory." And then you read the paper, and you say, "Well, where's the theory?" They've used methods that are associated with grounded theory or part of grounded theory, but they are not using grounded theory because they are not transforming the data to come up with a theory. So I think you have to keep up to date on all of those, and bottom line, you have to be a good manager.

What training and experience do you feel is necessary to become an effective researcher?

Well, there is really no replacement for doing. In a lot of training structures, especially in graduate and doctoral programs, all too often, it is sort of about research and not necessarily how to do it. A lot of books are written that way, too. Usually, qualitative research kind of gets the short end. Often, universities will throw in one qualitative class after a sequence of three statistics classes, and it is just difficult to be a good qualitative researcher based upon one class. The same thing is true where someone could be trained by all researchers, but none of them in their field. So they learn a nice generic research training, but they don't know what the basic questions are that are being asked in a particular field. The other thing is to get balanced. I think you should understand quanitative and how to collaborate with it and vice versa, to collaborate with qualitative. How do you fit it within the larger picture in even the evidence-based approach and so forth? In order to be an effective researcher, you have to have those kinds of experiences where you are really doing the more modern things. And the challenge of not only doing the research, being able to put those writings into effective written form is important, too. I think, to be an effective researcher, you have to work it all the way through.

What are your suggestions for students wanting to go into the field of research?

Probably to get a full mental examination to see why they would. No, I'm just kidding. Really, see if you like it. I guess there is the idea of research and there is research. There are a lot of people in our field that, I think, we could refer to as called leisure research—is that you do it on your own time. That is one style of research. Even in academia, often that's where a lot of faculties do that. They are not grant funded. They are expected to do a certain level of scholarship and research. And they may do it with their students in dissertations and so forth. But then, there are the researchers that get on the grant train and if you talk to them, you get a feel of the picture that they are under in terms of that they are constantly putting out—one part of the team is constantly putting out new responses to proposal and applications; the other part of the team is constantly generating the data, they're developing their models and so forth. And there are a lot of responsibilities that those people feel in terms of supporting a family. They may have two or three other researchers. They have teams and so forth. Secondly would be is to really seek out a mentor because you can read books and you can look from the outside but getting that tacit knowledge, that insider knowledge and someone who can help you. And it is very hierarchical—sometimes in publishing and sometimes in getting funded. And you really can't do it without a mentor. At the same time, don't get abused by a mentor. There are many good people out there, just select one wisely. And for a lot of people, it is very formal in that they really suggest that after your doctoral program is to seek out a postdoc appointment, where you can then work in one of these shops that I have described and just do pure research all the time. So a lot of people—I don't think that is a total requirement, but certainly if you are looking to eventually be an RO1-type funded NIMH and IH type of researcher, that's probably the career track you should follow. I think you have to become a connoisseur of research, too—is that something that has to be a desire that you really want to explore, different methodologies you want to explore, questions, and so forth; and so I think you have to do a gut check and see if that's what you want to do—it's something that you, I guess not to suggest that one has to become obsessive compulsive about it, but you have to really like doing it because it can be very competitive and most folks that you are competing with, they like doing it. And I just don't think you can do it halfway.

What role should research play in the therapeutic process?

About the therapeutic process . . . this is one I'm having the hardest time with because I think it is a very controversial question especially at this time. I was looking back at some stuff when I was going to school and instead of calling everything evidence based the word we used was empirical back then. And there was a bit of a tyranny to that, that people say well that's not empirical. And I never thought that they really understood the word *empirical*, because *empirical* is to know something through your senses. So a lot of times that was a term that was invoked that quantitative—good and qualitative—bad, that somehow qualitative was empirical. So now, it's the evidence-based practice and I don't think it's really being introduced in the most inviting manner as it's coming off from many directions. It's coming from science, it's coming from the federal government, and it's coming from regular old people. Therapists have abused clients for years using untested, unreviewed approaches, and a lot of bad has been done. And that may all be true, at the same time, I think the evidenced based . . . I think it is just like the empirical, if you understand the evidenced based and really adhere to the multiple levels of evidence. And that is as in the therapeutic process, you as a practitioner, you should look for the best evidence across all levels of evidence. So to just say, "I've got the best evidence and I'm going to blast forward with my clients." I don't think that's good science; I don't think that is good practice. So some people play at it as sort of a play on words when they talk about evidence-based practice and practice-based evidence. And they want to encourage that kind of balance, that which is learned in the lab versus that which is learned in the field. So I think that the other thing you need to look at is that the researchers need to get out of their labs and maybe sometimes, the therapists need to get out of their therapy offices and go to the library or look online to see what is going on and that for the researchers to go and see what's is actually working in therapy. So that's a long and involved way of saying that they are looking for a stronger connection, a stronger affinity between the two groups.

What are some important ethical issues that need to be addressed when doing family science research?

We had a question today about consent and assent, especially when you are working with children. And the actual question we were dealing with today at the university had to do more with the technical things in terms of date stamped and so forth and so on. So, with the general management issues, are you doing the things that you say you are doing? We do trainings in terms of institution review board training. We are going to be doing a new training on scientific misconduct. So ethics are always a matter of making choices and making sure you are making good choices. So, handling that well.

Second thing would be confidentiality, especially within families and especially with children that is a real issue. I always worry about the ethics of the nontreatment treatment. That therapists understand that an approach is really the best thing out there. And then to compare it to nothing, I don't think is very ethical. So the idea that there should be something that you are giving those participants that has some value for their time. And so I think those are kind of the general things.

In terms of qualitative research, you've got a real balancing act where, say, a case study or you are doing a discourse and you are having lots of quotes and so forth. You combine that with using lots of identifiers for your participants, even if it's a handful, you are really adding to the threat that someone can figure out who the person is, especially, say, if you are working in the divorce area or custodies and so forth. Another one I never thought of until we actually encountered this was when we were doing research on students who had submitted their materials and had been diagnosed and accepted as having a learning disability and so that there's reasonable accommodations. The idea is to adjust your methodology such that you are giving reasonable accommodations to someone with a learning disability.

Can you briefly discuss the pros and cons of quantitative and qualitative research when applied to marriage and family therapy? And, do you prefer one more than the other?

I always tell the joke about why I do qualitative research. I will say there are two kinds of people in the world: those who are good with numbers and those who aren't. I do the quantitative stuff; it is just that I like doing the qualitative stuff better. The basic thing with the two of them is [that] their strengths are their weaknesses. The strength of the quantitative approach is kind of the nomothetic where you are getting generalizable what can be said about from the sample to the population because that is the real focus.

You want to focus and be able to say something about the population, which means, of course, when you are dealing with NF1, the client who walks into the room, you have no idea where that person weighs out in terms of the range of that population. And so going from the population down to your NF1, there is always a degree of uncertainty in whether that is going to apply to your case. Qualitative research's, on the other hand, real strength is that in your graphic you are going to get that really thick description and understanding of that individual. But now that you have studied this individual, what can you say about other individuals like this individual? You're not so strong in that area. So I think the two of them balance each other off, and I think we've gotten to a point now where you are getting less of a prejudice toward either of the methodologies.

And I think the name of the game now is to really demonstrate that there's a fit between the question that you are asking and the methodology that you are using. So in that manner, I think that they are both very applicable for studying marriage and family therapy. If we take the example of evidence-based work and so you are developing a model that you are trying for an intervention or a program that you are trying to show its effectiveness and so forth, that there is a developmental model that goes. So you get to a degree of confidence and then so in the first part, you want to know more about what is happening in the room and you want to discover more about what's working in the room. You know what's working in the room; what seems to be happening, what are the active ingredients. Qualitative is great for that.

Then you get to the point where you feel that you've developed your manual and then you are trying to train people. Again you want to observe and see what's going on. And then it works out in the lab, you take it out into the real world. So the qualitative/quantitative can either be done concurrently or sequentially in that process. So I think you're seeing that again if you are looking at the overall enterprise of doing research and how it can help to understand marriage and family therapy better then I think that they work very well together.

Tell me about* The Qualitative Report, *what is its purpose and how beneficial is qualitative research in marriage and family therapy?
Well, the mission of *The Qualitative Report* is to improve the quality of qualitative research reporting and writing. And indirectly, we think that's going to help people to do better qualitative research and also to mentor qualitative researchers. And so you get a sort of quality with that. There's a lot of good books out there and so forth. But again, it's a big difference in reading about qualitative research and actually doing that. And so we have a sort of Rogerian approach in that if the paper that's submitted in *The Qualitative Report* fits the editorial mission, meaning it's either a qualitative inquiry or uses qualitative inquiry or critiques qualitative inquiry or something like that, then we will accept the author and the paper. Whether or not the paper ends up getting published is another matter because it's a very rigorous review process. So, we maybe accept 90% of the papers, but less than 40% actually end up being published. Because once they get the comments back, they say, "Oh, my gosh, this is too much," or that they just don't persist to working through the paper to make it of a quality paper. It's a very unique editorial mission. It's been adopted by some other journals in terms of its approach. But in terms of how beneficial it is for marriage and family therapy qualitative research, it really depends if you use it appropriately. So if you are looking for discovery-oriented work, if you are interested in focusing on the subjective experience of clients and therapists,

if you're really interested in description interpretation explanation, you'll want to look at something with that kind of qualitative study. Say you do your study and you discover things that you didn't expect, at least qualitative is really good for going back into the field to see what's going on. As I said earlier, I think it proves evidence-based developmental approaches, and I think it's inclusion in the systematic reviews and the metasummaries also give you a broader picture of the evidence that is out there about the particular phenomenon. And you'll see qualitative research I think really improving in this area. There's a researching team at the University of North Carolina, actually in nursing. A couple of years ago, they got a million dollar grant to look at qualitative work and to come up with some standardized ways of how to evaluate qualitative papers and to see how then to include that or how to do systematic reviews or metasummaries or whatever they call the metasynthesis of the literature. And the authors are Sandolowski and Barrasso. And they have written a series of papers. The actual study they did was in nursing and HIV. But what they've done, they've come up with this series of articles that really I think helped improve the quality. They wrote a really funny article called "Finding the Findings." You can't find the findings in qualitative studies sometimes. It could be in the intro, it could be in the findings section, [or] it could be in the analysis. So they gave suggestions of how to improve your reporting. And they had another one about being more accurate in describing the methodology you are using.

Can you identify and discuss recent publication trends in marriage and family therapy?
You're seeing a lot more emphasis on culture and diversity. And that is seen in a couple of different ways. One, it's seen in your specifically studying a particular population, by their race, their ethnic minority, racial minority, or gender, or sexual orientation, and so forth and so on. The other, and people are being very critical of the kinds of research are those saying—well I studied—you know, fill in the blank—I studied married couples. I studied families, or whatever. And saying that that holds for the whole population and not being sensitive to either what kind of diversity did you have in your sample and do you need to be a bit more careful with your language in terms of describing who you studied and what's your sample, what's your population? So that's a trend that we're definitely seeing. For the last couple of years at *JMFT*, we've seen an increase in the papers dealing with culture and diversity. I think you're seeing a methodological plurality that we, at *JMFT*, we still see more quantitative papers than qualitative. But we are seeing more research papers than nonresearch papers. So I think you are seeing more happening in marriage and family therapy. And so you're seeing some methodologies [coming in] that you may not have seen before—some of these are from medicine—like we talked about the systematic reviews and that. And then you are seeing some more mixed methodologies, which are a real challenge because it is sometimes hard to write up, especially if you did them sequentially, how to put that all into one paper.

Do you feel that certain subjects in the field are being neglected by researchers? If so, what are they? And how would marriage and family therapy benefit from increased research in these areas?
I think we have lost the family process in our research. One of major journals is called *Family Process*. You don't see that many of those kinds of articles that look at the basic science as you go back to Don Jackson's "The Study of the Family" and for those kinds of foundational articles. I get kind of concerned that maybe our foundation has become a bit stale. And maybe it's hard to get funding in there, I don't know. But I worry

about the kind of ongoing scientific foundation of how do families function. There were a flurry more in the 80s and maybe earlier looking at just the study of clinical communication—How do therapists talk? How do families talk when they are being clients? I think we are missing some of that. If everything's all about what's the outcome, what's the outcome, I think you miss out on the process. So I just think that it is a matter of balance. And the same thing is true if we just studied process. So, I think we've kind of gotten out of balance just a bit in terms of putting those together. And so I think that would be an area we need more research in. As for specific areas, if you look there are still huge gaps in terms of looking at families along the lines of couples and along the lines of culture and diversity. And that holds along the whole gamut with terms of just basic family studies research in child and marriage and so forth, research not just in the clinical areas. You see that what's not happened in our field but it's definitely something that has happened in medicine especially in the last 5 years is what they refer to as health care disparities. And when they talk about that in medicine, they talk about the prejudices on the part of a physician or health care professional in terms of what they will prescribe and not prescribe for clients based upon ethnic and racial minds and age and so forth, produce disparities in outcomes. So that you see more diabetes, you see more heart [problems], and that's not necessarily based upon genetic or biological, as far as we know, differences, a lot has to do with language differences, how directions are given, doctor–patient communication, and prejudices. And so the AMA and a number of other medical groups have just come up with this big campaign that talks about "One Doctor at a Time." And I think we're going to see that in the mental health areas, too.

Where do you see the future of family science research going?
What drives researchers are policy and political decisions or where the funding is. It's amazing before 9/11 how many people studied bioterrorism and what was the impact of terrorism in the United States. Terrorism has been going on a long time. People were studying it, but there was not a lot of money in the area. A lot of it will be policy decisions and where things are going. So, for example, when you have a presidential administration, which is supporting faith-based initiatives and community-based initiatives, you're going to find a rise in spirituality or a rise in looking at marriage. A lot of it will be where the money is. People will have to adjust in order to continue their work. And so maybe in the area of minority ethnic racial and so forth in culture, it may be in an area that is more identified in Washington. We are seeing a change in education research all based upon the "No child left behind" program. So I think that one of the things to track is to see policy changes, what's happening. For a lot of people, that's probably the most important part of their job is to actually work with the senators and the congressmen to be involved in terms of changing policy. One of the things that AAMFT does a lot of is to make sure that a family focus is built into a lot of these policies and a lot of these national reports, and that marriage and family therapy is seen on equal footing with different types of psychotherapy—individual, group, and family. It's a bit of a challenge because we want to maintain our distinctiveness as marriage and family therapist. We want to bring a difference but not be so different that we can't be considered on an even playing field, both in terms of a policy decision but also in terms of reimbursement and so forth. So, a lot of identifying where the future's going is making sure people understand where those policies are going.

RON CHENAIL'S 10 STEPS FOR CONDUCTING A CLINICAL RESEARCH STUDY

The following list is intended as a general set of guidelines for researchers to plan and execute a clinical research study. Investigators following specific clinical research approaches such as conducting clinical trials of behavioral treatments (e.g., Rounsaville, Carroll, & Onken, 2001) or synthesizing qualitative research findings (Sandelowski & Barroso, 2007) would be guided by more particular prescriptions, but as suggested by these guidelines, there are some actions which are common across most, if not all, research projects, including clinical ones.

1. *Reflect on what interests you clinically.* Think about the clinical population, participant, problem, phenomenon, policy, practice, process, or product about which you would like to learn more. For instance, are you interested in discovering more about couples considering divorce, MFT interns, domestic violence, therapist disclosure, prohibition of dual relationships, becoming culturally competent, therapist–client interaction, or patient satisfaction?

2. *Draft a statement identifying your preliminary area of interest and justifying its clinical importance.* Compose a simple sentence or two in which you state your beginning area of curiosity and explain why the topic is significant, clinically relevant, and worthy of study. By doing so, you begin to address the "so what" question right away. For instance, if you select "couple considering divorce" as your preliminary area of interest, you might cite demographics on the number of married couples who seek divorce and the challenges with working with such a clinical problem as reasons why the topic would be worthy of further study. In addition, reflect on your personal standpoint in relation to your preliminary area of interest and record your hopes, aspirations, and biases. As you progress through the rest of these steps, refer back to this record from time to time to assess if any of your personal perspectives are negatively shaping the research process (e.g., biasing data analysis or research design).

3. *Hone your topic focus.* Now that you have begun to articulate your area of interest, begin to hone your focus by considering the choices you need to make to design your study. For example, if you have selected "couples considering divorce" as your topic, explore the options you can exercise by deliberating on the following questions:

   - Who: Who do you want to study and from whose perspective do you want to learn about couples considering divorce (e.g., wives, husbands, both spouses, children, therapists, supervisors, participants, observers, younger couples, older couples, couples with children, couples without children, couples with specific demographics or characteristics like culture, race, religion, or ethnicity)?

   - What: What aspect of the couples considering divorce phenomenon would be your focus (e.g., couples' experiences, presenting problems, attempted solutions, in-session behaviors, therapist–client discourse, client stories, presession and postsession change)?

   - When: When would you focus on this phenomenon (e.g., pretreatment, during treatment, posttreatment, a combination of all of them)?

   - Where: Where would you observe this phenomenon (e.g., university-based clinics, homes, multiple sites, psychometric instruments, surveys)?

- Why: Why would you study this phenomenon (e.g., because you want to inform, perform, reform, transform, describe, interpret, explain, confirm, criticize, suggest, evaluate, assess)?

- How: How will you generate data to study this phenomenon (e.g., give a battery of tests, create a survey, conduct interviews, make observations, study therapy sessions, review case notes)?

4. *Compose your initial research question or hypothesis.* Based on your answers to the Who, What, Where, When, Why, and How questions, compose your initial research question or hypothesis for your study. For example, one research question could be, "What are the positive and negative experiences of African American wives considering divorce who participate in emotionally focused marital therapy (Johnson, 2004) conducted by graduate student therapists in a university-based clinic?" In composing this research question, envision what would be the clinical implications arising from the results of this study.

5. *Define your goals and objectives.* Focus on the overall goals of your potential research study and the objectives that you must accomplish to achieve these goals. For example, if a goal is to learn more about African American wives' experiences of their couples therapy, relevant objectives could be to (a) conduct a literature search to learn what has been previously published on this topic, (b) adjust the research question based on the literature review, (c) identify potential sites for collecting data, (d) prepare Institutional Review Board (IRB) protocol, and so forth. Make sure each goal and objective can be measured so you can track the progress you are making and identify where problems are arising.

6. *Conduct a review of the literature.* Some researchers start their research process with a review of the literature, some delay their reviews until after the study is completed, and some continually review the literature throughout the research process. Some researchers explore the literature to learn what is known about a phenomenon in question and then formulate hypotheses, which will guide a confirmatory-oriented inquiry to test whether or not evidence can be established supporting or rejecting what is believed to be known about the phenomenon in question. Some researchers explore the literature to learn what is not known about a phenomenon and then formulate questions, which will guide a discovery-oriented inquiry to uncover new evidence about the phenomenon in question. With any of these approaches, it is important that the researcher identify key terms (e.g., emotionally focused marital therapy, African American wives, divorce) to guide the electronic searchers of relevant databases (e.g., ProQuest, Medline, Google Scholar); in addition, the researchers must complement electronic searches with systematic reviews of the references cited in the articles collected to locate additional sources.

7. *Develop your research design.* Develop a research design, which will allow you to address your research question or hypothesis effectively and efficiently. To do so, you will need to make choices in the following areas:

- Participants: Who will participate in the study, how will I gain access and recruit them, and what precautions will I need to take to protect them from harm throughout the study?

- Research methodology: What will be my research methodology (e.g., experimental design, ethnography, survey, mixed methodology, action research, grounded theory); what will be the epistemological orientation (e.g., objectivism, constructionism, subjectivism) and theoretical perspective (e.g., postpositivism, interpretivism, critical theory, postmodernism) for my methodology; and what will be my procedures for generating, collecting, preparing, and analyzing the data (Crotty, 1998)?

- Quality control: How will I maintain rigor (e.g., reliability, validity, trustworthiness) throughout the study?

8. *Conduct a self-assessment to determine what strengths you have that will be useful in your study and what skills you will need to develop to complete your study.*

   Review your plan and identify what skills and knowledge base you will need to complete the study successfully. Develop a growth plan for helping you to master the competencies you will need throughout the study (e.g., open-ended interviewing, taking field notes, using statistical packages, writing). You may also consider creating a team or involve consultants to assist with your areas in need of development. Remember to reflect on your personal context and point of view, which may bias you during the study and record your plan for managing this perspective throughout the project.

9. *Plan, conduct, and manage the study.* Develop an action plan detailing the steps you need to take to begin and complete your study. Depending on the study, the elements you will need to address include people (including yourself), communication, data (including backup systems), analysis, results, technology, time, money, ethical concerns (including securing institutional approvals), and other resources. Maintain a chronicle of your research activities (e.g., lab notebook, journal, diary, audit trail, time and effort reports) and save supporting documentation.

10. *Compose and submit your report.* Depending on the vehicle you will use to report your study (e.g., dissertation, thesis, scholarly paper, poster, or conference presentation), identify the relevant policies and rules governing the form, substance, and submission of the report (e.g., school or departmental guidelines, journal article submission requirements, book prospectus elements, style manual of the APA) and report and submit your findings in compliance with these parameters. Even though there can be various outlets to make the results of your study public, a typical reporting format would be as follows:

- Introduction of the Problem
- Review of Literature
- Methodology
- Findings or Results
- Discussion of Implications and Limitations of the Results

It is important to think about the form in which you will present your study early and often, so do not wait until the end of your study to write up your report. Lastly, be prepared to write and rewrite your report several times until you have successfully represented the process and outcome of your research project.

The challenge of conducting a research study successfully is to manage choices well throughout the inquiry. In starting your first study, you will quickly realize that one decision made usually opens up multiple new decisions in which you will also have to address. For example, if you select a qualitative approach, then you will have to decide which qualitative research methodology will best fit your research question. Then if you select grounded theory (Glaser & Strauss, 1967), you next will need to figure out is what style of grounded theory works for the project. Then once you have chosen the Glaser variation (Glaser, 1994), you then will need to work on how you will actually carry out your clinical Glaserian grounded theory study. In making these methodological decisions, it is critically important that you document your actions and evaluate them to make sure that your choices made over time form a coherent plan. Refer regularly back to your research question and study plan to make sure that you are staying on track. Of course, you can make adjustments to your plan along the way; however, make sure you are aware when such calibrations need to be made; otherwise, your study will quickly go adrift. In navigating this sometimes-treacherous research sea, your best compass is your research question. Consult it often and let it be your guide so you keep your methodological bearings on an even keel and ultimately reach your investigative port of destination!

KEY TERMS

Descriptive research   Research that intends to describe what, where, when, and/or how a phenomenon occurs.

Empirically based research   Research involving a planned research design that attempts to accurately describe a phenomenon by basing its findings on direct or indirect observation.

Explanation research   Research that intends to explain why a phenomenon occurs.

Exploration research   Research that is intended to familiarize the researcher about a chosen topic.

Positivism   The philosophical belief that authentic knowledge can be acquired only through strict research following the scientific method with the goal of establishing scientific law.

Postmodernism   The philosophical belief that knowledge is constructed at the individual and interpersonal levels.

Postpositivism   The philosophical belief that human knowledge is not absent of human bias, and therefore, no single reality exists.

Qualitative research   Research that uses a descriptive means to analyze and interpret a phenomenon.

Quantitative research   Research that uses numbers and statistics to analyze a phenomenon.

REFERENCES

American Association for Marriage and Family Therapy. (n.d.). *Editorial policies & guidelines.* Retrieved from http://www.aamft.org/jmft/Authors/PoliciesGuidelines.asp
American Psychological Association. (2001). *Publication manual of the American Psychological Association* (5th ed.). Washington, DC: Author.
Babbie, E. R. (2004). *The practice of social research.* Belmont, CA: Thomson Wadsworth.
Bailey, C. E., & Sprenkle, D. H. (1997). JMFT publishing tips from an editor's perspective. *Journal of Marital and Family Therapy, 23,* 235–238.

Bold, M. (2005). [Statistics]. Unpublished class notes.

Cain, H. I., Harkness, J. L., Smith, A. L., & Markowski, E. M. (2003). Protecting persons in family therapy research: An overview of ethical and regulatory standards. *Journal of Marital and Family Therapy*, *29*(1), 47–57.

Crotty, M. (1998). *The foundations of social research: meaning and perspective in the research process.* Thousand Oaks, CA: Sage.

Davis, S. D., & Piercy, F. P. (2007b). What clients of couple therapy model developers and their former students say about change, part II: Model-independent common factors and an integrative framework. *Journal of Marital and Family Therapy*, *33*, 344–363.

Easterby-Smith, M., Thorpe, R., & Lowe, A. (1997). *Management research: An introduction.* London, United Kingdom: Sage.

Gale, J. (1993). A field guide to qualitative inquiry and its clinical relevance. *Contemporary Family Therapy*, *15*(1), 73–91.

Gehart, D. R., Ratliff, D. A., & Lyle, R. R. (2001). Qualitative research in family therapy: A substantive and methodological review. *Journal of Marital and Family Therapy*, *27*, 261–274.

Gilgun, J. F. (1992). Definitions, methodologies, and methods in qualitative family research. In J. F. Gilgun, K. Daly, & G. Handel (Eds.), *Qualitative methods in family research.* Newbury Park, CA: Sage.

Glaser, B. G. (1994). *Grounded theory: 1984–1994: Volumes I & II.* Mill Valley, CA: Sociology Press.

Glaser, B, G., & Strauss, A. (1967). *The discovery of grounded theory: Strategies for qualitative research.* Chicago, IL: Aldine Transaction.

Gold, R. L. (1958). Roles in sociological field observations. *Social Forces*, *36*(3), 217–233.

Goodman, E. S. (1973). Marriage counseling as science: Some research considerations. *The Family Coordinator*, *22*(1), 111–116.

Gurman, A. S., & Fraenkel, P. (2002). The history of couple therapy: A millennial review. *Family Process*, *41*(2), 199–260.

Gurman, A. S., & Kniskern, D. P. (1981). Family therapy outcome research: Knowns and unknowns. In A. S. Gurman & D. P. Kniskern (Eds.), *Handbook of family therapy* (pp. 742–776). New York, NY: Brunner/Mazel.

Gurman, A. S., Kniskern, D. P., & Pinsof, W. M. (1986). Research on the process and outcome of marital and family therapy. In S. L. Garfield & A. E. Bergin (Eds.), *Handbook of psychotherapy and behavioral change* (3rd ed., pp. 565–624). New York, NY: Wiley.

Hughes, J. A., Sharrock, W. W., & Hughes, J. A. (1994). *The philosophy of social research.* Essex, United Kingdom: Longman.

Johnson, S. M. (2004). *The practice of emotionally focused couple therapy.* New York, NY: Routledge.

King, G., Keohane, R. O., & Verba, S. (1994). *Designing social inquiry: Scientific inference in qualitative research.* Princeton, NJ: Princeton University Press.

Liddle, H. A., Bray, J. H., Levant, R. F., & Santisteban, D. A. (2002). Family psychology intervention science and practice. In H. A. Liddle, D. A. Santisteban, R. F. Levant, & J. H. Bray (Eds.), *Family psychology: Science-based interventions* (pp. 3–16). Washington DC: American Psychological Association.

Moustakas, C. E. (1994). *Phenomenological research methods.* Thousand Oaks, CA: Sage.

Mudd, E. H. (1957). Knowns and unknowns in marriage counseling research. *Marriage and Family Living*, *19*, 75–81.

National Commission for the Protection of Human Subjects of Biomedical and Behavioral Research. (1979). *The Belmont report: Ethical principles and guidelines for the protection of human subjects of research* (Department of Health, Education and Welfare Publication No. OS 78-0012). Washington, DC: U.S. Government Printing Office.

Olson, D. H. (1970). Marital and family therapy: Integrative review and critique. *Journal of Marriage and the Family*, *32*, 501–538.

Piercy, F. P., & Sprenkle, D. H. (1990). Marriage and the family therapy: A decade review. *Journal of Marriage and the Family*, *52*(4), 1116–1126.

Powell, W. E. (2001). Doing it better: On imaging the uses of information. *Families in Society*, *82*(6), 437–439.

Rodgers-Farmer, A. Y., & Potocky-Tripodi, M. (2001). Gender, ethnicity, and race matters. In B. A. Thyer (Ed.), *The handbook of social work research methods* (pp. 445–454). Thousand Oaks, CA: Sage.

Rounsaville, B. J., Carroll, K. M., & Onken, L. S. (2001). A stage model of behavioral therapies research: Getting started and moving on from stage I. *Clinical Psychology: Science & Practice, 8*(2), 133–142.

Sandberg, J. G., Johnson, L. N., Robila, M., & Miller, R. B. (2002). Clinician identified barrier to clinical research. *Journal of Marital and Family Therapy, 28*(1), 61–67.

Sandelowski, M., & Barroso, J. (2007). *Making sense of qualitative and quantitative findings in mixed research synthesis studies.* New York, NY: National Institute of Health. U.S. National Library of Medicine.

Sells, S. P., Smith, T. E., Coe, M. J., Yoshioka, M., & Robbins, J. (1994). An ethnography of couple and therapists experiences in reflecting team practice. *Journal of Marital and Family Therapy, 20*, 267–286.

Sexton, T. L., Ridley, C. R., & Kleiner, A. J. (2004). Beyond common factors: Multi-level process models of therapeutic change in marriage and family therapy. *Journal of Marital and Family Therapy, 30*(2), 131–150.

Smith, M. J. (1998). *Social science in question.* London, United Kingdom: Sage.

Sprenkle, D. H. (2003). Effectiveness of research in marriage and family therapy: Introduction. *Journal of Marital and Family Therapy, 29*(1), 85–96.

Thomas, R. M. (2003). *Blending qualitative & quantitative research methods in theses and dissertations.* Thousand Oaks, CA: Sage.

Woolley, S. R., Butler, M. H., & Wampler, K. S. (2000). Unraveling change in therapy: Three different process research methodologies. *The American Journal of Family Therapy, 28*(4), 311–327.

RECOMMENDED READING LIST

Books

Bogdan, R. C., & Taylor, S. J. (1975). *Introduction to qualitative research methods.* New York, NY: John Wiley.

Strauss, A., & Corbin, J. (1990). *Basics of qualitative research.* Newbury Park, CA: Sage.

Articles

Crane, D. R., & Law, D. D. (2002). Conducting medical offset research in health maintenance organizations: Challenges, opportunities, and insights. *Journal of Marital and Family Therapy, 28*, 15–20.

Davis, S. D., & Piercy, F. P. (2007a). What clients of couple therapy model developers and their former students say about change, part I: Model-dependent common factors across three models. *Journal of Marital and Family Therapy, 33*(3), 318–343.

National Institute of Mental Health. (1999). *Basic behavioral science research for mental health: A national investment.* NIH Publication No. 963682. Retrieved from http://www.nimh.nih.gov/publicat/baschap7.cfm//redir7

Sells, S. P., Smith, T. E., & Moon, S. (1996). An ethnographic study of client and therapist perceptions of therapy effectiveness in an university-based training clinic. *Journal of Marital and Family Therapy, 22*(3), 321–342.

Thomas, V. (2002). Conducting research with community agencies: Meeting recruitment and collaboration challenges. *Journal of Marital and Family Therapy, 28*(1), 9–14.

Ethical Issues in Marriage and Family Therapy

19

Beena Benny

The first step in the evolution of ethics is a sense of solidarity with other human beings.

—Albert Schweitzer

INTRODUCTION

Ethics is the discipline relating to right and wrong, moral duty and obligation, moral principles and values, and moral character. To many people, ethics and *morality* are synonymous. However, the Greek term "ethics" also implies character, whereas "mores" refers to social customs. Although Socrates and Plato discussed moral questions at length, it was Aristotle who first made a serious and systematic study of moral principles, which he termed ethics (Beck, 1987). Ethical decision making is an evolving process. The professional code of ethics governing marriage and family therapy was developed by the American Association for Marriage and Family Therapy (AAMFT) and was most recently revised in 2001. This chapter will provide the reader with background on common ethical issues—such as client confidentiality, informed consent, record keeping, technology, dual relationships, treating minors, and termination—and their applications in family therapy. Finally, this chapter concludes with a case study of an ethical complaint and interviews with two therapists known for their work and interest in ethical issues.

CONFIDENTIALITY

Trust between therapist and client is a vital part of the therapeutic alliance; clients must feel that whatever they disclose in therapy will be treated confidentially. For this reason, the therapist is not to disclose information unless required by law or authorized by the client to do so. Information obtained in the therapeutic relationship should be discussed with others for professional purposes only; when consulting with other colleagues, confidential information leading to identification should not be shared.

When may confidentiality be breached? If a client presents a danger to himself or herself or others, the therapist may be obligated to disclose such information to relevant third parties. Under a famous legal case, *Tarasoff v. Regents of the University of California* (1976), California therapists have a duty to warn and to protect the intended victim "when the client has communicated to the therapist a serious threat of physical violence against an identifiable victim or victims" (Corey, Corey, & Callanan, 2003, p. 210). State laws vary; some states, such as Texas (*Thapar v. Zezulka, 1999*), do *not* have a "duty to warn." In this case, it is the therapist's discretion to warn the intended victim. It is therefore a therapist's duty to find out what his or her state law dictates is proper and ethical in cases where the client has disclosed intent to harm another person.

Court decisions such as the *Tarasoff* case mandate that the therapist has a duty to protect the public in the case of imminent danger to self or others that overrides any obligation to maintain client confidentiality. Likewise, if a client is potentially suicidal, the therapist may break confidentiality.

When dealing with a potentially dangerous client, S. Campbell stresses the importance of documentation (personal communication, August 1, 2005). "Documentation should include a rationale for the action taken" (Corey et al., 2003, p. 217). Concerning child abuse, there is a duty to report suspected child abuse or neglect within 48 hours upon suspicion to the Department of Child Protective Services.

Confidentiality is a simpler issue when one client is involved in therapy (Watkins, 1989). "When a family is seen in therapy, the client is the family, not just a member of the family" (Watkins, 1989, p. 133). In couple or family therapy, it is up to the therapist's discretion whether he or she would like to keep issues disclosed by each family member individually confidential. Some therapists take the stance that confidentiality does not apply between couples and family members when seen for individual sessions. As a therapist, if you agree with this stance, you would want to include this in the confidentiality section of your informed consent document, which will be discussed later.

A clause within the informed consent form dealing with individual confidentiality might state, "In couple or family therapy, or when different family members are seen individually, confidentially and privilege do not apply between the couple or between family members" (Gawf, n.d.). This is intended to prevent a conflict of interest in the event that a person's goals are not consistent with the goals of the family (Leslie, 2003a).

Other therapists assert that anything shared in an individual session will not be disclosed with anyone else. Still, others take more of a middle ground approach, stating that information learned in individual sessions may be beneficial in the treatment of the family or couple and may be used by the therapist. Whatever approach is taken, it is up to the therapist's discretion.

A client with suicidal thoughts must be cared for appropriately by a therapist by checking to see if the client has a plan. If the client has such thoughts or a plan and is younger than the age of 18, confidentiality is lifted, and the therapist has a professional obligation to call the client's parent or guardian and not release the client from the therapist's office until the parent or guardian arrives. If the client is older than the age of 18 and is actively suicidal with a plan, the therapist has a professional obligation to call the police and wait until the police arrive to help escort the client to the nearest hospital. The therapist should document all actions taken to ensure the safety of the client.

Finally, confidentiality may be broken if the client himself or herself allows the release of his or her records. A sample authorization form is shown in Figure 19.1.

INFORMED CONSENT

Informed consent holds that "a patient should have access to all meaningful information in order to formulate an intelligent decision about whether to proceed with a particular course of treatment" (Caudill, 1998). It is important to educate clients about their rights and responsibilities, as well as the rights and responsibilities of the therapist, before embarking on treatment. "Before entering therapy, clients should be made aware to the purposes, goals, techniques, policies, and procedures involved" (Corey, 2001, p. 147). "Clients should be aware of both the possible benefits and risks associated with counseling before beginning a professional relationship" (Corey et al., 2003, p. 147).

Authorization to Release Records

Please Print All Information Unless Otherwise Noted

Client Name: _____   _____
             Last   First   M.I.   Date of Birth

Address: _____   Home phone: _____
         _____   Work phone: _____
         _____   Other phone: _____

I hereby authorize _____ to release information from my records to
_____ for the purpose of review/examination, and I further authorize
_____ to provide copies thereof as may be requested. The foregoing is subject to such limitations as indicated below:

Release: The entire chart _____   Verbal information _____
Specific Information:
_____

I give special permission to release any information regarding the following: (Initial on line[s] below). Mark **N/A** if nonapplicable.

_____ Substance abuse.
_____ Psychiatric/mental health information.
_____ HIV information.

This authorization will automatically expire one (1) year from the date signed. I understand that I may revoke this consent at any time except to the extent that action has been taken in reliance thereon.

Signed: _____   Date: _____
            (If not patient, state relationship)
Witness' Printed Name: _____
Witness' Signature: _____   Date: _____

FIGURE 19.1 ■ Sample authorization to release records.

Corey (2001) asserts the importance of keeping a balance between giving the client too much and too little information. The therapist should aspire to solicit and encourage the client's active cooperation in the counseling plan.

According to Haslam and Harris (2004), most informed consent documents will include the following information:

- *Qualification and background of the practitioner:* Therapist's licensure, education, experience, theoretical orientation, services offered, areas of specialty, and potential value conflicts.

- *Process of therapy:* General goals of counseling, length of treatment, frequency of sessions, benefits and risks of counseling, treatment planning or goal, the responsibilities of the client, and the clients rights.

- *Limitations and exceptions to confidentiality:* Standard exemptions where confidentiality *must be* compromised (e.g., child abuse, elder abuse, suicide); other situations where confidentiality *may be* compromised (e.g., insurance and court interactions, outside consultations, collection agencies). This relates to the earlier discussion about individual confidentiality within a couple or family counseling session.

- *Issues related to insurance:* Division of responsibility for setting up reimbursement or how to obtain preauthorization.
- *Fee structure:* Charges for specific services, payment expectation, policies on unpaid debts, and so forth.
- *Office information and emergency procedures:* Hours of operation, after-hours access to therapist, and emergency procedures.

A sample informed consent form is shown in Figure 19.2.

RECORD KEEPING

From an ethical, legal, and clinical perspective, "good record keeping is important both to clients and to therapists" (Leslie, 2003a). There are several reasons for maintaining thorough and accurate records. For one, the client may need to prove that he or she has completed court-ordered therapy sessions or prove that he or she attended therapy before if the client is involved in a lawsuit. Other reasons would be for the professional use of the therapist to review case notes, for billing purposes, for insurance company consultation about session lengths, and additional requests for sessions. Additionally, should a client move out of the area and request records for future therapists, it is helpful if the records are in proper condition.

The therapist may also need to prove that he or she took an acceptable standard of care, the degree of care a therapist would give in the circumstance, if a case is scrutinized. For example, in the event that a client attempts suicide, documentation of the precautions taken by the therapist can help demonstrate that the therapist did all that was clinically possible to help the client. For this reason, it is prudent for mental health practitioners to carefully document in crises, such as cases involving potential harm to self or others. "Failing to keep records deprives practitioners of evidence they will need to defend themselves should they become involved in a malpractice or disciplinary action. Likewise, lack of adequate records may deprive clients of data needed for treatment" (Corey et al., 2003, p. 164). Both the client and the therapist can be hurt if notes are not kept.

Types of Client Records

Records vary from agencies and practitioners, but they usually fall into one of the six following categories (1990):

1. *Identifying or intake information.* Personal and demographic data about the client; a sample intake information form is shown in Figure 19.3.
2. *Assessment information.* Psychological, social, and family vocational or educational assessments; drug and alcohol use assessment and health assessment.
3. *The treatment plan.* Presenting problem, goals of counseling; a sample treatment plan is shown in Figure 19.4.
4. *Case notes.* Documenting progress toward achieving the stated goal; a sample case notes template is shown in Figure 19.5.
5. *Termination summary or letter.* Outcome of treatment, reason for termination, and aftercare plan.
6. *Other data.* Informed consent, release of information, and no-harm contract.

Sample Informed Consent Form

Qualifications and Background of the Practitioner

Bea Happy is a licensed marriage and family therapist in Texas and is a national certified counselor. In 2001, she received her bachelor's degree in child development from Texas Women's University, and then received her master's degree in marriage and family therapy from Texas Women's University in 2005. She has primarily worked with adolescents, couples, and families.

Process of Therapy

Her theoretical orientation is solution-focused brief therapy. Using this model, the approximate length of the therapeutic process depends on what brings a client into therapy. Her role as the therapist is to help the client get "unstuck" by assisting the family in identifying its resources, building on what is working, and managing its problem. Therefore, questions, assignments, or tasks are designed to maintain and highlight positive changes that are already occurring within the family.

General Goals of Counseling

The goals of counseling set in the sessions are decided on by you, the client.

Length of Treatment

The approximate length of the therapeutic process depends on what brings you into therapy. On average, there are six to eight sessions; sessions last 50 minutes.

Frequency of Sessions

It is recommend that sessions are scheduled weekly or biweekly.

Benefits and Risks of Counseling

I understand that the counseling process involves working together with the therapist to achieve a desirable outcome. Participation in therapy can produce benefits in interpersonal relationships. However, it requires my active involvement. The outcome of therapy cannot be guaranteed; there is a possibility that the goals of therapy will not be met. I realize that things may become worse for a period before it gets better. I may experience levels of awareness that could lead to emotional discomfort.

Treatment Planning/Goal

We will collaborate together to establish the goals of therapy and monitor the progress of these goals frequently. The treatment plan will be based on the goals of therapy; if the treatment plan is not effective, then it may have to be altered. During the course of therapy, goals may change; therefore, the treatment plan will reflect these changes.

The Rights and Responsibilities of the Client

I am aware that my records are kept for my benefit, and I may inspect or obtain a copy of my records, unless it contains information that may be detrimental to my well-being. It is ultimately my responsibility to make decisions regarding my own health care. The choices that I make determine the outcome of therapy. It is the responsibility of the therapist to help me, the client, understand the consequences of my decisions. I understand that participation in therapy is voluntary, and I can terminate counseling services at any time, although consulting with my therapist will often provide a more beneficial termination. I am aware that I may choose an alternative to treatment, such as help programs, stress management, programs for personal-effectiveness training, peer self-help groups, bibliotherapy, 12-step programs, support groups, and crisis-intervention centers.

Confidentiality

I understand that all information shared within the counselor–client relationship is kept confidential, unless written permission is obtained by you, the client, stating what information is to be released and to whom.

Limitations and Exceptions of Confidentiality

I understand that there are certain limitations to confidentiality. By law, the therapist must break confidentiality in instances where I, the client, might do serious harm to myself or others. The therapist

FIGURE 19.2 ■ Sample informed consent form.

is legally bound to break confidentiality in instances of child abuse, elder abuse, suicide, and other instances of harm to self or others.

It is a standard of practice that there is a possibility that the therapist may discuss cases with colleagues and/or a supervisor. In the event that this occurs, I understand that my identifying information will not be revealed. Discussions may focus on what the therapist is doing rather than on the client. The therapist may be required to release information or records under a court order from a judge. If using managed care or insurance, I understand that the therapist will need to disclose confidential information about my case to my provider. I may receive a diagnostic classification as a requirement to receive reimbursement for psychology services. A diagnosis can become a part of my permanent file and may affect the cost of insurance, long-term insurability, and employment. I may avoid this by not involving a third-party reimbursement and paying directly for my therapy. By choosing to use my managed care benefits, I release my therapist to disclose all information needed by my managed care company to receive my benefits. Outstanding payments exceeding $200 will be delegated to a collection agency; I understand that my name, address, phone number, and the amount owed will be disclosed. The collection agency will not receive any information regarding the content of therapy.

Issues Related to Insurance
I understand that it is the client's sole responsibility to obtain preauthorization from the insurance company prior to the initial session and to file insurance claims.

Fee Structure
I understand that a 50-minute session is $80. Extended sessions cost $15 for each additional 10-minute increment. Sessions can be purchased at a reduced rate of $75, if purchased in advance for 6 sessions, totaling $450. A minimum of 24-hour notice is required to reschedule or cancel an appointment. The full fee will be charged for sessions missed without 24-hour notice. Fees are collected at the time of service. Payments can be made by cash or check. In the event that my account exceeds $200 of outstanding payments, your name, address, phone number and the amount owed will be passed on to a collection agency. In the event that this happens, I reserve the right to terminate counseling.

Office Information/Emergency Procedures
Office hours are Monday through Friday from 9 a.m. to 12 noon and 2 p.m. to 7 p.m. To reach my therapist during normal business hours, I should contact the main line at 800-555-5555. In case of a life-threatening circumstance after hours, I may page the therapist on call at 800-777-7777 or contact the County Crisis Line at 800-333-3333. If I need to talk to someone right away I can call the emergency National Hopeline at 800-784-2433 or 911.

Consent to Treatment
I agree to receive counseling from Bea Happy, LMFT. I understand that my participation is voluntary and that I may leave therapy at any time. I have read and understood the Informed Consent Form. I have been given the opportunity to ask questions to my satisfaction.

_____   _____
Client   Date

*According to House Bill 2036, a licensed sex-offender treatment provider must treat offenders. Bea is not licensed by the Council on Sex Offender Treatment, but is willing to suggest a referral to another therapist. Because of a potential conflict of interest, cases pertaining to abortion and end-of-life decisions may need to be referred out to another therapist. Additionally, cases involving drug and alcohol addiction may need to be referred out to another therapist because of Bea's limited experience in this area.

Portions of this sample informed consent form has been taken from The TWU Counseling and Development Clinic and from Dr. Patrick O'Malley's private practice.

FIGURE 19.2 ■ Sample informed consent form. *(Continued)*

Intake Information

Name: _____
          First   Middle Initial   Last

Address: _____
City:_____ State: _____ Zip:_____
OK to contact you by mail? _____
SSN:_____ DOB:_____ Age: _____
Home phone:_____ OK to leave message?_____
Cell phone:_____ OK to leave message?_____
Work phone:_____ OK to leave message?_____
E-mail:_____ OK to leave message?_____
Gender:_____ Race:_____
Please list everyone who is living at your address.

First Name	Last Name	Relationship	Age	Gender	Education Level

Please list any children who are not living at your address.

First Name	Last Name	Age	Gender	Education Level

Assessment Information

Have you had any previous counseling?_____When?_____
Are you currently seeing another counselor?_____Who?_____
Family History:
Are you single, married, or divorced?_____
If divorced with children, do you have joint legal custody?_____
If divorced with children, who has legal custody?_____
Is there any history of drug abuse in your family?_____
Is there any history of alcohol abuse in your family?_____
Is there any history of sexual abuse in your family?_____
Is there any history of domestic violence in your family?_____
Is there any history of suicide attempts in your family?_____
Vocation/Education:
Highest level of education completed:_____
Clients' occupation:_____
Clients' employer:_____
Drugs/Alcohol:
Are you or is anyone in your family currently using drugs or alcohol?_____
Medical History:
Please describe any current health problems:_____
_____
Please list any family member with health problems and his or her condition:_____
_____
Name of general physician:_____
Date of last physical exam:_____
Please list any medications and the dosage you currently taking:_____
For what conditions?_____
Prescribing doctor:_____

FIGURE 19.3 ▓ Sample intake information form.

The Treatment Plan

Name:_____ **Date**:_____

Presenting problem:_____
_____
_____
_____

Goal of counseling:_____
_____
_____
_____

Steps to be taken to reach the targeted behavior:_____
_____
_____
_____
_____

Please note specific therapeutic or behavioral changes that take place and the client's response and adjustments.

_____
_____
_____
_____
_____
_____
_____
_____

FIGURE 19.4 ■ Sample treatment plan.
Source: Bernstein & Hartsell, 2004.

Case Notes Template

Date:_____ Session #:_____ Payment:_____

Client's Name:_____

Attended the session:_____

Presenting problem:_____

Summary of session:_____

_____

_____

_____

_____

_____

_____

Assignment:_____

_____

Signed:_____

Sample Case Notes

Date: _September 1, 2005_ Session #: _2_ Payment: _$80_

Client's Name: Mr. & Mrs. Smith

Attended the session: Mr. & Mrs. Smith

Presenting problem: The Smiths would like to resolve marital problems. Mrs. Smith has been spending money impulsively over the course of the past year. Mrs. Smith complains of her husband being a workaholic and not being affectionate.

Mr. and Mrs. Smith arrived promptly for their 3:00 appointment. Mr. Smith and Mrs. Smith both complained about their marriage. When asked when the last time that their marriage was better, they commented that it had been 2 years ago when they were "happily married." When asked to describe what was different back then, they both reminisced about the weekend trips that they would take, evening walks/talks, and enjoying a football game. Throughout the session, Mrs. Smith looked directly at Mr. Smith, whereas the previous week Mrs. Smith would look downward. On a scale of 1 to 10, 1 being miserably married and 10 being happily married, Mrs. Smith reported that she was a "3." The previous week she reported a "1." When asked how she moved up two points on the scale, Mrs. Smith reported exceptions throughout the past week. When asked what it would look like soon when they were reliving their happily married relationship and small steps that they could take to move a little bit closer to being happily married, they came up with a list of three things they could try to improve their score on the scaling question. They could go for an evening walk, hold hands, and dance together.

Assignment: Select one of the activities discussed (i.e., evening walk, hold hands, or dance together) to do in the upcoming week.

Signed:_____

FIGURE 19.5 ■ Case notes.

Writing Effective Records

A common question of a beginning therapist is whether to keep minimal records to protect the privacy of the client. Marriage and family therapists should keep the client's best interest in mind while protecting themselves in the event of a disciplinary proceeding or investigation. "The file is the therapist's first line of defense" (Bernstein & Hartsell, 2000, p. 180). A good rule of thumb to keep in mind while writing progress notes is to take into consideration that it may be read in a courtroom someday. You would not want to document anything that would be detrimental to the client's well-being. Keep in mind that the client has the legal right to inspect his or her records and may request a copy anytime. In writing progress notes, it is important to note specific and concrete behavior instead of personal opinions or reactions to the client (Corey et al., 2003).

Records should provide a road map of the therapeutic process (Bernstein & Hartsell, 2000). Sallie Campbell, a trainer in ethics for marriage and family therapists, states that the essential components to a good record include

> what goes on in the therapy, the behavior, the treatment, your plan for the next session, presenting issues that are coming on in therapy, how the client behaved, the treatment provided, the client's response and your plan for going into the next session. Each note needs to tie to the note before and the notes need to tie to the treatment plan that is written. (Sally Campbell, personal communication, August 1, 2005)

Retaining and Destroying Records

Guidelines for record-keeping procedures vary from state to state, so it is vital to understand the requirements of your state. The length of time for retaining records also varies from jurisdiction to jurisdiction. In many locales, 7 to 10 years is the upper range to retain records after the last contact with a client (Leslie, 2003a). However, if the client is a minor, the clinician may be responsible for retaining records for a longer period.

There are several other ethical considerations to take into mind regarding records, such as how the records should be handled in the event that the therapist moves from an area, closes his or her practice, or passes away. Practitioners are responsible for making appropriate arrangement for the storage, transfer or disposal of client records in a way that maintains confidentiality (AAMFT, 2001). Therapists should keep files in a locked file cabinet and out of common areas that can be exposed to the general public.

TECHNOLOGICAL ISSUES AND CLIENT COMMUNICATION

E-mail, texts, cell phones, facsimiles, and computers have provided clinicians and their clients with convenience. However, many of these methods are not secure mediums of communication. When using any electronic devices to communicate with a client, keep the following guidelines in mind:

- Inform the client when you are calling from a cell phone.
- Limiting the content of e-mail and voicemail messages to general information not pertaining to the content of therapy (i.e., scheduling appointments).
- Avoid Internet contact, voicemails, and e-mail if there is any uncertainty that the intended recipient will not receive the information.

- Computer files may become accessible to others who use the same computer. Have some form of password protection to restrict access to confidential materials that are stored on the hard drive.

- Additionally, storing case notes on a computer can cause a dilemma if the hard drive were to crash. Routinely backing up files can serve as a preventative measure.

- Bernstein and Hartsell (2004) suggest obtaining the client's written consent before sending fax transmissions. Furthermore, they suggest asking the client to wait for the fax and confirm that he or she received it.

Internet, telephone, e-mail, chat-based, and videoconferencing therapy are fairly new to the industry; the existing AAMFT Code of Ethics does not yet address electronic therapies. However, they raise many ethical issues. For example, if a therapist practices in California and provides Internet therapy to a client in Texas, does that constitute unlicensed practice in another state? Other mental health professions, such as the American Counseling Association (ACA) have guidelines for Internet therapy; refer to the 2005 ACA Code of Ethics for more information.

DUAL RELATIONSHIPS

When a therapist has two or more roles with a client at the same time, this constitutes a *dual relationship* (Corey et al., 2003). Common dual relationships include friendships or sexual relationships with a client. Bernstein and Hartsell (2004) recommend that the relationship between the therapist and client should be limited to a therapeutic relationship. Furthermore, they exert that being up front with clients and explaining limitations of nontherapeutic personal contact can avoid dual relationship issues and boundary problems.

Bernstein and Hartsell (2000) also urge mental health professionals to maintain a clinical distance between themselves and clients. They further assert that therapists should raise and reinforce the wall of professionalism if there is any hint of compromising an ethical boundary.

In rural settings or small communities where dual relationships are difficult to avoid, therapists can provide clients with a contract that explicitly states boundaries to avoid an ethical dilemma.

It is inappropriate to engage in activities that would compromise the therapist's objectivity toward a client (Bernstein & Hartsell, 2000). Bernstein and Hartsell (2000) further state that when boundaries are violated, the therapeutic relationship will be jeopardized. Accepting gifts that have substantial value, including emotional or sentimental value, "runs the risk of compromising the boundaries that are imperative to the integrity of the therapeutic relationship" (O'Malley, 2001, p. 41). Boundary violations are sometimes subtle. These encounters may seem innocent at first glance but in reality are unethical (Bernstein & Hartsell, 2000). If the line is crossed, it is best for the therapist to deal with the issue immediately because it may be necessary to terminate and refer the client to another therapist.

TREATING MINORS

When a parent or guardian initiates therapy for a child, the therapist should check whether the parent has the right to do so. In instances where the initiating parent is divorced, the best practice is to "require a review of actual divorce decree or other legal document that describes the custody settlement, and to keep a file copy of that document" (p. 3).

Almost always, when a therapist provides services to a minor whose parents are married, the consent of one parent is sufficient for providing medical or mental health treatment. If the parents are separated or divorced and have custody, either parent may consent to treatment except in those cases where the divorce decree specifies which parent has the power to obtain psychological or psychiatric care for the children. In cases of sole custody, only the parent who has sole custody may consent to therapy. In order to act proactively when seeing minors with or without a parent, therapists must inquire at intake about the parents' marital status and, in the case of divorce, whether the parent requesting services has the right to authorize such treatment. (Haug, 2001, p. 25)

Engaging both adults (if possible) in the therapeutic process from the onset may resolve questionable matters concerning custody (Brock, 2001). Regardless of who has the legal right to make decisions regarding medical health care, it would be wise to obtain the written consent of both parents before treating the child (Leslie, 2004). Finally, it is a good practice to include these questions and issues on the informed consent form, which was discussed earlier in the chapter.

Working with minors raises issues of confidentiality, particularly if or when a parent asks the therapist about what is happening in the child's therapy. In *Issues and Ethics in the Helping Professions*, Corey et al. (2003) state that the parent has a right to general information regarding the child's progress. However, parents do not have rights to access their child's records. Involving parents in the initial session with their child and disclosing the nature of what the therapist will or will not disclose creates a clear understanding of the boundaries for sharing information (Corey et al., 2003). However, confidentiality may need to be breached when acting in the best interest of the minor's welfare, such as instances where the "... client reports of behaviors that may be dangerous to self or to others" (Isaacs & Stone, 2001, p. 342).

TERMINATION

Bernstein and Hartsell (2000) suggest several reasons for the termination of therapy. Therapy can end by mutual agreement if the client is no longer benefiting or if the therapist transfers the client's file because of a dual relationship or lack of expertise. Furthermore, therapy can also end because the client no longer has the financial capability to continue in therapy, or the number of sessions determined by his or her health insurance provider has been depleted.

Principle 1.11 of the AAMFT Code of Ethics states that therapists do not abandon or neglect clients without making adequate arrangements or providing referral sources (AAMFT, 2001). For example, in the event that a therapist retires, becomes ill, moves, or passes away, the therapist is responsible for making adequate arrangements.

Participation in therapy is voluntary and clients may terminate at anytime; however, it is beneficial to discuss with the therapist reasons for termination. "A therapeutic relationship should be maintained only as long as it is clear that the client is benefiting" (Corey et al., 2003, p. 147). Corey et al. (2003) advise the termination of therapy to be a collaborative process involving both the therapist and client. Developing contracts "during the final sessions involving actions to be taken between the termination and the follow-up session" (Corey et al., 2003, p. 441) can motivate clients to make continued progress toward their goals.

"Document the rational[e] for termination: why it is taking place, and how it is in the client's best interest" (Bernstein & Hartsell, 2000). They also suggest setting up termination interview and preparing a termination letter for the client to sign. In the event that the client discontinues therapy without notification, attempt a phone conference; if that is unsuccessful, mail two copies of the termination letter with a self-addressed stamped envelope, asking the client to sign and return one of the copies. The termination letter should include appropriate referral sources (Bernstein & Hartsell, 2000) and any alternative treatment methods. A sample termination letter is shown in Figure 19.6.

Termination Summary/Letter

Bea Happy, LMFT
3915 E. Boaz Ave., Suite 3000
Dallas, TX 76501
November 1, 2010

Mr. and Mrs. Smith
1505 Huntington Dr.
Dallas, TX 75203

Re: Termination of Treatment

Dear Mr. and Mrs. Smith,

This letter is to inform you that our therapist–client relationship is terminated effective November 1, 2010. After missing your last scheduled appointment on September 8, 2010, I have not heard back from you. I have left four messages with you, over the past month, to discuss this matter; however, you have not returned my phone calls. I assume that you no longer wish to continue therapy or have sought care from another practitioner.

Our work together began on August 25, 2010. During this time, we worked on establishing a happy marriage by doing shared activities that would move you closer toward a happier marriage. Because our work together ended prematurely and the goals of counseling were not met, it would be beneficial to seek further treatment.

Please feel free to contact me about future counseling session or about finding a new therapist. If you desire to return to counseling, I am available for future sessions. If you choose to work with another therapist, I will be willing to consult with your subsequent therapist on your written request. Your file will be made available to your future therapist with your written consent along with a $10.00 fee to handle administrative costs.

I wish you good luck and continued success.

Sincerely,

Bea Happy, LMFT

FIGURE 19.6 ■ Sample termination letter.

Case Study of an Ethics Complaint

The following is a case study of an ethics complaint from a client and the therapist response. Thanks to Dr. Patrick O'Malley for providing this example and allowing us to use it within this volume.

COMPLAINT

Dear Chair of the AAMFT Ethics Committee:

1	I have been married for 15 years. The last 5 years have been very difficult.
2	Last January, my husband said he wanted to get a divorce. I have two sons and a
3	daughter ages 5, 7, and 13. I love my husband and my family and did not want
4	our marriage to end. I got my husband to agree to not take any action until
5	we went through some counseling. I wanted to see our pastor, but my husband,
6	who is an attorney, insisted he knew someone good. I did not want to argue
7	the point since I was surprised he was willing to go to therapy in the first
8	place.
9	
10	We had our first appointment with Dr. Irene Care last February. Looking back
11	on that appointment, I should have known this marriage counselor was not the
12	right person for us. Although my husband had told me he knew of this person,
13	I had no idea he knew her so well. It turns out that my husband refers
14	a number of social security disability cases to Dr. Care for psychological
15	evaluations. He actually introduced me to her when she came to the waiting
16	room to get us for our appointment. In the first part of the session, they
17	joked about a mutual friend. Dr. Care also mentioned to him that she would
18	have the report done on a certain case at the end of the week. I thought it
19	was strange they were talking business in the session.
20	
21	When Dr. Care finally got around to asking what brought us to counseling, my
22	husband began to describe what a horrible wife, mother, and sexual partner I
23	had been. My husband is a very persuasive man. He argues for a living. I
24	hardly got a chance to say anything in the first session. Dr. Care said she
25	was a marriage therapist and a sex therapist so she thought she could help
26	us. She wanted us to come back for another session. I felt very defeated.
27	However, I did not want to give up so I agreed to come back for another
28	session, hoping I could give my side of the story when we returned. At the
29	end of the session, Dr. Care asked if we were going to file on our insurance.
30	My husband said that he had already called our managed care company and they
31	had authorized six sessions. Dr. Care said that she needed one of us to be
32	the patient for her to diagnose. I did not understand what this meant. My
33	husband said that I was the patient and to file the claim on me.
34	
35	In the second session, to Dr. Care's credit, she asked me to tell my side of
36	what needed to be changed in our marriage. I began to talk about how my
37	husband worked all of the time and was often angry and verbally abusive to me
38	and the children when he was home. My husband began to defend himself, but he
39	did not show the kind of anger he does at home. He was very reasonable and

40   calm when he spoke to Dr. Care. He claimed that he saw himself as a good
41   father and provider, and although he did admit he worked many hours, he did so
42   for the good of the family. This calm response infuriated me. I admit that I
43   lost my composure in this session. I usually keep my feelings to myself at
44   home so as not to make him mad. But I thought since we were here for
45   counseling, I might as well say what was on my mind. Maybe too many years of
46   not expressing my feelings caught up with me. Anyways, I began to scream at him
       about what a domineering jerk he was. Dr. Care became very aggressive
47   with me in this session and told me that if I wanted to stay in the office, I
48   needed to "get a grip" on myself. I was finally reduced to sobbing. It was
49   time for the session to end, and Dr. Care scheduled us for another session. I
50   ran out of the office. I was angry and embarrassed.
51
52   In the third session, Dr. Care asked if we wanted to address our sexual
53   problems. Although I thought we needed to work on our communication, I did
54   not want to upset anyone so I agreed. Dr. Care began to ask very personal
55   questions about our sexual relationship. This line of questioning made me
56   very uncomfortable, but I thought since she was a professional, she knew what
57   was best. At the end of the session, Dr. Care said we should take a couple of
58   evenings a week and do a massage on each other in order to get more
59   comfortable with each others' bodies. Again, I agreed to this although it
60   made me uncomfortable to think about being physical with my husband when we
61   could not talk.
62
63   We never did what Dr. Care suggested. I even asked my husband a couple of
64   times if he would like to but he ignored me. I was about to tell Dr. Care
65   about this in the fourth session when my husband dropped the bomb. He began
66   the session by stating that he did not believe there was any hope for us and
67   he wanted a divorce. He further stated that he had already filed and wanted
68   me to leave the house tonight. I was devastated. I pleaded with him to give
69   the counseling more time. I asked Dr. Care if she thought with some
70   counseling, we might have a chance. She said she thought our relationship did
71   have some serious problems, and that if my husband thought it was over that
72   we should probably go ahead and end the marriage. It was only 15 minutes
73   into the session but I was beginning to lose control again, and so I left the
74   office.
75
76   When I got home, the locks on the doors had been changed. I called my parents
77   who live close by and told them what had happened. They told me to come over
78   so I did. They found an attorney for me and we began a long battle over
79   property and the children. Our divorce and custody case was recently
80   settled. I ended up with the house but my husband got primary custody of our
81   children. I believe Dr. Care helped him do so.
82
83   In one of the many hearings we had while we were getting divorced, my
84   husband's attorney asked the court to not allow me to have overnight
85   visitation with my children. When the judge asked the attorney why he was
86   requesting this, the lawyer said he had our records from our marriage
87   counseling and the therapist said I was unstable. The judge denied the

88 request. I was furious that the attorney had our records from counseling.
89
90 My attorney then immediately requested the records so we could see what was
91 in them. In her notes, Dr. Care said I was unstable and possibly "Borderline
92 Personality Disorder." I did not know what this meant. My attorney's
93 assistant looked it up in a book. I know I was out of control in one session,
94 but I am not what that book says.
95
96 In our final hearing, my husband's lawyer called Dr. Care to testify. While
97 she did not outright say I was a bad parent, she did say she thought my
98 husband was more financially and emotionally stable. When the attorney asked
99 her who would be the better parent, she said "probably" my husband because of
100 those factors. When my attorney asked her if she was an expert in making
101 assessments for child custody, she said she had been involved in few
102 custody cases through the years. How could she know what is best for my
103 children when she never met them?
104
105 I have one other complaint against Dr. Care. Because of the divorce, I have
106 had to find a job to support myself. I am working for a small company as a
107 receptionist. The problem is that I cannot get on their insurance plan
108 because I have a "psychiatric diagnosis." This is from our marriage
109 counseling. I had no idea when we filed on our insurance that this meant I
110 was getting that kind of diagnosis.
111
112 I am filing this complaint with you because I believe Dr. Care messed my life
113 up. You want to believe when you see a professional that it will help. All
114 I can say is that my life is worse because I went to Dr. Care.

Sincerely,
Ms. Ann Gry

Response to the Charges

Dear Chair and Ethics Committee:

1   I am in receipt of your correspondence in which I have been charged with
2   several violations of the Code of Ethics of the American Association For
3   Marriage and Family Therapy. I value my membership in AAMFT and intend to
4   fully cooperate in this investigation. I have been a clinical member of this
5   organization for 10 years. I am dedicated to the highest standards of ethical
6   practice. I have never had a complaint lodged against me until this case.
7
8   I have included all of the material you requested. A couple of explanations
9   are in order before I respond to the charges. Although I am not certified as
10 a sex therapist, I have had 6 graduate hours in human sexuality and sex
11 therapy. I have intentionally not sought certification as a sex therapist
12 because of the increase in liability insurance when this credential is

13   listed.
14
15   I am not, nor do I hold myself, out to be an expert in child custody cases. As
16   you will see in my response to the charges, I was merely answering the
17   attorney's question.
18
19   I will respond to the question about my competency to diagnose Borderline
20   Personality Disorder later in my response to the charges.
21
22   There has been a complaint lodged against me with my licensing board. This
23   complaint has not proceeded beyond the initial letter[, which] informed me that an
24   investigation will take place.
25
26   Responses To The Charges:
27
28   Charge 1 (Subprinciple 1.2): Denied. Ms. Gry has greatly exaggerated the
29   circumstances of my relationship with Mr. Gry. I met Mr. Gry after a speech I
30   gave at a rotary meeting. We chatted a minute, and he asked for some of my
31   cards. He began sending me personal injury cases to evaluate for psychological
32   disability. We would often talk on the phone about these cases. I would send
33   him a report on each client. That is the extent of my relationship with him.
34   My work with the Grys was not influenced by my previous relationship with
35   Mr. Gry.
36
37   Charge 2 (Subprinciple 1.4): Denied. The statement I made regarding the future
38   of the Grys marriage was taken out of context. What I was trying to
39   communicate is that, if one person wants out of the marriage, then there is not
40   much the other person can do to stop it. At no time did I tell this couple to
41   end their marriage.
42
43   Charge 3 (Subprinciple 2.1): Denied. I did not willingly violate Ms. Grys
44   confidentiality. My records were subpoenaed. I had to turn them over to comply
45   with the subpoena.
46
47   It is at this point [that] I want to explain my misunderstanding about the
48   Diagnosis of Borderline Personality Disorder. Ms. Gry's actual diagnosis was
49   Adjustment Disorder with mixed Feature of Depression and Anxiety. On the
50   certification form for the managed care company that the Grys use, you are
51   asked to give the complete five axis diagnoses. On Axis II, I put R/O
52   Borderline Personality Disorder. I only suspected this disorder at the time I
53   made the initial report to the managed care company. I am qualified in my
54   state at the doctoral level to make diagnoses of personality disorders. Ms.
55   Gry's behavior had borderline features that I believe should be noted on her
56   insurance form. I now believe I was right in suspecting this diagnosis. Ms.
57   Gry has made me the target of her anger about her divorce. She was very
58   disruptive in my office while I was seeing her and her husband. She made
59   repeated attempts to talk to me by phone in-between sessions. She even began
60   to call me at home to ask me if I thought I could save her marriage.

61
62   Charge 4 (Subprinciple 3.8): Denied. I did say what Ms. Gry claims I said.
63   However, I do not believe I have violated the Code. The attorney asked me who
64   I thought the better parent would be. I gave the court my honest answer.
65
66   Charge 5 (Subprinciple 3.6): Denied. As I previously stated, I do not do child
67   custody evaluations in my practice. I have been involved in a few custody cases
68   like most experienced marriage and family therapists. Again, I was
69   simply answering the question based on the information I had.
70
71   Charge 6 (Subprinciple 7.4): Denied. Giving an individual diagnosis when
72   seeing a marital case is common practice. Perhaps I should have explained the
73   details of the managed care company's requirements for treatment in more
74   detail to Ms. Gry. I assume people who come to see me know what the
75   implications are of using their insurance.

          Please feel free to contact me if more information is needed.

          Sincerely,
          Irene Care, PhD

MASTER THERAPIST INTERVIEW

SALLIE CAMPBELL

Sallie Campbell is an assistant professor at the Medical University of South Carolina's (MUSC's) Department of Psychiatry and Behavioral Sciences. She was the chair for the AAMFT Ethics Committee and has done local, regional, and national presentations on various topics related to ethics. She served as South Carolina Association for Marriage and Family Therapy (SCAMFT) president from 2000 to 2001, and SCNASW President from 1990 to 1991.

What interested you in the field of ethics?
In 1989, I was president elect for South Carolina NASW (National Association of Social Workers) and I got interested in the board of social work examiners in our state, as they were making decisions that were very different than how the organization made decisions. A friend of mine was on the board so the two of us came together to start ethics trainings in the state to help people become more aware of the ethical dilemmas that people were getting caught in through the legal arm as well as the professional arm. I have continued to be interested in ethics ever since then, and I have done presentations across South Carolina, some in Georgia, and some on the national level.

What do you feel is the importance of ethics?
To me, it's something that we use every day in our practice. Learning how to think through ethical dilemmas is a good form of risk management so that you give better service to the clients and your agency has less risk.

Do you feel like there are any limitations in being ethical?

I think ethical dilemmas in and of themselves are not always black and white, and many times they are lots more complicated than what we think. One of the things that we have trouble [with] within our center is gift giving. People want to give menial gifts, and I have a real problem with how to think through those things. I know we aren't supposed to accept gifts but, at the same time, if we deal with children and adolescents and families, you hurt people's feelings sometimes if you don't accept something that is personally made.

So in that situation where you've been given a gift by a child that they've created for you, how do you handle that so they don't get their feelings hurt?

It's hard because based on what it is, if there is not a lot of cost involved, I may accept it, but if there's a good deal of cost, I encourage them to give what they've made to someone else and work with them to help them understand that that's a better use of their gift. Usually, it is someone else they know that would appreciate it, something that they've made. Big gifts are clearly a "no." For example, anything that has a substantial value that they have purchased needs to be returned.

What do you feel are some essential characteristics that a therapist should possess to be ethical?

They should have a sense of empathy for their client and the situation. Systems wise, I think it's very important for them to be able to think through the multilayers of a situation. A lot of people think in a particular family kind of context, but you have to think family, agency, bigger picture, organization. The therapist has to have good clinical skills to realize that they even have an ethical dilemma. For example, people across the country who get caught in just sexual misconduct know it's wrong, but once boundaries are crossed, its almost too late. A therapist needs to know how to recognize something early enough to be able to prove it is an ethical issue. So to sort of be able to see it ahead of time, the forethought is something that everybody needs to have. We are doing more continuing education on ethics and have noticed that across the country, the number of ethical complaints have actually decreased. When you are concentrated in teaching ethics in specific courses, it means you teach people how to think things through, and I think that's the absolute difference when you are showing them all the various areas where they can get caught in various quandaries and ethical dilemmas, and still that doesn't stop some people, which is amazing.

What do you feel are some common misconceptions about ethics?

Ethics are not black and white. It's clearly not as if I know the rules, then I can play by the rules. A lot of times you have two conflicting things that are very, very hard to think through. I've certainly been in the middle of a lot of ethical dilemmas in the sense that I am risk manager for the agency that I work in, and in the last several years, I've had two big ethical issues that involved me personally and neither of them were legitimate. Ethical issues are not always easy to solve, and I think that it's important to have that sort of plan in place and your back-up, and when you are in a situation where there's and ethical quandary, you go to your supervisor, you go to the agency head, and run it through an attorney.

In the ethical dilemmas that you've faced in the agency where you work, what are some common issues?

Divorce custody is an area where you see a great deal of contention. We do a lot of work with youth, and a lot of times, the parents are separating and divorcing, and we don't per se do child custody work but as a result of working with children, you find yourself in that position many times. Divorce custody has been probably our biggest issue in the last year, but across the country, sexual misconduct and crossing boundaries have been areas that have been prominent.

Of the ethical dilemmas that you have encountered, which one have you found the most difficult to handle?

In the work area, it was one against me. I work for an academic medical center, and one of my clients wrote the boss a five-page paper on what a horrible therapist I was. It was an awful case where the mother had been blocked from visitation by the court system and they were coming to therapy and we were trying to implement back visitation. I think one of the parents felt like the finger was beginning to be pointed in their direction. They retaliated and complained about me throughout the system. And then after that, they allowed me to go ahead and see them, the second letter was sent in and they then allowed me to transfer that client to someone else. I have felt awful about it because my gut told me something was happening and that I needed to protect those kids.

When would you say it is appropriate for the needs of an individual family member to take precedence over the family's need?

Well, in any family situation, you have to have an identified patient (IP) anytime you are taking insurance that you are billing on. So, in that situation, I would want to take care of that individual first, certainly within the context of the family, but your charting, etcetera, has to be reflective of the person who is coming in for treatment. I think that in a situation where there is an IP, we are ethically bound to deal with that, and if there are other kinds of abuse going on in the family and others are getting hurt and my patient is not, I still would make a report, but usually it's sort of child abuse or neglect. I think we look at the whole family, but usually it's the IP that we would look at first.

In regards to keeping session notes, I know some therapists advise colleagues to keep short notes for protection, and others write detailed notes for legal reasons. Which do you recommend?

I keep detailed notes, not to reveal intimate details, but notes regarding what was talked about, what was done and goals for the next session. We have treatment plans and reviews and keep notes and a chart on every patient. I am audited on every patient, so if my notes don't have certain things in them, I am downgraded in my audit. So, I also have the internal organization looking [at] my notes. We take Medicaid, so we get Medicaid audits and insurance audits.

You said that you keep detailed records. Is that primarily for the purpose of being audited, or is that your personal preference as well?

I think it's my preference in both. I review a lot of ethical complaints that come in across the country, and when a complaint comes in, that person's records are up for review. The record they did this, this, and this, and they are being accused of not doing this, and the record becomes their best defense. So while I have seen a detailed record save many people, the ones that are just kind of sketchy and don't really say anything don't let the therapist have a chance to really defend anything.

In your review of records, what would you say would be components that are essential to a good record?
What goes on in therapy, the behavior, the treatment, the plan for the next session, presenting issues, how the client behaved, the treatment you provided as a therapist, their response, and your plan for going into the next session . . . those are the issues that are in the notes. Since the new HIPAA law, we get releases when we have to chart up on one couple and we have to get a release that it's okay to talk to the other part of the couple about things. Last year, there was a situation where I had met with a woman where I had brought in the husband and met with them for a little while and then again later met with the woman for a little while, and then her husband came in again and she wanted him to be seen by himself. So I met with him and the woman was upset that he met with me alone, even though she had pushed for me to do that. So she made a complaint with the organization, and since I had clearly written in there that she had asked me to see her husband and that was arranged, my notes clearly saved me. I mean I even chart phone calls. I know it's hard but I chart all of them.

I know that many LMFT's are also seeking the LPC licensure. To your knowledge, are there any ethical codes that are conflicting between the two licenses?
I think the majority of most of the professional mental health codes are pretty similar. They all hold confidentiality, informed consent, termination, [and] statements about sexual misconduct in the same manner of ethics.

Would it be the safest option in regard to terminating and keeping case notes, if one license says 7 years, to keep it afterwards?
If the ethical code conflicts with the LPC and LMFT or the LISW, and the LMFT says to go with the higher of the two, to stay out of trouble, you have to adhere to the highest of the ethical codes if you are dually licensed.

Have you encountered any difficulties with your two licenses?
They do conflict at times. With LISW, once a client always a client, and with LMFT, it is a minimum of 2 years before you can enter into something. So, I tend to go more toward the social work view on that, once a client always a client. What I've done is to try to make the strongest of the three across the board for me.

If one of your interns came to you and said that they were sexually attracted to one of their clients, and they felt like it was interfering with their therapeutic relationship, what would you suggest as their supervisor?
Well, I would actually talk with them first about the sexual attraction and why they allowed themselves to go there. We would probably transfer that client to someone else. This actually happened recently to one of my interns in a little bit of a different way. The husband was saying that the wife was dressing up to come to therapy and the husband was jealous of the wife's position with the therapist. The wife was actually playing the husband against the therapist and we began to talk about the dynamics of that and put the family with a female therapist so that [there] could not be a complaint and it ended up working out fine. On the other hand, if the therapist is sexually attracted to

the client, I want that person talking to me about that. If you know the client is aware that the sexual attraction is there, then that is a huge liability and termination needs to occur. I think you have to [be] extremely proactive as the supervisor in those situations to help protect the supervisee and your client.

What are your thoughts on conducting Internet therapy?
I think Internet therapy is very risky. You lose a lot in not being able to see somebody and it's not protected confidentiality-wise. If anyone e-mails me, I always write them back and say that "this is an unprotected site and anything that you write me cannot be held in confidence because I don't know who has access to this." As far as keeping up with doctors, we use numbers rather than names. We never put names in e-mails or correspondence. I do telephone conference calls when I have families that live out of town and can't afford to come in town.

So in your documentation, you note that you were calling from a cell phone.
That is correct. If I e-mail anyone, I always keep a copy of the e-mail in the chart. I haven't seen an Internet complaint yet. But it's only kind of a matter of time.

What would you say are the most common reasons for suspension and termination of one's licensure?
Probably sexual misconduct and breach of confidentiality.

What are some suggestions that you have for students starting out, regarding common ethical mistakes?
I would suggest that if you are in an area where you think ethics are brewing, bring it up. Ask advice and seek help early. I've noticed that students often realize that they are in an area that they are unsure of but don't ask about it soon enough. The supervisor should create an atmosphere where the therapist feels comfortable to bring information and to work through it together. I think it is important to read the code of ethics early and reread it every year.

One of the things that stood out to me as I was reading the code of ethics is that there is a clause that says that family therapists shouldn't diagnos[e], advise, or treat for problems outside of their competency. I was wondering if you could just comment a little about that in regards to students and beginning therapists, because there is not a lot that you are very competent at as you are beginning to see clients.
First, you should not diagnos[e] or treat in areas outside of your competence. In recent years, marriage and family therapists have had to take a diagnostics course, psychopathology course, and an ethics course in our state. It may be that a student feels comfortable diagnosing an adjustment disorder, anxiety, or depression but may not feel competent in diagnosing autism or bipolar or schizophrenia. In that case, the new therapist would gather up that info and send the client to a psychologist who could make a more definitive diagnosis and then send it back to the therapist for more continued work in therapy. There are times where I'm not sure if I'm dealing with schizophrenia or psychosis, so I'll gather all the info and then send it and have a psychiatrist look at it and then have them determine which category that person falls into. I would encourage a student to keep a list of all the continuing education events and course work that they take; all that proves your area of competence in certain arenas. I've never trained as a child and adolescent person. I was trained on the job in the field and developed that

area of expertise in the field. When I first started ethics, I had to learn about it as I went, and I still study and read books and go to conferences in this area all the time. But you are right, a student does have to diagnose and treat, and they are developing their competence so their supervisor is an integral part of their training.

MASTER THERAPIST INTERVIEW

PATRICK O'MALLEY

Patrick O'Malley, PhD, is currently the chair for the AAMFT Judiciary Committee. He has held this position from 2003 to 2006. Dr. O'Malley has served in numerous other offices. He served as the AAMFT Judiciary Committee from 2001 to 2006, AAMFT Code Revision Task Force from 1998 to 2000, AAMFT Ethics chair from 1996 to 1997, AAMFT Ethics Committee member from 1994 to 1995, Family Political Action Committee Regional chair from 1990 to 1991 and from 1988 to 1989, Tarrant County AMFT president on 1987, Texas AMFT Board member from 1991 to 1995, TAMFT Nominating Committee from 1986 to 1988, and TAMFT Ethics Committee chair from 1982 to 1984. He has done ethics workshops on a local, regional, and national level and written several publications. Additionally, the TAMFT presented him with the Meritorious Service Award in 1995 and 1993. Dr. O'Malley has more than 25 years of practice as a marriage and family therapist. He has a private practice in Fort Worth, Texas.

What interested you in the field of ethics?

I had a primary professor in my first year of graduate school that I bonded with very tightly. He enlisted me to help him with an article. It was actually a public article that was exposing a therapist in town, who had been unethical and had a sexual relationship with a client. This was before licensures. The client released everyone to write the article. I helped him with the article, which went into a local magazine. I also worked with him on another article on ethics, looking at different ethical dilemmas. As a result, I got very interested in ethics early in graduate school. I became the TAMFT chair of ethics; from there I was elected to the AAMFT ethics board. I served on the board for several years and chaired that for 2 years. I got the opportunity to be on the group that wrote the latest ethics code. I was then elected to what is called the judicial appeals board, the judicial committee for AAMFT.

What are some of the cases that make it to the appeals board?

When someone comes to the appeals level, they believe they've gotten an unfair verdict. They may think that the committee was biased, or they didn't read all of the material, or they read the information in a biased manner, or that there was a procedural problem. Usually, they don't like the verdict or they thought the punishment was too harsh. They may agree on the violation, but the ethics committee hands down the consequence. So often times, they're not necessarily appealing the verdict, they are appealing the consequence. They have the right to do that. If they challenge our finding, they can go to the AAMFT board. Our job is to make sure that the process was followed well. Ethics cases for AAMFT are not handled in person; they are all done in writing. There's a process in which people submit material. The client submits material and it is reviewed. An appeal is handled in person, so a therapist almost always comes with an attorney. AAMFT has their attorney present; it is pretty intense because at that point, they've spent a lot of money and time trying to preserve their membership in AAMFT.

How long of a process is an appeals case?

Usually a day. As a chair, I say how long everyone can talk but there is a protocol for doing that. Usually half a day for the testimony and half a day for the appeals committee to meet and come up with a decision. Then the member will be informed in writing within 2 weeks. Preparation for it is probably a day and the actually appeals is a day, so a 2-day ordeal, because we'll meet before the case and go over the fine points of the case. The chair of the ethics committee represents the ethics committee. I was in that spot where I was defending our decision to the judicial committee, but now I've switched roles, and now, I'm chairing the judicial committee. So the two witnesses are the chair of the ethics committee and the therapist. The chair of the ethics committee has to represent the ethics committee's decision. The therapist usually represents himself or herself with an attorney. It's fascinating to read a case because you'll get the complaint from the client, and you'll read through all of that. I watch myself going, "I cannot believe this therapist did what he or she did," and then I'll read the therapist and think that [the] client was really out of line and then go back and forth. Now sometimes they're just clear-cut. But sometimes, the evidence is in the middle and so the ethics committee will ask more questions to get more information in writing.

And how long would you say that it takes for a case to get to the appeals process?

If it gets to appeals, there's a deadline. From the moment a client makes a complaint to when it gets to the ethics committee, could take anywhere from 4 months to a year. The ethics committee meets twice a year. If a client makes a complaint and notifies the AAMFT, then the ball starts rolling and it could be 3 or 4 months to get all the materials. Then in the next ethics meeting, we'll process that, and then the decisions will be made. The ethics committee decides to uphold the therapist if we don't see supporting evidence or uphold the client, and discipline the therapist. The discipline might be something like taking another ethics course or another year or two of supervision. Let's say that their offense was a dual relationship problem, so we'd have them go into supervision to work on dual relationship matters. In extreme cases, membership is terminated. Membership is terminated usually for sexual offenses. There's really two parts of the process that the committee has to do. One is to determine guilt or innocence, and then the other is to create consequence that is rehabilitative. We think about what the therapist needs in order to function better and where they are going to learn it. Maybe 1 out of 50 make it to the appeals level.

How does the board deem that a case is worthy to be appealed?

The board doesn't do it; the therapist does it. The therapist has the right to challenge the findings. If the therapist says, "I don't think my hearing was fair, or I don't think the process is fair, I don't think the outcome was justified," then they have the right to appeal. What they are taking on is a fair amount of time and expense, particularly if they hire an attorney, because they are going to have to travel to Washington for a meeting and pay an attorney for that, and that's pretty costly. Usually, that's the final version. What the association has to deal with is the fact that the therapist can sue. We are very careful to make sure the process and procedures are followed.

What's the importance of ethics?

I think it's really to protect the client, as a consumer need. Risk management is to protect the therapist. Ethics is the AAMFT code; any code in the state licensure is basically a consumer product. It basically says, "Here's our pledge to the consumer of how we will treat you and make sure that no harm is done to you." So risk management is where I'm protecting me. For instance, I can't think of anywhere in the ethics code where it says specifically how you should terminate a client. It talks about you shouldn't treat past effectiveness. It talks about making sure you keep good notes. It talks about making sure the contract work is followed.

Let's say a client no-shows and we're in a therapeutic process and I don't hear back from them. Well there's not necessarily a code issue that says, "I should do anything about that." A risk manager would say you need to send them a termination letter, or a risk manager would say you need to have a document that you hand to each client that says, "We've terminated and you're free to call me back." Basically, saying that you want to unhook responsibility from that client down the road that you're no longer providing treatment. Let's say that the client commits a crime, and somehow it's tied back to the therapist. If I terminate that relationship officially, then there's less chance that I'm going to have to deal with that further down the road. So when you go to an ethics workshop, you'll probably come out a little less scared than when you go to a risk management workshop. Every risk management workshop I go to, I think, "There's no longer a reason to practice therapy. It's way too risky." We should go to those because you're going to hear it from a lawyer's point of view. The importance of ethics is to protect the client, and in protecting the client, we're doing good work. We are making sure what we do, above all dues, do no harm.

You mentioned that the importance of ethics is to protect the client. Do you feel that there are limitations to being ethical? Do you feel that there are limitations from the therapist perspective?

Limitations in that nobody can do it perfectly. Risk managers will talk about standard of care. I occasionally get asked by lawyers to be a witness on an ethics case. When it gets into a civil court, the question that gets asked is, "Was standard of care followed?" Yes, there are limits because we can't do it perfectly. The aspiration should be to follow the licensure code as well as you can. But there are just human limitations to doing that. Some lawyers define standard of care not as perfection but I've heard one lawyer talk about it as a C+ level. You're doing about what your community does. When we were rewriting the code, we had a lot of input from rural communities because one of the big points in the code is not to have dual relationship when they are avoidable. Well in these small, small towns, that's almost impossible. So the standard of care may be different. A therapist in a small town couldn't have a practice if every dual relationship had to be eliminated. I'm being a little bit extreme for the example. So they have to be particularly careful that no exploitation occurs out and that that the two roles stay separate. The standard of care in a rural community doesn't change the code, but there's a bit different culture around that. In a big city like Fort Worth, Texas, I can pretty easily avoid a dual relationship, but if I live in a town of 500 or 1,000, how am I going to do that in practice?

What training and experience would you say is necessary to be an ethical therapist?

Certainly familiarity with licensure, statutes, and code. I think there are two or three things to practicing ethically and to learning ethics. You've got to know the professional code, like AAMFT, you need to know your state license and state law. I think ongoing education and reading. The good thing about state licensure is that they all require workshops. Having somebody to talk to when you're early in practice so you're not isolated. Even 26 years later, there's still folks I call and say, "I thought I'd seen it all but let me tell you about this one" and I try to get some consultation from colleges.

You mentioned earlier about being subpoenaed. I think that is something that is scary to a beginning therapist. What would you recommend to a therapist that is being subpoenaed as a witness?

If a client subpoenas a therapist, it is usually in custody cases with minors. That's every therapist's nightmare and prevention is a big piece of that. First of all, I think every therapist needs to have a lawyer on call that you can talk to who understands the code. Let's walk through a custody case. If you get a subpoena from the Mom's attorney that they want you in court on Monday for a hearing to testify on a custody matter, many things need to be in place for that to work. Let's say you've done therapy with a couple. They're going to get a divorce. I cannot respond to that subpoena by testimony or turning over my records unless I have permission from all parties involved or unless it's court ordered. So this is where therapists get themselves in trouble. They assume a subpoena means, "I've got to respond." Well you do have to respond, but you are not free without a release to turn over information. If you show up and Mom and Dad are there and you hand the records to the judge and attorneys and you get on the stand and you don't have the releases in place, you just set yourself up for a lawsuit because that father didn't give you permission to talk about him. Now if you get all the releases that you need, you may be in business. You may be ready to go. But if you don't and you sit there and refuse to hand over records and refuse to testify and look the judge square in the eyes and say, "Judge, I may not respond to these questions unless you order me to," the judge says, "You're so ordered," then you're free to do it. Now if you don't do it and you're ordered to do it, then you're in contempt. If you've done your work properly you should not, in my opinion, testify as to who the better parent is, because that's not your job, unless you're a forensic psychologist or forensic therapist who has interviewed all the children and administered certain tests. All I can witness to is what I know. I don't have any opinion about who's going to be a better parent. The minute I say so, I've set myself up, unless I've done a forensic evaluation. So, as a marital therapist, or even if I've seen the children, I'm not going to take a position on custody. I can only answer questions as to what's called a material witness as to what I witness in the therapy. But I've been on the stand many times. "Dr. O'Malley, what is your opinion on who is the preferable parent." I respond, "I'm not qualified to answer that question." "You saw these people. You had a relationship with them." I respond, "I'm not qualified to answer that question. I have not done the proper protocol to make that type of determination. I will not answer that question." In the new AAMFT code, we basically set out some protection on that. You've got a code here that states you aren't in a position to determine custody, in so many words, unless that's what you've been hired to do.

There's a Supreme Court case (*Abrams v. Jones Texas Supreme Court*, October 12, 1999) where the therapist refused to hand over the records of a child because the therapist believed the parents that wanted those records were not functioning in the best interest of the child. It went all the way up to the Texas Supreme Court. The Texas Supreme Court upheld that, and they said unless there is evidence that a parent wants those records for the best interest of the child, the therapist has the right to refuse. What the parent wanted was leverage against the other parent in a custody case. That's not in the best interest of a child. I've used it once since that court case came down. Protect yourself up to the point of it by making sure your records are good. Make sure the informed consent forms are clear about the limitations of your confidentiality. Know how to read a subpoena, and if you don't know how to read a subpoena, know how to get a hold of an attorney who can figure it out. I once had a grand jury subpoena for my records, and I'm calling my lawyer in Washington. I say, "All right, I've gotten a written request." He says, "Don't hand them over." I've gotten another request. "Don't hand them over." I call him back and say, "I have a grand jury subpoena and two marshals are on their way over to get them." He says, "Don't hand them over." It was so helpful to have that. I'm a fairly large guy, and two larger guys came to my office to get my records that night and said, "We're not leaving without them," and they left without them. That was a case where I ended up in court with my records and the judge said, "Why haven't you handed these over with these previous subpoenas?" I said, "I don't have the release," and I cited all the laws around that. I said, "Judge, I cannot release these records without your order." It's kind of coincidental, she was someone that I knew; she was actually a friend of mine. And she understood exactly. And she said, "You are so ordered to hand over your records." Then I handed them over. That's a situation where the pressure was really amazing, but attorney kept saying, "Don't do it, don't do it, don't do it." That's why it's important to understand the importance of having an attorney.

What do you think are some good things that should be included in an informed consent?
I cover confidentially. I talk about the limits of that in terms of the two laws of elder abuse and child abuse. I talk about risk. I also talk about working towards the goal, but it could get worse before it could get better or it could just get worse. I include the fee. I've got a little paragraph about our relationship. People look at it and say, "That's odd," you won't approach me in public. Absolutely not. If they approach me, I'll speak to them, but I will not, in any way, risk violating our relationship. I have consented to treat and consent to treat a child a little bit separate. I make sure that I agree that both parents are going to consent. I also state in there that I have the right to refuse to give over records if I deem it's not in the child's best interest. I've had some people upset at that. Now, this is an example of risk management if a parent calls me and says, "I need you to see my son or daughter." In the phone interview, I say, "Are you currently married to your son's or daughter's Mom or Dad?" They say, "No." Then I ask them to tell me about their arrangement for nonemergent mental health care. Before we can move forward I need you to fax or mail to me your divorced decree. Now I want you to know therapeutically, now this is ethics, I just moved from risk management. I don't want to treat somebody's kid without his or her permission. So we're going to need to talk, even if you have the right, about the importance of having your child's Mom or Dad also involved on some level. There's an example of protecting me and protecting the child. I need for them to take a copy of the informed consent when we're done. So they have a copy and I have a copy and that's our contract.

You have mentioned risk management versus ethics. What would you say are some common misconceptions of ethics?
I think subpoenas and understanding dual relationships. Confidentially, because we see more than one person in the room. How do you protect the individual's confidentiality

if there are other people in the room? When I was a chair in ethics, dual relationship was the biggest confusion. The way that the code reads, it doesn't say that you can't have a dual relationship; it says they should be avoided if possible and special care should be taken to protect the client if it occurs. I think that's a misconception. Avoid if possible and then take special precautions. For instance, I see this little kid in therapy. Random selection, he ends up on my YMCA basketball team; what are the chances? He didn't pick me, just random selection. So do I terminate him as a client? It's too late to get him on another team; by the time he showed up, it was well into the season. I guess I could. That dual relationship is in place; we both stumbled into it. So we just made sure we had a conversation between me and the child and me and the child's parents to say, "This is the thing. Let's make sure if there is any problem. Let's talk about it." None of us signed up for this, it just happened. I will not expose your relationship with me as a client, etcetera, etcetera. Technically, I could get him on another team. The family didn't want it; there was just no good way out of it. It could have been a case, where I would transfer him to somebody but we're in the middle of therapy.

Can you clarify about common misconceptions about confidentiality?
How to protect everybody's confidentiality? For instance, the subpoena. Because I had gotten a subpoena, I saw a couple; I handed over my notes, even though it has both. Some risk management people say, "Keep two separate sets of notes or you should black out anything that the other person says." I think that's too impractical. There may be some mechanical ways around that when you see a couple. I've never understood how you could do couples therapy and have separate notes because it's all systemic, talking about reactive loop. I think the whole issue of confidentially when here is an outside source, in a legal matter, is a misconception about ethics or just confusion about what to do.

How have you handled a situation where a secret is told, such as an affair?
That's been a long-time debate in the field. Do you expose that or do you not? My usual approach is to say, "Now that you've told me this, you need to understand the limits of what we are able to do and there is enough variance to talk about it. Is the affair active, and the person is about to leave? Or did it take place 10 years ago and nothing has happened since?" I know some therapists have that in their informed consent, I've been quite particular about it . . . anything that you tell me privately if we're doing couples work will be shared. So you've got a choice that sets them up, keeping a secret from you, or you have to expose the secret. For that reason, I will rarely see a couple apart. Many times, I'll see a couple and I'll smell it, you know you can tell that it's happening and sure enough it gets exposed later. From the rule of confidentiality, unless I have a very clear disclaimer and they've agreed to it, I can't take a secret and expose it. What I can do with an individual is to say that "this is greatly going to hamper what we're going to do here." What I might end up doing is say, "Either you're going to find some way to deal with this or I'm not sure I can go forward as your therapist." I won't see a couple if an individual comes and is interested in couple's therapy. I won't see an individual more than twice. Then the couple session has to come next. That's not in the code anywhere or in the law. That's just the level of practice. It's in the code in that you're trying to watch out for the best welfare of your client. My general rule with children is that if you tell me something that is dangerous, we're going to have to talk about how we're

going to talk about that with your parents. I tell them that up front. I tell the parents that not everything that your child tells me am I going to share with you. But you do have my pledge that I will never let it get to a place where it is dangerous.

What are some other ethical dilemmas that you've encountered?
Because referrals run into sort of a pattern I've been in spots where, for instance, I knew the person I was seeing had had an affair with another client. Piecing stories together, which I just find miserable. I hate it when it happens. Because they may not even know that I know, but I can figure it out. Then I've got to figure out if I am competent to do this work. It's very hard in my opinion to stop therapy without disclosing why. But sometimes you just have to say it's a conflict of interest. I had a call the other day and a woman was saying, "I need you to see my child," and she told me a little bit of the story and bells started going off. I wish I had said, "I've got a conflict of interest." She says, "Don't tell me you've seen my ex-husband. I just need you to hear that I've got a conflict of interest." I had seen her ex-husband, and I had worked with him on a court order case to deal with her about not reacting to her behavior.

Would you say that there are certain models of therapy that a therapist might have to be more flexible with in regards to ethics? Whitaker's approach is one that comes to mind.
We have an old joke on the ethics committee if Fritz Pearls, founder of Gastalt Therapy, were alive today, he'd be in front of the ethics committee. Carl Whitaker, cofounder of Experiential Family Therapy, certainly rode that line very tight. The answer is that I don't think a model supersedes ethics. There are certainly people within the bounds of ethics that may a bit outrageous. Pearls Fritz would have his chair right up to the client; his knees would be right up to the client's knees. He'd challenge and provoke you. Of course, boundaries are a hot word right now, but it hadn't always been a part of our conversation. I would shift that question to say that you could have a Pearls Fritz and Carl Whitaker model and be absolutely ethical, but what are you doing about risk management? Are you acting in such a way where you're not protecting yourself? Think about more primal therapies, screaming therapy, anger release therapy, and bataka bats with couples, there's not a law against that. The question we have to ask ourselves in ethical terms is, "Are we providing good quality care where no one can be harmed?" There is room to be creative and do things.

I look back on my ethics committee work, which was from '94 to '97; there was a huge movement on repressed memory. Repressed memory therapy hit its peak right in there. We had numerous cases. A classical case would be a parent brings a charge against a therapist, for provoking, their belief was provoking, false memories. So we had the full false memories syndrome. I bet we heard 20 cases during those years. False memory therapy, repressed memory was the model, and it exploded during those times. The critics were saying folks had memories that didn't exist. The supporters were saying, "Finally all the people with repressed memory are getting the help they need." It was a cultural phenomenon. When a new model comes along, you'd better be real sure that (a) it does no harm, (b) you can track what you're doing, and (c) you've got to decide what risk you're willing to take particularly if it's a new model that may be stranger by regular standards. Part of what happens in our field is we don't really get new standards of care for new models; it takes a while for that to happen. EMDR, eye movement desensitization, Francine Shapiro threw that thing out and everyone went crazy over it. I think she tried to keep pure research underneath it as best as she could. If I'm going to do EMDR, I've got to prove the validity of what I'm doing if I was in the court of law.

You mentioned documenting well. What would you say is best as far as taking progress notes? Some people say, "Take short notes to protect the client in case of a subpoena," and other people say, "Make longer notes for risk management purpose."

Again, I understand that with the HIPPA issue, you should do both, if you've got that kind of time. Certainly, you can protect your client with shorter notes, but you better be sure you can protect yourself with more. You need to look at your notes as doing both, how am I protecting the client, in that what am I writing that could end up in somebody else's hands? But the other question is how am I protecting me by what I'm writing? You have to look at your statute to see what note taking requires. That's going to be different by state licensure by some degree. I've battled this for 26 years, I've done little, I've done big, I've done dictation. I talk about the code; if there is a diagnosis, I put it on there. I do a session content, basically what we're talking about. I do a mini mental status exam. I do a progress towards goal. On the back of it, I write if I've given them something to do, so I can keep up with what we're doing. I note any medication changes. From a risk management point of view, Bart Bernstein, a Texas attorney and licensed social worker whose area of expertise is legal and ethical issues faced by mental health professionals, would probably say, "Write your notes in such a way to protect yourself." From an ethics point of view, what I am going to put in here [is something] that's not deceptive, but do I put every little detail?

What about therapists who encourage couples in a general direction, such as divorce busters. Is it okay to take that stance as long as you're up front with it?

Yeah, but I think that can be done in a way without saying, "Stay married." I think what you can say is, "You need to know this about me, I very much promote keeping folks together if at all possible. But I can't make that decision for you ultimately." But I think as long as you do that up front and folks know that going in and you're skilled at it. That just has to be handling well. You just don't get into a position of saying, "I don't think you should stay apart." Again, the ethical thing is you've got to treat everybody, but there may be a point where there is somebody who's safety needs or emotional need are such that you have to create a shift. That doesn't mean that you quit treating that person. If the child needs to get out of the house to go to the aunt's for a week to cool off, and the Dad disagrees and the Mom agrees and you think it's a safety issue, then you've got to take a risk on that, but not in a way that alienates the other parent. So much of it ethically is to inform people why you're doing what you're doing, when you're doing it.

Who's welfare is the therapist bound to protect?

Everyone that's there. You certainly may get into situation where the perception is that you're not protecting everybody. I saw a Mom yesterday that said, "I want to get my daughter in to see you." And I said, "Well I thought she was in pervious therapy." "Yes, we had court-ordered therapy but the therapist said they're finished, they can't do anything more to help us." "Was the Dad court ordered?" "Yes, he was. Well, I'll just bring her in next time," she says. "No, I want you to visit her dad to see how he feels about it."

The portrayal is he's an angry, difficult guy, and none of the kids want to see him. So I'm going to respect that up front and make sure he knows that I'm including him along the way. So if we get out here, and I've done my work here, I'm going to be less of that imbalanced position. I think that's a real subtlety to functioning ethically to be able to forecast, again a kind of risk management/ethics issue, of how can I provide the right quality of care? Because I don't want this little girl to come in and her dad to sabotage that down the road. And I don't want this Dad to look at me like I've alienated him. So I'm going to make sure he's going to sign off on the consent even though Mom has unilateral power to do so. I'm going to try to march him through this as much as possible. Now that's ideal and it doesn't always work out. That's the thing to be thinking of preventatively when you find yourself in a jam and you've got somebody mad at you and you backtrack and realize that you didn't really do a good job of marching forward. Some therapists are real advocacy oriented. If they can protect themselves and do that, I guess that'll work. But if you're going to do a family system approach the best we know how, you're going to pay attention to that along the way.

One of the trends that seem to be becoming more prominent among students is getting both their LMFT and LPC. To your knowledge, are there any conflicting ethical codes?
Not that I'm aware of. There are differences not that would create conflict. The rule of thumb on that is, if there is a conflict between licenses, you always follow the highest code. Do the one that's the most conservative. When I was doing committee work for ethics, our most common dual certification was AAPC (American Association of Pastoral Counselors) and AAMFT. And what would happen is we'd get a defense in which a pastor would get into a dual relationship that was damaging the client and then say, "I was functioning as a pastor then. I wasn't functioning as a marriage and family therapist." You can't do that. You can't say all [of a] sudden, "I'm not bound by this ethics code because I'm doing this kind of work."

Would the state code take precedent over the AAMFT code?
If it's higher. Again, you've got to protect yourself and the client based on all the various ways you could be held accountable. You're accountable to your professional association; you're accountable to your state license code. You're held accountable to state statute, which aren't necessarily in the license. So this case is not a licensing issue but it's now at the Texas Supreme Court level, where somebody could make a case that if you did do duty to warn, that your confidentiality in violation isn't protected. Let's say he or she was just venting, and now I've gone and warned. We used to be safe around that. But now since this case we're not. That's why it's so good to have someone look at that with you. So if I had that case, I would call an attorney and say, "Here's what's happening. What do you think I should do?" They might say, "Of course, you have duty to warn."

Can you comment a little about communicating or conducting therapy through electronic media?
We tried to tackle this when we were rewriting the code we ending up giving it up. It was so confusing. There were so many questions at that point. The code gets rewritten about every 10 years. We decided that we needed another 10 years of data to decide. We put that on our list to try to get some guidelines to telecommunications. AAMFT has a

website; almost all of the professional organizations have some guidelines on telecommunication. So the best thing to do is to read that and see what the updates are. We were dealing with things like, "If you live in Kansas and I'm in Texas, and I'm only doing Internet therapy with you, am I practicing in Kansas or in Texas?" "Am I practicing from where I come or where you live?" "Do I have a license to practice in Kansas?" On my intake sheet, I've got information on where to call clients. Can I leave you a message at home? yes/no; Leave you a message at work? yes/no; E-mail you? yes/no. Give me your e-mail address. May I contact you there? yes/no. Just from a private practice point of view, obviously on faxes, I just make sure that I have permission for any form of communication that I use and then I use that very, very conservatively. Protect the client. Protect yourself. Keep reading your association information.

What things would you suggest to a student or beginning therapist regarding common ethical mistakes?

I think the whole issue on confidentiality and subpoenas are probably the biggest ones. Not keeping good boundaries, being too loose. Kind of how you do things. Having right amount of rapport but formality. Then the other big issue is folks who get too isolated. If you're uncomfortable about telling a colleague about something that you have done, then you've probably done something you shouldn't have done it, it's just a great rule of thumb. And then go ahead and tell a colleague, unless it would put your colleague in a position, where they would have to report you or you cannot protect the identity of the client. If you are concerned that what you have done rises to that level, then speak with an attorney. And make sure your agency's procedures are in line with your ethical code. I can imagine there are circumstances where an agency takes a different point of view. There are cases where therapists were acting ethically, but they were getting some level of agency pressure to do it differently, maybe to turn over records. Hopefully, agencies are up-to-date on that. But that's something that you must be clear about if you're going to work in an agency. Is there anything in the policies or procedures here that [is] in any way compromising to that I've been taught, in terms of following the ethical code?

Do you have a protocol that you go through when you're trying to find people as referral sources?

Not a protocol really. It's informal in that I know them to do good work, or I've met with them or a colleague. Now if they get a bad report two or three times, I don't use them. Doctor so and so seemed distracted. I have a woman that I refer to that does biofeedback. That's very useful with anxious children and adults. I have and educational diagnostician that I use. I've got my little group that I'm comfortable with. Sometime, people will ask me to refer them to another therapist. I've got it on my phone message that I'll help you find a therapist. People will read me names off a list and, by definition, I would say, "I wouldn't recommend anyone on the list. What I'll say is you read me the names and if I hear someone I know, I'll say, 'Yes.'"

Is there anything else that you'd like to go over?

Again, I think again for licensed folks you're going to get 3 hours of training sometime in the year. Be mindful of that in terms of what you need to do therapy well. It's not that ethics changes that much but application changes. Think about electronics; there's always something that they didn't cover, that's important to deal with. I think the main themes are what I've been saying: Don't do it in isolation, be informed, and be preventative. In this stage of practice, I can most often see what's coming down the pike, but I occasionally get stuff and have to make a call to an attorney or colleague and say, "I don't know what to do on this, what do you think?" I think when you've done that and if you do get into a jam, you can back yourself up by saying, "Seek outside support or I did seek outside consultation." It doesn't matter how long you've been doing this. Complacency is your worst enemy when you're dealing with ethics or risk management.

KEY TERMS

Boundaries   A delineation of personal limits that outlines what is/are not permissible.

Confidentiality   An understanding between a therapist and client that any information revealed or discovered in connection with the treatment of a client will not be disclosed unless authorized by law or by the client.

Dual relationships   A relationship between a therapist and a client in which the clinician is functioning beyond his or her role as clinician (i.e., the clinician has another relationship with the client outside of the clinical setting).

Informed consent   When a client is informed of the benefits and risks of counseling prior to entering the therapeutic relationship and agrees to participate.

REFERENCES

American Association for Marriage and Family Therapy. (2001). *User's guide to the AAMFT Code of Ethics.* Washington, DC: Author.

Beck, Sanderson. (1987). *Life as a whole: Principles of education based on a spiritual philosophy of love.* Farmingdale, NY: Coleman Publishing.

Bernstein, B. E., & Hartsell, T. L. (2000). *The portable ethicist for mental health professionals: An a–z guide to responsible practice.* New York, NY: John Wiley & Sons.

Bernstein, B. E., & Hartsell, T. L. (2004). *The portable lawyer for mental health professionals: An a–z guide to protecting your clients, your practice, and yourself* (2nd ed.). Hoboken, NJ: John Wiley & Sons.

Brock, G. (2001). Subprinciples 1.1–1.6: Responsibility to clients. In American Association for Marriage and Family Therapy, *User's guide to the AAMFT Code of Ethics* (pp. 1–19). Washington, DC: AAMFT.

Boorhem, H., & Zygmond, M. J. (1989). Ethical decision making in family therapy. *Family Process, 28*(3), 269–280.

Caudill, B., Jr. (1998). Malpractice and licensing pitfalls for therapists: A defense attorney's list. In *Innovations in clinical practice: A source book* (Vol. 20). Sarasota, FL: Professional Resource Press.

Corey, G. (2001). Ethical issues in counseling practice. In G. Corey (Ed.), *Theory and practice of counseling and psychotherapy* (6th ed., pp. 42–62). Belmont, CA: Wadsworth.

Corey, G., Corey, M. S., & Callanan, P. (2003). *Issues and ethics in the helping professions* (6th ed.). Pacific Grove, CA: Wadsworth Group.

Gawf, L. (n.d.). *Terms of service.* Retrieved from http://www.licensedcounseling.com

Haslam, D. R., & Harris, S. M. (2004). Informed consent documents of marriage and family therapist in private practice: A qualitative analysis. *The American Journal of Family Therapy, 32*(4), 359–374.

Haug, I. E. (2001). Principle 2: Confidentiality. In American Association for Marriage and Family Therapy, *User's guide to the AAMFT Code of Ethics* (pp. 21–31). Washington, DC: AAMFT.

Isaacs, M. L., & Stone, C. (2001). Confidentiality with minors: Mental health counselors' attitudes toward breaching or preserving confidentiality. *Journal of Mental Health Counseling, 23*(4), 342–356.

Leslie, R. S. (2003a). Ethical and legal matters: Keeping clinical records part I. *Family Therapy Magazine, 2*(4), 43–45.

Leslie, R. S. (2003b). Ethical and legal matters: Using a "no secrets" policy when treating a couple or family. *Family Therapy Magazine, 2*(3), 45–47.

Leslie, R. S. (2004, March /April). Treating children-selected legal and ethical issues. *Family Therapy Magazine.*

O'Malley, P. (2001). Principle 3: Subprinciple 3.10 through 3.15 professional competence and integrity. In American Association for Marriage and Family Therapy, *User's guide to the AAMFT Code of Ethics* (pp. 41–48). Washington, DC: AAMFT.

Tarasoff v. Regents of the University of California, 17 Cal. 3d 425, 551 P.2d 334, 131 Cal. Rptr. 14 (Cal. 1976).

Thapar v. Zezulka, 994 S.W.2d 635 (1999).

Watkins, S. A. (1989). Confidentiality and privileged communications: Legal dilemma for family therapists. *Social Work, 34*(2), 133–136.

RECOMMENDED READING LIST

Books

Gladding, S. T. (2004). Ethical and legal aspects of counseling. In S. Gladding, *Counseling: A comprehensive profession* (5th ed., pp. 57–83). Upper Saddle River, NJ: Pearson Education.

Goldberg, I., & Goldberg, H. (2004). Professional issues and ethical practices. In I. Goldberg & H. Goldberg (Eds.), *Family therapy: An overview* (6th ed., pp. 428–447). Pacific Grove, CA: Brooks/Cole.

Articles

Kitchener, K. S. (1986). Teaching applied ethics in counselor education: An integration of psychological processes and philosophical analysis. *Journal of Counseling and Development, 64*(5), 306–310.

O'Malley, P. (1995, December). Confidentiality in the electronic age. *Family Therapy News.* Retrieved from http://www.aamft.org/members/Resources/lrmplan/Ethics/eth_ElectronicAge.htm

Piazza, N. J., & Baruth, N. E. (1990). Client record guidelines. *Journal of Counseling and Development, 68*(3), 313–316.

Website

American Counseling Association
http://www.counseling.org/PDFs/ACA_2005_Ethical_Code.pdf

The Family Therapist and Diversity

20

Kelly M. Taylor and Tiffany Nicole Smith

It is not for him to pride himself who loveth his own country, but rather for him who loveth the whole world. The earth is but one country and mankind its citizens.

—Baha'u'llah

INTRODUCTION

Although people of various cultures have sought counseling for many years, it is only in the last 40 years that multicultural counseling has been studied as its own field in the counseling arena. Now, more than ever, multicultural standards and competencies are needed for therapists who enter into practice. As marriage and family therapy begins to gain acceptance across various cultures, therapists are or will see clients of widely varying cultural backgrounds and worldviews. These worldviews affect not only the client's comfort level entering therapy but also his or her level of self-disclosure and expectation of the therapeutic process (Jordan, 2001).

It is important that therapists be prepared to work with various cultures as our population trends shift. Demographics of the United States have changed drastically since many of the family therapy theories and models discussed in this book were introduced. Projections by the U.S. Census Bureau suggest that by the year 2042, minority populations will become the majority (Christensen, 2009a). For example, the Hispanic/Latino population in the United States accounted for half of the nation's growth between 2000 and 2006, at 24.3%, 3 times the growth rate of the total population during this period (U.S. Census Bureau, 2002). Asian American and Pacific Islanders are two of the fastest growing communities in the United States (Maki & Kitaono, 2002; U.S. Bureau of the Census, 2002). It is also estimated that there are 8.8 million gays, lesbians, bisexuals, and transgendered people living in the United States (Johnson, 2010).

Therapists in training must consider their own cultural awareness and biases of themselves and their families and their knowledge, awareness, attitudes, and beliefs of different cultural groups distinct from their own. This chapter will briefly explore some key issues involved in cultural competence and counseling.

HISTORY AND LEADING FIGURES

Since the 1960s, waves of social movements have promoted the rights of various groups of Americans. For example, Title VI of the Civil Rights Act of 1964 was enacted to prohibit discrimination for reasons of race, color, religion, and national origin. The Older Americans Act of 1965 was passed to meet the needs of social services for older persons; issues of ageism and age discrimination continue to be explored in our society. During the 1960s and 1970s, the feminist movement began to demand equality for women. The gay rights movement promotes awareness, education, and equal rights for lesbian, gay, bisexual, transgender, and questioning (LGBTQ) individuals. The Americans With Disabilities Act of 1990 protects people with disabilities from discrimination and promoting their full inclusion into all other aspects of our society. More recent controversies over the rights of those of Islamic faith are testing our commitment to religious freedom.

The field of family counseling has followed suit to acknowledge the needs of an increasingly diverse population. In 1972, the Association for Non-White Concerns in Personnel and Guidance was formed as a charter of the American Counseling Association (ACA). In 1985, it was renamed as the Association for Multicultural Counseling and Development (AMCD). The purpose of the association is to provide global leadership, research, training, and development for multicultural counseling professionals with a focus on racial and ethnic issues, especially as it relates to the psychological health of people of all diversities and cultures (AMCD, n.d.).

In 1991, the AMCD developed an outline of competencies that are necessary for counseling professionals; they are listed on the AMCD website (http://www.counseling.org/Resources/Competencies/Multcultural_Competencies.pdf).

The following sections will briefly highlight the contributions of some leaders in the field of multicultural counseling.

Paul Pedersen

Paul Pedersen's teaching and lecturing career spans more than 40 years. He is currently professor emeritus for the Department of Counseling and Human Services at Syracuse University and visiting professor for the Department of Psychology at the University of Hawaii. Some of his recent books include *Counseling Across Cultures, Sixth Edition* (which he coedited with Juris G. Draguns, Walter J. Lonner, and Joseph E. Trimble) and *A Handbook for Developing Multicultural Awareness, Third Edition*. One of the contributions he is best recognized for is the triad model. The model uses role-plays as a means for counselors to work with diverse clients in a setting where they can discover differences. The triad model involves counselors of different ethnic backgrounds interviewing a single client. The model uses the three roles of counselor, client, and the "anticounselor," who personifies the problem held by the client and deliberately attempts to pull the client away from the counselor during the session to show how strong a cultural difference can be. The anticounselor continuously gives feedback to the counselor during the session.

Derald Wing Sue and David Sue

As a young boy living in Portland, Oregon, Derald Wing Sue and his brothers were teased by the Caucasian children in elementary school. This sparked their fascination with human behavior and interaction (Munsey, 2006). Today, Dr. Sue, a professor at Columbia University, is recognized for his groundbreaking writing and research in the area of multicultural counseling. He is coauthor (with his brother David Sue) of *Counseling the Culturally Diverse: Theory and Practice*, now in its 5th edition, and *A Theory of Multicultural Counseling and Therapy* (with Allen Ivey and Paul Pedersen). Both textbooks are staples in counseling programs. Dr. Sue was past president of the Society for the Psychological Study of Ethnic Minority Issues, the cofounder and first president of the Asian American Psychological

Association (AAPA), and is currently the president of the Society of Counseling Psychology (SCP). He has received numerous awards for his contributions to the field.

Dr. Sue is most famous for the theory of *microaggression*. Microaggression occurs when "subtle racial expressions" (as opposed to more overt expressions of racial hostility and/or violence) affect people of color (DeAngelis, 2009).

Allen Ivey

Dr. Allen E. Ivey has been a leader in multicultural counseling since the late 1960s, when he first began work on the multicultural implications of microskills for counselors. *Microskills* refers to a hierarchical interview process used when working with clients during psychotherapy and is based on ethics, multicultural competence, and wellness (Ivey & Ivey, 2007). He served as past president and fellow of the SCP of the American Psychological Association (APA), a fellow of the Society for the Psychological Study of Ethnic Minority Issues of the APA and the AAPA, and is a founding director of the National Institute for Multicultural Competence. Some of his books include *Intentional Interviewing and Counseling: Facilitating Client Development in a Multicultural Society* (with Mary Bradford Ivey and Carlos P. Zalaquett) and *Intentional Group Counseling: A Microskills Approach* (with Paul B. Pedersen and Mary Bradford Ivey). Most recently, Dr. Ivey has been appointed to serve on a committee of the APA to define competencies and practices for multicultural counseling and therapy (MCT).

Patricia Arredondo

A licensed psychologist, educator, and leader, Dr. Arredondo has contributed much to the Latino/Hispanic counseling community and the counseling profession as a whole. She has authored and coauthored numerous articles and books, including *Key Words in Multicultural Interventions: A Dictionary* (with Harold E. Cheatham, Jeffery Mio, and David Sue) and *Becoming Culturally Oriented: Practical Advice for Psychologists and Educators* (with Nadya A. Fouad). Her leadership positions include having served as president of the AMCD, president of the Society for the Psychological Study of Minority Issues, Division 45 of the APA, and president of the National Hispanic Psychological Association, among others. Outside of the counseling arena, she has contributed to areas such as business, government, and nonprofit agencies and is more of a consultant for diversity management. Additionally, she is founder and president of Empowerment Workshops, Inc., of Boston and has received numerous awards for her work in the field of multiculturalism.

Monica McGoldrick

In her vast experience as a family therapy educator, clinician, and researcher, combined with her awards and leadership positions, Monica McGoldrick has always emphasized the importance of becoming multiculturally competent. Her contributions include concepts such as family patterns and genograms (see Chapter 1). She has also published seminal works such as *Ethnicity and Family Therapy, Third Edition* and *Re-Visioning Family Therapy, Second Edition: Race, Culture, and Gender in Clinical Practice* with Kenneth V. Hardy that can help any family therapist learn how to work with culturally diverse families.

She currently serves as the director of the Multicultural Family Institute in Highland Park, New Jersey, which was founded in 1991. The institute is a nonprofit educational institution, which trains therapists to work with individuals, couples, and families while promoting social justice and provides clinical services to the community.

INTRODUCTION TO CULTURAL COMPETENCE

Multicultural counseling has been described as "counseling that takes place among individuals from different cultural backgrounds" (Jackson, 1995, p. 3 as cited in Vinson & Neimeyer, 2003). To truly understand this theory, we must define the term *culture*.

Certainly, it can be said that *culture* includes the shared beliefs and values of a group. Part of this may include ethnicity and race. Lee (1999) defines *ethnic identity* as "part of an individual's self-concept that comes from knowledge of membership in a social group and the value or emotional significance attached to that membership" (p. 48). However, Lee proposes that *culture* encompasses much more than all of this, including the "language, customs, values, beliefs, spirituality, sex roles, and sociopolitical history" of a group of people (p. 2).

It is also important to distinguish *cultural awareness*, *cultural sensitivity*, and *cultural competence*. "Awareness is primarily a cognitive function; an individual becomes conscious of a thought or action and processes it intellectually. Sensitivity, on the other hand, is primarily an affective function; an individual responds emotionally to stimuli with delicacy and respectfulness" (Hardy & Laszloffy, 1995, p. 227).

> *Cultural competence is a combination of clinical skill and knowledge and experience of a particular culture. When I think of cultural competence, I think of being a good clinician but also having sufficient familiarity with a specific culture, and to be able to attend to the process and perspective of the family and to be able to identify and relate with what those are. You have to have some experience in that realm so you aren't at a loss. (Hastings, 2002)*

It is not possible for marriage and family therapists to achieve total cultural competence, but they can continually learn and develop a personal awareness about various cultures to benefit the populations they serve (Hastings, 2002). It is also important to recognize that each therapist's various life experiences also determine his or her degree of cultural competence.

One of the first challenges in becoming a competent multicultural family therapist is to be able to recognize one's own cultural biases and to be aware of one's racial, ethnic, and cultural identity when working with a family culturally different from one's own family of origin (Nelson et al., 2001). By trying to understand where their clients have come from, marriage and family therapists can more readily recognize the cognitions that the clients may bring about themselves into the therapy setting.

Cultural competence assists family therapists in forming relationships based on their understanding of a family's culture, beliefs, and values. This relationship influences the therapy process and helps the therapist incorporate the family's culture into formulating solutions.

Much of the literature references two different perspectives within the multicultural counseling arena (Hays, 1996). The "etic" perspective studies topics that apply across many cultures whereas the "emic" perspective studies topics that are specific to a certain culture. A well-trained family therapist should be able to blend both perspectives. For example, although it is important to become knowledgeable about the various cultures that one will encounter, it is also necessary to be aware of the different issues that certain cultures face, such as discrimination, oppression, or in the case of recent immigrants, acculturation to a host country.

To become aware of these issues, students, practitioners, and researchers need to become aware of and/or overcome the role *ethnocentrism* plays in their lives. Defined as a psychological phenomenon characterized by the belief in the superiority of a set of values and a worldview that evolves from one's own cultural, ethnic, or racial group (Sue, Ivey, & Pedersen, 1996), ethnocentrism creates biases that are harmful to the counseling profession. These biases have both cognitive and affective dimensions. Cognitively, ethnocentrism affects the way people think about other cultures. The affective dimension of ethnocentrism describes the way people feel about themselves concerning their culture and other people from their culture (Sue et al., 1996). However, to deny the role ethnocentrism plays in counseling is to deny such realistic events in history—racism, oppression and prejudice—and some clients' realities.

MULTICULTURAL COUNSELING AND THERAPY

Multicultural therapy takes into consideration racial and ethnic diversity as well as a host of other issues such as spirituality, sexual orientation, disabilities, age, class, and the potential cultural bias of practitioners. Although there is no single multicultural therapy, multicultural theory has influenced many approaches to be more sensitive to the history of the oppressed and marginalized, acculturation issues, and the politics of power.

In *Multicultural Therapy Over Time* (APA, 2010), Dr. Melba J. T. Vasquez outlines her approach, which contains three elements:

1. Cultural sensitivity (an awareness and appreciation of human cultural diversity)
2. Cultural knowledge (including factual information about cultural variation)
3. Cultural empathy (the ability to connect emotionally with the patient's cultural perspective)

In this approach, one must make decisions about when and how a person's problems relate to or are mediated by cultural factors, because not every problem is necessarily related to or best treated by emphasizing culture.

In *A Theory of Multicultural Counseling and Therapy* (Sue et al., 1996) explains the six propositions of MCT, which are as follows:

1. MCT is a metatheory of counseling and psychology; that is, it is a theory about how counseling and psychology theories can integrate information on diverse populations.
2. Both counselor and client identities are formed and embedded in multiple levels of experiences (individual, group, and universal) and contexts (individual, family, and cultural milieu). The totality and interrelationships of experiences and contexts must be the focus of treatment.
3. Development of cultural identity is a major determinant of counselor and client attitudes toward the self, others of the same group, others of a different group, and the dominant group.
4. The effectiveness of MCT theory is most likely enhanced when the counselor uses modalities and defines goals consistent with the life experiences or cultural values of the client.

5. MCT theory stresses the importance of multiple helping roles developed by many culturally different groups and societies.

6. The liberation of consciousness is a basic goal of MCT theory. MCT theory emphasizes the importance of expanding personal, family, group, and organizational consciousness of the place of self-in-relation (Sue et al., 1996).

TECHNIQUES FOR COUNSELING DIVERSE CLIENTS

Although learning and researching the cultural norms of a client is one helpful way to prepare for a culturally different client, family therapists must not forget that the most important information will come directly from talking with the client family. Each family will inevitably have its own story or reality to tell. "In fact, reality is a perception field that is constructed and deconstructed by individuals depending, in part, on their cultural group memberships" (Constantine, 2002). The information imparted by the family will be immeasurable in helping the therapist (Sadeghi, Fischer, & House, 2003).

Culturally sensitive family therapists may take a cultural history of their clients, using the genogram, for example (see Chapter 1), before doing any assessments, forming judgments, or initiating interventions. The *culturagram* is a particular type of genogram, which tracks cultural issues such as immigration status; time in community; language spoken; health beliefs; cultural and religious institutions; oppression, discrimination, bias, and racism; and so forth (Congress, 2004).

It is important to realize that although the client's family setting before a family therapist may appear to be from a certain cultural or ethnic group, there are many differences within a cultural group as well that can only be ascertained by curious questioning of the family to see how they may veer from or align with their culture's majority belief systems. This can also involve religious beliefs. For example, a family may come to a therapist with a concern over their teenage daughter who is pregnant, seeking counseling and mention that they are Catholic. Rather than automatically assume the family has "traditional" religious views, it is important to the therapist to ask the family about their views on various options including that of abortion, adoption, and rearing the child as a single parent.

It is important, too, to find out who in the family embraces or does not embrace a cultural view. For example, a couple from Japan who wants to maintain their culture in America may see their adolescent daughter embrace more American ways and begin having a conflict. It is the wise family therapist who explores the parental beliefs about their culture and tries to understand how the daughter's stepping away from family beliefs can cause a problem. Then, exploring with the daughter, which cultural beliefs she may still hold on to, may help to reengage the family so that compromise can occur.

Commenting on the intersection of race, ethnicity, gender, and social class in counseling, Constantine (2002) proposed that counselors may be overwhelmed about their ability to help clients who bring in concerns based on societal forces, especially those who did not have a multicultural component in their training. With the lack of this component, there also comes the question of how to deal with ethical dilemmas (Sadeghi et al., 2003). For example, should a therapist encourage a client to end an abusive marriage if the client's culture considers divorce as heinous and grounds for banishment? Should a therapist encourage an ill client to seek Western medical treatments when they are not an accepted practice or belief in the client's culture? If counselors are trained or at least introduced to case studies involving these situations, it may prove to be invaluable in the future when these dilemmas possibly and likely will arise. It will spur them to at least think about what their course of action will be. Yan and Lam (2000) hold that if family therapists do not account for cultural differences when working with a family, as well as look at their own role in the therapy setting, then they are not truly helping their clients. They propose that the profession needs a cross-cultural model based on how clients define themselves culturally, not based on traditional models.

It is worth noting that there may be times when family therapists work with a client or family that appears to be from the same group (be it cultural, racial, ethnic, religious, etc.) as their own. In such cases, it is important not to assume that the family's beliefs will be the same as the therapist's. "A client working with a counselor who comes from the same ethnic group may still have different cultural identifications and orientations" (Tsang, Bogo, & George, 2003, p. 66). It is important for family therapists to always ask pertinent questions that will allow the client to tell the family therapist what his or her cultural beliefs are.

As a family therapist in training, it is also important to find a theory that fits with the client's view of how change occurs, as well as one that fits with the client's personality. Every therapist must be flexible enough to adjust his or her therapeutic style based on cultural necessity and the background of the client in actual practice (Yan & Lam, 2000). There are no specific therapeutic skills, techniques, or theoretical foundations that can be generalized to all cultures.

Therapist's Role

The role of the family therapist using a multicultural lens should be adaptable to the clients' cultural expectations regarding helping professions.

Sue and Sue (1990) describe various roles identified by Atkinson, Morten, and Sue (1989) that therapists may need to take to be effective in counseling multicultural clients. These are the "out-of-office" roles such as that of a consultant, providing psychoeducation; the outreach role, helping families in the community setting; the ombudsman role, advocating for the family; and the facilitator of indigenous support systems role, helping families find services and resources. Many of these are based on the belief that to work effectively with clients from another culture, more than just in-session therapeutic needs must be met. Families may need help obtaining services from the community at large or need their counselor to reach out to them in their own environment because of financial constraints.

McGoldrick and Giordano (1996) postulate that the therapist's role is to be a cultural broker to the client/family. This means that the therapist should help the family recognize their own ethnic and cultural values to work out their presenting problems. Behaviors acceptable in one culture are based within the context of one's values of family interaction patterns.

CULTURAL COMPETENCE WORKING TEMPLATE

The following template is meant to be used as a guideline when working with any family, and with any of the models discussed in this book. It provides a guideline for the beginning therapist on steps to take and questions to ask that might promote cultural competence. It embraces the Guidelines on Multicultural Education, Research, Training, Practice, and Organizational Change for Psychologists, which the APA established in 2002. It includes suggested questions under each heading to help start the process of an actual session with multicultural sensitivity. Although no one "script" exists for any therapy session, the author hopes that the template serves as an impetus to learning this family therapy model.

Tools for Change

As mentioned earlier in the chapter, the family therapist may wish to use a genogram when working with a diverse family. It allows the therapist to explore with the family who they are, what their culture means to them, and what their culture says to them about the problem. Additionally, the therapist should "check at the door" any preconceptions he or she possesses about the family's orientation, ethnicity, or culture.

The therapist should consider the following:

- *"How do I identify myself in terms of my own racial/cultural identity?"*
- *"What prejudices does my own racial/cultural group hold?"*
- *"Do I have any personal barriers, such as religious or cultural biases, that may prevent me from effectively working with the client family before me?"*
- *"Do I know enough about the family's culture or ethnicity, and if not, how can I learn so I am respectful and helpful?"*
- *"What is the client family's level of acculturation?"*
- *"Do I have any previous experiences with the client family's culture that I can draw from?"*
- *"What is the client family's socioeconomic status, and how will this affect therapy?"*
- *"What therapeutic model or intervention might be most helpful to the client family based on the family's cultural identity?"*
- *"Does the family therapy intervention planned match the worldview of the client family?"*

Phase 1: Joining and Building Rapport

The first phase should involve getting to know the client family. To do this, one must be authentic, honest, and curious about learning its values, beliefs, customs, and history (Sue, 2006). Listening is the paramount skill here. Let the family members tell you what they want to tell you.

Here are some areas into which a therapist might inquire during this phase:

- *"How do you identify yourselves in terms of your racial identity?"*
- *"How do you identify yourselves in terms of cultural identity?"*
- *"How is the presenting problem viewed in terms of your family's culture?"*
- *"How long has your family resided in this country?"*
- *"Who are the members of your family?"*
- *"What is your family's idea of why you are here?"*
- *"Are you open to working with a therapist of a different culture from your own?"*
- *"How does your family view therapists in your culture?"*

Phase 2: Understanding the Presenting Issue

After the therapist has gained some perspective on the client family's culture and the family's view of its presenting problem, the therapist should begin to explore how the presenting problem affects the family. The following questions may be helpful:

- *"Father, can you explain how this problem is interfering with your family's home life?"*

- *"Mother, can you tell me why it is important for you to work outside the home even though your mother did not?"*
- *"Daughter, can you tell me how it helps you to dress like the other students at school rather than in your native clothing?"*

Phase 3: Assessment of Family Dynamics

Family therapists constantly look for patterns of interaction so that they can intervene at appropriate times and guide the family into interactions that promote health. The therapist should watch for ways that the diverse family relates, and ask family members to explain their interaction in a way that is consistent with the family's cultural identity, level of acculturation, and level of respect for each other. For example, some cultures emphasize a patriarchal hierarchical structure where the father possesses authority and power. In such families, the therapist should address the father first when intervening or asking for explanations. Such an approach demonstrates cultural respect and is likely to be productive.

Questions such as the following are consistent with a respect for cultural identity, level of acculturation, and level of respect for each other:

- *"Father, can you explain to me what happens when you tell your son, "No," and your wife then gives him permission later?"*
- *"Daughter, can you tell me what happens in your family when you try to explain that you want to go away to college rather than stay at home and attend a junior college?"*
- *"Parents, when you talk to your daughter, how does she respond? Why does that bother you? What could she say to tell you something respectfully so that you would respond respectfully to her?"*
- *"Grandmother, would you explain what you think your grandson should do when you tell him what you think about his activities?"*

Phase 4: Goals

In this phase, the family therapist uses the family therapy model of choice, adapts it to the family, sets goals for the family, and structures behaviors to achieve them. At this point, various models may differ regarding specific questions and approaches; however, the consideration and respect for gender, culture, and ethnicity remain.

The following questions reflect that mandatory element of respect:

- *"Parents, when you think of how you want things to be with your son in school, what can we work on today that would be helpful to you?"*
- *"Father, what do you think your daughter needs to know about your culture as she grows into a young adult?"*
- *"Daughter, can you explain to your father what needs to happen so that you can communicate more freely with him, as you have expressed you want to do?"*

Phase 5: Amplifying Change

As change occurs in the multicultural family, the therapist should support whatever productive changes each family member makes. It is important in such families to commend any change, even if it feels slightly uncomfortable to the family, as growth yet also to support their adherence to their values, beliefs, and culture.

- *"Father, I am impressed that you took time to come home early to spend time with your daughter last week. Daughter, what did that mean to you?"*
- *"Mother, it seems that your efforts to spend more time with your husband at night are making a difference to him. What do you think the children see as a result?"*
- *"Jose, the changes you have made at school tell me that you want to succeed and make a good life for yourself and your girlfriend. I wonder what else you can continue to do to strengthen your dream."*

Phase 6: Termination

Therapy, with a multicultural family, may demand sensitive termination when the family meets its goals. Family therapy is a relationship, and cultures value relationships in different ways. Consequently, the therapist should ensure the family knows that once it resolves its presenting problem, therapy will end unless an additional problem reveals itself. Some cultures may find short, solution-focused therapy as a comfortable approach and will find "good-bye" relatively easy. Other cultures may require a less precipitous approach in which some sort of follow-up beyond that ethically required demonstrates the cultural respect on which this section has focused. The therapist should discover such cultural mores as he or she builds rapport and discuss openly with the family the best way to say "good-bye" as an appropriate point for termination approaches.

MASTER THERAPIST INTERVIEW

DERALD WING SUE

One of the most recognized and respected names in multicultural counseling, Dr. Derald Wing Sue holds many honors and awards for his works. He received his PhD from the University of Oregon and went on to begin a highly successful and prolific career as writer, researcher, and educator. In 1997, he was invited to address President Clinton's Race Advisory Board on the National Dialogue on Race and has been honored with many awards for his contributions to the field. He is currently a professor of psychology and education in the Department of Counseling and Clinical Psychology at Teachers College, Columbia University. When speaking with Dr. Sue, his passion for his work clearly shines through.

Can you tell me more about your professional background and what led to your interest in multicultural issues in counseling?

When I was first born, my father emigrated from China when he was very young, around 14 years old. My mother was born here but never had more than a third-grade education. When my father came, we lived as a family in Portland Chinatown that was relatively isolated from the rest of the community. In the Portland Chinatown, we were taught that the outer community was not particularly friendly toward ethnic, racial, [and] cultural differences. Subsequently in my young years, when I moved out, I found that to be the truth. I mean, my father moved us from Chinatown to the southeast district of Portland, Oregon, where we were the only Asian family, and my father did it to primarily give us a larger home to live in. There were never any homes in Chinatown. They were just stacked apartments, so when he moved us out there, we loved the space, but the experiences we had was one of high discrimination from fellow students. I remember that I, my brothers and I, often times would wonder what it was about us, because we were internalizing the blame that brought such teasing and negativism from my fellow classmates. It was just not the students in terms of making fun of our language, saying "Ching Chong Chinaman," teasing us for our physical differences. For instance, there was this game that they played, which is "Chinese–Japanese"—Chinese, they would pull their eyelids up, and Japanese, they would pull them down. I remember these times when they circled us and would chant that constantly. And so, our family became very close, as a means to ward off what we felt was a very invalidating and intolerant society.

I remember that as we grew older, my brothers and I would constantly spend hours just talking about these issues and our feelings associated with that. And while it was painful for us to be victims of stereotyping and bias by classmates, what was most painful was teachers and counselors and my experiences with them. One of my teachers—and I wrote about this, I recall specifically—as I'm talking to my brother Stan in Chinese in front of our classroom, and I think that it was maybe 5th or 6th grade or something of that nature, the teacher came out to close the door because class was about to start and overheard us speaking in Chinese and came up to me and said, "Derald, I don't ever want to hear you speak Chinese. You're in America, and in America, you speak English. Now get into your room now." And I felt totally humiliated not knowing in particular what I had done wrong. I ran into my classroom and slumped in my chair all that day. I suddenly realized, as I'm older now, the teacher might have meant well in terms of saying "if you want to be successful in the United States, you have to learn to speak good English," but the way she communicated was to make me feel that my language was deviant and a deficit. And when you realize that language is a carrier of your culture, to be made ashamed of your language is to be made ashamed of your culture. And since I am part of the culture, I became ashamed of myself and that lead me into later years to the study of what I called, at that time, *racial self-hatred*. That is because everyone reacts toward you being racially [and] culturally different as if there is something wrong. The real damage is that students of color [and] young children of color, may begin to internalize that and believe in that. That was the part of my early struggles, and it was really my ability to talk to my brothers who shared this that really got us over the hump and be able to deal with it. I have three brothers in psychology, with doctorates, all of them. So there are four of us with doctorates in the field. So I do think that something happened to us as a family that really made us begin to constantly try to understand what motivated people, what made them so intolerant. Why should we, as people of color, Asian Americans, feel ashamed of who and what we are? And that led my brother Stan and I to do the first major article and study on Asian American identity and mental health. But that is where the early crux of being oriented towards understanding psychology of what was happening and this issue of multiculturalism, racism, diversity . . . all of that sprung from those early childhood experiences.

I enjoyed hearing your description of that, and it gives me and other people a great picture of why you are so passionate and how you have come to be so scholarly in this field. Can you talk about which models fit particular cultures, ethnicities, [and] socioeconomic status groups best?

All theories and all models have something to offer. What I don't like about current models is that they don't acknowledge that they are culture bound. All theories of human behavior [and] development . . . all theories of counseling and psychotherapy originated from a cultural context. And as such, it is impossible for them to be culture free. And if indeed they are culture bound, they have various biases and assumptions about human behavior that guide their definitions of what is normal/abnormal. If we talk about, for example, family counseling or couple counseling, you have to look at the societal definitions of what is the traditional healthy family. Well, in all my research and work[s], there are five that come out on almost all family system models, and one of them is *that [it] is desirable and a sign of healthiness to be able to express emotions freely and openly*. If you watch family systems and family therapy operate, even individual counseling and therapy, you want the clients to be able to express their feelings. Well, most cultural groups that I know, specific ones like Asian Americans, value, for example, restraint of strong feelings. And a counselor or therapist who doesn't understand that may pathologize that this person or family is inhibited, restrained, [and] enmeshed . . . all negative terms that are going on.

A second aspect of what is considered a healthy family is that, *we say that members have the right to be their own person*. That is that, if you look at theories of human development, the healthy individual is one who individuates from the group. And that is the same . . . while the family is considered important in our society and Western society, there is a desire for the family to individuate from what we call the *emotional field of the family*. Now, that comes from the background of what we call the *psychosocial unit of operation* of Western society. And that is, you are healthier when you mature to be your own person, to be autonomous, and independent. Three quarters of the world [that] is psychosocial unit of operation is not the individual. It is the family, the group, or the collective society. In fact, among the Japanese, there is a saying that "the nail that stands up is considered an anomaly and is pounded back down again." You do not individuate. You are the family. And that is where a major clash occurs in terms of many of the counseling situations.

A third one is that *a healthy family has an equal division of labor*. Well, that is not necessarily shared. Division of labor in Latino families [and] Asian families is based upon how old you are and your gender. And while I know that in the United States, we talk about the women's movement, we treat each gender equally . . . but most of the cultures of the world are patriarchal. Now, does that make them abnormal or deviant? From the perspective of Western society, it may. But what I think that we've got to realize is that we cannot change the cultural dictate. It has to occur internally from the culture.

That leads to the fourth major difference . . . *Egalitarian role relationships are valued in this society in families and our relationships*. And I've said before, most cultures outside of the United States, if you look at Latino culture [and] Asian culture . . . it is patriarchal. Men are more valued over women. And I understand that a lot of feminists would get upset about that, but that is really a strong cultural dictate. Now, we can ask the question, does culture justify a practice? I don't have an answer to that.

And then the last thing that I see, the fifth major difficulty, is that, *one of the strongest values of this society is the belief in the nuclear family* even though statistically it is no longer operable. But most people believe that the nuclear family is the definition of the family. And again, Asian, Latino, African American, and Native Americans . . . the family is defined quite differently. In Asia, it is the extended family. Among Latinos, you have what we call *compadres* (i.e., coparents) in which you have the *madrina* and the *padrino*, who can be aunts or uncles. Among African Americans, uncles [and] neighbors can be defined as the family. And among African Americans, the absence of a father doesn't mean that there is an absence of a father figure. And among the greatest definition, broadest definition, of family are American Indians in which it is defined as a whole village. You know, when Hillary Clinton wrote that book, *It Takes a Village*? She really took that from both Native American and African American thinking, that is that the raising of children, the responsibility towards children, is that of the whole village. And the whole village is considered the family.

So when I see this, the theory, the model that I work with is to really understand that there is no such thing as a culture-free/universal application of a theory that applies. There are universal similarities that one has to be done, what I call a culture-specific approach to understanding [and] helping relationships.

How would you suggest therapists prepare for a client that is culturally very different from themselves?

First of all, *it would be very important for the helping professional to be aware of their own values, biases, and assumptions about human behavior.* As long as it is invisible to the helping professional, if it is invisible to me, I will inadvertently apply those to, let's say a culturally different client, or culturally different family that I work with unknowingly, and therefore engage in what I call a process of cultural oppression. So it is very important for me to understand what my worldview is and what are the values and assumptions that dictate my behavior. And I find that most counselors, most therapists, are unaware of that. They operate, almost intuitively, and when a difference occurs, they never question it.

The second one, really, is to begin to understand the worldview of the culturally different clients, or family, or groups that I'm going to work with. This is not simply reading books. Understanding cultural diversity and cultural differences does not come simply from academic or intellectual understanding. So, if I'm going to work with an African American family, for example, I need to not only understand intellectually what is going on, but experientially and affectively. I am equally at a loss to deal with an African American client or family if all I have is intellectual understanding. I mean, I can know about slavery; I can know about what playing-the-dozens is among African Americans. I understand what, intellectually, what I call is the *paranorm*. If I do not have experiential reality to supplement that, I am equally unable to relate to the family. So for me, it is very important that I have Black friends; that I frequent Black community forums; that I interact with them in working in this way.

And then the third thing that is truly needed is *a sociopolitical understanding of ethnic minority reality*. And that, if you talk about the four major groups, Asian American, Latino/Hispanic American, American Indian, and African Americans, all of them have a sociopolitical experience in reality that have commonalities, but are very different. A counselor or therapist who does not understand what it means to be a person of color and [of] a primarily monocultural society is at a loss about their ability to truly understand the worldview of a culturally different person. They have to understand, for example, historical trauma. I find that it is very difficult, for example, for Native Americans talk about the Soulwound that resulted in the oppression and the loss of land of American Indians. This historical trauma during the Trail of Tears is relived over and over by generations. It hasn't ended. It's like the Jews in the Holocaust. The Jews today still have this historical trauma of that particular incident. And for a therapist not to understand that handicaps them completely in their ability to deliver services and to understand where the paranorm comes from. That is a healthy, functional survival mechanism that is present. So that is the third thing—understanding the sociopolitical reality and how it indeed influences [not only] the person of color but [also] the helping professional as well. For example, most counselors or therapists don't realize that the nature of race relations is constantly operating and being reenacted in counseling and helping sessions. Their idea is that I'm a counselor, I'm a therapist, I'm here to help people, but they don't realize how it is structured and operates in the actual session itself.

And the fourth thing that I think in approaching and working with clients is to *have a high repertoire of helping or intervention strategies that you can use and not be bound by the formal professional definitions of what is a therapist and what is a counselor.* Because if you look at the codes of ethics and the standards of practice in APA and ACA, there is what we call therapeutic taboos:

1. A therapist does not give advice and suggestions.

2. A therapist does not serve dual-role relationships.

3. A therapist does not accept gifts from clients.

4. A therapist does not disclose their thoughts and feelings.

Now, those four therapeutic taboos are precisely the qualities that bind the helping relationship in other cultures. For example, a therapist who doesn't realize that an Asian client who gives them a gift, if they refuse the gift because it will unduly obligate them (that's the thinking—that Western thinking) they fail to understand that in essence, the gift represents an intimate part of that Asian individual, and to reject it and not accept it is to deny a part of that client's identity. If you look at African Americans, the therapeutic taboo of not playing dual-role relationships can cause problems because helping among African Americans . . . if you ask yourself this question, "What is the most powerful healing force besides the family in the African American community?" What is it? It is the African American church. The politicians know this now. Anytime they campaign, where do they go to speak to a Black community? The churches. And a person will likely seek help from a fellow member of the congregation, and this may be a dual-role relationship that is going on.

I can give numerous examples of this, so that, what I'm saying is that the role of the helper has to be expanded so that counselors and therapists feel comfortable in giving advice and suggestions and playing the role of not only the conventional therapist and counselor, but also serve the role as an advocate, a consultant, a facilitator of indigenous healing practices, and not to think about traditional healers as unscientific and supernatural types of . . . you got to have these bonds with the community. So it is those four things, I feel, all helping professionals need. As you can see, you never become culturally competent. You are constantly on a journey to cultural competence, but once you take those few steps, you are better for it in terms of being able to deliver these helping services to people.

Do you have any specific questions that you feel are good at eliciting information from your culturally diverse clients?
Well, one of the things that I generally do is to not be problem focused. That's one of those things that when I supervise and work with my graduate students, and we're talking about a situation. The traditional method in mental health and counseling and therapy, and very Western, is to identify the problem and solve it. And so often times, what I see is that when students are working with clients, they will start a session by focusing on the problem. "What brings you here? What is the problem?" That is a very offensive question for many cultural groups. "How come you are focusing on the task and the problem? Aren't you interested in me as a person?" So the way that I usually approach it is that . . . you know how in many of these mental health clinics or counseling centers, you fill out this intake form? What will happen is that I see many counselors and student trainees looking at the intake form and relating to the intake form rather than the client. So I'm more interested when someone comes in, to say, "Elaina, how are you? My name is such and such. Tell me something about yourself. Where were you born? What's going on? How many do you have in the family?" The task at hand is not the individual. It is related to the individual, but it is not the individual.

Now interestingly enough, when I first started modeling and demonstrating this, I overheard one of my graduate students talking to another new student who said that, "Dr. Sue really has given me hope and some insights into working with Latino clients and families, because before you can work with them, you have to make small talk first." It struck me that this is not small talk to the Latino, nor is it small talk for me. It is essential and important, and yet she understood technically what I was doing, but in her mind it was small talk, it was trivial, it was insignificant to the actual task and problem at hand.

What I try to do is to get my students to begin to understand that you have a real person and family before you. You need to bind with them. And to bind with them, you have to be authentic. And this is another thing that I try to communicate to people. Many of my trainees, when they get into a session and they know that I'm observing them or listening to their audiotape, they are so wrapped up in terms of what is the therapeutic thing to do or say. I find this to be almost an 80 something percent [80%] in counselors or therapists. What is the therapeutic thing to do or say to this client or this family? And I tell them that that creates a distance between you and your client. Don't think so much about the therapeutic thing to say. What do you feel is the authentic and honest response? Because the authentic and honest response is often times the therapeutic response. So what I see among a lot of people who are trained professionally is a degree, they are well-intentioned, but there is this degree of inauthenticity that comes across. And they don't recognize it. They think they are being professional, that they are operating from therapeutic guidelines. But

I try to say, what is missing from you, what is the human thing that is missing from you that binds together?

I give examples of this. If you begin to think about before counseling and therapy existed, which is a very Western concept, how did societies and cultures ever get along without counseling and therapy? Well, the true answer is that, well, there are several answers . . . maybe, what it might indicate is that counseling and therapy really isn't important or needed if all these societies have existed and survived without it. I don't believe that. What I am seeing is that all societies, all cultures have indigenous or intrinsic healing networks. They do not look like what our Western formal definitions of therapy are all about. But they are equally effective. And that we have lost something in terms of trying to look at our Western theories and imposing them and modifying them on different racial ethnic groups. I sometimes wonder, what would a system of healing, not a system of therapy, what would a system of healing look like if we took the indigenous, non-Western methods of healing and built up from them for the groups, rather than imposing a Western scheme and trying to adapt the Western method to these different groups? I think they would look quite differently. Because if you look at the non-Western methods of healing, they are very relationally oriented in an authentic way, and they are usually group oriented. That is, that you don't treat individuals apart from the group or the community. When someone suffers with a problem, it is not just an individual dysfunction. It indicates a group dysfunction, and it is a group responsibility to also be involved in the healing process that is going on. But to me, those are really very important things to do.

Have you or any of your colleagues attempted to look at different approaches or methods?

Yes, we have. Increasingly, we have been looking at things like Nikon therapy in Japan. A group of us, not a lot, are beginning to explore what we call UST, which is the acronym for the Universal Shamanic Tradition. Now when I talk about Shamans, when I talk about healers, witch doctors, fakers, who are healers in different communities, it is really quite strange that there are universal beliefs and concepts that are present. For example, there is a big movement in counseling in spirituality. I think that you've probably been up on it and have been reading about it. Spirituality has increasingly been explored and written about in the mental health literature. Well, spirituality has always been a part of indigenous healing, and I think that is part of what is going on there. Many of the indigenous groups feel strongly that it is a spirituality, not necessarily religion; spirituality and religion are two different things, but spirituality talks about a life force that connects everyone together, that there is a bond that goes through all of us together. And it is a belief that disorder is a falling out of synchrony with the spiritual bond that among Native Americans they call it the Red Path. The Red Path is part of the life journey of the spirit that placed us on this Red Path. Dysfunction is when an individual falls out of alignment or leaves that Red Path and begins to travel a different direction. That is where you get alcoholism, psychological disorder, [and] family dysfunction, and the goal of healing is to get that person to realize that they have ancestors that once placed them on that path, and they have journeyed off of it. And they have a responsibility that their future generations, their sons and daughters, will also be born on a path that is not on the Red Path, unless they come back on to it. So a part of healing is this leap that the spiritual bond is something that you have to get back in contact with. This is something that is very important. Another thing that I think that people are beginning to realize is that all these non-Western . . . you know, if you look at what is the most frequently used method of healing in the world? It is really meditation. I have a colleague, Carl Thoreson, who is doing a lot of research on meditation, non-Western methods of healing, and counseling and therapy. But meditation recognizes that there are alternative states of consciousness and in many cultures, it is believed that you journey to a different state of consciousness to seek answers. I mean Native Americans have always done this. In terms of whether they do it with certain plants and drugs that induce a journey into a different . . . you seek answers or you seek the aid of spirits to come back to help you. Or among Buddhists, the belief is that our current state of consciousness is not the normal state. That is why meditation . . . you journey to a different state—a state that is on a higher plane and level that allows you to see the world as it really is. Those are all concepts that now, I find, coming in to Western healing. Unfortunately, I don't think people who use it have this connection with indigenous or the past. This is not to say that Western counseling and psychotherapy doesn't have much to offer. It offers a lot. But what we've done is forgotten what indigenous healing has to offer that might be equally revealing.

So if we were to look more at utilizing different kinds of healing here in the United States, how do you see your involvement in the therapeutic process as the therapist?
Well, I think that as a therapist, I think that I operate from the four conditions that I said before. That is the way that I operate, and the ultimate goal of therapy has to be defined between you and the family or you and your client. And nothing, to me, is truly either/or. Because, when clients come to me . . . a lot of the issues that clients [bring] to me, especially racial/ethnic minority clients, are ones that deal with their sociopolitical relationship in this society. For example, if they have racial identity issues, they need to understand the sociopolitical base of where those racial identity conflicts come from. Just like it happened to me. They also have to begin to develop a set of thinking that society has built in them, that are either Western, or cultural conflicts or issues, that are often times brought [to the session] that make you feel stuck. Let me give you an example. If you have Asian American clients who are told one set of values by peers that you should express your feelings freely, that unless you do it, you're inhibited. Then you have your traditional parents who are telling you that you should restrain your feelings. You are caught in a cultural conflict. And they feel stuck. When they come to you, they have bought into an "either/or" dynamic. If you as a counselor buy into that type of "either/or," you are stuck as well. A client who is stuck and a therapist who is stuck . . . you are not going to be very helpful. There are gradations that you have to bring the client to begin to see in terms of what their choices are and to involve also the parents in terms of doing that.

What would you say are the necessary agents of change in multicultural family therapy?
To involve the entire family. And this is sometimes very difficult to do. First of all, let me say something, and that is that this really applies to White Western families. And I don't mean to broad stroke it in any way because most of the racial ethnic minority families . . . the psychosocial unit is the family and it is an extended family. Well, if you look at the history of White Europeans who immigrated to the United States, when

they immigrated, they operated from extended families as well. It is not that they were nuclear families or individuals. If you look at what they operated from, it was very similar to almost all of the racial ethnic minority beliefs in terms of interdependence among family members, among neighbors, [and] friends. And it was really a group feel.

Something happened historically that began to shift from a family focus to an individual focus in the United States. And part of that has been mobility, part of it was the Industrial Revolution, but families became separated and the issue of autonomy and independence began to become the norm here. I think that, and I've found this in working with even White families, there is what Eduardo Durand calls a *Soulwound*. That is that, I believe, that White Americans have a deep desire and know that they have lost something as Westernization has occurred. And one of those losses, this emptiness that is present, is a loss of the connection with other family members and with other people. And the only time that this begins to come up strongly in White families is that as they get older and begin to deal with their own mortality, that is when this emptiness of the inner spiritual connection with other family members and friends becomes very important. There are what I call critical stages, and I see that all the time. And when White family members are able to acknowledge that, they become stronger. It's almost like they've denied that. And so, this is a long way for me to say that when I deal with racial ethnic minority families, I almost always inevitably assume how important the family is. That it is not just an individual decision by one member of the family. It affects the whole, collective family. And that's what we talk about.

For example, parents often times say to their young children, minority children, that "you're becoming too Westernized," and the minority children get angry at the parents by saying that "you're too old-fashioned." I hear that all the time. What connects them, however, is that while they are on the surface making this battle, you begin to ask, "What are the parents fearing that will happen to their kids as they become more Westernized?" And I think if you look at that, their greatest fear is that their children, by virtue of what they are doing, [are] rejecting an intimate, important aspect of their family heritage. The children's perception is that the parents are old-fashioned; these are outdated things; that they are restraining them; that my parents are mean. So I try to get them to realize that, "Do you believe that your mother and father mean bad for you? Do they not love you anymore? Why do you think that they are so concerned that you adhere to the old ways?" Not that you have to, but what makes them so . . . when they see that their parents also have strong love, are fearful that they are going to be lost to the family, there is almost a binding that goes on. And when the parents are able to see that what their children are doing is not a rejection of them, they become more free to allow their children to do things that traditionally might not have been as acceptable.

That is what I work for in the family because you do indeed have these strong cultural conflicts, and you get them to realize that you will always be bound together. And that is something to be valued and something very spiritual that will occur here. Now children or youngsters frequently will understand on some level but what they will find out, and I tell the parents this, that as they grow older, they may think that they've given up some of these cultural values. But they are dormant but present there. And that they will come up as the children get older in critical points in their time. A critical point in the time of White Americans is when they face their mortality, and they begin to realize that family is important. Friendships are important. When these values occur in youngsters generally is if they get married. This happened to me. I had this big battle with my father. I thought he was old-fashioned. He thought I was too Westernized and disrespected him. My father forced us to go to Chinese school to learn the language. This was after regular school that we had to go to Chinese school. And I swore that I would never put my kids through Chinese school because that's old-fashioned. Well, what happens to me? I get married, still thinking that I'm very Westernized. I don't have these values. I had my son, and then I found myself, as my son got older, reached about 4 or 5 years old, I said to my wife, it came out of my mouth without me even realizing it, "Maybe we should put DP [son] into Chinese school?" It shocked me.

What I guess I'm saying is that almost all of the conflicts within the families when you're doing family systems are based in some sense between these classes of values. But the values aren't good or bad. They sometimes are dormant. And at critical periods, they will make their appearance. And when they make their appearance, that is when insight occurs to me, [meaning] you're not as Westernized as you really think. But being Westernized or being traditional is not one of good or bad. And I tell my students when I work with them, that there is nothing more unrewarding at times than to work in counseling and psychotherapy because the benefits and the changes aren't something that may occur immediately in your presence. But you are planting seeds that you may never see blossom 30 decades [30 years, 3 decades] from now. The blossoming was at this point the "aha, that's what my father meant . . . aha, that's what my mother meant." And you begin to see it quite differently.

And at this point, I find the battles with my son and daughter to be very much the same. It's being reenacted, but I have greater ability to accept what might be going on with them as opposed to demanding immediate compliance. And I guess that's one thing that I don't necessarily hope to expect immediate change, and I have to be satisfied. Maybe it's even a rationalization. But I'm satisfied with the feeling that the process has begun. That you start a process with a family. It's not that a cure occurs in 10 sessions. It's a lifelong process that will go on.

KEY TERMS

Acculturation   The modification of the culture of a group or individual as a result of contact with a different culture.

Anticounselor   From Pete Pedersen's triad training model; the anticounselor is a term used to mean the "problem" in matching a counselor from one culture with two people from contrasting cultures.

Assimilation   A term used to reference immigrants or other ethnic groups acquiring customs of their new culture.

Cultural competence   A set of congruent policies, behaviors, and attitudes that collaboratively work together in a system and allows that system to work successfully in cross-cultural conditions (Cross, Bazron, Dennis, & Isaacs, 1989; Isaacs & Benjamin, 1991).

Culture   The predominating attitudes and behavior that characterize the functioning of a group or organization.

Emic viewpoint   Emphasizes that each client is a person with individual differences.

Ethnicity   Common ancestry through which individuals have evolved shared values and customs.

Ethnocentrism   When a person uses his or her own culture as a standard of reference for measuring all other cultures and thus views self as superior.

Etic viewpoint   Emphasizes that humans are all alike, regardless of culture, and thus, same theories and techniques can be applied to all clients.

Hierarchy   An organization or group whose members are arranged in ranks (e.g., in ranks of power and seniority).

Immigration   The act of entering into and becoming established in a country that one is not a native for permanent residence.

Individualism   The pursuit of personal happiness and independence rather than collective goals or interests.

Kinship/kinfolk   A close connection marked by community of interests or similarity in nature or character; people descended from a common ancestor.

Metatheory   A set of interlocking rules, principles, or a story (narrative), that both describes and prescribes what is acceptable and unacceptable as theory; an overall theory about a theory.

Multicultural families   Relating to families of several cultures.

Multicultural identities   The culture that a person identifies himself or herself with and the way that he or she goes about formulating that identity.

Multiculturalism   Relating to, consisting of, or participating in the cultures of different countries, ethnic groups, or religions.

Nuclear family   Parents and their children living together as a unit.

Oppression   The state of being kept down by unjust use of force or authority.

Patriarchal   Relating to or characteristic of a culture in which men are the most powerful members.

Psychosocial   Involving aspects of social and psychological behavior.

Race   A group of people united or classified together on the basis of common history, nationality, or geographic distribution.

Racism   The prejudice that members of one race are intrinsically superior to members of other races; discriminatory or abusive behavior toward members of other races.

Sociopolitical   Relating to or involving both social and political factors.

Spirit   The vital force that characterizes a human being as being alive; also, having a soul.

Stigma   The shame or disgrace attached to something regarded as socially unacceptable.

Values   The accepted principles or standards of a person or a group.

REFERENCES

American Psychological Association (Producer). (2010). *Multicultural therapy over time* [DVD]. Available from http://www.apa.org/pubs/videos/4310877.aspx

Association for Multicultural Counseling and Development. (n.d.). Retrieved from http://www .amcdaca.org/amcd/default.cfm

Atkinson, D. R., Morten, G., & Sue, D. W. (Eds.). (1989). A minority identity development model. In *Counseling American minorities* (pp. 35–52). Dubuque, IA: W. C. Brown.

Christensen, J. (2009a). Cultural communication. *Counseling Today*, 40–45.

Christensen, J. (2009b). Multicultural considerations. *Counseling Today*, 28–39.

Congress, E. (2004). Cultural and ethical issues in working with culturally diverse patients and their families: The use of the *culturagram* to promote cultural competent practice in health care settings. *Social Work in Health Care*, *39*(3/4), 249–262.

Constantine, M. G. (2002). The intersection of race, ethnicity, gender, and social class in counseling: Examining selves in cultural contexts. *Journal of Multicultural Counseling and Development*, *30*(4), 210–215.

Cross, T., Bazron, B., Dennis, K., & Isaacs, M. (1989). *Towards a culturally competent system of care, Volume I*. Washington, DC: Georgetown University Child Development Center, CASSP Technical Assistance Center.

DeAngelis, E. (2009). Unmasking "racial micro aggressions." *Monitor*, *40*(2), 22.

Hardy, K. V., & Laszloffy, T. A. (1995). The cultural genogram: Key to training culturally competent family therapists. *Journal of Marital and Family Therapy*, *2*, 227–237.

Hastings, C. (2002, March/April). So, how do you become culturally competent? *Family Therapy Magazine*, *1*(2), 18–25.

Hays, P. A. (1996). Addressing the complexities of culture and gender in counseling. *Journal of Counseling & Development*, *74*, 332–338.

Isaacs, M., & Benjamin, M. (1991). *Towards a culturally competent system of care, volume II, programs which utilize culturally competent principles*. Washington, DC: Georgetown University Child Development Center, CASSP Technical Assistance Center.

Ivey, A., & Ivey, M. (2007). Intentional interviewing and counseling: Facilitating client development in multicultural society. Belmont, CA: Brooks/Cole.

Johnson, R. (2010). Interview with Gary Gates of The Williams Institute. *About.com*. Retrieved from http://gaylife.about.com/od/index/a/garygates.htm

Jordan, K. (2001, Summer). Promoting multicultural competence in marriage and family therapy supervisees *Supervision Bulletin*, 9–10.

Lee, W. M. L. (1999). *An Introduction to Multicultural Counseling*. Philadelphia, PA: Accelerated Development.

Maki, M., & Kitaono, H. (2002). Counseling Asian Americans. In P. Pedersen, J. Draguns, W. Lonner, & J. Trimble (Eds.), *Counseling across cultures* (pp. 109–131). Thousand Oaks, CA: Sage.

McGoldrick, M., & Giordano, J. (1996). Overview: Ethnicity and family therapy. In M. McGoldrick, J. Giordano, & J. K. Pearce (Eds.), *Ethnicity & family therapy* (pp. 1–27). New York, NY: Guilford Press.

Munsey, C. (2006). A family for Asian psychologists. *Monitor*, *37*, 60.

Nelson, K. W., Brendel, J. M., Mize, L. K., Lad, K., Hancock, C. C., & Pinjala, A. (2001). Therapist perceptions of ethnicity issues in family therapy: A qualitative inquiry. *Journal of Marital and Family Therapy*, *27*(3), 363–374.

Sadeghi, M., Fischer, J. M., & House, S. G. (2003). Ethical dilemmas in multicultural counseling. *Journal of Multicultural Counseling and Development*, *31*(3), 179–191.

Sue, D. W. (2006). *Multicultural social work practice*. New York, NY: Wiley.

Sue, D. W. & Sue, D. (1990). *Counseling the culturally different: Theory & practice*. New York, NY: John Wiley & Sons.

Sue, D. W., Ivey, A. E., & Pedersen, P. B. (1996). *A theory of multicultural counseling and therapy*. Pacific Grove, CA: Brooks/Cole.

Tsang, A. K. T., Bogo, M., & George, U. (2003). Critical issues in cross-cultural counseling research: Case example of an ongoing project. *Journal of Multicultural Counseling and Development, 31*(1), 63–78.

U.S. Census Bureau. (2002). Selected characteristics of the population by citizenship: 2001. Retrieved from http://www.census.gov/population/socdemo/race/api

Vinson, T. S., & Neimeyer, G. J. (2003). The relationship between racial identity development and multicultural counseling competency: A second look. *Journal of Multicultural Counseling and Development, 31*(4), 262–277.

Yan, M. C., & Lam, C. M. (2000). Repositioning cross-cultural counseling in a multicultural society. *International Social Work, 43*(4), 481–493.

RECOMMENDED READING LIST

Books

Aponte, J. A., & Wohl, J. (2000). *Psychological interventions and cultural diversity* (2nd ed.). New York, NY: Allyn & Bacon.

Atkinson, D. R. (Ed.). (2004). *Counseling American minorities* (6th ed.). New York, NY: McGraw-Hill.

Atkinson, D. R., & Hackett, G. (Ed.). (2003). *Counseling diverse populations* (3rd ed.). New York, NY: McGraw-Hill.

Barret, R. L., & Robinson, B. E. (2000). *Gay fathers: Encouraging the hearts of gay dads and their families.* San Francisco, CA: Jossey-Bass.

Cross, W. E., Jr. (2001). Encountering nigrescence. In J. G. Ponterotto, J. M. Casas, L. A. Suzuki, & C. M. Alexander (Eds.), *Handbook of multicultural counseling* (pp. 30–44). Thousand Oaks, CA: Sage.

Cross, W. E., Jr., & Vandiver, B. J. (2001). Nigrescence theory and measurements. In J. Ponterotto, J. M. Casas, L. A. Suzuki, & C. M. Alexander (Eds.), *Handbook of multicultural counseling* (pp. 371–393). Thousand Oaks, CA: Sage.

Edelman, M. W. (1987). *Families in peril: An agenda for social change.* Cambridge, MA: Harvard University Press.

Fontes, L. A., & Thomas, V. (1996). Cultural issues in family therapy. In F. P. Piercy, D. H. Sprenkle, J. L. Wetchler, & Associates. (Eds.). *Family therapy sourcebook* (2nd ed.). New York, NY: Guilford Press.

Garcia-Preto, N. (1996). Latino families: An overview. In M. McGoldrick, J. Giordano, & J. K. Pearce (Eds.), *Ethnicity & family therapy* (pp. 141–154). New York, NY: Guilford Press.

Hines, P. M., & Boyd-Franklin, N. (1996). African American families. In M. McGoldrick, J. Giordano, & J. K. Pearce (Eds.), *Ethnicity and family therapy* (pp. 66–84). New York, NY: Guilford Press.

Hines, P. M., Garcia-Preto, N., McGoldrick, M., Almeida, R., & Weltman, S. (1999). Culture and the family cycle. In B. Carter & M. McGoldrick (Eds.), *The expanded family life cycle: Individual, family, and social perspectives* (3rd ed.). Boston, MA: Allyn & Bacon.

Kliman, J. (1994). The interweaving of gender, class and race in family therapy. In M. P. Mirkin (Ed.), *Women in context: Toward a feminist reconstruction of psychotherapy.* New York, NY: Guilford Press.

Kliman, J., & Madsen, W. (1999). Social class and the family life cycle. In B. Carter & M. McGoldrick (Eds.), *The expanded family life cycle: Individual, family and social perspectives* (3rd ed.). Boston, MA: Allyn & Bacon.

Krestan, J. A. (Ed.). (2000). *Bridges to recovery: Addiction, family therapy, and multicultural treatment.* New York, NY: The Free Press.

Lee, E. (1996). Asian American families: An overview. In M. McGoldrick, J. Giordano, & J. K. Pearce (Eds.), *Ethnicity & family therapy* (pp. 227–248). New York, NY: Guilford Press.

Maslow, A. (1954). *Motivation and personality.* New York, NY: Harper & Row.

McGoldrick, M. (Ed.). (1998). *Re-visioning family therapy: Race, culture and gender in clinical practice.* New York, NY: Guilford Press.

McGoldrick, M., Anderson, C. M., & Walsh, F. (1989). Women in families and in family therapy. In M. McGoldrick, C. M. Anderson, & F. Walsh (Eds.), *Women in families: A framework for family therapy.* New York, NY: Norton.

McGoldrick, M., Giordano, J., & Pearce, J. K. (Eds.). (1996). *Ethnicity & family therapy*. New York, NY: Guilford Press.

Ng, K. (1998). *Counseling Asian families from a systems perspective*. Alexandria, VA: American Counseling Association.

Pedersen, P. B., Draguns, J. G., Lonner, W. J., & Trimble, J. E. (Eds.). (2002). *Counseling across cultures*. Thousand Oaks, CA: Sage.

Philpot, C. L., Brooks, G. R., Lusterman, D. D., & Nutt, R. L. (1997). *Bridging separate gender worlds: Why men and women clash and how therapists can bring them together*. Washington, DC: American Psychological Association.

Smith, R. L., & Montilla, R. E. (2005). *Counseling and family therapy with Latino populations: Strategies that work (family therapy and counseling)*. New York, NY: Routledge.

Sue, D. W., & Sue, D. (2003). *Counseling the culturally diverse: Theory and practice*. New York, NY: John Wiley & Sons.

Sutton, C. T., & Broken Nose, M. A. (1996). American Indian families: An overview. In M. McGoldrick, J. Giordano, & J. K. Pearce (Eds.), *Ethnicity & family therapy* (pp. 31–44). New York, NY: Guilford Press.

Wimberly, E. P. (1997). *Counseling African American marriages and families*. Louisville, KY: Westminster John Knox Press.

Articles

Brucker, P. S., & Perry, B. J. (1998). American Indians: Presenting concerns and considerations for family therapists. *The American Journal of Family Therapy*, 26(4), 307–319.

Cartwright, B. Y., & D'Andrea, M. (2005). A personal journey toward culture-centered counseling: An interview with Paul Pedersen. *Journal of Counseling & Development*, 83(2), 214–221.

Coleman, H. L. K. (1997). Conflict in multicultural counseling relationships: Source and resolution. *Journal of Multicultural Counseling & Development*, 25(3), 195–200.

Duncan, A. (2010). 20th anniversary of the Americans With Disabilities Act a cause for celebration and rededication to equal educational opportunity for students with disabilities. Retrieved from http://www.ed.gov/news/press-releases/20th-anniversary-americans-disabilities-act-cause-celebration-and-rededication-e

Healy, M. (1998, March 13). Study says poverty persists for kids of working poor. Los Angeles Times.

Keiley, M. K., Dolbin, M., Hill, J., Karuppaswamy, N., Liu, T., Natrajan, R., . . . Robinson, P. (2002). The cultural genogram: Experiences from within a marriage and family training program. *Journal of Marital and Family Therapy*, 28(2), 165–178.

Kim, E. Y., Bean, R. A., & Harper, J. M. (2004). Do general treatment guidelines for Asian American families have applications to specific ethnic groups? The case of culturally competent therapy with Korean Americans. *Journal of Marital and Family Therapy*, 30(3), 359–372.

Patterson, C. H. (2004). Do we need multicultural counseling competencies? *Journal of Mental Health Counseling*, 26(1), 67–73.

Schoen, A. (2005). Culturally sensitive counseling for Asian Americans/Pacific Islanders. *Journal of Instructional Psychology*, 0094–1956.

Websites

American Counseling Association
http://www.counseling.org/resources/

Association for Multicultural Counseling and Development
http://www.amcdaca.org/amcd/history.cfm
http://www.amcdaca.org/amcd/default.cfm

The Multicultural Family Institute
http://www.multiculturalfamily.org

Index

AAMC. *See* American Association for Marriage Counseling

AAMFT. *See* American Association for Marriage and Family Therapy

ABCDE model, *131, 138*

accountability, *72. See also* multidirected partiality

acculturation, *527*

acknowledgement of efforts, *72, 87. See also* multidirected partiality

affect, *3*

agency, *369–370*

Alexander, James, 98–99

alignments, *232*

All Out (Ellis), 130

AMCD. *See* Association for Multicultural Counseling and Develop ment

American Association for Marriage and Family Therapy (AAMFT), 28, 38, *411–413, 422*
  Ethics Code, 422–423, 458, 475, 486
  research, 459

American Association for Marriage Counseling (AAMC), *411*

American Association of Brief and Strategic Therapy, 259

American Counseling Association, 30, 38

American Family Therapy Association, 66

American Psychological Association (APA), 444–445, 461

American Society of Consultant Pharmacists, 366

amplifying the deviation, *265*

An Introduction to Family Therapy (Haley), 256

Anderson, Carol, 390

anticounselor, *510*

anxiety, *44*

APA. *See* American Psychological Association

Aponte, Harry J., 239–242, 247

approved supervisors, *412–413*

Aristotle, 92

Arredondo, Patricia, 511

article submission, 460

Ashby, W. Ross, 7

assessment, *160*

assimilation, *527*

Association for Multicultural Counseling and Development (AMCD), 510

asymmetrical relationship, *68*

attachment
  emotional cutoff, 47
  orientations, *342*
  theory, 342

attending, to build rapport, *182*

automatic thoughts, *93*

"awfulizing," *131–132*

Bailey, C. Everett, 459

Bandura, Albert, 92, 94–95

basic self, *60*

Bateson, Gregory, 4, 9, 201–202, 256–257, 288, 314, 367

Bateson Project, 157, 288

Battle for Initiative, *149*

Battle for Structure, *149*

Beavin, Janet, 202, 258, 259, 288

Beck, Aaron, 92–93

behavior analysis, *121*

behavior therapy, *91–92*

behavioral family therapy, 134

behavioral marital/couple therapy, *98,* 109–110

behavioral parent training, *97–98,* 108–109

behavioral regulation, *121*

behaviorism, *91*

beliefs about people, 26–27

beneficence, 458

Berg, Insoo Kim, 288–289, 301–303, 308

BFTC. *See* Brief Family Therapy Center

bias, *27*

biased explanations, *95*

bias-free psychotherapy, *22*

biopsychosocial model, *365, 367*

blamer, blaming stance, *177*

Boscolo, Luigi, 201–202, 208

Boszormenyi-Nagy, Ivan, 65–66

boundaries, *232, 485, 507*

Bowen Center, 40–41

Bowen family systems theory, 24
  change process, 49
  differentiation of self, *42–44*

CPSIA information can be obtained
at www.ICGtesting.com
Printed in the USA
BVHW01*0448310818
526144BV00010B/58/P